James H. Graff, George A. Sala

Gaslight and Daylight

with some London scenes they shine upon

James H. Graff, George A. Sala

Gaslight and Daylight
with some London scenes they shine upon

ISBN/EAN: 9783337270988

Printed in Europe, USA, Canada, Australia, Japan

Cover: Foto ©Andreas Hilbeck / pixelio.de

More available books at **www.hansebooks.com**

GASLIGHT AND DAYLIGHT

WITH SOME

LONDON SCENES THEY SHINE UPON

BY

GEORGE AUGUSTUS SALA

A NEW EDITION

London

CHATTO AND WINDUS, PICCADILLY

PREFACE.

THIS book is a re-issue of thirty-four Papers, mainly descriptive Essays on London streets and London people, originally published in the columns of *Household Words* between the years 1851 and 1856, and first put forth in collected form in 1858. The public in 1872 seeming to be calling for a new edition of *Gaslight and Daylight*, I am very glad to answer the summons conveyed to me through the intermediary of my publishers; and I am still more glad to be Alive, and able in the autumn of life to review the labours of my youth. Ignorance of books and crudity of style excepted, I do not, however, think that these papers, written when I was a very young man, bear much of the impress of juvenility. Indeed, I had served a very hard and bitter apprenticeship at the workbench of Life—since the age of fourteen, when I began to earn my own living—ere one line of *Gaslight and Daylight* was committed to paper. When I had attained the ripe age of twenty-one I was gaining my livelihood by letters; yet I think that literature was the fourth profession I. had taken up ; and it proved to be the only one in which I did not fail, miserably. Being now tolerably well known, I naturally receive every year numbers of letters from correspondents personally unknown to me — some of them literary aspirants, impetuously asking me to obtain immediate employment for them in the establishments of the *Times*, the *Saturday Review*, and *Punch :* others informing me that they are persons of the most commanding talents, that they have already published several volumes of poetry, travels, or fiction, of which friends well qualified to judge have spoken in the highest terms ; but that through an organised conspiracy on the part of the publishers and the critics — a plot, I fear, in which the public have a part—they have been deprived of that extended circulation, that handsome remuneration, and that universal fame which are their due. For the benefit of the first-named class of my correspondents, and for the consolation of the latter, I may mention, that for the first of my printed literary compositions I did not get one penny ; that for the second I was paid the sum of one shilling ; that some months afterwards I was much gratified at receiving half-a-crown for a poem of eighty-six lines ; and that at the age of eighteen I thought myself as rich as Crœsus on enjoying the salary of a pound a-week for editing a comic periodical. Nor have I the slightest doubt that my pecuniary reward at that period was on a precise par with my capacity. I was not worth more than a

pound a-week to anybody. Again, I should state that
after I had become a contributor to *Household Words*
I remained for a period of six long years in total anon-
ymity and obscurity; that I never dreamt of repub-
lishing the articles I had written; that I contentedly
saw them translated into foreign languages with another
person's name attached to them; and that it was not
until I returned from a journey to Russia in 1857 that
it occurred to me to seek an interview with a bookseller,
and ask him whether he thought that a volume from
my pen would have any chance of success.

That I was during the brightest years of life thus
stolidly unambitious may be due to two facts: first,
that I had (and have still, I hope, albeit in a modi-
fied degree) a profound mistrust of my own capacity;
secondly, that I looked (and still look to some extent)
upon literature as a means rather than as an end.
Never mind what that end may be. I have often heard
an eminent barrister declare that his sole desire in life
was to accumulate sufficient money to purchase the lease
and goodwill of a small roadside public-house. The
goal I propose to myself may be not dissimilar to my
friend the lawyer's. I may cherish hopes of one day
keeping an eligible chandler's shop, or of entering the
Church; of emigrating to Batavia, or of opening a cigar-
divan. Finally, as regards the question of literary fame, I
may remark that even at present nine-tenths of the papers
I write every year are published anonymously; and that

the notoriety I may have gained by my published writings has never failed to my being unmercifully abused by critics who hate and who envy me. This hatred and envy culminated last year in a gross and cruel attack made upon me by a person to whom I had never shown anything but kindness. I took the onslaught, however, as Colonel Quagg took his, not 'lying down' but 'fighting,' and I do not think that my assailant will meddle with me, or my Nose, any more.

I have not striven, in any way, to correct the manifold extravagances of style and diction which disfigure this book. Here and there I have appended an explanatory note; for the rest the book is Myself as I was; and whether it is better than Myself as I am is a matter for others to determine. Some little points of elucidation, however, which I have jotted down, may not be without interest to my readers. The theatre to which the article on pantomimes refers was the Princess's; the scene-painter was Mr. William Beverly; and the pantomime was one I wrote myself in 1850 in conjunction with a dear brother, now dead. In the papers bearing on the Musical World I meant, under the title of 'Octave and Piccolo's,' to shadow forth the renowned music-shop, in Regent Street, of Messrs. Cramer, Addison, and Beale—gentlemen who are all dead, but whose names I am glad to record as those of the kindest of friends to my mother, who was a member of the musical profession. Mr. Sims Reeves did *not* sit for the entire likeness of Basserclyffe, the tenor; but I hope the lady who was once Miss Louisa Pyne will not be angry with me when I hint that she *did* sit for the portrait of Miss Larke. Fripanelli is a wholly imaginary character; so is Panslavisco; Gaddi is or was a reality. By Polpetti I meant Rubini. Bompazek, the German bass, is a caricature — not an ill-natured one, I trust, of the famous German basso, Pischek. Madame Perigord and Mr. Saint Sheddle are nobody at all. Again, I may observe that when I wrote 'Tattyboys Rents,' I had in my mind's eye a cloudy combination of Blenheim Street, Oxford Street, and Carnaby Street, Golden Square, and that ere I wrote 'Gibbet Street' I had a very distinct impression on my mental retina of Charles Street, Drury Lane. I am glad at this time of day to look back at the words I wrote fifteen years since in this last-named paper concerning the dwellings of the poor and the reformation of juvenile criminals.

Glancing at a few other papers, I remember that Dumbledowndeary was Erith, in Kent; that the theatrical public-house was a compound of the Garrick's Head in Bow Street and the Crown in Vinegar Yard; and that the artistic tavern was the Sol's Arms in the Hampstead Road.

The remaining articles will speak for themselves. They are all, like their author, full of faults; but they were written in the frankness and with the earnestness of youth. Occasionally, in the midst of gossip and banter, I have ventured on the expression of some thoughts and some opinions on serious subjects. I do not find myself called upon to retract any of those thoughts or opinions, now. So far as my lights have led me, I hold them to be true. When I was a boy I was actually and physically Blind; and when I recovered my eyesight I began to strive to make up for lost time by looking very closely and earnestly about me. The truth had been so long hidden from me that, so soon as it became visible and palpable, I tried my hardest to clutch and hold it. I have erred, no doubt, in my endeavours, many times—have mistaken a phantom for a a reality, and worthless dross for unalloyed gold; but in perseverance of research I have not faltered; and although husk and rind may form the major part of that which I have gathered, here and there perhaps I may have lighted on that which Lord Bacon tells us is the grand desideratum in discovery—Fruit.

GEORGE AUGUSTUS SALA.

January 1872.

CONTENTS.

GASLIGHT AND DAYLIGHT.

THE KEY OF THE STREET.

It is commonly asserted, and as commonly believed, that there are seventy thousand persons in London who rise every morning without the slightest knowledge as to where they shall lay their heads at night. However the number may be over or understated, it is very certain that a vast quantity of people are daily in the above-mentioned uncertainty regarding sleeping accommodation, and that when night approaches, a great majority solve the problem in a somewhat (to themselves) disagreeable manner, by not going to bed at all.

People who stop up, or out all night, may be divided into three classes :—First, editors, bakers, market-gardeners, and all those who are kept out of their beds by business. Secondly, gentlemen and 'gents,' anxious to cultivate a knowledge of the 'lark' species, or intent on the navigation of the 'sprec.' Thirdly, and lastly, those ladies and gentlemen who do not go to bed, for the very simple reason that they have no beds to go to.

The members of this last class—a very numerous one—are said, facetiously, to possess 'the key of the street.' And a remarkably disagreeable key it is. It will unlock for you all manner of caskets you would fain know nothing about. It is the 'open sesame' to dens you never saw before, and would much rather never see again,—a key to knowledge which should surely make the learner a sadder man, if it make him not a wiser one.

Come with me, luxuriant tenant of heavy-draped four-poster —basker on feather bed, and nestler in lawn sheets. Come with me, comfortable civic bolster-presser—snug woollen-night-

cap-wearer. Come with me, even workman, labourer, peasant
—sleeper on narrow pallet—though your mattress be hard, and
your rug coarse. Leave your bed—bad as it may be—and gaze
on those who have no beds at all. Follow with me the veins
and arteries of this huge giant that lies a-sleeping. Listen
while with 'the key of the street' I unlock the stony coffer,
and bring forth the book, and from the macadamised page read
forth the lore of midnight London Life.

I have no bed to-night. Why, it matters not. Perhaps I
have lost my latch-key,—perhaps I never had one; yet am
fearful of knocking up my landlady after midnight. Perhaps
I have a caprice—a fancy—for stopping up all night. At all
events, I have no bed; and, saving ninepence (sixpence in
silver and threepence in coppers), no money. I must walk
the streets all night; for I cannot, look you, get anything in
the shape of a bed for less than a shilling. Coffee-houses,
into which—seduced by their cheap appearance—I have
entered, and where I have humbly sought a lodging, laugh
my ninepence to scorn. They demand impossible eighteen-
pences—unattainable shillings. There is clearly no bed for me.

It is midnight—so the clanging tongue of St. Dunstan's
tells me—as I stand thus, bedless, at Temple Bar. I have
walked a good deal during the day, and have an uncomfort-
able sensation in my feet, suggesting the idea that the soles of
my boots are made of roasted brick-bats. I am thirsty, too
(it is July, and sultry), and, just as the last chime of St.
Dunstan's is heard, I have half a pint of porter—and a ninth
part of my ninepence is gone from me for ever. The public-
house where I have it (or rather the beer-shop, for it is an
establishment of the 'glass of ale and sandwich' description)
is an early-closing one; and the proprietor, as he serves me,
yawningly orders the pot-boy to put up the shutters, for he is
'off to bed.' Happy proprietor! There is a bristly-bearded
tailor, too, very beery, having his last pint, who utters a
similar somniferous intention. He calls it 'Bedfordshire.'
Thrice happy tailor!

I envy him fiercely, as he goes out, though, God wot, his
bedchamber may be but a squalid attic, and his bed a tattered
hop-sack, with a slop great-coat—from the emporium of Messrs.
Melchisedech and Son, and which he has been working at all
day—for a coverlid. I envy his children (I am sure he has a
callow, ragged brood of them), for they have at least somewhere to sleep,—I haven't.

I watch, with a species of lazy curiosity, the whole process of closing the 'Original Burton Ale House,' from the sudden shooting up of the shutters, through the area grating, like gigantic Jacks-in-a-box, to the final adjustment of screws and iron nuts. Then I bend my steps westward, and at the corner of Wellington Street stop to contemplate a cab-stand.

Cudgel thyself, weary Brain,—exhaust thyself, Invention,—torture thyself, Ingenuity—all, and in vain, for the miserable acquisition of six feet of mattress and a blanket!

Had I the delightful impudence, now—the calm audacity—of my friend, Bolt, I should not be five minutes without a bed. Bolt, I verily believe, would not have the slightest hesitation in walking into the grandest hotel in Albemarle Street or Jermyn Street, asking for supper and a bootjack, having his bed warmed, and would trust to Providence and his happy knack of falling, like a cat, on all-fours, for deliverance in the morning. I could as soon imitate Bolt as I could dance on the tight-rope. Spunge again, that stern Jeremy Diddler, who always bullies you when you relieve him, and whose request for the loan of half a crown is more like a threat than a petition—Spunge, I say, would make a violent irruption into a friend's room; and, if he did not turn him out of his bed, would at least take possession of his sofa and his great-coats for the night, and impetuously demand breakfast in the morning. If I were only Spunge, now!

What am I to do? It is just a quarter past twelve; how am I to walk about till noon to-morrow? Suppose I walk three miles an hour, am I to walk thirty-five miles in these fearful London streets? Suppose it rains, can I stand under an archway for twelve hours?

I have heard of the dark arches of the Adelphi, and of houseless vagrants crouching there by night. But, then, I have read that police constables are nightly enjoined by their inspectors to rout out these vagrants, and drive them from their squalid refuge. Then there are the dry arches of Waterloo Bridge, and the railway arches; but I abandon the idea of seeking refuge *there*, for I am naturally timorous, and I can't help thinking of chloroform and life-preservers in connection with them. Though I have little to be robbed of, Heaven knows!

I have heard, too, of tramps' lodging-houses, and of the 'twopenny rope.' I am not prepared to state that I would not avail myself of that species of accommodation, for I am getting terribly tired and foot-sore. But I don't know where to seek for it, and I am ashamed to ask.

I would give something to lie down, too. I wonder whether that cabman would think it beneath his dignity to accept a pot of porter, and allow me to repose in his vehicle till he got a fare? I know some cabmen never obtain one during the night, and I could snooze comfortably in hackney-carriage two thousand and twenty-two. But I cannot form a favourable opinion of the driver, who is discussing beer and democratic politics with the waterman; and neither he nor any of his brother Jehus, indeed, seem at all the persons to ask a favour of.

It is Opera night, as I learn from the accidentally-heard remark of a passing policeman. To watch the departing equipages will, surely, help to pass the time on bravely, and with something almost like hope, I stroll to Covent Garden Theatre.

I am in the thick of it at once. Such a scrambling, pushing, jostling, and shouting! Such pawing of spirited horses, and objurgations of excited policemen! Now, Mrs. Fitzsomebody's carriage stops the way; and now, Mr. Smith, of the Stock Exchange, with two ladies on each arm, stands bewildered in a chaos of carriages, helplessly ejaculating 'Cab.' Now, is there a playful episode in the shape of a policeman dodging a pickpocket among horses' heads, and under wheels; and now, a pitiable one, in the person of an elderly maiden lady, who has lost her party in the crush, and her shoe in the mud, and is hopping about the piazza like an agonised sparrow. It is all over soon, however. The carriages rattle, and the cabs lumber away. The great City people, lords of Lombard Street, and kaisers of Cornhill, depart in gorgeous chariots, emblazoned in front and at the back. The dukes and marquises, and people of that sort, glide away in tiny broughams, and infinitesimal clarences. The highest personage of the land drives off in a plain chariot, with two servants in plain black, more like a doctor (as I hear a gentleman from the country near me indignantly exclaim) than a queen. Mr. Smith has found his party, and the sparrow-like lady her shoe, by this time. Nearly everybody is gone. Stay, the gentleman who thinks it a 'genteel' thing to go to the Opera, appears on the threshold carefully adjusting his white neckcloth with the huge bow, and donning a garment something between a smockfrock and a horsecloth, which is called, I believe, the 'Opera envelope.' He will walk home to Camberwell with his lorgnette case in his hand, and in white kid gloves, to let everybody know where he has been. The policemen and the night wanderers will be edified, no doubt.

Following him comes the *habitué*, who is a lover of music, I am sure. He puts his gloves, neatly folded, into his breast-pocket, stows away his opera-glass, and buttons his coat. Then he goes quietly over to the Albion, where I watch him gravely disposing of a pint of stout at the bar. He is ten to one a gentleman: and I am sure he is a sensible man. And now all, horse and foot, are departed; the heavy portals are closed, and the Royal Italian Opera is left to the fireman, to darkness, and to me.

The bed question has enjoyed a temporary respite while these proceedings are taking place. Its discussion is postponed still further by the amusement and instruction I derive from watching the performances in the ham and beef shop at the corner of Bow Street. Here are crowds of customers, hot and hungry, from the Lyceum or Drury Lane, and clamorous for sandwiches. Ham sandwiches, beef sandwiches, German sausage sandwiches—legions of sandwiches are cut and consumed. The cry is 'mustard,' and anon the coppers rattle, and payment is tendered and change given. Then come the people who carry home half a pound of 'cold round' or three-pennyworth of 'brisket;' I scrutinize them, their purchases, and their money. I watch the scale with rapt attention, and wait with trembling eagerness the terrific combat between that last piece of fat and the half-ounce weight. The half-ounce has it; and the beef merchant gives the meat a satisfied slap with the back of his knife, and rattles the price triumphantly. I have been so intent on all this, that I have taken no heed of time as yet; so, when custom begins to flag, glancing at the clock, I am agreeably surprised to find it is ten minutes past one.

A weary waste of hours yet to traverse—the silence of the night season yet to endure. There are many abroad still; but the reputable wayfarers drop off gradually, and the disreputable ones increase with alarming rapidity. The great-coated policeman, the shivering Irish prowlers, and some fleeting shadows that seem to be of women, have taken undisputed possession of Bow Street and Long Acre; and but for a sprinkling of young thieves, and a few tipsy bricklayers, they would have it all their own way in Drury Lane.

I have wandered into this last-named unsavoury thoroughfare, and stand disconsolately surveying its aspect. And it strikes me now, that it is eminently distinguished for its street-corners. There is scarcely a soul to be seen in the street itself, but all the corners have posts, and nearly all the posts are garnished with leaning figures—now two stalwart policemen holding municipal converse—now two women, God help them!—now a knot of lads with pale faces, long greasy hair, and short pipes. Thieves, my friend—(if I had a friend)— unmistakable thieves.

There are no professional beggars about—what on earth is there for them to be out for! The *beggees* are gone home to their suppers and their beds, and the beggars are gone home to *their* suppers and *their* beds. They have all got beds, bless you!

Some of the doorways have heaps of something huddled up within them; and ever and anon a policeman will come and stir the something up with his truncheon, or more probably with his boot. Then you will see a chaotic movement of legs and arms, and hear a fretful crooning with an Irish accent. Should the guardian of the night insist in the enforcement of his 'move on' decree—the legs and arms will stagger a few paces onward, and as soon as the policeman's back is turned, slink into another doorway—to be routed out perchance again in another quarter of an hour by another truncheon, or another boot.

Half-past one by the clock of St. Mary-le-Strand, and I am in Charles Street, Drury Lane. It is a very dirty little street this—full worthy, I take it, to challenge competition with Church Lane or Buckeridge Street. A feeling, however, indefinable, but strong, prompts me to pursue its foul and devious course for some score of yards. Then I stop.

'Lodgings for single men at fourpence per night.' This agreeable distich greets me, pictured on the panes of a window, behind which a light is burning. I step into the road to have a good look at the establishment that proffers the invitation. It is a villanous ramshackle house—a horrible cut-throat-looking den, to be sure:—but then the fourpence! Think of that, Master Brooke! There is a profusion of hand-bills plastered on the door-jambs, which 1 can read by the light of a gas-lamp a few paces off. I decipher a flattering legend of separate beds, every convenience for cooking, and hot water always ready. I am informed that this is the real model lodging-house; and I read, moreover, some derisive couplets relative to the Great Spitalfields Lodging-House, which is styled a 'Bastille!' I begin fingering, involuntarily, the eightpence in my pocket. Heaven knows what uncouth company I may fall into; but then, fourpence! and my feet are *so* tired. *Jacta est alea*, I will have fourpenn'orth.

You have heard ere now what the 'deputy' of a tramps'

lodging-house is like. I am received by the deputy—a short-haired, low-browed, stunted lout, sometimes, it is said, not over courteous to inquisitive strangers. As, however, I come to sleep, and not to inspect, I am not abused, but merely inspected and admitted. I am informed that, with the addition my company will make, the establishment is full. I pay my fourpence, without the performance of which ceremony I do not get beyond the filthy entrance passage. Then, the 'deputy' bars the door, and, brandishing an iron candlestick as though it were an antique mace, bids me follow him.

What makes me, when we have ascended the rotten stair-case, when I have entered my bedchamber—when the 'deputy' has even bid me a wolfish good-night—what makes me rush down stairs, and, bursting through the passage, beg him to let me out for Heaven's sake? What makes me, when the 'deputy' has unbarred the door, and bade me go out, and be something'd, and has *not* given me back my fourpence, stand sick and stupefied in the street, till I wake up to a disgusted consciousness in being nearly knocked down by a group of staggering roysterers, howling out a drunken chorus?

It was not the hang-dog look of the 'deputy,' or the cut-throat appearance of the house. It was not even the aspect of the score or more ragged wretches who were to be my sleeping companions. It was, in plain English, the smell of the *bugs*. Ugh!—the place was alive with them. They crawled on the floor—they dropped from the ceiling—they ran mad races on the walls! Give me the key of the street, and let me wander forth again.

I have not got further than Broad Street, St. Giles's, before I begin to think that I have been slightly hasty. I feel so tired, so worn, so full of sleep now, that I can't help the thought that I might have fallen off into heavy sleep yonder, and that the havoc committed by the bugs on my carcase might have been borne unfelt. It is too late now. The four pence are departed, and I dare not face the deputy again.

Two in the morning, and still black, thick, impervious night, as I turn into Oxford Street, by Meux's Brewery. The flitting shadows that seemed to be of women, have grown scarcer. A quarter past two, and I have gained the Regent Circus, and can take my choice, either for a stroll in the neighbourhood of the Regent's Park, or a quiet lounge in the district of the Clubs. Quite an epicure! I choose the Clubs, and shamble down Regent Street, towards Piccadilly.

I feel myself slowly, but surely, becoming more of a regular night skulker—a houseless, hopeless, vagrant, every moment. I feel my feet shuffle, my shoulders rise towards my ears; my head goes on one side; I hold my hands in a crouching position before me; I no longer walk, I prowl. Though it is July, I shiver. As I stand at the corner of Conduit Street (all night skulkers affect corners), a passing figure, in satin and black lace, flings me a penny. How does the phantom know that I have the key of the streets? I am not in rags, and yet my plight must be evident. So I take the penny.

Where are the policemen, I wonder? I am walking in the centre of the road, yet, from end to end of the magnificent street, I cannot see a single soul. Stay, here is one. A little fair-headed ruffian leaps from the shadow of Archbishop Tenison's Chapel. He has on a ragged pair of trousers, and nothing else to speak of. He vehemently demands to be allowed to turn head over heels three times for a penny. I give him the penny the phantom gave me (cheap charity!), and intimate that I can dispense with the tumbling. But he is too honest for that, and, putting the penny in his mouth, disappears in a series of somersaults. Then, the gas-lamps and I have it all to ourselves.

Safe at the corner (corners again, you see!) of what was once the Quadrant, where a mongrel dog joins company. I know he is a dog without a bed, like I am, for he has not that grave trot, so full of purpose, which the dog on business has. This dog wanders irresolutely, and makes feigned turnings up by-streets—returning to the main thoroughfare in a slouching manner; he ruminates over cigar-stumps and cabbage-stalks, which no homeward-bound dog would do. But even that dog is happier than I am, for he can lie down on any doorstep, and take his rest, and no policeman shall say him nay; but the New Police Act won't let me do so, and says sternly that I must 'move on.'

Hallo! a rattle in the distance—nearer—nearer—louder and louder! Now it bursts upon my sight. A fire-engine at full speed; and the street is crowded in a moment!

Where the people come from *I* don't pretend to say—but there they are—hundreds of them all wakeful and noisy, and clamorous. On goes the engine, with people hallooing, and following, and mingling with the night wind the dreadful cry of FIRE.

I follow, of course. An engine at top speed is as potent a spell to a night prowler, as a pack of hounds in full cry is to a Leicestershire yeoman. Its influence is contagious too, and the crowd swells at every yard of distance traversed. The fire is in a narrow street of Soho, at a pickle-shop. It is a fierce one, at which I think the crowd is pleased ; but then nobody lives in the house, at which I imagine they are slightly chagrined ; for excitement, you see, at a fire is everything. *En revanche* there are no less than three families of small children next door, and the crowd are hugely delighted when they are expeditiously brought out in their night-dresses by the Fire-brigade.

More excitement! The house on the other side has caught fire. The mob are in ecstasies, and the pickpockets make a simultaneous onslaught on all the likely pockets near them. I am not pleased, but interested—highly interested. I would pump, but I am not strong in the arms. Those who pump, I observe, receive beer.

I have been watching the blazing pile so long—basking, as it were, in the noise and shouting and confusion ; the hoarse clank of the engines—the cheering of the crowd—the dull roar of the fire, that the bed question has been quite in abeyance, and I have forgotten all about it and the time. But when the fire is quenched, or at least brought under, as it is at last ; when the sheets of flame and sparks are succeeded by columns of smoke and steam ; when, as a natural consequence, the excitement begins to flag a little, and the pressure of the crowd diminishes ; then, turning away from the charred and gutted pickle-shop, I hear the clock of St. Anne's, Soho, strike four, and find that it is broad daylight.

Four dreary hours yet to wander before a London day commences ; four weary, dismal revolutions on the clock-face, before the milkman makes his rounds, and I can obtain access to my penates, with the matutinal supply of milk !

To add to my discomfort and to the utter heart-weariness and listless misery which is creeping over me, it begins to rain. Not a sharp pelting shower, but a slow, monotonous, ill-conditioned drizzle ; damping without wetting—now deluding you into the idea that it is going to hold up, and now with a sudden spirt in your face, mockingly informing you that it has no intention of the kind. Very wretchedly indeed I thread the narrow little streets about Soho, meeting no one but a tom-cat returning from his club, and a misanthropic-looking policeman, who is feeling shutter-bolts and tugging at door-handles with a vicious aspect, as though he were disappointed that some unwary householder had not left a slight temptation for a sharp housebreaker.

I meet another policeman in Golden Square, who looks dull, missing, probably, the society of the functionary who guards the fire-eseape situated in that fashionable locality, and who hasn't come back from the burnt pickle-shop yet. He honours me with a long stare as I pass him.

'Good morning,' he says.

I return the compliment.

'Going home to bed ?' he asks.

'Y-e-es,' I answer.

He turns on his heels and says no more ; but, bless you ! I can see irony in his bull's-eye—contemptuous incredulity in his oilskin cape ! It needs not the long low whistle in which he indulges, to tell me that *he* knows very well I have no bed to go home to.

I sneak quietly down Sherrard Street into the Quadrant. I don't know why, but I begin to be afraid of policemen. I never transgressed the law—yet I avoid the 'force.' The sound of their heavy boot-heels disquiets me. One of them stands at the door of Messrs. Swan and Edgar's, and to avoid him I actually abandon a resolution I had formed of walking up Regent Street, and turn down the Haymarket instead.

There are three choice spirits who evidently have got beds to go to, though they are somewhat tardy in seeking them. I can tell that they have latch-keys, by their determined air— their bold and confident speech. They have just turned, or have been turned out from an oyster-room. They are all three very drunk, have on each other's hats, and one of them has a quantity of dressed lobster in his cravat.

These promising gentlemen are 'out on the spree.' The doors of the flash public-houses and oyster-rooms are letting out similar detachments of choice spirits all down the Haymarket ; some of a most patrician sort, with most fierce moustachios and whiskers ; whom I think I have seen before, and whom I may very probably see again, in jackboots and golden aiguillettes, prancing on huge black horses by the side of Her Majesty's carriage, going to open Parliament. The gentlemen, or rather gents on the 'spree,' call this 'life.' They will probably sleep in the station-house this morning, and will be fined various sums for riotous conduct. They will get drunk, I dare say, three hundred times in the course of a year, for about three years. In the last-mentioned space of time they will bonnet many dozen policemen, break some hundreds of gas-lamps, have some hundreds of 'larks,' and scores of 'rows.' They will go to Epsom by the rail, and create disturbances on the course, and among the 'sticks,' and 'Aunt Sallies.' They will frequent the Adelphi at half-price, and haunt night-houses afterwards. They will spend their salaries in debauchery, and obtain fresh supplies of money from bill-discounters, and be swindled out of it by the proprietors of gambling-houses. Some day, when their health and their money are gone—when they are sued on all their bills, and by all the tradesmen they have plundered—they will be discharged from their situations, or be discarded by their friends. Then they will subside into Whitecross Street and the Insolvent Debtors' Court—and then, God knows! they will die miserably, I suppose: of delirium tremens, maybe.

I have taken a fancy to have a stroll—save the mark!—in St. James's Park, and am about to descend the huge flight of stone steps leading to the Mall, when I encounter a martial band, consisting of a grenadier in a great-coat, and holding a lighted lantern (it is light as noon-day), an officer in a cloak, and four or five more grenadiers in great-coats, looking remarkably ridiculous in those hideous gray garments. As to the officer, he appears to regard everything with an air of unmitigated disgust, and to look at the duty upon which he is engaged as a special bore. I regard it rather in the light of a farce. Yet, if I mistake not, these are 'Grand Rounds,' or something of the sort. When the officer gets within a few yards of the sentinel at the Duke of York's Column he shouts out some unintelligible question, to which the bearer of Brown Bess gives a responsive, but as unintelligible howl. Then the foremost grenadier plays in an imbecile manner with his lantern, like King Lear with his straw, and the officer flourishes his sword; and 'Grand Rounds' are over, so far as the Duke of York is concerned, I suppose; for the whole party trot gravely down Pall Mall, towards the Duchess of Kent's.

I leave them to their devices, and saunter moodily into the Mall. It is but a quarter to five now; and I am so jaded and tired that I can scarcely drag one foot after another. The rain has ceased; but the morning air is raw and cold; and the rawness clings, as it were, to the marrow of my bones. My hair is wet, and falls in draggled hanks on my cheeks. My feet seem to have grown preposterously large, and my boots so preposterously small. I wish I were a dog or a dormouse! I long for a haystack, or a heap of sacks, or anything. I even think I could find repose on one of those terribly inclined planes which you see tilted towards you through the window of the Morgue at

Paris. I have a good mind to smash a lamp, and be taken to the station-house. I have a good mind to throw myself over Westminster Bridge. I suppose I am afraid; for I don't do either.

Seeing a bench under a tree, I fling myself thereon; and, hard and full of knots and bumps as the seat is, roll myself into a species of ball, and strive to go to sleep. But oh, vain delusion! I am horribly, excruciatingly wakeful. To make the matter worse, I rise, and take a turn or two—*then* I feel as though I could sleep standing; but availing myself of what I consider a favourably drowsy moment, I cast myself on the bench again, and find myself as wakeful as before!

There is a young vagrant—a tramp of some eighteen summers—sitting beside me—fast asleep, and snoring with provoking pertinacity. He is half naked, and has neither shoes nor stockings. Yet he sleeps, and very soundly, too, to all appearance. As the loud-sounding Horse-Guards clock strikes five, he wakes, eyes me for a moment, and muttering 'hard lines, mate,' turns to sleep again. In the mysterious freemasonry of misery, he calls me 'mate.' I suppose, eventually, that I catch from him some portion of his vagrant acquirement of somnolence under difficulties, for, after writhing and turning on the comfortless wooden seat till every bone and muscle are sore, I fall into a deep, deep sleep—so deep it seems like death.

So deep that I don't hear the quarters striking of that nuisance to Park-sleepers, the Horse-Guards clock—and rise only, suddenly *en sursaut*, as six o'clock strikes. My vagrant friend has departed, and being apprehensive myself of cross-examination from an approaching policeman (not knowing, in fact, what hideous crime sleeping in St. James's Park might be), I also withdrew, feeling very fagged and footsore—yet slightly refreshed by the hour's nap I have had. I pass the stands where the cows are milked, and curds and whey dispensed, on summer evenings; and enter Charing Cross by the long Spring Garden passage.

I have been apprised several times during the night that this was a market-morning in Covent Garden. I have seen waggons surmounted by enormous mountains of vegetable-baskets wending their way through the silent streets. I have been met by the early costermongers in their donkey-carts, and chaffed by the costerboys on my forlorn appearance. But I have reserved Covent Garden as a *bonne bouche*—a wind-up to my pilgrimage; for I have heard and read how fertile is the

market in question in subjects of amusement and contemplation.

I confess that I am disappointed. Covent Garden seems to
me to be but one great accumulation of cabbages. I am pelted
with these vegetables as they are thrown from the lofty
summits of piled waggons to costermongers standing at the
base. I stumble among them as I walk; in short, above,
below, on either side, cabbages preponderate.

I dare say, had I patience, that I should see a great deal
more; but I am dazed with cabbages, and jostled to and fro,
and 'danged' dreadfully by rude market-gardeners—so I
eschew the market, and creep round the piazza.

I meet my vagrant friend of the Park here, who is having a
cheap and nutritious breakfast at a coffee-stall. The stall
itself is a nondescript species of edifice—something between
a gipsy's tent and a watchman's box: while, to carry out the
comparison, as it were, the lady who serves out the coffee very
much resembles a gipsy in person, and is clad in a decided
watchman's coat. The aromatic beverage (if I may be allowed
to give that name to the compound of burnt beans, roasted
horse-liver, and refuse chicory, of which the 'coffee' is composed) is poured, boiling hot, from a very cabalistic-looking
caldron into a whole regiment of cups and saucers standing
near; while, for more solid refection, the cups are flanked by
plates bearing massive piles of thick bread and butter, and an
equivocal substance called 'cake.' Besides my friend the
vagrant, two coster-lads are partaking of the hospitalities of
the *café;* and a huge gardener, straddling over a pile of
potato-sacks, hard by, has provided himself with bread and
butter and coffee, from the same establishment, and is consuming them with such avidity that the tears start from his
eyes at every gulp.

I have, meanwhile, remembered the existence of a certain
fourpenny-piece in my pocket, and have been twice or thrice
tempted to expend it. Yet, on reflection, I deem it better to
purchase with it a regular breakfast, and repair to a legitimate coffee-shop. The day is by this time getting rapidly on,
and something of the roar of London begins to be heard in
earnest. The dull murmur of wheels has never ceased, indeed,
the whole night through; but now, laden cabs come tearing
past on their way to the railway station. The night policemen gradually disappear, and sleepy potboys now gradually
appear, yawning at the doors of public-houses—sleepy wait-
resses at the doors of coffee-houses and reading-room. There

have been both public-houses and coffee-shops open, however,
the whole night. The 'Mohawks' Arms' in the market never
closes. Young Lord Stultus, with Captain Asinus of the
Heavies, endeavoured to turn on all the taps there at four
o'clock this morning, but at the earnest desire of Frume, the
landlord, desisted ; and subsequently subsided into a chivalrous
offer of standing glasses of 'Old Tom' all round, which was as
chivalrously accepted. As the 'all round' comprised some
thirty ladies and gentlemen, Frume made a very good thing
of it ; and, like a prudent tradesman as he is, he still further
acted on the golden opportunity, by giving all those members
of the company (about three-fourths) who were drunk, glasses
of water instead of gin ; which operation contributed to dis-
courage intemperance, and improve his own exchequer in a
very signal and efficacious manner. As with the 'Mohawks'
Arms,' so with the 'Turpin's Head,' the great market-
gardeners' house, and the 'Pipe and Horse Collar,' frequented
by the night cabmen—to say nothing of that remarkably snug
little house near Drury Lane, 'The Blue Bludgeon,' which is
well known to be the rendezvous of the famous Tom Thug
and his gang, whose achievements in the strangling line, by
means of a silk handkerchief and a life-preserver, used *tour-
niquet* fashion, were so generally admired by the consistent
advocates of the ticket-of-leave system. I peep into some of
these noted hostelries as I saunter about. They begin to
grow rather quiet and demure as the day advances, and will
be till midnight, indeed, very dull and drowsy pothouses, as
times go. They don't light up to life, and jollity, and robbery,
and violence before the small hours.

So with the coffee-shops. The one I enter, to invest my
fourpence in a breakfast of coffee and bread and butter, has
been open all night likewise ; but the sole occupants now are
a dirty waiter, in a pitiable state of drowsiness, and half a
dozen homeless wretches who have earned the privilege of
sitting down at the filthy tables by the purchase of a cup of
coffee, and, with their heads on their hands, are snatching
furtive naps, cut short—too short, alas !—by the pokes and
'Wake up, there !' of the waiter. It is apparently his *consigne*
to allow no sleeping.

I sit down here, and endeavour to keep myself awake over
the columns of the 'Sun' newspaper of last Tuesday week—
unsuccessfully, however. I am so jaded and weary, so dog-
tired and utterly worn out, that I fall off again to sleep ; and
whether it is that the waiter has gone to sleep too, or that

the expenditure of fourpence secures exemption for me, I am allowed to slumber.

I dream this time. A dreadful vision it is, of bugs, and cabbages, and tramping soldiers, and anon of the fire at the pickle-shop. As I wake, and find to my great joy, that it is ten minutes past eight o'clock, a ragged little news-boy brings in a damp copy of the 'Times,' and I see half a column in that journal headed 'Dreadful Conflagration in Soho.'

Were I not so tired, I should moralize over this, no doubt; but there are now but two things on my mind—two things in the world for me—HOME and BED. Eight o'clock restores these both to me—so cruelly deprived of them for so long a time. So, just as London—work-away, steady-going London—begins to bestir itself, I hurry across the Strand, cross the shadow of the first omnibus going towards the Bank; and, as I sink between the sheets of MY BED, resign the key of the street into the hands of its proper custodian, whoever he may be—and, whoever he may be, I don't envy him.

II.

GETTING UP A PANTOMIME.

CHRISTMAS is coming. Cold weather, snow in the streets, mince-pies, and our little boys and girls home for the holidays. Kind-hearted people's donations for the poor-boxes. Turkeys from the country; Goose Clubs in town; plums and candied citron in the windows of the grocers' shops; hot elder wine; snap-dragon; hunt the slipper; and the butchers' and bakers' quarterly bills. The great Anniversary of Humanity gives signs of its approach, and with it the joyfulness, and unbending, and unstarching of white neckcloths, and unaffected charity, and genial hand-shaking and good fellowship, which, once a year at least, dispel the fog of caste and prejudice in this land of England. Christmas is coming, and, in his jovial train come also the Pantomimes.

Goodness! though we know their stories all by heart, how we love those same pantomimes still! Though we have seen the same Clowns steal the same sausages, and have been asked by the Pantaloon 'how we were to-morrow?' for years and years, how we delight in the same Clown and Pantaloon still! There can't be anything æsthetic in a pantomime—it must be deficient in the 'unities;' it has no 'epopœa,' or anything in the shape of dramatic property, connected with it: yet it must have something good about it to make us roar at the old, old jokes, and wonder at the old tricks, and be delighted with the old spangled fairies, and coloured fires. Perhaps there may be something in the festive season, something contagious in the wintry jollity of the year, that causes us, churchwardens, householders, hard men of business, that we may be, to forget parochial squabbles, taxes and water-rates, discount and agiotage, for hours, and enter, heart and soul, into participation and appreciation of the mysteries of ' Harlequin Fee-fo-fum ; or the Enchanted Fairy of the Island of Abracadabra.' Possibly there may be something in the shrill laughter, the ecstatic hand-clapping, the shouts of triumphant laughter of the little children, yonder. It may be, after all, that the sausages and the spangles, the tricks and coloured fires of Harlequin Fee-fo-fum may strike some long-forgotten chords ; rummage up long-hidden sympathies ; wake up kindly feelings and remembrances of things that were, ere parochial squabbles, water-rates, and discount had being ; when we too were little children ; when our jackets buttoned over our trousers, and we wore frills round our necks, and long blue sashes round our waists. Else why should something like a wateriness in the eye, and a huskiness in the throat (not sorrowful, though) come over us, amid the most excruciatingly comic portion of the ' comic business '? Else why should the lights, and the music, the children's laughter, and the spangled fairies conjure up that mind-picture, half dim and half distinct, of *our* Christmasses years ago ; of ' Magnall's Questions,' and emancipation from the cane of grandmamma, who always kept sweetstuff in her pockets ; of Uncle William, who was never without a store of half-crowns wherewith to ' tip ' us ; of poor Sister Gussey, who died ; of the childish joys and griefs, the hopes and fears of Christmas, in the year eighteen hundred and——; never mind how many.

Hip, hip, hip ! for the Pantomime, however ! Exultingly watch the Clown through his nefarious career ; roar at Jackpudding tumbling ; admire the paint on his face ; marvel at the ' halls of splendour ' and ' glittering coral caves of the Genius of the Sea,' till midnight comes, and the green baize curtain rolls slowly down, and brown holland draperies cover the ormolu decorations of the boxes. Then, if you can spare half an hour, send the little children home to Brompton with the best of governesses, and tarry a while with me while I discourse of what goes on behind that same green curtain, of what has gone on, before the Clown could steal his sausages, or the spangled Fairy change an oak into a magic temple, or the coloured fires light up the 'Home of Beauty in the Lake of the Silver Swans.' Let me, as briefly and succinctly as I can, endeavour to give you an idea of the immense labour, and industry, and perseverance—of the nice ingenuity, and patient mechanical skill—of the various knowledge, necessary, nay, indispensable—ere Harlequin Fee-fo-fum can be put upon the stage ; ere the green baize can rise disclosing the coral caves of the Genius of the Sea. Let us put on the cap of Fortunio, and the stilts of Asmodeus ; let us go back to when the pantomime was but an embryo of comicality, and, in its progress towards the glory of full-blown pantomime-hood, watch the labours of the Ants behind the Baize—ants, without exaggeration ; for, if ever there was a human ant-hill, the working department of a theatre is something of that sort.

And mere amusement—your mere enlightenment on a subject, of which my readers may possibly be ignorant, are not the sole objects I have in view. I do honestly think that the theatrical profession and its professors are somewhat calumniated ; that people are rather too apt to call theatres sinks of iniquity and dens of depravity, and to set down all actors as a species of diverting vagabonds, who have acquired a knowledge of their calling without study, and exercise it without labour. I imagine, that if a little more were known of how hard-working, industrious, and persevering theatricals, as a body, generally are,—of what has to be done behind the scenes of a theatre, and how it is done for our amusement,—we should look upon the drama with a more favourable eye, and look upon even poor Jack-pudding (when he has washed the paint off his face) with a little more charity and forbearance.

Fortunio-capped, then, we stand in the green-room of the Theatre Royal, Hatton Garden, one dark November morning, while the stage-manager reads the manuscript of the opening to the new grand pantomime of Harlequin Fee-fo-fum. The dramatic performers—the pantomimists are not present at this reading, the lecture being preliminary, and intended for the sole behoof of the working ants of the theatrical ant-hill—the fighting ants will have another reading to themselves. This morning are assembled the scene-painter, an individual bespattered from head to foot with splashes of various colours, attired in a painted, ragged blouse, a battered cap, and slipshod slippers. You would be rather surprised to see him turn out, when his work is over, dressed like a gentleman (as he is, and an accomplished gentleman to boot). Near him is the property-man, also painted and bespattered, and strongly perfumed with a mingled odour of glue and turpentine. Then there is the carpenter, who twirls a wide-awake hat between his fingers, and whose attire generally betrays an embroidery of shavings. The leader of the band is present. On the edge of a chair sits the author—not necessarily a seedy man, with long hair and a manuscript peeping out of his coat pocket, but a well-to-do looking gentleman, probably; with rather a nervous air just now, and wincing somewhat, as the droning voice of the stage-manager gives utterance to his comic combinations, and his creamiest jokes are met with immovable stolidity from the persons present. Catch them laughing! The scene-painter is thinking of 'heavy sets' and 'cut cloths,' instead of quips and conundrums. The carpenter cogitates on 'sinks' and 'slides,' 'strikes' and 'pulls.' The property-man ponders ruefully on the immense number of comic masks to model, and coral branches to paint; while the master and mistress of the wardrobe, whom we have hitherto omitted to mention, mentally cast up the number of ells of glazed calico, silk, satin, and velvet required. Lastly, enthroned in awful magnificence in some dim corner, sits the management—a portly, port-wine-voiced management, maybe, with a white hat, and a double eye-glass with a broad ribbon. This incarnation of theatrical power throws in an occasional 'Good!' at which the author colours, and sings a mental pœan, varied by an ejaculation of 'Can't be done!'—at which the dramatist winces dreadfully.

The reading over, a short, desultory conversation follows. It would be better, Mr. Brush, the painter, suggests, to make the first scene a 'close in,' and not a 'sink.' Mr. Tacks, the carpenter—machinist, we mean—intimates in a somewhat threatening manner, that he shall want a 'power of nails and screws;' while the master of the wardrobe repudiates, with respectful indignation, an economical suggestion of the management touching the renovation of some old ballet dresses by means of new spangles, and the propriety of cutting up an old crimson velvet curtain, used some years before, into costumes for the supernumeraries. As to the leader of the band, he is slowly humming over a very 'Little Warbler' of popular airs, which he thinks he can introduce; while the stage-manager, pencil in hand, fights amicably with the author as to the cuts necessary to make the pantomime read with greater smartness. All, however, agree that it will do ; and to each working ant is delivered a 'plot' of what he or she has to manufacture by a given time (generally a month or six weeks from the day of reading). Mr. Brush has a 'plot' of so many pairs of flats and wings, so many 'borders' and set pieces, so many cloths and backings. Mr. Tacks has a similar one, as it is his department to prepare the canvasses and machinery on which Mr. Brush subsequently paints. Mr. Tagg, the wardrobe keeper, is provided with a list of the fairies,' demons', kings', guards', and slaves' costumes he is required to *confectionner ;* and Mr. Rosin, the leader, is presented with a complete copy of the pantomime itself, in order that he may study its principal points, and arrange characteristic music for it. As for poor Mr. Gorget, the property-man, he departs in a state of pitiable bewilderment, holding in his hand a por- tentous list of properties required, from regal crowns to red- hot pokers. He impetuously demands how it's all to be done in a month. Done, it will be, notwithstanding. The stage- manager departs in a hurry (in which stage-managers generally are, twenty hours out of the twenty-four), and, entrapping the Clown in the passage (who is an eccentric character of immense comic abilities, and distinguished for training all sorts of animals, from the goose which follows him like a dog, to a jackass-foal which resides in his sitting-room), enters into an animated pantomimic conversation with him, discoursing espe- cially of the immense number of ' bits of fat ' for him (Clown) in the pantomime.

The author's name we need not mention ; it will appear in the bill, as it has appeared in (and across) many bills, stamped and unstamped, before. When the officials have retired, he remains a while with the management—the subject of con- versation mainly relating to a piece of gray paper, addressed to Messrs. Coutts, Drummonds, or Childs.

For the next few days, though work has not actually commenced in all its vigour, great preparations are made. Forests of timber, so to speak, are brought in at the stage door. Also, bales of canvas, huge quantities of stuffs for the wardrobe ; foil-paper, spangles and Dutch metal, generally. Firkins of size, and barrels of whiting, arrive for Mr. Brush ; hundred-weights of glue and gold-leaf for Mr. Gorget, not for- getting the ' power of nails and screws ' for Mr. Tacks. An- other day, and the ants are all at work behind the baize for Harlequin Fee-fo-fum.

Fortunio's cap will stand us in good stead again, and we

had better attach ourselves to the skirts of the stage-manager, who is here, there, and everywhere, to see that the work is being properly proceeded with. The carpenters have been at work since six o'clock this nice wintry morning : let us see how they are getting on after breakfast.

We cross the darkened stage, and, ascending a very narrow staircase at the back thereof, mount into the lower range of 'flies.' A mixture this of the between-decks of a ship, a rope-walk, and the old wood-work of the Chain-pier at Brighton. Here are windlasses, capstans, ropes, cables, chains, pulleys innumerable. Take care ! or you will stumble across the species of winnowing-machine, used to imitate the noise of wind, and which is close to the large sheet of copper which makes the thunder. The tin cylinder, filled with peas, used for rain and hail, is down stairs : but you may see the wires, or 'travellers,' used by 'flying fairies,' and the huge counterweights and lines which work the curtain and act-drop. Up then, again, by a ladder, into range of flies, No. 2, where there are more pulleys, windlasses, and counterweights, with bridges crossing the stage, and lines working the borders, and gas-pipes, with coloured screens, called 'mediums,' which are used to throw a lurid light of a moonlight on scenes of battles or conflagrations, where the employment of coloured fires is not desirable. Another ladder (a rope one this time) has still to be climbed : and now we find our-selves close to the roof of the theatre, and in the Carpenter's Shop.

Such a noise of sawing and chopping, hammering and chiselling ! The shop is a large one, its size corresponding to the area of the stage beneath. Twenty or thirty men are at work, putting together the framework of 'flats,' and covering the framework itself with canvas. Some are constructing the long cylinders, or rollers, used for 'drops,' or 'cloths ;' while others, on their knees, are busily following with a hand-saw the outline of a rock, or tree, marked in red lead by the scene-painter or profile (thin wood) required for a set piece. Mr. Tacks is in his glory, with his 'power of nails and screws' around him. He pounces on the official immediately. He must have 'more nails,' more 'hands ;' spreading out his own emphatically. Give him 'hands !' The stage-manager paci-fies and promises. Stand by, there, while four brawny car-penters rush from another portion of the 'shop' with the 'Pagoda of Arabian Delights,' dimly looking through canvas and whitewash !

A curious race of men these theatrical carpenters. Some of them growl scraps of Italian operas, or melodramatic music, as they work. They are full of traditional lore anent the 'Lane' and the 'Garden' in days of yore. Probably their fathers and grandfathers were theatrical before them; for it is rare to find a carpenter of ordinary life at stage work, or *vice versâ*. Malignant members of the ordinary trade whisper even that their work never lasts, and is only fit for the ideal carpentry of a theatre. There is a legend, also, that a stage-carpenter being employed once to make a coffin, constructed it after the Hamlet manner, and ornamented it with scroll-work. They preserve admirable discipline, and obey the master carpenter implicitly; but, work once over, and out of the theatre, he is no more than one of themselves, and takes beer with Tom or Bill, and the chair at their committee and sick-club *réunions*, in a perfectly republican and fraternal manner. These men labour from six in the morning until six in the evening; and, probably, as Fee-fo-fum is a 'heavy pantomime,' from seven until the close of the performances. At night, when the gas battens below the flies are all lighted, the heat is somewhat oppressive : and, if you lie on your face on the floor, and gaze through the chinks of the planking, you will hear the music in the orchestra, and catch an occasional glimpse of the performers on the stage beneath, marvellously foreshortened, and microscopically diminished. The morning we pay our visit, a rehearsal is going on below, and a hoarse command is wafted from the stage to 'stop that hammering' while Marc Antony is pronouncing his oration over the dead body of Cæsar. The stage-manager, of course, is now wanted down stairs, and departs, with an oft-iterated injunction to 'get on.' We, too, must 'get on' without him.

We enter another carpenter's shop, smaller, but on the same level, and occupying a space above the horse-shoe ceiling of the audience part of the theatre. A sort of martello of wood occupies the centre of this apartment, its summit going through the roof. This is at once the ventilator, and the 'chandelier house' of the theatre. If we open a small door, we can descry, as our eyes become accustomed to the semi-darkness, that it is floored with iron, in ornamented scroll-work, and opening with a hinged trap. We can also see the ropes and pulleys, to which are suspended the great centre chandelier, and by which it is hauled up every Monday morning to be cleaned. More carpenters are busily at work, at bench and trestles, sawing, gluing, hammering. Hark!

we hear a noise like an eight-day clock on a gigantic scale running down. They are letting down a pair of flats in the painting-room. Let us see what they are about in the painting-room itself.

Pushing aside a door, for ever on the swing, we enter an apartment, somewhat narrow, its length considered, but very lofty. Half the roof, at least, is skylight. A longitudinal aperture in the flooring traverses the room close to the wall. This is the 'cut,' or groove, half a foot wide, and seventy feet in depth, perhaps, in which hangs a screen of wood-work, called a 'frame.' On this frame the scene to be painted is placed : and, by means of a counterweight and a windlass, is worked up and down the cut, as the painter may require ; the sky being thus as convenient to his hand, as the lowest stone or bit of foliage in the foreground. When the scene is finished, a signal is given to 'stand clear' below, and a bar in the windlass being removed, the frame slides with immense celerity down the cut to the level of the stage. Here the carpenters remove the flats, or wings, or whatever else may have been painted, and the empty frame is wound up again into the painting-room. Sometimes, instead of a cut, a 'bridge' is used. In this case the scene itself remains stationary, and the painter stands on a platform, which is wound up and down by a windlass as he may require it—a ladder being placed against the bridge if he wishes to descend without shifting the position of his platform. When the scene is finished, a trap is opened in the floor, and the scene slung by ropes to the bottom. The 'cut' and frame are, it is needless to say, most convenient, the artist being always able to contemplate the full effect of his work, and to provide himself with what colours, or sketches, he may need, without the trouble of ascending and descending the ladder.

Mr. Brush, more bespattered than ever, with a 'double tie' brush in his hand, is knocking the colour about bravely. Five or six good men and true, his assistants, are also employed on the scene he is painting—the fairy palace of Fee-fo-fum, perchance. One is seated at a table, with something very like the toy theatres of our younger days, on which we used to enact that wonderful 'Miller and his Men,' with the famous characters (always in one fierce attitude of triumphant defiance, we remember) of Mr. Park before him. It is, in reality, a model of the stage itself ; and the little bits of pasteboard he is cutting out and pasting together form portions of a scene he is modelling 'to scale' for the future guidance of the carpenter. Another is fluting columns with a thin brush called a 'quill tool,' and a long ruler, or 'straight-edge.' Different portions of the scene are allotted to different artists, according to their competence, from Mr. Brush, who finishes and touches up everything, down to the fustian-jacketed whitewasher, who is 'priming' or giving a preparatory coat of whiting and size to a pair of wings.

Are you at all curious to know how the brilliant scenes you see at night are painted; you may watch the whole process of a pair of flats growing into a beautiful picture, under Mr. Brush's experienced hands. First, the scene, well primed, and looking like a gigantic sheet of coarse cartridge-paper on a stretcher, is placed on the frame; then, with a long pole, cleft at the end, and in which is stuck a piece of charcoal, Mr. Brush hastily scrawls (as it seems) the outline of the scene he is about to paint. Then, he and his assistants 'draw in' a finished outline with a small brush and common ink, which, darkening as it dries, allows the outline to shine through the first layers of colour. Then, the whitewasher, 'labourer,' as he is technically called, is summoned to 'lay in' the great masses of colour—sky, wall, foreground, &c., which he does with huge brushes. Then, the shadows are 'picked in' by assistants, to whom enters speedily Mr. Brush, with a sketch in one hand, and brushes in the other, and he finishes—finishes, too, with a delicacy of manipulation and nicety of touch which will rather surprise you—previously impressed as you may have been with an idea that scenes are painted with mops, and that scenic artists are a superior class of house-painters. Stay, here is the straight line of a cornice to be ruled from one part of the scene to the other, a space fifty feet wide, perhaps. Two labourers, one at either end, hold a string tightly across where the desired line is to be. The string has been well rubbed with powdered charcoal, and, being held up in some part, for a moment, between the thumb and finger, and then smartly vibrated on to the canvas, again leaves a mark of black charcoal along the whole length of the line, which being followed by the brush and ink, serves for the guide line of the cornice. Again, the wall of that magnificent saloon has to be covered with an elaborate scroll-work pattern. Is all this out-lined by the hand, think you? No; a sheet of brown paper, perforated with pin-holes with a portion of the desired pattern, is laid against the scene; the whole is then gently beaten with a worsted bag full of powdered charcoal, which, penetrating through the pin-holes, leaves a dotted outline, capable of repetition *ad infinitum* by shifting the pattern. This is called 'pouncing.' Then some of the outlines of decoration are 'stencilled;' but for foliage and rocks, flowers and water, I need not tell you, my artistical friend, that the hand of Mr. Brush is the only pouncer and stenciller. For so grand a pantomime as 'Fee-fo-fum,' a scene will, probably, after artistic completion, be enriched with foil paper and Dutch metal. Admire the celerity with which these processes are effected. First, an assistant cuts the foil in narrow strips with a penknife; another catches them up like magic, and glues them; another claps them on the canvas, and the scene is foiled. Then Mr. Brush advances with a pot, having a lamp beneath, filled with a composition of Burgundy pitch, rosin, glue, and bees-wax, called 'mordant.' With this and a camel-hair brush, he delicately outlines the parts he wishes gilt. Half a dozen assistants rush forward with books of Dutch metal, and three-fourths of the scene are covered, in a trice, with squares of glittering dross. The superfluous particles are rubbed off with a dry brush, and, amid a very Danaëan shower of golden particles, the outlines of mordant, to which the metal has adhered, become gradually apparent in a glittering net-work.

Around this chamber of the arts are hung pounces and stencils, like the brown-paper patterns in a tailor's shop. There is a ledge running along one side of the room, on which is placed a long row of pots filled with the colours used, which are ground in water, and subsequently tempered with size, a huge caldron of which is now simmering over the roomy fireplace. The colour-grinder himself stands before a table, supporting an ample stone slab, on which, with a marble muller, he is grinding Dutch pink lustily. The painter's palette is not the oval one used by picture painters, but a downright four-legged table, the edges of which are divided into compartments, each holding its separate dab of colour, while the centre serves as a space whereon to mix and graduate the tints. The whitewashed walls are scrawled over with rough sketches and memoranda, in charcoal or red lead, while a choice engraving, here and there, a box of water-colours, some delicate flowers in a glass, some velvet drapery pinned against the wall, hint that in this timber-roofed, un-papered, uncarpeted, size-and-whitewash-smelling workshop, there is Art as well as Industry.

Though it is only of late years, mind you, that scene-

painters have been recognised as Artists at all. They were
called 'daubers,' 'whitewashers,' 'paper-hangers,' by that
class of artists to whom the velvet cap, the turn-down collars,
and the ormolu frame, were as the air they breathed. These
last were the gentlemen who thought it beneath the dignity
of Art to make designs for wood-engravers, to paint porcelain,
to draw patterns for silk manufacturers. Gradually they
found out that the scene-painters made better architects, landscape painters, professors of perspective, than they themselves
did. Gradually they remembered that in days gone by, such
men as Salvator Rosa, Inigo Jones, Canaletto, and Philip de
Loutherbourg were scene-painters ; and that, in our own times,
one Stanfield had not disdained size and whitewash, nor a
certain Roberts thought it derogatory to wield the 'double
tie' brush. Scene-painting thenceforward looked up ; and even
the heavy portals of the Academy moved creakingly on their
hinges for the admittance of distinguished professors of scenic
art.

We have been hindering Mr. Brush quite long enough, I
think, even though we are invisible; so let us descend this
crazy ladder, which leads from the painting-room down
another flight of stairs. So : keep your hands out before you,
and tread cautiously, for the management is chary of gas, and
the place is pitch dark. Now, as I open this door, shade your
eyes with your hand a moment, lest the sudden glare of light
dazzle you.

This is the 'property-room.' In this vast, long, low room,
are manufactured the 'properties'—all the stage furniture and
paraphernalia required during the performance of a play.
Look around you, and wonder. The walls and ceiling are
hung, the floor and tables cumbered with properties :—
Shylock's knife and scales, Ophelia's coffin, Paul Pry's umbrella, Macbeth's truncheon, the caldron of the Witches, Harlequin's bat, the sickle of Norma, Mambrino's helmet, swords,
lanterns, banners, belts, hats, daggers, wooden sirloins of beef,
Louis Quatorze chairs, papier-mâché goblets, pantomime
masks, stage money, whips, spears, lutes, flasks of 'rich burgundy,' fruit, rattles, fish, plaster images, drums, cocked hats,
spurs, and bugle-horns, are strewn about, without the slightest
attempt at arrangement or classification. Tilted against the
wall, on one end, is a four-legged banqueting table, very
grand indeed,—white marble top and golden legs. At this
table will noble knights and ladies feast richly off wooden
fowls and brown-paper pies, quaffing, meanwhile, deep pota-

tions of toast-and-water sherry, or, haply, golden goblets full of nothing at all. Some of the goblets, together with elaborate flasks of exhilarating emptiness, and dishes of rich fruit, more deceptive than Dead Sea apples (for they have not even got ashes inside them), are nailed to the festive board itself. On very great occasions the bowl is wreathed with cotton wool, and the viands smoke with a cloud of powdered lime. Dreadfully deceptive are these stage banquets and stage purses. The haughty Hospodar of Hungary drinks confusion to the Bold Bandit of Bulgaria in a liquorless cup, vainly thirsting, meanwhile, for a pint of mild porter from the adjacent hostelry. Deep are his retainers in the enjoyment of Warden pies and lusty capons, while their too often empty interiors cry dolorously for three penn'orth of cold boiled beef. Liberal is he also of broad florins, and purses of moidores, accidentally drawing, perchance, at the same time, a Lombardian debenture for his boots from the breast of his doublets. The meat is a sham, and the wine a sham, and the money a sham; but are there no other shams, oh, brothers and sisters! besides those of the footlights? Have I not dined with my legs under sham mahogany, illuminated by sham wax-lights? Has not a sham hostess helped me to sham boiled turkey? Has not my sham health been drunk by sham friends? Do I know no haughty Hospodar of Hungary myself?

There is one piece, and one piece only, on the stage, in which a real banquet—a genuine spread—is provided. That piece is 'No Song, No Supper.' However small may be the theatre—however low the state of the finances—the immemorial tradition is respected, and *a real leg of mutton* graces the board. Once, the chronicle goes, there was a heartless monster, in property-man shape, who substituted a dish of mutton chops for the historical *gigot*. Execration, abhorrence, expulsion followed his iniquitous fraud, and he was, from that day, a property-man accursed. Curiously enough, while the leg of mutton in 'No Song, No Supper,' is always real, the cake, introduced in the same piece, is as invariably a counterfeit —the old stock wooden cake of the theatre. When it shall be known why waiters wear white neckcloths, and dustmen shorts and ankle jacks, the proximate cause of this discrepancy will, perhaps, be pointed out.

To return to the property-room of the Theatre Royal, Hatton Garden. Mr. Gorget, the property 'master,' as he is called, is working with almost delirious industry. He has an imperial crown on his head (recently gilt—the crown, not the head—and placed there to dry), while on the table before him lies a mass of modelling clay, on which his nimble fingers are shaping out the matrix of a monstrous human face, for a pantomimic mask. How quickly, and with what facility he moulds the hideous physiognomy into shape—squeezing the eyelids, flattening the nose, elongating the mouth, furrowing the cheeks! When this clay model is finished, it will be well oiled, and a cast taken from it in plaster of Paris. Into this cast (oiled again) strips of brown paper, well glued and sized, will be pasted, till a proper thickness is obtained. When dry, the cast is removed, and the hardened paper mask ready for colouring. At this latter process, an assistant, whose nose and cheeks are plentifully enriched with Dutch metal and splashes of glue, is at work. He is very liberal with rose pink to the noses, black to the eyebrows, and white to the eye. Then Mrs. Gorget, a mild little woman, who has been assiduously spangling a demon's helmet, proceeds to ornament the masks with huge masses of oakum and horsehair, red, brown, and black, which are destined to serve as their coiffure. Busily other assistants are painting tables, gilding goblets, and manufacturing the multifarious and bewildering miscellaneous articles required in the 'comic business' of a pantomime; the sausages which the Clown purloins, the bustle he takes from the young lady, the fish, eggs, poultry, warming-pans, babies, pint pots, butchers' trays, and legs of mutton, incidental to his chequered career.

Others besides adults are useful in the property-room. A bright-eyed little girl, Mr. Gorget's youngest, is gravely speckling a plum-pudding; while her brother, a stalwart rogue of eleven, sits on a stool with a pot full of yellow ochre in one hand, and a brush in the other, with which he is giving a plentiful coat of bright yellow colour to a row containing a dozen pairs of hunting-boots. These articles of costume will gleam to-night on the legs and feet of the huntsmen of his highness the Hospodar, with whom you are already acquainted. Their wearers will stamp their soles on the merry green sward—ha, ha!—waving above their heads the tin porringers, supposed to contain Rhine wine or Baerische beer.

Mr. Gorget will have no easy task for the next three weeks. He will have to be up early and late until 'Fee-fo-fum' is produced. The nightly performances have, meanwhile, to be attended to, and any new properties wanted must be made, and any old ones spoilt must be replaced, in addition to what is required for the pantomime. And something more than common abilities must have abiding place in a property-man, although he does not receive uncommonly liberal remuneration. He must be a decent upholsterer, a carpenter, a wig-maker, a painter, a decorator, accurate as regards historical property, a skilful modeller, a facile carver, a tasteful embroiderer, a general handy man and jack-of-all-trades. He must know something of pyrotechnics, a good deal of carving and gilding, and a little of mechanics. By the exercise of all these arts he earns, perhaps, fifty shillings a week.

Come away from the property-room, just a glance into that grim, cavernous, coal-holey place on the left, where all the broken-up, used-out, properties are thrown, and is a sort of limbo of departed pantomimes ; and peeping curiously also into the room, where, on racks and on hooks, are arranged the cuirasses, muskets, swords, spears, and defunct yeomanry helmets, of the pattern worn when George the Third was king, which form the armoury of the theatre. Time presses, and we must have a look at the proceedings in the wardrobe.

Mr. Baster is busily stitching, with many other stitchers (females), sedent, and not squatting Jagod-like, all of a row. His place of work is anything but large, and movement is rendered somewhat inconvenient, moreover, by a number of heavy presses, crammed to repletion with the costumes of the establishment. Mr. Baster has been overhauling his stock, to see what he can conveniently use again, and what must indispensably be new. He has passed in review the crimson velvet nobleman, the green-serge retainers, the spangled courtiers, the glazed-calico slaves, the 'shirts,' 'shapes,' 'Romaldis,' and 'strips' of other days. He has held up to the light last year's Clown's dress, and shakes his head ruefully, when he contemplates the rents and rivings, the rags and tatters, to which that once brilliant costume is reduced. Clown must, evidently, be new all over. Mr. Baster's forewoman is busy spangling Harlequin's patchwork dress ; while, in the hands of his assistants, sprites and genii, slaves and evil spirits, are in various stages of completion. So, in the ladies' wardrobe, where Miss de Loggie and her assistants are stitching for dear life, at Sea-nymphs', and Sirens', and Elfins' costume ; and where Miss Mezzanine, who is to play Columbine, is agonizingly inquisitive as to the fit of her skirt and spangles.

Work, work, work, everywhere ;—in the dull bleak morning, when play-goers of the previous night have scarcely finished their first sleep ; at night to the music of the

orchestra below, and amid the hot glare of the gas. Mr.
Tacks carries screws in his waistcoat pockets, and screws in
his mouth. Mr. Gorget grows absolutely rigid with glue,
while his assistants' heads and hands are unpleasantly enriched with Dutch metal and foil-paper ; and the main staircase of the theatre is blocked up with frantic waiters from
adjoining hostelries laden with chops and stout for Mr. Brush
and his assistants. The Management smiles approvingly,
but winces uneasily, occasionally, as Boxing-day draws
near ; the stage-director is unceasing in his 'get ons.' All
day long the private door of the Management is assailed by
emissaries from Mr. Tacks for more nails, from Mr. Brush for
more Venetian red and burnt sienna, from Mr. Baster for
more velvet, from Mr. Gorget for more glue. The Management moves uneasily in its chair. 'Great expense,' it says,
'If it should fail ?' 'Give us more nails, "hands," Venetian
red, velvet, and glue, and we'll *not* fail,' chorus the ants behind
the baize.

Nor must you suppose that the pantomimists—Clown,
Harlequin, Pantaloon, and Columbine—nor the actors playing
in the opening, nor the fairies who fly, nor the demons who
howl, nor the sprites who tumble, are idle. Every day the
opening and comic scenes are rehearsed. Every day a melancholy man, called the *répétiteur*, takes his station on the stage,
which is illumined by one solitary gas jet ; and, to the dolour-
music he conjures from his fiddle, the pantomimists, in over-
suits of coarse linen, tumble, dance, jump, and perform other
gymnastic exercises in the gloom, until their bones ache, and
the perspiration streams from their limbs.

Work, work, work, and Christmas-eve is here. Nails,
hammers, paint-brushes, needles, muscles and limbs going in
every direction. Mr. Brush has not had his boots cleaned for
a week, and might have forgotten what sheets and counterpanes mean. Mr. Brush's lady in Camden Villa is, of course,
pleased at the artistic fame her lord will gain in the columns
of the newspapers, the day after the production of the pantomimes, but she can't help thinking sometimes that Brush is
'working himself to death.' No man works himself to death,
my dear Mrs. B. 'Tis among the idlers, the turners of the
heavy head, and the folders of the hands to rest, that death
reaps his richest harvest. No snap-dragon for Mr. Tacks, no
hunt-the-slipper for Mr. Gorget. Pleasant Christmas greet-
ings and good wishes, though, and general surmises that the
pantomime will be a 'stunning' one. Christmas-day, and,

alas and alack! no Christmas beef and pudding, save that from the cook-shop, and perchance the spare repast in the covered basin which little Polly Bruggs brings stalwart Bill Bruggs, the carpenter, who is popularly supposed to be able to carry a pair of wings beneath each arm. Incessant fiddling from the *répétiteur*. 'Trip,' 'rally,' and 'jump,' for the pantomimists. Work on the stage, which is covered with canvas, and stooping painters, working with brushes stuck in bamboo walking-sticks. Work in the flies, and work underneath the stage, on the umbrageous mezzonine floor, where the cellar-men are busily slinging 'sinks' and 'rises,' and greasing traps. An overflow of properties deluges the green-room; huge masks leer at you in narrow passages; pantomimic wheelbarrows and barrel-organs beset you at every step. So all Christmas-night.

Hurrah for Boxing-day! The 'compliments of the season,' and the 'original dustman.' Tommy and Billy (suffering slightly from indigestion) stand with their noses glued against the window-panes at home, watching anxiously the rain in the puddles, or the accumulating snow on the house-tops. Little Mary's mind is filled with radiant visions of the resplendent sashes she is to wear, and the gorgeous fairies she is to see. John, the footman, is to escort the housemaid into the pit: even Joe Barrikin, of the New Cut, who sells us our cauliflowers, will treat his 'missus' to a seat in the gallery for the first performance of Harlequin Fee-fo-fum.

There—the last clink of the hammer is heard, the last stroke of the brush, and the last stitch of the needle. The Management glances with anxious approval at the elaborately funny bill—prepared with the assistance of almost every adult employed in the establishment, who is supposed to have a 'funny' notion about him, subject, of course, to the editorial supervision of the author, if he be in town, and the Management can catch him or he catch the Management—of the evening's entertainment. It is six o'clock in the evening. The Clown (Signor Brownarini, of the Theatres Royal) has a jug of barley-water made, his only beverage during his tumbling, and anxiously assures himself that there is a red-hot poker introduced into the comic business; 'else,' says he, 'the pantomime is sure to fail.' Strange, the close connection between the success of a pantomime and that red-hot poker. A pantomime was produced at a London Theatre—the Old Adelphi, I think—without (perhaps through inadvertence) a red-hot poker. The pantomime failed lamentably the first night.

Seven o'clock, and one last frantic push to get everything ready. Tommy, Billy, Mary, Papa and Mamma, arrive in flics, broughams, or cabs. The footman and housemaid are smiling in the pit; and Joe Barrikin is amazingly jolly and thirsty, with his 'missus' in the gallery. Now then, 'Music!' 'Play up!' 'Order, order!' and, 'Throw him over!' 'George Barnwell,' or 'Jane Shore,' inaudible, of course, and *then* 'Harlequin Fec-fo-fum, or the Enchanted Fairy of the Island of Abracadabra.' Fun, frolic, and gaiety; splendour, beauty, and blue fire; hey for fun! 'How are you to-morrow?' and I hope success and crowded houses till the middle of February, both for the sake of the author, the Management, and the Theatre Royal, Hatton Garden, generally.

The ants behind the baize have worked well, but they have their reward in the 'glorious success' of the pantomime they have laboured so hard at. They may wash their faces, and have their boots cleaned now; and who shall say that they do not deserve their beer to-night, and their poor salaries next Saturday?

Reader, as Christmas-time comes on, pause a little ere you utterly condemn these poor play-acting people as utter profligates, as irreclaimable rogues and vagabonds. Consider how hard they work, how precarious is their employment, how honestly they endeavour to earn their living, and to do their duty in the state of life to which it has pleased Heaven to call them. Admit that there is some skill, some industry, some perseverance, in all this, not misdirected, if promoting harmless fancy and innocent mirth.

III.

DOWN WHITECHAPEL, FAR AWAY.

It is natural that a metropolis so gigantic as the Empress-city of Britain should set the fashion to its provincial kinsfolk. It is, I believe, a fact not very much controverted, that London habits, London manners and modes, London notions and London names are extensively copied, followed, and emulated in the provinces. There is scarcely a village, not to say a town, in Great Britain where some worthy tradesman has not baptized his place of business London House, or the London Repository, where he pretends to sell London porter, London hosiery, or London cutlery. There are few **towns**

that do not number among their streets several whose appella-
tions are drawn from the street-lists of the London Post-Office
Directory. Regent Streets, Bond Streets, St. James's Streets,
Pall Malls, Drury Lanes, Strands, Fleet Streets, Ludgate
Hills, Covent Gardens, Cheapsides, and Waterloo Places
abound in great profusion throughout the whole of the United
Kingdom. There is sometimes a ludicrous incongruity
between the appearance, class, and species of streets familiar in
London, and the synonymous street presented in a country
town. A man, for instance, is apt to be puzzled when he
finds a little greasy cube of ill-favoured houses, resembling a
bar of soap just marked for cutting into squares figured down
as Belgrave Place or Wilton Crescent. He will not be
quite prepared to recognise Cheapside in a series of basket-
makers' cottages with small kitchen-gardens; nor will a
dirty thoroughfare, principally occupied by old clothes-
vendors and marine-store-dealers, quite come up to his ideas
of Bond Street or Regent Street. Islington—composed of a
long avenue of merchants' warehouses, each rejoicing in a
plurality of stories, with gaping doors where there should be
windows, and huge cranes from which perpetually balance
sacks of meal or hogsheads of sugar after the manner of
Mahomet's coffin—creates in the mind of the London-bred
Islingtonian a curious dissociation of ideas. And when he
comes upon a Grosvenor Street in the guise of a blind alley,
or upon a Holborn fringed with pretty suburban villas, or a
Piccadilly next to a range of pigsties, or a Fleet Street planted
with flowering shrubs, he cannot fail to doubt whether a street
is still a street 'for a' that.'

These topographical incongruities have lately been brought
under my notice in the great commercial port of Liverpool.
In Liverpool, which can show—its suburbs and dependencies
included—a population not much under four hundred thousand souls, I found Pall Malls, Fleet Streets, Covent Gardens,
Drury Lanes, Houndsditches, Islingtons, and other places, all
with London names, and all with a most opinionated want of
resemblance to their London sponsors. Islington I found to
be not a district, but a single street, the site of several public-
houses, one or two pawnbrokers', and numerous chandlers'
shops. Fleet Street is without bustle, Drury Lane without
dirt, and Covent Garden without an apple or an orange.
Park Lane—the very sound of which is suggestive of curly-
wigged coachmen, high-stepping carriage-horses (jobbed
mostly; but such is life), silver-studded harness, luxurious

carriages hung on feathery springs, ostrich feathers, diamonds, Danish dogs, blue ribbons, the ladies' mile, the Grenadier Guards, and the Duke of Somerset's coronet-tipped gas lamps, the whole pomp, pride, and circumstance of our glorious aristocracy—Park Lane I found to be filled with shops, pavement, and population; and devoted to the vending of marine-stores, the purveying of fiery gin, the receipt of miscellaneous articles in pledge, and the boarding, lodging, and fleecing—with a little hocussing, crimping, and kidnapping included—of those who go down to the sea in ships : in short, a West Coast Wapping.

There is, however, no rule without an exception; and I came ultimately upon a street, which, albeit possessing certain originalities of aspect and existence not to be found elsewhere, did nevertheless offer in its general character something approaching a resemblance to the London highway from which it has drawn its name. Whoever built this street was evidently a man impressed with a sufficient idea of the general fitness of things. He must have been a travelled, or, at least, a well-read man ; and he evidently had a keen remembrance of that great London artery which stretches from Aldgate Pump to Mile End Gate, London, when he called that Liverpool street, Whitechapel.

I am thankful to him for having done so ; for had the Liverpool Whitechapel not resembled in some measure the London Whitechapel, and thereby become exceptional, I should—having walked Down Whitechapel Way, in London, one Saturday night in eighteen hundred and fifty-one—not have walked down this Whitechapel Way (two hundred and twenty miles away) one Saturday night in eighteen hundred and fifty-three.

Whitechapel in Lancashire is so far like Whitechapel in Middlesex, that it is passably dirty, moderately thronged by day, and inconveniently crowded by night ; is resorted to by a variety of persons of a suspicious nature, and by a considerable number about whom there can be no suspicion at all : that, moreover, it has a kerb-stone market for the negotiation of fruit and small ware : that it is scoured by flying tribes of Bedouins, in the guise of peripatetic street vendors ; that it is sprinkled with cheap tailoring establishments, cheap eating and coffee houses, cheap places of public amusement, and finally, that it is glutted with gin-palaces, whisky-shops, taverns, and public-houses of every description.

Thus far the two streets run in concert, but they soon

diverge. The Liverpool Whitechapel is intensely maritime
(or what I may call 'Dockish'), intensely Hibernian—in its
offshoots or side-streets almost wholly so—intensely commercial, and during the daytime, not wholly unaristocratic ;
for it is intersected in one part by Church Street, the Eden of
the haberdashers' shops, and the pet promenade of the beauty
and fashion of the city of the Liver. Lord Street the proud
branches off from it, full of grand shops, and the pavement of
which is daily trodden by those interesting specimens of
humanity, 'hundred thousand pound men :'—humble-minded
millionaires who disdain carriages in business hours, and in
the humility of their wealth, condescend to pop at stray times
into quaint little taverns, where they joke with the landlady,
and ask for the 'Mail' or the 'Mercury' after you have done
with it, as though they were nothing more than wharfingers or
entering clerks. Nor are these all the high connections Whitechapel in Liverpool can claim. At the upper end branches
off a short thoroughfare, leading into Dale Street, likewise
patronised by the magnates of Liverpool. At its extreme
end, again, is the confluence of streets abutting on the stately
London and North-Western Terminus in Lime Street, and on
the great open space, where stands that really magnificent
building, St. George's Hall. The consequence of all this is,
that there is a constant cross-stream of fashionables mingling
with the rushing river of the *profanum vulgus.*

It is half-past ten o'clock ; for the early-closing system—on
Saturdays, at least—is not prevalent in Liverpool ; and thousands have yet their purchases to make on Sunday morning.
Before we enter Whitechapel, glowing with gas flowing from
enormous jets, we are attracted by an extra blaze of light, by a
concourse of people, and by a confusion of tongues, over which
one strident and resonant voice dominates ; all being gathered
round the booth of Messrs. Misture and Fitt, to which booth
we must turn aside for a moment.

In the left hand centre of a piece of waste land, these gentlemen have boldly pitched—among the potsherds, the dead cats,
and broken bottles—a monster marquee, gaily decorated with
pink and white stripes and variegated flags. Here Messrs.
Misture and Fitt have gone into the quack line of business, in
a Bohemian or travelling manner. They are herb doctors,
chiropodists, universal medicine vendors, veterinary prescri-
bers, and much more besides. A mob of men, women, and
children are talking, screaming, laughing, and jesting around
the temporary laboratory of these medical sages, before a long

counter which creaks beneath a bountiful spread of nasty-looking preparations, pills, pots of ointment, bottles of sarsaparilla, cases of herbs, blisters, plaisters, and boluses. The whole affair has the appearance of the stock in trade of half a dozen unsuccessful chemists and druggists, who had been burnt out or emigrated to the backwoods, or set up business in Canvas Town, and here clubbed the remainder of their goods as a last effort to sell off under prime cost. There are several gaily-decorated placards eulogistic of Misture's Epileptic Pills, and Fitt's Concentrated Essence of Peppermint. Fitt is haranguing his select auditory as we draw near. His style of eloquence is something beyond the old hocus-pocus diatribes of the old medical mountebanks. He is not so broad as Cheap Jack, not so lofty as Dulcamara, not so scientifically unintelligible as the quacks you see in the Champs Elysées or the Boulevard du Temple, in Paris. But he is astonishingly rapid ; and mingles with a little bit of sporting a snack of slang, and a few genteel anecdotes of the nobility and gentry. He has so fluent a delivery, such tickling jokes for the men and such sly leers for the ladies, that the former slap their legs and break forth into enthusiastic encomiums in the dialect of Tim Bobbin. The latter simper and blush delightfully. Some of his jokes apply forcibly to the personal appearance of a select few of his auditory, and provoke roars of laughter. A happy allusion to the neighbouring churchyard, being close to a doctor's shop, tells immensely. At the upper end of the drug-heaped counter the other partner, Misture—hard featured with a fox's face ; one of those men who will wear black clothes and white neckcloths, and who never can look respectable in them—is silently but busily engaged in handing over divers packets of the medicines his partner has been praising to eager and numerous purchasers. I see through Misture and Fitt in a moment. Fitt is the volatile partner, the fine arts professor. Misture is the sound practical man of business. Misture is the careful builder, who lays the foundation and gets up the scaffolding ; Fitt does the ornamental work, and puts on the fancy touches. Do you not remember when Geoffrey Crayon and Buckthorne went to the bookseller's dinner, that the latter pointed out the partner who attended to the carving, and the partner who attended to the jokes ? They are prototypes of Misture and Fitt.

The busy throng tends Whitechapel way, and down Whitechapel we must go. So great is the number of orange-sellers and oranges in Whitechapel, that it would seem as if the whole of one year's produce of St. Michael's and the Azores had been disgorged into the narrow street this Saturday night. The poor creatures who sell this fruit—desperately ragged and destitute—were formerly much harried and beset by the police, who in their over-zeal made descents and razzias upon them, put them to horrid rout and confusion, and made so many of them captives to their bows and spears (or batons), that the miserable creatures scarcely dared to venture into the light for grievous fear and trembling. They offered oranges in by-places and secret corners, as if they had been smuggled merchandise, prohibited under annihilating penalties. Latterly, however, some benevolent persons took their case in hand ; and, demonstrating to the authorities that to obstruct a thoroughfare was not quite high treason, nor to offer an orange for sale was not quite sufficient to warrant a human creature being hunted like a wild beast, the dread taboo was taken off, and some small immunities were conceded to the army of orange-vendors.

My Uncle's counting-houses, which abound here in Whitechapel, are all thronged to-night. As per flourishing gold letters on his door-jamb, he proposes to lend money on plate, jewellery, and valuables ; but he is not much troubled with plate, jewellery, or valuables on a Saturday night. If you enter one of these pawnshops—they are called so plainly, without reticence or diffidence, hereabout—and elbow your way through Vallambrosian thickets of wearing apparel and miscellaneous articles, you will observe these peculiarities in the internal economy of the avuncular life, at variance with London practice ; that the duplicates are not of card-board, but of paper having an appearance something between Dock-warrants and Twelfth-cake lottery-tickets, and that the front of each compartment of the counter is crossed by a stout wooden barrier ; whether for the convenience of the pledger to rest his elbows on while transacting business, or to restrain the said pledger from violently wresting from My Uncle's hands any article before he has legally redeemed it, I am unable to say. Furthermore, it will not be without emotion that you will become sensible that in very many of the pawnbroking warehouses my Uncle is for the nonce transformed into my Aunt—not simply figuratively, in the French sense—but substantially. The person who unties your package, names the extent of the investment therein by way of loan, fills up the duplicate, and hands you the cash is a Young Lady ;

sharp-eyed, quick-witted, and not to be done by any means.

I have said that my Uncle is troubled with few articles of any considerable value on Saturday nights. This is ordinarily the case; but not unfrequently a young lady of an inflamed complexion bears down on my Uncle, laden with the spoils of some galleon from the Spanish Main; the watch, chain, trinkets, and clothes of some unfortunate sailor fresh from abroad, whom she has plundered. Sometimes this tight craft disposes successfully of her booty, and sheers off with all her prize-money, and with flying colours; but occasionally, suspicions being awakened, and signals made to the Preventive, she is compelled to heave-to, and to tack, and to change her course, and even to proceed under convoy to a roadstead known as Bridewell; the harbour-dues of which are so considerable, that an overhauling before a stipendiary magistrate, and a lengthened sojourn in a graving dock near Kirkdale gaol, are absolutely necessary before she can get to sea again. Sometimes, again, a drunken sailor (they are every whit as apt to rob themselves as to be robbed) will drop in with a watch, or a gold thumb-ring, or even the entire suit of clothes off his back to pawn. One offered a five-pound note in pledge on a Saturday night; upon which my Uncle considerately lent him (he was very far gone) five shillings—taking care to ascertain to what ship he belonged—and the next morning, to Jack's great joy and astonishment, returned him four pounds fifteen shillings.

Here is a 'vault:' it has nothing to do with pallid death. It is, indeed, a chosen rendezvous for 'life,' in Whitechapel— such life as is comprised in spirituous jollity, and the conviviality that is so nearly allied to delirium tremens. The vault is large enough to be the presence-chamber of a London gin-palace; but lacks the gilding, plate-glass, and French polish, which are so handsomely thrown in with a London penny-worth of gin. The walls are soberly coloured; the only mural decorations being certain and sundry oleaginous frescoes, due, perhaps, to the elbows and heads of customers reclining there-against. The bar-counter is very high, and there are no enclosed bars or snuggeries; but there is one unbroken line of shop-board. The vault is very full to-night. A party of American sailors in red flannel shirts, and bushy whiskers, and ear-rings, are liberally treating a select party of ladies and gentlemen; hosts and guests being already much the worse for liquor. One mariner, to my personal knowledge, had been regaling for the last ten minutes on a series of 'glasses to follow,' of almost every excisable fluid, taken without any relation to their chemical affinities or proper order of succession. He is now reduced to that happy frame of mind, common I am told, in some stages of Bacchic emotion, which leads him to believe, and to state (indistinctly), that though he has spent his last sixpence, it is 'awright;' and that things generally must come round and be as satisfactory (in a rectified point of view) as a trivet. Next to the sailors and their guests are a knot of Irish labourers, gesticulating, quarrelling, and all but fighting, in their native manner, and according to the custom of their country. Next are ragged women and mechanics, who have already spent, prospectively, up to the Friday of the next week's earnings. Next, and next, and next, are sailors, and Irish, and women, and mechanics, over and over again.

We are arrested at the door by an episode of a domestic nature, which merits tarrying an instant to witness. A very broad Lancastrian chandler's-shop-keeper, speaking broad Lancashire, and of mature years, has been drinking in an adjoining apartment with a Sergeant and a couple of recruits of one of Her Majesty's regiments of militia. Arrived at that happy state in which the celebrated Willie may reasonably be supposed to have been when he had finished brewing the peck of malt, it has occurred to this eccentric tradesman to slip on one of the recruit's scarlet jackets, and to represent to the partner of his joys (who, according to the Hymeneal Statute in that case made and provided, has 'fetched' him) that he has 'listed;' at which she sheds abundant floods of tears, and besecches him to 'cast t' red rag off and coom awa.' 'Coom awa, Robert, coom awa,' she passionately says, 'yans nowt but jack-shappers (hangmen), yans nowt but "shepstering rads" (what ever can *they* be?) coom awa! The'll crop 'te pow, lad. They'll mak thee shouther arms, lad. Dunna go wi' 'em, Robert.' But her adjurations are vain. Her husband—who, however far gone he may be in liquor, is a long way too far North to 'list in reality—maintains the impossibility of violating the engagement he has recently entered into with Her Majesty the Queen. 'I'se geatten byounty, lass,' he represents, 'an I mun go wi Seargent!' At length, deeming further expostulation useless, she abandons the cause; 'Go thy ways, thou fool,' she exclains; Go thy ways and be hanged, thou *Plump Muck!*' with which last transcendant figure of rhetoric she sweeps into the street. Whether the

appellation of 'Plump-Muck' (pronounced 'ploomp-mook')
has touched some hidden chord in her husband's bosom, or
whether the bent of his inebriety takes suddenly another direction, I could not discover, but he presently falls into a fit
of grievous weeping, and to use his own words, 'whips off
t' skycarlet rag' and follows his spouse into Whitechapel, into
which we emerge likewise.

More gas, more music, and more crowds. Wax-work shows
where Monsieur Kossuth, Queen Elizabeth, and Gleeson
Wilson the murderer, may be seen for the small charge of one
penny. Raffles for fancy articles on the Sea-side bazaar plan,
with results nearly as profitable. Panoramas of Versailles,
the Himálaya Mountains, and the city of Canton. Shooting
Galleries (down cellar-steps), Dissolving Views, Dancing and
Singing Saloons. These, with shops for the sale of chandlery,
slop-clothing, hosiery, grocery, seamen's bedding, ships'
stores, and cheap literature (among which, I grieve to say it,
the blood-and-thunder school preponderates), make up the rest
of Whitechapel. It is the same in the continuation thereof:
Paradise Street, which, however, boasts in addition a gigantic
building known as the Colosseum : once used as a chapel, and
with much of its original ecclesiastical appearance remaining ;
but now a Singing Saloon, or a Tavern Concert, crowded to
the ceiling.

As we wander up and down the crowded, steaming thoroughfare, we catch strange glimpses occasionally of narrow streets.
Some occupied by lofty frowning warehouses ; others tenanted
by whole colonies of Irish ; ragged, barefooted, destitute ;
who lurk in garrets and swelter in back rooms, and crouch in
those hideous, crowded, filthy, underground cellars, which are
the marvel and the shame of Liverpool—warehouses and
cellars, cellars and warehouses without end—wealth, the
result of great commercial intelligence, rising up proudly
amidst misery, hunger, and soul-killing ignorance.

If I may be allowed to make a parting remark concerning the
Lancashire Whitechapel, it is with reference to its elasticity.
All the rags and wretchedness, all the huckstering merchandise, seem to possess a facility for expanding into gigantic commerce and boundless wealth. Not a cobbler's stall, a petty
chandler's shop, but seems ready to undertake anything in the
wholesale way at a moment's notice, and to contract for the
supply of the Militia with boots and shoes, or the British navy
with salt beef and tobacco immediately. Hucksters change
with wonderful rapidity into provision dealers, brokers into

salesmen, small shopkeepers into proprietors of monster emporiums. The very destitute Irish in this city of all cities of commerce, (the Great Liverpool runs even London hard in matter of fast trading!) after a preliminary apprenticeship to the begging and hawking business, become speculators and contractors on a surprising scale.

So may Whitechapel flourish all the year round, I say: may its dirt, when I next see it, be changed to gold, and its rags to fine linen, and its adjoining cellars to palaces. Although, to be sure, the one disastrous thing likely is, that, when the work of transmutation is completed, other rags, and cellars, and dirt, will take the place of what has been changed to fine linen, palaces, and gold. The ball *must* roll, and something *must* be undermost.

IV.

JACK ALIVE IN LONDON.

COMING from Greenwich or Blackwall, radiant with 'Badminton,' or 'Cider cup;' or, perchance, coming home very satiated and sea-sick from foreign parts, tired, jaded, used-up, as a man is apt to be under such circumstances, the Pool always pleases, enlivens, interests me. I pull out the trumpet-stop of my organ of veneration; my form dilates with the tall spars around me; I lose count of the wonders of the lands I have seen, of the coming cares and troubles—the worrying and bickering—awaiting me, perhaps, in that remorseless, inevitable London yonder. I forget them all in the Pool. If I have a foreigner with me, so much the better. 'Not in crimson-trousered soldiery,' I cry, 'oh! Louis or Alphonse —not in the constant shouldering of arms, and the drumming that never ceases,—not in orders of the day, or vexatious passports, are the glories of Britain inscribed. See them in that interminable forest of masts, the red sun lighting up the cupolas of Greenwich, the tarry hulls, the patched sails, the laden hay-boats, the trim wherries, the inky waters of the Pool. Read them in the cobweb rigging; watch them curling from the short pipes of red-capped mariners lounging on the bulwarks of timber ships! Ships upon ships, masts everywhere, even in the far-off country, among trees and churches; the commerce of the world jammed up between these cumbered wharves, and overflowing into these narrow creeks!'

I propose to treat, as shortly as I can consistently with accuracy, of maritime London, and of 'Jack' (alluding, under that cognomen, to the general 'seafaring' class) alive in London.

'Jack' is 'alive,' to my knowledge and experience, in East Smithfield, and in and about all the Docks; in Poplar, Limehouse, Rotherhithe, Shadwell, Wapping, Bermondsey, and the Island of Dogs. He is feebly alive in Fenchurch Street and the Minories; but he shows special and vigorous symptoms of vitality in Ratcliffe Highway. If it interest you at all to see him alive, and to see how he lives, we will explore, for some half-hour or so, this very muddy, tarry, salt-water-smelling portion of the metropolis.

You can get to Ratcliffe Highway through the Minories: you may attain it by a devious route through Whitechapel and Mile End New Town; but the way *I* go, is from London Bridge, down Thames Street, and through the Tower, in order to come gradually upon Jack alive, and to pick up specimens of his saline existence bit by bit.

London Bridge is densely crowded, as it has been, is, and always will be, I suppose. The wheels of the heavy waggons, laden with bales and barrels, creak and moan piteously; while the passengers, who are always certain of being too late (and never are) for a train on the South-Eastern Railway, goad cabmen into performing frantic *pas de deux* with their bewildered horses. The sportive bullocks, too, the gigs, knackers' carts, sheep, pigs, Barclay's drays, and cohorts of foot-passengers, enliven the crowded scene.

Comfortably corn-crushed, jostled, and dust-blinded, I descend the flight of stairs on the right of the King William Street side of the bridge. I have but to follow my nose along Thames Street to Ratcliffe; and I follow it. I elbow my way through a compact mass of labourers, porters, sailors, fishwomen, and spruce clerks, with their bill books secured by a leather-covered chain round their waists. Room there, for a hot sugar-broker tearing by, towards the Exchange, bursting with a recent bargain! Room for a spruce captain (he had his boots cleaned by one of the 'brigade' opposite Billingsgate Market) in an irreproachable state of clean shirtedness, navy-blue-broadclothedness, and chimney-pot-hattedness! He sets his big silver watch at every church, and dusts his boots with an undoubted bandanna. He has an appointment, doubtless, at Garraway's or the Jerusalem Coffee House, with his owner or broker.

A gush of fish, stale and fresh, stretches across Thames Street as I near Billingsgate Market. I turn aside for a moment, and enter the market. Business is over; and the male and female purveyors of the treasures of the deep solace themselves with pipes and jovial converse.

Jack is getting more lively all through Thames Street, and Tower Street, and is alarmingly vital when I emerge on Tower Hill. A row of foreign mariners pass me, seven abreast: swarthy, ear-ringed, black-bearded varlets in red shirts, light-blue trousers, and with sashes round their waists. Part of the crew of a Sardinian brig, probably. They have all their arms round each other's necks; yet I cannot help thinking that they look somewhat 'knifey,' 'stilettoey.' I hope I may be mistaken, but I am afraid that it would be odds were you to put an indefinite quantity of rum into *them*, they would put a few inches of steel into *you*.

But I enter the Tower postern, and am in another London —the military metropolis—at once. Very curious and wonderful are these old gray towers, these crumbling walls, these rotting portcullises, so close to the business-like brick and mortar of St. Katherine's Dock House hard by. What had the 'Devilin Tower,' the 'Scavenger's Daughter,' the 'Stone Kitchen,' to do with wholesale grocers, ship-chandlers, and outfitting warehouses? Is there not something jarring, discordant, in that grim, four-turreted old fortalice, frowning on the quiet corn and coal carrying vessels in the pool? What do the 'thousand years of war' so close to the 'thousand years of peace?' Is not the whole sombre, lowering old pile, a huge anachronism? Julius Cæsar, William the Third, and the Docks! Wharves covered with tubs of peaceful palm-oil, and dusky soldiers sauntering on narrow platforms, from whence the black mouths of honeycombed old guns grin (toothless, haply) into peaceful dwelling-houses. The dried-up moat, the old rooms, wall-inscribed with the overflowings of weary hearts; the weazen-faced old warders, with their strange, gone-by costume; the dinted armour, and rusted headman's axe; all tell—with the vacant space on the Green, where the four posts of the scaffold stood, and the shabby little church, where lie Derwentwater and Lovat, Anne Boleyn and Northumberland, the innocent and the guilty, the dupers and the duped—of things that *have been*, thank God !

I pass a lane where the soldiers live, (why should their wives necessarily be slatterns, their children dirty, and they themselves alternately in a state of shirt-sleeves, beer and tobacco, or one of pipeclay, red blanketing, and mechanical stolidity, I wonder?) and ask an artilleryman on guard where a door of egress is to be found. He 'dwoan't know:' of course not. Soldiers never do know. It isn't in the articles of war, or the Queen's regulations. Still, I think my friend in the blue coat, and with the shaving-brush stuck at the top of his shako, would be rather more useful in guarding a fortress if he knew the way into and the way out of it.

Patience, 'trying back,' and the expenditure of five minutes, at last bring me out by another postern, leading on to Tower Hill the less, East Smithfield, St. Katherine's Docks, and the Mint; very nearly opposite is a narrow street, where a four-oared cutter, in the middle of the pavement, in progress of receiving an outer coat of tar and an inner one of green paint, suggests to me that Jack is decidedly alive in this vicinity; while, closely adjacent, a monster 'union jack,' sloping from the first-floor window of an unpretending little house, announces the whereabouts of the 'Royal Naval Rendezvous.' You have perhaps heard of it more frequently as the house of reception for the 'Tower Tender.' The Rendezvous, and the Tender too, had a jovial season of it in the war-time, when the press was hot, and civilians were converted into 'volunteers' for the naval service by rough compulsion. The neighbourhood swarmed with little 'publics,' embellished with cartoons of the beatified state of Jack when alive in the navy. Jack was continually drinking grog with the port-admiral, or executing hornpipes with the first-lieutenant. The only labour imposed on him (pictorially) was the slaying half a dozen Frenchmen occasionally before breakfast; for which a grateful country rewarded him with hecatombs of dollars. At home, he was represented frying gold watches, and lighting pipes with five-pound notes. Love, liquor, and glory! King and country! Magnificent bounty, &c., &c., &c. But the picture has two sides; for Jack hung back sometimes, preferring to fry watches in the merchant service. A grateful country pressed him. He ran away from captivity; a grateful country flogged him. He mutinied; a grateful country hanged him. Whether it was the flogging, or the hanging, or the scurvy, or the French bullets, or the prisons at Verdun and Brest, I won't be certain; but Jack became at last quite a scarce article. So the Royal Naval Rendezvous, and the Tower Tender were obliged to content themselves with the sweepings of the prisons—thieves, forgers, murderers, and the like. These even grew scarce; and a grateful country pressed everybody she could lay her hands on. 'Food for powder,' was wanted—'mortal men' good enough to 'fill a pit,' *must* be had. Quiet citizens, cripples, old men were pressed. Apprentices showed their indentures, citizens their freedom, in vain. Britannia *must* have men. People would come home from China or Honolulu, and fall into the clutches of the press-gang five minutes after they had set foot on land. Bags of money would be found on posts on Tower Hill, left there by persons who had been pressed unawares. People would leave public-house parlours to see what sort of a night it was, and never be seen or heard of again. I remember, even, hearing from my nurse, during childhood, a ghostly legend of how the Lord Chancellor, going over Tower Hill one night with the great seal in a carpet bag, and 'disguised in liquor' after a dinner at Guildhall, was kidnapped by a press-gang, sent on board the Tower Tender, and not released until three months afterwards, when he was discovered on board the 'Catspaw' frigate, in the Toulon fleet, scraping the mizen-mast, under the cat of a boatswain's mate. Of course I won't be answerable for the veracity of the story; but we scarcely need its confirmation to find plenty of reasons to bless those glorious good old times when George the Third was king.

Times are changed with the Rendezvous now. Sailors it still craves; but good ones—A. B.'s; not raffish gaol-birds and useless landsmen. The A. B.'s are not so plentiful, though the times *are* so peaceful. The A. B.'s have heard of the 'cat;' and they know what 'holystoning' and 'black-listing' mean. There is a stalwart A. B., I watch, reading a placard in the window of the Rendezvous, stating that the 'Burster,' one hundred and twenty guns, fitting at Plymouth, wants some able-bodied seamen. 'Catch a weasel asleep,' says the A. B., walking on. He belongs to the 'Chutnagore,' A 1, under engagement to sail for Madras, and would rather not have anything to do with the 'Burster.'

A weather-beaten old quarter-master stands on the steps of the Rendezvous, and eyes the A. B. wistfully. The A. B. is the sort of man Britannia wants just now. So are those three black-whiskered fellows, swaggering along with a Yankee skipper, with whom they have just signed articles for a voyage to Boston, in the 'Peleg Whittle;' Coon, master. Poor old quarter-master! give him but his 'four-and-twenty stout young fellows,' his beloved press-gang; and the 'Chutnagore' would go one A. B. short to sea; while Captain Coon would vainly lament the loss of three of the crew of the

'Peleg Whittle.' The 'Burster' is very short of hands; but he has bagged very few A. B.'s yet. See, a recruit offers; a lanky lad in a torn jacket, with an air of something like ragged respectability about him! He wants to 'go to sea.' The quarter-master laughs at him—repulses him. The boy has, ten to one, run away from school or from home, with that vague indefinite idea of 'going to sea' in his mind. To sea, indeed! He has prowled about the docks, vainly importuned captains, owners, seamen, anybody, with his request. Nobody will have anything to do with him. The greatest luck in store for him would be the offer of a cabin-boy's berth on board a collier, where the captain would regale him with the convivial crowbar and the festive rope's-end, whenever the caprice seized him. Going to sea! Ah, my young friend, trudge home to Dr. Broombaek's seminary—never mind the thrashing—explain to *your* young friends, impressed as you have been with a mania for 'running away and going to sea,' that it is one thing to talk about doing a thing, and another to do it; that a ragged little landsmen is worse than useless aboard ship; and that there are ten chances to one even against his ever being allowed to put his foot on ship-board.

I leave the Royal Naval Rendezvous just as a dissolute Norwegian stops to read the 'Burster' placard. Now, I turn past the Mint, and past the soldiers on guard there, and pursue the course of a narrow little street leading towards the Docks.

Here Jack leaps into great life. Ship-chandlers, ship-grocers, biscuit-bakers, sail-makers, outfitting warehouses, occupy the shops on either side. Up a little court is a nautical day-school for teaching navigation. There is a book-stall, on which lie the 'Seaman's Manual,' the 'Shipmaster's Assistant,' and Hamilton Moore's 'Navigation.' There is a nautical instrument-maker's, where chronometers, quadrants, and sextants are kept, and blank log-books are sold. The stationers display forms for manifests, bills of lading, and charter-parties. Every article vended has some connection with those who go down to the sea in ships.

When we enter St. George's Street, where there are shops on one side of the way, and St. Katherine's Dock warehouses on the other, Jack becomes tremendously alive on the pavement. Jack from India and China, very sunburnt, and smoking Trichinopoly cheroots—thin cigars with a reed passed through them, and nearly a foot long. American Jack, in a red worsted shirt, and chewing indefatigably.

E

Swedish Jack, smelling of tallow and turpentine, but amazingly good-natured, and unaffectedly polite. Italian Jack, shivering. German Jack, with a light-blue jacket and yellow trousers, stolid and smoky; Greek Jack, voluble in petticoats and long boots. Grimy seamen from colliers; smart, taut men, from Green's or Wigram's splendid East India ships; mates in spruce jackets, and gold-laced caps, puffing prime Havannahs. Lastly, the real unadulterated English Jack, with the inimitable roll, the unapproachable hitch, the unsurpassable flowers of language. The pancake hat stuck at the back of the head, the neckerchief passed through a wedding-ring, the flaring yellow silk handkerchief; the whole unmistakable costume and demeanour—so unlike the stage sailor, so unlike the pictorial sailor—so like only what it really is.

This is the busiest portion of the day, and the Highway is crowded. Enthusiasts would perhaps be disappointed at the woful lack of nautical vernacular prevalent with Jack. He is not continually shivering his timbers; neither is he always requesting you to stand by and belay; to dowse the lee-scuppers, or to splice the main brace.

The doors of the public-houses disgorge great crowds of mariners; nor are there wanting taverns and eating-houses, where the sailors of different nations may be accommodated. Here is a '*Deutsches Gasthaus*,' a Prussian '*Bierhalle*,' a real 'Norwegian House.' Stay! Here we are at the Central Dock gates, and, among a crowd of sailors, hurrying in and out, swarm forth hordes of Dock labourers to their dinner.

A very queer company, indeed;—'navvies,' seafaring men, and individuals of equivocal dress and looks, who have probably taken to the 'two shillings' or half-crown a day awarded for Dock toil, as a last refuge from inevitable starvation. Discharged policemen, ruined medical students, clerks who have lost their characters, Polish and German refugees, might be found, I opine, in those squalid ranks. It is all equality *now*, however. The college-bred youth, the educated man, must toil in common with the navvy and the tramp. They seem contented enough, eating their poor meals, and puffing at the never-failing pipe with great gusto. Poor and almost destitute as these men are, they can yet obtain a species of delusive credit—a credit by which they are ultimately defrauded. Crafty victuallers will advance them beer and food on the security of their daily wage, which they themselves secure from the foremen They exact, of course, an

enormous interest. It is, after all, the old abuse, the old
Tommy-shop nuisance—the 'infamous truck system'—the
iniquitous custom of paying the labourers at the public-house,
and the mechanic late on the Saturday night.

I have not time to enter the Docks just now; and plunge
further into the Babel of Ratcliffe Highway. Jack is alive
everywhere by this time. A class of persons remarkably
lively in connection with him, are the Jews. For Jack are
these grand Jewish outfitting warehouses alone intended.
For his sole use and benefit are the swinging lamps, the
hammocks and bedding, the code of signal pocket-handkerchiefs, the dreadnought coats, sou-wester hats, telescopes,
checked shirts, pilot jackets, case bottles, and multifarious
odds and ends required by the mariner. For Jack does
Meshech manufacture the delusive jewellery; while Shadrach
vaunts the watch that has no works; and Abednego confidentially proposes advances of cash on wages-notes. Jewry
is alive, as well as Jack, in Ratcliffe Highway. You may
call that dingy little cabin of a shop, small; but, bless you!
they would fit out a seventy-four in ten minutes, with everything wanted, from a spanker-boom to a bottle of Harvey's
Sauce. For purposes marine, they sell everything;—biscuits
by sackfuls, bales of dreadnoughts, miles of rope, infinities
of fishing-tackle, shaving-tackle, running-tackle, spars, sextants, sea-chests, and hundreds of other articles. Jewry will
even supply you with sailors; will man vessels for you, from
a cock-boat to an Indiaman. Jewry has a capital black cook
inside. A third mate at two minutes' notice. A steward in
the twinkling of a handspike. Topmast men in any quantity,
and at immediate call.

A strange sound—half human, half ornithological—breaks
on the ear above the turmoil of the crowded street. I follow
a swarthy mariner, who holds a cage, muffled in a handkerchief in his hand, a few yards, until he enters a large and
handsome shop, kept also by a child of Israel, and which
literally swarms with parrots, cockatoos, and macaws. Here
they are, in every variety of gorgeous plumage and curvature
of beak: with their wicked-looking, bead-like eyes and crested
heads; screaming, croaking, yelling, swearing, laughing, singing, drawing corks, and winding up clocks, with frantic
energy! Most of these birds come from South America and
the coast of Africa. Jack generally brings home one or two
as his own private venture, selling it in London for a sum
varying from thirty to forty shillings. I am sorry to have to

record that a parrot which can swear well, is more remunerative to Jack than a nonjuring bird. A parrot which is accomplished enough to rap out half a dozen round oaths in a breath, will fetch you fifty shillings, perhaps. In this shop, also, are stuffed humming-birds, ivory chessmen, strange shells, and a miscellaneous collection of those foreign odds and ends, called 'curiosities.' Jack is very lively here with the rabbinical ornithologist. He has just come from the Gold Coast in a man-of-war, the captain of which, in consideration of the good conduct of the crew while on the station, had permitted each man before the mast to bring as many parrots home with him as he liked. And they did bring a great many, Jack says—so many, that the vessel became at last like a ship full of women; the birds creating such an astonishing variety of discordant noises, that the men were, in self-defence, obliged to let some two or three hundred of them (they didn't keep count of fifty or so) loose. Hundreds, however, came safe home; and Jack has two or three to dispose of. They whistle hornpipes beautifully. I leave him still haggling with the ornithologist, and triumphantly eliciting a miniature 'Joe Bee's Vocabulary of slang' from the largest of his birds.

You are not to suppose, gentle reader, that the population of Ratcliffe is destitute of an admixture of the fairer portion of the creation. Jack has his Jill in St. George's Street, Cable Street, Back Lane, and the Commercial Road. Jill is inclined to corpulence; if it were not libellous, I could hint a suspicion that Jill is not unaddicted to the use of spirituous liquors. Jill wears a silk handkerchief round her neck, as Jack does; like him, too, she rolls, occasionally; I believe, smokes, frequently; I am afraid, swears, occasionally. Jack is a cosmopolite—here to-day, gone to-morrow; but Jill is peculiar to maritime London. She nails her colours to the mast of Ratcliffe. Jill has her good points, though she does scold a little, and fight a little, and drink a little. She is just what Mr. Thomas Dibdin has depicted her, and nothing more or less. She takes care of Jack's tobacco-box; his trousers she washes, and his grog, too, she makes; and if he enacts occasionally the part of a maritime Giovanni, promising to walk in the Mall with Susan of Deptford, and likewise with Sal, she only upbraids him with a tear. I wish the words of all songs had as much sense and as much truth in them as Mr. Dibdin's have.

A hackney-coach (the very last hackney-coach, I verily

believe, in London, and the one, moreover, which my Irish maid-of-all-work always manages to fetch me when I send her for a cab)—a hackney-coach, I say, jolts by, filled inside and out! Jack is going to be married. I don't think I am mis-stating or exaggerating the case, when I say that the whole party—bride, bridegroom, bridesmaids, bridesmen, coachman and all—are considerably the worse for liquor. Is this as it should be? Ah, poor Jack!

And I have occasion to say 'Poor Jack!' a good many times in the course of my perambulations. It is my personal opinion that Jack is robbed—that he is seduced into extra-vagance, hoodwinked into spendthrift and dissolute habits. There is no earthly reason why Jack should not save money out of his wages; why he should never have a watch without frying it, nor a five-pound note without lighting his pipe with it. It cannot be indispensable that he should be con-tinually kept 'alive' with gin; that he should have no com-panions save profligate women, no amusements save low dancing-saloons and roaring taverns. The sailor has a strong religious and moral bias. He scorns and loathes deceit, dishonesty, and injustice, innately. He is often a profligate, and a drunkard, and a swearer (I will not say blasphemer), because abominable and vicious customs make him so; because, ill-cared for on board ship, he no sooner lands than he becomes the prey of the infamous harpies who infest maritime London. He is robbed by outfitters (I particularise neither Jew nor Gentile, for there are six of one and half a dozen of the other); he is robbed by the tavern-keepers, the crimps, and the boarding-masters. He is robbed by his associ-ates, robbed in business, robbed in amusement. 'Jack' is fair game to everybody.

The conductors of that admirable institution, the Sailors' Home, I understand, are doing their best to alleviate the evils I have lightly, but very lightly, touched upon. Jack is alive, but not with an unwholesome galvanic vitality, in the Home. He is well fed, well treated, and well cared for, generally; moreover, he is not wronged. The tailor who makes his clothes, and the landlord who sells him his beer, and the association that board him, do not conspire to rob him. The only shoal the managers of the Sailors' Home have to steer clear of, is the danger of inculcating the idea among sailors, that the institution has anything of a gratuitous or eleemosynary element in its construction. Sailors are high-spirited and eminently independent in feeling.

I have come by this time to the end of the straggling series of broad and narrow thoroughfares, which, under the names of East Smithfield, St. George's Street, Upper Shadwell Street, and Cock Hill, all form part, in the aggregate, of Ratcliffe Highway. I stand on the threshold of the mysterious region comprising, in its limits, Shadwell, Poplar, and Limehouse. To my left, some two miles distant, is Stepney, to which parish all children born at sea are, traditionally, said to be chargeable. No longer are there continued streets—'blocks,' as the Americans call them—of houses. There are swampy fields and quaggy lanes, and queer little public-houses like ship-cuddies, transplanted bodily from East Indiamen, and which have taken root here. The 'Cat and Fiddle' is a waterman's house—'jolly young watermen,' I am afraid, no more. At the 'Bear and Harp'—so the placard informs me—is held the 'Master Mariners' Club.' Shipbuilders' yards start suddenly upon me—ships in full sail bear down on me through quiet lanes; lofty masts loom spectrally among the quiet graves in the churchyard. In the church yonder, where the union jack flies at the steeple, there are slabs commemorating the bequests of charitable master-mariners, dead years ago; of an admiral's widow, who built an organ; of the six poor women, who are to be yearly relieved as a thank-offering for the release of some dead and gone Levant trader 'from captyvitie among the Turkes in Algeeres.' In the grave-yards, scores of bygone sea-captains, their wives and children, shipwrights, ropemakers, of the olden time, dead pursers, and ship-chandlers, sleep quietly. They have compasses and sextants, and ships in full sail, sculptured on their moss-grown tombs. The wind howls no more, nor the waves roar now for them. Gone aloft, I hope, most of them!—though Seth Slipcheese, the great ship-contractor, who sold terribly weevilly biscuit, and salted horse for beef, sleeps under that substantial brick tomb yonder; while beneath the square stone slab, with the sculptured skull and hour-glass, old Martin Flibuster may have his resting-place. He was called 'captain,' nobody knew why; he swore terribly; he had strange foreign trinkets and gold doubloons hanging to his watch-chain, and told wild stories of parboiled Indians, and Spanish Dons, with their ears and noses slit. What matters it now if he *did* sail with Captain Kidd, and scuttle the 'Ellen and Mary,' with all hands aboard? He died in his bed, and who shall say, impenitent?

The old sea-captains and **traders** connected with the sea

have still their abiding-places in quiet, cosy little cottages about here, mostly tenements, with green doors and bow-windows, and with a summer-house perched a-top, where they can twist a flag on festive occasions, and enjoy their grog and tobacco on quiet summer evenings. The wild mania for building—the lath-and-plaster, stucco-palace, Cockney-Corinthian frenzy—has not yet extended to Limehouse, and the old ' salts ' have elbow-room.

I must turn back here, however; for it is nearly four o'clock, and I shall be too late else for a peep into the Docks. The Docks! What a flood of recollections bursts through the sluice-gates of my mind, as I gaze on the huge range of warehouses, the swarms of labourers, the crowd of ships! Little as many of us know of maritime London, and of the habits of Jack alive, we have all been to the Docks, once in our lives at least. Was it to see that wonderful seafaring relation of ours who was always going out to the Cape with a magnificent outfit, and who always returned, Vanderdecken-like, without having doubled it—being also minus shoes and stockings, and bringing home, as a species of atonement-offering, the backbone of a shark? Was it to dine on board the ' Abercrombie, Jenkinson,' of I don't know how many hundred tons burden, which went out to Sydney with emigrants, and foundered in Algoa Bay? Was it with that never-to-be-forgotten tasting-order for twelve pipes, sixteen hogsheads, twelve barrels, of rare ports and sherries, when coopers rushed about with candles in cleft sticks, running gimlets into casks, and pouring out rich wines into sawdust like water? When we ate biscuits, and rinsed our mouths scientifically, and re-proached our companions with being uproarious; but coming out (perfectly sober, of course), could not be prevented from addressing the populace on general subjects, and repeatedly volunteering the declaration (with our hat on the back of our head and the tie of our cravat like a bag-wig) that we were ' All Right!'

I remember, as a child, always asking myself how the ships got into dock; a question rapidly followed by alarming incerti-tude as to how they got out. I don't think I know much more about the matter now, though I listen attentively to a pilot-coat and scarred face, who tells me all about it. Pilot-coat points to the warehouses, dilates on the enormous wells those gigantic brick-work shells contain; shows me sugar-bags, coffee-bags, tea-chests, rice-bags, tubs of tallow, casks of palm-oil. Pilot-coat has been everywhere, and every voyage has added a fresh scar to his face. He has been to sea since he was no higher than 'that'—pointing to a stump. Went out in a convict-ship; wrecked off St. Helena. Went out to Valparaiso; had a fever. Went out to Alexandria; had the plague. Went out to Mobile; wrecked. Went out to Jamaica; fell down the hatchway, and broke his collar-bone. Deserted into an American liner; thence into an Australian emigrant ship; ran away at Sydney; drove bullocks in the bush; entered for Bombay; entered the Indian Navy; was wrecked off the coast of Coromandel; was nearly killed with a Malay creese. Been in a South-Sea whaler, a Greenland whaler, a South Shields collier, and a Shoreham mackerel boat. Who could refuse the 'drop of summut' to an ancient mariner, who has such a tale to tell, were it only to curtail the exuberance of his narration? And it is, and always has been, my private opinion, that if the 'wedding guest' had given the real 'ancient mariner' sixpence for a 'drop of summut,' he would have had the pith of his story out of him in no time, whereby, though we should have lost an exquisite poem, the 'wedding guest' would not have been so unsufferably bored as he undoubtedly was, and some of us would have known better, perhaps, what the story was about.

You have your choice of Docks in this wonderful maritime London. The St. Katherine's Docks, the London, the West India Docks lie close together; while, if you follow the Commercial Road, the East India Docks lie close before you, as the Commercial Docks do after going through the Thames Tunnel. There are numerous inlets, moreover, and basins, and dry docks: go where you will, the view begins or ends with the inevitable ships.

Tarry with me for a moment in the Isle of Dogs, and step on board this huge East Indiaman. She is as big as a man-of-war, and as clean as a Dutch door-step. Such a bustle as is going on inside, and about her, nevertheless! She is under engagement to the 'Honourable Company' to sail in three days' time; and her crew will have a tidy three days' work. There are horses, pigs, bullocks, being hoisted on board; there are sheep in the launch, and ducks and geese in the long-boats. French rolls can be baked on board, and a perfect kitchen-garden maintained foreward. Legions of stores are being taken on board. Mrs. Colonel Chutney's grand piano; old Mr. Mango's (of the civil service) hookahs and black servants; harness, saddlery, and sporting tackle for

Lieutenant Griffin of the Bombay Cavalry. And there are spruce young cadets whose means do not permit them to go by the overland route, and steady-going civil and military servants of the Company, going out after furlough, and who do not object to a four months' sea-voyage. And there are black Ayahs, and Hookabadars, and Lascars, poor, bewildered, shivering, brown-faced Orientals, staring at everything around them, as if they had not quite got over their astonishment yet at the marvels of Frangistan. I wonder whether the comparison is unfavourable to us in their Brahminical minds, between the cold black swampy Isle of Dogs, the inky water, the slimy hulls, the squalid labourers, the rain and sleet; and the hot sun and yellow sands of Calcutta : the blue water, and dark maiden, with her water-pitcher on her head ;—the sacred Ganges, the rich dresses, stately elephants, half-naked Sircars of Hindostan ;—the rice and arrack, the paddy-fields and bungalows, the punkato, palankeen, and yellow streak of caste of Bengal the beloved ! Perhaps.

Passengers are coming aboard the Indiaman, old stagers wrangling as to the security of their standing bed-places, and young ladies consigned to the Indian matrimonial market, delightfully surprised and confused at everything. The potent captain of the ship is at the Jerusalem Coffee-house, or busy with his brokers ; but the mates are hard at work, bawling, commanding, and counter-commanding. Jack is alive, above, below, aloft, and in the hold, as usual, shouldering casks as though they were pint pots, and hoisting horses about manfully.

Shall we leave the Isle of Dogs, and glance at the West India Docks for a moment ? Plenty to see here at all events. Rice, sugar, pepper, tobacco ; desks saturated quite brown with syrup and molasses, just as the planks of a whaling ship are slippery. Jack, in a saccharine state, strongly perfumed with coffee-berries. Black Jack, very woolly-headed, and ivory-grindered, cooking, fiddling, and singing, as it seems the nature of Black Jack to cook, fiddle, and sing. Where the union-jack flies, Nigger Jack is well treated. English sailors do not disdain to drink with him, work with him, and sing with him. Take a wherry, however, to that American clipper, with the tall masts, and the tall man for skipper, and you will hear a different tale. Beneath the star-spangled banner, the allowance of halfpence for Nigger Jacks decreases wofully, while that of kicks increases in an alarming proportion. I would rather not be a black man on board an American ship.

In the London Docks we have a wonderful mixture of the ships of all nations : while on a Sunday the masts are dressed out with a very kaleidoscope of variegated ensigns. Over the ship's side lounge stunted Swedes and Danes, and oleaginous Russians ; while in another, the nimble Gaul, faithful to the traditions of his *cuisine*, is busy scraping carrots for a *pot au feu.*

Not in one visit—not in two—could you, O reader ! penetrate into a tithe of the mysteries of maritime London ; not in half a dozen papers could I give you a complete description of Jack alive in London. We might wander through the dirty mazes of Wapping, glancing at the queer, disused old stairs, and admiring the admirable mixture of rotting boats, tarry cable, shell-fish, mud, and bad characters, which is there conglomerated. We could study Jack alive in the hostelries, where, by night, in rooms the walls of which are decorated with verdant landscapes, he dances to the notes of the enlivening fiddle; we might follow him in his uneven wanderings, sympathise with him when he has lost his register ticket, denounce the Jews and crimps who rob him. Let us hope that Jack's life will be amended with the times in which we are fortunate enough to live; and that those who have the power and the means, may not long want the inclination to stretch forth a helping hand to him. Ratcliffe and Shadwell, Cable Street and Back Lane, may be very curious in their internal economy, and very picturesque in their dirt ; but it cannot be a matter of necessity that those who toil so hard, and contribute in so great a degree to our grandeur and prosperity, should be so unprotected and so little cared for.

V

THINGS DEPARTED.

I USE the parlour, I am not ashamed to say it, of the 'Blue Pigeon.' There was an attempt, some months since, headed I believe, by that self-educated young jackanapes, Squrrel, to prevail on the landlord to change the appellation of ' parlour ' into ' coffee-room ;' to substitute horsehair-covered benches for the Windsor chairs ; to take the sand off the floor, and the tobacco-stoppers off the table. *I* opposed it. Another person had the impudence to propose the introduction of a horribly seditious publication, which he called a liberal newspaper. I opposed it. So I did the anarchical proposition to rescind our standing order, that any gentleman smoking a cigar instead of a pipe, on club nights, should be fined a crown bowl of punch. From this you will, perhaps, sir, infer that I am a Conservative. Perhaps I am. I have my own opinions about Catholic Emancipation, Parliamentary Reform, and the Corn Laws.

I have nothing to do with politics, nor politics with me, just now; but I will tell you what object I have in addressing you. I can't help thinking, coming home from the club, how curiously we adapt ourselves to the changes that are daily taking place around us; how, one by one, old habits and old customs die away, and we go about our business as unconcernedly as though they never had been. Almost the youngest of us—if he choose to observe, and can remember what he observes—must have a catalogue of 'things departed;' of customs, ceremonies, institutions, to which people were used, and which fell gradually into disuse; which seemed, while they existed, to be almost necessaries of life, and for which now they don't care the value of a Spanish bond. There was a friend of mine, a man of genius, whose only fault was his continuous drunkenness, who used to say that the pith of the whole matter lay in the 'doctrine of averages.' I was never a dab at science and that sort of thing; but I suppose he meant that there was an average in the number of his tumblers of brandy and water, in the comings up of new fashions, and in the goings down of old ones; then of the old ones coming up again, and so *vice versâ*, till I begin to get muddled (morally muddled, of course), and give up the doctrine of averages in despair.

I have a copious collection in my memory of things departed. I am no chicken (though not the gray-headed old fogy that insulting Squrrel presumes to call me); but if I were to tell you a tithe of what I can remember in the way of departed fashions, manners, and customs, the very margins of this paper would be flooded with type. Let me endeavour to recall a few—a very few only—of what I call things departed.

Hackney-coaches, for instance. Why, a boy of twelve years of age can remember them; and yet, where are they now? Who thinks of them? Grand, imposing, musty-smelling, unclean old institutions they were. Elaborate heraldic devices covered their panels; dim legends used to be current amongst us children, that they had all been noblemen's carriages once upon a time, but falling—with the

princely houses they appertained to—into decay, had so come
to grief and hackney-coachhood. They had wonderful coachmen, too—imposing individuals, in coats with capes infinite
in number. How they drove! How they cheated! How
they swore! The keenest of your railway cabbies, the most
extortionate of your crack Hansoms, would have paled before
the unequalled Billingsgate of those old-world men, at the
comprehensive manner in which you, your person, costume,
morals, family, and connections were cursed. As all boatmen at Portsmouth have (or say they have) been Nelson's cox-
swain, so used I to believe every hackney-coachman I saw to
be the identical Jarvey who had been put inside his own
vehicle by the Prince of Wales, and driven about the metropolis by that frolicsome and royal personage, in company
with Beau Brummel, Colonel Hanger, and Philippe Egalité.
But the hackney-coach is now one of the things departed.
There is one—one still, I believe—stationed in the environs
of North Audley Street, Oxford Street. I have seen it—a
ghostly, unsubstantial pageant—flit before me, among cabs
and omnibuses, like a vehicular phantom ship. The coachman is not the rubicund, many-caped Jehu of yore. He is
a thin, weazened old man in a *jacket* (hear it!) and Wellington
boots. The armorial bearings on the coach-panels are defaced ;
the springs creak ; the wheels stumble as they roll. I should
like to know the man who has the courage to call that
hackney-coach off the stand, and to ride in it. He *must* be a
Conservative.

What have they done with the old hackney-coaches ? Have
they sent them to Paris as raw materials for barricades ? Are
their bodies yet mouldering, as in a vale of dry bones, in
some Long Acre coach-builder's back shop ? and some day,
mounted on fresh springs, fresh painted and fresh glazed,
newly emblazoned with heraldic lies, with flaunting hammer-
cloths and luxurious squabs, are they to roll once more to
courtly levée, or civic feast, to stop the way at ball or opera, to
rattle nobility to the portal of St. George's, Hanover Square,
to be married, or follow it, creeping, and with windows up, to
be buried ?

What have they done with the old cabriolets, too—the
bouncing, rattling, garishly-painted cabs, with a hood over the
passenger, and a little perch on one side for the driver ? They
upset apple-stalls often—their fares, too, frequently. Their
drivers were good whips, and their horses skittish. Where
are they now ? Do they ply in the streets of Sydney or San

Francisco, or have their bodies been cut up, years ago, for firewood and lucifer-matches?

Intimately connected, in association and in appearance, with the Jarveys, were the Charleys, or watchmen. They went out with oil-lamps, the Duke of Wellington's ministry, and the Bourbon family. Like the coachmen, they wore many-caped coats; like them, they wore low-crowned hats, and were rubicund in the countenance; like them, they were abusive. In the days of our youth we used to beat these Charleys, to appropriate their rattles, to suspend them in mid air, like Mahomet's coffin, in their watch-boxes. Now-a-days, there be stern men, Policemen, in oilskin hats, with terrible truncheons, and who 'stand no nonsense;' *they* do all the beating themselves, and lock us up when we would strive to knock them down. There is yet, to this day, a watch-box— a real monumental watch-box standing, a relic of days gone by—somewhere near Orchard Street, Portman Square. It has been locked up for years; and great-coated policemen pass it nightly, on their beat, and cast an anxious glance towards it, lest night-prowlers should be concealed behind its worm-eaten walls.

And, touching great-coats, are not great-coats themselves among the things departed? We have Paletôts (the name of which many have assumed), Ponchos, Burnouses, Sylphides, Zephyr wrappers, Chesterfields, Llamas, Pilot wrappers, Wrap-rascals, Bisuniques, and a host of other garments, more or less answering the purpose of an over-coat. But where is the great-coat—the long, voluminous, wide-skirted garment of brown or drab broadcloth, reaching to the ankle, possessing unnumbered pockets; pockets for bottles, pockets for sandwiches, secret pouches for cash, and side-pockets for bank-notes? This venerable garment had a cape, which, in wet or snowy weather, when travelling outside the ' High-flyer' coach, you turned over your head. Your father wore it before you, and you hoped to leave it to your eldest son. Solemn repairs—careful renovation of buttons and braiding were done to it, from time to time. A new great-coat was an event—a thing to be remembered as happening once or so in a lifetime.

There are more coaches and coats that are things departed, besides hackney-coachmen and long great-coats. Where are the short stages? Where are the days when we went gipsying, in real stage-coaches, from the ' Flower-Pot,' in Bishopsgate Street, to Epping Forest, or to Kensington, or to the

inaccessible Hampstead ? The time occupied in those memorable journeys now suffices for our transportation to Brighton —
fifty-two good English miles. Where is the Brighton coach
itself? its four blood-horses; the real live baronet, who coached
it for a livelihood; and, for all the 'bloody hand' in his
scutcheon, sent round his servant to collect the gratuitous half-
crowns from the passengers.

Things departed are the pleasant view of London from
Shooter's Hill, the houses on the river, and, over all, the
great dome of St. Paul's looming through the smoke. What
is the great North Road now? one of the Queen's highways,
and nothing more; but, in those days, it was the great coach-
ing thoroughfare of the kingdom. Highgate flourished; but,
where is Highgate now? I was there the other day. The
horses were gone, and the horse-troughs, and the horse-
keepers. Yet, from the window of the Gate-house I could
descry in one *coup d'œil*, looking northwards, *thirteen public-
houses*. The street itself was deserted, save by a ragged
child, struggling with a pig for the battered remnant of a
kettle. I wondered who supported those public-houses now;
whether the taps were rusty, and the pots dull; or whether,
in sheer desperation at the paucity of custom, the publicans
had their beer from one another's houses, and, at night,
smoked their pipes and drank their grog in one another's bar-
parlours. So, yet wondering and undecided, I passed through
Highgate Archway—where no man offered to swear me—
and came to the turnpike, where I saw a lamentable illustration
of the hardness of the times, in the turnpike-man being obliged
to take toll in kind; letting a costermonger and a donkey-cart
through for vegetables; and a small boy, going Islington-wards,
for an almost bladeless knife.

Where is Cranbourne Alley? where that delightful maze of
dirty, narrow, little thoroughfares, leading from Leicester
Square to St. Martin's Lane? There was an alley of bonnet-
shops—behind whose dusty windows faded Tuscans and
Leghorns were visible, and at the doors of which stood
women, slatternly in appearance, but desperate and accomplished touters. Man, woman, or child, it was all the same to
them; if they had made up their minds that you were to buy
a bonnet, buy one you were obliged to do, unless gifted with
rare powers for withstanding passionate persuasion and awful
menace. Piteous stories were told of feeble-minded old
gentlemen emerging from the 'courts,' half-fainting, laden
with bonnet-boxes, and minus their cash, watches, and jewel-

lery, which they had left behind them, in part payment for merchandise which they had bought, or had been compelled to buy. The Lowther Arcade was not built in those days ; and, in Cranbourne Alley, there were toy-shops, and cheap jewellery warehouses, and magazines for gimcracks of every description. Moreover, in Cranbourne Alley was there not Hamlet's—not Hamlet the Dane, but Hamlet, the silversmith ! How many times have I stood, wondering, by those dirty windows, when I ought to have been wending my way to Mr. Wackerbarth's seminary for young gentlemen ! Peering into the dim obscurity, dimly making out stores of gigantic silver dish-covers, hecatombs of silver spoons and forks— Pelions upon Ossas of race-cups and church services,—Hamlet was, to me, a synonyme with boundless wealth, inexhaustible credit, the payment of Consols—the grandeur of commercial Britain, in fact. Hamlet, Cranbourne Alley, and the Constitution ! Yet Cranbourne Alley and Hamlet are both things departed.

In the shops of this neighbourhood they sold things which have long since floated down the sewer of Lethe into the river of Limbo. What has become of the tinder-box ?—the box we never could find when we wanted it ; the tinder that wouldn't light ; the flint and steel that wouldn't agree to strike a light till we had exhausted our patience, and chipped numerous small pieces of skin and flesh from our fingers ? Yet Bacon wrote his ' Novum Organum,' and Blackstone his ' Commentaries,' by tinder-box-lighted lamps : and Guy Fawkes was very nearly blowing up the Legislature with a tinder-box-lighted train. The tinder-box is gone now ; and, in its place, we have sinister-looking splints, made from chopped-up coffins ; which, being rubbed on sand-paper, send forth a diabolical glare, and a suffocating smoke. But they do not fail, like the flint and steel, and light with magical rapidity ; so, as everybody uses them, I am obliged to do so too.

And, while I speak of lights and smoke, another thing departed comes before me. There is no such a thing as a pipe of tobacco now-a-days, sir. I see English gentlemen go about smoking black abominations like Irish apple-women. I hear of Milo's, Burns' cutty-pipes, Narghiles, Chiboucks, meerschaums, hookahs, water-pipes, straw-pipes, and a host of other inventions for emitting the fumes of tobacco. But where, sir, is the old original alderman-pipe, the churchwarden's-pipe, the unadulterated ' yard of clay ?' A man was wont to moisten the stem carefully with beer ere he put it to his lips ; when once it was alight, it kept alight ; a man could sit behind that pipe, but can a man sit behind the ridiculous figments they call pipes now? The yard of clay is departed. A dim shadow of it lingers sometimes in the parlours of old city taverns ; I met with it once in the Bull Ring at Birmingham. I have heard of it in Chester ; but in its entirety, as a popular, acknowledged pipe, it must be numbered with the things that were.

Where are the franks? I do not allude to the warlike race of Northmen, who, under the sway of Pharamond, first gave France its name ; neither do I mean those individuals who, rejoicing in the appellation of Francis, are willing to accept the diminutive of Frank—I mean those folded sheets of letter-paper, which, being endorsed with the signature of a peer, or of a Member of Parliament, went thenceforward post-free. There were regular frank-hunters—men who could nose a Member who had not yet given all his franks away, with a scent as keen as ever Cuban bloodhound had for negro flesh. He would give chase in the lobby : run down the doomed legislator within the very shadow of the Sergeant-at-Arms' bag-wig ; and, after a brief contest, unfrank him on the spot. They were something to look at, and something worth having, those franks, when the postage to Edinburgh was thirteen-pence. But the franks are gone—gone with the procession of the mail-coaches on the first of May ; they have fallen before little effigies of the sovereign, printed in red, and gummed at the back. English Members of Parliament have no franks now ; and the twenty-five (though of a metallic nature) allowed, till very lately, to the Members of the French Legislature, have even been abolished.

I never think of franks without a regretful remembrance of another thing departed—a man who, in old times, stood on the steps of the Post-office in St. Martin's-le-Grand, with a sheet of cartridge-paper, and whom I knew by the appellation of ' it forms.' ' It forms,' he was continually saying, ' now it forms a jockey-cap, now a church-door, a fan, a mat, the paddle-boxes of a steamer, a cocked hat ;' and, as he spoke, he twisted the paper into something bearing a resemblance to the articles he named. He is gone ; so is the sheet of fools-cap *we* used to twist into the semblance of cocked hats, silk-worm boxes, and boats, when boys at school. The very secret of the art is lost in these degenerate days, I verily believe, like that of making Venetian bezoar, or staining glass for windows.

Whole hosts of street arts and street artists are among the things departed. Where is the dancing bear, with his piteous brown muzzle and uncouth gyrations? Where is the camel? Where the tight-rope dancers? the performers on stilts? Where are these gone? Say not that the New Police Act has abolished them; for though that sweeping piece of legislation has silenced the dustman's bell, and bade the muffin-boy cry muffins no more, we have still the organ-grinders with, or without, monkeys, the Highland bagpipes, and the acrobats. The fantoccinis are almost extinct; and I suppose Punch will go next. It is all very well, and right, and proper, of course. Dancing bears and camels, monkeys and fantoccinis, are all highly immoral, no doubt; but I should just like to see what the British Constitution would be without Punch and Judy!

The small-coal man is gone; the saloop stall; the blind man and his dog are becoming *raræ aves;* the grizzled Turk with a dirty turban, and a box of rhubarb before him, is scarcely ever to be met with. In his stead we have a liver-coloured Lascar, shivering in white cotton robes, selling tracts of the inflammatory order of Piety, and occasionally offering them in exchange for gin. Age, caprice, the encouragement of new favourites, are driving these old-established ornaments of the streets away.

I do not quarrel so much with the ever-changing fashions in dress. I can give up without a sigh the leg-of-mutton sleeves, those dreadful pear-shaped monsters of silk and muslin, they wore about the year '30. I will not clamour for the revival of the bishop's sleeves—unwieldy articles that were always either getting squashed flat as a pancake in a crowd, or dipping into the gravy at dinner. I will resign the monstrous Leghorn hats—the short-waisted pelisses, the Cossack trousers, and flaming stocks in which we arrayed ourselves when George the Fourth was king; but let me drop one tear, heave one sigh, to the memories of pig-tails and Hessian boots.

Both are things departed. One solitary pig-tail, I believe, yet feebly flourishes in some remote corner of the agricultural districts of England. It comes up to town during the season; and I have seen it in New Burlington Street. The Hessians, though gone from the lower extremities of a nation, yet find abiding-place on the calves of the Stranger in Mr. Kotzebue's play of that name, and over the portals of some bootmakers of the old school. The Hessians of our youth are gone. The mirror-polished, gracefully-outlined, silken-tasselled Hessians exist no more — those famous boots, the soles of which Mr. Brummel caused to be blacked, and in the refulgent lustre of which the gentleman of fashion immortalised by Mr. Warren was wont to shave himself.

Of the buildings, the monuments, the streets, which are gone, I will not complain. I can spare that howling desert in the area of Leicester Fields, with its battered railings, its cat-haunted parterres, its gravel walks, usurped by snails, and overgrown with weeds. I like Mr. Wyld's Great Globe better. I can dispense with the old Mews of Charing Cross, and the bill-covered hoarding surrounding them, though I loved the latter, for the first announcement of the first play I ever saw was pasted there. I like Trafalgar Square (barring the fountains) better. I can surrender the horrible collection of mangy sheds, decomposed vegetables, and decaying baskets, which used to block up Farringdon Street, and which they called Fleet Market. I can renounce, though with a sigh, the Fleet Prison, acquiesce in the superiority of New Oxford Street over St. Giles's and the Holy Land, and of Victoria Street, as compared with the dirt and squalor and crime of Westminster. Yet let me heave one sigh for King's Cross, that anomalous little area where many roads converge, and many monuments have stood. There was a stone monster, an adamantine Guy Fawkes, which was traditionally supposed to represent George the good, the magnificent, the great; his curly wig, his portly mien, his affable countenance. Little boys used to chalk their political opinion freely on the pedestal, accompanied by rough cartoons of their parents and guardians, their pastors and masters; omnibus drivers and conductors pointed the finger of hilarity at it, as they passed by; it was a great statue. They have taken it away, with the Small-pox Hospital into the bargain, and though they have set up another George, stirrupless, hatless, and shoeless, in Trafalgar Square, and the Hospital is removed elsewhere, the terminus of the Great Northern Railway, and the pedestal with three big lamps now standing in their stead, are a dis-sight to mine eyes, and make me long for the old glories of King's Cross and Battle Bridge.

Smithfield is going. Tyburn is gone (I am not such an old fogy, Mr. Squrrel, as to be able to remember *that;* nor so stanch a Conservative as to regret it, now that it is gone). Bartholomew Fair is gone. Greenwich Fair going. Chalk Farm Fair a melancholy mockery of merriment. Let me ask a few more interrogations, and let me go too.

Where are the fogs? Light brumous vapours I see hanging over London, in December; but not the fogs of my youth. They were orange-coloured, substantial, palpable fogs, that you could cut with a knife, or bottle up for future inspection. In those fogs vessels ran each other down on the river; link-boys were in immense request; carriages and four drove into chemists' shops and over bridges; and in the counting-house of Messrs. Bingo, Mandingo, and Flamingo, where I was a small boy, copying letters, we burnt candles in the battered old sconces all day long. I saw a fog, a real fog, the other day, travelling per rail from Southampton; but it was a white one, and gave me more the idea of a balloon voyage than of the fog *de facto*.

Gone with the fogs are the link-boys, the sturdy, impudent varlets, who beset you on murky nights with their flaming torches, and the steady-going, respectable, almost aristocratic link-bearers, with silver badges often, who had the monopoly of the doors of the opera, and of great men's houses, when balls or parties were given. I knew a man once who was in the habit of attending the nobility's entertainments, not by the virtue of an invitation, but by the grace of his own indomitable impudence, and by the link-boys' favour. An evening costumo, an unblushing mien, and a crown to the link-boy, would be sufficient to make that worthy bawl out his name and style to the hall-porter; the hall-porter would shout it to the footman; the footman yell it to the groom of the chambers; while the latter intoning it for the benefit of the lady or gentleman of the house, those estimable persons would take it for granted that they *must* have invited him; and so bowing and compli-menting, as a matter of course, leave him without restriction to his devices, in the way of dancing, flirting, *écarté*-playing, and supper-eating. Few and far between are the link-boys in this present 1860. The running footmen with the flambeaux have vanished these many years; and the only mementos surviving of their existence are the blackened extinguishers attached to the area railings of some old-fashioned houses about Grosvenor Square. With the flambeaux, the sedan-chairs have also disappeared; the drunken Irish chairmen who carried them; the whist-loving old spinsters, who delighted to ride inside them. I have seen *disjecta membra*—venerable ruins, here and there, of the sedan-chairs at Bath, at Cheltenham, at Brighton; but the bones thereof are marrowless, and its eyes without speculation.

The old articles of furniture that I loved, are things

departed. The mirror, with its knobby gilt frame, and stunted little branches for candles, the podgy eagle above it, and its convex surface reflecting your face in an eccentric and distorted manner; the dumb waiter, ugly and useful; the dear old spinnet, on which aunt Sophy used to play those lamentable pieces of music, the 'Battle of Prague' and the 'Caliph of Bagdad;' * the old cheffonnier, the 'whatnot,' and the 'Canterbury;' the workbox, with a view of the Pavilion at Brighton on the lid; the Tunbridge ware, (supplanted now by vile, beautifully-painted, artistic things of papier-mâché, from Birmingham, forsooth,)—gone, and for ever.

Even while I talk, whole crowds of 'things departed' flit before me, of which I have neither time to tell, nor you patience to hear. Post-boys, 'wax-ends from the palace,' Dutch pugs, black footmen, the window-tax, the Palace Court, Gatton, and Old Sarum! What will go next, I wonder? Temple Bar, Lord Mayor's Day,† or the 'Gentleman's Magazine?'

Well, well: it is all for the best, I presume. The trivial things that I have babbled of, have but departed with the leaves and the melting snow—with the hopes that are extinguished, and the ambition that is crushed—with dear old friends dead, and dearer friendships severed. I will be content to sit on the milestone by the great road, and, smoking my pipe, watch the chariot of life, with Youth on the box and Pleasure in the dicky, tear by till the dust thrown up by its wheels has whitened my hair, and it shall be my time to be numbered among the things departed.

VI.

PHASES OF 'PUBLIC' LIFE.

CHAPTER I.

WHEN the race of this huge London World-City shall be run —when the millstone shall have been cast into its waters, and the word has gone forth that Babylon the great is fallen, is fallen—when the spider shall weave his web amidst the broken columns of the Bank; the owl shriek through the deserted arcades of the Exchange; and the jackal prowl through labyrinths of ruins and rubbish, decayed oyster-shells,

* Temporarily resuscitated lately.
† It is well nigh gone. The man in armour is a myth, and his place knows him no more.

and bleached skeletons of the dogs of other days, where once was Regent Street—I should very much like to know what the 'Central Australian Society for the Advancement of Science,' or the 'Polynesian Archæological Association,' or the 'Imperial New Zealand Society of Antiquaries,' would be likely to make of a great oblong board which glares at me through the window at which I am writing this present paper —a board some five-and-twenty feet in length perchance, painted a bright resplendent blue, and on which are emblazoned in glittering gold the magic words, 'Barclay, Perkins, and Co.'s Entire.'

One of these boards will, perchance, be disinterred by some persevering *savant* from a heap of the relics of old London antiquities; wheel-less, shaft-less, rotting Hansom's cabs, rusted chimney-cowls, turnpike-gates of ancient fashion and design, gone-by gas-lamps and street-posts. And the *savant* will doubtless imagine that he will find in the mysterious board—the once glittering characters—some sign, some key, to the secret freemasonry, some shibboleth of the old London world. Learned pamphlets will be written, doubtless, to prove a connection between Barclay and Perkins, and Captain Barclay the pedestrian, and Perkins' steam-gun, who and which, joined together by some Siamese bond of union, became thenceforth and for ever one entire 'Co.' Other sages, haply, will have glimmering notions that Barclay and Perkins have something to do with a certain XXX.; others stoutly maintain that the words formed but Christian and surnames, common among the inhabitants of old London, even as were the well-known 'Smiths,' and the established 'Jones.' 'We know,' they will say, 'that the great architect of the most famous buildings in old London was called "Voluntary Contributions;" we know that a majority of the citizens of that bygone city were addicted to the creed of Zoroaster, or sun-worship; for we find on the ruins of their houses votive plates of brass, of circular form, bearing an effigy of the sun, with a reference to fire-insurance—these things have been demonstrated by learned doctors and professors of ability; why may we not, then, assume that Barclay and Perkins were names possessed in an astonishingly prolific degree by London citizens, who, proud of belonging to so respectable a family, were in the habit of blazoning the declaration of their lineage in blue and gold on an oblong board, and affixing the same to the front of their houses?' The Emperor of China has upwards of five thousand cousins, who are distinguished from the tag-rag and bobtail of the Celestial Empire by wearing yellow girdles. ' Why,' these sages will ask, 'may not the parent Barclay Perkins have been a giant, blessed with hundreds of arrows in his quiver, whose thousand thousand descendants were proud to be clad like him in a livery of blue and gold ?'

Then the sages will squabble, and wrangle, and call each other bad names, and write abusive diatribes against each other by magnetic telegraph, just as other sages were wont to squabble and wrangle about the Rosetta Stone, the Source of the Niger, and Bruce's discoveries ; or, as they do now, about the North-West passage and the *percement* of the Isthmus of Suez, the causes of the cholera and diphtheria, and the possibility of aërial navigation. As it has been, so it is, and will be, I suppose ; and if we can't agree nowadays, so shall we, or rather our descendants, disagree in times to come, and concerning matters far less recondite or abstruse than Barclay Perkins.

I know what Barclay and Perkins mean, I hope ;—what Combe and Delafield—what Truman, Hanbury, and Buxton— what Calvert and Co.—what Reid and Co.--what Bass—what Allsopp—what Broadwood, Mundell, and Huggins. *You* know, too, gentle, moderate, and bibulous reader of the present age. They all mean BEER. Beer, the brown, the foaming, the wholesome, and refreshing, when taken in moderation ; the stupefying, and to-station-house-leading, when imbibed to excess. That oblong board, all blue and gold, I have spoken of as visible from my parlour window, has no mystery for me. Plainly, unmistakably, it says *Beer :* a good tap ; fourpence a pot in the pewter ; threepence per ditto if sent for in your own jug.

And if you admit (and you will admit, or you are no true Englishman) that beer be good—and, being good, that we should be thankful for it—can you tell me any valid reason why I should not write on the subject of Beer ? Seeing how many thousands of reputable persons there are throughout the country who live by the sale of beer, and how many millions drink it,—seeing that beer is literally in everybody's mouth, it strikes me we should not ignore beer taken in its relation towards the belles lettres. Tarry with me, then, while I discourse on Beer—on the sellers and the buyers thereof—and of their habitations. I will essay to navigate my little bark down a river of beer, touching, perchance, at some little spiritcreek, or gently meandering through the ' back-waters ' of neat wines.

When the Spanish student—immortalised by Le Sage—was inducted into the mysteries of the private life of Madrid, he availed himself of a temporary aërial machine, in a person of diabolical extraction, called Asmodeus—who further assisted him in his bird's-eye inspection, by taking the roofs off the houses. When the nobility and gentry frequenting the fashionable circles of the Arabian Nights, were desirous of travelling with extraordinary rapidity, they were sure to be accommodated with magical carpets, or swift-flying eagles, or winged horses. Then they could be rendered invisible, or provided with telescopes, enabling them to see through every obstacle, from stone walls to steel castles; but things are changed, and times are altered now. One can't go from London to Liverpool without buying a railway-ticket, and being importuned to show it half a dozen times in the course of the journey. If you want to study character in the Stock Exchange, you can get no more invisible suit to do it in than a suit of invisible green, and run, moreover, the risk of hearing a howl of '201!' and feeling two hundred pair of hands, and two hundred pair of feet to match, bonneting, buffeting, hustling, and kicking you from the high place of Mammon.

So, then, in the study of Beer and Beerhouses, I have had no adventitious aid from accommodating demons, obliging genii, invisible caps, carpets, or cloaks. '*Experientia*'—you know the rest. I have graduated in Beer; I have mastered its mysteries; and I will now assume, for your benefit, a magic power, which I devoutly wish I had possessed during my Beery researches. Come with me, then, in the spirit, to Bankside; and, after a cursory stroll round the fountain-head of beer, let us seat ourselves (still in the spirit) at the tail of one of these big drays, drawn by big horses, and, fearing no cries of 'whip behind!' from jealous boys (for, being spiritual, we are, of course, invisible), perambulate the metropolis, rapt in the contemplation of Beer. Surrounded with Barclay and Perkins's beer-barrels, our steeds conducted by Barclay and Perkins's red night-capped draymen, we will go in this, our magic chariot, from public-house to public-house: 'The latent tracks, the giddy heights explore;' 'shoot folly as it flies, and catch the manners living as they rise;' attempt a mild classification of the peculiar social characteristics of the different metropolitan 'publics;' give, in short, a view and a description, however lame and incomplete it may be, of 'London on Tap.'

I do not purpose, in these pages, at least, to enter minutely into the consideration of the aspect of a London Brewery, or of the manufacture of the great English beverage ; so, then, our stay will be but short in this huge brick beer emporium. I make remark, *en passant*, that an odour prevails in and about the establishment, resembling an amalgamation of several washing-days, a few cookshops, and a stable or two. To cursory spectators, such as you and I are, the brewery will offer very little besides this, and a general impression of ' bigness,' length, height, breadth, rotundity. The premises are large, the vats are large ; the stables, the strong, stalwart, horses, the provisions of hay and straw, of malt and hops, of smoke and steam, are all large. Large, also, to almost Titanic extensiveness, are the draymen—gladiators of the Beery arena, with Phrygian caps of scarlet hue, and wide-spread leathern aprons. Large are *their* labours ; larger still their appetites ; largest and mightiest of all, their thirst of beer. Grocers and pastry-cooks, they say, give their apprentices and shopmen the run of all the delicacies they deal in, for the first month of their service—*carte blanche* to the plums, and figs, and tarts, of which—to the ultimate benefit of the tradesmen—they speedily get very sick and tired ; but with the drayman-neophyte it seems quite different ; for I never heard—nor, did I hear, should I credit the assertion—that any of Barclay and Perkins's men ever got tired of Barclay and Perkins's tap. Largely impressed, therefore, with their pervading largeness, we will leave the brewhouse for the present.

Privately, we may be allowed, and confidentially, to surmise, that the profits of the proprietors are also large—very large, indeed ; but goodness forbid that we should venture to hint (aloud at least) that the prices they demand and obtain for beer are large, and—considering malt, and hops, and grain, and Free Trade, and that sort of thing—a great deal too large, and not quite just.

The heavy wheels of our chariot have been rumbling, while I spoke, through the great thoroughfare which commences at Charing Cross, and ends at Mile End—somewhere about where there was, once on a time, a Maypole. It diverges, going westward ; and we are in a trice in a street, in which *I* never was in a vehicle in my life without being blocked up, and in which, in the present instance, we are comfortably wedged with a timber-laden waggon, a hearse, and an advertising-van in front, and a Hansom cab or two, a mail-phaeton, and Mr. Ex-Sheriff Pickles's elegant chariot behind. Leaving the respective drivers to exchange compliments, couched in language more or less parliamentary, we will descend for a moment — for the neighbourhood is thickly studded with public-houses—and we shall have time, ere our chariot be extricated, to investigate numerous varieties of 'London on Tap.'

Here, first—blatant, gay, and gaudy—is a GIN PALACE—a 'ginnery,' in full swing.

The Palladio or the Vitruvius who built this palace, has curiously diversified the orders of architecture in its construction. We have Doric shafts with Corinthian capitals—an Ionic frieze—Renaissance panels—a Gothic screen to the bar-parlour. But French polish and gilding cover a multitude of (architectural) sins; and there is certainly no lack of either the one or the other here. Tier above tier surround the walls, supporting gigantic casks, bearing legends of a fabulous number of gallons contained within. Yet are they not dummies; for we may observe spiral brass pipes, wriggling and twisting in snake-like contortions till they reach the bar, and so to the spirit-taps, where they bring the costly hogshead of the distiller home to the lips of the humblest costermonger, for a penny a glass. Beer is sold, and in considerable quantities—a halfpenny a pint cheaper, too, than at other hostelries; but it is curious beer—beer of a half-sweet, half-acrid taste, black to the sight, unpleasant to the taste, brown in the froth, muddy in consistence. Has it been in delicate health, and can that shabby old man, in close confab with the landlord at the door, at the steps of the cellar, be the 'Doctor?' Or has it been adulterated, 'fined,' doctored, patched, and cobbled up, for the amusement and instruction of amateurs in beer—like steam-frigates, for instance, or Acts of Parliament?

The area before the bar, you will observe, is very spacious. At this present second hour of the afternoon, there are, perhaps, fifty people in it; and it would hold, I dare say, full twenty more, and allow space, into the bargain, for a neat stand-up fight. One seems very likely to take place now between the costermonger, who has brought rather an inconvenient number of 'kea-rots' and 'turmuts' into the bar with him, and a peripatetic vendor of fish—the quality of whose wares he has (with some show of justice, perhaps) impugned. So imminent does the danger appear, that the blind match-seller —who was anon importuning the belligerents—hastily scuttles off; and an imp of a boy, in a man's fustian jacket, and with a dirty red silk 'kerchief twisted round his bull neck, has

mounted the big tub, on which he sits astride, pipe in hand—
a very St. Giles's Bacchus—declaring that he will see 'fair
play.' Let us edge away a little towards the bar—for the
crowd towards the door is somewhat too promiscuous to be
agreeable ; and it is not improbable that in the *mêlée*, some
red-'kerchiefed citizen, of larger growth, whose extensor and
flexor muscles are somewhat more powerfully developed, may
make a savage assault on you, for his own private gratification,
and the mere pleasure of hitting somebody.

This ginnery has not only a bar public, but divers minor
cabinets, bibulous loose boxes, which are partitioned off from
the general area ; and the entrances to which are described in
flowery, but somewhat ambiguous language. There is the
'Jug and Bottle Entrance,' and the entrance 'For Bottles
only.' There is the 'Wholesale Bar,' and the 'Retail Bar ;'
but, wholesale or retail, jug or bottle, the different bars all
mean Gin ! The long pewter counter is common to all. A
counter perforated in elaborately-pricked patterns, like a
convivial shroud, apparently for ornament, but really for the
purpose of allowing the drainings, overflowings, and out-
spillings of the gin-glasses to drop through, which, being
collected with sundry washings, and a dash, perhaps, of fresh
material, is, by the thrifty landlord, dispensed to his customers
under the title of 'all sorts.' Your dram-drinker, look you,
is not unfrequently paralytic, wofully shaky in the hand ; and
the liquor he wastes, combined with that accidentally spilt,
tells up wonderfully at the close of the year. There are cake-
baskets on the counter, patronised mostly by the lady votaries
of the rosy (or livid ?) god ; but their tops are hermetically
sealed, and their dulcet contents protected by a wire dome, or
cupola, of convex form. Besides what I have described, if
you will add some of my old friends the gold-blazoned boards,
bearing the eulogies of various brewers, together with sundry
little placards, framed and glazed, and printed in colours,
telling, in seductive language, of 'Choice Compounds,' 'Old
Tom,' 'Cream of the Valley,' 'Superior Cream Gin,' 'The
Right Sort,' 'Kinahan's LL,' 'The Dew off Ben Nevis,' the
'Celebrated Balmoral Mixture, patronised by his Royal
Highness Prince Albert' (the illustrious personage, clad in
full Highland costume, with an extensive herd of red deer in
the distance, is represented taking a glass of the 'Mixture'
with great apparent gusto) ; besides these, I repeat, you will
need nothing to 'complete the costume,' as the romancers have
it, of a Gin Palace.

Except the landlord, perhaps, who is bald and corpulent, who has a massive watch-chain, and a multiplicity of keys, and whose hands seem to leave the pockets of his trousers as seldom as his keen eye does the gin-drawing gymnastics of his barmen. Gymnastics they are, *tours de force*, feats of calisthenics as agile as any performed by the agile professor whom I have just seen pass, all dirt, flesh-coloured drawers, and spangles. A quick, sharp, jerking twist for the spirit tap, allowing to run till the liquor is within a hair's breadth of the top of the measure, and no longer; a dexterous tilt of the 'two,' or 'three out' glasses required; an agile shoving forward of the pewter noggin with one hand, while the other inevitable palm is presented for the requisite halfpence; and oh! such a studious carefulness that one hand is not emptied before the other is filled. It is not everybody can serve in the bar of a Gin Palace. The barman wears a fur cap—generally —sometimes a wide-awake. He is addicted to carrying a piece of straw, a pipe-light, or the stalk of a flower in his mouth, diversifying it occasionally by biting half-crowns viciously. When he gives you change, he slaps it down on the counter in a provocatory manner; his face is flushed; his manner short, concise, sententious. His vocabulary is limited; a short 'Now then,' and a brief 'Here you are,' forming the staple phrases thereof. I wonder what his views of human nature—of the world, its manners, habits, and customs—can be like! Or what does the barmaid think of it? I should like to know: the young lady in the coal-black ringlets (like magnified leeches), the very brilliant complexion, and the coral necklace. Mercy on us! what can she, a girl of eighteen, think of the faces, the dress, the language of the miserable creatures among whom she spends sixteen hours of her life every day—every mortal day throughout the year—once in every three weeks (her 'day out') excepted?

One word about the customers, and we will rejoin our chariot, which must surely be extricated by this time. Thieves, beggars, costermongers, hoary-headed old men, stunted, ragged, shock-haired children, blowzy, slatternly women, hulking bricklayers, gaunt, sickly hobbledehoys, with long greasy hair. A thrice-told tale. Is it not the same everywhere? The same pipes, dirt, howling, maundering, fighting, staggering gin fever. Like plates multiplied by the electro process —like the printers' 'stereo'—like the reporter's 'manifold'—you will find duplicates, triplicates of these forlorn beings everywhere. The same woman giving her baby gin; the same haggard, dishevelled woman, trying to coax her drunken husband home; the same mild girl, too timid even to importune her ruffian partner to leave off drinking the week's earnings, who sits meekly in a corner, with two discoloured eyes, one freshly blacked—one of a week's standing. The same weary little man, who comes in early, crouches in a corner, and takes standing naps during the day, waking up periodically for 'fresh drops.' The same red-nosed, ragged object who disgusts you at one moment by the force and fluency of his Billingsgate, and surprises you the next by bursting out in Greek and Latin quotations. The same thin, spectral man who has no money, and with his hands piteously laid one over the other, stands for hours gazing with fishy eyes at the beloved liquor—smelling, thinking of, hopelessly desiring it. And lastly, the same miserable girl, sixteen in years, and a hundred in misery; with foul, matted hair, and death in her face; with a tattered plaid shawl, and ragged boots, a gin-and-fog voice, and a hopeless eye.

Mr. Ex-Sheriff Pickles's carriage no longer stops the way, and the big draymen have conducted the big horses and the big dray to its destination. Beer has to be delivered at the sign of the 'Green Hog Tavern;' whither, if you have no objection, we will forthwith hie.

The Green Hog is in a tortuous but very long street—a weak-minded street indeed, for it appears unable to decide whether to go to the right or to the left, straight or zigzag, to be broad or to be narrow. The Green Hog participates in this indecision of character. It evidently started with the intention of having a portico, but stopping short, compromised the matter by overshadowing the street door with a hideous excrescence between a verandah, a 'bulk,' and a porch. Contradictory, also, is the Green Hog; for it calls itself, over the door, the Green Hog Tavern, over the window, a Wine Vaults, and round the corner (in the Mews), a Spirit Stores. The bar is shamefaced, having run away to the end of a long passage; and even then, when you *do* get to it, it is more like a bow-window than like a bar, and more like a butler's pantry than either. Very few customers do you see standing at the bar of the Green Hog; yet does its verdant porcinity considerable business with Barclay Perkins.

The truth is, the Green Hog is one of a class of publics, becoming rapidly extinct in London. It is a tavern—one of the old, orthodox, top-booted, sanded-floored taverns. It does a good business, not by casual beer-drinkers, but in 'lunch, dinner, and supper beers.' A better business, perhaps, in wines and dinners; for to the Green Hog resort a goodly company of the customers of the 'old school,'—men who yet adhere to the traditional crown bowl of punch, and the historical 'rump and dozen,' who take their bottle of wine after dinner, and insist upon triangular spittoons. They are behind the times, perhaps, and the Green Hog is a little behind them too. The Green Hog can't make out competition, and new inventions, and fresh blood, and new resources. 'My father kept this house afore me,' says the Green Hog, 'and my son'll keep it after me.' So, within his orthodox and time-honoured precincts, a 'go' of sherry is still called a bottle of sherry—a glass of brandy and water is charged a shilling. 'Bell's Old Weekly Messenger' is taken in; and the Green Hog goes to bed at midnight—winter or summer—week-day or Sabbath.

The parlour (or common room) of the Green Hog is a sight. The ceiling is low and bulging, and is covered with a quiet, gray-patterned paper. There is a sanded floor, a big fireplace, 'settles' on either side thereof, long substantial tables, and a chair on a dais nailed against the wall. No newfangled portraits hang on the walls, of race-horses, Radical Members, of performers at the Theatres Royal. There is, however, Mr. Charles Young, in mezzotint, Roman costume, and toga. There is the best of monarchs in Jack-boots and a pig-tail, reviewing two hundred thousand volunteers in Hyde Park. There is the next best of monarchs in his curliest wig, smiling affably at the fur collar of his surtout. There is the portrait of the late landlord, and the portrait of the present one. There is, finally, Queen Caroline, looking deeply injured in an enormous hat and feathers, and an aquatint view of the opening of Blackfriars Bridge.

To this comfortable and old-fashioned retreat come the comfortable and old-fashioned customers, who 'use' the Green Hog. Hither comes Mr. Tuckard, a round old gentleman, supposed to be employed in some capacity at the Tower of London, but whether as a warder, an artilleryman, or a gentleman-gaoler—deponent sayeth not. He appears regularly at nine o'clock every morning, eats a huge meat-and-beer breakfast, orders his dinner, reappears at six o'clock precisely, eats a hearty dinner, drinks a bottle of port, and smokes nine pipes of tobacco, washed down by nine tumblers of gin and water. He invariably finishes his nine tumblers just as John the waiter (of whom no man ever knew the surname, or saw the bow to his neck-tie) brings in tumbler of brandy and water, number four, for Mr. Scrayles, the eminent corn-chandler (reported to be worth a mint of money). The door being opened, Mr. Tuckard rises, looks round, nods, and without further parley, makes a bolt through the door and disappears. This, with but few interruptions, he has done daily and nightly for five-and-thirty years. He rarely speaks but to intimate friends (with whom he has had a nodding acquaintance for twenty years, perhaps). He occasionally condescends to impart, in a fat whisper, his opinions about the funds and the weather. It is reported that he cannot read, for he never was known to take up a newspaper—that he cannot write—that he never sleeps. No one knows where he lives. He is Tuckard, employed in the Tower of London; that is all. Sometimes, on high days and holidays, he hands round a portentous golden snuff-box, purporting, from the engraving on its lid, to have been presented to Thomas Tuckard, Esquire, by his friends and admirers, members of the Cobb Club.' Who was Cobb? and what manner of Club was his?

Besides the mysterious possessor of the snuff-box, and the wealthy corn-chandler, there are some score more grave and sedate frequenters of the parlour, all 'warm' men, financially speaking, all quietly eloquent as to the funds, and the weather, and all fond of their bottle of wine, and their tumbler of grog. Time and weather, changes of ministry, births, deaths, and marriages, seem to have but little effect on them, nor to ruffle, in any sensible degree, the even tenour of their lives. They will continue, I have no doubt, to 'use' the Green Hog as long as they are able to use anything; and when the grog of life is drained, and the pipe of existence is extinguished, they will quietly give place to other old codgers, who will do, doubtless, as they did before them.

Don't suppose that Barclay and Perkins's dray, or Barclay and Perkins's men, have been idle or unprofitably employed while I have been poking about the parlour of the Green Hog. No: theirs has been the task to raise the cellar-flap on the pavement and to lower, by means of sundry chains and ropes, the mighty butts of beer required for the lunches, dinners, and suppers of the Green Hog's customers. Curious evolutions, both human and equestrian, were performed during the operation. Small boys took flying leaps over the prostrate barrels; the stalwart steeds cut figures of eight in the narrow thoroughfare, occasionally backing into the chandler's shop opposite, to the imminent peril of the Dutch cheeses, balls of twine, screws of tobacco, and penny canes there exposed to

view, and the loudly-expressed consternation of the proprie-
trix; the pavement on one side was rendered temporarily
impassable by a barricade of tightly-strained cordage, and
the otherwise equable temper of the servant-maid from No. 4,
seriously ruffled, as, emerging from the door with a foaming
jug of half-and-half, a dirty rope came right across her clean
white stocking. Then, after all this, have the gigantic draymen rested and refreshed themselves. A temporary game of
hide-and-seek has taken place—each red-capped butt-twister
wandering about anxiously inquiring for his 'mate;' but the
lost have been found; and, when from the dark and poky
parlour we re-enter the bow-windowed bar (where the sweet-
smelling thicket of lemons, and the punch-bowls, the punch-
ladles, with William and Mary guineas soldered in them, and the
bright-eyed landlord's daughter are)—we find the mighty yeomen discussing huge dishes of beefsteaks and onions, and swallowing deep draughts from the Pierian spring of Barclay's best.

Take with me, I entreat, a glass of Dutch bitters from that
pot-bellied, quaint-shaped bottle with the City shield and dagger
on it, for all the world like one of the flasks in Hogarth's
Modern Midnight Conversation. Then as the draymen have
finished their repast, and our chariot awaits us, let us sally forth
into London again, and seek a fresh tap.

What have we here? A pictorial 'public.' Lithographic
prints, wood engravings in the windows; Highland gentlemen,
asseverating, in every variety of attitude, that their names are
Norval—that their pedigrees are pastoral, and that their last
past places of residence were the Grampian Hills; Hamlet
declaring his capacity to tell a hawk from a handsaw; Job
Thornbury vindicating the rights of the Englishman's fireside:
Lady Macbeth lamenting the inutility of all the perfumes of
Arabia to sweeten 'this little hand'—which looks large;
clowns bewailing the loss of a 'farden,' grinning hideously
meanwhile—all as performed by Messieurs and Mesdames So-
and-so, at the Theatres Royal. The little glazed placards in
the window, telling of chops, steaks, and Schweppe's soda-
water, are elbowed, pushed from their stools, by cartoons of
the 'Bounding Brothers of the Himalaya Mountains;' Signor
Scapino and his celebrated dog Jowler; Herr Diavolo Buffo,
the famous corkscrew equilibrist (from the Danube), and tight-
rope dancer; or Mademoiselle Smicherini the dancer, with
undeniable silk fleshings, and very little else. Lower down,
bills of theatrical benefits, tournaments at tea-gardens, 'readings' from Shakspeare, and harmonic meetings, dispute the

pavement with the legitimate possessors of the soil—the brewers and distillers. Within is a grove—a forest rather, of play-bills, waving their red and black leaves in Vallambrosan density. Patent theatres, minor theatres, country theatres—even Transatlantic temples of the drama. This is a theatrical 'public'—a house of call for Thespians. Over the way is the Theatre Royal, Barbican; round the corner, up the court and two pair of stairs, Mr. Wilfred Grindoff Belville, has his theatrical agency office; here meet the Sock and Buskin Club; and here, in days gone by, the great Konks, the tragedian, was wont to imbibe that bottle and a half of gin, without the aid of which he disdained to perform his famous character of 'The Robber of the Hills.'

To the theatrical public come the actors of the Theatre Royal, Barbican, their friends and acquaintances, being actors at other theatres, and that anomalous class of persons who hunt for orders, and scrape acquaintance with theatrical people, of which and of whom they afterwards discourse voluminously in the genteel circles. Hither, also, come comedians, dancers, and pantomimists who are for the time out of engagements, who have placed their names on Mr. W. G. Belville's 'list,' and expect situations through his agency. A weary-looking, heart-sick with hope deferred body they are. There, intently studying the bill of the Bowie-knife Theatre, New York, is Mr. Montmorency de Courcy (*né* Snaggs) in a mulberry-coloured body-coat and gilt basket buttons, check trousers, and a white hat. He is from the Northern Circuit, and hopes, please the pigs and Mr. Belville, to do second low comedy in London yet, though he has been a long time 'out of collar.' At the door, you have Mr. Snartell, the low comedian from Devonport, and Mr. Rollocks, the heavy father from the Bath Circuit, who affects, in private life, a low-crowned hat with a prodigious brim (has a rich though somewhat husky bass voice), and calls everybody 'My son.' These, with many more dark-haired, close-shaven, and slightly mouldily-habited inheritors of the mantles of Kean, Dowton, or Blanchard, wait the live-long day for the long-wished-for engagements.

Inside, at the bar, Signor Scapino, *in propriâ personâ*, is exercising his celebrated dog Jowler at standing on the hind legs, placing a halfpenny on the counter, and receiving a biscuit instead; two or three stage-carpenters are enjoying themselves over the material used to 'grease the traps,' *i. e.*, half a crown's worth of stimulants placed to their credit by the author of the last new piece over the way; while tho author himself, a mysterious individual in spectacles, and clutching an umbrella, eagerly scrutinizes the pile of country play-bills, in the hope of discovering among them some theatre at which one of his pieces has lately been performed, and on which he can be 'down' for half a crown an act for each representation. Then there is a little prematurely-aged man, Dr. Snaffles, indeed, as he is called, who did the 'old man' line of business, but who does very little to speak of now, except drink. Drink has been his bane through life; has thrown him out of every engagement he ever had, has muddled his brain, rendered his talent a shame and a curse, instead of a credit and a blessing to him; made him the ragged, decrepit, palsied beggar-man you see him now. He asks the barmaid piteously for a pinch of snuff, which she never refuses him—and returns him in addition, sometimes (when he can find no old theatrical friend to treat him) half a pint of porter. He is never seen to eat, and sleeps nowhere in particular, and has not washed within the memory of man.

There's a little snuggery or private parlour behind the bar, to which are only free the actors of the adjacent theatre, of a certain standing, and their friends. In the intervals of re-hearsals before and after the performance this little snuggery is crammed. The heavy tragedian makes jokes that set the table in a roar, and the low comedian is very dismally and speechlessly drawing lines in beer with his finger on the Pembroke table. In the chimney corner sits Mr. Berrymax, a white-haired old gentleman, with a pleasant expression of countenance, who, though not an actor, enjoys prodigious consideration in the profession, as a playgoer of astonishing antiquity, who is supposed to remember Mrs. Bracegirdle, Peg Woffington—nay, Betterton, almost; whose opinions on all points of reading, business, and stage traditions, are looked upon as oracles, whose decisions are final, and whose word is law.

The landlord of the theatrical public-house is, very probably, a retired actor—a prompter who has made a little money—or, sometimes, even an unsuccessful manager. His daughter may be in the ballet at the adjacent theatre; or, perhaps, if he be a little 'warm,' she may have taken lessons from Signor Chiccarini, wear a black velvet dress, carry an oblong morocco music-case, like a leathern candle-box, and sing at the Nobility's Concerts, and in the choruses of Her Majesty's Theatre. There are other theatrical publics, varying however in few particulars from the one into which we have peeped. There is the 'public' over the water,

G

whither the performers at the Royal Alexandrina Theatre (formerly the old Homborg) resort; where Jobson, the original Vampire of 'Venice, reigns supreme, and where you may see a painted announcement, that—'Bottles are lent for the Theatre,' meaning that any thirsty denizen of the New Cut, who may choose to patronise, on a given night, the Royal Alexandrina Theatre, with his wife, family, and suite, may here buy beer, and borrow a bottle to hold it, wherewith to regale himself between the acts, the standing order of the theatre as to 'No bottles allowed,' notwithstanding. Then there is the equestrian theatrical house, also, over the water, where you may see fiercely moustachioed gentlemen, who clank spurs, and flourish horsewhips, after the manner of life-guardsmen off duty; who swear fearfully, and whose grammar is defective; who affect a great contempt for actors, whom they term 'mummies,' and who should be in polite parlance denominated 'equestrian performers,' but are generally, by a discerning but somewhat too familiar public, known as 'horse-riders.' There are, of course, different cliques and coteries holding their little discussions, and conserving their little prejudices and antipathies, their likings and dislikings, in the various classes of theatrical publics; but there is common to them all a floating population of old play-goers, superannuated pantomimists, decayed prompters, actors out of engagement, and order-haunters and actor-hunters.

Ramble on again, wheels of Barclay's dray; clatter, ye harness, and crack, ye loud-sounding whips; and let us leave the world theatrical for the world pictorial. Let us see the Arts on tap!

VII.

PHASES OF 'PUBLIC' LIFE.

CHAPTER II.

IN a suburban locality, mostly, shall you find the artistic public-house. There is nothing essentially to distinguish it from other houses of entertainment. Indeed, by day, were it not for the presence, perhaps, of an old picture or two in the bar, and a bran new sacred piece by young Splodger, 'Madonna col Bambino' (models Mrs. Splodger and Master W. Splodger), with an intensely blue sky, a preternaturally fat Bambino, and a Madonna with a concentrated sugar-candyish sweetness of expression—were it not for these, you would be puzzled to discover that the arts had anything to do with this class of public. But after eight o'clock at night, or so, the smoking-room is thronged with artists, young and old : gray-headed professors of the old school, who remember Stothard, and have heard Fuseli lecture ; spruce young fellows who have studied in Paris, or have just come home from Italy, full of Horace Vernet, Paul Delaroche, the *loggie* and *stanze* of the Vatican, the Pitti Palace, and the Grand Canal; moody disciples of that numerous class of artists known as the 'great unappreciated,' who imagine that when they have turned their shirt-collars down, and their lips up, grown an enormous beard and moustache, and donned an eccentric felt hat, all is done that can be done by art, theoretical, practical, and æsthetical, and that henceforward it is a burning and crying shame if their pictures are not hung 'on the line' in the Exhibition of the Royal Academy, or if the daily papers do not concur in a unanimous pæan of praise concerning their performances. Very rarely condescends also to visit the artists' public that transcendant genius Mr. Cimabue Giotto Smalt, one of the P.P.P.B. 'Præ-painting and Perspective Brotherhood.' Mr. Smalt, in early life, made designs for 'The Ladies' Gazette of Fashion,' and was suspected also of contributing the vigorous and highly-coloured illustrations to 'The Hatchet of Horrors'—that excellent work published in penny numbers by Skull, of Horrorwell Street. Subsequently awakening, however, to a sense of the hollowness of the world, and the superiority of the early Italian school over all others, he laid in a large stock of cobalt, blue, gold leaf, small wooden German dolls, and glass eyes, and commenced that course of study which has brought him to the proud position he now holds as a devotional painter of the most æsthetic acerbity and the most orthodox angularity. He carefully unlearned all the drawing and perspective which his kind parents had been at some trouble and expense to have him taught ; he studied the human figure from his German dolls, expression from his collection of glass eyes, drapery from crumpled sheets of foolscap paper, colour from judiciously selected *morceaux* (in panel), such as Barclay and Perkins's blue board, and the 'Red Lion' at Brentford. He paints shavings beautifully, sore toes faultlessly. In his great picture of St. Laurence, the bars of the gridiron, as branded on the saint's flesh, are generally considered to be masterpieces of finish and detail. Some critics prefer his broad and vivid treatment of the boils in his picture of 'Job scraping himself' (the potsherd exquisitely rendered), exhibited at the Academy last year, and purchased by the Dowager Lady Grillo of Pytchley. He dresses in a sort of clerico-German style, cuts his hair very short, sighs continually, and wears spectacles. No Mondays, Tuesdays, or Wednesdays, are there in his calendar. The days of the week are all Feasts of St. Somebody, or Eves of something, with him. When he makes out his washing-bill, his laundress is puzzled to make out what 'shyrtes' and 'stockynges' mean, for so he writeth them down; and when he wanted to let his second floor, not one of the passers-by could for the life of them understand the wondrous placard he put forth in his parlour window, the same being an illuminated scroll, telling in red, blue, and gold hieroglyphics of something dimly resembling this:

FVRNISHED CHAMBERES MAIE ON YE UPPER FLOOR BEE HADDE.

Pipes are in great request in the smoking-room of the artists' public—fancy pipes of elaborate workmanship and extraordinary degrees of blackness. The value of a pipe seems to increase as its cleanliness diminishes. Little stumpy pipes, the original cost of which was one halfpenny, become, after they have been effectually fouled and smoke-blackened, pearls beyond price—few content themselves with a simple yard of clay—something more picturesque—more *moyen âge*. Chrome, who paints 'still life' nicely, fruit and flowers, and so on (his detractors say, apples, oranges, and bills of the play), smokes a prodigious meerschaum, warranted to be from the Danube, crammed with Hungarian tobacco, and formerly the property of the Waywode of Widdin. Scumble (good in old houses and churches) inhales the fumes of a big pipe with a porcelain bowl, purchased in the Dom-Platz of Aix-la-Chapelle, and having Saladin and all his paladins depicted thereon. The black cutty, patronised by Bristley (son of Sir Hogg Bristley, R.A.), has been his constant companion in the adventurous sketching journeys he has undertaken—was with him when under sentence of fusillation for sketching a droschky in the Nevski Perspective at Petersburgh; when lion-hunting in Caffreland; nay, it is suspected, even lay quiescent in his pocket when hunted as a lion here, on his return.

In the further corner, sits, as perpetual vice-chairman, the famous Nobbs. Nobbs was gold medallist and travelling student of the Royal Academy in the year Thirty-four. He has been a blockhead ever since. He has never painted a picture worth looking at; nor, I seriously believe, were you to lock him in a room with a pencil and a piece of paper, could he draw a pint pot from recollection. Yet hath he covered roods, perches, acres of tinted paper, with studies from the antique and the life; set him before a statue, with drawing-board, crayons, compasses, and plumb-line complete, and he will give you every hair of Moses' beard, every muscle of the Discobolus; give him a Raphael or a Titian to copy, and he will produce a duplicate so exact that you would be puzzled to tell the ancient from the modern.

Storyteller in ordinary, historiographer, and undisputed nautical authority, is Jack Bute, who is supposed, once upon a time, to have painted Lord Nelson's portrait, and who, on strength of that one achievement, has been a famous man ever since. Who would not be proud of standing fourpenn'orth to Jack Bute? Jack has been a sailor, too, a gallant sailor. ' I was at Algiers, sir,' he says, ' and *fit* there '—he always says *fit.* ' I was among the boarders, and the only difficulty I had was in shaking the Algerine blackguards off my boarding-pike, I spitted so many of them.' Sometimes an over-sense of his dignity, and an over-dose of gin and water, make Jack quarrelsome and disagreeable; sometimes he is maudlin, and can only ejaculate ' Nelson '—' Fourpenn'orth '—amid floods of tears.

The artists' ' public ' is generally hard-by a ' life school,' or institution where adult artists meet nocturnally to study the human figure, animals, &c., from the life. One of the standing patterns or text-books of the school is quietly standing in front of the house now, in the shape of a symmetrically-shaped donkey, which Bill Jones, its master, the costermonger, is very happy (for a consideration) to lend to the life school to be ' drawed ' at night, after the patient animal has been draw-ing all day. Another pattern is refreshing himself with mild porter at the bar, being no other, indeed, than the well-known Caravaggio Potts, *Artiste-modèle*, as he styles himself. He began life as Jupiter Tonans, subsequently passed through the Twelve Apostles, and is now considered to be the best Beli-sarius in the model world. His wife was the original Venus Callipyge, of Tonks, R.A., but fluctuates at present between Volumnia and Mrs. Primrose.

The landlord of the artists' inn knows all about the exhibi-tions, what days they open, and what days they shut—who ought to have been hung ' on the line,' who the prize-holders in the Art Union are, and what pictures they are likely to select for their prizes. Were you to enter the sitting-room, you would be astonished at the number of portraits, full-length, half-length, three-quarter-length, in oil, water-colour, and crayons, of himself, his wife, children, and relations generally, which adorn that apartment. Has the blushing canvas blotted out the sins of the slate?

Between art and literature there is a very strong band of union (becoming stronger every day, I trust), and I would step at once from the artists' tavern to the literary tavern, were I not enabled to save time and our chariot steeds by remaining a while in Camden Town, where two or three varieties of Public life yet remain to be noticed; for, in this locality, uplifts its lofty head 'The Railway Tavern;' here, also, is the 'house' frequented by veterinary surgeons; here, the hostelry affected by medical students. A brief word we must have with each of them.

Hope—wild, delusive, yet comfortable hope—baked the bricks and hardened the mortar of which the Railway Tavern was built. Its contiguity to a railway station appeared to its sanguine projector a sufficient guarantee for immense success. He found out what the fallacies of hope were, before he had done building. *He* hanged himself. To him enters an enterprising licensed victualler, formerly of the New Cut, who obtained a transient meed of success by an announcement of the sale within of 'Imperial black stuff, very nobby.' Everybody was anxious to taste the 'Imperial black stuff,' and for some days the Railway Tavern was thronged; but the public found out that the mixture was not only very nobby, but very nasty, and declined a renewal of the draught. The next proprietor was a fast gentleman, which may account for his having gone so very fast into 'The Gazette;' although he always attributed his ruin to his having had a many pewter great pots stolen, which he subsequently unwittingly received again in the guise of bad half-crowns. For years the Railway Tavern stood, big, white, deserted-looking, customerless; but a new neighbourhood gradually arose round the station; front streets gradually generated back streets; back streets begot courts and alleys. There is a decent assemblage of customers, now, at the bar; a fair coffee-room connection, and a very numerous parlour company, composed of guards and engine-drivers; strongly perfumed with lamp-oil, who call the locomotives 'she,' the company 'they,' and each other 'mate.' Though it has been built some years, the Railway Tavern has yet an appearance of newness. The paint seems wet, the seats unworn, and the pots unbattered. The doors have not that comfortable, paint-worn manginess about the handle common to public-house portals in frequented neighbourhoods. The Railway Tavern always reminds me of the one hotel in a small Irish town—that square, white, many-windowed, uncomfortable-looking edifice, frowning at the humble, ramshackle little chapel, awing the pigs and embellishing the landscape; but seldom troubled with custom or customers.

Out of the way, lumbering drink-dray of ours, and let this smart gig, with the fast-trotting mare braced up very tight in the shafts thereof, rattle by! In the vehicle sits a gentleman with a very shiny hat, a very long shawl, and an indefinite quantity of thick great-coats, from the pocket of one of which peep a brace of birds. The gig is his 'trap,' and the fast-trotting mare is *his* mare Fanny, and he himself is Mr. Sandcracks, of the firm of Sandcracks and Windgall, veterinary surgeons. He is going to refresh Fanny with some meal and water, and himself with some brandy and ditto, at the Horse and Hocks, a house especially favoured and frequented by veterinary surgeons, and the walls of whose parlour (the H. and H.) are decorated with portraits of the winners of ever so many Derbys, and some curious anatomical drawings of horses. The frequenters of the H. and H. are themselves curious compounds of the sporting character and the surgeon. You will find in the bar, or behind it (for they are not particular), or in the parlour, several gentlemen, with hats as shiny, shawls as long, and coats as multifarious, as Mr. Sandcrack's, discoursing volubly, but in a somewhat confusing manner, of dogs, horses, spavins, catch-weights; the tibia and the fibula, handicaps, glanders, the state of the odds, and comparative anatomy. They will bet on a horse and bleed him with equal pleasure—back him, dissect him, do almost everything with him that can be done with a horse. They must work hard and earn money; yet to my mind they always seem to be driving the fast-trotting mare in the smart gig to or from the Horse and Hocks.

Medical men don't enter into my category of 'public' users. They have their red port wine at home. The Medical students' public is never known by its sign. It may be the Grapes, or the Fox, or the Magpie and Stump, but it is always distinguished among the students as Mother So-and-so's, or Old What-d'ye-call-him's. The students generally manage to drive all other customers away. Nor chair, nor benches—nay, nor settle, are required for the students' parlour. They prefer sitting on the tables ; nor do they want glasses—they prefer pint pots ; consuming even gin and water from those bright flagons : nor do they need spittoons, nor pictures on the walls, nor bagatelle boards.

If I wonder how the veterinary surgeon finds time to practise, how much greater must be my dubiety as to how the medical students find time to study ! The pipe, the pot of half and half, the half-price to the theatre, the Cider-cellars to follow, and the knocker-twisting gymnastics to follow *that* (with, sometimes, the station-house by way of rider), appear to fill up their whole time—to leave not a point unoccupied upon the circle of their daily lives. Yet, work they must, and work they do. The smoking, drinking, fighting life, is but an ordeal —somewhat fiery, it is true—from which have come unscathed Doctor Bobus, rolling by in his fat chariot ; Mr. Slasher, ready to cut off all and each of my limbs, in the cause of science, at St. Spry's Hospital ; but, from which have crawled, singed, maimed, blackened, half-consumed, poor Jack Fleam (he sang a good song did Jack, and was a widow's son), now fain to be a new policeman ; and Coltsfoot, the clinical clerk at Bartholomew's, who died of *delirium tremens* on his passage to Sydney.

On again we roll, and this time we leave the broad suburban roads, furzed with trim cottages and gardens—white cottage bonnets with green ribbons—for crowded streets again. If you want to back Sally for the Chester Cup, or Hippopotamus for the double event, or to get any information on any sporting subject, where can you get it better, fresher, more authentic, than in one of the sporting-houses, of which I dare say I am not very far out if I say there are a hundred in London ? Not houses where sporting is casually spoken of, but where it is the staple subject of conversation, business, and pleasure to the whole of the establishment, from the landlord to the potboy.

Let us take one sporting-house as a type. Dozens of pictures —Derby winners, Dog Billys, the Godolphin Arabian ; Snaffle, the jockey ; Mr. Tibbs, the trainer (presented to him by a numerous circle of, &c., &c.). Nailed against the wall are a horse-shoe, worn by Eclipse, and a plate formerly appertaining to Little Wonder. In a glass case behind the bar is a stuffed dog—Griper ; indeed, the famous bull-dog formerly the property of that enthusiastic sporting character, Jack Myrtle, who having had rather too decided a settling day with one Mr. Ware, was done to death at Aylesbury ; the body of Mr. Ware having been found in a pond, and twelve ignorant jurymen having concurred in a verdict that the bold Jack Myrtle put him there. The landlord of the sporting-house is a sporting character you may believe me. Such a chronological memory he has of all the horses that have won races, for goodness knows how many years! Such bets he makes touching these same chronological questions!—such crowns, half-crowns, and ' glasses round' he wins! When he has been lucky on an ' event,' he stands unlimited champagne. He had a Derby Sweep, and a St. Leger Sweep, and a Great Northamptonshire Sweep, and a great many other sweeps, or ticket lotteries, at his house ; of which sweeps I only know that I never drew the highest horse in any of them, and never knew the sporting character who did.

Horses are A 1, of course, at the sporting public, but dogs are not despised. The Screwtail Club have a ' show' meeting every Friday night, followed by an harmonic meeting. At the ' show,' comparisons take place, and the several qualifica- tions are discussed of spaniels, terriers, greyhounds, and almost every other kind of canine quadruped. Dark-whiskered men in velveteen shooting-coats, loom mysteriously about the bar on show nights. In their pockets they have dogs ; to them enter ' parties,' or agents of ' parties' who have lost the said ' dogs '—flagons of beer, and noggins of Geneva without number, are discussed to bind bargains, or ' wet ' bargains, or as portions of the ' regulars,' to which the agents or their assigns are entitled.

Who comes to the sporting public-house ? Who drinks in its bar and parlour ? Who puffs in its smoking-room ?—who, but the sallow-faced little man, with the keen black eye and the bow-legs—swathed in thick shawls and coats—who, every Derby-day, bursts on your admiring gaze, all pink silk, snowy buck-skins, and mirror-like tops, as a jockey ? Who but ' Nemo,' who offers you an undeniable ' tip,' and ' Mendax,' with his never-failing ' pick ?' who come *incog.*, indeed, but still come to see without being seen ? Who, but that fool of all fools—that dupe of all dupes—that gull of all gulls—the sporting fool, the sporting dupe, the sporting gent ! He (brain- less youth) who has ' good information ' about Hawkeye, who ' lays out his money ' upon Buster ; who backs Pigeon for the ' double event ;' who ' stands to win ' by every horse, and loses by them all ; who is so stupendously knowing, and is so stupidly and grievously plucked by the most transparent sharpers upon earth !

London, the great city of refuge for exiles of all nations, the home or place of sojourn for foreign ambassadors, foreign merchants, foreign singers, cooks, artists, watchmakers, sugarbakers, organ-grinders, and hair-dressers, has necessarily also its public-houses, favoured by the more especial and peculiar patronage of foreigners temporarily or permanently resident in the metropolis. The foreigner can take his glass, and imbibe his 'grogs' with as much pleasure as the true Briton; although, perhaps, with somewhat more moderation, and less tablethumping, glass-replenishing, waiter-bullying, and subsequent uneven and uncertain locomotion. It is a great mistake to imagine that foreigners cannot appreciate and do not occasionally indulge in conviviality; only they generally content themselves with the 'cheering' portion of the cup, eschewing its 'inebriating' part.

Let us essay a pull at the beer-engine of one of the foreign hostelries of London—the refugees' house of call. Herr Brutus Eselskopf, the landlord, is a refugee himself, a patriot without a blot on his political scutcheon. He has been a general of brigade in his time; but he has donned the Boniface apron, and affiliated himself to the Boniface guild, and dispenses his liquors with as much unconcern as if he had never worn epaulettes and a cocked hat, and had never seen real troops with real bands and banners defile before him. Where shall his house be? In the purlieus of Oxford Street, near Leicester Square, or in the centre of that maze of crooked, refugee-haunted little streets between Saint Martin's Lane and Saint Anne's Church, Soho? Go for Soho! Go for a mean unpretending-looking little house of entertainment at the corner of a street, a Tadmor in the wilderness, set up by Herr Brutus Eselskopf for the behoof of his brothers in exile.

No very marked difference can at first be discerned, as regards fittings up and appurtenances, between the refugees' and any other public-house. There is a bar and a barmaid, there is a beer-engine and there are beer-drinkers; and were it not that the landlord wears a Turkish cap, with blue tassels, and a beard and moustachios of prodigious magnitude, all of which are rather out of the common or Britannic order of things, you might fancy yourself at an English public-house. But five minutes' sojourn therein, and five minutes' observation of the customers, will soon convince you to the contrary. Herr Eselskopf's little back parlour is filled, morning, noon, and night, with foreigners under political clouds of various degrees of density, and in a cloud of uniform thickness and of strong tobacco, emitted in many-shaped fumes from pipes of eccentric design. By the fire, reading the 'Allgemeine Zeitung' or 'Ost-Deutsche Post,' and occasionally indulging in muttered invectives against the crowned heads of Europe, generally, and the Emperor of Austria in particular, is that valiant republican Spartacus Bursch, erst P.H.D. of the University of Heidelberg, then on no pay, but with brevet rank, behind a barricade formed of an omnibus, two water-carts and six paving-stones at Frankfort; subsequently and afterwards of the *Charité* Hospital at Berlin, possessor of a broken leg; afterwards of the fortress of Ehrenbreitstein, condemned to imprisonment for life; afterwards of Paris, France, Red Republican, manufacturer of lucifer-matches, *affilié* of several secret societies, chemical lecturer, contractor for paving roads, usher in a boarding-school; then of Oran, Algeria, private soldier in the Foreign Legion; then of Burgos, Santander, St. Sebastian, and Passages, warrior in the Spanish service, Carlist or Christino by turns; then of Montevideo; then of the United States of America, professor in the Colleges of Gougeville, Va., and Ginslingopolis, Ga.; barman at a liquor store, professor of languages, and marker at a New Orleans billiard-room; subsequently and ultimately of London, promoter of a patent for extracting vinegar from white lead, keeper of a cigar-shop, professor of fencing, calisthenics, and German literature; and latterly out of any trade or occupation.

There is likewise to be found here the Polish colonel, with one arm, Count Schottischyrinkski, playing draughts with Professor Toddiegraff, lately escaped from Magdeburg; Captain Scartaffaccio, who has fought bravely under Charles Albert, at Novara, and for the Danes in Schleswig Holstein, and against the French on the battlements of Rome, and under Manin, at Venice, against the Austrians; also there may be encountered sundry refugees of the *vielle souche*—the old style, in fact—men who can remember the Grand Duke Constantine, the knout, nose-slitting, and Siberia; who have been St. Simonians, and Carbonaros, and Setembrists; who can tell you grim stories of the *piombi* at Venice, of Prussian citadels, and Italian galleys, of the French cellular vans, and the *oubliettes* of Spielberg. But the last few years, and the almost European revolt that followed the Revolution of 1848, has brought to England a new class of refugees, somewhat looked down upon, it must be said, by the old hands, the matriculated in barricades, and those who have gone in for honours in street combats, but still welcomed by them as brothers in adversity. These are enthusiastic young advocates, zealous young sons of good families, patriotic officers, who have thrown up their commissions under despot standards to fight for liberty, freedom-loving literary men, republican journalists, Socialist workmen. These poor fellows have been hunted from frontier to frontier on the Continent, like mad dogs. Half of them have been condemned to death in their own country, many of them forced to fly from home, and kindred, and friends, and occupation, for deeds or thoughts expressed in print or writing, which ministers or governments would take, here, more as compliments than otherwise. They manage things differently abroad ; and so there are in London many public-houses and coffee-shops always full of refugees. Harmless enough they are, these unfortunate *forestieri*. There are black sheep among them certainly ; but St. Wapshot's sainted fold itself has, sometimes, muttons of suspicious hue amongst its snowy fleeces. There are refugees who cheat a little sometimes at billiards, and who rob their furnished lodgings, and attempt to pass bad half-crowns, and forge Prussian bank-notes [I never could find out how *they* could pay for forging, for their value appears to vary between twopence-halfpenny and sixpence]. There are refugees who get up sham testimonials, and are connected with swindling companies and gambling cigar-shops ; but consider how many thousands of them here in London, born and bred gentlemen, who have lost everything in the maintenance of what they conscientiously believed to be the right against might, live quietly, honestly, inoffensively, doing no harm, existing on infinitesimal means, working hard for miserable remuneration, willing to do anything for a crust, teaching languages for sixpence a lesson, painting portraits for a shilling a-piece, taking out lessons on the flute or pianoforte in bread or meat ! We give them foot-room, to be sure, but little more ; and stout John Bull, with all his antipathy to foreigners, may sometimes melt at the sight of a burly Polish major of heavy dragoons, explaining the intricacies of an Italian verb to the young ladies in a boarding-school, or a Professor of moral philosophy selling cigars on commission for his livelihood. They live, somehow, these poor foreigners, much as the young ravens do I opine ; yet they meet sometimes at Herr Eselskopf's, in Soho, or at some French or Polish or Italian public-house in the same refugee neighbourhood, and take their social glass, drinking to better times, when they shall enjoy their own again. Meanwhile, they accommodate themselves, as best they may, to the manners and customs of their step-fatherland, forgetting Rhine wines and Bavarian beer, and such foreign beverages for the nonce, and living humbly, industriously, contentedly, good-humouredly, on such poor meats and drinks as they can get.

I call these refugees (and they form the great majority of the exiles in London) the quiescent ones; but there are also the incandescent ones, the roaring, raging, rampaging, red-hot refugees; the amateurs in vitriol, soda-water bottles full of gunpowder, and broken bottles for horses' hoofs; the throwers of grand pianofortes from first-floor windows on soldiers' heads, the cutters-off of dragoons' feet, the impalers of artillerymen. There are some of these men in London. Where do *they* meet? Not at Herr Eselskopf's, certainly. They did frequent his establishment; but since Hector Chalamot, ex-silkweaver from Lyons, attempted to bite off the nose of Captain Sprottleowski, on the question of assassinating the King of Prussia : which little *rixe* was followed by Teufelshand, delegate of the United Society of Brother Butchers, demanding the heads of the company : and by little Doctor Pferdschaff insisting on singing his ' *Tod-lied*,' or Hymn to the Guillotine, to the tune of the Hundredth Psalm, — since these events, good Herr Eselskopf would have none of them. They met after that at a little *gasthaus* in White-chapel, formerly known as the ' *Schinkenundbrod*,' or German sandwich-house ; but Strauss, the landlord, in compliment to the severe political principles of his guests, re-christened it under the title of the ' Tyrants' Entrails.' Liberty, equality, and fraternity were here the order of the day, until Dominico Schiavonne was stabbed by an Italian seaman from the docks, because he was a Roman ; the assassin being subsequently knived himself by another seaman, because he was a Tuscan.

Well, well ! Can ever a pot boil without some scum at the top ? There is bellow and black smoke as well as a bullet to every blunderbuss.

VIII.

PHASES OF 'PUBLIC' LIFE.

CHAPTER III.

SHOULD the readers of these pages have formed or expressed any opinion on the subject of Barclay's Dray, formerly herein adverted to, I should not wonder if they opined that the

wheels of that vehicle stood grievously in need of lubricating;
inasmuch as the spokes and axles thereof have ceased revolv-
ing for some time ; a dead lock being thereby created, and a
crowded literary thoroughfare blocked up.   Weighty and
sufficient reasons are not wanting to be alleged in excuse for
this temporary stoppage.   The writer could, if he chose,
plead as many pleas as the defendant in an action at law—
from 'never indebted,' to 'leave and licence ;' yet he is of
opinion that it would be far more graceful and respectful in
him to follow the example of that Mayor of Boulogne, who
of the four-and-twenty sufficient reasons he had provided to
account for the non-firing of a salute to Henry the Eighth,
put forward as the first reason, that he had no gunpowder.
So I may say, humbly, that the third chapter of this essay
was not sooner printed, because it was not written;—a thoroughly logical and conclusive reason, reminding me of the
Spanish fleet, which could not be seen, because it was not in
sight; or, to come nearer home, of some worthy men—Con-
servatives, ratepayers, vestrymen, and other residents of a
country town I know—who petitioned lately against the
introduction of gas-lamps into the streets; for which they
alleged as a reason—not that gas was atheistical, or papistical,
or subversive of Church and State—but solely that, as they
expressed it with beautiful simplicity, 'they didn't want no
gas.'
    The world has grown older, and the Registrar-General has
written a good many columns in the 'Times' since we sat in
the dray together among the beer-barrels.   The May sun was
shining and the birds were singing, when I sat down to write
chapter the first ; but now, as I bend over chapter the third,
the trees are strewing dead leaves on the grave of summer,
and the October blast moans lamentably through the branches
as though it were a dog, howling by night before a house for
the year that is to die.
    The public life of Israel ; Judaical conviviality ; that shall
be my theme.   The publics used by the peculiar people are
marked with distinctive characteristics, like everything else
appertaining to that curious race.   When Holywell Street
was more old clothesy than literary ; and, when children of
the Tribes lay in wait at the shop-doors behind cloaks and
paletôts, like wild beasts in ambush, frowsy little public-
houses nestled among the old-clothes shops pretty numerously.
They were not cheerful nor gaily-decorated establishments.
Mostly with semicircular counters, mostly without forms or

settles (for it is a peculiarity of the 'persuasion' to take its refreshment almost invariably standing): they smelt intolerably of stale tobacco-smoke—that of bad cigars which the landlord and his customers continually smoked. No pipes were ever seen, and no cigar-cases or cigar-boxes were ever produced. All smoked cigars, yet no man ever seemed to light a fresh 'weed,' but kept on, from morn to dewy eve, continuously puffing at the same stump or fag-end of rolled tobacco or cabbage, or lettuce-leaf, as the case might be. They appeared to possess some magical property of indefinite prolongation.

The 'Jews' Harp' stood somewhere between Old Castle Street, Holywell Street, and Lyons Inn. There was an old clothes shop, wholesale, retail, and for exportation, on either side. Early in the morning, winter and summer, the gentlemen clothesmen of the vicinity called in for a cigar before they started on their habiliment-collecting rounds. Liquor they never consumed before business, and they even went trust (till the afternoon) for the cigar: it being a maxim among the people never to part with money, where disbursement could by any means be avoided, before some bargains had been made, and some profit, however small, secured. Towards twelve o'clock the clothesmen would return with heavily-laden bags; and then the space before the bar became so crowded with Jews and their sacks that it resembled a granary of old clothes; then was the foaming pot quaffed, and the fried flounder eaten; then were racy anecdotes told of keen bargains and unwary customers, and clothes-vendors who 'didn't know the value of things, no more than a child, my dear.' Towards evening the bar would be crowded again, but always with Jews. They betted on every imaginable topic—horses, dogs, the various lengths of cigars, theatricals, politics,—anything, in short, on which a variety of opinion could possibly exist, and could consequently offer a field for a wager. And then they played—these jovial Jews —at cribbage, at all-fours, or any game at which sixpences could be won or lost. The card-tables were the top of the counter, the crown of a hat, the knees of the players, a pair of bellows, or any other object offering a plane surface. The card-playing at the 'Jews' Harp' grew to such a pitch, that at last Moss lost his licence. He goes under the name of Montmorency now; has a brougham, and handsome chambers in Waterloo Place; and, I am given to understand, does little bills for the Guards, horse and foot.

If you would see a genuine Jewish public (since Holywell
Street has been un-Israelitised), our dray must rumble us
through the narrow straggling City streets *via* Aldgate Pump
to the heart of Jewish London. We could have taken St.
Mary Axe as a nearer approach to it; but Bevis Marks, Mitre
Street, Duke's Place, Cree Church Lane, St. Anne's Square,
half a dozen choked-up little streets running into the broad
channel of Houndsditch, are more redolent of Jewish life.
The sign of the people is everywhere. The air is heavy with
the fumes of Minories-made cigars. Old—very old—Old
Jewry is puffing lazily from open windows, or lounging on
door-steps, or chatting at street corners—apparently idle, but
trust me, doing keen strokes of business. It is Sunday morning, and the New Police Act notwithstanding, I can find half
a dozen publics, not wide open, but still in the full swing of
business. Sunday not being the Sabbath of the peculiar
people, they have, of course, none of the scruples connected
with working on that day that we have; so the Nemesis of
the blue uniform, the lettered collar, and the glazed hat
slumbers in Jewry on Sunday morning; won't see that beer
is sold, won't remember that Church service is proceeding,
won't hear the gurgling of beer-engines, or the murmurs of
spirit-taps. Our Judaical public-house lies in Aminadab
Street, close to Talmud Square, and hard by the Marks. It
used to be known as Duke's Place. On one side resides Mr.
Reuben Sheeny, dealer in old gold and silver, who displays
nothing more valuable in his shop window than a wooden
bowl with two anchor buttons, within, a ragged tarnished
epaulette; but who, I dare say, has the wealth of the Indies
inside, somewhere. On the other side is a little squeezed-up
sandwich of a shop; which, at first sight, I mistook for a stall
for the repair of Hebrew soles and upper leather; imagining
that the Hebrew inscription over the window and on the door-
jambs related to the mysteries of the crispinical art. But I
have since found out my error. The grave old man with
goggle-eyed spectacles and a flowing white beard is not a
cobbler. He is a scribe, a public letter-writer, an *écrivain
public*. He will write love-letters, draw contracts and agree-
ments, make severe applications for little bills, and conduct
the general correspondence of Jewry. Unchanging Jewry!
Here, among the docks and screaming factories, to find a
scribe. Writing, perhaps, with a reed pen, and possessing
very probably the rolls of the law in his corner cupboard.
Between those two tenements is the Bag o' Rags. The

shutters are up, and the front door is closed; but, by the side door, free ingross and egress are afforded. Not less than fifty persons are in the narrow parlour and scanty bar, and your humble servant the only Nazarene. Behind the counter is Miss Leah, a damsel of distracting beauty, but arrayed for the moment in a gown of cotton print. Probably Miss Cosher adheres to the principle that beauty, when unadorned, is adorned the most, although yesterday, had you seen her walking to Synagogue, you would have seen the rainbow-tinted produce of the Chinese insect on her 'fair bodye;' the *chef-d'œuvre* of the looms of India on her symmetrical shoulders; the sparkling treasures of the mines of Golconda and of the Brazils on her neck and fingers; and with surely 'enough gay gold about her waist' in the way of watches, Trichinopoly chains, chatelaines and waist-buckles, to purchase that landed estate in the county of Northumberland alluded to by the proud young porter of Lord Viscount Bateman. Old Cosher sits smilingly by his blooming daughter, smoking; old Mrs. Cosher (very fat, and with a quintuple chin), is frying fish in a remarkably strong-smelling oil in the snuggery behind the bar, and Master Rabshekah Cosher, aged eight, is officiating as waiter, and pocketing the perquisites or royalties attached to his office with amazing rapidity, and with a confidence beyond his years. On the muddy pewter counter sits a huge tom-cat—a cat of grave and imposing mien, a feline Lord Chancellor—sitting, solemnly blinking from out of his robes of three-piled fur.

I may say of the customers of this hostelry, of the neighbouring public 'The Three Hats,' and of 'The Sheenies Arms' round the corner, that the chief object of their Sunday morning's sojourn is the buying or selling of some articles of merchandise. From old Simon Rybeck of Bremen, who from his dress and piteous look you would not take to be worth twopence-halfpenny, but who from the depths of his greasy overcoat produces dazzling bracelets, and rings of price and necklaces such as a princess might covet, and as you, my dear sir, would like to present to your bride that is to be; from Mr. Levi, who wants to dispose of a broeaded petticoat formerly in the wardrobe of Queen Anne; from Mr. Belasco, who has some humming-birds, unstuffed, to sell; and brings them out by handfuls, till the table is covered with iris-tinted feathers; from these down to Jewish lads and striplings, willing to swop, buy, sell, or speculate on anything in a small way—bargaining is the rule, quiet consumption of grog or beer with

H

no reservation the exception. Old Mr. Rybeck has just brought out of his waistcoat pocket (after much fumbling and diving, and bringing up rusty keys and bladeless penknives) a dirty screw of paper which you would take, haply, to contain a pennyworth of tobacco, but which, unscrewing, Mr. Rybeck shows to contain loose diamonds—four or five hundred pounds' worth perhaps. From dirty hands to dirty hands are passed about massive golden chains and weighty arguments ; and in some of the greasy, frayed, battered pocket-books, which are from time to time produced, lurk several of those autographs of Mr. Matthew Marshall, the sight of which is so good for sore eyes.

One parting glance we give at these strange Sunday customers—these olive faces and glistening eyes, and moist, red, pulpy lips. Look around, ere you leave, at an engraving on the parlour wall, of the new Synagogue and the Jews' Asylum ; at the passover cakes over the mantelpiece, kept there from year's end to year's end ; and, finally, into the dim snuggery in which Mrs. Cosher fried the fish. It is very dark and very narrow ; but there is a rich Turkey carpet and handsome furniture, and a great cupboard, making a brave show of plate and linen. Among the dinner-party damask you would find, I dare say, a significant garment—Mr. Cosher's shroud, which he wears over his clothes, and walks about City streets in on the day of the ' White Fast.'

A sporting public-house. Have you any curiosity, gentle reader and student of beer in its varieties, to peep at the interior of a ' fighting-house ?' You have : then let us stop our chariot before the sign below depicted.

It is evening. The ' mill' between Lurky Snaggs and Dan Pepper (the ' Kiddy '), for one hundred pounds a side, is due on the proximate morning. The parlour of the fighting-house, where the whereabouts of the fight is to be notified, is thronged by professional and amateur members of the Fancy. Hard talking has rendered these gentlemen's throats rather dry. Beer is indignantly repudiated as something too drouthy and thin-bodied by these noble sportsmen ; and steaming ' fours ' of gin, and ' sixes ' of brandy troop into the room on the waiter's tray in succession, as rapid as the flowers from the inexhaustible hat of Herr Louis Döbler. The parlour itself is a pugnacious-looking apartment, grimed with smoke, the paper torn from the walls in bygone scuffles and punchings of heads. Belcher, Mendoza, and Molyneux the black, spar ominously at the spectator from muddled mezzotinto plates in shabby black

frames; while a tarnished gilt frame, on the surface of which
a thousand flies had given up the ghost, surrounds a portrait,
in oils, of Mr. Coffin himself, his muscles spasmodically developed, murderous highlows on his feet, and a gay Belcher
handkerchief twisted round his waist; the whole painted by
Archy M'Gilp (a clever man, but given to drinking). This
work of art is flanked by a shadowy, evanescent engraving of
Mr. Figg the gladiator, stripped to box for the championship
in the reign of Queen Anne. There is a door, on the back of
which divers accusations of unpaid drams are scored in chalk
against members of the Prize Ring. There is, wheezing before the fire, an elderly bull-dog, blind of one eye, and with a
face so scratched and scarred, and beaten out of shape in
former combats, so crafty, savage, and villainous of aspect, that
were I to see it on human shoulders and in a felon's dock, a
thought very like 'fifteen years across the water for you, my
man,' would pass through my mind. The parlour tables are
dinted by angry pewter pots; the parlour chairs are dislocated
by angry men who have used them as weapons of offence and
defence, or who have exhibited feats of dexterity and strength
with them; such as balancing them on the tips of their noses
—swinging them on their little fingers at arms' length, or
holding them between their teeth. The parlour company is
numerous and not select. In a corner, tossing for half-crowns
in a hat with Spanks the omnibus proprietor, is a lord—a live
lord, ye knaves! one of the few live lords who yet support the
P.R. He is in a rough great-coat, every hair of which stands
on end like quills upon the fretful porcupine, and known in
sporting circles, I believe, from its resemblance to the outer
envelope of a shaggy dog, as a 'bow-wow coat.' This is Lord
Shortford, Lurky Snaggs's 'backer.' His noble father, the
Earl of Absentaroo (whose broad lands were recently brought
to the judicial hammer in the Encumbered Estates Court, in
the island of Ireland), is a zealous admirer of the 'noble art
of self-defence,' even at this time of day; he being on the
wrong side of seventy, and very paralytic. At his lordship's
Villa-Fisterati, near Cufficina, Tuscany, his lordship's grooms
frequently have a 'set-to' on the lawn for his lordship's
amusement: with the gloves on, of course; though, if they
happen to fall off after the third or fourth round, his lordship
is not unappeasably incensed. Next to the lord is a cada-
verous, wild-haired man, 'all tatter'd and torn.' He is an
author, and cultivates literature upon small 'goes' of grog.
He has written handbooks to the ring, memorabilia of boxers,

ana of sporting characters without end. He has the chronology of every event in every fight, from the days of Figg and Broughton to the last fight, at his fingers' ends. His toilette is on his back; his dressing-case (in the shape of a felting comb with all the back teeth knocked out) is in his pocket, cheek-by-jowl with his library (a torn copy of 'Boxiana') and his writing-desk (a tattered pad), an iron pen lashed on to the stump of a tobacco-pipe by a piece of twine, and a penny bottle of ink with a paper plug, formed from a defunct screw of bird's eye tobacco, instead of a cork. He is as strong as a bull, but never fights. He is an oracle, but is too timid to bet, and too honest to go into the prophetic line of business. He is content to write his literary compositions on tap-room tables for the meagre wages doled out to him by cheap sporting periodicals, to get drunk at those said tables afterwards, and to sleep peaceably beneath their Pembroke canopies, when he falls. He has a pretty turn for poetry, and will write you an acrostic on any subject from geology to gaiters, for sixpence. He was a compositor once, and even works occasionally now, being able to set up in type the rounds of a fight right off, without any manuscript. Lord Shortford patronises him, from time to time: and he is fond of reciting an ode, in the Alcaic measure, composed by him in honour of his lordship, in which he (the peer) is celebrated as the 'Mæcenas of the ring,' and for which Mæcenas stood two dozen of champagne. The room is, besides, thronged by fighting men, all with close-cropped hair, flattened noses, discoloured faces, wide mouths, short within of the natural allowance of teeth; and all addicted to the wearing of coats with big buttons, cloth boots, and staring shawls. Then, there are young gentlemen in loose and slack garments, who were lately flogged at Eton, and are now in the Guards—old gentlemen who have been a considerable time on town, and know, I am led to believe, every move thereon—seedy gentlemen living on their wits, and, seemingly, not thriving much on that course of diet. There are gentlemen who, from top to toe, are as plainly and clearly dupes as though they carried 'pigeon' inscribed in legible characters on their hat-bands; and gentlemen in nose, whisker, and pervading appearance, as unmistakably hawks. There are some meritorious public characters decorated with a profusion of chains and rings, who know several Inspectors of the Metropolitan Police by sight, are on bowing terms with the stipendiary magistrates sitting at the London Police Offices, and who, I dare say, were you to

ask them, could tell you which was the snuggest corner on
Brixton treadmill, and the warmest cell in Coldbath Fields
prison. There is the landlord, in a decent suit of black and a
white neckcloth, which costume, superadded to his bonifacial
apron and his eminently prize-fighting face, would tend to
create a confused idea in your mind that, after he had been a
gladiator, he had had a call and had gone into the ministry;
but, finding that not to agree with him, had taken, eventually,
to the public line. Finally, there is Lurky Snaggs himself,
the hero of to-morrow's fray. Mr. Coffin has had him in
training for the last two months; and the devoted Snaggs has
worn spiked shoes, and carried dumb-bells, and taken long
country walks in heavy great-coats, and eaten semi-raw beefsteaks, all for the more effectual bruising, pounding, and
mutilating of Dan Pepper, the 'Kiddy,' to-morrow morning.
He broke away from his training a fortnight since, and was
found in an adverse house solacing himself with a pint of raw
rum, which aberration caused some terrible fluctuations in
the betting-market; but, all things considered, he has been
very docile and abstemious, and is, as Mr. James Coffin
triumphantly asseverates, 'in prime condition, with flesh as
firm as my thumb.'

Betting, laughing, smoking, fierce quarrelling, snatches of
roaring songs are the entertainments at the Bottleholder and
Sponge. But Lurky Snaggs is off to bed, and we must be off
with him. Whither shall this much-enduring dray convey us
now? Let us go down to Flunkeyland, to a Servants'
Public.

No low neighbourhoods for you now—no narrow streets or
swarming courts. Hie we to Belgravia; nay, that is too new
—to Tyburnia; nay, the mortar is scarcely dry there, either.
Let it be time-honoured Grosvenoria, the solemn, big-wigged,
hair-powdered region, where the aristocracy of this land have
loved to dwell time out of mind. Tyburnia and Belgravia
may be very well for your yesterday nobility—your mushroom
aristocrats—millionnaires, ex-Lord Mayors, and low people
of that sort; but for the heavy swells of the peerage, those
of the blue blood and the strawberry-leaves, and who came
over with the Conqueror, Grosvenoria is the place. There
seems to be a natural air of fashion and true gentility about
it. Yet things do change, and streets will decline. The
Earl of Craven lived in Drury Lane once; Sir Thomas More
resided down Bishopsgate way; the Duke of Monmouth's
address was Soho Square; and, who knows, some day or

other, perhaps I shall engage a garret in the mighty Lower Grosvenor Street itself.

Out of Crinoline Square runs, parkwise, as all men know, Great Toppleton Street. Where that thoroughfare intersects with Tip Street is, as you well know, Wangwidgeon House—a big mansion in the rustic style, of brick, with stone dressings, standing in a court-yard—where dwells that mighty prince, the Duke of Pampotter. Next door to him, down Tip Street, is the bachelor's mansion of the Honourable Tom Sardanapalus, M.P. Then comes Mrs. Zenobia, the rich Indian widow (worth two lacs: husband was in council: eats too much mulligatawney: a great tract distributor, and horsewhips her maid-servants). Then is the noble mansion, a double house, of old Sir Fielding Framboise, of the firm of Framboise, Verditter, and Plum, bankers, and a sleeping partner in a great brewery. And then, sir, come Toppletoton Mews, and down Toppletoton Mews is the Cocked Hat and Smalls, used by all the gentlemen servants in the neighbourhood.

Checks, the landlord, who was the Bishop of Bosfursus's butler, and married Mrs. Crimmins, his grace's housekeeper, has a very delicate and difficult task to perform, I can assure you, to keep on friendly terms with all his customers—to oblige all and offend none. Some of the gentlemen are so very particular, so very scrupulous as to precedency and professional etiquette. There's the duke's gentleman, Mr. Lapp. Well, once upon a time, he was not too proud to step round and take a glass with Checks—in his private snuggery, be it understood—and even to smoke a pipe with Binns, Mrs. Zenobia's butler, and Truepenny, the Honourable Tom Sardanapalus's man, who reads all his master's blue-books, and is crushingly erudite on the case of the Ameers of Scinde. But, bless you, Mr. Lapp happening to see a groom—a low stockbroker's groom—in Checks's parlour, dandling Mrs. Crimmins' sister's child, there and then cut and repudiated Checks and his establishment for ever. He told Mr. Wedgewood, Prince Knoutikowski's groom of the chambers, that he 'would never enter that man's house again.' Checks, when he heard of it, said in great wrath, that, 'nobody wanted him so for to do,' that he was 'a hupstart;' and that he, Checks, had kicked him many a time, when they both lived at Sir John's—where Checks was under-butler, and the duke's gentleman was a knife-boy. Then, the footmen rebelled, because Doctor Philblister's coachman used the coffee-room. Then, even the grooms revolted, because a man of stably appearance, supposed, to be an ostler out of place, used the tap-room; and, as he sat, made a hissing noise as though he was rubbing down horses. Poor Checks was very nearly out of his mind; at last he bethought him of the expedient of dividing his coffee-room into two, by a movable wooden partition. In one of these he put the butlers, and in another the footmen. The great men among the former, and the tip-top valets were free of his snuggery; the grooms and coachmen had the tap-room; and the common helpers and stable-folk and the general public the bar.

Our dray has brought us from Mr. Checks's establishment to the brewery. We may, perhaps, by-and-by, look in upon it again, to inspect its home—the head-quarters of every one of the Phases of Public life we have already described.

IX.

POWDER DICK AND HIS TRAIN.

THE Surrey shore of the Thames at London is dotted whit damp houses of entertainment. The water-side public-house, though, perchance, hard by an archiepiscopal residence, and over against a legislative palace, is essentially watersidey. Mud is before, behind, around, about it: mud that in wet weather surges against its basement in pea-soup-like gushes, and that in summer cakes into hard parallelograms of dirt, which, pulverised by the feet of customers, fly upwards in throat-choking dust. The foundations of the water-side public-houses are piles of timbers, passably rotten; timbers likewise shore up no inconsiderable portion of its frontage. It is a very damp house. The garrets are as dank and oozy as cellars, and the cellars are like—what?—well: mermaids' caves. The pewter pots and counters are never bright; the pipe splints light with a fizzy sluggish sputter; an unwholesome ooze hangs on the wall; the japanned tea-trays are covered with a damp rime; the scanty vegetation in the back garden resembles sea-weed; the rickety summer-house is like the wreck of a caboose. The landlord wears a low-crowned glazed hat, and the pot-boy a checked shirt; the very halfpence he gives you for change are damp, so is the tobacco, so are the leaves of last Saturday's 'Shipping and Mercantile Gazette.' They don't wash the water-side public-house much,

but let it fester and ooze and slime away as it lists; neither
do they attempt to clear away the muddy sort of moat surrounding it; although, for the convenience of customers
wishing to preserve clean boots, there is a species of bridge or
pontoon leading from the road to the public door, formed of
rotten deck planks, and stair rails. One side of the door is
guarded by a mop as ragged and as tangled as the unkempt
head of Peter the wild boy; the other by a damp dog,
looking as if he had been in the water too long, had not been
properly dried when he came out, and had so got chapped and
mangy.

Rollocks is the landlord of the water-side public-house, the
Tom Tug's Head. Rollocks was a jolly young waterman
once, and used for to ply at Blackfriars and elsewhere in the
days when the waters of the Thames were ruffled by oars
feathered with skill and dexterity; and not by the paddle-
wheels of the Citizen and Waterman steamboats. Rollocks
won Dogget's Coat and Badge twenty years ago. Afterwards,
when by the introduction of steam-vessels aquatics had
become more a sport than an avocation, Rollocks won many
hard-contested matches. He beat Sammon the Newcastle
coaley, by three lengths, and was subsequently matched to
row Jibb, the famous sculler, from Execution Dock, for a
matter of two hundred pounds. On the evening of the payment of the last deposit (made good at Thwaits's, the Trim-
built Wherry, Fishgaff Stairs) it so fell out that Jibb and
Rollocks quarrelling as to who fouled whom in some previous
match, Jibb broke both Rollocks' shins with an oar; which,
coupled with his getting exceedingly inebriated that night
and sleeping in a six-oared cutter, half full of water, brought
on lameness and rheumatism, broke off the match (Jibb paid
forfeit), and moved Rollocks to retire into the public line.
He is a damp mildewed man now, with bow-legs and very
long arms; to exhibit the symmetry and muscle of which he
is, seemingly, much addicted—if one may judge from his
shirt-sleeves being always rolled up to his armpit.

Rollocks has, behind his bar, the silver cups he has won
during his aquatic career; his Dogget's Coat and Badge,
with his portrait wearing ditto; the silver oar presented to
him by the Barge Club (Viscount Billingsgate, chairman), the
mahogany model of his wager-boat, and a neat collection of
oars and sculls of various shapes and dimensions. Likewise
the identical cushion on which Her Mellifluous Highness the
Grand Duchess Dowager of Kartoffelshausen-Stoubenfeldt sat

when he, Rollocks, had the honour to row her from Vauxhall to Whitehall Stairs, during the visit of the Allied Sovereigns to England in 1815. Rollocks's parlour is decorated with various coloured engravings of crack scullers in crack wager-boats, all bearing (the boats, I mean) in their sharp-nosedness, slim-shapedness, and eager, straining attitudes, a certain curious, inanimate, yet striking resemblance to so many race-horses, winning memorable Derbys. There is a screen before the fire, on which are pasted sundry pictorial illustrations of the songs of Mr. Thomas Dibdin ; notably Jolly Dick the lamplighter, in a full curled wig, lighting a large lamp with an enormous flambeau, in so jaunty a manner, that his tumbling off his ladder seems an event anything but problematical of occurrence.

When a rowing-match is on the *tapis*—or, more appropriately, on the water—the parlour of the Tom Tug's Head is searcely large enough to contain the eager crowd of fresh-water sportsmen, watermen, bargees, backers, and amateurs in aquatics. On these occasions, it is by no means unfrequent to see the happy class of society, known among the commonalty as ' swells,' muster strongly within Rollocks's damp walls. The *alumni* of the two great seats of Academic education are here in great numbers, their costumes presenting a sumptuary medley, in which the fashions of the wild-beast menagerie mingle with those of the stable. At present, they come to Rollocks's (which is close to Hook's, the great boat-builder); they drink out of his pots and clap him on the back, and are hail-fellows well met with the decayed tapsters and discarded serving-men ; the river weeds, and slime, and scum. They meet here, not because they like it, but because some of their associates who have been two terms longer than they have at ' Keys,' or ' Maudlin,' say that it is very 'jolly' to go to old Rollocks's 'crib,' that it is 'life, my boy,' that it is 'the thing,' and so on.

Apart from the parlour of the Tom Tug's Head connected with aquatics as a sport, I must enumerate a miscellaneous population who are of the water and watery, though they run no races and win no cups. Here by night smoke their pipes and drink their grog, captains of river steamboats : silent, reserved men, mostly, lost in fogs of fluvial metaphysics, perhaps ; or forming mental charts of shoals in the river yet undiscovered. These aquatic omnibus drivers, if I may call them so, puzzle and disconcert me mightily. They are inscrutably mysterious. Where do they live ? What were

they before the steamboats were started? Do their wives (if
they have wives) call themselves Mrs. Captain So and So?
Are the call-boys their sons? Have they studied steam?
Could they stoke? Would they be sea-sick if they were to go
to sea? They are nautical men, yet why do they always wear
frock coats, round hats, and half-boots? When shall we see a
'Citizen' captain in a cocked hat?

Not so much parlour customers, but chiefly frequenters of
the bar, or hangers about the door and muddy bridge, are
knots of damp, silent, deep-drinking men, surrounding whom
there is a halo of deep and fearful interest. I know what
they wear those huge leathern aprons and thigh boots for.
I know why they carry at times that weird apparatus of
hooks and cordage. I know what lies sometimes in the long,
low, slimy shed at the bottom of the garden, with a padlock
on the door, blue, swollen, stiff, stark, dead! These be the
searchers of the river, the finders of horrors, the coroner's
purveyors, the beadle's informants, the marine-storekeeper's
customers. When a man is no longer a man, but a body, and
drowned, these seek and find him. The neighbouring brokers'
stalls and rag-shops have dead men's boots and dead men's
coats exposed for sale. These men are quiet, civil, sober men
enough, and passing honest—only there never was a drowned
man found with any money in his pockets.

Homogeneous to the bar and purlieus of the Tom Tug's Head
are casual half-pint-of-porter customers, mudlarks, sewer
gropers, rat-catchers, finders, river thieves, steamboat touters,
waterside beggars, waterside thieves, I am afraid, sometimes.
They pick up a living, nobody knows how, out of the mud and
soppy timbers, as men will pick up livings from every refuse;
as a teeming population and an advanced civilization only can
have such livings to be picked up.

I don't know whether I am justified—before coming to
Powder Dick—in describing the house I am about, now,
lightly to touch upon as a waterside 'public,' inasmuch as it is
less by the waterside than on the water itself—an hostelry
permanently floating on the muddy bosom of the Thamesian
stream. In good sooth this 'public' hath its *habitat* on a
barge: its basement and cellar are keel and ribs. During
the week it is moored by the muddy shore; but on Sundays
it casts anchor a good score of yards therefrom; and the proprietor may, if he list, join in the exulting chorus of the
piratical navigator whose bark was his bride, who was afloat,
afloat! and, being a rover, free. I will call the proprietor

Mr. Rover; for his hair is red, and he has a jovial, roving
delivery and a roving eye (one), and, according to the
centilingued Rumour, has roved a great deal in his time—to
the Antipodes once on compulsion. Mr. Rover's bride, the
Barge and Buttons, has attained a green old age—to judge
by the rankly aqueous vegetation clinging to her mildewed
sides. For aught I or Mr. Rover know, she may have been
once, as a single barge or lady, first cousin to, if not herself the
very identical, Folly on the Thames, at which our great-grand-
fathers and grandmothers halted sometimes in their wherries on
their way to a Vauxhall masquerade. The Barge and Buttons
may have beheld the 'nice conduct of a clouded cane,' the
surrounding waters may have rippled reflectively with the
dazzling brightness of Belinda's diamonds, of the still more
dazzling brightness of Belinda's eyes. The Barge's rotten
timbers may have been mute witnesses of the humours of
Lieutenant Lismahago, of the fopperies of Beau Tibbs, of the
assurance of Ferdinand Count Fathom, of the fashionable airs
of Miss Caroline Arabella Wilhelmina Skeggs; for the Folly
on the Thames was the resort of highly fashionable company,
and if bears were danced there they were never danced but to
the very genteelest of tunes. I only hazard this, nothing more.
I am not certain.

Rover is a cunning man. Sunday, the *dies non* (comparatively speaking) of the publican, of the financier (though beer
can be sold in church hours and bargains made at church doors),
is a harvest day for him. On week-days, as I have said, his
boat is on the shore; but, hebdomadally, his bark is on the
sea, or rather on the river; and, being there, Rover is extra-
parochial, and can sell all sorts of excisable commodities. So
can, and do, as all men know, the river steamboats. All sorts
of benches of magistrates, parochial and municipal authorities,
have tried to do all sorts of things with the astute landlord;
but in vain. The Rover is free and licensed. You have, to be
sure, to pay a small augmentation of price on the liquors you
consume, owing to the necessity of taking a wherry or a ferry-
boat to put you on board the Barge and Buttons; but what is
a penny to a man who must and will have his drink, week-day
or Sunday, fair weather or foul?

Touching Sunday, I am moved to advert here, cursorily, to a
class of bibulous philosophers, who unite the wisdom of the
serpent to the subtilty of the fox, and who, drunken dogs as
they mostly are, have been wary and expert enough to baffle
persons and powers of no meaner note than the Houses of

Lords and Commons. These are the Sunday 'dram-waiters.'
The legislature has said to the dram-waiter, 'John Smith,
during such and such hours, when divine service is performed, you shall not buy beer of Thomas Swypes.' To the
publican it has said, 'Swypes, you shall not, during the
aforesaid hours, sell any beer to John Smith; and if you do,
I, the Law, will send my lictors, or "bobbies," after you, and
I will mulct you of golden pounds and take away your licence,
and bring you very low, and, in fact, play the devil with you.'
But the 'dram-waiter,' wiser, subtler, and warier than even
the collective wisdom of the nation, forthwith sets to study
parochial law and parochial regulations. He finds, that in one
parish, afternoon service begins at one hour, and in another
at another; that in the one street in the county of Middlesex,
called the Strand, there are houses that close from two till four,
from three till five, from three till eight, from six to seven, P.M.,
respectively: that some publics are extra-parochial. The
'dram-waiter' will do without his Sunday-morning drink by
taking as much home over-night as he wants, or he will introduce himself surreptitiously into a 'public' with the connivance
of a lawless licensed victualler; but he is not to be balked of
his post-prandial potations. He knows to a moment when the
Bag o' Nails opens, and when the Elephant and Shoestrings
closes. He can roam from bar to bar, suck sweets from
every noggin, and keep himself all the time within the strict
limits of legality. He is never hard up for a drink. He may
get as drunk as an African king between litany and sermon,
and endanger no man's licence. So much will perverted
human ingenuity do. The glutton studies Latin to be able
to read the beastly messes of Apicius in the original. We
learn to paint in order to blacken, to write in order to
libel. Heaven gives us the talents, and—somebody else their
application.

But, *revenons à nos* Buttons. This barge-tap offers, both on
week-days and Sundays, many features of social peculiarity
worthy of entrance into the commonplace book of the philosophic observer. Analogically thinking, I perpend that this
beery vessel has many points in common with the dark,
stifling mouldy cheese, and rancid rat, and raw rum-smelling
store-room of an emigrant-ship, or to the worst class of bar in
the worst class American steamer. This reeking smell of
bad spirits, this lowering roof, these sticky stains of beer,
this malty mildew, these haggard or crimsoned customers—
these, the accessories more or less of almost every public-

house, but here denuded of the adventitious concomitants of light and glitter and gilding, stand forth in hideous and undisguised relief. They mean drink and drunkenness without excuse or extenuation; the cup that inebriates and does not cheer; the bowl that is wreathed with no flowers of soul, but with the crass dockweeds of intemperance. Bacchus is dismounted here, and lies wallowing in the thwarts of a bumboat. Sir John Barleycorn staggers about disknighted, with his spurs hacked off his heels. It is convivial life, but life seen in a Claude Lorraine glass, and that glass a pothouse rummer blackened with the smoke of a pipe of mundungus.

'Love levels ranks,' Lord Grizzle says, but intemperance has pre-eminently the power of levelling and confounding ranks and ages and sexes, and species even. And thus it happens that from so levelling a system there will result a terrible sameness of feature and expression, of habit, manner, and custom; even as drill makes ploughboys, mechanics, and vagabonds all machines, as similar to each other as the sequent spikes in an area railway; even as slavery makes all negroes alike as one parched pea to another; even as judicious flogging will train a pack of hounds to run and cry and stop as one dog. Tyranny is most potent for exacting and maintaining conformity; and there is no tyranny so strong as that of the King of Drink, no conformity so abject and so universal as that of drunkards. Which must be my excuse, gentles, if I find no very novel characters among the bibbers at the Barge and Buttons.

Stay! one, a man; nay, half a man; nay, a quarter man; nay, less than that, a trunk—a drunken trunk. As I live, a miserable little atomy, more deformed, more diminutive, more mutilated than any beggar in a bowl, any *cul-de-jatte*, than that famed Centaur-beggar who, as Charles Lamb phrased it, appeared to have had his equestrian half hewn off in some dire Lapithæan conflict. This wondrous abortion's name, if he have a name, is doubtful. Men call him 'Powder Dick,' whether in remembrance of some terrible Dartford or Hounslow explosion, by which his limbs were (supposititiously) blown off, or because his chest and face are ceaselessly covered with the black powdery refuse of coal-barges, or because he was so actually baptized, who can say? Powder Dick he has been for years: blasted, blown up, crushed, torn up, or amputated he must have been at one time or another; but he cares not to say, and no man cares to ask him; for, though an atomy, he blasphemes like an imp of Acheron, and, though he cannot

fight he can bite and spit, and with one maimed arm his accidents have left him, hurl pewter pots, and broken glasses, and
hot tobacco ash, with unerring aim. His occupation is that of
a ferryman ; and he ferries fares 'cross river from six in the
morning till nine in the evening all the year round.

Not, of course, that he rows himself. He sits at the stern
of the boat like a hideous pagod, and steers, swearing meanwhile, and craunching a monstrous plug of tobacco, in the
manner of a wild beast over a shin-bone of beef. His wife
plies the oars—a tall, bony, ay, and a strong-boned woman—
quick of action—quicker of imprecation and vituperation, who
on a disputed copper would not scruple to paint your eyes as
black as Erebus with the fire out. She is called Mrs. Dick,
but whether that be her right name, or she have her ' marriage
lines ' to prove her legitimate connection with Mr. Dick, I
should advise you not to be too curious in inquiring. She is
communicative, however, when unruffled. ' My fust,' she vouch-
safed to tell your correspondent, ' was a life-guardsman, and I
kep him, for he carried on dreadful, and his pay wouldn't a kep
him in blacking. My second was a navvy, and I kep him. So
then I took up along with Powder Dick, here, and, rabbit him,
I a'most keeps him, for though the boat is his hown, and the
hoars hare his hown, my harms is my hown, and they keeps us
all afloat. A penny, please, sir.'

Every evening at nine Mrs. Dick marches into the bar of
the Barge and Buttons with Powder Dick, pickaback ; which
mode of conveyance she adopts and he acquiesces in with the
utmost coolness and complacency. Powder Dick is then set
up on end in a corner of the bar, propped up by emptied
measures ; and there he remains, on end, guzzling fiery compounds, and roaring forth obscene songs, till his wicked old
trunk is suffused with drink to the very stumps, and he
tumbles or rolls on to the floor, at which period of time his
wife, who has been drinking rum and porter mixed all the
evening, with an inflexible countenance raises him, replaces
him in the pickaback posture, and so exit with him towards
that unknown slum of the purlieus of Lambeth, which may
contain his home—if he have a home—or den.

Powder Dick has engrossed so much of my space, has caused
me to digress in what is itself but a long digression, because I
consider him to be in some measure not only an original but a
meritorious deformity—most *cul-de-jettes* contenting themselves
with existing upon charity—wheeling themselves about on
small trucks like cockhorses ; sitting on kerbstones with rude

oil paintings spread before them, pictorially explaining how they came by their mutilation; being conveyed about as riders to perambulating organs; or simply crouching on the cellar flaps of public-houses, holding hats in their mouths much in the fashion of poodle dogs, with an associate (unmutilated) posted close handy to give timely intimation of the approach of the police. But Powder Dick, inasmuch as he is the owner and exploiter of a flourishing ferry-boat (albeit the *feme coverte*, his wife, rows it), inasmuch as he makes an honest living and gets drunk on his proper earnings, may almost be considered in the light of a Mister Biffin, working as he does, though so horribly foreshortened.

I knew another meritorious deformity once (he is dead now), who positively became independent through his deformed industry, coupled with ingenuity. This worthy, being born endowed with qualities combining ignorance the most crass and most persistent, with idleness the most steadfast and persevering, is reported (I speak from report, for I knew him not in his perfect manhood) to have wilfully cast himself three separate times beneath the wheels of three separate carriages belonging to the nobility and gentry. Three mutilations of the most appalling nature, obtained from the charitable and wealthy occupants of the carriages three separate though trifling annuities, amounting in the aggregate to twenty-eight pounds a year. I believe he enacted the part of a votary of Juggernaut a fourth time; but the vehicle turning out to be a yellow hackney coach with a prodigious coat of arms on each panel, he gained little this time, save a five-pound note from the coach proprietor and two months' eleemosynary treatment in St. Bartholomew's hospital. He then retired upon his annuities, and, feeling naturally lonely and in want of comfort, fixed his eyes and affections on a young and ugly vender of fruit in the public thoroughfares, to whom he was shortly after united, but who does not appear to have had that regard and consideration for the trunk of her husband, to which his talents and well-earned competence would have seemed to entitle him. At the commencement of my acquaintanceship with him (he had then been married two years), it was patent and notorious that his unfeeling partner was in the frequent habit of leaving him for days together without sustenance, on-end in his chair, from which, owing to his infirmity, he was, it is needless to say, unable to move. Nay, as a refinement of brutality, she has been known to place at the foot of the chair a large footbath of mustard and water, thus insultingly and derisively taunting him with his inability to avail himself of that useful adjunct to the toilet. But his sufferings were speedily terminated. My unfortunate friend was one morning found dead, drowned, his stumps uppermost, and his head in the footbath. It was conjectured that, after a too copious dose of snuff (to which he was much addicted, and to which he was wont to help himself by a dexterous extension and elongation of his upper lip, between a bag of snuff suspended round his neck and his nose—thus quite rivalling the elephant and his trunk)—he had fallen into a violent fit of sneezing; and, in the midst of his convulsive movements, had been precipitated from his chair into the bath, and so asphyxiated. His annuities died with him, and I hope his unworthy widow went to the workhouse.

One more variety of the waterside public, and I will go inland. Farther, much farther down river must you sail with me (our dray hath masts and sails now) before you come to the Trinchinopoly Crab. Far down below Woolwich, with its huge Dockyard and Field of the Balls of Death, or Arsenal, and hideous convict hulks—spruce men of war once, but now no more like men of war than I to Hecuba! far down below Dumbledowndeary, the already-sung (which charming water-port had lately been endowed with a garrison of fourteen real coast-guardsmen—called by the natives ' perwenters,'— armed with real muskets and cutlasses: and who shall say the coast's in danger now?);—far, even below Bluehithe, where the gentleman hung his harriers, and Grays, and Purfleet, and Raidham, where the gentlemen fight for money —in a reach, a lonely reach, a swampy-shored reach—the grim sedgy banks of Essex staring from over the way, the salt marshes of Kent behind and on each side—here is the Trinchinopoly Crab, a lone white house, approached from the shore by a bridge over a slough of worse than Despond; approachable from the western side of Kent by ferry only, other communication being cut off by a sludgy miry little estuary—Dead Man's Creek.

The Trinchinopoly Crab is dismally white. Its frame might be taken for the bones of a house, bleached by the wind. The rickety bridge is painted white, so is the door of entry, with ghastly, skeleton-like chequers on either jamb, that remind you of the pips on the Dice of Death. The outward aspect of the Trinchinopoly Crab is, decidedly, not canny; yet within it is a very haven of maritime joviality and jollity. From the ships in the river come skippers, pilots, mates, supercargoes; from the adjacent villages come river-pilots, ship-chandlers, shop-dealers. From, no man knows whither —going, no man knows where—come strange mysterious men, who seem to know everything and everybody, who smoke cigars of inconceivable fragrance, *moucher* themselves with rainbow-hued bandannas, and must be either smugglers (none of your London street 'duffers,' but real smugglers— fellows who could run a cargo of Hollands in the teeth of all my lords mustered in the Long Room at the Custom House), or else aquatic detective policemen.

If you put your head, and subsequently your corporeality, into the long low coffee or tap-room (for it serves for both) of the Crab, you will first of all be sensible that the tobacco smoked by the majority of the company is of a far better and more fragrant quality than that vended by your lordship's tobacconist. Your olfactory nerves will be greatly titillated by the pungent fumes of the genuine molasses-mixed Cavendish; by the incense-like suavity of the pure Oronooko; by the manly, vigorous smoke of unadulterated Virginia, and the dream-like languor of Varinhas and Latakia. Next you shall observe pipes, strange in form and fashion—not alone meerschaums and cherry-sticks of foreign make, but also yards of clay with outlandish bowls and tubes. Lastly, you are to be struck by the fact, that, although three-fourths of the company present are nautical men, you cannot detect any one nautical item in any portion of their attire. *Sic vos non vo is.* The stout little man in the rough brown coat and wide-awake has just come home from Smyrna, and is going back again in ballast, which, in the shape of sand, he is come down river to load himself with, from this portion of the Kentish coast. The tall, lean, wiry, sallow-faced man, wearing a fluffy white hat, a brown frock-coat, light cord trousers, very much pulled up over his Wellington boots, and a steel watchguard exactly like a patent corkscrew, is a Yankee skipper, come on shore to see if he can pick up some sea-stores advantageously for the return voyage. Observe that he has whittled away a considerable portion of the circular wooden platter on which the pewter pots are placed, and has spat his and his neighbour's spittoon quite full, and is now sowing expectoration broadcast on the boots of the company underneath the table. His ship is a temperance ship, and he is a temperance man; for, although he has to all appearances consumed two or three tumblers of grog already (judging from the rubicund hue of the bumpers supplied to him), his refreshment is, in reality,

I

nothing more than a harmless compound, or temperance
cordial called raspberry. All publics frequented by those who
' go down to the sea in ships' keep a store of this, and similar
cordials, such as gingerette, lemonette, orangette, all mixing
with sugar and hot water in a duly groggy manner, but all
perfectly innocuous and teetotal. There are snuggeries in
Liverpool, frequented almost solely by American captains—
temperance captains be it understood—which have no sale at
all for malt or alcoholic liquors.

The fat, gray-headed, farmer-like man in the body coat,
pepper-and-salt trousers, and brown gaiters, with a heavy
bunch of watch-seals at his fob and a broad-brimmed hat, is
a pilot; not one by any means you will say resembling the
interesting individual with bushy whiskers, snowy ducks,
varnished hat, telescope, and black neckerchief tied in a
nautical knot, who very properly enjoined the impertinent
passenger to go below to his berth and trust in Providence
on a certain fearful night : for which *vide* the song and Mr.
Brandard's lithographed frontispiece thereto. The pilot I have
first introduced you to does not answer to the lithographed
pilot. He is not at all like him. *I* never saw one like him :
I never even saw a pilot in a pilot-coat, though I have seen
one in a hat like a London dustman's, in a Jerry hat, in a
costermonger's fur cap, and in a red nightcap. Never a one
like him of the lithograph. But, my dear sir, is anything in
life like the lithograph, or the book, or the canvas, or the proscenium picture thereof? Is a Royal Academy brigand like
a Calabrian brigand?—a Royal Italian Opera Swiss maiden
like a young girl of any one of the thirteen Cantons ? Are
poet-shepherdesses like women who tend sheep ? Are stage
peasants like Buckinghamshire labourers ? Is any imitation,
reproduction, or representation of life, like life ?—of man, like
man ? All men are liars. Put pencils or pens, or 'broidering
needles in our hands, we straightway fall a-lying, and lie our
heads out of shape, calling that imagination, fiction, forsooth !

The long low room of the Trinchinopoly Crab, though by
day a very Lybian desert of sandy floor, tenantless settles, and
pyramid-spittoons, and drawing, perhaps, scarcely a butt of
beer per month, does a roaring trade at night; for there are
always ships in the river, and boats to row, and skippers who
have used the Crab before, and nautical tradesmen eager to
meet them ; though this river-side house is a good mile and a
quarter from any village, or even inhabited house. Decent,
honest, civil, God-fearing men are these seamen-captains—the

nobly great majority of them that is—of every port and nation. From the blunt whaling captains at Hull and Glasgow, to the mighty mail steamers skippers at Liverpool or Southampton, they are almost invariably the same : civil of speech, quiet of demeanour, modest of assertion, and incapable of grandilo-quence, almost to a fault. They will tell you diffidently of the Isles of Greece that they 'were down Cerigo way once with fruit ;' whereas young Swallowpounce of the Treasury, whose Mediterranean travels I verily believe have never extended beyond Malta, is for ever bragging of and quoting

'Eternal summer gilds them yet,
But all except their sun is set.'

Have they been to India? Um, yes : Calcutta, and so on, said as easily as 'Chelsea.' The terrible Patagonian promon-tory, the awful and inhospitable land of Terra del Fuego is to them merely The Horn ; and Venice, the Adriatic, Dalmatia, Styria, are all summed up in a simple 'Up the Gulf as far as Tryeast with hides.' Farewell, ye seamen-captains, honest men, who as pertinaciously persist in wearing chimney-pot hats and frock-coats, as your pictorial and literary delineators are incorrigible in delineating you in large-buttoned peacoats, wide ducks, and flat hats. Simple-minded men, making the little parade you do of your travelling lore and nautical learn-ing—leaving the first only to be guessed at in your mahogany cheeks and sun-crimsoned foreheads and embrowned hands ; the second only to be known in the hour of danger and peril, when the sea runs mountains high, and the masts bend like whips, and the rigging writhes like the tresses of a woman possessed.

X.

MY SWAN.

THERE was once a great Italian painter—the same who had a hand in building Saint Peter's—who, when he came to be nearly eighty years of age, when he was justly considered and renowned throughout Europe as the most learned artist living, as a man who knew by heart every bone, ligament, muscle, and vein, and could portray them with the most recondite foreshortening and the most crudite symmetry—which, indeed, he could—designed a rough pencil sketch, representing a very old man (himself) seated in a go-cart,

I 2

drawn by a little child; while underneath the drawing these words were written : ' *Ancora impara* '—' Still he learns.' The octogenarian sage—the oracle of art—was wise and modest enough to confess how little he knew, and how much he had yet to learn.

Now, though I do not pretend to the learning of Michael Angelo, or—I say it in all modesty—to know much about anything, I did flatter myself that I was passably well read in ' public ' lore—that, as I once foolishly boasted, I had graduated in beer. Flippantly, as men of superficial acquirements are prone to do, I summed up the phases of ' public ' life in three chapters. Fatuitous scribe! I had but broken the ground with the point of my spade. Insensate! I had thought to do in a day what it would take years to accomplish a moiety of. Impotent! I had essayed to dip the Mississippi dry with a salt-spoon.

Consider the contemplative man's recreation. The fishing public-house! On the banks of a suburban stream, or by the towing-path of a canal, or by the mud-compelling, stream-restraining portals of a lock shall we find the piscatorial public : the Jolly Anglers, maybe, or the Izaak Walton, or very probably the Swan. What connection there can be between a Swan and the gentle craft I know not; but it is a fact no less strange than incontrovertible, that the Swan is the favourite sign for fishing-houses : the White Swan, the Old Swan, the Silver Swan, the Swan and Hook, but the Swan, always.

The Swan, my Swan—on the little fishing river Sprec (which has been playing some astonishing freaks of late—overflowing its banks and depositing roach and dace in back kitchens and dustbins)—always puts me in mind of a very old man with very young legs ; for whereas it is above, as far as regards its upper and garret story, a quaint, moss-covered, thatched-roofed edifice with crooked gable ends, and an oriel window with lozenge-panes, it is below an atrociously modern erection of staring yellow brick with an impertinent stuccoed doorway, and the usual rhetorical conventionalities in golden flourishes about neat wines, fine ales, good accommodation, and the rest of it. This doorway faces the high omnibus road, and is a sixpenny ride from the Bank—a great convenience to anglers whose everyday occupations are of a City or commercial cast. The sign of the Swan formerly stood in this high road, or at least creaked and swung within an iron frame affixed to a post standing there. This Swan was a brave bird with a neck like a corkscrew, and a head like the griffin's in the City Arms. There were faint vestiges of a gold-laced cocked hat, and a rubicund red nose gleaming through the whity-brown plumage of the bird, and old folks said that before the house had been the Swan, it was known as the General Ligonier. Other old folks held out stoutly that the cocked hat and rubicund nose belonged to the publican's friend, the Marquis of Granby, while a third party swore hard that they were the property of Admiral Byng, and that he was dissignified after they had shot him. When Groundbait, the present landlord of the Swan, took the house, he caused the sign to be removed as too shabby and tarnished, and agreed with Joe Copal, the journeyman decorator, to paint a new one for a crown and a bottle of wine. Unfortunately he paid the money and the liquor in advance, and Joe soon after emigrated to Texas, leaving not only the sign unpainted, but a considerable score for malt liquors and tobacco unsettled ; whereupon Groundbait grew moody and abstracted on the subject of signs ; refusing to have a new one painted, and replying haughtily to such friends as pressed him on the subject that 'the gentlemen as used the Swan knew his 'ouse was the Swan without a swan being painted up outside like a himage ; and that if they didn't they might go to any other swan or goose :' after which he was wont to expel several vehement whiffs from his pipe, and knitting his brows, gaze ruefully at Joe Copal's unliquidated score, which to this day remains in full chalk characters behind the parlour door ; it being as much as Dorothy the pretty barmaid's place is worth to meddle with, or hint about effacing it. Groundbait has looked at it a good many times since the discovery of the gold-fields in Australia, as he has an idea that Texas may be somewhere that way ; and that Joe, coming back repentant some day with a store of nuggets, may call in and settle it.

The Swan has been a fishing-house for years, not only as in the neighbourhood of a fishing stream and the resort of metropolitan anglers, but also as a species of house-of-call for freshwater fishermen—a piscatorial clearing-house—a fishing news-exchange, a social club-house for the amateurs of the rod and line.

The little bar parlour of the Swan, which is of no particular shape, and has a paper ceiling, has a door covered on the inner side half by a coloured mezzotint of George the Third in jack-boots, on a horse like a gambolling hippopotamus, reviewing one hundred thousand volunteers in Hyde Park : half by the famous *abacus*, or slate—the tabular record of scores. Dorothy, the ' neat-handed Phillis ' of the Swan, albeit a ready reckoner and an accomplished *artiste* in stewing carp and frying smelts, is not a very apt scholar; so she has devised a system of financial hieroglyphics to cover her want of proficiency in the delineation of the Arabic numerals. Thus in her money alphabet, a circle (o) stands for a shilling; a half-moon (☾) for sixpence, a Maltese cross for a penny, and a Greek ditto for a halfpenny. Farthings are beneath the calculations of the Swan ; and pounds are represented by a very large O indeed ; the agglomeration of a score of circles into one circumference. The room is hung round with badges and trophies of the piscatorial craft. Rods of all shapes and sizes, eel-spears, winches, landing-nets, Penelopean webs of fishing-tackle, glistering armouries of hooks, harpoons, panniers, bait-cans ; and in a glass case a most wonderful piscatorio-entomological collection of flies—flies of gorgeously tinted floss silk, phea-sants' feathers, and gold and silver thread—flies warranted to deceive the acutest of fish ; though if, viewed through a watery medium, the flies come no nearer Nature than these do, I have no great opinion of the fishes' discernment—with all due reverence for the Eleusinian mysteries of fly-fishing, which I do not understand, be it said. Over the fireplace is the identical rod and line with which J. Barbell, Esq., hooked the monstrous and European-famed jack in the river Dodder, near Dublin, and in the year of grace eighteen hundred and thirty-nine ; in one corner are the shovel and bucket with and in which at the same place and time the said jack, after being walked seven miles down the banks of the Dodder, and cracking the rod into innumerable fissures (though the supe-rior article, one of Check's best would not break), was ultimately landed. Conspicuous between the windows is the portrait of J. Barbell, Esq., a hairy-faced man, severely scourging a river with a rod like a May-pole ; beneath that, the famous jack himself *in propriâ personâ*, in a glass case, stuffed, very brown and horny with varnish, with great staring glass eyes (one cracked), and a mouth wide open grinning hideously. He is swimming vigorously through nothing at all, and has a neat foreground of moss and Brighton-beach shells, and a backing of pea-green sky. There are very many other glass cases, containing the mummies of other famous jacks, trout, roach, dace, and carp, including the well-known perch which was captured after being heard of for five years in the back waters of the Thames near

Reading, and has a back fin nearly as large as Madame de Pompadour's fan. Not forgetting a well-thumbed copy of dear old Izaak's 'Complete Angler;' a price-list of fishing materials sold at the Golden Perch or the Silver Roach in London, with manuscript comments of anglers as to the quality thereof pencilled on the margin, and the contributions of the ingenious Ephemera to 'Bell's Life in London,' cut from that journal and pasted together on the leaves of an old cheesemonger's day-book; not forgetting these with a certain fishy smell prevalent, I think I have drawn the parlour of the Swan for you pretty correctly. The first thing you should do on entering this sanctuary of fishing is to keep your skirts very close to your person, and to duck your head a little—the air being at times charged with animal matter in the shape of dried entrails twisted into fishing-lines, which flying about, and winding round your clothes or in your hair, produce a state of entanglement more Gordian than pleasant. The chairs and other articles of furniture are also more or less garnished with hooks of various sizes, dropped from the parchment hook-books of the gentlemen fishermen. These protrude imperceptibly, but dangerously, like quills upon the fretful porcupine; and it is as well to examine your chair with a magnifying glass, or to cause a friend to occupy it preliminarily, before you sit down in it yourself.

If you come to the Swan to fish you cannot do better than tackle (I do not use the word with the slightest intention of punning) Groundbait, the landlord, immediately. That Boniface will be but too happy to tell you the latest fishing news, the most approved fishing places, the neighbouring gentry who give permissions to fish. He knows of fish in places you would never dream of: he has cunningly-devised receipts for ground-bait: his butcher is the butcher for gentles, his oil-shops are the shops for greaves; he has hooks that every fish that ever was spawned will gorge, lines that never break, rods that never snap. If you would go farther a-field after an essay at the mild suburban angling of the River Spree, he will put you up to rare country fishing spots, where there are trouts of unheard-of size, eels as big as serpents, pikes so large and voracious that they gnaw the spokes of water-wheels; of quiet Berkshire villages, where the silver Thames murmurs peacefully, gladsomely, innocently between sylvan banks, through a green thanksgiving landscape, among little islets, quiet, sunny, sequestered as the remote Bermudas; where the river, in fine, is a river you may drink and lave in and rejoice over, forgetting the bone factories and gas works and tanneries, the sweltering sewerage, inky colliers, and rotting corpses below Bridge.

If you come to the Swan merely as an observer of the world, how it is a-wagging as I do, you may take your half-pint of neat port with Groundbait, or shrouding yourself behind the cloudy mantle of a pipe, study character among the frequenters of the Swan. Groundbait does not fish much himself. The engineer has an objection to see himself hoist with his own petard. Doctors never take their own physic. Lawyers don't go to law. Groundbait, the *arbiter piscatorium*, the oracle, the *expert juré* of angling, seldom takes rod in hand himself. He has curiously a dominant passion for leaping, darting the lancing pole, swinging by his hands, climbing knotted ropes, and other feats of strength and agility. He has quite a little gymnasium in his back garden, leading to the river—a kind of gibbet, with ropes and ladders, an erection which, when he first took the Swan, and set up his gymnastic apparatus, gave his neighbour and enemy, the Reverend Grieax Typhoon, occasion to address several stinging sermons to the congregation sitting under him at little Adullam, touching the near connection between publicans and the most degraded of mankind, such as public executioners, with a neat little historical parallel concerning Mordecai and Haman.

The angling company frequenting the Swan are varied and eccentric. Rarely, I am of opinion, is eccentricity so prevalent as among anglers. Take Mr. Jefferson Jebb, among his intimates known as Jeff. He is something in the City, that mysterious place, the home of so many mysterious avocations. Every evening during the summer months, and every Sunday throughout the year, he comes to the Swan to fish or to talk of fishing. He is intensely shabby, snuffy, and dirty, and wears a beaver hat brushed all the wrong way, and quite red with rust. On one finger he wears a very large and sparkling diamond ring. His boots are not boots but bats—splay, shapeless, deformed canoes, with bulbous excrescences on the upper leather. When he sleeps at the Swan, and you see the boots outside his door, they have an inexpressibly groggy, wall-eyed, shambling appearance, and sway to and fro of their own accord like the Logan or rocking-stone in Cornwall. I think Jeff must be in the habit of drinking coffee at breakfast, and, purchasing dried sole-skins wherewith to clear the decoction of the Indian berry, be continually forgetting to take his purchases out of his pockets, for there is a fishy smell about him, constant but indescribable. He never catches any fish to speak of. He does not seem to care about any. His principal delight is in the peculiarly nasty process of kneading together the compound of gravel, worms, and soaked bread, known as groundbait, small dumplings of which ordinarily adhere to his hands and habiliments. He smokes a fishy pipe, and frequently overhauls a very greasy parchment-covered portfolio filled with hooks. His line or plan of conversation is consistent and simple, but disagreeable, consisting in flatly contradicting any assertion on angling, or, indeed, any other topic advanced by the surrounding company. This peculiarity, together with a general crustiness of demeanour and malignity of remark, have earned for him the *sobriquets* of the 'hedgehog,' 'old rusty,' 'cranky Jeff,' and the like. If he be not a broker's assistant, or a Custom House officer in the City, he must certainly be a holder of Spanish bonds, or Mexican scrip, or some other description of soured financier.

The arm-chair immediately beneath the portrait of J. Barbell, Esq., is the property, by conquest, by seniority, and by conscription, of Mr. Bumblecherry, Captain Bumblecherry, who has been a brother of the angle, and a supporter of the Swan for twenty years. For the last five he has boarded and lodged beneath Groundbait's hospitable roof. In his hot youth he was an exciseman; for some years he has been a gentleman, existing on the superannuation allowance granted him by a grateful country. He keeps a vehicle which he calls a 'trap,' but which is, in reality, a species of square wickerwork clothes-basket on wheels, drawn by a vicious pony. Bumblecherry is a very square, little old man with a red scratch wig, a bulbous nose, and a fangy range of teeth. He looks very nearly as vicious as his pony. He bids you good morning in a threatening manner; scowls when you offer him a light for his pipe, and not unfrequently takes leave of the parlour company at night with the very reverse of a benediction. He is a very bad old man; and when he speaks to you looks very much as if he would like to bite you. He does not believe in anything, much, except fishing, at which recreation he is indefatigable; fishing at all times and all seasons when it is possible to fish, singing the while, in a coffee-mill voice, a dreary chaunt, touching 'those that fish for roach and dace.' In the evening, when he is in a decent humour, he will volunteer an equally dismal stave called 'The Watchman's nervous,' and a certain song about a wheelbarrow, of whose twenty-four verses I can only call to mind one, running, I think,

'The Mayor of Hull come in his coach,
Come in his coach so slow—
And what do you think the Mayor come for?
Why, to borrow my wheelbarrow—oh, oh, oh!'
                                        Ad libitum.

It is a sight to see the captain savagely fishing in all weathers, fair or foul ; pouring maledictions on all who dare to meddle with his tackle ; gloomily cooking the fish he has caught, or driving doggedly along in the basket-cart with the vicious pony—which brute anon attempts to bite crossing passengers, anon stands stock still, whereat Bumblecherry gets out and kicks him till he moves again. He abuses Dorothy very frequently, but as he occasionally makes her presents of odd hanks of floss-silk he uses in fly-making, meat-pies, and other confectionery, and once attempted to kiss her, in disengaging a double-barbed hook from her dress, there is a report that he means to marry her, and at his decease endow her with the fabulous wealth he is supposed to have accumulated during his connection with the British excise.

A frequent visitor to the Swan is a tall, high-dried French gentleman in a short cloak, decorated with the almost obsolete poodle collar. Nobody knows his name, so he is generally called, with reference to his foreign extraction, as the 'Moossoo.' He is a very assiduous, but pensive and melancholy, fisherman, and, sitting on a stump, with the poodle collar turned up over his countenance, looks very like 'Patience on a monument.' In hot weather he will not disdain to take off his stockings, and, rolling up his trousers, fish barelegged at a considerable distance from the bank. He is an amateur in the breeding and care of gentles and wormbait, and generally carries about with him a box of lob-worms, which, he laments to Mrs. Groundbait (who speaks a little French), are continually getting loose, and walking up and down the stairs of his house '*la canne à la main*'—an anecdote I venture to relate with a view to signalling a peculiarity, hitherto unknown, in the natural history of lob-worms.

In summer weather a great crowd of dandy fishermen invade the Swan. These gay young brothers of the angle—bucks of Cheapside and exquisites of the Poultry — come down on afternoons and Sundays in the most astonishing fishing costume, and laden with the most elaborate fishing-tackle. Wide-awake hats of varied hue, fishing-jackets of curious cut, veils, patent fishing-boots, belts, pouches, winches like small steam-engines, so complicated are they; stacks of rods, coils of lines, bait-cans painted the most vivid green : such are the panoplies of these youths. Tremendous is the fuss and pother they make about bait and hooks, elaborate are their preparations, bold and valorous their promises, but, alas! frequently and signally lame and unsatisfactory their performances. With all their varied armament and intricate machinery, I have seen them, many a time and oft, distanced and defeated by a stick and a string, a worm at one end, and a little barelegged boy at the other.

XI.

THE BOTTLE OF HAY.

I AM a retired publican, and date from the days when publicans *were* publicans. I kept the Bottle of Hay, in Leather Lane, when public-houses were worth keeping. I have a tidy penny in the funds now, a neat little box at Hoxton, am an elder of my chapel, one of the committee of my Literary and Scientific Institution, and a governor of the Licensed Victuallers' Association. If I had kept my house as houses are kept now, I might have a villa at Ealing, and be a Middlesex magistrate, perhaps; or, just as probably, I should be occupying apartments in the Licensed Victuallers' Almshouses. I prefer my tidy funded penny and my box to both. Altogether I may claim to be a respectable man, for I have a very snug little trap (under tax) and my pony, Barrett (he was a butcher's before he was mine, and a swell's before he was a butcher's), can do something considerable in the trotting line.

My trap and I and my friend Spyle, who has a neat superannuation on the Customs, go about a goodish deal among public-houses now. You see I have a kind of liking for the old trade; and there is no amusement I like so much as tasting the beer at a new house, or dropping in at stated times, and in rotation, on an old one, or looking about as to the next probable owner of a shut-up house, or attending public-house auctions and the like. Something might turn up some day, you know, where a party could invest his little savings profitably; and that is why I like to keep in with my distillers, Porcus and Grains, and with my old brewers, Spiggot, Buffle, and Bung, for business reasons, over and above the drop of something comfortable that they are sure to ask me if I will take this morning. In fact, if you could put me up to any snug concern drawing a reasonable number of butts a month, that a party could drop into reasonable, I think I might hear of a bidder.

This doesn't interfere a tittle, however, with my firm and settled opinion that the public line is going to ruin. To rack and ruin. The teetotallers, of course, have done a deal of harm; but still they take a decent quantity medicinally, and the very fierce ones, they generally break out very fierce about once a month, and make up for lost time. It's the publicans themselves that do the injury by introducing all sorts of innovations and new-fangled enticements to drink to their customers. As if a man wanted leading on to drink! He never did in my time. The landlords themselves are their own enemies, and with their plate-glass and gilding and rosewood fittings and the rest of it, they are making the line disrespectable. At least, I think so. A public-house isn't a public-house now, but something quite different.

Now, there's my old house in Leather Lane—the Bottle of Hay. I sold the lease, stock, goodwill, and fixtures to old Berrystack. He was one of the old school, as I am, and if he hadn't taken it into his senses to go out of them, and to be now in a lunatic asylum and a padded room, he would have carried the house on in the old, and my manner, to this day, I have no doubt. Before he went mad, however, he had sense enough to sell the house to young Bowley, whose father was a gauger in the docks. The licence and Berrystack's pretty daughter Louisa were transferred to Bowley at the same time; and as man and wife (Louisa was the prettiest hand at mixing a twopenn'orth, hot, and saying a civil word to the old gentlemen that used the house, that ever you saw) they went on for a year or two as comfortable as may be. But what did young Bowley but go to cards, and then to horse-racing and betting, and to wearing a horseshoe pin in his neckerchief, and trousers much too tight for him about the legs? And where did he go afterwards but into Whitecross Street, and afterwards to the Insolvent Court; and where did Mrs. Bowley go but off to Boulogne with the cash-box and the military chap (I never could abide him with his mustachios and his airs) that was always hanging about the bar-parlour. A pretty piece of business this for a respectable house! But, bad as Bowley was, the next tenant was worse. He had plenty of money, and all that; but I have no hesitation in saying that he was a fellow. A fellow. He was ashamed of his apron. Nothing but a full suit of black would suit my gentleman; and he would stand behind the bar twiddling his Albert guard-chain, and, if he were asked for change, pull it out of a thing like a lady's reticule, which he called his 'port-money.' He'd better have looked to his port wine. He shut his house up all day Sunday, and actually tried to put his pot-boy into a white neckcloth; but he, being a pot-boy that knew his business, and wasn't above it, told him plainly that he wasn't used to it, and that he had better look out for another young man.

His bar, instead of being covered with the decent piles of halfpence and trays full of silver, that a right-minded publican loves to accumulate towards Saturday, was tricked out with all sorts of bulbs and roots, and trumpery—nasturtiums, helio-tropes, ranunculuses, and the like; and there wasn't an Italian image-man out of Leather Lane that came in to take a drop but he'd buy a Venus, or a Jenny Lind, or a Holy Family of; and these he'd stick up on gim-crack brackets under his tubs, and ask me with a simpering grin if I didn't think the rubbish classical? Classical! What business has a licensed victualler with the classics? I could not stand this; I turned to Pruff-well (this was the classical gentleman's name), and said I to him—'Mr. Pruffwell, it's my belief that you're not acting becoming. If you're a landlord, say so; if you're not, the sooner you say so, or go out of the business, the better;' and thereupon I paid for what I had had and walked out. He said I was an old fool; but Mr. Batts, of Liquorpond Street, and Mr. Crapper, of Gray's Inn Lane, and little Shoulderblade, the sheriff's officer—all respectable warm men, who used the house—went out with me, and all said I had done the thing that was right. I never set my foot in Pruffwell's house again till he left it; but I heard that he went on from bad to worse afterwards: that he took a wife who was all curls and conceit, and was nervous and musical, bless us; and that the choruses at the Wednesday Evening Free and Easy in the tap-room used to be drowned by Madam's piano-forte up stairs jangling such variations upon Auld Robin Gray that his mother wouldn t have known him. At last he got a fellow with long hair and spectacles, and a turn-down collar, and a tuft, to lecture upon the 'Od force,' and 'Things not Seen,' or things never heard of in his coffee-room; and another (in a cloak and more spectacles, green this time) to demonstrate the 'theory of the earth's movement,' with a piece of string, a copper disc, like the bottom of a stew-pan knocked out, and an old clock dial-plate. He couldn't demonstrate it, it seemed, without a great deal of gin and water first, and turning off the gas afterwards; and there were two great-coats and seven spoons missing the next morning. When I heard Pruffwell was countenancing such proceedings as these, I thought he was coming to a bad end; and, sure enough, to a very bad one he came shortly afterwards. He got into some scrape about defrauding the gas company out of their dues, falsifying the meter and tapping the main himself; but somehow he was too clever, and the gas got into the gin, and the water into that, and the sewer into that; and the gas company came in and tore up the flooring, and spoilt the beer-engines, and sued him dreadfully. He ran away very quickly did Mr. Pruffwell after this, Albert chain, port-money, and all. I did hear that he went to America, where he turned schoolmaster, lecturer, and got into some trouble about the notes of a bank that had stopped payment; and, besides that, Mrs. Pruffwell was not Mrs. Pruffwell after all, and after P.'s disappearance, had taken to drinking dreadfully.

All this while the Bottle of Hay was becoming dingier and dingier, and more dilapidated in appearance every day. The pots had lost their brightness, and the pewter-covered bar counter, which should have been clean and glistening, became stained and discoloured with sticky rings of treacly porter. When the handles of the taps got loose and unscrewed they were never replaced; the glasses lost half their feet, and the pewter measures half their capacity of containing by dinting and battering. The letters and numbers wore off the gin-tubs; the till contained nothing but broken tobacco-pipes, and pock-marked, defaced, advertisement-branded and perforated halfpence, which even the neediest of the customers had indignantly refused; and little Ruggs, the tipstaff of the Sheriff's Court, now pretty nearly the only regular customer that remained, declared that really he must use some other house, for that on three separate days the Bottle of Hay had been out of gin and bitters. The harp, piano, and violin that used to come regularly every Saturday night and give a musical performance in front of the door, removed to the Coach and Horses up the lane; and really if it had not been for the sign, and the old portrait of myself in the coffee-room (kitcat, half length three-quarter face, representing me with my hand in my waistcoat, backed by a crimson velvet curtain and a Grecian column, and flanked by an inkstand, a hat and gloves, four books and an orange cut in halves) I really should not have recognised my old house, where I had worked hard for so many years, and realised such a neat little bit of property. Then the sheriff came in with his levy and his men in possession ; and for a week or so what little beer was required was drawn by hooked-nosed men of the Israelitish persuasion. Then they hung the carpets out of the window, and had a sale ; and three weeks afterwards I recognised my old arm-chair, bar-flap and beer-engine at a second-hand shop in Brokers' Row, Long Acre, higgledy-piggledy with tin tea-canisters, sham bookshelves, dummy chemists' drawers, bandy-legged counting-house desks and empty jars, labelled ' tama-rinds ' and ' leeches.'

I wish they had pulled down my old house after this. I wish they had built a Methodist Chapel, or Baths and Wash-houses, or a Temperance Hall upon its site. Anything rather than it should have become what it is now. It was shut up a long time ; and I certainly had a slight twinge of melancholy when, passing it occasionally, I saw its doors fast closed and bolted and barred with the doors that had been for so many years on the swing, and of which the paint about the handles had been worn off by the hands of so many good fellows who had got ' comfortable ' in my house so many Monday morn-ings and so many Saturday nights. At last the Bottle of Hay was let.

The new landlord was a young, beardless man, in a coloured shirt and a wide-awake hat. He was one of three brothers, and they had public-houses all over London ; one at Ber-mondsey, one large gin-palace somewhere over the water at a corner where six crowded thoroughfares met ; one in a sub-urban neighbourhood, very new and very improving, which was an omnibus house ; and an establishment in the City in a dark alley down Dockway, where prime ports and sherries were drawn from the wood, and sold at an extraordinarily low price per imperial quart, and white-headed old gentlemen whose only occupation it seemed to be to drink (I do a good deal in that way), went to taste the prime wines and eat nuts and cheese-crumbs. Fishtail was this new young landlord's name, and his wide-awake hat was a green one. No other symptom of that colour was there in him, however, for he was as wide awake as his hat or a detective policeman, as cun-ning as a fox, as pert as a magpie, and as avaricious as a Jew. He wasn't above his business. He and the wide-awake were scudding, poking, peeping, scampering morning noon and night about the house during its renovation (doing up, I should call it). He began by pulling the house half down. Then he threw the ground and first floor into one, and filled the window with plate glass and tremendous gilt gas-burners. Then he raised an ornamental balustrade above the coping of the roof, and a vase above that, and a statue of Hercules or somebody defying something above that, and a huge flag above all—to say nothing of a big gilt clock surrounded with stucco cornucopias and emblems, and which had an illuminated dial, the letters of 'B.O.T.T.L.E. O.F. H.A.Y. O.' instead of numerals, and hands like ornamental fire-shovels. Not content with this, the second floor front middle window was blocked up with a large gas star with V.R. and the crown, and the rose, shamrock, and thistle, and Heaven knows what besides, all in gas. The house was painted from top to bottom in as gaudy colours as could be procured, and wherever it was feasible plastered over with compo mouldings and flourishing ornaments. His name, Fishtail, was painted upon almost every imaginable part of the building, in all sorts of colours, and in letters so big that it was almost impossible to read them. The inside of the house was as much transmogrified as the outside.

It was all mahogany—at least, what wasn't mahogany, was gilt carving and ground glass, with flourishing patterns on it. The bar was cut up into little compartments like pawnbrokers' boxes ; and there was the wholesale entrance, and the jug and bottle department, the retail bar, the snuggery, the private bar, the ladies' bar, the wine and liqueur entrance, and the lunch bar. The handles of the taps were painted porcelain, and green and yellow glass. There were mysterious glass columns, in which the bitter ale, instead of being drawn up comfortably from the cask in the cellar below, remained always on view above ground to show its clearness, and was drawn out into glasses by a mysterious engine like an air-pump with something wrong in its inside. There were carved benches in the private bar, with crimson plush cushions aerated and elastic. There were spring duffers, working in a tunnel in the wall, which you were to strike with your fist to try your muscular strength. There were machines to test your lifting power, and a weighing-machine, and a lung-testing machine, or 'vital-power determinator.' There were plates full of nasty compounds of chips, saw-dust, and grits, called Scotch bannocks, which were to be eaten with butter, and washed down by the Gregarach Staggering old Claymore

or Doch an' Dorroch ale ; but which never should have shown
its face in my old house, I warrant you. There were sausages, fried in a peculiar manner, with barbecued parsley, and
a huge, brazen sausage chest, supported on two elephants,
with a furnace beneath, from which sausages and potatoes
were served out hot and hot all day long. There were sandwiches cut into strange devices ; and cakes and tarts that
nobody ever heard of before ; and drinks and mixtures concocted that, in my day, would have brought the exciseman
about a landlord pretty soon, I can assure you. The soda-
water bottles had spiral necks like glass corkscrews, and zigzag labels. The ginger beer was all colours—blue, green,
and violet. Every inch of the walls that was not be-plastered
with ornaments and gilding, or bedizened with gilt announcements of splendid ales and unrivalled quadruple stouts I never
heard of, was covered with ridiculously gaudy-coloured prints,
puffing the 'Cead Mille Failthe Whisky,' the 'Phthisis
Curing Bottled Beer,' recommended by the entire faculty ;
the Imperial Kartoffelnsfell-hopfbrunnen Waters bottled at
the celebrated mineral springs of Kartoffelnsfell under the
immediate superintendence of the Kartoffelnsfell Government,
all of which were to be had in splendid condition, and for
which J. Fishtail was the sole agent. This was a nice beginning. But the worst was to come. The house was opened,
and J. Fishtail was as busy as a bee with an opening dinner,
which he bragged and boasted a great deal of having reported
in the press. He did, to be sure, get a seedy chap with an
umbrella and a hat full of old newspapers and red comforters,
who did fires and murders, and the Lord Mayor's state footmen's liveries at three-halfpence a line ; and he certainly
came to the dinner, and, when the toast of 'the press' was
given, prefaced by the appropriate glee of 'When winds
breathe soft,' made a neat speech, rendered rather indistinct
by hot liquids, in acknowledgment ; but, though he borrowed
half a pound and stuck up an unlimited score, and though
Fishtail became a quarterly subscriber to 'The Weekly Murder
Sheet,' price threepence, stamped, I never heard of any account
of his grand initiatory banquet being published therein, or in
any other newspaper. Meanwhile, his business went on
apace. The harp, flute, and violin would have been glad to
come back and play outside ; but they were far too low for
the Bottle of Hay, now. Nothing would suit Fishtail but a
real German green-baize band, composed of six dumpy,
tawney-haired musicians from Frankfort, all with cloth caps,

K

like shovels of mud, thrown on their heads, and falling over
on the other side ; all with rings in their ears and on their
thumbs ; and all born barons, at least, in their own country.
These gentry put their fists into their horns, and drew out
their trombones to amazing lengths, playing such wonderfully
complicated tunes, and singing, meanwhile, such long-winded
choruses, all ending with 'tra la la, tra la la, tra la-a-a-a !'
that a dense crowd would gather round them during their
performances, and the very policeman would refrain from
ordering them to move on, to the great disgust of the Alabama
Ethiopian Serenaders (from Cork Buildings, Gray's Inn Lane)
who were, in truth, only the harp, flute, and violin fallen into
evil days, and disguised in lamp-black, pomatum, Welsh wigs
dyed black, paper shirt collars, white calico neckcloths, ban-
joes, tambourines, and bones.   The gas star, too, and the
illuminated clock, brought a great many customers—but what
sort of customers were they ?   Italian image-men and organ-
grinders, and Irish hodmen, and basket-women.   The Irish
and the Italians fell to fighting immediately (of course about
the Pope), which was bad for themselves ; and then they
complained that the bar had been so altered that they hadn't
room to fight, which was worse for the house : for the Italians
you see, when fighting, were accustomed to tramp in a circle,
their knives pointing towards the centre, ready for a lunge,
whereas the Irish always wanted a clear stage and no favour
—at least plenty of space convenient for a spring, and ample
room to jump upon a man, or beat his head in with a quart
pot, or bite his nose off.   The nooks and corners into which
the bar had been cut up rendered this very difficult of
accomplishment ; and the consequence was, that the fine
ground-glass panels and lustres, the porcelain tap-handles,
the crystal ale columns, the gold-fish fountain (I don't think I
mentioned that), the fine gilt and rosewood mouldings, soon
came to be knocked off, smashed, and spoilt past mending.
J. Fishtail was very savage at this, you may be sure, and,
striving to turn the noisy customers out, the wide-awake hat
was perpetually being flattened on his head with pewter
measures, and his cut-away coat ripped up with clasp knives
—for he was full of pluck, and did his best to keep order.
The police naturally appeared on the scene in these disturbances, and a great deal of expense was entailed upon him in
'squaring' these functionaries, particularly when the Italians,
being prevented from fighting, took to gambling on the tubs,
at dominoes, moro, or 'buck-buck, how many fingers do I hold

up ?' and stabbing each other quietly when they lost. The police had to be 'squared' so often under these circumstances, that the little court by the side door was half lined with pots of half and half, which the municipals slipped off their beat to drink on the sly ; and as it was, Fishtail—albeit, as harmlessly inclined as any landlord—was always in trouble with the magistrates, and having his licence endorsed, and being fined. He grew into awful disfavour with the licensing authorities at Clerkenwell Green, where Major Blueblasis, of Tottenham, once stated his conviction that the Bottle of Hay was an 'infamous den;' and if Inspector Buffles had not stood Fishtail's friend he would have lost his licence, and the spite of his enemy Ditcher, who keeps the Italian Stores beershop in the lane, and has been trying after a spirit licence these five years, would have been gratified.

Then he got into trouble' about his dry skittle-ground. When my old house was near, I had as neat, and as good, and as dry a skittle-alley as any in Clerkenwell parish. Many and many have been the respectable tradesmen that have played there—good warm men—moral men, and ex-churchwardens. The 'setter up' made fifteen shillings a week clear, all the year round. Many, too, have been the rumps and dozen ordered in my house after matches, aye, and paid for. J. Fishtail of course was too go-ahead a young gentleman to be contented with a dry skittle-ground with plenty of sawdust and one gas jet, and the pins and balls (like wooden Dutch cheeses) painted on the door-jambs. Oh no ! he must have an American Bowling Alley, with more mahogany, more gilding, more ground-glass shades to the gas-burners, more crimson-covered benches, a scorer or marker, who played tricks with a grand mahogany board like a railway time-table instead of using the old legitimate chalk, and a flaring transparency outside, representing General Washington playing skittles with Doctor Franklin. Of course there was an additional bar for the use of the skittle-players, where the scorer, who wore a very large shirt collar and a straw hat, and was at least a General in America—mixed and sold 'American Drinks:' brandy cock-tails, gin-slings, egg-noggs, timber-doodles, and mint-juleps, which last tasted like very bad gin and water, with green stuff in it, which you were obliged to suck through a straw instead of swigging in the legitimate manner. A fine end for my dry skittle-ground to come to !

It hadn't been open a month before Dick the Brewer, Curly

K 2

Jem Simmons and Jew Josephs, all notorious skittle-sharps, found it out and made it a regular rendezvous for picking up flats. They soon picked up young Mr. Poppinson, the rich pawnbroker's son, who had twenty thousand pounds and water on the brain, and has since gone through the Court. They picked him up to some tune. It wasn't the games he lost on the square (which were few), or the games he lost on the cross (which were many), or the sums he was cheated of at the fine slate billiard-table up stairs, or the bottles of champagne he stood (champagne at my old house in Leather Lane!); it was the dreadful deal of money he lost at betting : —fifties that Dick the Brewer couldn't cross the alley in three jumps, ponies that Curly Jem couldn't name the winners of the Derby and Oaks for ten years running—even fives that Jew Josephs couldn't turn up a Jack four times out of four. Poor young Mr. Poppinson! He ruined himself and his poor child of a wife (a little delicate thing you might blow away with a puff at most) and his poor old widowed mother who sold herself up, and pawned her comfortable little annuity for her wayward son. I met him the other day—he is but a boy still—flying in rags ; and said I to myself, there are not many people who pass this scarecrow who would believe, were they told it, that in two or three years he managed to squander away twenty thousand golden pounds, not in horse-racing, not at Crockford's, not on actresses and dancing-girls, not even in foreign travel, but between the skittle-alleys and billiard-tables and tap-rooms of three or four low public-houses. I have seen life and a many phases of it, and know how common these cases are. It is astonishing how often those who spend the most enjoy and see the least for their money. I met a man the other day ragged, forlorn, with no more fat upon him than would grease a cobbler's bradawl. Now I had known this man when he was worth ten thousand pounds. He had spent every penny of it. 'How on earth did you manage it?' I asked him, for I knew that he never drank, or had any ambition to be what you call a swell. 'Ah,' said he, with a sigh, 'I played.' 'What at?' I asked again, thinking of rouge-et-noir, roulette, or chicken hazard. 'Bagatelle,' says he. Ten thousand pounds at bagatelle—at a twopenny-halfpenny game of knocking a ball about with a walking-stick, and that a child could play at! Yet I dare say he told the truth. Just similarly young Mr. Poppinson went to ruin in J. Fishtail's American Bowling Alley ; and when in desperation he gave Curly Jem

Simmons and Jew Josephs in charge for swindling him (and they were discharged, of course), people did say that J. Fishtail was in league with Jew Josephs; stood in with the whole gang, and had as much to do with cheating Mr. Poppinson as anybody. At all events he got a very bad name by the transaction.

Just at this time, I think, I was taken very bad with the rheumatism, and, lying up at Hoxton, lost sight of J. Fishtail. I expected to find him in 'The Gazette' by the time I was able to be on my feet and about again; but the next time I looked in at my old house I found him still in Leather Lane, and heard that he was carrying on worse than ever. He had been satisfied with barmaids for some time, and saucy minxes they were too, all ribbons and airs, together with a very fast young barman, who was always making up his betting-book when he should have been attending to the customers; and had run matches, so I heard—the wretch—upon a turnpike-road in pink drawers, with a ribbon tied round his head. But what do you think J. Fishtail's next move was? To have a Giant as a barman! As I live, a Giant.

He was a great, shambling, awkward, bow-legged, splayfooted brute, considerably more than seven feet high, and as great a fool as he was a creature. He had a head like an ill-made slack-baked half-quartern loaf, inclining to the sugar-loaf form at the top; or perhaps a bladder of lard would be a better comparison. His little lack-lustre eyes were like two of No. 6 shot poked into the dough anyhow. His mouth was a mere gash, and he slobbered. His voice was a shrill squeak, with one gruff bass note that always turned up when it wasn't wanted, and oughtn't to have been heard. He had at least four left hands, and spilt half the liquids that he drew, and was always breaking his long shins over stools or anything that came handy—as almost everything seemed to do, in that sense. To see him in his huge shirtsleeves, with his awkward beefy hands hanging inanely by his side, and his great foolish mouth open, was disgusting: he was a pillar of stupidity, a huge animated pump with two handles, and not worth pumping. He took to wearing a little boy's cloth cap at the back of his monstrous ill-shaped head, which made him look supremely ridiculous. What his name was I never knew or cared to inquire; but he was generally known as 'Big Bill,' or the 'Giant Barman.' Of course he had been exhibited before the Queen and the principal Courts of Europe, and was patronised by all the royal families extant;

and a gigantic lithographic representation of him in a full
suit of black with a white neckcloth, exhibiting his bigness in
the private parlour of Windsor Castle, before her Majesty and
a select assembly, all the ladies of which wore feathers and all
the gentlemen stars and garters, was framed and glazed in
J. Fishtail's bar ; while a copy of it in coarse wood engraving
was placarded half over London. He had been Professor
Somebody once on a time I believe ; and had squeezed up
quart pots, lifted hundred weights of iron with his little
finger, and held bars of lead in his teeth ; but where Fishtail
picked him up was not known : some said in a caravan at a
fair, some sweeping a crossing, some in a ferry steamboat at
Liverpool, where he amused the company who crossed from
the landing stage at Birkenhead. He 'drew'—as the play-
acting people say—rather satisfactorily, at first, and was
goaded on by J. Fishtail to ask everybody to treat him to sixpenn'orth of brandy and water for the good of the house—the
consumption of which sixpenn'orths made him maudlin drunk ;
staggering on his long legs, crying to go home to Worcester-
shire (where he came from originally, I suppose), and at last
falling all of a huge heap in a corner. His admirers, however,
were soon confined to people who had half a pint of beer and
stared stupidly at him for half an hour together ; and as he
was totally useless as a barman, and broke more glasses than
he was worth, J. Fishtail soon gave him his travelling ticket
and started him.

J. Fishtail had not done enough to degrade my old house
yet. Not a bit of it. 'You'd better have a dwarf, Fishtail,'
I said to him in my quiet chaffing way (I always had a turn
for satire). 'P'raps a Miss Biffin would suit you, or a pig-
faced lady for a barmaid. What do you think of a " What is
it ?" or a spotted girl. You had better have a Rumtifoozle,
and put my old house on wheels, and hang my old portrait
outside for a placard, and stand at the door yourself and cry,
" Walk in, walk in and see the Rumtifoozle, two thousand
spots on his body, no two alike ; two thousand spots on his
tail, no two alike ; grows a hinch and a half every hanimal
year, and has never yet come to his full growth ; the Rumtifoozle which the proprietor wouldn't sell to George the
Fourth, saying : ' No, George the Fourth, you shall not have
our Rumtifoozle ; for the Rumtifoozle has a foot like a warm-
ing-pan, and a body like the keel of a vessel, and a tail that
would astonish a donkey !' " Try that, Fishtail.' 'Wait a bit,'
says he. Three days afterwards he came out with the fat barmaid.

Ugh! the monster. Sho was a lump of suet. She was a dollop of dripping, a splodge of grease. The poor thing was so helplessly fat that she could neither stand nor walk without difficulty; and all she could do was to crouch languidly in a wide chair, baring her horribly fat arms to the curious customers. She drew at first a little, and was profitable, and people turned faint directly they saw her layers and creases of fat and her quintuple chin, and were obliged to have three penn'orths of brandy; but they never came again, oh, no! and the fat barmaid soon followed the giant.

After this there came a bit of a lull in the way of monsters: but J. Fishtail was not tired. The cholera was very bad, and Leather Lane being a nice, teeming, no-washing neighbourhood, they just died off in it and about it like sheep. Out comes J. Fishtail with an infallible specific for the cholera—brandy and something, which took wonderfully and paid, for it made people very ill immediately, and compelled them to have more brandy, without anything, to set them all right again. The cholera died away, and Fishtail was hesitating between another giant who could sing beautifully, and a bearded lady, and an innocent-looking young lady, with pink eyes and long flaxen hair like floss silk, and was reported to have killed a man with a chopper, and would have been a great catch, if she would have come down to his terms, when the bloomer costume came out. Straightway, Fishtail put his two barmaids into variegated satin trousers and broad-brimmed hats. I rejoice to say that this move turned out an egregious failure. The increase of frequenters to the Bottle of Hay was confined to blackguard boys, who blocked up the doorways, whooping, and performing on the bones or pieces of slate; but, as they could see no more of the costume than the broad-brimmed hats, they grew disgusted, and made irreverent remarks, till the poor girls did nothing but take refuge in the bar-parlour and cry, and Fishtail was compelled, sorely against his will, to allow them to assume their proper attire.

More monsters; and such a monster this time. James Fishtail had the audacity, the impiety, the indecency, to engage and set up in a Christian bar a painted savage. Whether the wretch was a Caffre, or a Zooloo something, or a Hottentot, or a Krooman, or an Ashantee, it matters not; but there he was, all dirt and cock's feathers, and paint and leopard skin. He was a miserable, deformed creature, with bones through his nose, and ears, and chin, of course, and eyes which he was instructed to roll, and teeth to chatter

continually. At first he was allowed to go through his national performances of the chace, war, &c., before the bar,
with a hatchet, and a bow and arrows, and a string of beads;
but he lost his temper so frequently, and tried to bite Fishtail,
and to make ferocious love to the barmaids, that his sphere
of action was limited. So J. Fishtail had him penned up in a
corner of the bar with stools and pots, where he subsided into
a state of helpless stupidity; but he was wont at times to
howl so piteously, and to make such frantic efforts to escape,
that people cried shame, and Fishtail sent him back to the
showman who called himself his guardian, and had bought
him for two cows and a yard of red cloth somewhere out at
the Cape of Good Hope.

I was so out of patience with this last want of common
propriety on the part of Fishtail, that I solemnly discarded
him, and have never entered his house since.

XII.

CITY SPECTRES.

In the Royal Exchange there always were, and are, and will
be, rows of gaunt men, with haggard countenances, and in
seedy habiliments, who sit on the benches ranged against the
walls of the arcades; sit, silently, immovably, with a stern
and ghostly patience, from morn till dusk. These shabby
sedentaries have long haunted me. I call them City Spectres.
I have passed through 'Change as early as nine o'clock in the
morning, and found the Ghosts there; I have passed through
it just as it was about to close, and found them there still—
silent, unalterable in their immobility; speechless in the
midst of the gabble and turmoil, the commercial howls, and
speculative shrieks of high 'Change. I have gone away from
England, and, coming back again, have found the same Ghosts
on the same benches. They were on the Old Exchange;
they were on the 'Burse' in Sir Thomas Gresham's time, I
have no doubt; and when the 'coming man'—the Anglo-New-
Zealander of Thomas Babington Macaulay—arrives to take his
promised view of the ruins of St. Paul's, he will have to place
in the foreground of his picture, sitting on crumbling benches,
in a ruined Exchange, over-against a ruined Bank, the City
Spectres, unchangeable and unchanged.

What do they do on Sundays and holidays, and after 'Change

hours? What did they do when the Exchange was burnt down, and the merchants congregated first at the Old South-Sea House, and then in the courtyard of the Excise Office, in Broad Street? Are they the same men, or their brothers, or their cousins, who sit for hours on the benches in St. James's Park, staring with glazed, unmeaning eyes at the big Life-Guardsmen and the little children? Are they the same men who purchase half a pint of porter, usurp the best seat (upon the tub, and out of the way of the swing-door) before the bar, to the secret rage of the publican? Are they connected with the British Museum spectres—the literary ghosts—who pass the major part of the day in the Reading-room, not reading—for their eyes always seem to me to be fixed on the same spot, in the same page of the same volume, of the Pandects of Justinian—but snuffing, with a grimly affectionate relish, the morocco-leather-laden atmosphere, and silently hugging the comfortable chairs and tables, luxuriating in the literary hospitality of Britain—the feast of paper-knives and eleemosynary quill-pens, the flow of well-filled and gratuitous leaden inkstands?

Yet these City Spectres must live in their spectral fashion. They must eat. They must drink, even; for I have observed that not a few of them have noses of a comfortable degree of redness. Who supplies them with food and raiment? Who boards and lodges them? Who washes them?—no; that last interrogation is certainly irrelevant; for the City Ghosts, both as regards their persons and their linen, appear to be able to do without washing altogether.

I used to ask myself, and I still do ask myself, these questions about the City Spectres with distressing pertinacity; I form all sorts of worrying theories concerning them. By dint, however, of considerable observation, of unflagging industry in putting 'this and that together,' and, perhaps, of a little stretching of possibilities into probabilities, and probabilities into certainties, I have managed to cover the dry bones of the Spectres of the Royal Exchange with a little commercial flesh and blood. I have found local habitations and names for them. I assume avocations which occupy them even as they sit in idle ghostliness on the benches. I discover incomes which cover their meagre limbs with mildewed raiment; which find some work for their lantern jaws in the way of mastication; and which give a transient rubicundity to their sometimes livid noses. I have found out—or at least think I have found out—who the City Ghosts are;

how and where they live ; what they were before they were
ghosts ; and how they came to bench-occupying and to ghost-
hood.

Take that tall Ghost who sits in the portion of the arcade
called the Wallachio-Moldavian walk, on the bench between
the advertisements setting forth the approaching departure of
the ' Grand Turk, A. 1, and copper-bottomed for Odessa,' and
the pictorial chromo-lithographic placard, eulogising, in so
disinterested a manner, the virtues of Mr. Alesheeh's magic
strop. See him once, and forget him if you can. His countenance is woebegone : his hat is battered in the crown, torn
in the brim, worn away in the forepart, by constant pulling
off ; napless long since ; but rendered factitiously lustrous by
the matutinal application of a wet brush ; his satin stock—
black once, brown now—fastened at the back with a vicious
wrench and a rusty buckle ; his sorry body-coat (Spectres
never wear frock-coats), tesselated on the collar and elbows
with cracked grease-spots ; torn at the pockets with continuous
thrusting-in of papers ; dotted white with the tombstones of
dead buttons : his shrinking, withered, shame-faced trousers :
his boots (not Bluchers, but nearly always Wellingtons)
cracked at the sides and gone at the heel, the connection still
preserved by the aid of a red-hot poker and gutta percha. I
know all about that Ghost. He passed to the world of spectres
in 1825. He must have been that head clerk in the great
banking firm of Sir John Jebber, Jefferson, and Co., which
speculated somewhat too greedily in the Patent Washing,
Starching, Mangling, and Ironing Company ; in the Amalgamated Dusthole, Breeze Exportation, and Cinder Consumption
Company ; in the Royal Rat, Cat, and Rabbit Fur Company
(Incorporated by Royal Charter) ; in the Imperial Equitable
Spontaneous Combustion Association for Instantaneous Illu-
mination (in connection with the Northern Lights Office) ;
in the Anglico-Franco-Mexico Mining Company for the Rapid
Diffusion of Quicksilver all over the World ; in Baratarian
(deferred) Bonds. When the panic of '25 came, and there
was a rush on Jebber's bank, and a line of carriages extended from Lombard Street to Ludgate Hill (for most of
the aristocracy banked at Jebber's), it was the Spectre who
enacted the bold stroke of policy, of having heavy coal-
waggons driven artfully into the line of vehicles between
Birchin Lane and Nicholas Lane ; and of raising an alarm of
' mad dog' at the corner of Pope's Head Alley, whereby the
stream of customers, rabid to draw out their deposits, was

arrested for hours. 'Twas he who suggested to the firm the artful contrivance (first practised by a larger establishment) of paying heavy cheques in sixpences; but all, alas! in vain. The firm had to be removed from Lombard Street to the Bankruptcy Court, in Basinghall Street. Jebber went into a lunatic asylum; the Miss Jebbers went out (poor things!) as governesses; and Jefferson with the Co. emigrated—some people said with the cash-box—to the land of freedom; where he became principal director of that famous banking company, the five-dollar notes of which were subsequently in such astonishing demand as shin-plasters and pipe-lights. Their head clerk went, straightway, into the Ghost line of business, and has never given it up. The other clerks found easily and speedily berths in other establishments; but, malicious people said that the Ghost-clerk knew more about that bundle of bank notes, which was so unaccountably missing, than he chose to aver. He did not give satisfactory information, either, about the shares in several of the companies we have enumerated, and no one would employ him; so he became an accountant, with no accounts to keep; and an agent, with no agencies. Then he was secretary to that short-lived association, 'The Joint-Stock Pin-Collecting Company.' Then he got into trouble about the subscription for the survivors of the 'Tabitha Jane,' Mauley, master; his old detractors, with unabated malice, declaring that there never was a 'Tabitha Jane,' nor a Mauley, master. He sells corn and coal on commission now—not at first-hand; but for those who are themselves commission agents. He is a broker's 'man in possession,' when he can get a job. He does a bit of law-writing, a bit of penny-a-lining, a bit of process-serving;—an infinity of those small offices known as 'odd jobs.' He picks up a sorry crust by these means, and is to be heard of at the bar of the Black Lion. He is sober; but upon compulsion I am afraid. If you give him much beer, he weeps, and tells you of his bygone horse and gig; of his box at Shooter's Hill; of his daughter Emily, who had the best of boarding-school educations (and married Clegg, of the Great Detector Insurance Office), and who won't speak to her poor old father now, sir: of his other daughter, Jenny, who is kind to him; although she is mated with a dissolute printer, whose relations are continually buying him new founts of type, which he is as continually mortgaging for spirits and tobacco Poor old Ghost! Poor old broken-down, spirit-worn hack! When great houses come toppling down, how many slender balustrades and tottering posts are crushed along with the massive pillars!

Here is another Spectre of my acquaintance, who has been a ruined man any time these twenty years; but is a very joyous and hilarious Ghost, notwithstanding. Though utterly undone, he sits cheerfully down all day on his accustomed bench in the Bengalee walk, beating the devil's tattoo with mirthful despair on the Exchange flags. Bless you, he has thriven on ruin. He lives on it now. Burnt out four times—broken both legs—bed-ridden wife—child scalded to death—execution on his poor 'sticks,' at this very moment. He is, you will please observe, no begging-letter writer; he would scorn the act. You can come round to his 'place' now, if you like, and judge of his total wreck for yourself; here is the letter of Alderman Fubson, condoling with him; and, *could* you lend him half a crown?

Turn round another arcade into the Austro-Sclavonian walk, and sympathise with this melancholy Spectre in the hat pulled over his brows, and the shabby cloak with the mangy fur collar. No clerk, cashier, or stock-broker's assistant has he been; but, in times gone by, a prosperous merchant, one who walked on 'Change, rattling his watch-chain; who quoted prices with a commanding, strident voice; who awed the waiters at Garraway's, at the Cock in Threadneedle Street, at the New England, and at the Anti-Gallican; whose name was down in every charity and on every committee; who carried a gold snuff-box in his hand, and his gloves and silk handkerchief together with his bank-book, in his hat. He failed; and his brother allows him a small stipend. His hat is now crammed with the records of defunct transactions; memoranda of mythical bargains; bills of lading referring to phantom ships that never were loaded; old blank bills of exchange, with the name of his firm (when it had a name) curiously flourished thereon in copper-plate; his former seal of office; a greasy cheque-book, with nothing but tallies telling of sums long since drawn from his banker's; bits of sealing-wax; his bankrupt certificate; his testimonials of integrity from his brother merchants. These have an abiding place in his pockets. He has a decayed pocket-book, too, bulging out with prospectuses of dead companies full of sound and flourish, signifying nothing. He sits alone, and aloof from his brother Ghosts; not indulging even in the silent freemasonry of these commercial phantoms. The greatest favour you could do him would be to send him to get a cheque cashed for you (he is perfectly honest), or to leave a bill for acceptance. The trembling eagerness with which he would present the magic document, and answer the bland inquiry of the cashier as to 'how he would have it;' the delirious semblance of business he would put into the mere act of dropping 'this first of exchange' into the box appointed to receive it, would be quite affecting. When he is not sitting on 'Change, I can picture him wandering furtively about Lombard Street, peering anxiously through the half-opened doors when customers go in and out; or sauntering along Cheapside; glancing with melancholy looks at the forms of bills of lading, charter-parties, and policies of insurance, displayed in the windows of the stationers' shops; scrutinising the strong-backed ledgers, day-books, and journals, in their brave binding of vellum and red, thinking meanwhile— miserable man—that their glories are no longer for him; that he hath done with ink, black, red, and blue; that 'cash —debtor—contra—creditor,' have no longer music for his ears. In the evening, at the shabby coffee-house where he takes his meal, nought strikes him in yesterday's 'Advertiser,' save the list of bankrupts. In bed he is haunted—ghost as he is—by the ghosts of buried hopes, by tipstaffs, by irate Commissioners, and by fiats to which he has neglected to surrender.

As the late Mr. Rothschild was called the 'Pillar of the Exchange,' so seemeth this other old phantom. He has been an Exchange Spectre since ever there were Exchanges or Ghosts at all. He puzzles me. I can weave histories, find genealogies, dovetail circumstances for all the other mysterious Bourse-haunters; but this silver-haired apparition is a mystery inscrutable. Centuries of commercial ghostliness seem hovering in the innumerable furrows of his parchment face, in the multitudinous straggling locks of his dull, lustreless white hair. Some garment he has on—whether a coat, a cloak, or a gaberdine, I will not be bold enough to say—which, reaching from his neck to his heels, allows you to see nothing but his furrowed face, and lean, long hands clasped before him. How long has he haunted the city of London? Did he linger in Paul's Walk, or in the Roundhouse of the Temple Church in Charles's days, when business, intrigue, and devotion were so curiously mingled in Christian temples; when mountebanks vended their wares by clustered pillars, and dirty-surpliced choristers pursued jingling cavaliers for 'spur-money?' Was he a City Ghost when ladies in sacks, and gallants in cut

velvet and embroidery, came to gamble South Sea shares in
'Change Alley? Did he haunt 'Change when merchants appeared thereon, who had had their ears cut off by the Spaniards
in Honduras : when bargains were made for cash in negro flesh ?
Does he remember Lord Mayor Beckford, Fauntleroy, and
Rowland Stevenson? Can he have been the broker for the
Poyais Loan ? I should not be surprised to hear that his recollection extended to Alderman Richard Whittington, thrice
Lord Mayor of London ; or to that topping wine-merchant who
' in London did dwell,' and ' who had but one daughter, he loved
very well.'

City Spectres, like the rest of their order, are, for the most
part, silent men. Their main object seems to be to impress
the spectator, by the inert force of taciturnity, with an idea
of the weighty business they have on hand. A few, however,
are talkative ; some, as I know to my sorrow, are garrulous.
Woe be unto you if you have ever been in the company of, or
have the slightest acquaintance with, the talkative Ghost !
Although, to say the truth, when he wants to talk, he *will* talk,
and is not even solicitous of an introduction : he thinks he
knows you ; or he knew your father, or he knows your wife's
second cousin, or he knows somebody very like you ; and,
upon the strength of that knowledge, he takes you quietly,
but firmly, by the button—he holds you in his ' skinny hand '
as tightly as if you were the wedding guest and he the Ancient
Mariner ; and, for all that you beat your breast, you cannot
choose but hear. You listen like a three-years' child, while
this ancient bore speaks on, discoursing of his grievances ; of
his losses ; of the ' parties ' he knows, or has known ; of his
cousin, who—would you believe it, my dear sir ?—drives into
the City every morning in a carriage and pair, with a powdered
footman in the rumble. All this, he speaks in a low and earnest,
though distressingly rambling tone ; and his brother Ghosts in
the distance—as if believing he had really business to transact
with you—clutch their umbrellas, and bend their dull eyes on
both of you with looks of jealous curiosity.

That substantial Spectre, who holds me in spirit-wearying
conversation ; who speaks in a low, hoarse, secret kind of
voice, with long and bitter words, was an attorney—a City
attorney—in large practice ; and, for some alleged malprac-
tices, was struck off the Rolls. He has been a Spectre and a
bore ever since. You *must* hear his case ; you must hear the
scandalous, the unheard-of manner in which he has been
treated. Read his statement to the public, which the newspapers

would not insert; read his letter to Mr. Justice Bullwiggle, which that learned functionary never answered; read his memorial to Lord Viscount Fortyshins, which *was* answered, and that was all. Only wait till he has the means to publish a pamphlet on his case. Meanwhile, read his notes thereupon. Never mind your appointment at three; what's that to justice?

Even as he speaks, a slowly gibbering army of Ghosts who have grievances start before you; Ghosts with inventions which they can't afford to patent, and which unscrupulous capitalists have pirated; Ghosts who can't get the Prime Minister to listen to their propositions for draining Ireland in three weeks, or for swamping the National Debt in a day; Ghosts against whose plans of national defence the War Office door has been more than once rudely shut; Spectres who, like Dogberry, have had losses; Ghosts who when in the flesh (but they never had much of that) were shrunk and attenuated, with interminable stories of fraudulent partners; Ghosts who have long been the victims of fiendish official persecutions: lastly, and in particular, that never-to-be-forgotten and always-to-be-avoided Ghost, who has had a Chancery suit on and off for an incalculable number of years; who has just been with his lawyers, and is going to file a bill to-morrow. Alas, poor Ghost! 'Be still, old mole; there is no hope for thee!'

There is a genealogical Ghost, eyeing me with devouring looks, that bode no conversational good. He only wants one baptismal certificate to prove that he is somebody's great-great-grandson, and to come into twenty thousand a year. Let him but earn, beg, or borrow a crown, and forthwith in the 'Times' comes out an advertisement, 'to parish clerks and others.'—There is a sporting Ghost, with a phantom betting-book, who tells you, in a sepulchral voice, of 'information' about 'Job Pastern's lot;' and that he can give you a 'tip' for safe odds on such and such an 'event.'—A Ghost there is, too, in mustachios, who is called, on the strength of those appendages, 'Captain,' and is supposed to have been embodied in some sort of legion in Spain, at some time or another.

Talkative or taciturn, however, here these poor spectres sit or loiter during the day, retiring into dark corners when genuine business begins, and the merchants and brokers come on 'Change; always, and without intermission, seeming to be here, yet prowling by some curious quality of body or spirit

in other City haunts ;—in Garraway's, and in the Auction
Mart ; in small civic coffee-houses and taverns ; in the police-
courts of the Mansion House ; in Guildhall and the Custom
House.

In Bartholomew Lane wander another race of perturbed
spirits, akin in appearance and mysterious demeanour to the
Exchange Spectres ; yet of a somewhat more practical and
corporeal order. These are the ' lame ducks ;' men who have
once been stockbrokers—wealthy ' bulls,' purse-proud ' bears ;'
but who, unable to meet certain financial liabilities on a
certain settling day, have been compelled to retire—who have
' waddled,' as is the slang of Cambists—from the parliament
of money-brokers. Yet do they linger in the purlieus of the
beloved Capel Court, even as the Peri waited at the gates of
Paradise : yet do they drive small time bargains with very
small jobbers, or traffic in equivocal securities and shares in
suspicious companies. They affect the transaction of business
when they have none to transact ; and, under cover of con-
sulting the share-list of the day, or the City intelligence in a
newspaper, they furtively consume Abernethy biscuits and
' Polony ' sausages.

Once, however, in about five-and-twenty years, do they cast
off their slough of semi-inactivity ; once even in that period do
the Spectres of the Royal Exchange start forth into life and
action. For, look you, once in every quarter of a century—
sometimes more frequently—do the men, women, and children
run stark, staring, raving, ranting mad. They have a MANIA.
Now for gold-digging in American Dorados ; now for South
Sea fisheries ; now for joint-stock companies, for doing everything for everybody ; now for railways ; now for life assurance.
Everybody goes crazed for shares. Lords, ladies, divines,
physicians, chimney-sweeps ; all howl for shares. They buy,
sell, barter, borrow, beg, steal, invent, dream of shares. Bank-
notes and prospectuses fly about thick as the leaves in Vallam-
brosa ; men are no longer mere human beings ; but directors,
provisional committee-men, auditors and trustees. The MANIA
continues, and the SPECTRES arise. They become STAGS. Capel
Court resounds with their shrill bargains ; and, the spectre of a
moment before stands erect, blatant, defiant, a stag of ten tynes.
Away with the appointment with the man who never comes ;
away with the delusive commission on corn and coals; away
with the phantom bill in the mythical Chancery ; away with
the air-drawn entail, and the twenty thousand a year ! Shares,
real shares, are what they hunger and thirst for. While

orthodox speculators sell their shares through their brokers, and at the market price, the bold dealers—no longer Spectres, but Stags —will sell their letters of allotment for fourpence, or anything, premium (so that it be current coin) per share. They personate directors; they get up impromptu provisional committees in the tap-room of the Black Lion; their references are bishops, Queen's counsel, fellows of the Royal Society; their substance sham shares in sham companies. For a while they are attired in purple and fine linen; they consume rich viands and choice wines in expensive taverns; they drive high chariots, and prance on blood-horses. For six weeks they live at the rate of ten thousand a year: they ride the whirlwind of Fortune! But after a storm comes rain; and after a mania, a *panic!* Then comes a run on the banking-houses; consternation darkens Capel Court; ruin is rampant on 'Change. And, as I speak, the old Ghosts come creeping back to the old benches, and begin listlessly to wait for the man so punctual in his unpunctuality. The hats are more crammed with papers, the rusty pocket-books more plethoric, the pockets more loaded, the button-holding talks are resumed as earnestly and as lengthily as ever; yet the flesh and blood of Staghood have departed, and the figures crouching on 'Change, and growling about Capel Court, are no longer *men*, but City Spectres.

XIII.

HOUSELESS AND HUNGRY.

In the city of London, in two contiguous thoroughfares—the shabbiest, dingiest, poorest of their class — there are two Houses of Poverty. To the first, entrance is involuntary, and residence in it compulsory. You are brought there by a catchpole, and kept there under lock and key until your creditors are paid, or till you have suffered the purgatory of an Insolvent Court remand. This house is the Debtors' Prison of Whitecross Street. I know it. I have seen the mysteries of the Middlesex side, and have heard the lamenting in the Poultry Ward. Its stones have sermons; but it was not to hear them that I travelled, one gloomy winter evening, Cripplegate Ward. My business in Whitecross Street was of no debtor or creditor nature; for I was there to visit another house of poverty, the asylum of the Society for affording Nightly Shelter to the Houseless,

L

Let me, in the first instance, state briefly what this Society professes to do. The manner in which it is done will form a subject for after-description. 'It is the peculiar object and principle of this charity' (I quote the Report), 'to afford nightly shelter and assistance to those who are really houseless and destitute during inclement winter seasons, and the occasional suspension of out-door work, in consequence of the rigour of the weather. To fulfil this intention, it is provided that an asylum shall be open and available at all hours of the night, without the need, on the part of the applicant, of a ticket, or any other passport or plea but his or her own statement of helpless necessity.' The relief afforded is limited to bread in a sufficient quantity to sustain nature, warm shelter, and the means of rest. Thus, little inducement is offered to those removed in the slightest degree from utter destitution, to avail themselves of the shelter for the sake of the food. But, in all cases of inanition or debility from exhaustion or fatigue, appropriate restoratives, such as gruel, wine, brandy, soup, and medicine, are administered under medical superintendence. 'Many have been thus rescued,' says the Report, 'from the grasp of death.'

I have two friends who do not approve of institutions on the principle stated above. My good friend Pragmos objects to them as useless. He proves to me by figures, by tables, by reports from perspicacious commissioners, that there is no need of any destitution in London; and that, statistically, tabularly, honourable-boardically-speaking, there is no destitution at all. How can there be any destitution with your out-door relief, and your in-door relief, your workhouse test, relieving officers, and your casual ward? Besides, there is employment for all. There are hospitals and infirmaries for the sick, workhouse infirmaries for the infirm. Prosperity, the war notwithstanding, is continually increasing. None but the idle and the dissolute need be houseless and hungry. If they are, they have the union to apply to; and, consequently, asylums for the houseless serve no beneficial end; divert the stream of charitable donations from its legitimate channels; foster idleness and vice, and parade, before the eyes of the public, a misery that does not exist.

So far Pragmos. He is not hard-hearted; but simply, calmly conscious (through faith in Arabic numerals, and in the Ninety-ninth Report of the Poor Law Commissioners) that destitution cannot be. But he has scarcely finished quoting schedule D, when my other and sprightlier friend, Sharplynx,

takes me to task, humourously, jocularly. He rallies me.
'Destitution, my boy,' says Sharplynx, familiarly, 'gammon!
How can you, a shrewd man of the world' (I blush), 'an old
stager' (I bow), 'be taken in by such transparent humbug?
Haven't you read the "Times?" Haven't you read the "Jolly
Beggars?" Did you never hear of cadgers, silver-beggars,
shallow-coves? Why, sir, that fellow in rags, with the imitation paralysis, who goes shivering along, will have veal for
supper to-night: the kidney end of the loin, with stuffing,
and a lemon squeezed over it. That woman on the doorstep
has hired the two puny children at fourpence a day; and she
will have a pint and a half of gin before she goes to bed.
That seemingly hectic fever flush is red paint; those trem-
blings are counterfeit; that quiet, hopeless, silent resignation
is a dodge. Don't talk to me of being houseless and hungry!
The impostors who pretend to be so, carouse in night cellars.
They have turkey and sausages, roast pork, hot punch, para-
mours, packs of cards, and roaring songs. Houseless, indeed!
I'd give 'em a night's lodging—in the station-house, and send
'em to the treadmill in the morning.' Whereupon Sharplynx
departs, muttering something about the good old times, and
the stocks, and the whipping-post.

So they go their separate ways—Pragmos and Sharplynx—
yet I cannot blame either of them. It is but the old story of
the many punished for the faults of a few. You, I, thousands
are coerced, stinted in our enjoyments, comforts, amusements,
liberties, rights, and are defamed and vilified as drunkards and
ruffians, because one bull-necked, thick-lipped, scowling beast
of a fellow drinks himself mad with alcohol, beats his wife,
breaks windows, and roams about Drury Lane with a life-preserver. Thousands—whose only crime it is to have no money,
no friends, no clothes, no place of refuge equal even to the
holes that the foxes have in God's wide world—see the hand
of charity closed, and the door of mercy shut, because Alice
Grey is an impostor, and Bamfylde Moore Carew a cheat; and
because there have been such places as the Cour des Miracles,
and Rats' Castle. 'Go there and be merry, you rogue!' says
Mr. Sharplynx, facetiously. So the destitute go into the
streets, and die. They do die, although you may continue
talking and tabulating till doomsday. I grant the workhouses,
relieving officers, hospitals, infirmaries, station-houses, boards,
minutes, and schedules, the Mendicity Society, and the Guildhall Solomons. But I stand with Galileo: *Si muove!* and
asseverate that, in the City paved with gold, there are people

who are destitute, and die on doorsteps, in the streets, on stair-cases, under dark arches, in ditches, and under the lees of walls. The police know it. Some day, perhaps, the Government will condescend to know it too, and instruct a gentleman at a thousand a year to see about it.

Thinking of Pragmos and Sharplynx, I walked last Tuesday evening through Smithfield and up Barbican. It is a very dreary journey at the best of times; but, on a raw February night—with the weather just hesitating between an iron frost and a drizzling thaw, and, not making up its mind on either subject, treating you to a touch of both alternately—the over-land route to Whitecross Street is simply wretched. The whole neighbourhood is pervaded with a miasma of grinding, unwholesome, sullen, and often vicious poverty. Everything is cheap and nasty, and the sellers seem as poor as the buyers. There are shops whose stock in trade is not worth half a dozen shillings. There are passers-by, the whole of whose apparel would certainly be dear at ninepence. Chandlers' shops, marine-stores, pawn-shops, and public-houses, occur over and over again in sickening repetition. There is a frowsy blight on the window-panes and the gas-lamps. The bread is all seconds; the butchers' shops, with their flaring gas-jets, expose nothing but scraps and bony pieces of meat. Inferior greengrocery in baskets chokes up the pathway; but it looks so bad that it would be a pity to rescue it from its neighbour the gutter, and its legitimate proprietors the pigs. The air is tainted with exhalations from rank tobacco, stale herrings, old clothes, and workshops of noxious trades. The parish coffin passes you; the policeman passes you, dull and dingy—quite another policeman compared to the smart A. 67. The raw night-breeze wafts to your ears oaths, and the crying of rotten merchandise, and the wailing of neglected children, and choruses of ribald songs. Every cab you see blocked up between a costermonger's barrow and a Pickford's van, appears to you to be conveying some miserable debtor to prison.

Struggling, as well as I could, through all this squalid life, slipping on the greasy pavement, and often jostled off it, I came at last upon Whitecross Street, and dived (for that is about the only way you can enter it) into a forlorn, muddy, dimly-lighted thoroughfare, which was the bourne of my travels—Playhouse Yard. I have not Mr. Peter Cunningham at hand, and am not sufficient antiquary to tell when or where-abouts the playhouse existed in this sorry place. It is but a melancholy drama enacted here now, Heaven knows!

I was not long in finding out the Refuge. About half-way up the yard hung out a lamp with a wire screen over it, and the name of the asylum painted upon it. I made my way to an open doorway, whence issued a stream of light; and before which were ranged, in a widish semicircle, a crowd of cowering creatures, men, women, and children, who were patiently awaiting their turn of entrance. This was the door to the House of Poverty.

I need not say that the object of my visit was promptly understood by those in authority, and that every facility was afforded me of seeing the simple system of relief at work. It was not much in a sight-seeing point of view that the Society's officers had to show me. They had no pet prisoners; no steam-cooking apparatus; no luxurious baths; no corrugated iron laundry; no vaulted passages, nor octagonal court-yards gleaming with whitewash and dazzling brass-work; no exquisite cells fitted up with lavatories and cupboards, and conveniences of the latest patent invention. Everything was, on the contrary, of the simplest and roughest nature; yet everything seemed to me to answer admirably the purpose for which it was designed.

I entered, first, an office, where there were some huge baskets filled with pieces of bread; and where an official sat at a desk, registering, in a ledger, the applicants for admission as they presented themselves for examination at the half-door, or bar. They came up one by one, in alternate sexes, as they had been summoned from the semicircle outside. Now it was a young sailor-boy in a Guernsey frock; now a travel-stained agricultural labourer; now a wan artisan; now a weary ragged woman with a troop of children; now, most pitiable spectacle of all, some woe-begone, shrinking needle-woman—young, but a hundred years old in misery—comely, but absolutely seamed and scarred and macerated by famine. The answers were almost identical: They had come up from the country in search of work; or they were London bred, and could not obtain work; or the Union was full, and they could not get admission; or they had no money; or they had had nothing to eat; or they did not know where else to go. All this was said not volubly; not entreatingly; and with no ejaculations or complaints, and with few additions; but wearily, curtly, almost reluctantly. What had they to tell? What beyond a name, a date, a place, was necessary to be extracted from them? In their dismal attire, in their death-like voices, in their awful faces, there was mute eloquence enough to fill five hundred ledgers such as the one on the desk. I am no professed physiognomist. I believe I have sufficient knowledge of the street-world to tell a professional beggar from a starving man; but I declare I saw no face that night passing the hatch but in which I could read : Ragged and Tired—Dead Beat—Utterly Destitute—Houseless and Hungry. The official took down each applicant's name, age, and birthplace; where he had slept the night before; what was his vocation; what the cause of his coming there. The ledger was divided into columns for the purpose. I looked over it. To the causes for application there was one unvarying answer—Destitution. In the ' Where slept the previous night ?' the answers ran : St. Luke's ; Whitechapel ; in the streets ; Stepney ; in the streets, in the streets, and in the streets again and again, till I grew sick. Many men are liars, we know ; and among the five hundred destitute wretches that are nightly sheltered in this place there may be—I will not attempt to dispute it—a per-centage of impostors ; a few whose own misconduct and improvidence have driven them to the wretchedest straits ; yet, I will back that grim ledger to contain some thousand more truths than are told in a whole library of Reports of Parliamentary Committees.

There was a lull in the admissions, and I was inquiring about the Irish, when the official told the doorkeeper to ' call the first female.' By luck, the ' first female ' was Irish herself. She was a very little woman, with the smallest bonnet I ever saw. It was, positively, nothing more than a black patch on the back of her head, and the frayed ends were pulled desperately forward towards her chin, showing her ears through a ragged trellis-work. As to her dress, it looked as if some cunning spinner had manufactured a textile fabric out of mud ; or, as if dirt could be darned and patched. I did not see her feet ; but I heard a flapping on the floor as she moved, and guessed what sort of shoes she must have worn. She was the sort of little woman who ought to have had a round, rosy, dumpling face—and she had two bead-like black eyes ; but face and eyes were all crushed and battered by want and exposure. Her very skin was in rags. The poor little woman did nothing but make faces, which would have been ludicrous, if—in the connection of what surrounded and covered her, and her own valiant determination not to cry—they had not been heartrending. Yes ; she was Irish (she said this apologetically) ; but, she had been a long time in Liverpool. Her husband had run away and left her. She had no children. She could have borne it better, she said, if she had. She had slept one night before in the ' Institution ' (she prided herself a little on this word, and used it pretty frequently), but she had been ashamed to come there again, and had slept one night in the workhouse and three nights in the streets. The superintendent spoke to her kindly, and told her she could be sheltered in the Refuge for a night or two longer ; and that then, the best thing she could do would be to make her way to Liverpool again. ' But I can't walk it, indeed,' cried the little woman ; ' I shall never be able to walk it. O, dear ! O, dear !' The valorously screwed-up face broke down all at once ; and, as she went away with her ticket, I heard her flapping feet and meek sobs echoing through the corridor. She did not press her story on us. She did not whine for sympathy. She seemed ashamed of her grief. Was this little woman a humbug, I wonder.

A long lank man in black mud came up afterwards, whose looks seemed fluttering between the unmistakable ' ragged and tired ' and an ominous ' ragged and desperate.' I shall never forget his hands as he held them across on the doorsill—long, emaciated, bony slices of integument and bone. They were just the hands a man might do some mischief to himself or some one else with, and be sorry for. I shall never forget, either, the rapt, eager gaze with which he regarded, almost devoured, the fire in the office grate. He answered the questions addressed to him, as it were mechanically, and without looking at his interlocutor ; his whole attention, wishes, thoughts, being centred in the blazing coals. He seemed to hug himself in the prospective enjoyment of the warmth ; to be greedy of it. Better the fire there than the water of the dark cold river. I was not sorry when he received his ticket ; and, looking over his shoulder at the fire, went shuffling away. He frightened me.

I was informed by the superintendent (a frank-spoken military man, who had lost a leg in the Caffre war), that, as a rule, the duration of the shelter extended by the Society is limited to three nights to Londoners, and to seven nights to country people. In special cases, however, special exceptions are made ; and every disposition is shown to strain a point in favour of those weary wanderers, and to bear with them, as far as is consistent with justice to others. A ration of eight ounces of bread is given to each admitted person on entrance, another ration when they leave between eight and nine the next morning.

Accompanied by the secretary and the superintendent, I was now shown the dormitories. We visited the men's side first. Passing a range of lavatories, where each inmate is required to wash his face, neck, and arms—hot water being provided for the purpose—we ascended a wooden staircase, and came into a range of long, lofty, barn-like rooms, divided into sections by wooden pillars. An immense stove was in the centre, fenced in with stakes; and, in its lurid hospitable light, I could fancy the man in black and some score more brothers in misery, greedily basking. Ranged on either side were long rows of bed-places, trough-like, grave-like, each holding one sleeper. In the early days of the Society (it has been in existence for more than thirty years) the inmates slept on straw; but, as this was found to possess many drawbacks to health, cleanliness, and to offer danger from fire, mattresses stuffed with hay and covered with waterproofing, which can be washed and aired with facility, have been substituted. Instead of blankets, which harbour vermin and are besides less durable, there are ample coverlets of Basil leather, warm and substantial. With these; with the ration of bread; with genial warmth, the objects sought for are attained. It is not an hotel that is required. The slightest modicum of luxury would corroborate Pragmos, and be an encouragement to the worthless, the idle, and the depraved. The Refuge competes with no lodging-house, no thieves' kitchen, no tramps' boozing-cellar; but it is a place for a dire corporeal necessity to be ministered to, by the simplest corporeal requisites. A roof to shelter, a bed to lie on, a fire to warm, a crust to eat—these are offered to those who have literally nothing.

By the flickering gas, which is kept burning all night, I stood with my back to one of the wooden pillars, and looked at this sad scene. The bed-places were rapidly filling. Many of the tired-out wayfarers had already sunk into sleep; others were sitting up in bed mending their poor rags; many lay awake, but perfectly mute and quiescent. As far as the eye could reach, almost, there were more ranges of troughs, more reclining heaps of rags. I shifted my position nervously as I found myself within range, wherever I turned, of innumerable eyes,—eyes calm, fixed, brooding, hopeless. Who has not had this feeling, while walking through an hospital—a lunatic asylum—a prison? The eyes are upon you, you know, gazing sternly, moodily, reproachfully. You feel almost as if you were an intruder. You are not the doctor to heal, the priest to console, the Lady Bountiful to relieve. What right have you to be there, taking stock of human miseries, and jotting down sighs and tears in your note-book?

I found the surgeon at a desk by the fire. He had just been called in to a bad case; one that happened pretty frequently, though. The miserable case was just being supported from a bench to his bed. He had come in, and had been taken very ill; not with cholera, or fever, or dysentery, but with the disease—my friend, Sharplynx, won't believe in —Starvation. He was simply at death's door with inanition and exhaustion. Drunk with hunger, surfeited with cold, faint with fatigue. He did not require amputation nor cupping, quinine, colchicum, nor sarsaparilla; he merely wanted a little brandy and gruel, some warmth, some supper, and a bed. The cost price of all these did not probably amount to more than sixpence; yet, curiously, for want of that sixpennyworth of nutriment and rest, there might have been a bill on the police-station door to-morrow, beginning, ' Dead Body Found.'

I asked the surgeon if such cases occurred often. They did, he said : Whether they ever ended fatally? Occasionally. Only the other night a man was brought in by a police sergeant, who had found him being quietly starved to death behind a cart. He was a tall, athletic-looking man enough, and was very sick. While the sergeant was stating his case, he suddenly fell forward on the floor—dead! He was not diseased, only starved.

Seeking for information as to the general demeanour of the inmates, I was told that good conduct was the rule, disorderly or refractory proceedings the exception. ' If you were here at eight o'clock, sir,' said the superintendent (it was now half-past seven), ' you wouldn't hear a pin drop. Poor creatures ! they are too tired to make a disturbance. The boys, to be sure, have a little chat to themselves ; but they are easily quieted. When, once in a way, we have a disorderly character, we turn him out, and there is an end of it. I was told, moreover, that almost anything could be done with this motley colony by kind and temperate language, and that they expressed, and appeared to feel, sincere gratitude for the succour afforded to them. They seldom made friends among their companions, the superintendent said. They came, and ate, and warmed themselves, and went on their way in the morning alone. There is a depth of misery too great for companionship.

Touching the boys, those juveniles were relegated to a plantation of troughs by themselves, where they were plunging and tumbling about in the usual manner of town-nursed Bedouins. I learnt that the Institution—to use a familiar expression—rather fought shy of boys. Boys are inclined to be troublesome; and, whenever it is practicable, they are sent to the ragged-school dormitories, where, my guide said, 'they make them go to school before they go to bed, which they don't like at all.' More than this, some parents, to save themselves the trouble of providing supper and bedding for their children, will send one or more of them to the Refuge; and where space is so vitally valuable, the introduction of even one interloper is a thing to be carefully prevented.

The Refuge is open after five in the evening, and a porter is on duty all night for the admission of urgent cases. The fires and gas are also kept burning throughout the night, and a male and female superintendent sit up, in case of need. Those who have been in the Refuge on Saturday night have the privilege of remaining in the Institution during the whole of Sunday. They have an extra ration of bread and three ounces of cheese, and divine service is performed in the morning and afternoon. There are many Sabbaths kept in London : the Vinegar Sabbath, the Velvet and Satin Sabbath, the Red-hot Poker Sabbath, the Carriage-and-pair Sabbath, the Gloomily-lazy Sabbath, the Pipe-and-pot Sabbath ; but I doubt if any can equal the Sabbath passed in this wretched Playhouse Yard, as a true Sabbath of rest, and peace, and mercy.

We went up, after this, to the women's wards. The arrangements were identical with those of the men ; save, that one room is devoted to women with families, where the partitions between the troughs had been taken away that the children might lie with their mothers. We passed between the ranges of bed-places ; noticing that the same mournful, weary, wakeful silence was almost invariable, though not, I was told, compulsory. The only prohibition—and safety requires this —is against smoking. Now and then a gaunt girl, with her black hair hanging about her face, would rise up in her bed to stare at us ; now and then some tattered form amongst those who were sitting there till the ward below was ready for their reception, would rise from the bench and drop us a

curtsey; but the general stillness was pervading and unvarying. A comely matron bustled about noiselessly with her
assistant, who was a strange figure among all these rags,
being a pretty girl in ringlets and ribbons. One seemed to
have forgotten, here, that such a being could be in existence.
I spoke to some of the women on the benches. It was the
same old story. Needle-work at miserable prices, inability
to pay the twopenny rent of a lodging, no friends, utter
destitution; this, or death. There were a few—and this
class I heard was daily increasing—who were the wives of
soldiers in the Militia, or of men in the Land Transport and
Army Works Corps. Their husbands had been ordered away;[*]
they had no claim upon the regular Military Relief Association, they had received no portion of their husbands' pay—
and they were houseless and hungry.

I stopped long to look down into the room where the women
and children were. There they lay, God help them! head to
heel, transversely, anyhow for warmth; nestling, crouching
under the coverlets; at times feebly wailing. Looking down
upon this solemn, silent, awful scene made you shudder;
made you question by what right you were standing up,
warm, prosperous, well-fed, well-clad, with these destitute
creatures, your brothers and sisters, who had no better food
and lodging than this? But for the absence of marble floors
and tanks, the place might be some kennel for hounds; but
for the rags and the eyes, these might be sheep in the pens in
Smithfield Market.

I went down stairs at last; for there was no more to see.
Conversing further with the secretary, I gleaned that the
average number of destitute persons admitted nightly is five
hundred and fifty; but that as many as six hundred have
been accommodated. Looking at the balance-sheet of the
Society, I found the total expense of the asylum (exclusive of
rent) was less than one thousand pounds.

A thousand pounds! we blow it away in gunpowder; we
spend it upon diplomatic fools' caps; we give it every month
in the year to right honourable noblemen for doing nothing,
or for spoiling what ordinary men of business would do
better. A thousand pounds! It would not pay a deputy-
sergeant-at-arms; it would scarcely be a retiring pension for
an assistant prothonotary. A thousand pounds! Deputy-
chaff-wax would have spurned it, if offered as compensation

---

* This paper was written during the Crimean war-time.

for loss of office. A thousand pounds! the sum jarred upon my ear, as I walked back through Smithfield. At least, for their ten hundred pounds, the Society for Sheltering the Houseless save some hundreds of human lives a year.

I abide by the assertion, that men and women die nightly in our golden streets, because they have no bread to put into their miserable mouths, no roofs to shelter their wretched heads. It is no less a God-known, man-neglected fact, that in any state of society in which such things can be, there must be something essentially bad and rotten.

XIV

THE SECRETS OF THE GAS.

The Gas has its secrets, and I happen to know them. The Gas has a voice, and I can hear it—a voice beyond the rushing whistle in the pipe, and the dull buzzing flare in the burner. It speaks, actively, to men and women of what is, and of what is done and suffered by night and by day; and though it often crieth like Wisdom in the streets and no man regardeth it, there are, and shall be some to listen to its experiences, hearken to its counsels, and profit by its lessons.

I know the secrets of the gas, but not all of them. Some secrets it has, which are hidden by land, and stream, and sea —by accident, position, and authority—even from my sight, but not from my ken. The gas has its secrets in palaces, on whose trebly-piled carpets my plebeian feet can never tread. It may be burning now,* to the heavy blow and great discouragement of bearded and sheep-skinned purveyors of tallow and lamp-oil—burning in a Ural gilt candelabrum, chastely decorated with double eagles in the den—the private cabinet, I mean—of some grim bear or autocrat, who lies not amidst bones and blood, far away with the weeds and shells at the bottom of the Inner Sea, but lies amidst protocols and diplomatic notes—unlighted fusees to the shells of destruction. That gas may be shining on minims and breves of Te Deums, fresh scored and annotated in appropriate red ink—to be sung by all orthodox believers, when the heretical fleets of the West shall have followed the Moslem three-deckers to their

* Temp. Bell. Taurid. Scrip.

grave in Sinope Bay. That gas may be flickering now—who knows?—in the lambent eyes of some tyrant as he peers greedily over the map of Europe, and settles in his own mind where in England this Off shall cat his first candle, or where in France that Owsky shall apply the knout. Permeating in pipes beneath the well-drilled feet of thousands of orthodox serfs, this same gas may be glimmering in the lamps of the *Nerskoi Prospekt*, and twinkling in the bureau of the Director of Secret Police as he prepares pass-tickets for Siberia, or cancels them for bribes of greasy rouble notes; it may be glowering at the Moscow railway station, as thousands of human hundred-weight of great-coated food for powder, leave by late or early trains for the frontier; it may be illumining the scared and haggard face of the incendiary when, on the map he is scanning, the names of the countries he lusts to seize, turn to letters of blood and dust, and tell him (as the handwriting told Belshazzar) that the Medes and Persians are at his gate, and that his kingdom is given to another. I say, this gas, with the glowing charcoal in the stove, and the ceremonial wax candles on the malachite mantelpiece, may be the only spectator of the rage in his eyes, and the despair in his heart, and the madness in his brain. Though, perhaps, he burns no gas in his private cabinet after all, and adheres to the same orthodox tallow fat and train oil, by the light of which Peter plied his adze, Catherine plundered Poland, Paul was strangled, and Alexander was poisoned!

The gas may have its secrets unknown to me (now that English engineering has been favoured with the high privilege of illumining the Eternal City), in the strong casemates of the Castle of St. Angelo. Yes, may derive deeper shadows from it; and it may light up tawny parchments with heavy seals, which attest that the Holy Office is yet little more than a name. There is gas in Venice; every tourist has had his passport examined by its light; and who shall say that the gas has not its secrets in the Palace of the Doges; that it burns not in gloomy corridor, and on stone winding staircase, lighting some imperial gaoler in his tour of inspection; or that by its unpitying light some wretched prisoner who has dared to violate the imperio-regal Lombardo-Venetian edicts by thinking, or speaking, or writing, in the manner of one who walks on two legs instead of four, is not brought forth to have some state secret (which he knows nothing of) extorted from him by the imperial and royal stick. Royal Neapolitan generosity may yet permit some streaks of prison gas to penetrate into the Sicilian dens where gentlemen are chained to felons, to show them the brightness of their fetters, and the filthiness of the floor, and the shadow of the sentry's bayonet through the heavy bars outside. Mighty secrets, dread secrets, dead secrets, may the gas have, abroad and at home. Strange stories could the dark lantern of old have told—the lantern by the light of which Fawkes laid his train, and D'Enghien was led into the ditch of Vincennes to be shot, and Pichegru was murdered, and Fletcher Christian whispered with John Adams; but the light of the lantern pales before the mystery of the gas. The gas saw the blood that was brought from the shambles and smeared over the pavement of the Paris Boulevards—the blood on which, next day, the dynasty of Orleans stumbled and came headlong down to ruin and death. The gas shone broadly, brightly, in hall and corridor and antechamber of the Elysée on the eve of the second of December. It penetrated into an inner chamber where one silent man sat, his feet on the fender, smoking a cigar, who to fears and questions, and remonstrances, and doubts, and counsels, had but this one answer, ' *Qu'on exécute mes ordres !*' The same gas saw those orders obeyed as the stealthy hackney-coaches went about with the stealthier Commissaries of Police, to kidnap the representatives and generals. I remember passing the Palace of the Elysées on the night of the third of December, and seeing the courtyard and windows of this palace of successful power, one blaze of gas—blazing on the green liveries of the lacqueys, and the uniforms of the aides-de-camp, and the hands and faces of the soldiers hardly yet cleansed from blood and gunpowder. What secrets that gas of the Rue St. Honoré—the same starting from the pert little Cupids quivering in the bonnet-shop opposite—must have been a trusty listener to, within those three December nights !

If any man doubt the secrets of the gas, not only abroad but at home—not only supposititious and probable but actual—let him remember that recent miserable inquiry into the cruelties and tyrannies of some of our vaunted philanthropy-purified English gaols. Let him remember among the list of wretches tied to walls, and strapped to railings, and whipped, and half throttled with collars, let him remember those who—as the official memorandum ran—were to be 'deprived of their bed and gas.' Bless you, the gas heard all these things while the good Birmingham people (may there never be worse people in England !) slept soundly. The gas knew how many turns of the crank prisoner No. 50 was short; of how many meals

51 had been mulcted ; how many lashes epileptic 52 was to receive ; how often 54 was to be deprived of his bed and gas !

As I walk about the streets by night, endless and always suggestive intercommunings take place between me and the trusty, silent, ever-watchful gas, whose secrets I know. In broad long streets where the vista of lamps stretches far far away into almost endless perspective ; in courts and alleys, dark by day but lighted up at night by this incorruptible tell-tale ; on the bridges ; in the deserted parks ; on wharves and quays ; in dreary suburban roads ; in the halls of public buildings ; in the windows of late-hour-keeping houses and offices, there is my gas—bright, silent, and secret. Gas to teach me ; gas to counsel me ; gas to guide my footsteps, not over London flags, but through the crooked ways of unseen life and death, of the doings of the great Unknown, of the cries of the great Unheard. He who will bend himself to listen to, and avail himself, of the secrets of the gas, may walk through London streets proud in the consciousness of being an Inspector—in the great police force of philosophy—and of carrying a perpetual bull's-eye in his belt. Like his municipal brother, he may perambulate the one-half world, while

> 'Nature seems dark, and wicked dreams abuse
> The curtain'd sleep.'

Not a bolt or bar, not a lock or fastening, not a houseless night-wanderer, not a homeless dog, shall escape that searching ray of light which the gas shall lend him, to see and to know.

The gas on the river. Has it no secrets to tell there ? On bridge after bridge, the long rows of lamps mirror themselves in the dark, still pool of the silent highway, and penetrate like arrows into the bosom secrets of the Thames. The gas knows of the ancient logs of timber, It—and Wisdom—only know how many centuries old, strong and seasoned in their gray rottenness, the logs which the bargemen and lightermen of Erith and Greenhithe bring home for fuel, or for garden-fences, and which, for aught we know, may have been in dead ages remnants of Danish ships. of Roman galleys, of the primitive skiffs of the old Britons, maybe. Down beneath, where the glittering arrow of the gas points, there may be shields, and arrows, and collars of barbaric gold. There may be the drinking-cup of Vortigern, the crown of Canute, the golden bracelets that Alfred hung up on the highways, the rings of Roman knights, and the swords of the Consuls, the amulets of the Druids, and the jewels of the Saxon kings. The gas knows of shoals which the cunningest harbour-masters, the best conservators of the river, and the mightiest hydrographers, cannot point out. The gas knows the weak points of the tunnel; and where the waters broke in years ago, and where they may break in again. Down where the gas points, may be the bones of men and women drowned before our great grandsires were born. There, may be Henry the Fourth, flung coffin and all from the boat in which his remains were being conveyed for sepulture. There, may be sailors slain in sudden broils on board ship, and flung into the river. There, may be bodies of men murdered by river pirates, plundered by longshore-men and lighthouse-men, and thrown from boats with heavy weights tied to them, into the pit where the water and the gas tell no tales. There, may be mangled corpses brought by assassins on horseback, as Cæsar Borgia brought his brother the Duke of Gandia, to the Tiber, and thrown into the dull plashing stream, with stones in their cloaks to make them sink. There, may be dead men, drowned in stepping from one ship to another, or who have slipped off planks, drunk, or fallen from mast-heads, or who have leaped into the river to escape press-gangs, or robbers, or river policemen. There, may be 'run' cargoes of contraband goods, tobacco, fiery spirits, rich silk or delicate lace; there, may be bales of goods plundered by fresh-water thieves from foreign ships, and sunk by bullets and iron weights until the time shall serve for fishing them up again. There, may be the suicide of yesterday; the wayward boy, once the pride and hope of the family; the girl, once loved and prized; the ruined spend-thrift; the hopeless bankrupt; the desperate man, driven by an intolerable misery and utter hunger and nakedness to cast himself into these jaws of death as into a bed of slumber and soft repose. Oh you gas upon the bridges! how many times have the garments of forlorn women gleamed in your unpitying light as they flung themselves from the high parapet into the abyss beneath. Oh you gas! how many sighs and prayers and words of despairing farewell! There was a shriek, a plunge, a plash, the vertical reflection of the gas was for a moment broken into zigzag sparkles by a body combating with the re-morseless river. Then, the waters of death went over the head of mortality, and all was still and all was over. O Gas! Where are they now? The hope of the family, the focus of tender love, and anxious care, and fond aspirations. The advertisements which entreat them to return are yet in the

'Times;' the bills which describe their appearance are yet on
the walls; the watchers at home are waiting; the river men
are out with drags; but the water holds them fast, and the gas
shines secretly above them, and they shall no more appear in
the comeliness of life and love. If we ever hear of these, O
Gas! it will be, at best, at the grim dead-house by the water-
side, and their only epitaph will be the awful placard on the
wall of the Police Station, 'Dead body found.'

Fast does the gas keep the secrets of the river. They cannot escape. The janitor gas lamps guard either side. They
watch over long lines of docks, and see that no light, save
their own, appear about gaunt-masted ships, and strong bricken
warehouses where the old wines ooze into toping casks, and
muddle them with vinous fumes; where the sawdust is purpled
with emptied glasses; where the spiral threads which the
coopers' gimlet has made, dance; where the great wreaths of
cobwebs hang lazily from the roof as if quite gone in liquor
and overcome with the tasting-orders of years; where floors
A and B, and cellarages C and D, are pungent with pepper
and tobacco, and fragrant with coffee and spices, and sickly
with oranges and grapes, and sticky with figs and muscovado
and molasses, and aromatic with crisp teas and chicory and
pemmican, and ammoniacally nauseous with horns and hoofs
and untanned skins and guano, and oleaginous with tallow and
palm oil, and hive-smelling with bees'-wax, and drowsy and
vapid with huge chests of opium, packed by Turkish rayahs
or Hindoo ryots, and in its black flabby cakes concentrating
Heaven knows how much madness, and misery, and death,
strangely mingled with soothing relief from pain and with
sparkling gaiety. The gas hems in the stealthy dockyard
watchman going his rounds, the beetle-browed convict in the
dismantled grated-ported hulks, the swift galleys of the
Thames Police, the moaning sufferers in the Dreadnought
hospital-ship; the gas throws into skeleton relief the ribs and
timbers of half-demolished ships, the stripped and spectral
hulks of condemned and broken-up vessels rotting in the mud.
The gas twinkles on the trellised panes of the Gothic windows
in the great Parliament Houses, and listens slily to the late
debates. The gas feebly illumines the blackened coal-barges and
lighters, full of bricks and huge paving-stones. It shines at the
end of the landing stages, and at the feet of the slimy river stairs,
upon moored wherries and river steam-boats so bustling and
busy by day, so hushed and quiet by night. The gas gleams
on the time-worn bastions of the Tower; tho gas knows the

M

secrets of the honeycombed old cannon better than do their
tompions; the gas knows the password and the countersign;
the gas is aware of the slow-pacing sentinel; the gas mirrors
itself in the darkling stream which gurgles about the heavy
timber barricades, with which the better feeling of the age
has blocked up the Traitor's gate. The gas is too young to
relate to you the secrets of the Tower in days gone by. It
lighted not Elizabeth climbing the slimy stairs, and sitting
down defiant of her gaolers, at the top; it has no knowledge
of Jane Grey creeping to her doom; it has not seen the furtive wherries with the warders and halberdiers in the stern,
and the prisoners in the midst, rowing towards the gate of
death. It has not seen the courtly mien of Surrey; the
gallant gray hairs, the toil and travel and trouble furrowed,
but yet handsome face of Raleigh; the fierce white locks of
the Countess of Pembroke; the sneers and sarcasms and
wicked wrinkles of Simon Lord Lovat; the blue eyes and
gentle smile of Derwentwater; the stern heroism of Charles
Radcliffe; the crazy fanaticism of George Gordon; the Spa
Fields and Cato Street enthusiasm of the poor feeble traitor
Thistlewood. The Tower gas knows not where the posts of
the scaffold stood, or how many stones have been bedewed
with blood. It cannot point out the spot where the ghost of
Ann Bullen was said to walk. It lighted not to their work
Dighton and Forrest creeping to murder the princes. It
shone not on the brazen countenance of the King-honoured
Blood, as, arrayed in sham canonicals, he compassed the
plunder of the crown. The gas knows not where Jane saw
the headless body of her husband, or how much good, and
gentle, and pious, as well as guilty and ambitious, dust
moulders beneath the chancel flags of the little church of
Saint Peter ad Vincula. Yet has the Tower gas seen the
hideous range of brick armouries built by the third William,
with their tens of thousands of swords and bayonets and
muniments of war, blazing up into one grand conflagration,
and driving it, potent gas as it is, into obscurity for a time.
It has seen the slow but absorbing footstep of the blessed bygone years of peace dismantle ramparts and brick up portcullises, and rust the mouths of the howling dogs of war and fill
up the mouth. Its mission is more peaceful now. It glistens
on the gold and crimson of the warders as the ceremony of
delivering the Queen's keys is nightly performed. It winks
at the spruce young Guardsmen officers as they dash up to the
gates in Hansom cabs just before shutting-up time, or saunter

jauntily to mess. It lights up the clean pots and glasses in the stone kitchen, and glows upon the rubicund countenances of thirsty grenadiers. It has an eye—a silent, watchful eye—upon a certain strong room where there is a great cage, and in that cage scintillating the precious stones of the Imperial Crown of England, the gold and silver and jewels of the sceptre, the orb, the ampulla, the great saltcellar, and all the stately regalia. The gas is a guardian of all these, and defies the Colonel Bloods of '60. (Oh degenerate '60, where are the good old Bloods, and where the good old monarchs who were so fond of them?) An impartial gas, it shines as brightly on the grenadier's quart pot as on the queenly crown. A convivial gas, it blazes cheerfully in the mess room of the Beauchamp Tower. A secretive gas, it knows that beneath the curtains and flags of that same mess-room there are dark words and inscriptions cut into the aged wall—the records of agony and hopeless captivity, anagrams of pain, emblems of sorrow and hopes fled and youth and joy departed.

So, from where the town begins to where it ends; from the twinkling lights of Putney and Kew, to the marshy flats below Deptford; the gas shines through the still night, and is the repository of secrets known to few, but which all who choose to make the gas their friend, may read, to the softening of their hearts, perhaps, even as they run.

XV

PERFIDIOUS PATMOS.

THE natural place of refuge for a haunted man is an island. None but those who have known what it is to be pursued from place to place, who have been aware of such and such blood-hounds upon their track, of such and such scouts waiting at given points to lead them down to death or captivity, can form an idea of the feeling of security engendered by the knowledge that there is between them and their enemies a bulwark far more impregnable than any gabion, glacis, bastion, or counterscarp, that Vauban ever dreamed of, in the shape of a ring of blue water. So islands have been, in all ages and circumstances, the chosen places of refuge to men who could find no rest elsewhere for the soles of their feet. Patmos was the elected asylum of St. John the Apostle. In Malta, the last Christian knights of Palestine driven from their first island refuge—Rhodes—found a haven of safety, and founded a city of strength against the infidels. The expiring embers of the Druidical priesthood smouldered away in the impenetrable groves of the island of Anglesey. The isles of Greece were the eyries of poetry, and art, and liberty, when the mainland groaned beneath the despotism of the thirty tyrants. The Greeks located their paradise in the islands of the blest. Madeira spread forth pitying, protecting arms to two fugitive lovers. Charles Edward hid in Skye. Once within the pleasant valleys of Pitcairn's Island, Jack Adams and the mutineers of the 'Bounty' felt secure and safe from courts-martial and yard-arms. There is a hiding-place for the pursued of sheriffs in the island of Jersey and in the Isle of Man; in which latter insular refuge, Charlotte de la Tremouille, Countess of Derby, sheltered the last remnants of the cause of the Stuarts against Oliver Cromwell. The dogs of Constantinople found protection from the sticks and stones of the men of Stamboul, in an island in the Bosphorus. The last of the London marshes staunchly defy drainage from the strongholds of the Isle of Dogs; and there is a wall of strength for the choicest London fevers, and the dirtiest London lodging-houses, against Inspectors Reason and Humanity and their whole force, in and about the mud embankments of Jacob's Island.

But, chief and pre-elect of islands on which camps of refuge have been built, is the one we are happy enough to live in, the Island of England. There are other islands in the world, far more isolated, geographically speaking, far more distant from hostile continents, far more remote from the shores of despotism. Yet to these chalky cliffs of Albion, to this Refuge, misnamed the perfidious, come refugees from all quarters of the world, and of characters, antecedents, and opinions, pointing to every quarter of the political compass. The oppressor and the oppressed, the absolutist and the patriot, the butcher and the victim, the wolf and the lamb, the legitimist as white as snow, and the *montagnard* as red as blood, the *doctrinaire* and the socialist—men of views so dissimilar that they would (and do) tear each other to pieces in their own lands, find a common refuge in this country, and live in common harmony here. The very climate seems to have a soothing and mollifying influence on the most savage foreign natures. South American dictators, who have shot, slaughtered, and outraged hecatombs of their countrymen in the parched-up plains of Buenos Ayres and Montevideo, roar you as mildly as any sucking doves as soon as they are in the Southampton Water—make pets of their physicians, and give their barbers silver shaving-dishes; pachas of three tails, terrible fellows for bowstringing, impaling, and bastinadoing in their Asiatic dominions, here caper nimbly in ladies' chambers to the twangling of lutes; hangers of men and scourgers of women forego blood-thirstiness; demagogues forget to howl for heads; and red republicans, who were as roaring lions in the lands they came from, submit to have their claws cut, and their manes trimmed, drink penny cups of coffee, and deliver pacific lectures in Mechanics' Institutes.

England, then, is the Patmos of foreign fugitives—a collection of Patmoses, rather : almost every seaport and provincial town of any note having a little inland island of refuge of its own ; but London being the great *champ d'asile*, the monster isle of safety, a Cave of Adullam for the whole world. It is with this Patmos that I have principally to do.

Years ago, Doctor Johnson called London 'the common sewer of Paris and of Rome;' but at the present day it is a reservoir, a giant vat, into which flow countless streams of continental immigration. More so than Paris, where the English only go for pleasure : the Germans to become tailors and boot-makers ; and the Swiss, valets, house-porters, and waiters. More so than the United States, whose only considerable feed-pipes of emigration are Irish, English, and Germans. There is in London the foreign artistic population, among which I will comprise French, and Swiss, and German governesses, French painters, actors, singers, and cooks ; Italian singers and musicians ; French hairdressers, milliners, dressmakers, clear-starchers, and professors of legerdemain, with countless teachers of every known language, and professors of every imaginable musical instrument. There is the immense foreign servile population : French and Italian valets and shopmen, and German nurses and nursery-maids. There is the foreign commercial population, a whole colony of Greek merchants in Finsbury, of Germans in the Minories, of Frenchmen round Austin Friars, of Moorish Jews in Whitechapel, and of foreign shopkeepers at the west end of the town. There is the foreign mechanical, or labouring population : French, Swiss, and German watchmakers, French and German lithographers, Italian plaster-cast makers and German sugar-bakers, brewers, and leather-dressers. There is the foreign mendicant population : German and Alsatian buy-a-broom girls, Italian hurdy-gurdy grinders, French begging-

letter writers (of whose astonishing numbers, those good
associations, '*La Société Française de Bienfaisance à Londres*,'
and 'The Friends of Foreigners in Distress,' could tell some
curious tales, maybe), Lascar street-sweepers, and tom-tom
pounders. There is the foreign maritime population: an
enormous one, as all men who have seen Jack alive in London
can vouch for. There is the foreign respectable population,
composed of strangers well to do, who prefer English living
and English customs to those of their own country. There is
the foreign swindling population: aliens who live on their
own wits and on the want thereof in their neighbours: sham
counts, barons, and chevaliers; farmers of German lotteries,
speculators in German university degrees, forgers of Russian
bank-notes, bonnets at gaming-houses, touts and spungers to
foreign hotels and on foreign visitors, bilkers of English taverns
and boarding-houses, and getters-up of fictitious concerts and
exhibitions. There is the foreign visiting or sight-seeing
population, who come from Dover to the Hôtel de l'Europe,
and go from thence, with a cicerone, to St. Paul's, Windsor, and
Richmond, and thence back again to France, Germany, or
Spain. Lastly, there is the refugee population; and this be
mine to descant upon.

The Patmos of London I may describe as an island bounded
by four squares ; on the north by that of Soho, on the south by
that of Leicester, on the east by the quadrangle of Lincoln's Inn
Fields (for the purlieus of Long Acre and Seven Dials are all
Patmos), and on the west by Golden Square.

The trapezium of streets enclosed within this boundary are
not, by any means, of an aristocratic description. A maze of
sorry thoroughfares, a second-rate butcher's meat and vegetable market, two model lodging-houses, a dingy parish
church, and some 'brick barns' of dissent are within its
boundaries. No lords or squires of high degree live in this
political Alsatia. The houses are distinguished by a plurality
of bell-pulls inserted in the door-jambs, and by a plurality of
little brass name-plates, bearing the names of in-dwelling
artisans. Everybody (of nubile age and English extraction)
seems to be married, and to have a great many children,
whose education appears to be conducted chiefly on the out-
door principle.

As an uninterested stranger, and without a guide, you
might, perambulating these shabby streets, see in them
nothing which would peculiarly distinguish them from that
class of London veins known inelegantly, but expressively,

as 'back slums. At the first glance you see nothing but dingy houses teeming with that sallow, cabbage-stalk and fried fish sort of population, indigenous to back slums. The pinafored children are squabbling or playing in the gutters; while from distant courts come faintly and fitfully threats of Jane to tell Ann's mother; together with that unmeaning monotonous chant or dirge which street-children sing, why, or with what object, I know not. Grave dogs sit on door-steps —their heads patiently cocked on one side, waiting for the door to be opened, as—in this region of perpetual beer-fetching —they know must soon be the case. The beer itself, in vases of strangely-diversified patterns, and borne by Hebes of as diversified appearance, is incessantly threading the needle through narrow courts and alleys. The public-house doors are always on the swing; the bakers' shops (they mostly sell 'seconds') are always full; so are the cookshops, so are the coffee-shops: step into one, and you shall have a phase of Patmos before you incontinent.

Albrecht Lurleiberg, who keeps this humble little *Deutsche Caffee und Gasthof*, as he calls it, commenced business a few years ago with a single coffee-pot and two cups and saucers. That was a little before February, 1848. Some few foreigners dropped in to visit him occasionally; but he was fain to eke out his slender earnings by selling sweetstuff, penny dolls, and cheap Sunday newspapers. After the first three months' saturnalia of revolution in '48, however, exiles began to populate Patmos pretty thickly. First, Barbès' and Albert's unsuccessful riot; then the escapade of Ledru-Rollin and Louis Blanc; then the wholesale proscriptions of Hungary, Italy, Austria, Russia, and Baden—all these contributed to swell the number of Herr Lurleiberg's customers a hundred-fold, and to fill Patmos to overflowing. The sweetstuff and dolls disappeared 'right away,' and the coffee-pots and cups and saucers multiplied exceedingly. In addition to this, the Herr caused to be stretched across the single window a canvas blind, on which his name, and the style and title of his establishment, were painted in painfully attenuated letters, with which, not yet content, he incited young Fritz Schiftmahl, the artist, with dazzling prospects of a carte-blanche for coffee and tobacco, to depict beneath, in real oil colours, the counterfeit presentments of a Pole, a Hungarian, and a German embracing each other in a fraternal accolade, all smoking tobacco like volcanos of sulphur; the legend setting forth that true, universal, and political brotherhood are only to be found at Albrecht Lurleiberg's.

In the Herr's back parlour—he once designed in the flush of
increased business to enlarge it by knocking it into the back
yard, till warned, by a wary neighbour, of the horrible pains
and penalties (only second to *præmunire*) incurred by meddling
with a wall in England—in this dirty back parlour with rings
made by coffee-cups on the ricketty Pembroke tables, and on
the coarsely papered, slatternly printed foreign newspapers
and periodicals, are a crowd of men in every variety of
beard and moustache and head-dress, in every imaginable phase
of attire more or less dirty and picturesque—figures such as,
were you to see them in the drawings of Leech, or Daumier,
or Gavarni, you would pronounce exaggerated and untrue to
nature ; hooded, tasselled, and braided garments of unheard-of
fashion ; hats of shapes to make you wonder to what a stage
the art of " squeezability " had arrived ; trousers with unnumbered plaits ; boots made as boots seemed never made
before ; finger and thumb-rings of fantastic fashion ; marvellous
gestures, Babel-like diversified tongues ; voices anything but
(Englishly) human ; the fumes as of a thousand brick-kilns ;
the clatter as of a thousand spoons : such are the characteristics
of this in-door Patmos.

Here are Frenchmen—ex-representatives of the people, ex-
ministers, prefects and republican commissaries, Prolétaires,
Fourierists Phalansterians, disciples of Proudhon, Pierre le
Roux and Cahagnet, professors of pantheism, socialism, phalan-
sterianism, all the 'isms' in ismdom ; men yet young, but
two-thirds of whose lives have been spent in prison or in
exile.   Here are political gaol-birds who have been caged in
every state prison of Europe ; in the citadels of France, the
cachots of Mont St. Michel, the *secrets* of the Conciergerie, the
piombi of Venice, the gloomy fastnesses of Ehrenbreitstein
and Breslau and Spandlau, the *oubliettes* of the Spielberg and
Salzburg.   Here are young men—boys almost—of good
families and high hopes, blasted by the sirocco of civil war.
Here are German philosophic democrats—scientific conspirators
—who between Greek roots and algebraical quantities, tobacco
smoke and heavy folios in German text upon international
law, have somehow found themselves upon barricades and in
danger of the fate of Robert Blum.   Here are simple-minded
German workmen—such honest-faced, tawny-bearded young
fellows as you see in the beer-cellars of Berlin—who have
shaken off their dreams of German unity to find themselves in
this back slum Patmos far away from home and friends.
Here are swarthy Italians, eyeing the Tedeschi (though

friendly ones) askance, cursing Radetzky and Gyulay, and
telling with wild gesticulations how Novara was fought and
Rome defended. Here, and in great numbers, are the poor,
betrayed, cozened Hungarians, with glossy beards, and small
embroidered caps and braided coats. They are more woe-
begone, more scared and wild-looking than the rest, for they
are come from nearly the uttermost corner of Europe, and
have little fellowship save that of misfortune with their continental neighbours. Lastly, here are the Poles, those historical
exiles who have been so long fugitives from their country
that they have adopted Patmos with a will, and have many of
them entered into and succeeded in business, but would, I
think, succeed better if the persons with whom they have commercial transactions were able to pronounce their names—those
jaw-breaking strings of dissonant letters in which the vowels
are so few that the consonants seem to have compassed them
round about, like fortifications, to prevent their slipping out.

There are many of these poor refugees (I speak of them in
general) who sit in coffee-shops similar to Herr Lurleiberg's
from early morning till late at night, to save the modicum of
fire and candle they would otherwise be compelled to consume
at home (if home their garrets can be called), and which, God
knows, they can ill spare. About one o'clock in the day,
those who are rich enough congregate in the English cook-
shops, and regale themselves with the cheap cag-mag there
offered for sale. Towards four or five the foreign eating-
houses, of which there are many in Patmos of a fifth or sixth-
rate order of excellence, are resorted to by those who yet
adhere to the gastronomic traditions of the land they have
been driven from; and there they vainly attempt to delude
themselves into the belief that they are consuming the *fricassées*
and *ragouts*, the suet puddings and *sauerkraut*, the *maccaroni*,
risotto, and *stuffato* of France or Germany or Italy—all the delightful messes on which foreigners feed with such extreme
gusto and satisfaction. But, alas! these dishes, though compounded from foreign recipes and cooked by foreign hands, are
not, or, at least, do not taste like foreign dishes. Cookery,
like the *amor patriæ*, is indigenous. It cannot be transplanted.
It cannot flourish on a foreign soil. I question if the black
broth of Sparta would have agreed with the Lacedæmonian
palate if consumed in an England *à la mode* beef shop.

Patmos is likewise studded with small foreign tobacco shops
—limited to the sale of tobacco mostly, for the cigar is a luxury
in most cases beyond the reach of the exile. You must re-

member that abroad you may obtain a cigar as large as an Epping sausage (and as damp), as strong as brandy and as fiery as a red-hot poker for a matter of two sous—in some parts of Belgium and Germany for one sous ; and that in England the smallest Cuba of Minories manufacture, smoked in a minute and of no particular flavour, costs three halfpence : a sum! There is, to be sure a harmless milk-mild little roll of dark brown colour, the component parts of which, I believe, are brown paper, hay, and aromatic herbs, vended at the charge of one penny. But what would be the use of one of those smoke-toys to an exile who is accustomed to wrap himself in smoke as in a mantle : to smoke by the apertures of his mouth, nostrils, eyes, and ears ; to eat cigars, so to speak ? Thus Patmos solaces itself with cut tobacco (good and cheap in England), which it puffs from meerschaums or short clays, or rolls up into fragments of foreign newspapers and makes cigarettes of.

If there exist a peculiarity of Patmos which I could not, without injustice, avoid adverting to, it is the pleasure its inhabitants seem to feel in reading letters. See, as we saunter down one of Patmos's back streets a German exile, in a pair of trousers like a bifurcated carpet bag, stops a braided Hungarian with a half quartern loaf under his arm. A sallow Italian (one of Garibaldi's men) enters speedily unto them, and the three fall greedily to the perusal of a large sheet of tissue paper, crossed and re-crossed in red, and black, and blue ink, patchworked outside with postage marks of continental frontiers and Government stamps. Few of these missives reach their destination without some curious little scissor marks about the seal, some suspicious little hot-water blisters about the wafers, hinting that glazed cocked hats, and jack-boots, and police spies have had something to do with their letters between their postage and their delivery. Indeed, so well is this paternal solicitude on the part of foreign governments to know whether their corresponding subjects write and spell correctly, known among the refugees, that some wary exiles have their letters from abroad addressed to 'Mr. Simpson Brown,' or 'Mr. Thomas Williams,' such and such a street, London ; and as foreign governments are rather cautious as to how they meddle with the families of the Browns and the Williams's—who grow refractory sometimes and post their letters in the paddle-boxes of war-steamers— the Brown and Williams letters reach London untampered with.

More exiles reading letters. One nearly falls over a dog's-meat cart, so absorbed is he in his correspondence; another, bearded like the pard, and with a fir cap like an Armenian Calpack, is shedding hot tears on his outstretched paper, utterly unconscious of the astonishment of two town-made little boys, who have stopped in the very middle of a 'cart-wheel' to stare at the 'furriner a crying.' Poor fellows! poor broken men! poor hunted wayfarers! If you, brother Briton well clothed, well fed, well cared for—with X 99 well paid to guard you—with houses for the sale of law by retail on every side, where you can call for your half-pint of habeas corpus or your Magna Charta, cold without, at any hour in the day—if you were in a strange land, proscribed, attainted, poor, unfriended, dogged even in your Patmos by spies; could *you* warrant yourself not to shed some scalding tears, even in a fierce fur cap, over a letter from the home you are never to see more?

My pencil may limn an individual portrait or so in the per-fidious refuge, and then I must needs row my bark away to other shores. Stop at forty-six, Levant Street, if you please, over against Leg-bail Court.

Up four flights of crazy stairs, knocking at a ricketty door, you enter a suite of three musty attics. They are very scantily furnished, but crowded with articles of the most heterogeneous description; *mes marchandises*, as the proprietor calls them. Variegated shades for lamps, fancy stationery, *bon-bon* boxes, lithographic prints, toys, cigar-cases, nicknacks of every description are strewn upon the chairs and tables, and cumber the very floor; at one window a dark-eyed mild-looking lady, in a dark merino dress, is painfully elaborating a drawing on a lithographic stone; at another a slender girl is bending over a tambour frame; at a desk a round-headed little boy is copying music, while in an adjoining apartment—even more denuded of furniture and littered with *marchandise*—are two or three little children tumbling among the card-board boxes. All these movables, animate and inanimate, belong to a Roman Marquis —the Marchese del Pifferare. He and his have been reared in luxury. Time was he possessed the most beautiful villa, the finest equipages, the most valuable Rafaelles in the Campagna of Rome; but *la politique*, as he tells you with a smile, has brought him down to the level of a species of unli-censed hawker, going with his wares (to sell on commission) from fancy warehouse to fancy warehouse, often rebutted, often insulted; yet picking up an honest livelihood somehow.

His wife has turned her artistic talent, and his eldest daughter her taste for embroidery to account; his son Mithridates copies music for the orchestra in a theatre, for living is dear in London, and those helpless little ones among the card-board boxes must be looked after. He has been an exile for five years. The Holy Father was good enough to connive at his escape and to confer all his confiscated estates on a Dominican convent. No one knows what the *politique*, which has been his ruin, exactly was; nor, I am inclined to think, does the good man know very clearly himself. 'We got away from Rome,' he tells you mildly, 'with a few hundred scudi, and our plate and a picture or two, and went to Marseilles; but when we had "eaten" (*avevamo mangiati*) what we had brought with us, we came to England. It was very hard at first; for we had no friends, and could speak nothing but French and Italian, and the English are a suspicious people, whose first impulse, when they see a foreigner for the first time, is to button up their pockets as if he must necessarily be a thief.' But the marquis went to work manfully, forgot his coronet, and is now doing a very good fancy commission business. He has an invention (nearly all refugees have inventions) for curing smoky chimneys, which, when he has money enough to patent it, he expects will bring him a fortune. In the days of his utterest and most dire distress, he always managed to pay three shillings every Sunday for the sittings of himself, his wife, and daughter at a foreign Catholic chapel, and to wear every day the cleanest of white neckcloths, fastened no man knows how, for no man ever saw the tie thereof.

Within these sorry streets—these dingy slums—are swept together the dead leaves, the rotten branches, the withered fruits from the tree of European liberty. The autumn blast of despotism has eddied them about from the ends of Europe, has chased them from land to land, has wafted them at last into this perfidious Patmos, where there is liberty to act, and think, and breathe, but also, alas! liberty to Starve.

O England, happily unconscious of the oppressions and exasperations that have driven these men here, try sometimes to spare some little modicum of substantial relief, some crumbs of comfort, some fragile straws of assistance to the poor drowning exiles! Their miseries are appalling. They cannot dig (for few, if any, Englishmen will call a foreigner's spade into requisition), to beg they are nobly ashamed. They do not beg, nor rob, nor extort. They starve in silence. The French and Hungarian refugees suffer more, perhaps, than those of other nations. The former have by no means an aptitude for acquiring the English language, and are, besides, men mostly belonging to the professional classes of society—classes wofully overstocked in England; the latter seldom know any language but their own—a language about as useful and appreciated here as Cochin-Chinese. Only those who have wandered through Patmos, who have watched the gates of the London Docks at early morning when the chance labourers apply for work, who have sat in night coffee-houses, and explored dark arches, can know what awful shifts some of these poor refugees, friendless, foodless, houseless, are often put to.

XVI.

DID Archimedes square the circle? The legend (I have a great respect for legends, mendacious though they often be) says that he did. The confident legend has it that he really, truly, and completely succeeded. That, chalk in hand, heedless in his scientific pre-occupation of the sack of Syracuse, he bent over the magic diagram he had traced on the floor of his humble domicile, contemplating with joy and exultation the glorious end by which his labours had been crowned. That then, however, a Soldier entered, hot with plunder and blood-spilling. That with his murderous javelin he smote the sage to death; and that the blood of Archimedes flowing in a sluggish stream effaced the diagram (which was to the ruthless warrior an unmeaning assemblage merely of lines curved and straight). And the circle remains unsquared to this day.

Many have experimentalised on the mighty problem since the legendary days of the Greek philosopher; but the failures have been as numerous as the attempts. Not that the thing is impossible; oh no! All of us have, more or less, friends and acquaintances on the very verge—the extremest point— of squaring the circle, as also of discovering perpetual motion, paying the National Debt, and accomplishing some trifling little undertakings of that description. Only, they never do. They resemble somewhat the poor little 'punters' one sees at Hombourg and Baden-Baden—the men with 'systems'— infallible 'martingales,' believers in *masse en avant*, who would always have won fifty thousand florins to a dead certainty, in one *coup*, my dear sir, if red had only turned up again. But it didn't. Red never does turn up when you want it. So with the circle squarers, perpetual motion discoverers, National-Debt liquidators, and inventors of directing power to balloons. Something always occurs at the very ace and nick of time—the critical moment—to nip their invention in the bud. My friend A. would have squared the circle, years ago, if he had not been sentenced to six months' imprisonment in one of Her Majesty's gaols for writing threatening letters to the Earl of Derby, in which the the Circle was mixed up, somehow, with a desire to have his lordship's life. B. is only deterred from terminating his experiments by the want of a loan (temporary) of one pound five. C.'s landlady, in the neighbourhood of Red Lion Square, has impounded for un-paid rent his philosophical apparatus, without which it is impossible for him to complete his discoveries. D., on the very eve of success, took it into his head to preach the Mil-lennium, as connected with the New Jerusalem and the Latter-day Saints, in the vicinity of Rotherhithe; and as for E., the only man who they say has squared the circle these few hundred years, he is at present so raving mad in a lunatic asylum, that we can't make much of the desperate diagrams he chalks on the walls of his day room, mixed as are his angles, arcs, and diameters, with humorous couplets and caricatures of public characters. I might, if I chose, enumerate initials which would use up the alphabet twice over; from M., who combined philosophy with the manufacture of Bengal lights, and blew himself, and half his neighbourhood, up one day, down to Z., who, impressed with a conviction that the circle was only to be squared in the interior of Africa, went out to the Gold Coast in a trader, and was supposed to have been eaten up by the natives, somewhere between Timbuctoo and the Mountains of the Moon. Still, the circle remains un-squared.

I, who am no mathematician, and would sooner throw my-self off the parapet of the *pons asinorum*, or go to sleep in one of the dry arches underneath, than trudge over it, not pre-suming to attempt squaring a circle, humbly intend to see if I cannot circle a square. Say Leicester Square, in the county of Middlesex.

In my opinion Leicester Square, or Leicester Fields, or 'the Square,' as its inhabitants call it, or '*Laystarr Squarr*,' as the French have it, offers in many of its features some striking points of resemblance to an institution expatiated upon by Monsieur Philippe de Lolme, called the British Constitution.

The Square, like the Constitution, has been infinitely patched, and tinkered, and altered. Some of its bulwarks have been broken down, some of its monuments have been utterly destroyed; and coaches-and-six may now be driven where edifices were. But in their entirety both institutions are unchanged. The Square and the Constitution have yet their Habeas Corpus and their Bill of Rights. Much has been abolished, changed, improved; but the Square is the Square, and the Constitution is the Constitution; and the Briton may point to both with pride, as immutable evidence of the stability of the institutions of a free country.

Before I commence circling seriatim this square—which I may call the liver of London, often spoken of but little known —let me say a few words of its history. This quadrangle of houses once went by the name of Leicester Fields. These fields (now partially covered by Mr. Wyld's great globe) were built round, three sides of them, about 1635, what time Charles the First was in difficulties about ship-money, and thirsting for Mr. Pym's ears. During the civil wars and Commonwealth, the powers that were, occupied themselves rather more with pulling down mansions than with building them; and the south side remained uncovered with houses until the days of that virtuous and exemplary monarch, who passed the bill for the better observance of the Sabbath, and murdered Algernon Sydney. From 1671 to the middle of the eighteenth century, Leicester Fields were Leicester Fields. Then the royal German gentleman, second of his name, endowed the enclosure in the centre with an equestrian statue of his gracious self (brought from Canons, the seat of the Duke of Chandos), and the fields became thenceforward a square, and fashionable.

Fashionable, to a certain extent, they had been before; since Charles the Second's time, Leicester Fields had boasted the possession of a palace. Yes, between where there are now sixpenny shows and *cafés chantants* with a Shades beneath, and where there is a cigar-shop, once stood Leicester House, built by Robert Sydney, Earl of Leicester, the father of poor Algernon Sydney, of Henry Sydney (the handsome Sydney of De Grammont's Memoirs), and of Lady Dorothy Sydney, the Sacharissa of Waller the poet. Here, when the Sydneys had come to grief, lived and died the Queen of Bohemia. Here resided the great Colbert, Louis the Fourteenth's ablest minister of finance and commerce, when on an embassy to King Charles the Second. Here, in 1703, lived (hiring the house from

Lord Leicester) the ambassador from the Emperor of Germany.
Prince Eugene lay at Leicester House, and courtiers (no
doubt) lied there in 1713. In 1718, no less a personage than
the Prince of Wales bought Leicester House, and made it his
town residence. Pennant, that sly old antiquary—whose wit,
though dry, like old port, is as nutty and full-flavoured—calls
it the 'pouting house for princes;' for here, when the next
Prince of Wales, Frederick, quarrelled with his papa (who
had quarrelled with his), he, too, removed to Leicester House
and kept a little sulky Court there.

Of Leicester House, palatially speaking, what now remains?
Of that princely north-east corner of the square, what is there,
save a foreigner-frequented cigar-shop? Stay, there is yet the
Shades, suggestive still of semi-regal kitchens, in their underground vastness. And haply there is, above Saville House, a
palace once, for George the Third's sister was married from
thence—so says the 'European Magazine' for 1761—to a
German prince, and to her misfortune, poor soul, as her German
prison-cell shall tell her in years to come. And Saville House
is a palace still, far more palatial than if kings sat in its upper
rooms, and princes in its gates. It is the palace of showmanship. It is the greatest booth in Europe.

Saville House! What Londoner, what country cousin who
visited the metropolis twenty-five years ago, does not immediately connect that magic establishment with the name of Miss
Linwood and her needlework? It was very wonderful. I, as
a child, never could make it out much, or settle satisfactorily to
my own mind, why it should not, being carpeting, have been
spread upon the floor instead of being hung against the wall.
I did not like the eyes, noses, and lips of the characters being
all in little quadrangles; and I was beaten once, I think, for
saying that I thought my sister's sampler superior to any
of Miss Linwood's productions. Yet her work was very
wonderful; not quite equal to Gobelin tapestry, perhaps,
but colossal as respects patience, neatness, and ingenuity.
Of and concerning Miss Linwood I was wont in my nonage
to be much puzzled. Who and what was this marvellous
being? I have since heard, and I now believe that Miss
Linwood was a simple-minded, exemplary schoolmistress, somewhere near Leicester—a species of needleworking Hannah
More; but at that time she was to me a tremendous myth—a
tapestry-veiled prophetess—a sibyl working out perpetual
enigmas in silk and worsted.

The shows at Saville House remained alive o! What show

of shows came after Miss Linwood ? There were some clumsy caricatures of good pictures and good statues, enacted on a turn-table by brazen men and women, called *Poses Plastiques*. I, your servant, assisted once at a representation of this description, where I think the subject was Adam and Eve in the garden of Eden. Adam by Herr Something, Eve by Madame Somebody, and the serpent by *a real serpent*, a bloated old snake quite sluggish and dozy, and harmless enough, between his rabbits, to be tied in a knot round the tree. The most amusing part of the entertainment was the middle thereof at which point two warriors, arrayed in the uniform of Her Majesty appeared on the turn-table, and claimed Adam as a deserter from the third Buffs ; which indeed he was, and so was summarily marched off with a great-coat over his fleshings, and a neat pair of handcuffs on his wrists—the which sent me home moralizing on the charming efficiency of the Lord Chamberlain and his licencers, who can strike a harmless joke out of a pantomime, and cannot touch such fellows as these, going vagabondizing about with nothing to cover them. I think I went the same evening to a certain theatre, where I saw the most magnificent parable in the New Testament parodied into a gew-gaw spectacle—a convention between the property-man, the scene-painter, and the corps de ballet— which made me think that the Lord Chamberlain and his licencers did not dispense their justice quite even-handedly ; that they strained at the gnats a little too much, maybe, and swallowed the camels a little too easily.

Serpents both of land and sea ;—panoramas of all the rivers of the known world ; jugglers ; ventriloquists ; imitators of the noises of animals ; dioramas of the North Pole, and the gold diggings of California ; somnambulists (very lucid) ; ladies who have cheerfully submitted to have their heads cut off nightly at sixpence per head admission ; giants ; dwarfs ; sheep with six legs ; calves born inside out ; marionnettes ; living marionnettes ; lecturers on Bloomerism ; expositors of orrery—all of these have by turns found a home in Saville House. In the enlarged cosmopolitanthrophy of that mansion, it has thrown open its arms to the universe of exhibitions. One touch of showmanship makes the whole world kin ; and this omni-showing house would accommodate with equal pleasure, Acrobats in its drawing-rooms, Spiritual Rappers in its upper rooms, the Poughkeepsie Seer in the entrance hall, and the Learned Pig in the cellar.

But I shall be doing foul injustice to Saville House were I

N

to omit to mention one exhibition that it has of late years adopted. The assault of arms! Who has not seen the adventurous life-guardsman effect that masterly feat, the 'severisation' of the leg of mutton ; and that more astonishing exploit, the scientific dissection at two strokes of the carcase of a sheep ? Who has not applauded the masterly cutting asunder of the bar of lead ; the 'Saladin feat ;' the terrific combat between the broadsword and bayonet ; the airy French fencing and small-sword practice (like an *omelette soufflée* after solid beef and pudding)? And then the wind up, when Saville House, forgetting its antecedents of the drama (slightly illegitimate), and puppets and panoramas, takes manfully to fisticuffs! I am reminded of that company of Athenian actors, who, in the earlier days of the Greek drama, essayed a performance before an Athenian public ; but who, finding their efforts not by any means appreciated or understood by their audience, took refuge in some gladiatorial acquirements they were lucky enough to possess, and 'pitched into' each other manfully, to the intense delight of the Areopagus. I am reminded, too, by the way, during this 'wind-up,' of the propinquity of certain gentlemen, whose bow-legs, green cut-away coats, flattened noses, fancy shawls, scarred lips, chameleon-coloured eyes, swollen mottled hands, Oxonian shoes (tipped), closely-cropped hair, bull necks, large breast-pins, &c., remind me, in their turn, that I am in the antechamber of the Ring; which leads me to descend into the street, foregoing the pleasure of witnessing the ' Grand exhibition of wrestling between two Southerners,' wherein I am promised a living illustration of the genuine Devonshire kick, and the legitimate Cornish hug. Formerly I was wont to linger, by the peristyle of Saville House, at the foot of its wide exterior staircase ; though Mr. Cantelo's acolyte next door, mellifluously invited me to ascend and see how eggs were hatched by steam ; though there was a rival lady with her head undergoing the very process of decapitation next door to him ; with a horned lady, a bearded lady, and a mysterious lady, on the other side. Saville House has yet charms for me which I cannot lightly pass by. There are the Shades, a remnant of the old London night cellars, bringing to mind Tom King's Coffee-house, and the cellar where Strap had that famous adventure, and the place where the admired Captain Macheath and his virtuous companions first heard 'the sound of coaches.' Saville House boasts also of a billiard-room, where there are celebrated professors in moustachios, who will give you eighty out of the hundred and beat you; who can do anything with the balls and cues save swallowing them; who are clever enough to make five hundred a year at billiards, and do make it, some of them; where there are markers who look like marquises in their shirtsleeves and difficulties. I have nought more to say of the palace of my square, save that the Duke of Gloucester lived at Leicester House, in 1767, previous to its final decadence as a royal residence; that Sir Ashton Lever formed here the collection of curiosities known as the Leverian Museum; and that New Lisle Street was built on the site of the gardens of Leicester House in 1791.

To resume the circling of my square may I beg you to pass Cranbourne Street, also a large foreign hotel, also a hybrid floridly eccentric building of gigantic dimensions, where the Pavilion at Brighton seems to have run foul of the Alhambra, and repaired damages with the temple of Juggernaut: splicing on a portion of a Chinese pagoda as a jury-mast, and filling up odd leaks with bits of the mosque of St. Sophia.

Passing this enigmatical habitation (now a circus for horse-riders), tarry, oh _viator_! ere you come to Green Street, by Pagliano's Sablonière Hotel, a decent house, where there is good cheer after the Italian manner. The northern half of this hotel was, until 1764, a private dwelling-house—its door distinguished by a bust made of pieces of cork cut and glued together, and afterwards gilt, and known as the 'Painter's Head.' The painter's head was cut by the painter himself who lived there; and the painter was that painter, engraver, and moralist, that prince of pictorial philosophers,

> Whose pictured morals charm the mind,
> And through the eye correct the heart;

the King's Sergeant Painter, William Hogarth.

I would give something to be able to see that merry, sturdy, bright-eyed, fresh-coloured little fellow in his sky-blue coat, and bob-wig, and archly cocked hat, trudging forth from his house. I would hypothecate some portion of my vast estates to have been in Leicester Square the day Will Hogarth first set up his coach; to have watched him writing that wrathful letter to the nobleman who objected to the too faithful _vraisemblance_ of his portrait, wherein he threatened, were it not speedily fetched away, to sell it, with the addition of horns and a tail, to a wild-beast showman, who doubtless had his show in Leicester Fields hard by; to have seen him in his painting-room putting all his savage irony of colour and expression into the picture of the bully-poet Churchill; or 'biting in' that grand etching of sly, cruel, worthless Simon Fraser, Lord Lovat, counting the forces of the Pretender on his fingers; or correcting the proof-sheets of the Analysis of Beauty; or scarifying Jack Wilkes on copper; or, haply, keeping quiet, good-humoured company with his gentle lady wife, Jane Thornhill, telling her how he engraved pint pots and masquerade tickets in his youth, and how he painted his grandest pictures for the love of her. We have painters, and engravers, and moralists now-a-days, and to spare, I trow; but thy name will long smell sweet as violets, Will Hogarth, though thou wert neither a Royal Academician nor a 'Sir.'

Yet, circling round about, stand momentarily at the corner of a little street—Green Street by name—full of musty little book-stalls and fugacious shops. Fugacious I call them, for their destinies are as fleeting as their proprietors. They are everything by turns, and nothing long: now betting-offices, now print-shops, now cigar-shops, anon oyster-shops, coffee-shops, brokers' shops. In Green Street shall you be sensible also of an odour very marked, of the cookery of the various foreign boarding-houses and cook-shops of the neighbourhood; and, towering above the dingy little houses, shall you see the Elizabethan chimney-shaft of the St. Martin's baths and wash-houses: a beacon of cleanliness to the neighbourhood; a Pharos of soapsuds; a finger-post to thrift and comfort.

We pass St. Martin's Street—street of no thoroughfare, but remarkable for Mr. Bertolini's restaurant, and formerly famous as the residence of Sir Isaac Newton. We pass the Soup-kitchen Association's Offices, Star Street, a score of private houses, and, halting at number forty-seven, we descry a mansion of considerable dimensions, formerly the property of Lord Inchiquin, afterwards the Western Literary and Scientific Institution, then the resting-place, I think, of a panorama of the Australian Gold Diggings; but, before all these, residence of Sir Joshua Reynolds, Knight, the first President of the Royal Academy.

It is something to think, gazing at this plain house from the shabby cab-stand opposite (where there are always six cabs, and apparently never any one to hire them) that to number forty-seven came, sixty years ago, all that was great, noble, and beautiful—all that was witty, learned, and brave—in this land. It is something to think that the plain awkward country lad, poor in purse and pauper in influence in the beginning, should in this number forty-seven, from 1761 to

1792, have held his state undisputed, undisturbed as the *pontifex maximus* of portrait-painting—the Merlin of his art —that the steps of his house should have been swept by the ermine of judges, the lawn of prelates, the robes of peers, the satin and brocade of princesses; that there should have been about his ante-rooms, thrown into corners like unconsidered trifles, of as little account as the gew-gaws of a player's tiring-room, the fans of duchesses, the batons of victorious generals, the badges of chivalry, the laurels of poets, the portfolios of ministers. It is something to think that if *some* spooney lords, some carpet warriors, some tenth transmitters of a foolish face, have mingled with the brilliant crowd at forty-seven, Leicester Fields, its rooms have re-echoed to the silvery laughter of Georgina, Duchess of Devonshire, to the commanding tones of Chatham, and Mansfield, and Camden. It is more to, think that to this house came, to hold familiar converse with its master, the wise men of England.

Come back, shades of the mighty dead, to number forty-seven! Come back from Beaconsfield, Edmund Burke! Come back, Percy, scholar and poet; Joe Warburton; lively, vain, kind-hearted David Garrick, courtly Topham Beauclerc, staunch old General Oglethorpe, drawing diagrams of the fields of Belgrade and Peterwardein with filberts, and nut-crackers, and port wine! Come back, stout-hearted Pasquale di Paoli; gossiping, toadying, boozy Boswell. Come back, oh, thou leviathan of literature, with the large wig and larger heart, with the rolling gait and voice of thunder, come back, Samuel Johnson!

Do thou also return, sprightly, kindly spectre in suit of Filby-made Tyrian bloom—poet and novelist and essayist and dramatist, for whom, wert thou alive and hard up for paper, I would send my last shirt to the paper-mill to make Bath post. Return, if for a moment, Oliver Goldsmith! Sins and follies there may be posted against thee in the Book, but surely tears enough have been shed over the ' Vicar of Wakefield ' to blot them out, and airs of light-hearted laughter have been wafted from ' She Stoops to Conquer ' to dry the leaves again a thousand times!

But they cannot come back, these shades, at my poor bidding. Beaconsfield and Poet's Corner, St. Paul's and Dromore, will hold their own until the time shall come. I cannot even wander through the genius hallowed rooms of Reynolds's house. Literary and scientific apparatus, and panorama, have effaced all vestige thereof. I can but muse in the spirit on the dining-room where these great ones met—on the octagon painting-room with the arm-chair on a dais, with the high window looking to the northward darkened on the day of Goldsmith's death, with the palette and pencils laid by for the day when Johnson was buried, and on every Sunday afterwards, according to his dying wish.

My square is nearly circled.   When I have stated that David Loggan, the engraver immortalised by Pope, lived next door to Hogarth, and that next door on the other side resided (after the painter's death) John Hunter, the surgeon, who here formed the famous anatomical museum, called the Hunterian collection, and gave every Sunday evening, during the winter months, medical *soirées*, where matters germane to the scalpel and lancet were pleasantly discussed over coffee and muffins, I think I have named all that Leicester Square offers of remarkable, historically speaking.   I am not aware that any nobleman ever had his head cut off here ; that Lord Rochester ever said anything witty from any of its balconies ; or that any patriot, from Jack Cade to Mr. Hunt, ever addressed British freeholders within its precincts.

The diameter I proposed to myself is well-nigh completed ; but there is yet the centre of my self-traced circle to be visited.   I shall say no more of Mr. Wyld's globe, save that it is a very excellent *vivâ voce* course of lessons in geography. I will not touch upon the bazaar that was to have been built there once ; but I must, for the benefit of my untravelled readers, say a word about the centre of the square before it was built upon.

Where now is a lofty dome was once, O neophyte in London, a howling desert enclosed by iron railings.   There was no grass, but there was a feculent, colourless vegetation like mildewed thatch upon a half-burnt cottage.   There were no gravel-walks, but there were sinuous gravelly channels and patches, as if the cankerous earth had the mange.   There were rank weeds heavy with soot.   There were blighted shrubs like beggars' staves or paralytic hop-poles.   There were shattered marble vases like bygone chemists' mortars which had lost their pestles, half choked with black slimy mould like preparations for decayed blisters.   The earth seemed to bring forth crops, but they were crops of shattered tiles, crumbling bricks, noiseless kettles, and soleless boots. The shrubs had on their withered branches strange fruits— battered hats of antediluvian shape, and oxidised saucepan lids.   The very gravel was rusty and mixed with fragments of willow-pattern plates, verdigrised nails, and spectral horse-shoes. The surrounding railings, rusty, bent, and twisted as they were, were few and far between. The poor of the neighbourhood tore them out by night, to make pokers of. In the centre, gloomy, grimy, rusty, was the Statue—more hideous (if such a thing may be) than the George the Fourth enormity in Trafalgar Square—more awful than the statue of the Commendatore in Don Giovanni.

There were strange rumours and legends current in Leicesterian circles concerning this enclosure. Men told, holding their breath, of cats run wild in its thickets, and grown as large as leopards. There was no garden, and if any man possessed a key to the enclosure, he was too frightened to use it. People spoke of a dragon, a ghoule, a geni, who watched over the square, and for some fell purpose kept it desolate. Some said, the statue was the geni; but in 1851, when the Globe was proposed, he showed himself to the world, howled dismally, and did furious battle to keep his beloved Square intact in all its ruin and desolation. This geni, or dragon's name was, if I remember right, Vested Interests. He was vanquished.

XVII.

DAYBREAK.

IT is but a narrow thread of grayish hue, streaking the murky horizon in the quarter the sun comes from, that I take to spin my feeble web from. Fragile it is, and of as little account as the long, slender, attenuated filament I have seen stretching from the limbs of an oak (whose frame has grown gaunter, but whose muscles seem to grow stronger in its rigid, iron knots, like those of an old athlete) down to the cowslips in a field beneath: the aërial suspension bridge of the spider. Break of day is my slender, gray, flickering thread; but Day and Night are the strong oak and the wide field they connect; and my thread may serve as a humble link between two mighty subjects.

And my thread—daybreak—should it not be a chord in the harp on which Nature at least for ever sings hymns of praise; if men do sometimes fail to pray? And daybreak, is it not a bell, a marriage-bell to millions—a passing-bell to dying millions too—a joy-bell and a knell of death? And daybreak, is it not the main, from which tend smaller pipes of light?

And daybreak, is it not the chandelier at which both wise and foolish virgins kindle their lamps, to light them their day's work through? The night may seem lifelong; but daybreak comes : it must come—like Death.

Yet, omnipresent as it is, how many children of humanity there be who rise, and work, and go to bed again, through a lifetime, without once beholding my thread. ' Does one man in a million,' asks Paley, in the Natural Theology, ' know how oval frames are turned?'—Is there one man in a thousand, I will less boldly ask, who has seen the break of day? If all had seen it, what would there be left for me to write about? If everybody knew everything, how many, many days the poor schoolmasters and philosophers would have to wait for the bread they had cast on the waters!

What aspect, observation, has daybreak on a railway? We have left London by the night mail for Liverpool. It is August weather, and day breaks just after we have passed Crewe. With a rasping, shattering express motion have we come over the rails. Reading was out of the question. A pale gentleman in spectacles essayed it at Watford; but the letters danced up and down in all manner of ways against his gold-rimmed pebbles, as though the matrix they (the letters) had descended from had been a maniac ; and they, in consequence, mad type, wholly unsuitable for so grave a work as ' The Architectural Psychology of the Middle Ages, as Exhibited in Flying Buttresses,' which the pale gentleman essayed to peruse but gave up at last in despair.

Another traveller, a political-looking man with gray whiskers and a determined neckcloth—the sort of man, I warrant, who looks sharply after the member for his borough, and heads a requisition to him to resign his seat two or three times in the course of a session—tried also to read a leader in that day's ' Times ;' but, in spite of the large, bold type, and of his folding the paper into a small, fierce compass, and holding it with both hands, with a paper-knife pressed over the line immediately below the one he read, and so moved downwards, and nearly gluing his eyes to it in the bargain ; in spite of this he had no better success : and muttering ' Unprincipled print ' (doubtless because he couldn't read it), went austerely to sleep, and dreamed, probably, of the brisk rubbing up he will give the honourable member for Throttlebury, shortly, concerning his infamous tergiversation about that poor burked little bill which was to have given sewers to Throttlebury. A commercial gentleman, with his great-coat full of gold pencil-cases,

vainly attempted at Rugby to jot down an order in his note-
book, and failing to make anything but incoherent zigzag
diagrams, bound a railway rug round his head till it assumed
the semblance of a grenadier's cap that had been stencilled at
a paper-stainer's, and went to sleep, too. Somebody (I hope
he didn't sit near me), not being able to read, or to sleep, or to
snore and gasp and bark like the ball of something with a
wide-awake hat in the left-hand off corner, and afraid to sing,
presumed to smoke, swallowing the major part of the fumes
through modesty, and tilting the ashes cautiously out of the
little Venetian *jalousies* above the window.

We all got out at Wolverton, where the commercial traveller
disappeared—perhaps to take an order for pork pies ; and the
pale gentleman in spectacles was indignant (and justly so, I
think), that he could not have threepenn'orth of brandy in his
tea. So, through the black night have we rushed fiercely
through black county after county. At Stafford, the ball of
something (which has turned out to be camlet cloak), speaking
for the first and last time, has remarked ' that it is a long train '
(which it is not). At some intermediate station—whose name,
as it was yelped forth by a porter as he hurried by thrusting
grease into the hot greedy maw of the axle-box, might just as
well have been cried in Chaldee or Sanscrit for anything I
could make of it—a simpering gentleman with a gold chain
peeping even from among his many coats, and a Fez cap,
proposed to enter the carriage ; but, drawing back, declared
that ' somebody had been smoking,' and that it was a ' disgrace ;' whereupon the guard asked nobody in particular if
anybody had been smoking, and, seeming perfectly satisfied
with the assurance that nobody had, remarked that ' it was
the engine—maybe,' and popped my simpering gentleman into
the next carriage, in which there were two old maids, one
purple satin lady of Lambertian or Armitagian bulk, a young
child (querulous), a black nurse, and a gentleman subject to
fits—having them, too, every other station or so. No smoking
there !

Far behind lies Crewe, though but a minute passed. I draw
down the window, and the keen morning breeze charges in at
the aperture like a Cossack. And in the eastern horizon Day
breaks. How many cocks, I wonder, in all the lands day
breaks upon are singing their morning hymn now ? I listen
for one Chanticleer ; but the engine has a crow of its own, and
a yell for going into tunnels, and a howl for coming out of
them, and hideous noises for all seasons and every inch of the

road. All the cocks in Lancashire might crow themselves hoarse ere I could hear them amid this din.

Day breaks fast, and the slender gray thread expands into a wide sheet of pale light. Against it the coldly violet clouds are defined in sharp and rigid relief. These are the fragments of the veil of night yielding slowly, and, as it were, reluctantly, to daylight. Slower and slower, almost imperceptibly, as day gains on night, one great bank of cloud sinks in nearly a horizontal line into Erebus, like a pair of flats in a theatrical spectacle; but the side pieces of clouds—the wings and set pieces, if I may call them so—split up into jagged, obstinate, refractory cloudlets over the sky, which by this time has turned from ashy pallid gray to silver blue—not sky-blue, as we generally understand it, yet—but a blue like that we see in the shadow part of silver lace. These clouds are of fantastic shapes : some are dark slices, long, and almost mathematically straight; others torn and zigzag-shaped; some take the semblance of fiendish heads, and hideous animals with more legs than were ever dreamt of in the philosophy of Buffon or Cuvier. Fast as the day breaks, and broad daylight as it is by this time, the genial, warming influence of the blessed sun is yet wanting. The guests are bidden and the banquet is spread ; but the bride and bridegroom are not come home from church yet. The contract is drawn up, but lacks the signature. The pyre is heaped up and needs only one friendly torch to set it in a blaze.

Coldly garish yet is the white, sunless day. Funereally black and dismal loom tufted masses of tall trees—their umbrageous mantles chequered here and there by diamond flashes of the sunlight coming up behind them. Coldly gray are the wide leas and ploughed fields. Coldly black are the hedgerows, and hayricks, and stunted pollard willows, and lonely cow-shippons. Coldly dark and dismal, rear their heads, the roofed posts of the electric telegraph—looking, in the dubious light, like gibbets. Coldly the wind keeps blowing in at the window ; so at least tells me my fellow-traveller in the gold pencil line—tells me so, too, in a remarkably discourteous tone, with some nonsensical allusion to the ear-ache. I shut the window and pity him. *He* thinks nothing of the break of day—thinks about it no more, nay, not so much as that flapping crow overhead—no more than that rustic in the clay-soiled fustian, who has been up since three to fodder the cows and lead Ball and Dapple to the pond to drink, and who now leans over a gate on the line, smoking his break-of-day pipe, and whistling bewhiles. And yet, perhaps, I libel this clay-stain d man. Perchance he *does* think of day and of its Maker —in his own rough untutored way, sees in the clouds, and the sky, and the light, as clear a connection between the varied Nature and the varied God, as he knows to exist between the two plain sets of iron rails on the gravel road before him, and the mighty terminus at Euston Square —two hundred miles away.

Wra-a-a-ah! the train enters a tunnel. All is black for half a dozen minutes—then emerging, we see the sun getting up in the East like a refreshed generous giant, scattering gold over the world.

Break of day after the Honourable Mrs. Plover's *soirée dansante*. The Honourable Mrs. Plover was the youngest and seventh daughter of General the Earl of Duxandraques of Liverwing Hall. The footmen at Liverwing have had for some years a somewhat Hebrew-Caucasian cast of countenance, and evil-minded men do say they are bailiffs in disguise. The noble lord's solicitor and heirs male do not dare to trust him, if they can help it, with as much wood as would serve for a lucifer match—so addicted is he to cutting down the timber on his estate, and afterwards ' cutting away ' with the ligneous proceeds to Hombourg or Baden-Baden. The Honourable Miss de Bressbohun (that is the family name of the Duxandraques) had for her fortune only a remarkably pretty face, and an assortment of the most captivating blonde ringlets you ever saw; so she married Mr. Rufus Plover, who is ambiguously known to be ' on 'Change ' and brings fabulously large sums of money off it. They have a grand country house at Gunnersbury, and a sweet little marine villa at Brighton—all Venetian blinds and dazzling stucco; and, to crown all, a jewel of a house, Number 402 (A), Toppletoton Street, Crinoline Square. In this Elysian mansion (Madame de Pompadour could not have spent more in upholstery upon it than did Mrs. Plover), the enchanting *soirées dansantes* of the Honourable Mrs. P are held.

This had been a grand night for the P. family. Half Long Acre in the way of carriages. Half the Heralds' College in the armorial bearings on the coach panels. Quite a Zoological Gardens of lions rampant, couchant, and passant, griffins sparring wildly with their paws at inoffensive shields, and birds', beasts', and fishes' heads drawn and quartered in every imaginary way. Quite a little course of ' Latin without a master ' in the heraldic mottos.

And such company! No merchants, nor ship-owners, nor

people of that sort—not even one of Mr. Plover's 'Exchange' friends. *Their* exclusion was won from Mr. P. after a hard battle the very morning of the ball, and only after the concession on the part of his lady of two trifles and a model of the Great Exhibition in confectionery, to be withdrawn from the *menu* of the supper. The nearest approach to commerce among the guests was the great Sir Blanke Cheque, the banker of Lombard Street, who has three daughters married to peers of the realm, and one to the Russian Count Candleatevich, who is immensely rich, but dare not return to Russia, where he would infallibly be knouted, have his nose and ears slit, and be sent to Tobolsk, for daring to overstay the time allowed him by the Czar for a continental trip, and for presuming to go to a concert where Miss Crotchet sang the 'Fair Land of Poland;' a due minute of which last crime was made the very next day by little Juda Benikowski, the Muscovite* Jew spy, and duly recorded against the count in the archives of the Russian Consulate General. Among the company were the noble Duke and Duchess of Garternee; the Earl and Countess of Anchorshect, and Ladies Fitzfluke (2); Field-Marshal Count Schlaghintern; the Ban of Lithuania; the Waywode of Bosnia; the Hospodar of Thrace; the new Bishop of Yellowjack Island, West Indies, the Mac Kit of that ilk in full Highland costume, with a dirk in his stocking worth five hundred pounds—having come to Mrs. Plover's straight from the anniversary of the Tossancaber Highland Association, where he danced more strathspeys on the table, emptied more mulls of snuff, and drank more glasses of whisky than I care to name. Then there was Chibouck Pasha, in a light frock-coat like that of an inspector of police, but with a blister of diamonds on his breast, a red cap, and a gorgeous beard.

There was Mr. Vatican O'Phocleide, M.P. for Barrybugle, Ireland, who had a slight dispute with the Hansom cabman who brought him to Toppletoton Street, and threatened to inflict personal chastisement on Berkely Montmorency, Mrs. P.'s sergeant-footman, for not rightly announcing his style and titles. There was old General Halberts, who served in the Prussian army at Leipsic, who was about sixty

---

* Nous avons changé tout ça—will say my Russian friends, who have so improved in civilisation within the last two years, that happening to turn over the leaves of a book called the "Journey due North" the other day at a stall—[the "Journey" was marked eightpence]—I thought I was reading the narrative of a nightmare.

years of age when that battle was fought, but is about fifty-one or two now, has very black hair and whiskers and moustachios, but being rather shaky and tremulous (not with age, of course), got nervous at the great confusion of carriages at the top of the street, and chose to dismount and walk to 402 (A), whereby he became entangled between one of Mr. Bunter's pastry-cook's men, and Ludovico Scartafaccio from Modena (with his orchestra on wheels, drawn by a pony of a Modenese cast of countenance), and unluckily hooked himself on to an area railing by his diamond-hilted sabre, and the collar of the Golden Fleece, from which unpleasant position he was at length extricated by policeman P. 95, and Silver Sam, the link-boy.

Finally, to mention a few more notabilities, there was Bohwanie Lall, from Calcutta, a being strongly resembling a cocoa-nut candle swathed in a pair of white muslin curtains, bound round with bell-ropes of diamonds, pearls, and emeralds, and surmounted by a *toupée* of birds-of-paradise feathers. There was the author of the last new novel, and the last new painter, and the last new preacher, and the last new lion of whatever shape or degree he might be. There was Professor Oxalicacides, from Breslau, who, in his lectures on *hygiène* lately, gravely hinted his suspicions that the English sweet-stuff makers adulterated Everton toffee with sugar of lead and *aqua tofana*. There was Madame Sostenuta, and Mademoiselle Orphea Sospianti, and Signor Portamento from the Italian Opera, engaged to sing professionally; and with them Herr Bompazek, the great German basso, with a voice from the tombs, and hair dreadfully long and dishevelled. There were battalions of grand old dowagers in various stages of velvet and satin, more or less airy. There were frigid chaperons, so awful in their impressiveness that they seemed to possess the capacity of doing the office of Medusa's head for you at once. There were anxious mammas; and simpering young dandies in colossal white neckcloths, and feet so tiny as to endanger their centre of gravity, and to render their tumbling over in the midst of a quadrille anything but unlikely. There were flushed-faced old papas. There was Jullien's band; and there were cohorts, Pyrrhic phalanxes, of the dear English girls, the forms, the faces, the bright eyes, the red lips, the laughing lips that I will defy you to match— Mademoiselle Eulalie, or Signora Bianca, or Fräulein Trudschen, or Donna Inez, or Sudarinia Nadiezda, or Khanoum Haidee, Gulnare, or Dudu, any summer or winter's day the whole year through. And so, through the noise of the night season, the Hon. Mrs Plover's *soirée dansante* proceeded.

How many quadrilles, and polkas, *valses à deux temps*, Schottisches and mazurkas there were ; how the ' lamps shone o'er fair women and brave men ;' how ' a thousand hearts beat happily,' and ' eyes looked love to eyes which spoke again ;' how hands were squeezed in conservatories, and soft nothings whispered in balconies ; how crushed white roses were ravished from unresisting Sabines by impetuous dragoons, and tulle ribbons purloined by Cupid-struck undergraduates of the University of Oxford, tell, philosopher in the ill-washed neckcloth and the dress-coat, to whose appearance candle-light was a decided advantage—philosopher, too awkward to dance, too timid to play whist, too moody to do aught else save lounge against door-posts and observe. How Lord Claude Pettitoes proposed (over strawberry ice) to Mrs. Vanilla, the Cuban widow ; how rude General Halberts made a dash at a model of Osler's crystal fountain in barley-sugar, and ate the fluted column up bodily. How Chibouck Pacha quaffed champagne till his face shone again ; and Lady Blanche Pettitoes (sister of Lord Claude and daughter of the Marchioness of Dayryfedde) complained to her mamma, that he, the Pacha, squeezed her ; how Mr. Remanet, M.P., insisted on talking agricultural statistics to his partner ;—how the various lions—literary, artistic, and scientific—howled, roared, and were stirred up with poles of different lengths, and were trotted out in different corners of the different *salons*. How dancing commenced again after supper ; how Mrs. Plover was here, there, and everywhere, with a smile for everybody and a frown for nobody, save that sad fellow the member for Barrybugle, who tried to get a circle together in the boudoir, to discuss the wrongs of Ireland. How Bohwanic Lall from Calcutta, being strictly of the Brahminical persuasion, rigidly refused to partake of supper with unbelievers, and was served with a light repast of pistachio nuts and water-ice in an adjoining apartment,—though my private opinion is that he subsequently devoured a trayful of real patties on the staircase. How the professional singers sang like syrens, and Herr Bompazek shook the very chandeliers with his sepulchral tones. How all these things were done, tell, fashionable Muse of *soirées dansantes*, if, Muse, thou wert honoured with a card for Mrs. Plover's, which I was not !

When daybreak came at last, how garish the yellow candle-light looked against the strong beams of the morning, the stalwart workers, the early-to-bed goers, and early risers. How they beat down the flickering wax-ends in their sockets. And the pretty girls—pretty still—yet looking pale, and a trifle draggled, and a thought sickly. There was a faint odour through the crowded rooms of faded roses and spilt perfumes, and spent champagne corks. The Honourable Mrs. Plover's *soirée* was over. Slowly down the grand stair-case came the company, looking, if I may be permitted the use of vulgarism, 'seedy.' Slowly the yawning footmen opened the carriage-doors, and the sleepy horses clattered off. This was break of day—the day the grubs have to earn their daily bread by—and it was time for the butterflies to be in bed.

XVIII.

ARCADIA.

Arcadia !—what a nice place it must have been to be sure ! A perpetual pic-nic, without wasps or thunder-storms, and with nothing to pay. A smiling landscape, all gently undulating —no fierce rocks or yawning chasms. Banks on which wild thyme and violets continually grow. Eternal summer. Fruits, flowers, and odoriferous herbs. Innocent flocks of more inno-cent sheeplings; soft, mild, benignant, undesigning bleaters with dainty coats of whitest wool, hanging in worsted ringlets, unsmirched by the red ochre or cinnabar of mercenary grazier ; yet when the sun rises or sets, gleaming with iris tints from Nature's prism, making of each a mutton-rainbow—like Mr. Hunt's sheep in his picture of our English Coasts. And then the shepherds with their long hair confined by an azure ribbon ; their abundance of clean linen, and guilelessness of braces ; their silken hose, and shoon with purple heels ; their harmless sports consisting in shooting at a stuffed bird on a highly decorated Maypole with a cross-bow bedecked with ribbons. And the shepherdesses, with auburn tresses and wide-spread-ing straw hats, with golden crooks, and wreaths of flowers, and petticoats of gold and silk and satin brocade. And the old women—the Dorcases and Cicelys—dear old dames with silvery hair, scarlet cloaks, and ebony crutch-sticks ; but who never scolded, oh no, nor had the rheumatism, nor groaned about their precious bones and the badness of the times. There were no Game Laws in Arcadia, no union workhouses, no beer-shops, no tally-men, no police. There wer **balls every** and all day long in Arcadia; endless country dances. No shepherd beat another shepherd or shepherdess with his crook, or a poker, or pewter pot; for there was no quarrelling—save here and there a trifle of bickering, a transient fugacious jealousy when Celia detected Corydon kissing of Phyllis, or if Sacharissa in a pet broke Damon's pipe. But these fleeting differences would soon be reconciled; all would kiss and be friends; and banquets to re-united friendship would take place in cool grottoes on carpets of fair flowers; the viands (fruits, syllabubs, and cakes of finest flour), cooled by murmuring, rippling, pebbly, sparkling streamlets, and by fragrant boughs outside the cave, drooping with foliage and luscious fruit, and waved by the pitying summer breeze; sheltering the grotto's inmates from the burly sun's too bold salute. And the sky was very blue, and the birds sang carols continually.

Yet, though the golden age be gone, and there are no more picturesque shepherds or shepherdesses, save in the canvasses of Watteau and Laneret, Arcadia still exists. It lives in the very heart of London.

The prototype of the London arcade was, undoubtedly, the Oriental Bazaar. There is not a town in Turkey or Hindostan, without some dirty, stifling, covered passage, both sides of which overflow with amphitheatres of knick-knackery for sale. The Bezesteen of Stamboul is a genuine arcade, with all the crowding and confusion, the kaleidoscopic arrangement and gossip-bargaining of the Arcadia of England.

The French, who manage so many things better than we ourselves do, and not a few so much worse, have long had an Arcadia of their own. As a special measure of relief for their legionary *flâneurs* or street-pacers—driven, in wet weather, from the much-sauntered-over Boulevards—there were devised the unrivalled galleries and passages which are the delight of Paris, the admiration of strangers, and the bread-winners of unnumbered artificers, factors, and retailers of those heterogeneous odds and ends known as *articles de Paris*. To the Passage de l'Opéra, des Panoramas, du Saumon, Jouffroy; from the Galeries Vivienne, Colbert, and Véro-Dodat; the caricatures of Gavarni and Grandville, the classic lithographs of Jullien, the novels of Paul de Kock, the statuettes of Danton, and the ballads of Mademoiselle Eloïsa Puget owe their chief celebrity. Beneath those glass roofs literary and artistic reputations have been won and lost.

Milan followed in the wake of Paris, and the city of the Duomo boasts many plate-glass-adorned and knick-knack-crowded covered thoroughfares. Vienna and Berlin followed; but England knew not arcades before the present century. Some inventive genius accomplished a great feat in conjunction with certain shopkeepers and the Cork and Burlington estates. He brought Arcadia into Piccadilly, and built the Burlington Arcade.

At first the shops of this Arcade were small and dark. They sold no articles of positive necessity: the useful arts were repellent to Burlingtonian notions of industry: and luxury was almost exclusively purveyed for. Burlington (as became a comital godfather) was intensely aristocratic. Boots and shoes and gloves were certainly sold; but they fitted only the most Byronically small and symmetrical hands and feet; none but the finest and most odoriferous leathers were employed in their confection, and none but the highest prices charged for them. The staple manufactures of this Arcade have been in turns jewellery, fans, feathers, French novels, pictorial albums, annuals, scrap-books, caricatures, harps, accordions, quadrille music, illuminated polkas, toys, scents, hair-brushes, odoriferous vinegar, Rowlands' Macassar Oil, zephyr paletôts, snuff-boxes, jewelled whips, clouded canes, lemon-coloured gloves, and false whiskers. Scarcely a fashionable vice, an aristocratic frivolity, or a Belgravian caprice, but had (and has) a representative in the Burlington Arcade. It was a little Vanity Fair. I have walked it many and many a time for years, thinking of John Bunyan, and wondering which was Britain Row and Portugal Row.

There was but one active handicraft exercised in the Arcade, and that was hair-cutting. The handicraftsmen cut your hair in sophisticated saloons, decorated with fallacious mural paintings of impossible Grecian landscapes, with flaming Greeks and Turks fighting. Below they inveigled you to buy drugs and potions wherewith to dye the gray hairs you should be proud of, blue black; and stuffs to make you emulate the smell of the civet, or the musk rat, and hogs' lard condimented into bears' grease, and wigs;—woven lies made from dead men's hair to thatch live fools. Further on, there were boots to pinch feet, corsets to tighten waists, and gloves to cramp hands. Boys with bundles were rigidly excluded from the precincts. Smoking was not allowed through its length or breadth. It was paraded by padded, tight-booted, tight-girthed, wigged old beaus striving to look like boys of twenty; by boys aping the vices of old men; by carpet warriors, and by knights fresh from Almack tournaments.

The department of Arcadia to which I have just (and it may seem to you rather harshly) alluded, has not been free from the vicissitudes, humiliations, and mutabilities common to buildings and thoroughfares, as well as to men. Yet, on the whole, it may be said that the Burlingtonians have been a prosperous and well-to-do community. If Burlington had appealed to the wisdom, learning, good taste; or to the scientific or philosophic tendencies of humanity, it might have been bankrupt long ago, and its traders gone barefoot. But Burlington has calculated, like the quack doctor, that of every fifty passers-by forty are fools. With Robert Macaire, it has studied the immortal axiom delivered by that sage to Bertrand, ' The day passes, but the fools remain ;' and has occupied itself with what is co-existent with the world and with humanity— human folly. But for such customers, the booths in Vanity Fair, wherever its tents be pitched, would drive a poor trade indeed.

I will leave the province of Burlington, and direct my attention to that of Exeter. One was of comital rank; but this is the fief of a marquisate. A word as to its antecedents.

Where now stands the street that forms the approach to Rennie's magnificent bridge—the Bridge of Waterloo ; the bridge of gorgeous sunset views—the Bridge of Sighs—the Rialto of transpontine theatricals, industrials of the New Cut, Elephant and Castle omnibuses, and women without names, without hope, without lives (save a certain dog-like existence), there stood, before I was born, certain dingy brick houses. One of them was the old office of the old (and now dead) ' Courier ' newspaper ; and many may be old enough to remember the bulletin of the great victory of Waterloo being pasted up on the ' Courier ' windows on the 21st of June, 1815. Another was the old Lyceum Theatre ; a third was Mr. Day's trunk-shop. Close beside these buildings, stood two mighty elephants' tusks and a burly Beefeater, directing the eager sight-seer, the impatient country cousin, the enthusiastic holiday-maker, to the Museum or Menagerie of Wild Animals, known throughout the United Kingdom as Crosse's Wild Beast Show. Here had the lord of ' aitches ' and the Patent Theatres—the great John Philip Kemble—borrowed of Mr. Crosse the rhinoceros on which he took his ever-memorable ride through Covent Garden Market—in the early morning, when the sun was bright, and saloop-stalls were yet about—as dignified as a lord, playing the fool as only wise men can. Here had the howlings of unnumbered savage brutes, the rugged Russian bear, the armed rhinoceros, like the Hyrcanian beast, shook

the bricks of Exeter Change. Ye spotted snakes, ye dwelt
there; hyenas, ye have laughed; jackals, ye have wept
deceivingly; blue-faced monkeys, ye have shown your cerulean visages in those byegone Arcadian precincts. Here the
" White Milliner," supposed to have been the Duchess of Tyr-
connel fallen upon evil days, sold ribbons and gauzes. There
held out against the united forces of Apothecaries' Hall and
His Majesty's foot-guards Chunee, unconquered of refractory
elephants. There he laughed at pounds of calomel and bales of
drugs, and shook his sides with elephantine scorn at guns and
pistols; till the great, embrowned regulation muskets of His
Majesty's foot-guards cracked his leviathan skin and let his
giant life out. Crosse's *must* have been an exhibition. Why
wasn't I alive when Exeter Change was extant, and the admission ' up stairs ' one shilling, or under?

But Arcadia was fated to come again; and Exeter Change,
though it retains its name, has changed its locale, and is no
more what it was. It is a changed change. It had a transition
state—a sort of chrysalis-like grubhood as a bad bazaar—a
very bad and lame imitation of those Margate and Ramsgate,
and general watering-place knick-knack shops, where there are
countless assemblages of trifles, unconsidered, because really
useless, and where you may, perhaps, (if you have great good
luck) win, after the investment of from seven to fifteen shillings,
such a prize as a German silver pencil-case, or a tea-pot stand
of plaited rushes. And then Exeter Change became a wilderness of bricks and mortar, scaffold-poles, hods, ladders and
ropes, and it and its neighbourhood went mad on the building
question, after which and (up to 1853) ultimately, the Change
changed its site, and burst on the world as an arcade—an
Arcade of desolation, silence, despair.

What can I compare it to? The street of the tombs at
Pompeii—the Via Sacra with all the shops shut up and half
a dozen funerals of Sextus Quintilius Somebody winding their
way through its mournful lengths? A street in Tripoli or
Algiers at mid-day when the sun is very hot and the plague is
very bad about? The ' dark entry ' in Canterbury Cathedral
Yard multiplied by two? Lawrence Pountney Hill (about the
dreariest of thoroughfares I know) of a Sunday afternoon?
Anything, anywhere, in any climate, country, age, or circumstance that is gloomy, dismal, heart-depressing, unventilated,
graveyard-smelling—dull. This gloomy avenue leads from
one and into another of the merriest London streets you would
wish to find : one the bustling Catherine Street with its noisy

News Exchange, and Old Drury (though to be sure that is not
so very gay) at the top; the other the lively Wellington
Street, embellished as it is with one of the most abusive cab-
stands in the metropolis, and the sprightly Lyceum Theatre.
But the Arcade is *so* dull. Some ghastly artist undertook, on
its construction, to decorate it with mural arabesques.   He
has succeeded in filling the spaces between the shop-windows
with some skeleton figures;—dripping, faded funerealities.
These 'arabesques' ('mauresques' would be more appropriate,
for they are very mortuary) twist themselves into horrible
skeleton presentments, all in a leaden, deadened, dusky tone of
colour; and, high over gas-lamps and grimly clambering about
shop-fronts, are melancholy dolphins and writhing serpents,
and attenuated birds of paradise; all looking intensely wretched
at the positions in which they find themselves.   Likewise
there are scrolls, which the Furies might twist in their hair;
and leaves which seem ready to drop off for very deadness, and
sepulchral beadings, and egg-and-tongue fillets like rows of
coffin nails.

And are there shops in this Arcadia? There are. And are
these shops tenanted? Well; they *are* tenanted; but not
much.   A great many of the shops have had occupants; but
somehow or other the occupants are continually vacating.
They never stopped. Doubtless they had many good and
sufficient reasons for so persistently continuing not to remain.
They went abroad, relinquished business, made their fortunes
—perhaps.   I can remember in this changing Change, house
and estate agents, servants' registry offices, coal-mine offices
(with neat little hampers of Wallsend in the window—a
novelty which would answer well, I opine, with a horse-
dealer, if he were to put a few pasterns and fetlocks and a
horse-shoe or two in *his* window), booksellers, newsvenders
and publishers (news and publicity here!), cigar-shops, tailors
and habit-makers, milliners, dressmakers, and bonnet-builders,
architects and surveyors, and a toy-shop: *that* didn't last.
The drums and trumpets, the miniature guns and swords
sounded and wielded there must have been of the same sort
as those used at Napoleon's midnight review; the Tombolas
must have had death's heads; the Jacks must have sprung,
not of boxes, but of sarcophagi; the kaleidoscopes must have
shown nothing but prismatic goblins; the accordions played
nothing but the Dead March in Saul.

I knew a French bookseller who established himself in
Exeter Arcadia, with his wife and olive-branches round him,

vainly thinking to live by vending the lively *nouvellettes* and *vaudevilles* of the Land of the Gaul. But his little children pined among the brumous shades of the 'Cade, and sighed, like Mary Queen of Scots, for the fair land of France again— so the Frenchman vamosed. I also knew a confident foreigner who came here in the Exhibition year of '51, with two stools, a desk, and a Nugent's dictionary, on a vague speculation of interpreting, translating for, or verbally assisting foreigners visiting London during the Exhibition season. ' Informations-Bureau ' he called his shop, if I am not mistaken. But, as he spoke no English, and nobody came to make any inquiries who spoke any foreign language, his bureau came to nothing, and he vamosed too.

Desolate, dreary, weary, as any grange with any number of moats, art thou, Arcadia of Exeter ! Yet there is hope for thee. ' Hope comes to all,' says Milton, and may I live to see the day when thy shops shall overflow with merchandise, when thy outlets shall be blocked up with customers, when thy fame shall be spread among the nations, and excursion trains start from the uttermost ends of the earth to visit thee. Till then, farewell, or be, as heretofore, a desert—not howling, for there are no wild animals to howl in thee—an empty sepulchre, a deserted wine-cellar, an abandoned quarry, an exhausted coal-mine, a ruined temple, or ' Ninny's Tomb,' meet only for the nocturnal rendezvous of some Pyramus of the Strand with some Thisbe of Adam Street, Adelphi ; be anything thou listest, for of a verity, Exeter, I (and, doubt- less, my readers) am weary of thee.

The Lowther Arcade—I seek not to disguise it under any plausible incognito, for I am proud of it—is a tube of shops running from St. Martin's Churchyard into the Strand, very nearly opposite Hungerford Market. There is, frequently, very much noise in this tube as in that far-famed one across the Menai Straits that Mr. Stephenson built ; and there are collisions and signals—but here my railroad similes end ; for, in lieu of being a pitch-dark colour with grim iron-ribbed sides, with a flooring of slippery rails on which huge locomo- tive dragons with many jointed tails of carriages glide, this tube is light and airy, and roofed with glass. It is noisy ; but not with the screaming and snorting, and panting of engines, the rattling of wheels, and the jangling of chains : it is resonant with the pattering of feet, the humming of voices, the laughter of children, the rustling of silken dresses, and buying, selling, bargaining, and chaffering.

The commodities vended in the Lowther Arcade I may classify under three heads : Toys, Jewellery, and Minor Utilities, about each of which I have a word to say.

Imprimis of toys. Enormous, preposterous, marvellous is Lowther in respect of toys. She possesses amphitheatres, rows upon rows, galleries upon galleries : Great Pyramids of Egypt, Great Towers of Belus, Great Tuns of Heidelberg, Great Beds of Ware, Great Dragons of Wantley, Giant Helmets of Otranto—of what ? Of toys. Birmingham is the toyshop of Europe ; Blair's Preceptor and Pinnock's Treasury of Knowledge say it is. But no : Lowther is. Look around, if you are sceptical, upon the toys of all nations, and for children of all ages, which give children such exquisite delight in playing with them—which give papa and mamma delight scarcely less exquisite in buying them. Cosmopolitan toys, too. Look at the honest, hearty, well-meaning toys of old England. The famous cockhorses of such high blood and mettle, that the blood has broken out all over their skins in an eruption of crimson spots ; so full of spirit that their manes stand bolt upright, and their tales project like comets ; such high and mighty cockhorses, that they disdain to walk, and take continual carriage exercise on wooden platforms, running on wheels. The millers' carts, so bravely painted, so full of snowy sacks, supposed to contain best boulted flour ; but, in reality, holding sawdust. The carriers' carts, the mail phaetons, the block-tin omnibuses, the deal locomotives with woolly steam rushing from the funnels, the brewers' drays, and those simple, yet interesting, vehicles of plain white deal—exact models, in fact, of the London scavengers' carts—so much in request at Brighton and Margate for the cartage of sand, pebbles, and sea-weed, and sometimes used as hearses for the interment of a doll, or as Bath chairs for the exercise of an unwilling poodle.

Can you look unmoved, although you _be_ a philosopher and your name Zeno, Plato, or Socrates, on the great Noah's arks —those Edens of wooden zoology, where the mouse lies down with the cameleopard (and is nearly as big), where the lion is on such familiar terms with the jackass as to allow him to stand atop of him, with his hoofs in his jagged mane ; where the duck is neatly packed (for more commodious stowage) in the bosom of the tigress, and then stands on his head between the fore feet of the elephant ? Can you passively inspect the noble fluffy donkeys, with real fur, and the nicely equipoised panniers, and harness of softest, brownest leather ? And those desirable family mansions, the dolls' houses, with the capital modern furniture, plate, glass and linen, which commands to sell which Messrs. Musgrove and Gadsden are not likely to be honoured. And the glorious kitchens, with that bottle-jack and meat-screen and dripping-pan, at which was roasted the wooden sirloin of beef, painted and varnished. The boxes of red-handled carpenters' tools, which cut, and sawed, and chiselled nothing but children's fingers. The boxes of tea-things—now of wood, now of more ambition, tin and lead. The dolls—from Missey's flaxen-headed beauty, with the movable blue eyes and the elegant pink leather extremities, swathed in silver tissue-paper, to Master Jackey's favourite policeman, A. 1, very blue in attire, and very stiff, with a very glazed hat, an intensely legible number, and varnished wooden boots. The fierce Hungarian hussar on horseback, with that cruel curved wire and counter-weight stuck through his entrails, with which he maintains an unceasing see-saw. The drummer with movable arms. The musical toys, the accordions, the marvellous kaleidoscopes regarded at first as phantasmagoria of delight; but, breaking, or being broken, soon disclosing to our great disappointment and disgust, nothing but a disc of tin, a fragment of smoked glass, and some tawdry coloured chips? And such is life.

Hoops, nine-pins, drums covered with real parchment, innocently white above, but which, were you to tear them, and look at the underpart, would, I gage, be found to be fragments of old deeds and indentures—such is life again : French toys, fierce toys, warlike toys, smelling of Young France, and glory, and blood—such as miniature cannon, lancers, sabretasches, war steamers armed en flûte, sabres, muskets, shakos, and tricoloured flags surmounted by the resuscitated Eagle of France. German toys, which like everything else coming from Deutschland, are somewhat quaint, and somewhat eccentric, and a thought misty : for example, queer old carved men and women, in queer attitudes, and animals whose anatomy is likewise of the queerest kind, and who yet have a queer expression of life and animation about them. Tortuous games, played with hammers and dice, and bells, and little men, which remind you somehow, you know not why, of Rhine Schlosses, and Gnomes and Undine, and Albert Dürer's mailed knights. Then the Germans have monks and hermits who open, like the dolls' houses, cupboard-door fashion, and show you (where gentlemen are generally supposed to accommodate

—well, there is no harm in it—their insides) little chapels and oratories, with little altars and candles and priests. And who but the Germans too, would make long panoramas and dioramas opening in the accordion and collapsing manner, and strange monsters in boxes? An infinity of other *jou-joux*, such as India-rubber balls, whips of all shapes and capacities for chair or cock-horse flagellation, skipping-ropes, flutes, spades, rakes and hoes : all these are to be found in the toy department of the Lowther Arcade.

These toys are sold by bright-eyed damsels, and they are bought by plump married couples, and pretty cousins, and prim yet benignant old aunts, and cross yet kind old grandmothers—yea and by cross-grained bachelors and sulky mysogynists, and crabbed City men. I have seen a man—one of those men who were he but five-and-twenty you would immediately feel inclined to call, mentally, an old fellow—enter Lowther Arcadia by the Strand, looking as savage, as ill-tempered, as sulky as the defendant in a breach-of-promise case, dragging rather than leading a child ; but I have seen him emerge ten minutes afterwards with an armful of toys, looking sunny with good humour.

And they are bought, these toys, for that marvellous little people who are the delight and hope and joy, the sorrow, solace, chief anxiety, and chief pleasure, of grown-up man and womankind :—for those little manuscripts of the book of life yet unsent to press, unset up in stern uncompromising type, as yet uncirculating in proof-sheets for the inspection of the judge : to be bound and published and criticised at the last ;— for those innocent little instruments of even-handed justice— the justice that makes of our children the chief punishment or reward to us—a heaven or a torment about us here in life. And whether Arcadia live or die, and whether those ruddy children and these plump parents continue or surcease, there will be toy-shops and toys and parents and children to purchase them to the end, I hope ; for I believe toys to be the symbolic insignia of the freemasonry of childhood—as aprons and mallets, adzes and jewels are to the older freemasons of Lincoln's Inn Fields—and that they are bonds of union, pledges of affection, from the man-child to the child-man ; and that they are substantial lectures on useful arts and useful recreations ; and although of course I would exclude from my Tommy's or Emily's play-box every toy that could suggest or hint at cruelty, intolerance, injustice, or wrong, I do think that

English toys (I speak not of tho Gallic and bellicose ones) are mainly honest and well-meaning, and even moral playthings. I love toys.

The second department of Lowther Arcadia of which I would wish, cursorily, to treat, is that connected with the sale of jewellery. The Lowther *bijouterie* is certainly unique. It may want the intrinsic value of the productions of Howell and James or Hunt and Roskell. The Lowtherian brilliants may not be of a water so fine as those of Regent Street or Cornhill; but the jewellery of my Arcade is as sparkling and as showy, as gay and as variegated, as any assemblage of gems you like to mention—the jewel-house in the Tower of London, or the Queen of Spain's jewels, or Mr. Hope's. The gold is as yellow; though, perhaps, not quite so valuable as any Brown and Wingrove have to refine. The emeralds are green, the rubies red, the turquoises blue : and what other colours would you have emeralds, and rubies, and turquoises to be ? Lowther shines, too, in cameos—none of your shrinking, shamefaced, genuine Roman ones—but great, bold, bouncing, pictorial pancakes : heads of Minerva as big as Bristol Channel oysters, and trios of Graces vying in size with bread-and-butter plates. Lowther hath, in its huge glass cases and beneath glass domes, good store of necklaces (the pearl ones like strings of varnished plovers' eggs), bracelets, agraffes, buckles, shirt-pins, hair ornaments ; but it is in the article of brooches that she chiefly shines : brooches with a vengeance. Geological brooches, comprising every variety of strata, from blue clay to red sandstone, genteelly cut, polished, and set. Pictorial brooches, forcing on you the counterfeit presentments of a heterogeneous assemblage of celebrated female characters : Mary Queen of Scots, Madame de la Vallière, Marie Antoinette, and Jenny Lind ; with a more cautious selection from among the gentlemen, ranging from Oliver Cromwell to Buffon the naturalist, or from Henry the Eighth to M. Kossuth. Brooches for hair, and simple jet or cornelian brooches. Landscape brooches, where the lake of Chamouni, and Mont Blanc—the monarch of mountains, who was crowned so long ago—are depicted in a vivid blue and green manner—astonishing to the eyes of Professor Forbes, or Mr. Brockedon. Brooches for all ages, from that blushing girl of eighteen yonder—for whom the fond youth in the astonishing coat and the alarming waistcoat is purchasing a gigantic oval half-length of Charles the Second set in elaborate filigree—down to the white-headed old grandmamma, doubly widowed and doubly childless, who will here provide herself with a cheap yet handsome locket-brooch wherein to preserve a lock of sunny brown hair, all that is left (save a ciphering-book) to remind her of that gallant nephew Harry, who went down in the war-steamer 'Phlegethon,' with all hands, far in the Southern Seas.

Nor is it the worse for being unreal—sham is hardly the word; for Lowther says boldly, 'Here is my jewellery; I will sell it to you at a price. If you choose to believe my half-crown cameo-moons are made of green cheese, my eighteen-penny bracelets sapphires or opals, my three-and-sixpenny necklaces barbaric pearl and gold, believe and be blest. We do not attempt to deceive you; if our price be too cheap, don't buy.' It may seem inconsistent in me, who have so lately borne rather hard upon the arcade of Burlington, that I should defend the fictitious gems that have their abode in the arcade of Lowther. But I consider this : that there is a difference between a sham deliberate, a wilful sophistry or wanton piece of casuistry, and a lie confessant; a work of fiction for instance—a novel, a fable, or a pleasant tale. As such, I consider the jewels of Lowther. Is it because my pretty trades-man's daughter, my humble milliner or sempstress; even my comely cook, housemaid, or damsel-of-all-work cannot afford the real barbaric pearl and gold—the real rose and table diamonds—that they are to be debarred from wearing innocent adornments, wherewith to accomplish the captivation (which their bright faces have begun) of their respective swains and sweethearts? No. Leaving their aristocratic sisters to disport themselves in real Cashmeres from Delhi and Allahabad, and real lace shawls from Brussels and Malines, they are content with humble Paisleys, and unobtrusive Greenocks; so, abandoning genuine precious stones, genuine guinea gold, genuine pearls and cameos, to perhaps not the happiest, but at least the more fortunate of their sex, they shall revel as it pleases them in the eighteenpenny finery of this Arcadia ; and Samuel or William walking 'along with them,' or 'keeping of 'em company' in the smartest of surtouts and the whitest of Berlin gloves, on crowded steamboats, or amid the velvetty glades of the metro-politan parks, shall be as proud of them and of their jewels as though they were duchesses.

One more department of Arcadia yet remains to be explored. This is the section devoted to what I may call minor utilities. and though minor, they occupy a very considerable portion of the Lowther Arcade. Heaped in wild confusion—though not worse confounded—on the estrades of half a dozen merchants, are different ranges of shelves ; grades on grades of such articles as cakes of Windsor soap, shaving-dishes, shaving-brushes, pocket-combs, snuffer-trays, bronze candlesticks, lucifer-boxes, pipe-lights, sealing-wax : hair, tooth, clothes, and blacking-brushes, French coffee-pots, tea-canisters, workboxes, nutmeg-graters, paper-weights, pencil-cases, china mantel-shelf ornaments, knick-knacks for drawing-room tables, artificial flowers, watch-chains, perfumery, hair-pins, plaster statuettes, penknives, scissors, dog-chains, walking-sticks, housewife-cases, knives, forks, and spoons, china plates, cups and saucers, wine-glasses, decanters, presents from Brighton, tokens from Ramsgate, letter-clips, portfolios, music-cases, reticules, scent-bottles, and fans. There is scarcely a minor want, an everyday wish in the catalogue of everyday wants and wishes, but which can be supplied from the delightfully egregious farrago of fancy hucksteries here collected. It is the Bagdad of housekeeping odds and ends, the very place I should advise all those about to marry to visit when they have found that besides the household furniture, plate, linen, bedding, pots, and pans they have discovered indispensable in fitting up their bridal mansion, there are yet a thousand and one things they cannot do without, and which nothing but a walk through Arcadia will satisfy them that they really want.

The most wonderful thing connected with the cosmopolitan merchandise displayed in the Lowther Arcade, is the apparent recklessness with which the commodities are exposed to the touch of the passers-by, and the enormous apparent confidence which their proprietors appear to place in their customers. The toys are tested, and the minor utilities examined ; the musical instruments are sounded at the good pleasure of those without, whether they mean buying or not buying ; but be assured, O man of sin—pilferer of small wares and petty larcener—that there is an eye within keenly glancing from some loophole contrived between accordions and tin breast-plates that watches your every movement, and is ' fly,'—to use a term peculiarly comprehensible to dishonest minds—to the slightest gesture of illegal conveyancing.

The Lowther Arcade should, to be properly appreciated and admired, be viewed at three widely distant periods of the day. First, in the early morning, when the bells of St. Martin's have just commenced carilloning the quarter-chimes to eight. Then the myriad wares that Lowther has to sell are scattered about in a manner reminding you of the parti-coloured chaos of one of the Lowther's own kaleidoscopes indefinitely magnified and blown to pieces, or of the wardrobe and property room of a large theatre combined, when the *employés* are ' taking stock.' In the midst of this chaotic olla podrida of oddities pick their way, with cautious steps yet nimble, the Arcadian shepherds and shepherdesses, wearing mostly over their pastoral garments large aprons and pinafores of brown holland and gray calico. With feather brooms or gauzy dusters they dust and cleanse and furbish and rub up and brighten all the multifarious paraphernalia of their calling ; and, swift the amphitheatrical benches or grades are crowned with rainbow toys, or glittering glass cases symmetrically arranged, artistically displayed to catch the eye and provoke the appetite of taste. Some pilgrim from the west may, at such times, fortuitously be found gliding among the fancy goods that corruscate the pavement, nervously apprehensive of stepping an inch to the right or to the left, lest he should ' fall into a bit of property ' his own might not be sufficient to replace.

I have no room for statistics, so I will not enter into any calculation as to the numerical quantities of fancy wares vended in the Lowther Arcade ; the gross amount of money received, the average number of visitors, or matters of that kind. I may passingly observe that there are toys, and gems, and knick-knacks here, that are things of great price to-day, and positive drugs in the market to-morrow. At one time the public toy-taste runs upon monkeys that run up sticks, or old gentlemen that swing by their own door-knockers, squeaking dreadfully the while : at another period the rage is for the squeezeable comic masks and faces (at first and fallaciously supposed to be made of gutta-percha, but ultimately discovered through the agency of a precocious philosopher, aged seven—who ate one of them—to be formed from a composition of glue, flour, and treacle). Now, horrible writhing gutta-percha snakes are up, and now they are down; now pop-guns go off and now hang fire.

There are certain toys and fancy ornaments that always, however, preserve a healthy vogue, and command a ready sale. Of the former, the Noah's arks, and dolls' houses, and India-rubber balls, may be mentioned ; although their nominal nomenclatures are sometimes altered to suit the exigencies of fashion. Thus we are enticed to purchase Uncle Buncle's Noah's ark, Peter Parley's balls, or Jenny Lind's Doll's mansion. Of the fancy goods, I may hint fugitively that some attenuated vases of artificial flowers under glass shades, I have known as Queen Adelaide's Own, Victoria's Wreath, The Jenny Lind Bouquet, and the Eugenie Vase. These flowerets are much cultivated as chimney ornaments by maiden ladies in the neighbourhoods of Peckham Rise and Muswell Hills. Lastly, there is a model, or sample piece of workmanship, of which copies are to this day sold, principally to the ladies, which I have known for nearly twenty years. It consists of a hollow cottage of latitudinarian architecture, composed of plaster-of-Paris, with stained glass windows, and with a practicable chimney. In the hollow part of the edifice an oil-lamp is nocturnally placed ; and the light pouring through the windows, and the smoke curling up the chimney (not altogether inodorously), produce a charming and picturesque effect. This building has had many names. When I knew it first, it was, I think, William Tell's Châlet. Then it was the Birthplace of the Poet Moore. Then it was Shakspeare's House. Then Her Majesty's Highland Hut or Shieling, near Balmoral, in Scotland. And now it is the Birthplace of Mrs. Harriet Beecher Stowe. House of many names ! farewell ! and thou, too, Arcadia ! till at some future day I wander through thy spangled glades again.

XIX.

TRAVELS IN CAWDOR STREET.

To the unobservant peripatetic, Cawdor Street is merely a thoroughfare, leading from Soho to Oxford Street, just as the ' Venus de Medici ' would be the stone figure of a lady, and nothing more, and the ' Transfiguration ' of Raphael simply so much canvas, covered with so much paint. To the ordinary street-lounger, even Cawdor Street can only offer a few musty shops, filled with ancient furniture ; half a dozen dingy bookstalls, some brokers' shops, and a score or more receptacles for cloudy-looking oil pictures in tarnished frames.

And, perhaps, this is the most sensible way of looking, not only at Cawdor Street, but at things generally. Why the plague should we always be making painful and blue-looking anatomical preparations, when we should be satisfied with the nice, wholesome-looking, superficial cuticle ? Why should we insist on rubbing the plating off our dishes and sugar-basins, and on showing the garish, ungenteel-looking copper beneath ?

Why should we lift up the corner of the show and pry out who pulls Punch's legs, and causes Shallabalah to leap ? Why can't we take Cawdor Street, its old curiosity-shops, brokers, book-stalls, and picture-dealers, the world generally, for granted ?

We ought to do so, perhaps ; but we can't. I am sure that I cannot. Cawdor Street is to me a fearful and wonderful country to be explored. There are mysteries in Cawdor Street to be unravelled, curiosities of custom and language to be descanted on, causes to be ascertained, and effects to be deduced. Though from eight to ten minutes' moderately rapid exercise of the legs with which Nature has provided you would suffice to carry you from one end of Cawdor Street to the other, I can sojourn for many hours in its mysterious precincts. I am an old traveller in Cawdor Street, and it may not be amiss to impart to you some of the discoveries I have made during these my travels.

I will spare you the definition of the geographical boundaries of Cawdor Street. I will be content with observing that its south-westerly extremity is within a hundred miles, as the newspapers say, of Princes Street, Soho. The climate may, on the whole, be described as muggy ; fogs appear to have a facility in getting in, and a difficulty of getting out of it. The coy and reserved Scotch mist, and the bolder and more *prononcé* pelting snow, linger pertinaciously on its pavements ; and when it is muddy in Cawdor Street—it *is* muddy.

Cawdor Street has public-houses, and butchers' shops, and dining-rooms, as other streets have. It has the same floating population of ragged children, policemen, apple-women, and domestic animals. The inhabitants, I have reason to believe, pay rent and taxes : cabalistic metallic plates point out the distance of the fire-plug from the foot-pavement ; and the banners of Barclay and Perkins, conjointly with those of Combe and Delafield, of Truman, Hanbury, and Buxton, and of Sir Henry Meux, hang out, as in other streets, upon the outward walls.

The intelligent reader will, I dare say, by this time begin to ask, why, if Cawdor Street resembles, in so many points, hundreds of other streets, I should be at the trouble of describing it ? Patience ; and I will unfold all that Cawdor Street has of marvellous, and why it is worth travelling in. It is the seat of a great manufacture ;—not of cotton, as is Manchester the grimy and tall-chimneyed ;—not of papier-maché, as is Birmingham the red-bricked and painfully-paved ;

—not of lace, as is Nottingham the noisy and pugilistic, but of Art. Those well-meaning but simple-minded men who, two or three years since, set about making spoons and dishes, bread-baskets and cream-jugs, after artistic designs, and which they called art-manufactures, thought, in their single-heartedness, they had originated the term. Why, bless them! Cawdor Street has had extensive art-manufactures for scores of years. It has been manufacturing Art, artistic furniture, and artists to boot, almost since the time that Art came into England.

For in Cawdor Street, be it understood, dwell the great tribe of manufacturers of spurious antiques, of sham *moyen-age* furniture, of fictitious Dresden china, of delusive Stradivarius violins. In Cawdor Street abide the mighty nation of picture-dealers, picture-forgers, picture 'clobberers,' picture-pawners, and other picture-traffickers, whose name is legion. In Cawdor Street are sellers of rare Rembrandt etchings, etched a year ago ; of autographs of Henry the Eighth, written a week since ; in Cawdor Street, finally, are gathered together (amongst many respectable and conscientious dealers) some rapacious gentry, who sell, as genuine, the things that are not, and never were ; who minister to the folly and credulity of the ignorant rich, on whom they fatten ; who hang on the outskirts of Art, seeking whom they may devour ; who are the curse of Art, and the bane of the artist.

I often wonder what Raphael Sanzio of Urbino, Gerretz van Rhyn, commonly called Rembrandt, Michael Angelo Buonarotti, and other professors of the art of painting would think, if, coming with a day-rule from the shades (Elysian, I trust), they could behold the daubs to which their names are appended. I often wonder how many hundred years it would have taken them to have painted, with their own hands, the multitudinous pictures which bear their names. Nay, if even the most celebrated of our living painters could see, gathered together, the whole of their 'original' works which Cawdor Street dealers have to sell, they would, I opine, be sore astonished. Canvases they never touched, compositions they never dreamed of, effects of colour utterly unknown to them, would start before their astonished gaze. For every one white horse of Wouvermans, five hundred snowy steeds would paw the earth. For every drunken boor of Teniers, Ostade, or Adrien Brouwer, myriads of inebriated Hollanders would cumber Cawdor Street. Wonderful as were the facility and exuberance of production of Turner, the dead

Academician would stare at the incalculable number of works imputed to him. Oh, Cawdor Street, thoroughfare of deceptions and shams! Oh, thou that sulliest bright mirrors with ignoble vapours! thou are not deceitful, but deceit itself!

Here is the collection of ancient furniture, armour, old china, cameos, and other curiosities and articles of *vertu*, forming the stock in trade of Messrs. Melchior Saltabadil and Co. A magnificent assemblage of rare and curious articles they have, to be sure. Not a dinted breastplate is there but has its appropriate legend; not a carved ebony crucifix but has its romance; not a broadsword or goblet of Bohemian glass but has its pedigree. That china monster belonged to the Empress Maria Louisa; that battered helmet was picked up on the field of Naseby; that rusted iron box was the muniment-chest of the Abbey of Glastonbury; that ivory-hafted dagger once hung at the side of David Rizzio; and that long broadsword was erst clasped by one of Cromwell's Ironsides. Come to the back of the shop, and Messrs. Melchior Saltabadil and Co. will be happy to show you a carved oak and velvet-covered *prie-dieu* once belonging to the oratory of Ann of Austria. That shirt of mail, yonder, hanging between the real Damascus sabre and the superb specimen of point lace, dates from the Crusades, and was worn by Robin de Bobbinet at the siege of Acre. Step up stairs, and Melchior Saltabadil and Co. have some exquisite needlework for your inspection, of a date coeval with that of the Bayeux Tapestry. An astounding collection of curiosities have they, from worked altar-cloths, and richly-stained glass of the fourteenth century, to Dresden shepherds and shepherdesses, and dazzling tea and dessert-services of genuine *Sèvres* china.

Chasuble Cope, dealer in Ecclesiastical Antiquities, has his *magasin* just opposite to that of the before-mentioned merchants. Mr. Cope is great in altar-candlesticks, pyxes, rochets, fald-stools, elaborately carved or brazen lecterns, mitres of the Middle Ages, illuminated missals, books of 'hours,' and other specimens of the paraphernalia of Romish ecclesiology. He has the skeleton of a mitred abbot in the cellar, and Bishop Blaise's crosier up stairs. Next door to him, the Cawdor Street traveller will find, perhaps, the copious and curious collection of Messrs. Pagoda and Son, who more specially affect Egyptian, Chinese, and Indian curiosities. Curiously-painted shells and fans, ivory concentric balls, wonderful porcelain idols, tear-bottles, bags of mummy wheat, carved

Hindoo sceptres, brocaded draperies of astonishing antiquity
—these form but a tithe of the Oriental relics detailed to
view. Farther up Cawdor Street are establishments teeming
with old furniture, and crowding the pavement with their
overplus of carved chairs, and bulky tables with twisted legs,
the boards of which glistened, in Harry the Eighth's time,
with those sturdy flagons and long spiral-columned glasses
now resting quietly on the dusty shelves ; and there are Queen
Elizabethan cabinets, and stools on which Troubadours and
Trouvères rested their harps when they sang the ' Roman du
Rou,' and the legend of King Arthur, in goodness knows how
many ' fyttes.' There are small curiosity-merchants in Cawdor
Street, as well as extensive ones ; humble dealers, whose stores
resemble more the multifarious odds-and-ends in brokers' shops
than collections of antiquity and *vertu*. These bring home the
savage tomahawk, the New Zealand boomerang, the rosary of
carved beads, to the poorest door ; and render old armour, old
furniture, old lace, and tapestry, comprehensible to the meanest
understanding.

And why should not all these be genuine—real, undoubted
relics of ages gone by ? To the man of poetical imagination,
what can be more pleasant than to wander through these
dingy bazaars of the furniture, and armour, and knick-
knackery of other days ? The sack, and malvoisie, and hypo-
cras are gone ; but there are the flagons and beakers that held
them. The mailed knights, and pious monks, have been dust
these five hundred years ; but there is their iron panoply,
there are their hauberks, and two-handed swords ; there are
the beads they counted, the roods before which they prayed,
the holy volumes they were wont to read. Cromwell's name
is but a noise ; but those ragged buff-boots may have enclosed
his Protectorial extremities. The mattock, and the spade, and
the earthworm have done their work with Diane de Poitiers
and Gabrielle d'Estrées ; yet in that quaint Venetian mirror
they may have dressed their shining locks, and mocked the
glass with sunny glances. That should have been the Black
Prince's surcoat ; that pearl and ivory box, the jewel-casket
of Ninon de l'Enclos ; that savage club, carved, beaded, and
ornamented with tufts of feathers, who shall say it was not
wielded once by Montezuma, or was an heirloom in some far
South American forest, ere Columbus was born, or Cortez and
Pizarro heard of ? Besides, are not the dealers in these
curiosities respectable men ? Are not little labels affixed to
some of the rarer articles, announcing them to have formed

P

part of the Stowe collection, of that of Strawberry Hill, of
Fonthill Abbey, of Lansdowne Tower—to have been bought
of the Earl of Such-a-one's executors, or acquired at the Duke
of So-and-so's sale ?   My friend, when you have travelled as
long in Cawdor Street as I have, your poetical imaginings
will have cooled down wofully; and your faith in Oliver
Cromwell's boots, Edward the Black Prince's surcoat, and Ninon
de l'Enclos's jewel-casket, will have decreased considerably.
Some of the furniture is curious, and much of it old ; but, oh!
you have never heard, you have never seen (as I have) the
art-manufactures that are carried on in Cawdor Street garrets,
in frowzy little courts, and mysterious back slums adjoining
thereon.   You do not know that wily armourers are at this
moment forging new breastplates and helmets, which, being
battered, and dinted, and rusted, shall assume the aspect of
age—and ages.   You do not know that, by cunning processes,
new needlework can be made to look like old tapestry ; that
the carved leg of an old chair, picked up in a dusty lumber-
room, will suffice, to the Cawdor Street art-manufacturer as a
matrix for the production of a whole set of carved, weather-
stained, and worm-eaten furniture—chairs, tables, stools, side-
boards, couches, and cabinets enough to furnish half a dozen
houses of families of the Middle Ages, 'about to marry.'   You
have not heard that corpulent man in the fur cap, and with the
pipe in his mouth—and who eyed you slily just now, as you
were handling those curious silver-mounted pistols—tell the
swart artisan by his side that there is rather a run for inlaid
Spanish crucifixes just now, and bid him make a dozen or two
according to the model he gives him.   How many of those
Dresden shepherds and shepherdesses are of Saxon origin,
think you?   On how many of those squat, grinning, many-
coloured Pagods did Indian sun ever shine?   The *bric-à-brac*
shops of the Quai Voltaire, in Paris, swarm with spurious
antiquities ; the dealers in antiques, in Rome, make harvests
out of credulous 'milords,' in the way of cameos, produced at
the rate of about two scudi, and sold at ten guineas each ; in
fragments of marble urns, statues, and rilievi, purposely
mutilated, buried in the environs of the Eternal City, and
then dug up to be sold as ancient originals.   How, then, should
Cawdor Street be exempt from the suspicion of deception ?—
Cawdor Street, standing, as it does, in the midst of that land,
and of that city, so bursting, so running over, with commercial
competition, that, panting to do business at any price, it
cannot refrain from vending counterfeit limbs, spurious gar-

ments, sham victuals and drink even. The worst of it is, that knowing how many of the curiosities and rarities in these seeming shops are cunning deceits, a man is apt to grow sceptical as regards them all. For my part, I would rather, were I a collector of curiosities, rummage in old country public-houses (I would I could remember the whereabouts of that one where, as I live, I saw in the tap-room a genuine and a beautiful Vandyck, smoke-grimed and beer-stained!) or search in obscure brokers' shops, where, among rusty lanterns, beer-taps, bird-cages, flat-irons, fishing-rods, powder-flasks, and soiled portraits of Mrs. Billington in 'Mandane,' one does occasionally stumble on an undoubted relic of the past, and say, 'here is Truth.'

But it is in the article of pictures that the art-manufacturers of Cawdor Street have astonished the world, and attained their present proud pre-eminence. Pictures are their delight, and form their greatest source of profit. Take, for example, the lion of Cawdor Street, the great Mr. Turps, 'Picture-dealer, liner, and restorer. Pictures bought, sold, or exchanged. Noblemen and gentlemen waited upon at their own residences.' To look at Mr. Turps' shop, you would not augur much for the magnitude or value of his stock in trade. A small picture panel of a Dutch Boor, boozy, as usual, and bestriding a barrel of his beloved beer; this and a big picture of some pink angels sprawling in, or rather on, an opaque sky; these are pretty nearly all that is visible above the wire-wove blinds which veil the penetralia of Mr. Turps' domicile. But only walk in—arrive well-dressed—come, above all, in a carriage—and the complaisant, the voluble Turps will show you stacks, mountains of pictures. He deals only in dead masters. He has nothing to say to the moderns. There is an original Sebastiano del Piombo, formerly in the Orleans collection; there a Madonna col Bambino of Raffaelle, which my Lord Bricabrac offered to cover with golden sovereigns, would he, Turps, only sell it to him. There is the 'Brigand Reposing,' by Salvator Rosa, formerly in the Boggotrotti Palace, and smuggled out of Rome in an extraordinary manner. The Prince Cardinal Boggotrotti, Turps tells you, had been prohibited by the Papal Government from selling any of his pictures; but being deeply in debt, and wanting ready money sadly, he ceded to the importunities of the adventurous Turps, who purchased the picture; but had *another picture*, 'St. Bartholomew, flayed alive,' painted over the original, *in distemper*. With this he triumphantly eluded discovery ; and though St. Bartholomew's great toe was nearly rubbed out by a careless porter, he passed the Custom House and the Police, and brought his treasure to England. But here is a gem of gems, Turps' almost priceless picture—a little, old, shabby panel, on which you can discover something dimly resembling a man's head, blinking through a dark-brown fog. This is THE Rembrandt 'Three-quarter Portrait of the Burgomaster Tenbroeck,' painted in 1630. Wonderful picture ! wonderful !

I have a great respect for Mr. Turps (who has a pretty house at Stamford Hill, and can give you as good a glass of pale sherry, when he likes, as ever you would wish to taste); but I must tell the honest truth. The Sebastiano del Piombo was bought at Smith's sale, hard by, for three pounds seven ; and Turps knows no more who painted it, or where or when it was painted, than the Cham of Tartary does. The Boggotrotti Raffaelle was 'swop,' being bartered with little Mo Isaacs, of Jewin Street, for a Wouvermans, a millboard study by Mortimer, and two glasses of brandy and water. As for the famous Rembrandt, Turps, in good sooth, had it painted himself on a panel taken from a mahogany chest of drawers he picked up cheap at a sale. He paid Young M'Gilp (attached to a portrait club, and not too proud to paint a sign occasionally,) just fifteen shillings for it; and a very good Rembrandt, now it is tricked up and smoked down, it makes, as times go.

At the top of Mr. Turps' house he has two large attics, where some half-dozen of his merry men manufacture pictures to order. According to the state of the market, and the demand for the works of particular painters, so do they turn out counterfeit Claudes, Murillos, Poussins, Fra Bartolomeos, Guidos, Guercinos, Giulio Romanos, Tenierses, Ostades, Gerard Dows, and Jan Steens. If the pictures they forge (a hard word, but a true one) are on canvas, they are, on completion, carefully lined so as to resemble old pictures restored ; if on panel, the wood is stained and corroded so as to denote antiquity. Little labels of numbers, bearing reference to sale catalogues, are carefully pasted on, and as carefully *half* torn off again. Sometimes the canvas is taken off the stretcher, and rolled backwards, so as to give it a cracked appearance ; anon, the panel is covered with a varnish, warranted to dry in a very network of ancient-looking cracks. Then the painting is tricked or 'clobbered' with liquorice-water, and other artful mixtures and varnishes, which give it a clouded appearance. Chemical substances are purposely mixed with the colours to make them fade; whites that dry yellow, and reds that turn brown. And then this picture, painted for the hire of a mechanic, is ready to be sold at a princely price to any British nobleman or gentleman who will buy it. Herein lies Mr. Turps' profit. The price of one picture will pay the expenses of his establishment for a twelvemonth, and leave him heavy in purse besides. His victims—well, never mind who they are—perhaps mostly recruited from the ranks of the vulgar with money, who purchase fine pictures as a necessary luxury, just as they buy fine clothes and carriages and horses. There are magnates of this class, who will absolutely buy pictures against each other; Brown becoming frantic if Jones possess more Titians than he does; Robinson running neck and neck with Tomkins in Claudes, and beating him cleverly sometimes with a Canaletto. These competitions do good, you may believe me, to Mr. Turps, and bring considerable quantities of grist to his mill. From his extensive collection also are the ' original *chef d'œuvres* of ancient masters,' which, from time to time, are brought to the auctioneer's hammer, both in private houses and in public sale-rooms. The 'property of a gentleman going abroad;' the ' collection of a nobleman, deceased;' the ' gallery of an eminent amateur;'—all these Mr. Turps will supply at per dozen, and many score of his brethren in London are ready to do the same.

Not that I wish to insinuate that there are no honest picture-dealers, and no *bonâ fide* picture auctions, in London. There are many—and there need be some, I am sure, to counteract the swarms of those which are impudent swindles.

Of the same kindred as Mr. Turps, and having his abode in the same congenial Cawdor Street, you will find the well-known Mr. Glaze, who turns his attention almost entirely to modern pictures. His art-manufactures consist of Turners, Ettys, Mulreadys, Landseers—in short, of all the favourite masters of the English school. He has a band of artists, who, for stipends varying from a pound to thirty shillings weekly, produce counterfeits of the works of our Royal Academicians by the yard or mile. These forgeries have their sale principally on the continent, where English pictures (notwithstanding the doubts sometimes expressed by our neighbours as to whether we can paint at all) are eagerly sought after, and where a genuine

Landseer is a pearl beyond price. Occasionally, though very rarely, Mr. Glaze buys original pictures by unknown artists— Snooks of Cleveland Street, perhaps, or Tibbs of Cirencester Place. He gives a few shillings for one—rarely half a sovereign. Then, according to the *genre*, or to some faint analogy in style or colour, the name of some celebrated living master is, without further ceremony, clapped on the unresisting canvas, and as a Mulready, a Webster, or a Creswick, the daub goes forth to the world.

Travelling yet through Cawdor Street, we come upon yet a lower grade of traffickers in pictures. These ingenious persons devote themselves to the art of picture-dealing, insofar as it affects pawnbroking. They employ artists (sometimes— daubers more frequently) to paint pictures for a low but certain price. These occasionally they pawn, selling the tickets subsequently to the unwary for whatever they will fetch; or, they buy tickets themselves, and remove them from one pawnbroker to another, who, as their knavish experience teaches them, gives a better price for pictures. 'My Uncle,' however, it must be admitted, has grown rather wary lately with respect to pictures and picture-pawners. He has been 'done' by apparent noblemen driving up to his door in carriages and pair, and by the footman bearing a carefully-veiled picture into his private office, and telling him that 'my Lord' *must* have fifty pounds this evening. He has been surfeited with pictures, new from the easel, painted by necessitous artists in their extremity, and known in the trade as 'pot-boilers.' So that, now, he 'would rather not' lend you anything on a picture; and would prefer some more convertible article—say a flat-iron, or a pair of boots—to all the Titians or Rembrandts you could bring him.

You might go on travelling up and down Cawdor Street for days, and find out some fresh proof of the deception and duplicity of this picture-dealing business at every step. It makes me melancholy to do so. And I think sometimes that not a few painters, who have had R.A. appended (and worthily) to their names, and have dined at the tables of live Dukes and Duchesses, may have thought of their old Cawdor Street days with a sort of tremor. More than one of them, I will be bound, as he has passed through Cawdor Street, has recognised an ancient master, or a modern original, in the painting of which he had a hand, and a considerable one, too. Our own Wilkie, we know, had no other employment for a long time save that of counterfeiting Tenierses and Ostades; and he is not the only great painter who has done grinding-work for the picture-dealers, and who has travelled wearily and sorrowfully through Cawdor Street.

Meanwhile,

> 'The Thane of Cawdor lives,
> A prosperous gentleman!'

XX.

HOUSES TO LET.*

I HAVE often heard conjectures hazarded, as to who and what manner of people they may be that read the supplement of the 'Times' newspaper. That a very fair proportion of the subscribers and readers of that journal do so, is a fact, I take it, apparent to, and acknowledged by, the frequenters of parlours, coffee-houses, club-rooms, and hotel snuggeries. Admitting always that it *is* read, it is not by any means so certain *who* reads it. The advertisers may do so, wishing, like careful men of business, to make sure that they have had their pennyworth for their penny. The proof-reader reads it *bongré, malgré*, though, very likely, while toiling down the dreary columns of uninteresting announcements, he may say, with Ancient Pistol, in the Great Leek Consumption Case,—'I read and eke I swear.' But do you or I affect the perusal of that portentous broad-sheet? From time to time we may glance at the Education near London column; at the New Discoveries in Teeth; at the Sales by Auction; and the Horizontal Grand Pianofortes; but we know that the really interesting 'ads.' are in the body of the paper; that the profligate initials are entreated to return to their parents, or to send back the key of the tea-caddy in the second or third column of the front page; and that the unfathomable hieroglyphics hold sweet converse in the same locality. In that Pactolean front page, who knows, from morning to morning, but that Messrs. Wouter, Gribble, and Sharp, of Gray's Inn, may publicly express their wish to communicate something to our advantage to us? In that front page, conscientious cab-

---

* This article was written before the abolition of the stamp duty on newspapers. There is now no supplement at all to the 'Times;' the whole concrete mass of advertisements and news being sold as an aggregate for fourpence.

men have found the wearing apparel and jewellery we have
lost, or dog-fanciers (more conscientious still) the dogs which
have been st——well, mislaid. In that same page we can
put our hands on all the announcements we want:—the Steam
Navigation, which is to waft us to Rotterdam and the Rhine,
or to Paris, *viâ* Calais, in eleven hours; of the exhibitions
and dioramas we delight in witnessing; of the charitable
associations it so pleaseth us (kind souls!) to subscribe to;
of horses and carriages, we buy or sell; of the commodious
travelling-bags, replete with every *nécessaire de voyage*, from
a bootjack to a toothpick, which Mr. Fisher of the Strand
exhorts us to purchase ere we set out on the grand tour; of
Mr. Bennett's watches; and Mr. Sangster's umbrellas, and
Mr. Tucker's lamps; and of the oats, which good Mary
Wedlake so pertinaciously desires to know if we bruise yet.
If we want clerks or governesses, or, as clerks and governesses, are ourselves wanted; if we wish to borrow or to
lend money, or to see what new books or new music appeal
to our taste, literary or musical, we find them, if not in the
front page, still almost invariably in the main body of the
'Times;' it is only on special occasions—when the honourable Member for Mugborough divides the house at two
o'clock in the morning; or the Crushclod Agricultural Society
holds a meeting, unusually stormy or lengthy; or my Lord
Centipede gives a dinner, at which everybody drinks everybody's health, and returns thanks into the bargain,—that the
really interesting advertisements are crowded into the Supplement. On other occasions, that document remains a dreary
acceptance for the education, teeth, pianoforte, and auctioneer
advertisements, with the addition, perhaps, of a few camphine
lamps, liquid hair-dyes, and coals at nine shillings per chal-
dron. Yet the Supplement is read by thousands,—not merely
by that pale man in the brown cloak and the discontented face
opposite to me, who has engaged the 'Times' *de facto* after
me, and is only, I can plainly see, affecting to read the *de jure*
Supplement; having rage in his heart, caused by the conviction (wherein he is right) that I intend to keep the paper till
I have read the 'leaders' through;—not merely by him, but by
the numerous and influential class of persons who are interested in a phalanx of advertisements, which I have hitherto
omitted to enumerate, as among the contents of the dullest
Supplement; and which have reference to Houses to Let.
This is, at least, *my* theory. If ever I see a man really
mentally immersed in the perusal of the 'Times' Supplement,

and appearing to derive any genuine interest therefrom, I make pretty sure that he has either a House to Let, or that he wants to take one.

Houses to Let! The subject is fraught with speculative interest for those philosophers who are content to leave the sun, the moon, the pre-Adamite dynasties, the Mosaic theory of creation, the Æolic digamma, and the perpetual motion, to their betters ; and can find sufficient food for philosophy in the odds and ends, the sweeping of the House of Life—who can read homilies in bricks and mortar, sermons in stones, the story of a life, its hopes and fears, its joys and woes, in the timbers of a dilapidated pigstye, in the desolation of a choked-up fountain, or the ruins of a springless pump !

We change our dresses, our servants, our friends and foes—how can our houses expect to be exempt from the mutabilities of life ? We tire of the old friend, and incline to the new ; the old baby is deposed in favour of the new baby ; the fat, turnip silver watch our father gave us, gives place to a gold Geneva—we change, and swop, and barter, and give up, and take back, and long for, and get tired of, all and everything in life—why not of houses too ? So the Supplement of the ' Times ' can always offer Houses to Let ; and wo are continually running mad to let or hire them, as vice versâ, six months hence, perhaps we shall be as maniacally eager to hire or to let.

Subdivision, classification, and elaboration, are certainly distinguishing characteristics of the present æra of civilisation. The house-agents of the ' Daily Courant,' of the ' Public Ledger,' or the ' Evening Intelligencer,' would have been coupled with the announcement pur et simple, that in such and such a street, or part of the court, there was a House to Let. They might, perhaps, have added, at the most, that it was over-against the Bear Garden, or that it formerly belonged to a tradesman possessing an infallible cure for the scurvy, and who ' made the very best purle that ever was brewed ;' but there they would stop. Catch us doing anything of the sort in these enlightened days. Where our benighted grand-fathers had boys' and girls' schools, we have seminaries, academies, lyceums, and colleges, for young ladies. Where they had sales ' by inch of candle,' we had Mr. George Robins, and have now Messrs. Musgrove and Gadsden, and Frederick Jones, who are always being ' honoured with instructions' to sell things for us or to us. A spade isn't a spade in 1860, but something else ; and with our house-agents, a house is not only a house, but a great many things besides.

A House to Let may be a mansion, a noble mansion, a family mansion, a residence, a desirable residence, a genteel residence, a family residence, a bachelor's residence, a distinguished residence, an elegant house, a substantial house, a detached house, a desirable villa, a semi-detached villa, a villa standing in its own grounds, an Italian villa, a villa residence, a small villa, a compact detached cottage, a cottage ornée, and so on, almost ad infinitum. Rarely do the advertisements bear reference only to a house, a villa, or a cottage : we must call the spade something in addition to its simply agrarian title.

Now, are all these infinitesimal subdivisions of Houses to Let merely intended as ingenious devices to charm the house-hirer by variety, in the manner of Mr. Nicoll, with regard to his overcoats, and Messrs. Swan and Edgar with reference to ladies' cloaks and shawls ; or do there really exist subtle distinctions, minute, yet decidedly perceptible, between every differently-named house ? Can it be that the desirable residence has points calculated to satisfy desire in a different degree to the elegant predilections to be gratified by the elegant residence ? Can it be that a residence, after all, isn't a house, nor a house a residence ? It may be so. People, in the innocence of their hearts, and unaccustomed to letting or hiring houses, may imagine that there can be no very material difference between a villa, a genteel villa, and a compact villa ; but in the mind of the astute house-agent, and equally intelligent house-hirer, differences, varieties of size, aspect, and convenience, immediately suggest themselves ; and to their experienced eyes there are so many points of distinction between the genteel and the compact, the desirable and the distinguished, as to the visual organs of those learned in horses between a cob and a hack, a racer and a screw ; or to the initiated in dog-lore, between a greyhound and a setter.

I do not pretend to any peculiarly nice perception as to things in general. I cannot tell to this day a hawk from a falcon (between the former bird and a handsaw I might be able to guess). It was a long time before I could distinguish between a leveret and a rabbit, or tell very high venison from decomposed shoulder of mutton ; and I will not be certain, even now, if I could tell from the odour (being blindfolded), which was pitch and which tar. So, the immense variety of Houses to Let has always been to me a mystery, the subtle distinctions in their nomenclature sources of perplexed speculation. There may be those who are more learned than I am

—those who, with similar acuteness as the gentlemen mentioned in Hudibras, who had been beaten till they could tell to a splinter of what wood the cudgel was composed, and kicked till they knew if the shoe were 'calfskin or neat's leather'—can mark the strong connections, the nice dependencies, the gradations just of houses, mansions, villas, and residences, and with their 'pervading souls look through' the wondrous variety of Houses to Let.

I can only theorise. I have studied the 'Times' attentively, and gazed wearily at the elongated crimson baize-covered panels in the house-agents' windows, on which, written on slips of foolscap, the announcements of Houses to Let are secured with parti-coloured wafers. Goodness knows how far from the actual mark I may be; but you shall hear what my ideas are on this very open House question.

First, of the Mansion. What manner of house would you imagine that to be? I take it to be situate at Kew, possibly at Chiswick, peradventure at Putney. Red brick, stone window casings, a great many chimney-pots, a steep flight of steps before the door. Perhaps the advertisement says that it is 'approached by a carriage drive.' I can see that carriage drive, the mangy gravel, weeds and grass springing up between; the brown ragged lawn in the middle; the choked-up flower-beds, with pieces of broken bottles and fractured tobacco-pipes, where once were geraniums, and heliotropes. There must be a wall in front, and a pair of rusty iron gates, or more probably a paint-destitute portal, scored over with drawings in crayons of unpopular churchwardens, and fierce denunciations of the Pope of Rome, the College of Cardinals, and the New Police Act. This door is blistered with the sun, dinted by the peg-tops and hockey-sticks of savage boys. In the centre you may see a parallelopipedal patch, where the paint is of a lighter colour, and where there are marks of bygone screws. That was where the brass plate was, when the mansion was occupied by the Reverend Doctor Brushback. It was called 'Smolensko House' then, and on Sundays and holidays a goodly procession of youths educated therein issued from it. A small confectioner's ('sock-shop,' the boys called it) was started in the adjacent lane, on the sole strength of the school custom; and Widow Maggle, the greengrocer, who supplied the establishment with birch-brooms, actually started her boy Dick in a cart with a live donkey from her increased profits. But the Reverend Doctor Brushback, at the age of fifty-seven, and in a most unaccount-

able manner, took it into his head to turn the wife of his
bosom out of doors. Then he flogged three-fourths of his
scholars away, and starved the remainder. Then he was
suspected of an addiction to strong drinks, and of breaking
Leather's (the shoe, knife, and general errand boy's) head,
because he could not tell him what was Greek for a boot-jack.
Smolensko House speedily presented that most melancholy
spectacle, a bankrupt school; and the last time I heard of
Doctor Brushback, it was on a charge (unfounded, of course)
at the Public Office, Bow Street, of being drunk and disorderly in the gallery of Drury Lane Theatre. Was not our
mansion, after this, Minerva House Finishing Academy for
Young Ladies? Surely so. The Misses Gimp devoted themselves to the task of tuition with a high sense of its onerous
duties, and strenuously endeavoured to combine careful ma-
ternal supervision with the advantages of a finished system of
polite education (*vide* ' Times '). But the neighbourhood was
prejudiced against the scholastic profession, and the Misses
Gimp found few scholars, and fewer friends. Subsequently,
their crack scholar, Miss Mango, the heiress, eloped with Mr.
De Lypey, professor of dancing, deportment, and calisthenics.
The resident Parisienne married Mr. Tragacanth, assistant to
Mr. Poppyed, the chemist, and the Misses Gimp went to ruin
or Boulogne. I lost sight of my mansion about here—for a
time at least. It must, however, have been rented by Captain
Vere de Vere Delamere, and his family, who paid nobody,
and owing innumerable quarters for rent, were eventually
persuaded to remove by a bribe from the landlord. Or was
the mansion ever in the occupation of the celebrated Mr. Nix,
who said he belonged to the Stock Exchange, and removed in
the midst of winter, and at the dead of night, taking with him,
over and above his own furniture, a few marble mantel-pieces,
register stoves, and other trifles in the way of fixtures? Or
was this mansion the one taken by Mr. Pluffy, immensely
rich, but very eccentric, who turned his nephews and nieces
out of doors, painted all the windows a bright red, kept a
tame hyæna, and persisted in standing outside his gate on
Sunday mornings with nothing on, to speak of, save a leather
apron and a meerschaum, assuring the public generally that
he was Peter the Great?

I glance again at the advertisement, and find my mansion
described as a ' noble ' one. In that case I should say it was
in some nice marshy, swampy, reedy part of Essex, where
the owls scream, and the frogs croak blithely at night. There

are two stone hawks sculptured above the gates ; a garden, as tangled and savage-looking as an Indian jungle ; a dried-up fountain ; and maimed, broken-nosed, mildewed statues, tottering on moss and weed-covered pedestals. In the old time, the Earl of Elbowsout lived at the ' noble ' mansion ; but his lordship afterwards resided in sunny Italy for many years. deriving immense benefit (not pecuniary, of course) from a judicious consumption of Professor Paracelsus's pills. He left an heir ; and whenever Inspector Beresford was wont to force open the door of some harmless house in Jermyn Street, with sledge-hammers, you would be pretty sure to find, among the list of prisoners, conveyed to Vine Street, on a suspicion of indulging in the forbidden game of chicken-hazard, the names of Robert Smith or of John Brown ; one of whom, you might have been as certain, was no other than Lord Viscount Hawker, his lordship's son.

' Convenient Mansion,' says the ' Times ' again. Ah! I know. A big, square block of a house, very small windows, iron-barred, and a high wall inside. Just suitable for Doctor Muffles's asylum for the insane ; plenty of cold water laid on. Very convenient!—Family Mansion, Plenty of bed-rooms, high gate on the nursery stairs, stables, coach-house, and detached room, for the gardener.—' Picturesque Mansion.' Decidedly picturesque, but damp. Picturesque in proportion to its ruin, and out of all habitable repair. Thomas Hood wrote a beautiful poem once, of a Picturesque Mansion —A Haunted House—and which has haunted me ever since. The choked-up moat ; the obscene birds, that flapped their wings on the roof; the foul insects, that wove webs inside ; the gaunt rats, that held unholy gambols in the kitchen ; the weed-grown courtyard, window-sills, and door-steps; the damp feculence, dust, dirt, rust, about all or everything; the one Sunbeam, coming through a grimed window, and illuminating a bloody hand. There had been a murder done there, and the house was haunted. I can well believe it. I, too, saw, once upon a time, a mansion, where a foul and wicked murder had been done. I saw labourers searching the muddy moat for the weapons of the assassins ; I was taken to see the corridor where the deed had been done ; and I followed the footsteps of the murderer through mud and slush, snow and straw, from the mansion to the farm he lived at. I never read poor Hood's plaintive poem without thinking that Stanfield Hall—shut up, untenanted, moat-dried—would be a very counterpart, now, of the house he shadowed forth.

Not, however, to forget Houses to Let. Shall I take the Bachelor's Residence ?   An invisible hand points to Highgate —an inward feeling suggests Mitcham.   *I* go for Crickle-wood : Kilburn is too near, and Edgeware too far ; but Crickle-wood holds a *juste milieu* between them.   I can see the Bachelor's Residence—a pert, smart, snug, little habitation, standing alone, mostly ; for your bachelor is incorrigible (steady or fast) with regard to musical instruments.   Your fast bachelor will manage the Redowa on the cornet-à-piston ; and your steady one, set 'Ah ! non giunge,' to hard labour on the flute—but all *will* practise ; and—should their bachelors' quarters happen to be supported, right and left, by family residences—the inhabitants of Acacia Terrace or Plantain Grove are apt to become remarkably disagreeable in their reclamations to the bachelor himself.   The bachelor is a bank clerk, very likely, or a stock-broker, not over-plethoric just yet with profits ; or a young fellow with a small independence. He has a front garden and a back garden ; both, ten to one, provided with a trim little summer-house, where he is very fond of sitting on fine afternoons with his friends, clad in bachelor-like deshabille, consuming the grateful beer of Bass, and gently whiffing the cutty pipe of Milo, or the meerschaum. He has flowers, but has a faint idea that the tobacco-smoke does not do them any good.   He has a housekeeper—generally middle-aged, and frequently deaf—many friends, more pipes, and frequently an anomalous kind of little vehicle, drawn by an eccentric pony, and which he calls his ' trap.'   Sunday is his great day.   All his fly-rods, fishing-tackle, gardening im-plements, guns, rabbit-hutches, and pipe-racks, are overhauled on that day ; grave judgments are passed on the dogs and horses of his friends ; and an impervious cloud of Bird's-eye or Oronooko hangs about the little summer-houses.   But the bachelor marries ; goes a little too fast, perhaps, or dies (for, alas ! even bachelors must die) ; and so his Bachelor's Resi-dence is To Let.

The Desirable Residence.   I have the secret of that ' House to Let,' I will be bound.   A lodging-house !   What could there be more desirable, in the way of a residence, than that, I should like to know ?   Twelve-roomed house, in Manchester Street, Manchester Square.   Blue damask curtains in the first-floor windows ; red ditto in the parlour windows ; a never-disappearing placard, of Apartments Furnished (for however full the lodging-house may be, it always seemed to have a marvellous capacity for holding more) ; and area railings, frequently enlivened and ornamented by the three-quarter portrait of a pretty servant-maid. Whenever you see the butcher, or the baker, or the grocer's man, at the door of the Desirable Residence, you will be sure, if you watch, to see him produce a red account-book ; for people who keep lodging-houses invariably run bills with tradesmen, probably to give an air of veracity and colourable truth to the persevering assertion made to their lodgers, that they have a little bill to pay to-morrow. If the lady who keeps the Desirable Residence is married, you will not be very far out, if you assert that her husband has something to do with the Docks, or that he is a barrister's clerk, in good practice. You can't be wrong, if you set him down as an indifferently-dressed man, with an umbrella, who, whenever he speaks to you, calls you 'Sir.' If your landlady should happen to be a widow, take my word for it, that '-she was not always in these circumstances ;' that her late husband's executors have used her shamefully ; and that she has a pretty daughter or niece.

Unless I am very far out in my theory, the 'Substantial Residence' is a lodging-house too, and the 'Genteel Residence' not very far from it. Cecil Street, Strand, for the former, and Camberwell for the latter, would not be very wide of the mark. Cecil Street is full of substantial houses, in which lodgers, sometimes not quite so substantial as the houses, continually dwell. The prices of provisions are high in Cecil Street, and the quantity of nourishment they afford far from considerable. Penny loaves are twopence each, and you can't get more than one dinner off a leg of mutton. The profits arising from the avocations of the landladies of substantial residences must be so large, that I wonder they ever come to be advertised as ' to let ' at all. Perhaps it is that they make their fortunes, and migrate to the ' elegant residence,' or the ' distinguished residence.'

Am I wrong in placing the *locale* of these two last species of ' Houses to Let ' in Belgravia and Tyburnia ? They may, after all, be wasting their elegance and their distinction in Golden Square, Ely Place, or Kennington Oval. Yet I am always coming across, and reading with great unction, paragraphs in the newspapers, setting forth that, ' after the marriage of Miss Arabella Constantia Tanner, daughter of Hyde Tanner, Esq., of the firm of Bender, Cooter, and Tanner, of Lombard Street, to the Honourable Captain Casey, son of Lord Latitat, the happy couple partook of a magnificent *déjeûner* at the elegant residence of the bride's father in Hyde

Park Gardens;' or else it is, that 'last evening the Earl and Countess of Hammersmith and Ladies Barnes (2), Sir John Bobcherry, Pillary Pacha, &c., &c., honoured Sir Styles and Lady Springer with their company to dinner at their distinguished residence in Eaton Place.' I can always imagine tall footmen, magnificent and serene in plush and embroidery, lolling at the doors of elegant and distinguished residences. I don't think I can be very far wrong. I reside, myself, over a milk-shop, and I know that to be neither an elegant nor a distinguished residence ; but are there not both elegance and distinction in the stately Belgrave Square, and the lofty Westbourne Grove ?

Coming, in the pursuit of this superficial examination of ' Houses to Let,' I stop puzzled at the word ' House,' simple, unadulterated, unaccompanied with eulogy, or explanatory prefix. I have my theory about it, though it may be but a lame one. The lone, silent ' House ' must be like that celebrated one at the corner of Stamford Street, Blackfriars, which, with its two companions, everybody has seen, and nobody knows the history of—a house unlet, unletable, yet always to let. Now, a house-agent having any bowels whatsoever, could not call this a desirable house, nor a convenient house, nor an elegant house. So, being too good a man of business to call it an ill-favoured house, a dirty house, and a villanous house, as it is, he calls it a ' House.' A house it is, sure enough, just as a horse, albeit spavined, wind-galled, glandered, staggered, lame, blown, a kicker and a roarer, is a horse still. But what a horse, and what a house !

A ' Genteel House ' seems to me different to a genteel residence. The latter's use I have elsewhere hinted at ; the former I take to be situate somewhere in Gower Street, Keppel Street, or Guildford Street, or in some of those mysterious thoroughfares you are always getting into when you don't want them, and never can find when you do. In the genteel house, I should think, two maiden ladies must have lived—sisters probably ; say, the Miss Twills, whose father was Twills of Saint Mary-Axe, sugar-baker ; and whose brother, Mr. Twills, in partnership with Mr. Squills, can be found in Montague Place, Bedford Square, where the two carry on a genteel business as surgeons and apothecaries. The Miss Twills kept a one-horse fly (not one of your rakish-looking broughams, be it understood), with a corpulent horse (serious of disposition, and given to eating plum-cake when he could get it), and a mild-looking coachman, who carried a hymn-book in his pocket. One day, however, I surmise, Miss Jessy Twills, the youngest and prettiest sister (she did not mind owning to forty) married the Reverend Felix Spanker, of Saint Blazer's Chapel, in Milman Street. Miss Betsy Twills went to live with her married sister (the two lead the poor parson a terrible life between them, and Felix is more irate in the pulpit against the Pope than ever), and the genteel residence took its place in the category of 'Houses to Let.'

The 'Detached House' bears its peculiar characteristic on its front; it stands alone, and nothing more can be said about it; but with the 'semi-detached house' there is a subtle mystery, much to be marvelled at. Semi-detached! Have the party-walls between two houses shrunk, or is there a bridge connecting the two, as in Mr. Beckford's house in Lansdown Crescent, Bath? A semi-detached house may be a house with a field on one side and a bone-boiling factory on the other. Semi-detached may mean half-tumbling to pieces. I must inquire into it.

The 'mansion,' the 'residence,' and the 'house,' seem to indicate dwellings of some considerable degree of importance and extent; the 'villa,' the 'cottage,' and the 'lodge,' seem to indicate smaller places of abode, though perhaps equalling, if not surpassing, their contemporaries in elegance, gentility, distinction, convenience, desirableness, substantiality, &c., &c. There is one thing, however, certain about the villa —one sound basis to go upon, which we do not possess as regards the 'house.' The 'house' is ambiguously situated, it may be, in Grosvenor Square, in Pall Mall, or in Brick Lane, Spitalfields, or Crown Street, Seven Dials; but the villa is necessarily suburban. You could not call a house (however small it might be) situated between a pie-shop and a public-house, a 'villa.' A four-roomed house in Fleet Street would be a novelty, and if you were to call it a Gothic lodge, would be a greater novelty still; while Covent Garden Market, or Long Acre, would scarcely be the *locale* for a cottage *ornée*, or an Italian villa. I recognise cottages, villas, and lodges, with the addition of 'hermitages,' 'priories,' 'groves,' 'boxes,' 'retreats,' &c., on all suburban roads;—in Kensington, Hammersmith, and Turnham Green; in Kingsland, Hackney, and Dalston; in Highgate, Hampstead, and Hornsey; in Camberwell, Peckham, and Kennington; in Paddington, Kilburn, and Cricklewood; their roads, approaches, and environs, inclusive. And a fair proportion do these suburbs contribute to the 'Houses to Let' in the Supplement of the 'Times.'

Q

The 'villa standing in its own grounds' is generally suggestive of stockbrokers. Great people are these stock-brokers for villas; for driving mail-phaetons, or wide-awake looking dog-carts; for giving capital dinners and wine. The young man who has a stockbroker for a friend, has need but to trouble himself only concerning his lodging and washing; his board will take care of itself, or, rather, will be amply taken care of in the villa of his Amphitryon. Next, I should say, to a decided *penchant* for giving and taking the longest of odds, and a marked leaning towards the purchase and sale of horseflesh, hospitality is the most prominent charac-teristic of a stockbroker. He is always 'wanting to stand' something. His bargains are made over sherry and sand-wiches; he begins and ends the day with conviviality. What a pity it is that his speculations should fail sometimes, and that his clients should lose their money, and himself be 'sold up'—ostracised from 'Change, driven to dwell among the tents of Boulogne-sur-Mer, or the cities of refuge of Belgium, the boorish and the beery! Else would he be living in his own ground-surrounded villa to this day, instead of its being confided to the tender mercies of Messrs. Hammer and Rapps, auctioneers and house-agents, as a 'Villa to Let.'

'An Italian Villa to Let.' Pretty, plausible, but deceptive. The house-agent who devised the Italian prefix was a humbug. Start not, reader, while I whisper in your ear. The Italian villa is a shabby little domicile, only Italian in so much *as it possesses Venetian blinds.* I know it; for I, who speak, have been egregiously sold, lamentably taken in, by this mendacious villa.

'A Villa to Let,' again. Not elegant, desirable, distin-guished, nor Italian; but a villa. It has bow-windows, I will go bail. A green verandah over the drawing-room window, for a trifle. *Two bells*, one for visitors, and one for servants. The villa is suitable for Mr. Covin (of the firm of Feraud and Covin, solicitors), who has been importuned so long by Mrs. Covin to abandon his substantial residence in Bedford Row, that he has at last acceded to her wishes. Covin is a portly man, with a thick gold chain, a bald head, and a fringe of black whisker. He is fond of a peculiarly fruity port, like black-currant jam diluted with treacle and water: and his wife's bonnet-box is a japanned tin-coffer, labelled 'Mr. Soldoff's estate.' He won't live in the villa long, because he will get tired of it, and long for Bedford Row again, with its pleasant odour of new vellum and red tape. *He* will let it to

Mr. Runt, the barrister, in 'chamber' practice, or Mr. Muscovado, the sugar-broker of Tower Street, or Mrs. Lopp, the
comfortably-circumstanced widow, who was so staunch a friend
to the Reverend Silas Chowler; the same who, in imitation of
the famous Mr. Huntingdon, S.S., called himself H.B.B., or
Half-Burnt Brand.

What should the 'cottage *ornée*' be like, I should wish to
know (to jump from villas to cottages), but that delightful
little box of a place at Dulwich, where a good friend of mine
was wont (wont, alas!) to live? The strawberries in the
garden; the private theatricals in the back parlour; the
pleasant excursions on week days to the old College—(God
bless old Thomas Alleyne and Sir Francis Bourgeois, I say!
Had the former done nothing worthier of benediction in his
life than found the dear old place, or the latter not atoned for
all the execrably bad modern pictures he painted in his lifetime, by the exquisitely beautiful ancient ones he left us at
his death);—the symposium in the garden on Sundays; the
clear church-bells ringing through the soft summer air; the
pianoforte in the boudoir, and Gluck's 'Che faro senza Euri-
dice?' lightly, gently elicited from the silvery keys (by
hands that are cold and powerless now), wreathing through
the open window; the kind faces and cheerful laughter, the
timid anxiety of the ladies concerning the last omnibus home
at night, and the cheerful recklessness with which they subsequently abandoned that last omnibus to its fate, and conjectured impossibly fortuitous conveyances to town, conjectures
ultimately resolving themselves into impromptu beds. How
many a time have I had a shake-down on the billiard-table of
the cottage *ornée*? How many a time——but my theme is of
Houses to Let.

And of 'Houses to Let,' I have been unconsciously garrulous, without being usefully communicative. I have said
too much, and yet not half enough. In houses, I am yet at
fault about the little mushroom-like rows of flimsy-looking
tenements that spring up on every side in and about the
suburbs; in brick-fields, in patches of ground where rubbish
was formerly shot, and vagabond boys turned over three
times for a penny. I have yet to learn in what species
of 'House to Let' the eccentric gentleman formerly resided,
who never washed himself for five-and-forty years, and
was supposed to scrape himself with an oyster-shell after
the manner of the Caribbees; where it was, whether in a
house, a villa, a residence, or a cottage, that the maiden lady

entertained the fourteen tom cats, that slept each in a four-post bedstoad, and were fed, all of them, on turtle soup. I want to know what 'every convenience' means. I should like to have some further information as to what a 'select number' actually implies. I am desirous of ascertaining in what category of 'Houses to Let' a house-agent would rank a tenantless theatre, a chapel without a congregation or a minister, an empty brewery, or a deserted powder-mill.

Finally, I should like to know what a 'cottage' is. Of the cottage *ornée* I have spoken ; the compact cottage, the detached cottage, the semi-detached cottage, speak for themselves ; but I am as much puzzled about the simple cottage as about the simple house, mansion, or villa. In my youth I had a chimera of a cottage, and drew rude outlines thereof on a slate. It had quadrangular tiles, a window immediately above the door, palings at the side, and smoke continually issuing from the chimney. Its architecture was decidedly out of the perpendicular ; afterwards, perusing works of a rural and pastoral description, a cottage became to me a little paradise of ivy, and honeysuckles, and woodbine. It had a pretty porch, where a young lady in a quilted petticoat, and a young gentleman in a flapped waistcoat, both after the manner (and a very sweet one it is) of Mr. Frank Stone, made first and last appeals to each other all the year round. That was in the time of roses. The times have changed, and I, so I suppose, have changed with them. The roses that remain to us, brother, when our hair becomes inclined to the grizzly, we feel disposed to look commercially upon, and to make money of. Yes ; the fairest rose-leaves from Damascus's garden will we sell to Messrs. Piesse and Lubin for the making of attar ; even as Olympia, at sixty, sells the love letters of her youth to Messrs. Hotpress and Co., publishers, to make three volumes octavo of 'memoirs.' I am sceptical, ignorant, undecided, about the cottage now. Sometimes it is the slate-pencil cottage, sometimes the Frank Stone one, sometimes the cottage of the sixpenny valentines, quitting which, by a bright yellow serpentine path, a gentleman in a blue coat, and a lady in a pink dress, wend their way to the altar of Hymen. Sometimes, O reader of mine ! I see other cottages, dreadful cottages, squalid cottages, cottages in Church Lane, Saint Giles's, where frowsy women in tattered shawls crouch stolidly on the door-step ; where ragged, filthy children wallow with fowls and pigs amidst the dirt and squalor. Sometimes I see cottages in my fondly pictured rural districts—

cottages dilapidated, half unroofed, where gaunt agricultural labourers are sullenly wrangling with relieving officers ; where white-headed, brickdust-faced children cry for bread ; where mother is down with the fever, and grandmother bedridden, yet querulously refusing to go into the dreaded ' House.'

Perhaps I am wrong in all this. Perhaps all these theories about mansions, residences, houses, villas, and the inexplicable cottages, after all may be but wild and improbable theories — crude, vague, purposeless speculations. But I have said my say, and shall be wiser some day, I hope, in other matters besides ' Houses to Let.'

XXI.

TATTYBOYS RENTS.

IN Tattyboys Rents the sun shines, and the rain rains, and people are born, and live and die, and are buried and forgotten, much as they do in Rents of greater renown. And I do not think that the obscurity of the Tattyboysians, and the lack of fame of their residence, cause them much grief, simply because it is to be believed that they are unconscious of both fame and obscurity. That happy conformation of the human mind which leads us firmly and complacently to think that the whole world is ceaselessly occupied with our own little tinpot doings—that serenity of self-importance which lends such a dignity of carriage to little Mr. Claypipkin, as he sails down the street in company with big, burly Mr. Brazenpot—these, I dare say, set my friends in the locality that gives a name to this paper, quite at their ease in regard to the place they occupy, in the estimation of the universe, and engender a comfortable indifference as to whether the eyes of Europe (that celebrated visionary) are continually fixed upon Tattyboys Rents or not.

To tell the plain truth about them, nevertheless, the Rents and the Renters are alarmingly obscure. Beyond the postman, the tax-collectors, and those miracles of topographical erudition who deliver County Court summonses, and serve notices for the Insolvent Court, I doubt if there are a hundred persons in London, exclusive of the inhabitants themselves, who know anything about Tattyboys Rents, or even whereabouts they are. It is to be surmised that the names of the magnates of the Rents are inscribed in that golden book of commerce, the Post-Office London Directory, but the place itself finds no mention there.

By internal evidence and much collation of the work in question, it may be conjectured that Tattyboys Rents is not even the proper name of the score of houses so called, and that it is legally known—no, not known, for it isn't known—but that it should be designated as—Little Blitsom Street. Plugg, of the water-rates, says that in his youth he well remembers a small stone tablet on the corner wall of number nineteen, running thus, 'Little Blitsom Street, 1770,'—and old Mrs. Brush, the charwoman, who, in the days of King James the First, would infallibly have been burnt for a witch, but is now venerated as the oldest inhabitant, minds the time 'when a ferocious band of miscreants,' whether forgers, burglars, or murderers is not stated, were captured in Tattyboys Rents by that bold runner Townshend, and his red-waistcoated acolytes, and by him conveyed before Sir Richard Birnie : the wretches being known as the 'Little Blitsom Street Gang.' Mogg's Map of the Metropolis, with the later charts of Richard and Davis, passes the Rents by, in contemptuous silence. Blitsom Street, and long, dirty Turk's Lane, into which it leads, are both set down in fair characters, but beyond a nameless little space between two blocks of houses, there is nothing to tell you where Tattyboys Rents may be. It is no good asking the policeman anything about them. I have my doubts whether he knows ; but even granting his sapience, I have my suspicions that unless he knew your position and character well, he would affect entire ignorance on the subject. He has his private reasons for doing so. Tattyboys Rents are far too snugly situated, peaceable, and well-behaved, for its locality to be divulged to strangers— possibly of indifferent character. Therefore my advice to you is, if you understand navigation, which I do not, to take your observations by the sun and moon, and by the help of your 'Hamilton Moore,' chronometers, quadrant, compass steering due north, and a guinea case of mathematical instruments, work out Tattyboys Rents' exact place on the chart,— and then go and find it. Or, 'another way,' as the cookery- book says, follow Turk's Lane, till you come to Blitsom Street, up which wander till you stumble, somehow, into Tattyboys Rents.

The last you are very likely to do literally, for the only approach to the Rents is by a flight of steps, very steep and very treacherous, their vicinity being masked by a grove of posts, and the half-dozen idlers whom you are always sure to find congregated round Chapford's beershop. And it has

often happened that, of the few strangers who have travelled in Tattyboys Rents, the proudest and sternest: men who would have scorned to perform the ceremony of the Kotou in China, and would have scouted the idea of salaaming to the Great Mogul: have made their first entrance into the Rents with the lowliest obeisances, with bended knees, and foreheads touching the pavement.

If Miss Mitford had not written, years ago, 'Our Village,' it is decidedly by that name that I should have called this paper. For, Tattyboys Rents form not only a village as regards their isolation, and the unsophisticated nature of their inhabitants, but they resemble those villages, few and far between, now-a-days, where there is no railway-station —cross-country villages, where the civilising shriek of the engine-whistle is never heard; where the building mania in any style of architecture is unfelt; where the inhabitants keep themselves to themselves, and have a supreme contempt for the inhabitants of all other villages, hamlets, townships, and boroughs whatsoever; where strangers are barely tolerated and never popular; where improvements, alterations, and innovations, are unanimously scouted; where the father's customs are the son's rule of life, and the daughters do what their mothers did before them. The Metropolitan Buildings Act is a dead letter in Tattyboys Rents, for nobody ever thinks of building—to say nothing of rebuilding or painting —a house. The Common Lodging-House Act goes for nothing, for there are no common lodging-houses, and the lodgers, where there are any, are of an uncommon character. No one fears the Nuisances Removals Act, for everybody has his own particular nuisance, and is too fond of it to move for its removal. The Health of Towns Act has nothing in common with the health of Tattyboys Rents, for fevers don't seem to trouble themselves to come down its steep entrance steps, and the cholera has, on three occasions, given it the cut direct. It is of no use bothering about the drainage, for nobody complains about it, and nobody will tell you whether it is deficient or not. As to the supply of water, there is a pump at the further extremity of the Rents that would satisfy the most exigent hydropathist; and, touching that pump, I should like to see the bold stranger female who would dare to draw a jugful of water from it, or the stranger boy who would presume to lift to his lips the time-worn and water-rusted iron ladle attached by a chain to that pump's nozzle. Such persons as district surveyors and inspectors of nuisances have been

heard of in Tattyboys Rents, but they are estimated as being
in influence and authority infinitely below the parish beadle.
There was a chimney on fire once at number twelve, and with
immense difficulty an engine was lifted into the Rents, but
all claims of the Fire Brigade were laughed to scorn, and the
boys of the Rents made such a fierce attack on the engine, and
manifested so keen a desire to detain it as a hostage, that the
helmeted men with the hatchets were glad to make their
escape as best they could.

The first peculiarity that will strike you on entering the
Rents is the tallness of the houses. The blackness of their
fronts and the dinginess of their windows will not appear to
you as so uncommon, being a characteristic of Blitsom Street,
Turk's Lane, and the whole of the neighbourhood. But,
Tattyboys houses are very tall indeed, as if, being set so
closely together, and being prevented by conservative tendencies from spreading beyond the limits of the Rents, they
had grown taller instead, and added unto themselves storys
instead of wings. I can't say much, either, for their picturesque aspect. Old as the Rents are, they are not romantically old. Here are no lean-to roofs, no carved gables,
no old lintels, no dormer or lattice windows. The houses
are all alike—all tall, grimy, all with mathematical dirty
windows, flights of steps (quite innocent of the modern
frivolities of washing and hearthstoning), tall narrow doors,
and areas with hideous railings. One uncomprisingly taste-
less yet terrible mould was evidently made in the first instance
for all the lion's-head knockers: one disproportioned spear-
head and tassel for all the railings. I can imagine the first
Tattyboys, a stern man of inflexible uniformity of conduct and
purpose, saying grimly to his builder : ' Build me a Rents of
so many houses, on such and such a model,' and the obedient
builder turning out so many houses like so many bricks, or so
many bullets from a mould, or pins from a wire, and saying,
' There, Tattyboys, there are your Rents.' Then new, painted,
swept, garnished, with the mathematical windows all glistening in one sunbeam, the same lion's-head knockers grinning
on the same doors, the regularity of Tattyboys Rents must
have been distressing ; the houses must all have been as like
each other as the beaux in wigs and cocked hats, and the
belles in hoops and hair powder, who lived when Tattyboys
Rents were built; but age, poverty, and dirt have given as
much variety of expression to these houses now, as hair,
whiskers, wrinkles, and scars give to the human face. Some

of the lion-headed knockers are gone, and many of the spear-headed railings. Some of the tall doors stand continually open, drooping gracefully on one hinge. The plain fronts of the houses are chequered by lively cartoons, pictorially repre-senting the domestic mangle, the friendly cow that yields fresh milk daily for our nourishment, the household goods that can be removed (by spring vans) in town or country; the enlivening ginger beer which is the favourite beverage (ac-cording to the cartoon) of the British Field-Marshal, and the lady in the Bloomer costume. Variety is given to the windows by many of their panes being broken, or patched with parti-coloured paper and textile fabrics; and by many of the windows themselves being open the major part of the day, disclosing heads and shoulders of various stages of mus-cular development, with a foreground of tobacco-pipes and a background of shirt-sleeves. Pails, brooms, and multifarious odds and ends, take away from the uniformity of the areas, while the area gates (where there are any left) swing cheer-fully to and fro. Groups of laughing children bespangle the pavement, and diversify the door-steps : and liveliness, colour, form, are given to the houses and the inhabitants by dirt, linen on poles, half-torn-off placards, domestic fowls, dogs, decayed vegetables, oyster tubs, pewter pots, broken shutters, torn blinds, ragged door-mats, lidless kettles, bottomless saucepans, shattered plates, bits of frayed rope, and cats whose race is run, and whose last tile has been squatted on.

Tattyboys originally intended the houses in his Rents to be all private mansions. Of that there can be no doubt: else, why the areas, why the doorsteps and the lion-headed knockers? But, that mutability of time and fashion which has converted the monastery of the Crutched Friars into a nest of sugar-brokers' counting-houses, and the Palace of Henry the Eighth and Cardinal Wolsey into a hair-dresser's shop, has dealt as hardly with the private houses in Tatty-boys Rents. The shopkeeping element has not yet wholly destroyed the aristocratic aspect of the place; still, in very many instances, petty commerce has set up its petty wares in the front-parlour windows, and the chapman has built his counters and shelves on the groundfloors of gentility.

I have spoken so often of Tattyboys Rents, that the ques-tion might aptly be asked, Who was Tattyboys? When did it occur to him to build Rents? By what fortunate in-heritance, what adventitious accession of wealth, what pros-perous result of astute speculations, was he enabled to give

his name to, and derive quarterly rents from, the two blocks
of houses christened after him? So dense is the obscurity
that surrounds all the antecedents of the locality, that I do not
even know the sex of the primary Tattyboys.
The estates, titles, muniments, and manorial rights (whatever they may be) of the clan Tattyboys, are at present enjoyed by a black beaver bonnet and black silk cloak of antediluvian design and antemundane rustiness, supposed to contain
Mis Tattyboys herself. I say supposed, for though the cloak
and the bonnet are patent in the Rents on certain periodical
occasions, the ancient female (she *must* be old) whom they
enshroud is facially as unknown as the first Odalisque of the
Harem to Hassan the cobbler, or as the Veiled Prophet of
Khorassan was to the meanest of his adorers. No man has
seen Miss Tattyboys, not even Mr. Barwise, her agent; nay,
nor old Mr. Fazzle, the immensely rich bachelor of number
thirteen; but many have heard her stern demands for rent,
and her shrill denunciation of the 'carryings on' of her
tenants. It is said that Miss Tattyboys resides at Hoxton, and
that she keeps her own cows. Men also say that she discounts
bills, and is the proprietor of a weekly newspaper. It is
certain that she is in frequent communication with Mr. Hemp,
the officer of the Sheriff's Court; and many are the proclama-
tions of outlawry made against sprigs of nobility, with tremendously long and aristocratic names at the 'suit of Bridget
Tattyboys.' Likewise she arrested the Honourable Tom
Scaleybridge, M.P., at the close of the last session, before
the advent of the present administration, but was compelled
to release him immediately afterwards, he claiming his privilege. There are many solicitors of my acquaintance, who
in their mysteriously musty and monied private offices have
battered tin boxes with half-effaced inscriptions relative to
'Tattyboys Estate, 1829;' 'Tattyboys Trust, 1832;' 'Tattyboys *versus* Patcherly;' and 'Miss Bridget Tattyboys.' She
is mixed up with an infinity of trusts, estates, and will cases.
She is the subject of dreary law-suits in which the nominal
plaintiff is the real defendant, and the defendant ought not
to be a party to the suit at all. Time is always being given to
speak to her, or communicate with her, or to summons her to
produce papers which she never will produce. Law reports
about her cases begin with 'So far back as eighteen hundred
and ten;' 'it will be remembered that;' 'this part heard case;'
and the daily newspapers occasionally contain letters denying
that she made a proposition to A, or sued B, or was indebted

to C : signed by Driver, Chizzle, and Wrench, solicitors for Miss Tattyboys. She got as far as the House of Lords once, in an appeal case against Coger Alley Ram Chunder Loll, of Bombay : but how this litigious old female managed to get out, physically or literally, to Hindostan, or into difficulties with a Parsee indigo broker, passes my comprehension. A mysterious old lady !

Meanwhile, Miss Bridget Tattyboys is the landlady of Tattyboys Rents. There is no dubiety about her existence *there*. Only be a little behindhand with your rent, and you will soon be favoured with one of Mr. Barwise's ' Sir, I am instructed by Miss Tattyboys ;' and close upon that will follow Mr. S. Scrutor, Miss Tattyboys' broker, with his distraint, and his levy, and his inventory, and all the sacraments of selling up. I should opine that Miss Tattyboys is deaf, for she is remarkable in cases of unpaid rent for not listening to appeals for time, and not hearing of a compromise Gilks, the chandler's shopkeeper of number nine, whose wife is always in the family-way, and himself in difficulties, once ' bound himself by a curse ' to seek out Miss Tattyboys at Hoxton, to beard her in her very den, and appeal to her mercy, her charity, her womanhood, in a matter of two quarters owing. He started one morning, with a determined shirt-collar, and fortified by sundry small libations at the Cape of Good Hope. He returned at nightfall with a haggard face, disordered apparel, and an unsteady gait ; was inarticulate and incoherent in his speech ; shortly afterwards went to bed ; and to this day cannot be prevailed upon by his acquaintances, by the wife of his bosom even, to give any account of his interview, if interview he had, with the Megæra of Hoxton. Mrs. Gilks, a wary woman, who has brought, and is bringing, up a prodigious family, has whispered to Mrs. Spileburg, of the Cape of Good Hope, that, on the morning after Gilks's expedition, examining his garments, as it is the blessed conjugal custom to do, she found, imprinted in chalky dust, on the back of his coat, *the mark of a human foot !* What could this portend ? Did Gilks penetrate to Hoxton, and was he indeed *kicked* by Miss Tattyboys ? or did he suffer the insulting infliction at the foot of some pampered menial ? Or, coming home despairing, was he led to the consumption (and the redundancy of coppers, and the paucity o silver, in his pockets would favour this view of the case) of more liquid sustenance of a fermented nature than was good for him ? And was he in this state kicked by outraged landlord or infuriated pot-companion? Gilks lives, and makes no sign. Pressed on the subject of Miss Tattyboys, he reluctantly grumbles that she is an 'old image,' and this is all.

Dear reader (and the digression may be less intolerable, seeing that it takes place in what is but a digression itself), I do wonder what Miss Tattyboys is like. Is she really the stern, harsh, uncompromising female that her acts bespeak her? Does she sit in a rigid cap, or still accoutred in the black bonnet and veil in a dreary office-like parlour at Hoxton, with all her documents docketed on a table before her, or glaring from pigeon-holes, shelves, and cupboards? Or is she a jolly, apple-faced, little woman, in a cheery room with birds and plants and flowers, liking a cosy glass and a merry song: a Lady Bountiful in the neighbourhood, a Dorcas to the poor, the idol of all the dissenting ministers around? Perhaps. Who knows? Ah! how unlike we all are to what we seem! How the roar of the lion abroad softens into the bleat of the lamb at home! How meekly the fierce potent schoolmaster of the class-room holds out his knuckles for the ruler in the study! He who is the same in his own home of homes as he is abroad, is a marvel.

Miss Tattyboys has a carriage and a horse, but for certain reasons upon which I briefly touched in allusion to the parish engine, her visits to the Rents are made perforce on foot. Monday mornings, black Mondays emphatically, are her ordinary visiting days; and on such mornings you will see her dusky form looming at Mr. Fazzle's door, or flitting through the Rents as she is escorted to her carriage by Barwise, her agent. Communications may be made direct to her, but they always come somehow through Barwise. He may be described as the buffer to the Tattyboys train; and run at her ever so hard, Barwise receives the first collision, and detracts from its force. If Gilks wants time, or Chapford threatens to leave unless his roof is looked to, or Mrs. Chownes asks again about that kitchen range, or Spilcburg expresses a savage opinion that his house will tumble in next week, and that there'll be murder against somebody, Barwise interposes, explains, promises, refuses, will see about it. Which Barwise never does. You try to get at Miss Tattyboys, but you can't, though you are within hand and earshot of her. The portentous black veil flutters in the wind; you are dazzled and terrified by her huge black reticule bursting with papers; you strive to speak; but Miss Tattyboys is gone, and all you can do is to throw yourself upon Barwise, who throws you over.

The carriage of the landlady of the Rents is an anomalous vehicle on very high springs, of which the body seems decidedly never to have been made for the wheels, which on their part appear to be all of different sizes, and shriek while moving dreadfully. Much basket-work enters into the composition of Miss Tattyboys's carriage, also much rusty leather, and a considerable quantity of a fabric resembling bedticking. There are two lamps, one of which is quite blind and glassless, and the other blinking and knocked on one side in some by-gone collision, to a very squinting obliquity. A complication of straps and rusty iron attaches this equipage to a very long-bodied, short-legged black horse, not unlike a turnspit dog, which appears to be utterly disgusted with the whole turn out, and drags it with an outstretched head and outstretched legs, as though he *were* a dog and the carriage a tin kettle tied to his tail. There have been blood and bone once about this horse doubtless; but the blood is confined at present to a perpetual raw on his shoulder, artfully veiled from the Society's constables by the rags of his dilapidated collar, and the bone to a lamentably anatomical development of his ribs. To him, is Jehu, a man of grim aspect and of brickdust complexion, whose hat and coat are as the hat and coat of a groom, but whose legs are as the legs of an agricultural labourer, inasmuch as they are clad in corduroy, and terminate in heavy shoes, much clayed. He amuses himself while waiting for his mistress with aggravating the long-bodied horse with his whip on his blind side (he, the horse, is wall-eyed) and with reading a tattered volume, averred by many to be a book of tracts, but declared by some to be a 'Little Warbler,' insomuch as smothered refrains of 'right tooral lol looral' have been heard at times from his dreary coachbox. It is not a pleasant sight this rusty carriage with the long horse and the grim coachman jolting and staggering about Blitsom Street. It does not do a man good to see the black bonnet and veil inside, with the big reticule and the papers, and overshadowed by them all, as though a cypress had been drawn over her, a poor little weazened diminutive pale-faced little girl, in a bonnet preposterously large for her, supposed to be Miss Tattyboys's niece, also to be a something in Chancery, and the 'infant' about whose 'custody' there is such a fluster every other term, the unhappy heiress of thousands of **disputed pounds.**

I cannot finally dismiss Miss Tattyboys without saying a
word about Barwise, her agent. Barwise as a correspondent
is hated and contemned, but Barwise as a man is popular and
respected. His letters are dreadful. When Barwise says he
will ' write to you,' you are certain (failing payment) of being
sued. Barwise's first letters first begin, ' It is now some time
since ;' his second missive commences with the awful words,
' Sir, unless ;' and after that, he is sure to be ' instructed by
Miss Tattyboys,' and to sell you up. It is horrible to think
that Barwise not only collects Miss Tattyboys's rents ; but
that he collects debts for anybody in the neighbourhood,
takes out the abhorred ' gridirons,' or County Court summonses, is an auctioneer, appraiser, valuer, estate, house, and
general agent. Dreadful thought for Barwise to have a
general agency over you ! Yet Barwise is not horrible to
view, being a sandy man of pleasant mien, in a long brown
coat. He is a capital agent, too, to employ, if you want to
get in any little moneys that are due to you ; and then it is
astonishing how you find yourself egging Barwise on, and
telling him to be firm, and not to hear of delay. I think
there is but one sentiment that can surpass the indignation a
man feels at being forced to pay anything he owes—and that
is the *sæva indignatio* with which he sets about forcing people
to pay, who owe him anything.

Barwise sings a good song, and the parlour of the Cape of
Good Hope nightly re-echoes to his tuneful muse. I don't
believe he ever went farther seaward than Greenwich, but he
specially affects nautical ditties, and his plaintive ' Then
farewell, my trim-built wherry,' and ' When my money was all
spent,' have been found occasionally exasperating to parties
whose ' sticks ' he has been instrumental in seizing the day
before. On festive occasions I have however heard his health
proposed, and the laudatory notes of ' For he's a jolly good
fellow !' go round.

There are three notable institutions in Tattyboys Rents.
I am rather at a loss which first to touch upon. These are
the posts, the children, and the dogs—and all three as connected with the steps. Suppose, in reverse order of rank, I
take the brute creation first. Tattyboys Rents, if it were
famous for anything, which it is not, should be famous for
its dogs. They are remarkable, firstly, for not having any
particular breed. Gilks, the chandler's shopkeeper, had a
puppy which was ' giv' to him by a party as was always
mixed up with dogs,' which he thought, at first, would turn

out a pointer, then a terrier, then a spaniel; but was miserably disappointed in all his conjectures. He had gone to the expense of a collar for him, and the conversion of an emptied butter-firkin into a kennel, and, in despair, took him to Chuffers, the greengrocer, and dogs'-meat vendor, in Blitsom Street, and solemnly asked his opinion upon him. 'There hain't a hinch of breed in him,' was the dictum of Chuffers, as he contemptuously bestowed a morsel of eleemosynary paunch upon the low-bred cur. Charley (this was the animal's name) grew up to be a gaunt dog of wolf-like aspect, an incorrigible thief, a shameless profligate, a bully, and a tyrant. He was the terror of the children and the other dogs; and as if that unhappy Gilks had not already sufficient sorrows upon his head, Charley had the inconceivable folly and wickedness to make an attack one Monday morning upon the sacred black silk dress of Miss Tattyboys. You may imagine that Barwise was down upon Gilks the very next day, like a portcullis. Charley thenceforth disappeared. Gilks had a strange affection for him, and still cherished a fond belief that he would turn out something in the thorough-bred line some day; but the butter-firkin was removed to the back yard, and Charley was supposed to pass the rest of his existence in howling and fighting with his chain in that town house amid brickbats, cabbage-stalks, and clothes-pegs, having in addition a villegiatura or country house in an adjacent dust-bin, into which the length of his chain just allowed him to scramble, and in the which he sat among the dust and ashes, rasping himself occasionally (for depilatory purposes) against a potsherd.

There is a brown dog of an uncertain shade of mongrelity, who (they are all of such decided character, these dogs, that I think they deserve a superior pronoun) belongs to nobody in particular, and is generally known in the Rents as the Bow-wow. As such it is his avocation and delight to seek the company of very young children (those of from eighteen months to two years of age are his preference) whose favour and familiarity he courts, and whom he amuses by his gambols and good-humour. The bow-wow is a welcome guest on all door-steps, and in most entrance-halls. His gymnastics are a never-failing source of amusement to the juvenile population, and he derives immense gratification from the terms of endearment and cajolement addressed by the mothers and nurses to their children, all of which expressions this feeble-minded animal takes to be addressed to himself, and at which he sniggers his head and wags his stump of a tail tremendously. I have yet

to learn whether this brown, hairy, ugly dog is so fond of the
little children, and frisks round them, and rolls them over
with such tender lovingness, and suffers himself to be pulled
and pinched and poked by his playmates, all with immovable
complacency—I say, I have yet to learn whether he does all
this through sheer good-humour and fondness for children, or
whether he is a profound hypocrite, skilled in the ways of the
world, and knowing that the way to Mother Hubbard's cupboard, when there are any bones in it, is through Mother
Hubbard's motherly heart. I hope, for the credit of dog nature
and for my own satisfaction, loving that nature, that the first
is the cause.

The only dog in the Rents that can claim any family or
breed is an animal by the name of Buffo, who was, in remote
times, a French poodle. I say *was*, for the poodleian appearance has long since departed from him, and he resembles
much more, now, a very dirty, shaggy, white bear, seen
through the small end of an opera-glass. He was the property,
on his first introduction to the Rents, of one Monsieur
Phillips—whether originally Philippe or not, I do not know—
who, it was inferred, from sundry strange paraphernalia that
he left behind him on his abrupt departure from his residence,
was something in the magician, not to say conjuror and
mountebank line. Buffo was then a glorious animal, half-
shaved, as poodles should be, with fluffy rings round his legs,
and two tufts on his haunches, and a coal-black nose, due
perhaps to the employment of nitrate of silver as a cosmetic,
and a pink skin. He could mount and descend a ladder ; he
could run away when Monsieur Phillips hinted that there was
a 'policeman coming ;' he could limp on one leg ; he could
drop down dead, dance, climb up a lamp-post at the word of
command. It was even said that he had been seen in James
Street, Covent Garden, on a ragged piece of carpet, telling
fortunes upon the cards, and pointing out Monsieur Phillips
as the greatest rogue in company. Monsieur Phillips, however, one morning suddenly disappeared, leaving sundry
weeks' rent owing to his landlord, Chapford, of the beer-shop ;
his only effects being the strange implements of legerdemain
I have noticed, and the dog Buffo, whom he had placed at
livery, so to state, at least at a fixed weekly stipend for his
board and lodging. I need not say that in a very short time
the unfortunate dog 'ate his head right off ;' the amount of
paunch he had consumed far exceeding his marketable value.
Chapford, after vainly debating as to the propriety of turning

the magician's cups into half-pint measures, and his balls into bagatelle balls, sold them to Scrutor, the broker, and Buffo himself to Joe (surname unknown), who is a helper up Spavins's yard, the livery and bait stables, in Blitsom Street. Joe 'knowed of a lady down Kensington wot was werry nuts upon poodles;' and Buffo, prior to his introduction to the lady amateur, was subjected to sundry dreadful operations of dog farriery, in the way of clipping, staining, and curtailing, which made him from that day forward a dog of sullen and morose temper. He soon came back from Kensington in disgrace, the alleged cause of his dismissal being his having fought with, killed, and eaten a gray cockatoo. He was re-sold to Mrs. Lazenby, old Mr. Fazzle's housekeeper; but he had either forgotten or was too misanthropic to perform any of his old tricks, regarded policemen unmoved, and passed by the whole pack of cards with profound disdain. A report, too, founded on an inadvertent remark of Chapford, that he (Buffo) had once been on the stage, and had been fired out of a cannon by the clown in a pantomime, succeeded in ruining him in the opinion of the Rents, who hold all 'play-actors' in horror : he passed from owner to owner, and was successively kicked out and discarded by all, and now hangs about Chapford's, a shabby, used-up, degraded, broken-down beast.

Is there anything more pitiable in animal nature than a thoroughly hard-up dog? Such a one I met two Sundays back in a shiningly genteel street in Pimlico. He was a cur, most wretchedly attenuated, and there in Pimlico he sat, with elongated jaws, his head on one side, his eyes wofully up-turned, his haunches turned out, his feet together, his tail subdued, his ribs rampant : an utterly worn-out, denuded, ruined old dog. If he had taken a piece of chalk, and written 'I am starving,' fifty times on the pavement in the most ornamental caligraphy, it could not have excited more sympathy than the unutterable expression of his oblique misery, propped up sideways as he was against a kitchen railing. I had no sooner halted to accost him, than, taking it for granted that I was going to kick or beat him because he was miserable, he shambled meekly into the gutter, where he stood, shivering; but I spoke him fair, and addressing him in what little I knew of the Doggee language, strove to reassure him. But how could I relieve him? What could I do for him? It was a stern uncompromising shining British Sunday; there was no back slum nigh; no lowly shop, whither I could convey him to regale on dogs'-meat. Moreover it was church time, and I could not even purchase licensed victuals for his succour. It was no good giving him a penny. I might as well have given him a tract. He was unmistakably mangy, and I dared not convey him home; and I knew of no dog-hospital. So I exhorted him to patience and resignation, and left him reluctantly; persuaded that the greatest charity I could have extended to him would have been to blow his brains out.

You are not to think that these I have mentioned are all the dogs of which Tattyboys Rents can boast. Many more are they, big dogs and little dogs: from that corpulent Newfoundland dog of Scrutor's, the broker, whose sagacity is so astounding as to lead to his being trusted with baskets and cash, to purchase bread and butchers' meat—the which he does faithfully, bringing back change with scrupulous exactitude—and whose only fault is his rapid rate of locomotion, and defective vision, which cause him to run up against and upset very nearly everybody he meets in his journeys—to Bob Blather, the barber's, cock-tail terrier, which can kill a 'power of rats,' and has more than once been matched in 'Bell's Life' (familiarly called by the sporting part of the Rents, 'The Life') to do so. I may say, to the honour of the dogs of Tattyboys Rents, that they seldom stray beyond its limits; and that if any strange dog descend the steps leading thereunto, they invariably fall upon, and strive to demolish him with the utmost ferocity.

The children of the Rents are so much like other street children, that they preserve the same traditions of street games and songs common to other localities. They are remarkable, however, for a certain grave and sedate demeanour, which I have never failed to observe in children who are in the habit of sitting much upon flights of steps. Such steps are the beach of street life, and the sea of the streets rolls on towards the stony shore. The steps of Tattyboys Rents are to the children there a place of deliberation, recreation, observation, and repose. There, is to-morrow's lesson studied; there, does the baby learn a vivâ-voce lesson in walking; there, is the dirt-pie made, and the sharp-pointed 'cat' constructed; there, does the nurse-child rest, and the little maid achieve her task of sewing; there, are tops wound, and marbles gambled for, and juvenile scandals promulgated; there, is the quarrel engendered, and the difference adjusted. It is good to see this La Scala of Tattyboys Rents on a sunshiny day; its degrees sown with little people, whose juvenile talk falls cheerfully on the ear after the ruder conversation at the posts.

The posts are immediately behind the steps, forming a grove
of egress,—a sort of forest of Soignies, behind the Mont Saint
Jean of the Rents,—into Blitsom Street. At the posts, is
Chapford's beer-shop ; pots are tossed for at the posts, and bets
are made on horse-races. Many a married woman in the Rents
' drats ' the posts, at whose bases she lays the Saturday night
vagaries of her ' master ;' forgetting how many of her own sex
are postally guilty, and how often she herself has stood a-gossip-
ing at the posts and at the pump.

XXII.

TATTYBOYS RENTERS.

THAT gregarious tendency common to men, as well as to the
inferior orders of animation, that leads the devouring lion to
howl in company with his fellows, minnows to flow together
into the net of the snarer, herrings to be taken in shoals
of thousands, blacklegs to horde with blacklegs, lords with
lords, children with children, birds of a feather, in fact,
human as well as ornithological, to flock together—has
brought a considerable number of eccentric parties together
in Tattyboys Rents. For the Rents being decidedly eccentric
of themselves as Rents, it was but natural and to be expected
that at least one party of eccentric character should, in the
first instance, come to reside in them. After this it was not
of course surprising, carrying out the birds-of-a-feather theory,
that other eccentric parties should come and join party number
one ; and the glorious yet natural result has been, that we
possess in Tattyboys Rents perhaps as queer a lot of parties
as you could find (though we are perfectly solvent) out of
Queer Street.

I strove so hard, *remis atque velis*, in the first instance, to
give you as sufficient an idea of the Rents, architecturally
speaking, that I had little space to dilate on the characteristics of the inhabitants. You might have been able to
discern something like eccentricity in Miss Tattyboys, but I
cannot bring her forward with anything like certainty as a
character ; she is so unsubstantial, so mythic. As it has
been often and bitterly complained of by her tenants—you
don't know where to have her. But the Rents can boast
other characters about whom there is no mistake, who stand

out in bold and well-defined relief, and who, whether tradesmen or dealing at one another's shops, are emphatically rum
customers. Will you allow me to introduce you to a few?
You will? Mumchance, stand forth!

Right up at the further end of the Rents, where the
thoroughfare is blockaded by the high frowning walls of
Smelt and Pigg's foundry, dwells, in a house—one of the
dingiest, shabbiest, queerest houses in Tattyboys Rents—
P. R. Mumchance. Would you know for what stand the
initials P. R.? For Peter Robert, haply? For Peregrine
Reuben, or Pietro Rolando, or Paul Ralph? Not at all.
Mumchance's father (commonly known as Old Nutcrackers,
from the strong development of his facial muscles) was a great
admirer—some say friend and creditor—of that virtuous, illustrious, and magnanimous prince, the penultimate possessor of
the British throne; and young Mumchance, being born about
the year eighteen hundred and eleven, was christened, in a
moment of loyal enthusiasm, Prince Regent Mumchance. This
curious Christian name is a sore point and grievous stumbling-
block with Mumchance. The Prince Regent is his old man
of the sea, his white elephant of Ava. He is fond of political
discussion. What could an individual bearing so illustrious
a name be but an out-and-out, an ultra-cerulean Conservative? So Mumchance is a Tory of the bitterest and bluest
description; and as the majority of the Renters are as bitter
Radicals, opposing rates, taxes, rents, or indeed any other
imposts, vehemently, the discussions that nightly take place
in the parlour of the Cape of Good Hope are not of the
pleasantest description. Moreover, Mumchance is fond of his
glass; and could you expect an individual bearing the august
name of the great champion of rare beverages (it is whispered,
even, the inventor of hock and soda water) to consume such
vulgar liquids as porter, or gin, or rum? No. P. R. Mumchance never asks you if you will take a glass of ale, or a
'drain' of gin. 'Glass of sherry wine, sir?' is the Prince
Regent's hospitable interrogatory; and a good many glasses
of sherry wine does the Prince Regent take in the course of
the twenty-four hours.

Mumchance keeps a shop—a stationer's shop. He sells
stationery, account-books, slates and slate-pencils, tops,
marbles, string, paste, and, by some curious idiosyncracy,
pickles. How he got into that line, or how he can reconcile
pickles with writing-paper, I cannot imagine; but there are
the pickles—walnut, onion, and mixed—in big earthen jars:

and at all hours of the day you may see small brigades of children bearing halfpence and cracked teacups or gallipots bound to Mumchance's for ' a penn'orth of pickles, please.'

But pray don't think that although Mumchance is a stationer and account-book manufacturer, his shop is at all like a stationer's. Not at all. It is considerably more like the warehouse of a wholesale tobacconist who has sold his stock out; and it has, if I must be candid, a considerable dash of the marine-store and of the rag-shop. There is a ghostly remnant of a whilom gigantic pair of scales; there are mysterious tubs and packing-cases, and bulging parcels tied with rotten cord. Mumchance does not deny that he buys waste-paper; the evil-minded whisper that he buys and sells rags: nay, old Mrs. Brush, the veteran inhabitant alluded to in a former paper, minds the time when a doll—a real black doll—swung backward and forward in the wind over the door of Toby, commonly hight Old Nutcrackers, the father of Prince Regent Mumchance.

That Mumchance is mad many have declared; but I, for one, do not believe it. That Mumchance is queer, very queer in manners, appearance, and general character, no one can deny. He is an undersized man, whose portrait can be succinctly drawn if I tell you that he is an utter stranger to the brush. By the brush I mean the clothes-brush, and the hat-brush, the hair-brush, the tooth-brush, the nail-brush, and, I may add, the flesh-brush. Buhl-work is a beautiful style of ornamentation, so is marqueterie, so is Venetian mosaic; but when you happen to find buhl, marqueterie, and mosaic, all represented in a gentleman's face and hands by a complicated inlaying and ingraining of dirt, the spectacle will hardly be so pleasant, I fancy, as examples of the same arts in a cabinet, an escrutoire, or the cupola of St. Mark's Church. So mosaicised is Mumchance. Bets have been freely made that he never washes; but he has been observed to rub his face occasionally with a very mouldy pocket-handkerchief of no discoverable size or colour, conjectured to be either a fragment of an old window-blind, or one of the ancient rags purchased by his father Toby in the way of business. Even this occasional friction of his countenance, however, is not supposed to advance in Mumchance the cause of that state which is said to be next to godliness; he wipes his face indeed; but he only removes the impurities of the day, of the hour, to show, in all its distinctness, the inlaid dirt of perchance years. It is just as when examining an old picture you pass

a wet cloth over its surface; and lo! the mellowness of centuries becomes visible to you beneath.

Mumchance's head is, if I may use the expression, rhom-
boidal. His hair is, as before stated, utterly unbrushed,
somewhat of the colour of an unbaked brick, and generally in
a state which I may characterise as fluffy. In fact, minute
particles of straw, paper, cotton, bread, and other foreign
substances, may freely be detected on its surface by the naked
eye alone, which may partially be accounted for, by his
carrying most of his purchases, sometimes his letters, and
always his lunch, in his hat. His whiskers, which are of the
same colour, or the same state of discoloration, as his hair, do
not appear to have made up their minds yet as to where they
shall settle, and have grown irregularly about his face, just as
hirsute things happened to turn up. His complexion I may
describe heraldically as a field gules, semé (I believe that is the
word) with sable or dirt. No sign of shirt appears in the entire
Mumchance. A big black stock confines his neck, and to his
chin rises his closely-buttoned blue swallow-tailed coat—that
woeful blue coat with the odd buttons once gilt, and once
tightly sewn on, but now drooping like Ophelia's willow,
askant the brook; the sleeves too short, the tails too long, the
coat with many darns, and the nap all turned the wrong way.
Add to this coat (without the connecting isthmus of a waistcoat)
a pair of corduroy trousers, of which the pockets, apparently
disgusted with their long seclusion, have burst forth to see
the world, and stand agape, on Mumchance's hips, at that
world's wonders; suppose these trousers to be much frayed at
the bottom, much inked (he makes calculations on their knees
frequently), and much too short, and conclude them with
Wellington boots, patched till they resembled that knight's
silk stockings that were darned so frequently that they
changed their texture from silk to worsted—and you have
Mumchance before you, all but his shamble, his watery eye,
his rich though somewhat husky voice.

For all his shabby appearance, however, once a year Mumchance throws aside his chrysalis garb, and comes forth a full-
blown butterfly. Once a year he dines with his Company—
the Stationers—at the grand old hall in the dim regions of the
City; for Mumchance is a citizen, a liveryman, a worshipful
stationer—who but he—and so was Toby his father before him.
He goes to the dinner of his Company, clean, rosy, shaven,
with a shirt, aye, and a shirt frill, a blue coat and gilt buttons,
but new, glossy, well brushed, a shiny hat, and shiny boots.

Thus he goes ; but how he comes back no inhabitant of Tattyboys Rents has ever been able to discover. The policeman
should know ; but he affects ignorance ; and though I do not
wish to impute corruption to that functionary, it is certain that
Mumchance is always leaving private drains of liquor for him
at the bar of the Cape of Good Hope, for at least a week following his Company's dinner.

Some of the renters have affirmed that they have heard with
the chimes at midnight dismal ditties trolled forth in incoherent accents ; and these are surmised to have issued from
Mumchance while in a state of conviviality, and to have been
occult Stationers' songs, taught him along with the other arts
and mysteries of the worshipful craft in his earliest youth.
Mrs. Mumchance (an elongated female of an uncertain age,
with a vexed cap and a perturbed gown) is a lady with a fixed
idea. That idea is Fisher. Fisher, whether he be the family
doctor, lawyer, nearest kinsman, dearest friend, or most valued
adviser, is at all events Mrs. Mumchance's Law and Prophet.
Fisher recommends her change of air. Fisher has inexorably
prophesied her dissolution within six calendar months, if she
continues worreting herself about her family. Fisher warned
her against the second floor lodger, who ran away without
paying his rent. Fisher advises her to stand it no longer with
Mr. Mumchance's recalcitrant debtors, but to employ Barwise,
and summons them all forthwith. When Fisher said Mrs. Mumchance, said he, beware of Mrs. Tuckstrap, were not those the
words of truth ? On all emergencies, in all difficulties and
dilemmas, Mrs. Mumchance throws herself upon Fisher. He
is intimately mixed up with the whole family. Mumchance
professes the highest respect and veneration for him. Mr. Fisher
he says, a man of the first, of the very first. Coat buttoned
up to here, sir. Great friend of poor father's, sir. Frequently
does he escape curtain lectures on late and vinous returns to
his Lares and Penates on the plea that he has been ' along with
Fisher.' If you ask Charley, Mumchance's youngest, who his
godfather was, he will answer, ' Missa Fisser ;' if you ask him
who or what Missa Fisser, or Fisher may be, he will answer,
a ' chown ;' from which, however, it is not to be inferred absolutely that Fisher is connected with the stage in a red ochre
and bismuth view as a clown ; Charley's ideas of trades and
professions being necessarily vague as yet ; and his whole
bump of admiration having been so engrossed by a pantomimic performance of which he was lately the spectator,
that he applies the epithet chown, or clown, to everything

great, or good, or pleasant ; being even known to address as chown, horses, sweetstuff, hoopsticks, fenders, and halfpence.

I never had the pleasure of seeing Fisher ; but Mrs. Brush, the oldest inhabitant, has seen him, and describes him as a pleasant-spoken body. Mrs. Spileburg, of the Cape of Good Hope, declares him to be a born gentleman, as takes his drink quite hearty like, which it would do you good to see. I should like to know Fisher.

Mumchance has an indefinite number of children. I say indefinite, for they are always being born and going out to service, and walking out with Tom or Dick So-and-so, and marrying, and so on. There is always, however, an eldest daughter Annie, tall, lanky, and fourteen, who must begin to do something for herself shortly, and a youngest boy, at present Charley ; but the whole family have such a curious way of shooting up and growing into maturity suddenly, that I should not be at all surprised on my next visit to the Rents to learn that Annie was suckling her second, or that Charley had enlisted in the Life Guards.

Mumchance's trade and manner of doing business puzzle and amaze me sorely. Men repute him to be wealthy : I know he spends a great deal of money, yet I seldom see him sell anything more considerable than a ha'porth of slate pencil, a sheet of writing-paper, a penn'orth of wafers, or a penny bottle of ink. The man who could purchase a quire of foolscap, or half gross of steel pens, was never yet known, I opine, to enter Mumchance's. He tries to force the market sometimes, and to create a factitious excitement about his wares, by displaying in front of his establishment placards in pen and ink, containing such announcements as ' Cheapest wafers in the world !' ' Paper down again !' ' Great news !' ' Ink a penny a bottle !' but the passers-by regard these notifications irreverently, and point to the inferior quality of the paper and ink of the placard, in depreciation of the stationery within : nay, even raise objections against Mumchance's pens, because Mumchance's writing is none of the best, and his orthography none of the most correct.

Mumchance puts the coldness of the public all down to the fault of the times. What's the good of painting the shop, sir ? he asks. Poor father never did, sir, and we had nobility here. Nobility, sir. But look at the times. Would nobility come here now, sir ?

I generally admit, when Mumchance asks me this puestion, that nobility would not.

'That's it, sir,' says Mumchance triumphant (he always says sir, even to the ragged little boys who come in for a penn orth of pickles). 'That's it, it's the times. Nobody buys stamps now a days. In poor father's time, we sold millions of stamps, sir. Lord Cabus, sir. Proud man, sir. Coat buttoned up to here, sir. Sit on the counter, sir. All in black, sir, with his coat buttoned. Mumchance, he'd say to poor father, Mumchance, bless your eyes, fifty pounds' worth of bill stamps. Proud man, sir, Lord Cabus; never would take hold of the handle of the door with his hand; always took the tail of his coat to it, like this, sir,' and Mumchance suits the action to the word.

I may remark as one of the most eccentric among Mumchance's idiosyncracies that the very great majority of his titled or celebrated acquaintances are always dressed in black, and have their coats buttoned up to here, meaning the chin. Thus, when Mumchance went to see Edmund Kean, and there was, in consequence of a certain trial, a violent commotion in the house against the tragedian, Mumchance described Kean as coming forward to address the audience attired in black, with his coat buttoned up to here. Similarly attired, according to Mumchance, was wont to be the famous Jack Thurtell, who was a great customer of poor father's for bill stamps. Likewise all in black, with coats buttoned up to here, were a mysterious company of four-and-twenty forgers who, according to Mumchance, were discovered sitting round a long table with a green baize cover (forging with all their might and main, I presume), by Townshend the officer (vide Little Blitsom Street gang). I can imagine Townshend with his coat buttoned up; but with the traditions of his white hat, red waistcoat, and top boots, still in my mind, I cannot form to myself an idea of him —all in black.

The number of extraordinary characters with whom Mumchance has been acquainted and connected, and whose little peculiarities he descants upon, is astonishing. His anecdotes bearing upon Colonel Bubb alone, would fill a volume. The Colonel is to Mumchance what Fisher is to Mrs. M. On all political, parochial, financial, and social questions, he is his chief adviser, and his heroic advice is ordinarily, 'Mumchance, be firm.' I met Mumchance once, just before the opening of a session of Parliament by her gracious Majesty. There had been some silly mares-nests found about that time by some sillier politicians, and grim whispers circulated about an illustrious personage, treason, the Tower, tampering with treaties, and such twopenny trash. Mumchance was full of it. He had scarcely time to gasp out his customary invite of ' glass of sherry wine, sir, and a crust ?' and to dive into a previously invisible public-house (he knows all the slip-in and slip-out public-houses in London), before he had me fast with Colonel Bubb on the illustrious question. Saw him this morning, sir. Got his leathers on, sir (I conjecture the Colonel to be in the cavalry). Got his cloak over his leathers, sir (a cloak this time, but well buttoned up you may be sure of it). Mumchance, he says, I've got my army in the park. Drawn up (in their leathers, I suppose). Mumchance, blood before night. Blood ! With which horrifying conclusion, Colonel Bubb departed in his leathers, as Mumchance took care supplementarily to inform me, to rejoin his army. I did go down to the park that day, where I saw the usual number of big life guardsmen ; but I missed Colonel Bubb, his cloak, and his leathers, and I saw no blood either that night or the next.

I cannot part with Mumchance without telling you that in his crazy, dingy, unpainted house in Tattyboys Rents he has something else besides slate-pencils, pickles, and penny bottles of ink. Up stairs, amid much dirt, and dust, and flew, he has some nobly carved oaken bedsteads and rare old cabinets filled with real porcelain, yet rarer, and yet older. Also down in his cellar Mumchance has stores of considerable value. Here, among the dirt and dust, and above a sort of subsoil of the rags in which Mumchance was libellously supposed to deal, lie hundreds of books, many of them bygone and worthless pamphlets and tracts, but many rare and beautiful copies of expensive works. How he came by these Mumchance vouchsafes not to tell ; neither will he explain how he became possessed of the copper plates engraved in line and mezzotinto and aquatint, which lumber the floor, and on whose dusky surfaces I can observe dim shadowings of landscapes after Wilson, and beauties after Sir Joshua Reynolds. Poor father would appear to have had something to do with the original acquisition of these rarities, and the hardness of the times to prevent their conversion into money ; so here they remain, and proofs from the plates themselves, and the books, and papers, and rags, all mildew and rot in Mumchance's cellar.

Rummaging among the heap one day I found a huge oak-bound, iron-clasped volume, written in black and red letter on vellum, in Saxon and Latin. It was the Rent Roll of Glastonbury Abbey ! I confess that I immediately broke the tenth commandment, and began to covet my neighbour's goods ; in **fact,**

I offered Mumchance several small sums, increasing in amount
at every bid, for the volume. He seemed at first disposed to
acquiesce, but requested time in order that he might consult
Fisher. The upshot of it was that Fisher (seconded no doubt
by Colonel Bubb) strongly advised him not to sell the book
until the arrival of a lady—name unknown—then sojourning
at Jerusalem, who knew all languages, and could read the
volume, as easy as a glove. As I never saw the oak-bound
volume again, and as I heard that Mumchance had sold it to
the trustees of a public library for forty guineas, I concluded
either that the lady possessing the lingual accomplishments
had come back from Jerusalem rather sooner than was expected,
or that Mumchance was not so mad as his neighbours took him
to be.

Thus have I drawn the portrait of Prince Regent Mumchance,
en pied, yet still grossly, broadly, sketchily. Were I to stay
to define, to detail, to stipple the little points of his character,
as Mr. Holman Hunt does his faces, I should weary myself and
you ; nay, more than that, I should leave no space for a three-
quarter portrait of another eccentric party in the Rents, old
Signor Fripanelli.

What Gian Battisto Girolamo Fripanelli of Bologna, professor of singing and the pianoforte, could have been about
when he came to lodge at Miss Drybohn's, number eighteen
in the Rents, I am sure I don't know, yet with Miss Drybohn
he has lodged for very nearly twenty years. They say that
he came over to England at the Peace of Amiens, that he was
chapel-master to Louis the Sixteenth, and that he only escaped
the guillotine during the reign of terror, by composing a
Sonata for the fête of the Goddess of Liberty. At any rate he
is of a prodigious age, although his stature is but diminutive.
I regret to state that the boys call him Jacko, and shout that
derisive appellation after him in the street. These unthink-
ing young persons affect to trace a resemblance between the
venerable Signor Fripanelli, and the degraded animal which
eats nuts and grins between the bars of a cage in the Zoological Gardens. To be sure, the Signor is diminutive in
stature. His head is narrow and long, his ears are large, his
eyes small, his cheekbones high, his complexion sallow and
puckered into a thousand wrinkles ; to be sure his hands are
singularly long and bony, and he walks with a sort of stumbling hop, and is generally munching something between his
sharp teeth, and has a shrill squeaking voice, and gesticulates
violently when excited ; but is a gentleman to be called

Jacko—to be likened to a low monkey for these peculiarities? Signor Fripanelli wears, summer and winter, a short green cloak, adorned with a collar of the woolly texture, generally denominated poodle ; a white hat stuck at the very back of his head, threadbare black pantaloons, and very roomy shoes with rusty strings. This costume he never varies. In it he goes out giving lessons ; in it, less the hat, he sits at home at Miss Drybohn's ; in it he goes twice every Sunday, in his own simple, quiet, honest fashion to the Roman Catholic Chapel in Lateran Street, out of Turk's Lane.

It would seem to favour the insolent Jacko theory concerning the poor Signor that Miss Drybohn, who it is generally acknowledged has the worst tongue in her head of any spinster in the Rents, and who, though Fripanelli has lodged with her for twenty years, and has never been a fortnight behind-hand with his rent—that Miss Drybohn, I say, declares that when the Signor returns home at night and retires to his bed-room, which is immediately above hers, she always hears (though she knows that he is alone) the noise of four feet pattering above. She accuses·nobody, she states nothing, but such (she says) it is—and the by-standers shake their heads and whisper that the Signor, on return home, fatigued with teaching, assumes his natural position—in other words, that he crawls about on all-fours, like a baboon on the branch of a tree. Horror!

Seriously, although the little man is like a monkey, he is one of the bravest, worthiest, kindest creatures alive. He has very little money ; none but those who know what the life o an obscure foreign music-master is can tell how difficult it is for him to live, much less to save, in England ; but from his scanty means he gives freely to his poor fellow-countrymen, yea, and to aliens of other climes and other creeds. Fifteen years ago, the Signor had a fine connection among the proudest aristocracy of this proud land. Yes, he taught singing at half a guinea a lesson, in Grosvenor Square, and Park Lane and Mayfair. You may see some of his old songs now yellow-tattered and fly-blown on the music book-stalls : Cabaletto, dedicated by permission to the Most Noble the Marchioness of Antidiloof, by her obliged, faithful, and humble servant, Gian Battisto Girolamo Fripanelli. Aria, inscribed with the most devoted sentiments of respect and reverence to Her Grace the Duchess of Fortherfludd, by Her Grace's etcetera, etcetera, etcetera. There have been scores of the fairest and noblest young English ladies, whose taper

fingers have been taught by poor old Jacko to fall harmoni-
ously upon the ivory keys, whose ruby lips and pearly teeth
he has tutored with much stress of sol-fa-ing, to give due and
proper, and gentle, and impassioned utterance to the silver
strains of Italian song. Gian Battisto has been asked to
lunch by Dukes—aye, and to dinner too, and has sat next
to Ambassadors and Plenipotentiaries—parties to the Holy
Alliance and hung with stars and crosses, as that patient
gentleman near the Bank of England (who also sells pocket-
books) is with dog-collars. He has played the grandest of
grand sonatas and symphonies on the grandest of pianofortes,
at fashionable soirées ; the fairest of the fair have brought him
ices and macaroons ; Lords, Baronets, and Chief Justices have
called him Fripanelli, and given him to snuff out of their gold
and jewelled boxes ; and the list of his pupils, with their half-
guinea lessons, has been at times so swollen, that, work from
morning till night, however hard he might, some were sure to
be in arrear.

But, ah me ! what changes take place in fifteen months—
what Worlds are upheaved, demolished, and built up again in
fifteen years ! Fripanelli did not change ; he had always
been, or seemed to be, as old and as ugly as he was before ;
but fashion changed—time changed. The fifteen years in
their remorseless whirl have caught him up scornfully from
Grosvenor Square and the half-guinea lessons and have dropped
him in Tattyboys Rents, to give lessons in singing, in instrumental music, in French, and even Italian, should the latter
be required, in tenth-class schools, to the daughters of small
tradesmen about the Rents and Blitsom Street, and Turk's Lane,
for a shilling a lesson, for sixpence a lesson, for seven shillings
a quarter, for anything that poor Gian Battisto can get to buy a
crust with.

Such is life for Art in the world's Rents, as well as Tattyboys' The educated and titled mob, which is ten times more
fickle, false, and capricious than the grossest Flemish rabble
that ever idolized an Artevelde, or massacred a De Witt, will
quietly drop you, when it has had enough of you, and will
let you starve or die, or go hang, with admirable indifference
and composure. And it serves you, and all other lions,
thoroughly right, who have not had the modest manhood to
be quietly superior to such mob, and to let it go its way. I
do not say this of poor old Fripanelli, for he was a stranger
in the land before he came to the Rents, and he may easily
have taken its surface for its core.

XXIII.

DOWN WHITECHAPEL WAY.

'Sir,' said Samuel Johnson to the Scotch gentleman—'sir, let
us take a walk down Fleet Street.' If I had not a thousand
other reasons to love and revere the memory of the great and
good old Doctor, I should still love and revere it for his preference of Fleet Street to the fields—of streets generally to
sylvan shades—of the hum of men and the rattling of wheels,
to the chirp of the cricket or the song of the skylark. It may
be prejudice, or an unpoetic mind, or so on ; but I am, as I
have observed five hundred times before ; and my critics may
well ask, 'why observe it again ?' of the streets, streety. I
love to take long walks, not only down Fleet Street, but up
and down all other streets, alleys, and lanes. I love to loiter
about Whitehall, and speculate as to which window of the
Banqueting House it was, and whether at the front, or at the
back,* that Charles Stuart came out to his death. I see a vivid
mind-picture of the huge crowd gathered together that bleak
January morning, to witness the fall of that 'grey discrowned
head.' Drury Lane I affect especially, past and present—the
Maypole, Nelly Gwynne, and the Earls of Craven, dividing
my interest with Vinegar Yard, the costermongers, the pawn-
brokers, and the stage door of the theatre round the corner.
Holborn, Cheapside, the Old Bailey, the great thoroughfares on
the Surrey side of the water, have all equal charms for me.

I will take a walk ' down Whitechapel way.'

How many thousands of us have lived for years—for a third
part of our lives, probably, in London—and have never been
down the Whitechapel Road ? I declare that there are not
half a dozen persons in the circle of my acquaintance who can
tell me where Bethnal Green is. As to Ratcliffe Highway,
Shadwell, Poplar, Limehouse, and Rotherhithe, they are entirely *terræ incognitæ* to shoals of born-and-bred Londoners.

'Down Whitechapel way.' Have you ever been 'down

* At the back for five hundred pounds, despite Mr. Peter Cunningham,
who maintains that it was at the front towards the park. I have law and
prophecy, book and broadside, mint and cumin to prove it, and I will—
some day.

that way, reader ? Ten to one you have not. You have heard, probably, of Whitechapel needles ; and the costermonger from whom you may occasionally have condescended to purchase vegetables would very likely inform you, were you to ask him, that he lives 'down that way.' Perhaps your impressions connected with Whitechapel refer vaguely to butchers, or, probably, to Jews, or possibly to thieves. Very likely you don't trouble yourself at all about the matter. You had an aunt once who lived at Mile End : but she quarrelled with everybody during her lifetime, and left her money to the London Hospital when she died, and you never went to see her. You see scores of omnibuses pass your door daily, with Aldgate, Whitechapel, Mile End, painted on their panels ; but you have no business to transact there, and let the omnibuses go on their way without further comment.

Those who care to know a little about what their neighbours in the Far East are doing this Saturday night, are very welcome to accompany me in the little excursion I am about to make. A thick pair of boots, and perhaps a mackintosh, or some light covering of that sort, would not be out of place ; for it is as rainy, slushy, and muddy a Saturday night as you would desire to have (or not to have) in the month of October. Stay, here is a friend with us who has known Whitechapel and its purlieus any time this five-and-twenty years, on all sorts of days and nights. Here is another who is an enthusiast in the noble art of self-defence, and who insists on forming one of our party, on the principle that a night excursion to Whitechapel must necessarily involve a ' scrimmage,' and an opportunity to develop the celebrated tactics of the prize-ring on a grand scale. Those who patronise the deleterious weed may light cigars ; and so onward towards Whitechapel !

On, through Fleet Street—passing St. Dunstan's as eight strikes ; noting the newspaper offices blazing with gas from basement to garret ; jostled occasionally by the well-looking (though ruined) agricultural gentlemen, with massy watch-chains (and bankrupt purses), who have been discussing port and Protection * after an ample dinner at Peele's or Anderton's. On, and up Ludgate the lofty, watching the red and blue lights of the doctors' shops as they are mirrored in the wet pavement ; and thinking, perhaps, that, after all, there may be some good in that early closing movement which has fastened the portals of all those magnificent palaces of linen-

* Written ere ' Protection, as an idea, died a natural death, and became a ' shadow of the shadow of smoke.'

drapery, and sent those shoals of spruce clerks and assistants
forth for health and recreation—many, it is to be hoped, to
the Literary and Scientific Institute, the class-room, and the
singing lesson, and not *all* (as some kind souls would insinuate)
to the tap-room or the cigar-shop.   On, round the solemn
dome of St. Paul's, and by that remarkable thoroughfare on
the left hand side, where, to my mind, the odours of a pastry-
cook's shop, of a tallow-manufactory, of the defunct, yet
promising to be phœnix-like Chapter Coffee House, and all the
newly-bound books in Paternoster Row are irrevocably, combined and blended.   On, by Cheapside, the magnificent, where
rows of dazzling gas-reflectors illumine shop fronts, teeming
with yet more dazzling stores of watches, rich jewellery, and
bales of silver spoons and forks.   There are desolate ragged
wretches staring wistfully at the glittering heaps of baubles, the
clocks, the tiny ladies' watches rich in enamel and jewels, the
repeaters, the chronometers, the levers jewelled in ever so
many holes, the trinkets, and châtelains, and 'charms,' and
Albert guard chains, which Mr. John Bennett, a doughty
watchmaker he, exposes to public admiration, just as they
would at the pennyworth of pudding in the window of a
cook's shop.   Are they speculating on the possibility of a gold
watch filling a hungry belly? or are they haply contemplating one bold dash through the frail sheet of glass—one hasty
snatch at the watches, and rings, and bracelets—one desperate
throw for luxury and riot at the best ; or at the worst, for the
comfortable gaol, the warm convict's dress, and the snug cell
with its hot-water pipes ?

Leaving Cheapside, the magnificent ; avoiding the omnibuses
in the Poultry as best we may ; skirting the huge Mansion
House, where a feeble gleam from an office in the basement
suggests that Messrs. John and Daniel Forrester are yet wide
awake, while the broad glare of light from the windows in
Charlotte Row proclaims jolly civic festivities in the Egyptian
Hall ; striking through Cornhill, the wealthy ; crossing Grace-
church Street, and suppressing a lingering inclination to take
a stroll by the old Flower Pot, and older South Sea House,
into old Bishopsgate Street, just to have a vagabond quarter
of an hour or so of thought about Baring Brothers, Crosby
Hall, Great St. Helen's, Sir Thomas More, and Mr. Ross the
hairdresser :—Supposing this, I say, our party boldly invades
Leadenhall Street.   Opposite the India House I must stop for a
moment, however.   Is there not Billiter Street hard-by, with
that never-dying smell of Cashmere shawls and opium chests

about the sale-rooms ? Is there not St. Mary Axe, redolent
of Hebrew London ? Is there not the great house itself, with
all its mighty associations of Clive and Warren Hastings,
Nuncomar, and Lally Tollendal, Plassy, Arcot, and Seringa-
patam— Sheridan, thundering in Westminster Hall on the case
of the Begums—and the mighty directors, with their millions
of subjects, and their palaces in Belgravia and Tyburnia, who
were once but poor hucksters and chapmen of Trichinopoly
chains and indigo balls—mere buyers and sellers of rice, sugar,
and pepper ? But my companions are impatient, and, dropping
a hasty tear to the memory of Mr. Toole, the great toastmaster
and beadle—(dost thou remember him, Eugenio, in that magnificent cocked hat and scarlet coat ? and Eugenio replies
that he lives again in his son)—we leave Leadenhall Street
the broad for Leadenhall Street the narrow ; and where the
tortuous Fenchurch Street also converges, emerge into the
open space by Aldgate pump. We have no time to dilate
on the antiquity of the pump. A hundred yards to the left
and here we are, not absolutely in Whitechapel itself, but at
the entrance of that peculiar and characteristic district, which
I take to be bounded by Mile-end gate on the east, and by the
establishment of Messrs. Moses and Son on the west.

First, Moses. Gas, splendour, wealth, boundless and im-
measurable, at a glance. Countless stories of gorgeous show-
rooms, laden to repletion with rich garments. Gas everywhere.
Seven hundred burners, they whisper to me. The tailoring
department ; the haberdashery department ; the hat, boots,
shawl, outfitting, cutlery department. Hundreds of departments. Legions of ' our young men ' in irreproachable coats,
and neckcloths void of reproach. Corinthian columns, enriched
cornices, sculptured panels, arabesque ceilings, massive chandeliers, soft carpets of choice patterns, luxury, elegance, the
riches of a world, the merchandise of two, everything that
anybody ever could want, from a tin shaving-pot to a Cashmere
shawl. Astonishing cheapness—wonderful celerity—enchanting civility ! Great is Moses of the Minories ! Of the Minories ? of everywhere. He pervades Aldgate ; he looms on
Whitechapel ; an aërial suspension bridge seems to connect
his Minorial palace with his West End Branch. Moses is
everywhere. When I came from Weedon the other day, his
retainers pelted me with his pamphlets as I quitted the railway
station. Moses has wrenched the lyre and the bays from our
laureate's hands ; he and his son are the monarchs of Parnassus.
His circulars are thrown from balloons and fired out of cannon.

S

I believe they must grow in market gardens somewhere out of town—they are so numerous. Of course, Moses is a great public benefactor.

Crossing the Minories, and keeping on the right-hand side of the road, we are in the very thick of 'Butcher Row' at once. A city of meat! The gas, no longer gleaming through ground-glass globes, or aided by polished reflectors, but flaring from primitive tubes, lights up a long vista of beef, mutton. and veal. Legs, shoulders, loins, ribs, hearts, livers, kidneys, gleam in all the gaudy panoply of scarlet and white on every side. ' Buy, buy, buy !' resounds shrilly through the greasy, tobacco-laden, gas-rarefied air. There are eloquent butchers, who rival Orator Henley in their encomia on the legs and briskets they expose ; insinuating butchers, who wheedle the softer sex into purchasing, with sly jokes and well-turned compliments ; dignified butchers (mostly plethoric, double-chinned men, in top-boots, and doubtless wealthy), who seem to think that the mere appearance of their meat, and of them-selves, is sufficient to insure custom, and seldom condescend to mutter more than an occasional ' Buy !' Then there are bold butchers—vehement rogues, in stained frocks—who utter frantic shouts of ' Buy, buy, buy !' ever and anon making a ferocious sally into the street, and seizing some unlucky wight, who buys a leg of mutton or a bullock's heart, *nolens volens !*

Bless the women ! how they love marketing ! Here they are by scores. Pretty faces, ugly faces, young and old, chaf-fering, simpering, and scolding vehemently. Now, it is the portly matron—housekeeper, may be, to some wealthy, retired old bachelor ; she awes the boldest butcher, and makes even the dignified one incline in his top-boots. And here is the newly-married artisan's wife—a fresh, rosy-cheeked girl, delightfully ignorant of housekeeping, though delighted with its responsibilities—charmingly diffident as to what she shall buy, and placing implicit, and it is to be hoped, not misplaced, confidence in the insinuating butcher, who could, I verily believe, persuade her that a pig's fry is a saddle of mutton. Poor thing ! she is anxious to be at home and get Tom's supper ready for him ; and as for Tom, the sooner he gets away from the public-house, where his wages are paid him every Saturday night, the better it will be for his wife and for him, too, I opine. There are but few male purchasers of butchers' meat. Stay, here is one—a little, rosy man, in deep black, and with a very big basket, and holding by the hand a little rosy girl, in black as deep as his. He is a widower, I dare say, and the little girl his daughter. How will it be, I wonder, with that couple, a dozen years hence? Will the little girl grow big enough to go to market by herself, while father smokes his pipe at home? or, will father marry again, and a shrewish stepmother ill-treat the girl, till she runs away and——Well well! we have other matters besides Butcher Row to attend to. We can but spare a glance at that gaunt old man, with the bristly beard and the red eyelids, who is nervously fingering, while he endeavours to beat down the price of those sorry scraps of meat yonder. His history is plain enough to read, and is printed in three letters on his face. G. I. N.

On the pavement of this Butcher Row, we have another market, and a grand one too. Not confined, however, to the sale of any one particular article, but diversified in an eminent degree. Half-way over the kerbstone and the gutter, is an apparently interminable line of 'standings' and 'pitches,' consisting of trucks, barrows, baskets, and boards on tressels, laden with almost every imaginable kind of small merchandise. Oysters, vegetables, fruit, combs, prints in inverted umbrellas, ballads, cakes, sweetstuff, fried fish, artificial flowers (!), chairs, brushes and brooms, soap, candles, crockeryware, ironmongery, cheese, walking-sticks, looking-glasses, frying-pans, bibles, waste-paper, toys, nuts, and fire-wood. These form but a tithe of the contents of this Whitechapel Bezesteen. Each stall is illuminated, and each in its own peculiar manner. Some of the vendors are careless, and their lamps are but primitive, consisting of a rushlight stuck in a lump of clay, or a turnip cut in half. But there is a degree of luxury in not a few; 'Holliday's lamps,' green paper shades, 'fishtail' burners, and, occasionally, camphine lamps, being freely exhibited. I don't think you could collect together, in any given place in Europe, a much queerer assortment than the sellers of the articles exposed, were it not the buyers thereof. Here are brawny costermongers by dozens, in the orthodox corduroys, fur caps, and 'king's man' handkerchiefs. Lungs of leather have they, marvellous eloquence, also, in praising carrots, turnips, and red herrings. Here, too, are street mechanics, manufacturers of the articles they sell, and striving with might and main to sell them; and you will find very few, or rather, *no* Irish among this class. I see women among the street sellers, as I move along—some, poor widow souls—some, who have grown old in street trading—some, little puny totter-

ing things, sobbing and shivering as they sell. The buyers
are of all descriptions, from the middle to the very lowest
class, inclusive. Ruddy mechanics, with their wives on their
arms, and some sallow and shabby, reeling to and from the
gin-shops. Decent married women, and comely servant girls,
with latch-keys and market-baskets. Beggars, by dozens.
Slatternly, frowsy, drabs of women, wrangling with wrinkled
crones, and bating down the price of a bunch of carrots
fiercely. Blackguard boys, with painted faces, tumbling head
over heels in the mud. Bulky costers, whose day's work is over,
or who do not care to work at all. Grimy dustmen, newly
emancipated from the laystall. The bare-headed, or battered-
bonneted members of the class called (and truly) unfortunate,
haunt the other side of the road. There is too much light and
noise here for them.

But the noise! the yelling, screeching, howling, swearing,
laughing, fighting saturnalia; the combination of commerce,
fun, frolic, cheating, almsgiving, thieving, and devilry; the
Geneva-laden, tobacco-charged atmosphere! The thieves, now
pursuing their vocation, by boldly snatching joints of meat from
the hooks, or articles from the stalls; now, peacefully, basket
in hand, making their Saturday night's marketing (for even
thieves must eat). The short pipes, the thick sticks, the mildewed umbrellas, the dirty faces, the ragged coats! Let us
turn into the gin-shop here, for a moment.

It is a remarkably lofty, though not very spacious, edifice—
the area, both before and behind the bar, being somewhat
narrow. There are enormous tubs of gin, marked with an
almost fabulous number of gallons each; and there are composite columns, and mirrors, and handsome clocks, and ormolu
candelabra, in the approved Seven Dials style. But the company are different. They have not the steady, methodical,
dram-drinking system of the Seven Dials, Drury Lane, and
Holborn gin-shop *habitués*; the tremulous deposition of the
required three halfpence; the slow, measured, draining of the
glass; the smack of the lips, and quick passing of the hand
over the mouth, followed by the speedy exit of the regular
dram-drinker, who takes his 'drain' and is off, even if he be
in again in a short time. These Whitechapel gin-drinkers
brawl and screech horribly. Blows are freely exchanged, and
sometimes pewter measures fly through the air like Shrapnell
shells. The stuff itself, which in the western gin-shops goes
generally by the name of 'blue ruin' or 'short,' is here called
indifferently, 'tape,' 'max,' 'duke,' 'gatter,' and 'jacky.'

Two more peculiarities I observe also. One is, that there are no spruce barmaids, or smiling landladies—stalwart men in white aprons supply their place. The second is, that there is a multiplicity of doors, many more than would at first seem necessary, and for ever on the swing; but the utility of which is speedily demonstrated to me by the simultaneous ejection of three 'obstropelous' Irish labourers, by three of the stalwart barmen.

The trucks and barrows, the fried fish and artificial flowers, are not quite so abundant when we have passed a thoroughfare called Somerset Street. They become even more scarce when we see, on the other side of the road, two stone posts, or obelisks on a small scale, marking at once the boundaries of the City, and the commencement of that renowned thoroughfare now politely called Middlesex Street, but known to Europe in general, and the nobility and gentry connected with the trade in old clothes in particular, as Petticoat Lane. It is no use going down there this Saturday, for the Hebrew community, who form its chief delight and ornament, are all enjoying their 'shobbhouse,' and we shall meet with them elsewhere. We will, if you please, cross over, leaving the kerbstone market (which only exists on one side), and allured by the notes of an execrably played fiddle, enter one of those dazzling halls of delight, called a 'penny gaff.'

The 'gaff' throws out no plausible puffs, no mendacious placards, respecting the entertainment to be found therein. The public take the genuineness of the 'gaff' for granted, and enter by dozens. The 'gaff' has been a shop—a simple shop—with a back parlour to it, and has been converted into a hall of delight, by the very simple process of knocking out the shop front, and knocking down the partition between the shop and parlour. The gas-fittings yet remain, and even the original counters, which are converted into 'reserved seats,' on which, for the outlay of twopence, as many costers, thieves, Jew-boys, and young ladies, as can fight for a place, are sitting, standing, or lounging. For the common herd—the οἱ πολλοὶ —the *conditio vivendi* is simply the payment of one penny, for which they get standing-room in what are somewhat vaguely termed the 'stalls,'—plainly speaking, the body of the shop The proscenium is marked by two gas 'battens' or pipes, perforated with holes for burners, traversing the room horizontally, above and below. There are some monstrous engravings, in vile frames, suspended from the walls, some vilely coloured plaster casts, and a stuffed monstrosity or two in glass cases. The place is abominably dirty, and the odour of the company generally, and of the shag tobacco they are smoking, is powerful.

A capital house though, to-night : a bumper, indeed. Such a bumper, in fact, that they have been obliged to place benches on the stage (two planks on tressels), on which some of the candidates for the reserved seats are accommodated. As I enter, a gentleman in a fustian suit deliberately walks across the stage and lights his pipe at the footlights ; while a neighbour of mine of the Jewish persuasion, who smells fearfully of fried fish, dexterously throws a cotton handkerchief, containing some savoury condiment from the stalls to the reserved seats, where it is caught by a lady whom he addresses by the title of 'Bermondsey Bet.' Bet is, perhaps, a stranger in these parts, and my Hebrew friend wishes to show her that Whitechapel can assert its character for hospitality.

Silence for the manager, if you please !—who comes forward with an elaborate bow, and a white hat in his hand, to address the audience. A slight disturbance has occurred, it appears, in the course of the evening ; the Impresario complains bitterly of the 'mackinations' of certain parties 'next door,' who seek to injure him by creating an uproar, after he has gone to the expense of engaging 'four good actors' for the express amusement of the British public. The 'next door' parties are, it would seem, the proprietors of an adjacent public-house, who have sought to seduce away the supporters of the 'gaff,' by vaunting the superior qualities of their cream gin, a cuckoo clock, and the 'largest cheroots in the world for a penny.'

Order is restored, and the performances commence. 'Mr. and Mrs. Stitcher,' a buffo duet of exquisite comicality, is announced. Mr. Stitcher is a tailor, attired in the recognised costume of a tailor *on* the stage, though, I must confess, I never saw it *off*. He has nankeen pantaloons, a red nightcap —a redder nose, and a cravat with enormous bows. Mrs. Stitcher is 'made up' to represent a slatternly shrew, and she looks it all over. They sing a verse apiece ; they sing a verse together ; they quarrel, fight, and make it up again. The audience are delighted. Mr. S. reproaches Mrs. S. with the possession of a private gin-bottle ; Mrs. S. inveighs against the hideous turpitude of Mr. S. for pawning three pillow-cases to purchase beer. The audience are in ecstacies. A sturdy coalheaver in the 'stalls' slaps his thigh with delight. It is *so* real. Ugh ! terribly real ; let us come away, even though murmurs run through the stalls that 'The Baker's Shop' is to be sung. I see, as we edge away to the door, a young lady in a cotton velvet spencer, bare arms, and a short white calico skirt, advance to the foot-lights, I suppose she is the Fornarina, who is to enchant the dilettanti with the flowery song in question.

We are still in Whitechapel High Street; but in a wider part. The kerbstone market has ceased; and the head quarters of commerce are in the shops. Wonderful shops, these! Grocers who dazzle their customers with marvellous Chinese paintings, and surmount the elaborate vessels (Properties for a Pantomime) containing their teas and sugars with startling acrostics—pungent conundrums. Is it in imagination only, or in reality, that I see, perched above these groceries, an imp—a fantastic imp, whose head-dress is shaped like a retort, who has a Lancet in his girdle, and a microscope in his hand, and on whose brow is written '*Analysis?*' —that when I read the placards relative to 'Fine young Hyson,' 'Well-flavoured Pekoe,' 'Strong family Souchong,' 'Imperial Gunpowder,' this imp, putting his thumb to his nose, and spreading his fingers out demoniacally, whispers, 'Sloe-leaves, China-clay, Prussian-blue, yellow-ochre, gum, tragacanth, garbage, poison?'—that, pointing to Muscovado, and 'Fine West India,' and 'superfine lump,' he mutters, 'Sand, chalk, poison?'—that, when I talk of cocoa, he screams, 'Venetian-red, and desiccated manure?'—that, when I allude to coffee, he grins mocking gibes of 'burnt beans, chicory, poison?'—that he dances from the grocer's to the baker's, next door, and executes maniacal gambadoes on the quartern loaves and French rolls, uttering yells about chalk, alum, and dead men's bones?—that he draws chalk and horses' brains from the dairyman's milk; and horse-flesh, and worse offal still, from sausages?—that he shows me everywhere fraud, adulteration, and poison! Avaunt, imp! I begin to think that there is nothing real in the eating and drinking line—that nothing is but what is not—that all beer is *cocculus Indicus*—all gin, turpentine, in this delusive Whitechapel. And not in Whitechapel alone. Art thou immaculate, Shoreditch? Art thou blameless, Borough? Canst thou place thy hand on thy waistcoat, Oxford Street, the aristocratic, and say thy tea knows no 'facing or glazing,' thy sugar no potato starch, thy beer no doctoring?

But one of my friends is clamorous for beer; and, to avoid adulteration, we eschew the delusive main thoroughfare for a moment and strike into a maze of little, unsavoury back streets, between Whitechapel Church and Goodman's Fields. Here is a beer-shop—a little, blinking, wall-cyed edifice, with red curtains in the window, and a bar squeezed up in one corner, as though it were ashamed of itself. From the door of the tap-room which we open, comes forth a thick, compact body of smoke. There are, perhaps, twenty people in the room, and they are all smoking like limekilns. From a kiln at the upper extremity, comes forth the well-remembered notes of the old *trink-lied*, 'Am Rhein, am Rhein.' We are in Vaterland at once. All these are Teutons—German sugar-bakers. There are hundreds more of their countrymen in the narrow streets about here, and dozens of low lodging-houses, where the German emigrants are crimped and boarded and robbed. Here, also, live the German buy-a-broom girls. There are little German public-houses, and German bakers, and little shops, where you can get sauer-kraut and potato-salad, just as though you were in Frankfort or Mayence. Dear old Vaterland! pleasant country of four meals a day, and feather-bed counterpanes—agreeable land, where you can drink wine in the morning, and where everybody takes off his hat to everybody else! Though thy cookery is execrable, and thy innkeepers are robbers, I love thee, Germany, still!

My experienced friend, when we have refreshed ourselves at this hostelry, brings us, by a short cut, into Union Street, and so into the broad Whitechapel Road. Here the kerbstone market I have alluded to, crosses the road itself and stretches, in a straggling, limping sort of way, up to Whitechapel Workhouse. We come here upon another phase of Saturday-night Whitechapel life. The children of Jewry begin to en-compass us, not so much in the way of business; for though their Sabbath is over, and work is legal—though Moses, at the other extremity, is in full swing of money-making activity, yet the majority of the Israelites prefer amusing themselves on a Saturday night. They are peculiar in their amusements, as in everything else. The public-house—the mere bar, at least—has no charms for them; but almost all the low coffee-shops you pass are crowded with young Jews, playing domi-noes and draughts; while in the publics, where tap-rooms are attached, their elders disport themselves with cards, bagatelle, and the excitement of a sing-song meeting. Smoking is universal. Cigars the rule—pipes the exception. Hounds-ditch, the Minories, Leman Street, Duke's Place, St. Mary

Axe, Bevis Marks, and Whitechapel itself, have all contributed their quota to fill these places of amusement; and here and there you will see some venerable Israelite, with long beard and strange foreign garb, probably from Tangier or Constantinople, on a visit to his brethren in England. There are legends, too, of obscure places in this vicinity, where what the French call '*gros jeu*,' or high play, is carried on. In Butcher Row, likewise, are Jew butchers, where you may see little leaden seals, inscribed with Hebrew characters, appended to the meat, denoting that the animal has been slaughtered according to the directions of the Synagogue. In the day time you may see long-bearded rabbins examining the meat, and testing the knives on their nails.

What have we here? 'The grand Panorama of Australia, a series of moving pictures.' Admission, one penny. Just-a-going to begin. Some individuals, dressed as Ethiopian serenaders, hang about the door; and one with the largest shirt-collar I have ever seen, takes my penny, and admits me, with some score or two more, where, though it *is* 'just a-going to begin,' I and my friends wait a good quarter of an hour. There are two policemen off duty beside me, who are indulging in the *dolce far niente*, and cracking nuts. There is a decent, civil-spoken silkweaver from Spitalfields, too, whose ancestors, he tells me, came over to England at the time of the revocation of the Edict of Nantes, and who has a romantically French name. He has the old Lyons indentures of his ancestors at home, he says.

We give up the panorama in despair; and, for aught we know, is 'jest a-going to begin' at this moment. In our progress towards the Gate, however, we look in at a few more public-houses. Here is a costermongers' house, where the very truck and baskets are brought to the bar. Here is that famous hostelry, where is preserved an oil painting, containing authentic portraits of three Whitechapel worthies, who once drank one hundred and one pots of beer at one sitting. The name of the captain of this gallant band was 'Old Fish.' Here, again, is a thieves' house—thievish all over, from the squint-eyed landlord to the ruffianly customers. Go in at one door, and go out at another; and don't change more five-pound notes at the bar than you can help, my friend. Here are houses with queer signs—'The Grave Morris,' supposed to be a corruption of some dead-and-gone German Landgrave, and 'The Blind Beggar,' close to Mile-end Gate.

Another 'gaff' on the right-hand side of the road—but on

a grander scale. The Effingham Saloon, with real boxes, a real pit, and a real gallery; dreadfully dirty, and with a dirtier audience. No comic singing, but the drama—the real, legitimate drama. There is a bold bandit, in buff-boots, call-ing on 'yon blew Ev'n to bring-a down-a rewing on ther taraytor's ed.' There is nothing new in him, nor in the young lady in pink calico, with her back hair down, expressive of affliction. Nor in the Pavilion Theatre over the way, where 'Rugantino the Terrible' is the stock piece, and where there are more buff-boots, rusty broad-swords, calico-skirts, and back hairs.

Shops, Gin-palaces, Saloons—Saloons, Gin-palaces, Shops; Costermongers, Thieves, and Beggars—Beggars, Thieves, and Costermongers. As we near the Gate, the London Hospital looms heavily on one side, while on the other the bare, bleak walls of Whitechapel Workhouse stretch grimly along, with a woful skirting-board of crouching Irish paupers, who have arrived too late for admission into the Workhouse, and are houseless for the night.

Going along, and still anxious to see what is to be seen, I look, curiously, at the portraits hanging on the walls of the coffee-houses and bar-parlours. The democratic element is not very strong in Whitechapel, it would seem; for the effigies of Her Majesty and Prince Consort are as a hundred to one of the effigies of the Cuffies and Meaghers of the sword. One portrait, though, I see everywhere; its multiplications beating all royal, noble, and democratic portraits hollow, and far out-numbering the Dog Billys, and winners of memorable Derbys. In tavern and tap-room, in shop and parlour, I see everywhere the portrait or the bust of Sir Robert Peel.

Mile-end Gate at last, and midnight chimes. There is a 'cheap-jack,' on a rickety platform, and vaunting wares more rickety still, who gets vehemently eloquent as it gets later. But his auditory gradually disperse, and the whole road seems to grow suddenly quiet. Do you know why? The public-houses are closed. The pie-shops, it is true, yet send forth savoury steams; but the rain comes down heavily. Therefore, and as I (and I fear you, too, dear reader) have had enough of Whitechapel for one while, let us jump into this last omnibus bound westwards, reflecting that if we have not discovered the North-West Passage, or the source of the Niger, we have beheld a strange country, and some strange phases of life.

XXIV.

THE MUSICAL WORLD.

It is a world of highly ancient lineage, having existed thousands of years ago, 'ere heaving bellows learned to blow.' Old Timotheus was its master (sub Jove), before divine Cecilia came to invent the vocal frame, and add length to solemn sounds; to wrest the lyre from Timotheus, or divide the crown with him. He could but raise a mortal to the skies. She drew an angel down.

Thus far (in somewhat different language) glorious John Dryden in praise of music. I must not tarry to sing the praise of ancient music, for I have not Dr. Burney's big book by me : and who knows where or when I should stop if I were to touch upon Orpheus and the beasts, Ulysses and the Syrens, Nebuchadnezzar with his lutes, and harps, and sackbuts, and all kinds of psaltery ; or if even I were to get middle-aged in music, and tell of the troubadours, trouveres, minne-singers, or glee-maidens ; or more modern yet, and gossip about Stradella, Purcell, Raymond Lulli and Father Schmidt, Paesiello, Handel, and Doctor Blow : the harmonious blacksmith, Cremona fiddles, and the Haarlem organ ?

The musical world of England of to-day, for to such place and time will I confine myself, contains in itself three worlds —the fashionable world of music, the middle-class world, and the country world.

Fashion first. What so fashionable as the Opera ? whose many tiers of boxes glitter with bright lights, and brighter eyes, with youth and beauty, and high birth ; where divinities in diamonds, and divinities in blue ribbons, hedge kings and queens (poor hedges ! how wofully tired, and ditchwatery dull they look, hedging royalty on one leg, or leaning wearily against chairbacks or brackets) ; where dandies in the stalls, in excruciating white neckcloths, turn their backs to the stage between the acts, and scrutinize the occupants of the grand tier, with their big lorgnettes; where gray-headed peers and habitués who can remember Nourri and Donzelli, Catalani and Pasta, Armand Vestris and Anatole, crouch in shady pit-boxes, and hear the music with palled ears, and watch the ballet with sated eyes ; where dilettanti in the back rows of the pit

(mostly admitted with orders, and cleaned white kid gloves)
are so particular in crying Brava when a lady is singing, and
Bravi, when a duet is sung ; where honest Tom Snugg, who
fancies himself a complete man about town and opera frequenter, is so proudly delighted in pointing out, to his friend
Nooks, the neophyte, a respectable stockbroker from Camberwell Grove, as the Duke of Tiransydon, or the lady of a
Hebrew sheriff's officer, covered with diamonds, as the Dowager Marchioness of Memphis ; where simple-minded English
people from the provinces, finding themselves in the amphitheatre stalls and at the Opera for the first time, make desperate efforts to understand the words of the songs and re-
citatives ; and failing signally, appeal to the sixpenny 'books
of the opera,' and find confusion worse confounded by the
librettist of the theatre ; who translates Italian into English
with about the same facility that French hotel-keepers trans-
late their advertisements into the same language ; where oleaginous foreigners, of the back settlements of the gallery,
gloat over every bar of the overture, and every note of the
opera, and keep time with their heads, and lick their lips at
a florid passage, or a well-executed cadence, and grind their
teeth savagely at a note too flat or too sharp, and scowl at you
if you cough or sneeze, or move your feet. This English land
has not been without its white days—its high and glorious
festivals. I say has been ; for, alas ! of the opera as a grand,
glorious, national, fashionable institution, we may say, as of
him whose sword is rust, and whose bones are dust,—It was.
The Grand Opera exists no more. I know there is an establishment in the vicinity of Covent Garden—a sumptuous, commodious, brilliant, and well-managed theatre, where the best
operas are given by the best singers and instrumentalists.
But I cannot call it THE Opera. It can never be more to me
than Covent Garden Theatre—the conquered, but never to be
the naturalised domain of Italian music. The ghost of Garrick
jostles the ghost of Farinelli in Bow Street, and from Mr. May,
the costumier's shop, in Wellington Street, the indignant voices
of Colman, Sheridan, Kenney, and O'Keefe, seem to be crying
to Bellini and Donizetti, Meyerbeer and Mozart, 'What do ye
here ?' What have the traditions of maestri and macaroni,
violins and Vellutis, bassi and ballet-girls to do with a locality
hallowed by the memory of the Great Twin Brethren, the two
mighty English theatres of Covent Garden and Drury Lane ?
I can fancy, drawn up in shadowy line opposite the grand
entrance and sadly watching the carriages disgorging their aris-

tocratic tenants, the by-gone worthies of the English stage. Siddons thrilling, O'Neil melting, Munden exhilarating, Dowton convulsing, Kemble awing, Kean astounding, Woffington enchanting, Young soothing, and Macready—not dead, haply, nor forgotten, nor unthanken, but gone for all that—teaching and elevating, and humanising us. About such a scene might flit the disembodied spirits of the ' O. P.' row; of those brave days of old, when people went to wait for the opening of the pit door, at three P.M., and took sandwiches and case bottles with them; when the engagement or non-engagement of a public favourite weighed as heavily in the balance of town curiosity as the siege of a fortress, or the capture of a fleet; when Shakspeare's scenes found gorgeous reflections in Stanfield's magic mirror; when actors (though rogues and vagabonds by act of parliament) were wonderfully respected and respectable, and lived in competence, and had quiet cosy houses in Bloomsbury and Marylebone, paying rates and taxes, serving on juries, and when they died found no mortuary eulogium in the columns of some slang periodical, but were gravely alluded to in the decent large type of a respectably small-sized journal, with a fourpenny stamp, as ' at his house in Buskin Street, Mr. So-and-so, many years of the Theatre Royal, Covent Garden, and one of the overseers of the parish of Saint Roscius. Universally lamented. An attached husband and a tender father.' No! The Opera cannot be in Covent Garden to my mind. The Opera should, and can only be in the Haymarket, over against palatial Pall-Mall. Come back then, Mr. Costa, whom I honour, to those *cari luoghi!* Come back, bâton, souffleurs' cavern, loud bassoon, and all! Let us have, once more, the linkman with his silver badge, and the guard of grenadiers (I mind the time when it was a subaltern's guard, and the officer had a free admission to the pit, and lounged tremendous in Fop's Alley in his bearskin and golden epaulettes). Come back to the Haymarket, carriages that stopped the way, and struggling footmen, and crowded crush room! Come back, and let not the walls of the grand opera be desolate, or the spider weave her web in the yellow satin curtains—though I believe they were taken down and sold in the last disasters!*

* The Haymarket Opera—Her Majesty's Theatre—has been born again and has again died, since I wrote these lines. May the courteous Mr. Lumley be again enabled to inscribe ' Resurgam ' on the hatchment, made from an old pass-check, which should properly decorate the architrave of this theatre!

Only one section of the musical world, however, was on view in the audience part of the opera. Its working members were to be found behind the footlights; nor could you learn much of their private or social habits even there. There are few duller, prosier, more commonplace scenes than the green-room of a theatre; and the artist's foyer at an opera-house is ordinarily the dullest of the dull. A prima donna swallowing sherry-negus with an egg in it preparatory to her grand scena; a basso stretching himself on the cushions of an ottoman, and yawning in an ectasy of fatigue; a tenor sulking in a corner because his aria has not been encored; a baritone suffering from hoarseness, and expectorating and swallowing cough lozenges with distressing pertinacity; a crowd of mysterious, snuffy, musty old Frenchwomen with handkerchiefs tied round their heads, pottering in corners with second-hand foreigners, who snuff more than they speak, and spit more than they snuff: these are the principal features of an operatic green-room. Yet, in the palmy days of opera-hats and opera-tights, there were few privileges more valued by the distinguished frequenters of the omnibus-box than that of the *entrée* behind the scenes. A door of communication used to exist between the omnibus-box and the penetralia of the coulisses; and an attempt to lock it once caused a riot of the most fashionable description, in the time of manager Laporte, and the demolition of the door itself by a prince of the blood. There are dandies yet who would give—not exactly their ears, but still something handsome—for the estimable privilege of wandering in a dingy ruinous desert of wings and set pieces and cobwebby rafters; of being hustled and ordered out of the way by carpenters and scene-shifters in their shirt-sleeves; of stumbling over gas-pipes, tressels, and pewter pots; and of being uncomfortably jammed up among chairs and tables, supernumeraries bearing spears and banners at one shilling per night, property-men with blazing pans of red and blue fire, and pets of the ballet gossiping the flattest of flat gossip, or intent upon the salutary, but, to a near bystander, rather inconvenient exercise known as 'pumping,' which, for the benefit of the uninitiated, I may mention consists in standing upon one leg, while another pet of the ballet pulls the other leg violently up and down—such pumping giving strength and elasticity to the muscles.

Hie we away, therefore, to where we can see the operatic world to greater advantage. Here is Messrs. Octave and Piccolo's Music Warehouse. Let us enter and behold.

In Regent Street is Messrs. Octave and Piccolo's establishment, the great Bourse or High Change of the Ars Musica. Hard by, on one side, is Messrs. Rowdeypoor, Cutchempoor, and Weaverbad's India shawl warehouse, which keeps so many native artists at Delhi and Lahore employed day and night in designing fresh patterns.* Hard by, on the other side, is Miss Bricabrac's great knick-knack shop, where a marquis might ruin himself in the purchase of porte-monnaies, smelling-bottles, tooth-picks, dressing-cases, blotting-books, French clocks, point lace, diamond pens, jewelled penwipers, amethyst card-cases, and watches no bigger than fourpenny pieces.† About four o'clock during the height of the London season, the road in front of these three shops—the shawl shop, the music shop, and the knick-knack shop—is blockaded by a crowd of carriages, the very study of the armorial bearings on whose panels is as good as a course of Clarke's Introduction to Heraldry, or Mr. Planché's Pursuivant-at-Arms. The pavement is almost impassable for mighty footmen gravely lounging, as it is the wont of mighty footmen to do ; the air is perfumed with pomatum and hair-powder, and the eye dazzled with plush, vivid aiguillettes, and gold lace.

In Messrs. Octave and Piccolo's shop, among the grand, semi-grand, square, cottage, and cabinet pianofortes, the harmoniums, melodions, accordions, concertinas, and flutinas, the last new ballads, polkas, mazourkas, gems of the last opera, &c., decorated with flaming lithographs in colours ; the shelves groaning beneath music-books and opera-scores, and pianoforte exercises, and treatises upon sol-faing ; among Erard's harps, and huge red and yellow concert posters, and plans of the boxes of the Opera and seats at the Philharmonic ; among circulars from professors of music, who beg to inform the nobility, gentry, their friends, and the public that they have just returned from the continent, or have removed their residence to such and such a street, where they have resumed their course of instruction, or have some equally interesting instruction to give ; among portraits of musical celebrities, lithographed by the accomplished M. Baugniet, and concert tickets stuck in the frames of looking-glasses ; among all these multifarious objects there circulates a crowd of countesses in lace, yea, and of duchesses oftentimes, together with representatives of musical wealth (chiefly female) of every degree, from the Princess Perigordowski, who has come to Messrs.

---

* They are bankrupt.　　　　† She is dead.

Octave and Co. to negotiate engagements with the stars of the
Italian stage for her grand ball and concert next week; from
tho Dowager Marchioness of Screwdown, who wants some one
at Octave's to recommend her a first-rate Italian singing-
master, who will teach the juvenile Ladies Harriet and
Georgina Skinflint for five shillings a lesson, she having
recently dismissed their former instructor, Signor Ravioli,
for gross misconduct—*a pawnbroker's duplicate* for some de-
grading article of wearing apparel, we believe boots, having
fallen from the wretched man's hat, on the occasion of his
last visit to Skinflint House; from these pillars of the titled
world to plump, rosy Mrs. Chippendale, who has 'musical
evenings' in the Alpha Road, and wants a good accompanyist,
moderate, a German not preferred. They breathe so hard,
and smell so strong of smoke, and have such long hair, Mrs.
C. says. Besides, they injure the piano so, and will insist at
last upon playing a 'sinfonia,' or a 'motivo,' or a 'pensée' of
their own composition, goodness knows how many hundred
bars or pages long. Then there is Miss de Greutz, who is
long, lean, pale, and spectacled. She is a governess is Miss
de Greutz, but has views towards professing singing on an
independent footing, and wishes to ascertain Signor Pappadaggi's terms (he is the singing-master in vogue), for a
series of finishing lessons. Pappadaggi will have fifteen
shillings a lesson out of her, and bate never a stiver; 'it soud
be zi gueeni,' he says; and valiant Miss de Greutz will hoard
up her salary, and trot, in her scanty intervals of leisure, to
the signor's palatial residence in Hyde Park Gardens; and
should you some half-holiday afternoon pass the open windows
of Belinda House, Bayswater, it is pretty certain that you
will hear the undulating of a piano in sore distress (not the
jangling one—*that* is the schoolroom piano where Miss Cripps
is massacreing the Huguenots worse than ever they were on
St. Bartholomew's day), and some feeble, though highly ornamental cadenzas, the which you may safely put down as Miss
de Greutz's repetition of her last, or preparation for her next
lesson.

You may observe that the gentlefolks, the customers who
come here to buy, naturally resort to the counters, and be-
siege the obliging assistants; those urbane persons, who are
not in the least like other shop assistants, being singularly
courteous, staid, and unobtrusive in demeanour, and not
without, at the same time, a reasonable dash of independence,
being in most cases sons of partners in the firm, or of wealthy

proprietors of other music warehouses, who send them here, as the great restaurateurs in France do their sons, to other restaurants, to acquire a knowledge of the business. They have a hard time of it among their fair customers ; a dozen voices calling at once for works, both vocal and instrumental, in three or four different languages : one lady asking for the 'Odessa Polka,' another for the 'Sulina Waltz,' a third for 'Have Faith in one Another ;' a fourth for ' L'Ange Déchu,' a fifth for an Italian aria, ' Sulla Poppa del mio Brik,' and a sixth for Herr Bompazek's new German ballad, 'Schlick, schlick, schlick.' Yet Messrs. Octave and Piccolo's young men contrive to supply all these multifarious demands, and take money, and give change, and indulge their customers with commercially scientific and sentimental disquisitions upon the merits of the last new song, and answer—which is the hardest business of all—the innumerable questions on subjects as innumerable, addressed to them not only by the customers, but by the professionals who throng the shop.

The professionals ! Where are they ? They gesticulate behind harps, or declaim from music stools, or congregate at the angles of Erard's grands. They may be heard of in the back shop fantastically torturing musical instruments, in the hope, perhaps, that some English marquis, enraptured by their strains, may rush from the titled crowd, and cry, ' Herr, signor,' or ' monsieur,' as the case may be, ' write me six operas, teach all my family at five guineas per lesson, and at the end of a year, the hand of my daughter, Miss Clarissa, is yours.' They waylay the courteous publishers, Messrs. Octave and Piccolo, in counting-houses—at doors—everywhere. Octave is a pleasant man, tall, an undeniable judge of port wine, and rides to the Queen's hounds. Piccolo is a dapper man, who speaks scraps of every European language, and is supposed to have been madly in love, about the year eighteen hundred and twenty-seven, with the great contralto, Madame Rostolati, who married, if you remember, Prince Popadochoff : he who broke the bank at Baden Baden, just before he shot himself at Ems, in the year '33.

Here is a gentleman just stepped out of a handsome brougham at Octave and Piccolo's door. His hair is auburn, curling and luxuriant ; his beard and moustache ample, and a monument to the genius of his hairdresser ; he is covered with jewellery ; his clothes are of the newest cut, and the most expensive materials. He is perfumed ; the front of his shirt—lace and studs—is worth twenty guineas, and leaning from the window of his brougham, you can descry a kid-gloved hand, with rings outside the glove, a bird-of-paradise feather, and the head of a King Charles's spaniel. The hair, the beard, the moustache, the jewellery, the shirt, the brougham, the bird of paradise, and the King Charles all belong to Orpheus Basserclyffe, fashionable singer of the day.

Snarling people, envious people, crooked-minded people, of course, aver that Basserclyffe roars; that he sings out of tune; that he doesn't sing as well as formerly; that he can't sing at all; that he has a fine voice, but is no musician; that he can read at sight well enough, but has no more voice than a jackdaw. What does Basserclyffe care? What do people *not* say about professionals? They say Joe Nightingale's mother (he preceded Basserclyffe as fashionable), kept a coal and potato shed in Bermondsey; yet he made twenty thousand pounds, and married a baronet's daughter. They say Ap Llewellyn, the harpist's name is not Ap, nor Llewellyn, but Levi, that he is not a Welshman at all, and that he used to play his harp in the streets, sitting on a little stool, while his sister went round with a hat for the coppers. They say that Madame Fioriture, the prima donna, does not know a note of music, and that old Fripanelli, the worn-out music-master of Tattyboys Rents, has to teach her every part she plays. Let them say on, says Basserclyffe. So that I sing on and sing well, what does it matter? He is right. If he had sung at the Italian Opera—as William, in 'Black-eyed Susan,' was said by Douglas Jerrold to play the fiddle—like an angel, there would have been soon found worthy people and astute critics to whisper—'Ah, yes, very sweet, but after all, he's not an Italian!' He is too sensible to change his name to Bassercliffi or Basserclifficini. He is content, perfectly content, with making his four or five thousand a year by singing at concerts public and private, oratorios, festivals, and philharmonic associations, in town and country. It is perfectly indifferent to him at what species of entertainment he gets his fifteen guineas for a song. It may be at the Queen's palace, or in the large room of some vast provincial music hall. I will say this for him, however, that while he *will* have the fifteen guineas (and quite right, if those who employ him can pay), he will sing gratuitously, and cheerfully, too, where real need exists, and, for the benefit of a distressed anybody, will pipe the full as melodiously as when his notes are exchanged by those of the Governor and Company of the

Bank of England. He has a fine house; he gives grand
dinner parties; he is an exemplary husband and father; he
has no serious care in the world, except for the day when his
voice will begin to fail him. 'He is beast like that,' says
Bambogetti, the cynic of the musical world, striking the sound-
ing-board of a pianoforte.

But there has sidled into the shop, and up to the polite
Mr. Octave, and held whispered converse with him, which
converse has ended in a half shake of the head on Octave's
part, a shrug of the shoulder, and a slipping of something
into the creature's hand, a dirty, ragged, shameful old man, in
a trailing cloak, and with an umbrella that would seem to have
the palsy as well as the hand that holds it. This is Gaddi.
About the time that the allied sovereigns visited England,
just before the battle of Waterloo, Teodoro Gaddi was the great
Italian tenor, the king of tenors, the emperor of tenors. He
was more largely paid than Farinelli, and more insolent than
Cuzzoni. They talked scandal about queens in connection with
Gaddi. Sovereigns sent semi-ambassadors to tempt him to
their courts. He sang, and the King's Theatre was in rap-
tures. He was the idol of routs, the admired of ladies in chip
hats and leg-of-mutton sleeves; he spent weeks at the country
seats of lords who wore hair-powder and Hessian boots, or
high-collared coats and Cossack trousers. He was praised in
the 'Courier,' the 'Day,' the 'News,' and the 'Belle Assemblée.'
There is no King's Theatre now. There are no routs, leg-of-
mutton sleeves, or chip hats left. No 'Couriers' to praise, no
ladies to admire, no lords to invite. There is no Teodoro
Gaddi, nothing but old Gaddi, the shabby, broken-down, old
beggarman, who hangs about the music-shops and haunts professional people's houses. If you ask Gaddi the cause of his
decadence, he lifts up his hands, and says piteously, ' Ma famille,
my dear, ma famille;' but as he notoriously turned all his sons
out of doors, and broke his daughters' hearts, you can't exactly
believe that story. Gaddi's voice is quite broken and ruined
now; he is immensely old, and pitiably feeble, but he is full
of galvanic vitality, and is as shameless a beggar as the Spanish
mendicant with the arquebus, that Gil Blas met. If you happen to know Gaddi, it is very probable that, descending your
stairs some morning, you will find him, cloak, umbrella, and
all, sitting somewhere on the bottom flight. ' I have come,'
he says, 'I, Gaddi. I die of hunger. I have no charbons,
my dear; give me twopence;' or, reposing quietly in your
bed, you may find the curtains at the bottom thereof drawn

on one side, and be aware of Gaddi, and of his voice mumbling, 'Twopence, *charbons*, Gaddi. I knew your father, I have supped with Georges Quatre; I, Gaddi.' It is singular that though Gaddi is always complaining of hunger, he is almost as continually eating a pie—a large veal pie; and as he munches, he begs. 'Tis ten to one that half an hour after you have relieved him, you will meet with a friend who will tell you 'old Gaddi called on me this morning, and asked for twopence. He was eating a pie. He said that he was starving, and had no coals, and that he knew my father.' Gaddi has known everybody's father.

A quiet-looking gentleman with a sallow countenance, and bearing a roll of music in his hand, has entered the music warehouse while we have been considering Gaddi. He has a profoundly fatigued, worn-out, *ennuyé* expression pervading his whole appearance. His lustreless black hair is listless, so are his small hands, on one of which glisten diamonds of price. His limp hat is negligently thrown rather than posed on the back of his head. He dangles a listless glove, and plays with a limp watch-chain ornamented with dully valuable breloques; his eyes are half closed, and he yawns wearily. His chief care seems to be for the butt-end of a powerful cigar, which he has left, in deference to English prejudices but evidently with much reluctance, on the railing outside the shop. He casts a lingering look at this remnant through the plate-glass windows, and twiddles his listless fingers as though the beloved weed were yet between his digits. Who may this be? Who but Polpetti, not the great English, nor even only the great Italian, but the great European tenor; the finest Edgardo in the world; the unrivalled Elviro; the unapproached Otello; the pride of the Scala and the Fenice, the Pergola, and the Italiens; the cynosure of Berlin and Vienna, and St. Petersburg; the decorated of foreign orders; the millionnaire; the Gaddi of to-day.

So much glory (more than a conqueror's), so much gold (more than a Hebrew banker's), has this listless person earned by his delightful art. I am not about to say that he is overpaid. I would walk ten miles fasting to be present at one opera in which he performs. You cannot resist him. You hang on his notes, and your heart keeps time with them. And when he has finished you must needs clap your hands till they be sore, and yell bravos till you be hoarse, for you can't help it.

Polpetti will **not** go the way of Gaddi. He has bought a

fine estate in Italy, some say an island, some say a province, whither in a few months he will retire to enjoy the ample fortune he has amassed in strange lands—from the banks of the Neva to those of the Thames—from the Po to the Potomac —from Liverpool to Lisbon. Twenty years since, and Giacinto Polpetti was an olive-faced lad, running meanly clad among the vines and olives and staring white houses, and dusty lanes of an Italian county town. He had an uncle, perhaps—a snuffy old abbate, fond of garlic, and olives, and sour wine, who wore a rusty soutane, and carried a sky-blue umbrella, and could read nothing but his breviary, and not much of that. His uncle's cross old housekeeper may have taught him to read, and at ten he may have been consigned to the shop-board of a tailor, or the farm-house of a vine-grower, till it was discovered that he had a voice—and a beautiful voice too—which caused his promotion to a badly-washed surplice and the choir of the church; his vocal duties being varied by swinging a censer and tinkling a bell, and making the various genuflexions which the service of the mass demands. He might have grown up, and gone back to the tailor or the vinegrower, or have degenerated into a sacristan, a dirty monk, with bare feet and a cowl, full of black bread and sausages, or an abbate like his uncle, with a rusty soutane and a sky-blue umbrella, but for a neighbouring magnifico, the Count di Nessuno-Denaro, who had no money, but considerable influence; who condescended to patronise him, and procured his admission into the Conservatoire of Milan. A weary time he had of it there. A wearier still when singing for starvation wages at the smaller provincial towns of Italy. A weariest when he fell into the hands of a grasping speculator who 'starred' him at Paris, and Milan, and Venice, paying him niggardly, and forcing him to work the rich mine of his youthful voice as though the ore would never fail. But he emancipated himself at last, and went to work in earnest for himself. The last ten years have been one long triumph, and Jupiter Success has found in him no unwilling Danaë. He will retire with his millions (of francs) to his own village in the sunny South, among the olives, and vines, and staring white houses. He will make his uncle the abbate (who lives still) as rich as an English bishop, and build a mausoleum over the grave of the cross old housekeeper, and lead a jovial, simple-minded, happy life among his old kindred and friends: now exhibiting the diamond cross that the Czar of Russia gave him, and now the golden snuff-box presented to him by the Kaiser of Austria.

Do not let us be too hard upon the 'confounded foreigners' who come here to sell their crotchets and quavers for as much gold as they will fetch. Only consider how many million pounds sterling a year we make by spinning shirts and welding iron for the confounded foreigners; how many millions of golden pennies our travelling countrymen turn by cutting canals, and making railroads, steamers, suspension-bridges, in lands where we ourselves are but 'confounded foreigners.'

If I have dwelt somewhat too lengthily and discursively upon the male illustrations of the musical world, I beg that you will not suppose that the fairer denizens of that harmonious sphere neglect to visit Messrs. Octave and Piccolo's shop. Prime Donne abound, even more than Primj Uomini. Every season produces a score of ladies, Signoras, Madames, Mademoiselles, and Fraus, who are to do great things : who come out and go in with great rapidity. Yonder is Madame Digitalis. She sings superbly ; but she is fifty, and fat, and ugly. ' Bah !' yawn the *habitués*. ' The Digitalis is passed. She is rococo. Give us something new.' Whereupon starts up Mademoiselle Crimea Okolska from Tartary (said to be a runaway serf of the Czar, and to have been thrice knouted for refusing to sing duets with the Grand Duke Constantine) the new soprano. But Mademoiselle Crimea (she with the purple velvet mantle and primrose bonnet bantering Polpetti in the corner), screams, and sings sharp, and pronounces Italian execrably ; and the *habitués* declare that she won't do, and that she is nothing after all but the same Miss Crummins of the Royal Academy, who failed in Adelgisa six years ago, and has been abroad to improve and denationalise her name. The rage among the ladies who can sing for being Prime Donne is greater than that among attorneys' clerks for playing Hamlet. Octave and Piccolo are besieged at the commencement of every season by cohorts of foreign ladies, all with the highest recommendations, all of whom have been mentioned in the most enthusiastic terms by M. Berlioz, M. Fétis, and the other great musical oracles of the continent, and all of whom desire ardently to sing at the Philharmonic or before her Majesty. The manager of the Opera plays off half a dozen spurious Prime Donne during the months of March and April, keeping the trumps for the height of the season. And not only to the continent is this prima donna rage confined. Staid and decorous English parents hearing their daughter singing ' Wapping old Stairs,' prettily, send her forthwith to the Royal Academy of Music. She comes back and sings florid Italian scenas. 'Send her to Italy,' cry with one voice her relations and friends. To Italy she goes, and from Italy she returns, and comes out at the Opera, or at one of the fashionable morning concerts. She sings something with a great deal of ornament, but in a very small voice: you may hear the rustling of the music-paper, as she turns the leaves, with far more distinctness than her song. She goes in again, after this coming out, and is heard of next year at the Snagglesgrade Mechanics' Institution; and soon afterwards she sensibly marries Mr. Solder, the ironmonger, and gives up singing altogether.

Prima donna upon prima donna—never ending, still beginning, none of them can oust from their thrones the four or five blue ribbons of melody, who go on from year to year, still electrifying, still enchanting, still amazing us: none of them can touch the Queen: the Semiramis of Song: whose voice no more declines than her beauty, whose beauty than her grace, whose grace than her deep pathos, and soulful declamation and glorious delivery. Ah, lovers of music, your aviaries may be full of nightingales and swans, English and foreign, black, white, and pied; but, believe me, the woods will be voiceless for long, long after the Queen of Song shall have abdicated her throne and loosened the silver cords of her harp of glory.

For all, however, little Miss Larke, the fair-haired English prima donna, holds her own manfully. Her name is Larke, and she sings like one; and her voice is as pure as her fame. This brave little woman has run the gauntlet through all the brakes and thickets, and jungles and deserts, where 'devouring tygers lie,' of the musical world. Lowliness was her young ambition's ladder, and now that she has attained the topmost round, she does not turn her back on the ladder,

> 'Scorning the base degrees
> By which she did ascend. So Cæsar did—'

But so does not Miss Larke. She is honourably proud of the position she has gained by her own merits and good conduct; but she sings with as much equanimity before royalty as she was wont to do at the Snagglesgrade Institution, and has ever a helping hand for those beneath her who are struggling and weak. There is my darling little Larke by the grand pianoforte blooming in pink muslin, with a neat morocco music-case in her hand. Mr. Piccolo has a whole list of engagements, metropolitan and provincial, for her; from aristocratic

soirées to morning concerts; and she has a list at home of engagements she has herself received, which she must consult
before she can accept more. Go on and prosper, little Larke!
May your sweet voice last a thousand years!

But the crowd thins in Messrs. Octave and Piccolo's shop;
the carriages drive away to the park; the professionals go
home to dinner or to dress for evening concerts; and as I
saunter away, and listen to the strains of a German band in
Beak Street, mingling with the jarring minstrelsy of some
Ethiopian Serenaders in Golden Square, I am obliged to
confess that the cursory view I have taken of the musical
world, is but an opuscular one after all—that I have but
described a worldling having a dozen worlds within it.

XXV.

MUSIC IN PAVING-STONES.

IN the Stones of Venice—their Sea Stories and Foundations—
Mr. Ruskin could find elaborate theories; could weave from
them fantastic tissues of Art-thought; could raise upon them
cunning superstructures of argument, illustration, dogmatism,
and beautiful description. Let me try, if, striking the paving-
stones with my iron heel, I cannot elicit some music from
them. Let the stones of Regent Street, London, be my rock
harmonicon, and let me essay to play upon them some few
bars more of the musical tune.

Regent Street is the only boulevard of which London can
boast; and though the eight-storied houses, the shady trees,
the gay cafés, the peripatetic journal-mongers, the bustling
stalls, the glittering passages, the broad asphalte pavement,
which give so pleasant and lively an aspect to that magnificent
promenade which extends from the Madeleine, in Paris, to the
Bastille—though these are wanting, there is sufficient crowd,
and bustle, and gaiety, in our Regent Street, sufficient wealth
and architectural beauty, to enable it, if not to vie with, at
least to compensate a foreigner for his temporary exile from
his beloved Boulevard des Italiens.

Between three and six o'clock every afternoon, celebrities
jostle you at every step you take in Regent Street. The
celebrities of wealth, nobility, and the mode, do not disdain
to descend from their carriages, and tread the flags like

ordinary mortals. Science, Literature, and Law, walk arm-in-arm three abreast. Dethroned kings, expatriated generals, proscribed republicans, meet on a neutral ground of politics, and paving-stones. It is pre-eminently in a crowded street, that you see that equality which will assert itself at times—etiquette, William the Conquerer, and Burke's Peerage and Baronetage, notwithstanding. The Queen of Spain has legs in Regent Street, and uses them. The Duke of Pampotter cannot usurp a larger share of the pavement than the plebeian in a velveteen shooting-jacket who sells lap-dogs. Every gent in a Joinville tie, irreproachable boots, and a successful moustache, can be for the nonce the shepherd Paris, and adjudge the golden apple to the most beautiful bonnet, and the most beautiful face, whether their possessor be a fashionable marchioness or a fashionable milliner.

Those good friends of ours, the foreigners, who need only to know and visit England to take kindly to its streets, people, viands, liquors, and import of bullion, have taken at least nine points of the law in Regent Street, these twenty years agone. It is refreshing to see these worthy fellows in the most eccentric hats, the wildest pantaloons, the craziest extravagancies of braiding, the most luxuriant beards ; glistening with pomatum, electro-plated jewellery, and boot-varnish ; swelling down Regent Street, making the air redolent with foreign perfumes and the smoke of foreign cigars ; their wives and daughters giving *vivâ voce* lessons in the art of wearing a bonnet, holding up a dress, and scragging the hair off the temples, *à l'Impératrice,* and all gazing approvingly at the numerous indications which Regent Street presents, of England being the place for foreigners after all, and Regent Street the locality, *par excellence,* for foreigners to open brilliant shops for the sale of perfumes, gloves, cambric pocket-handkerchiefs, Vanille chocolate, ormolu clocks, Strasburg pies, St. Julien claret, and patent leather boots.

Music, above all, hath charms in Regent Street ; and its paving-stones unceasingly echo beneath the feet of the denizens of the musical world. Music-masters and mistresses hurry to and fro from their lessons ; singers to concerts or into Messrs. Octave and Piccolo's music-warehouse ; and a considerable number of the stars of the musical hemisphere, walk in this harmonious boulevard, merely to see and to be seen. It is as incumbent on a musical notoriety, on his return from the continent, or the provinces, on the eve or the morrow of a success, to show himself in Regent Street, as for a betting-man to clink his boot-heels upon the nobbly stones of Messrs. Tattersall's yard. Musical reputations have been won and lost in Regent Street; and the reigning prima donna dares not despise the opinions of its paving-stones.

What gleams in the distance so snow-white, what is found to be on nearer inspection so elaborately embroidered, so faultlessly plaited, so free from crease or wrinkle? What but the shirt of the great German basso; and who can the great basso be but Bompazek?

No braces disturb the equanimity of that unrivalled shirt, no waistband visits its snowy expanse. In deference to established prejudices, Bompazek wears a coat—a coat, mulberry in colour, lined with watered silk, and marvellously tagged and braided; but were he entirely a free agent we have no doubt that the sleeves and wristbands, the seams, gussets, and bands, of that shirt of shirts would be made fully manifest to Regent Street. He must grieve that he is not a Whiteboy and cannot wear his shirt over his clothes; for the shirt is Bompazek, and Bompazek is the shirt. If ever he had a palace with stained glass windows, he might paraphrase the Cardinal of York's proud motto, and write up, *Ego et indusium meum*—I and my shirt. There is much virtue in a clean shirt—a good, fine, well-got-up shirt: showing plenty of collar, front, and wristbands. Many a man has been indebted to his washerwoman, not only in the amount of her little bill, but for subsequent fame and fortune. They say that Tom Gills, who was renowed for wearing the finest collars in Europe, and positively devoted a considerable portion of his time to cutting out models of shirt-collars in pasteboard for the guidance of his registered shirt-maker, obtained his colonial appointment mainly through his collars. I wish myself that colonial appointments were obtained from the virtuous government of this enlightened country for no worse reasons. Should we get on much worse than we do, I wonder, if we chose our governments themselves for their collars?

I have said that Bompazek wears not braces. In lieu thereof he is girt with an embroidered belt,—a belt thickly sown with rich beads—the gift and work, perchance, of some fair Fraulein in Germany, the lady of his love, whom, like the Standard Bearer, he dare not name. Bompazek has a beard that the Emperor Julian, the apostate, he who boasted of his *barba longa et populata*, would have been proud of. His mouth is of an affable, good-humoured cut; his blue eye suggests not violence, pride, ambition, but is suggestively eloquent of mild beer and milder pipes. In both does Bompazek mildly delight.

Yes. This big, barbated, spicated basso, with the beard of a sapeur, the stature of a Colossus, the strength of a Tauridor, the lungs of a Stentor, is the mildest, meekest, most placable, soft-hearted creature that you can imagine. He is a great friend of little children ; and though they are frightened at first at his tremendous bass voice, they soon venture to climb on his knees, and play with the breloques of his watch-chain, and make use of his beard for prehensile purposes, and listen to the little lieds he sings them in the biggest voice that ever you heard. He is the victim, milch cow, and *bête de souffrance* of herds of hungry, ragged, disreputable foreigners, who come to him with torn and greasy passports, and letters of introduction from people he never heard of; who drink his beer, smoke his pipes, eat his suet-puddings, sleep in his drawing-room, borrow his money, wear even his sacred shirts, and call him Dummerkopf for his pains. He is always giving or lending money, singing for nothing, subscribing to charities. He has always some *baufre eggzile* whose rent he pays, and whose *lit* is always being taken from under him and redeemed by Bompazek.

It is reported that Bompazek cannot go back to the Grand Duchy of Schloss-Schinkenstein, his native place, as he was seriously implicated in the revolutionary movement of '48 ; and the Grand Duke is furious against him. I cannot for the life of me conceive to what greater extent this big, harmless man could have compromised himself in a political sense than by drinking beer out of a conspirator's glass, or giving a pipe-light to a democrat. Perhaps his beard went against him. It is decidedly the most revolutionary thing about him.

Bompazek lodges in Great Blenheim Street, where he occupies the first-floor, and has irretrievably ruined four carpets with expectorations. His drawing-room and bed-room are one large pipe. The whitewashed ceiling is smoked to a golden colour, the walls are covered with the marks left by lucifer-matches rubbed against them for ignition ; tobacco-ash lurks in the chairs, the keys of the pianoforte, the curtains, and the music-books. The smell of tobacco is overpowering, but not offensive : it has no time to grow stale—fresh pipes being continually lighted. When Bompazek says, ' Gom and bipe vid me dis evedig,' you find a table covered with pipes of every imaginable form and size, a bottle of hollands, a huge porcelain jar of tobacco, and an armoury of pewter pots. Six

or seven Germans, including Bompazek, range themselves
round the fire-place, each man wrapped in a dry blanket of
smoke, and gravely spit the fire out ; the loudest sound that
is heard being the coughing of Mrs. Pickwinkle, the landlady,
and her servant 'Melia in the kitchen below.

Mrs. Pickwinkle does not object to the smoke or the expectoration.   Mr. Bompazek is so good a lodger, and pays so
liberally and regularly, says she.   But by one of those inexplicable caprices, peculiar to the feminine organization, she
has taken violent exception to Bompazek's suet-puddings.
He is inordinately fond of those indigestible delicacies.   So
are his friends.   He eats them for breakfast, luncheon, dinner,
supper,—for Bompazek, as befits a true child of Fatherland, is
a four-meals-a-day man.   So are his friends, the silent men
who help to spit the fire out.   Mrs. Pickwinkle has been on
the point several times of giving him warning on this irrita-
ting account.   She leads 'Melia a dreadful life about the
puddings.   She explodes on the subject in back kitchens and
areas, on staircases and landings, to friends and neighbours.
I called on Bompazek once.   He was out, but was expected
to return to dinner almost immediately ; Mrs. Pickwinkle was
in a fury on the pudding grievance.   She took me into his
sitting-room, where, on a table garnished with a cloth burnt in
several places by hot tobacco-ash, I found a stew and seven
puddings.   ' There,' she cried, ' seven mortal puddings for a
party as calls himself a Christian !   Now, Mr. Penn, can flesh
and blood stand that ?'   Landladies have curious likings and
antipathies.   One begged me to suit myself elsewhere, once,
because I objected to having four pounds of bacon at a time,
and didn't like it streaky.   She remarked that she had let
lodgings for five-and-twenty years, and wished to know if I
considered myself a gentleman.   I know of a landlady who
gave her lodger warning—not because he was backward with
his rent, nor for keeping late hours, or smoking, or carrying
on—but because he wore such large buttons.   She had bore
with it as long as she could, she said, but she was certain
them buttons could be no good.

As Bompazek comes sailing majestically down Regent
Street, you may remark that there hangs upon his arm, talking
very loudly and vivaciously, and looking round with a complacently defiant air, as if to say ' This is Bompazek, the great
basso, and I am his friend,' a very little man in a tremendously tall hat, which seems perpetually to be on the point of
overbalancing him.   This is little Saint Sheddle, who, as I

have remarked in a former paper, knows and is intimate with, everybody in the musical world. Saint Sheddle is one of the fifty thousand living enigmas who walk and talk, and wear good hats and boots, without any ostensible means of existence. Nobody knows how Saint Sheddle lives. He was known as Captain Saint Sheddle at Brighton ; as Dr. Saint Sheddle at Bath ; and I saw his name myself in the 'Vienna Fremden Blatt,' as Le Comte de Saint Sheddle, rentier from London. I should not be surprised to hear of him, some of these days, as the Venerable Archdeacon Saint Sheddle in Torquay, or as Shedalli Pasha at Erzroum.

Meanwhile, Saint Sheddle goes everywhere, and puts his legs under innumerable mahoganies. He walks out in the park with Madame Perigord's children. He fetched home Poskoggi's niece from school in the Avenue Marigny in Paris. He dines with Octave and Piccolo when they entertain the musical stars at Greenwich or Richmond ; he is at all Papadaggi's grand Soirées ; he is admitted to Lady Tremoloso's musical evenings ; stays whole weeks at her palatial country seat, Chromatic Park, and went to Vienna with the well-known amateur and friend of artists, Sir Peddler Fugue. He is a member of the Jolly Scrapers' Club, a réunion of the members of the principal orchestras, held at the Bass-viol, Vinegar Yard ; it is even reported that he is employed to pawn Madame . Garbanati's jewellery when that lady, as it frequently happens, is in difficulties ; and that he writes all Tifferari's letters. It is certain that he has admission to all the green-rooms, tickets for all the concerts, and is intimate with the mysterious Panslavisco. But how does the man live ? What hatter, what bootmaker, what tailor, supplied the habiliments ? Where does the massy gold chain come from ? Is Saint Sheddle something in the wine trade, or the coal trade ? Does he deal in pictures, or sell snuff on commission ?

The only business operation in which Saint Sheddle was ever positively known to be engaged was when he took the Saint Sepulchre's theatre for the performance of Burmese operas. We all remember how many nights his season lasted, who didn't get their salaries, and what a melancholy failure the whole speculation was. Saint Sheddle ran to Portugal Street as if he had been running a race. Somehow he didn't 'go through the court ;' the discovery of his multifarious addresses might perhaps have been fatal to him ; but he has been going through ever since. If you speak about debts or difficulties to Saint Sheddle, he says, 'Debts ! pooh, my boy !

Look at me. Five judgments out against me. What's that? Got my protection in my pocket.' And he shows it you.

The little man is very popular in the musical world. He negotiates engagements, arranges with music-sellers for the publication of sentimental ballads by the Honourable Miss A——, and polkas by captains in the Life Guards; is the general peacemaker, mediator, and go-between of the profession. When Poskoggi, the composer, maddened by the unfounded jealousy of madame his spouse, emptied a plate of macaroni upon the piano, and fled his home and household gods for ever, Saint Sheddle interposed, sought out the unhappy husband at the hotel in Lisle Street, Leicester Square, where he had taken refuge, and was playing billiards with the despair of Napoleon after Waterloo, and reconciled Madame Poskoggi to her 'horsepond'—as she called her husband. When Mademoiselle Shaddabacco broke her engagement with the management of the Italian Opera, and retired to Dieppe in the sulks, ostensibly because Packerlickey, the manager, refused to pay for the expense of a foot-page to attend to her poodles, but really because Mademoiselle Baracouta, that upstart parvenue—that prima donna of yesterday—had created a furore in Nabucodonosore; it was Saint Sheddle who started off to Newhaven by the express train. crossed the briny ocean, cleared away all difficulties, and brought the Shaddabacco back in triumph. His evidence on the great trial of Packerlickey *versus* Guffler, on the disputed question of the copyright in the music of the ballet 'Les mille et une Jambes,' was of the greatest value. He has just taken the affairs of Madame Garbanati (who has been living too fast) in hand. When malicious people began to whisper ugly things about Miss Linnet in connection with Captain de Prance of the Harpooners; who but Saint Sheddle went about, defending the young lady everywhere? Who but he vowed he was present when Miss Linnet boxed the Captain's ears, and when old Linnet, her papa (a worthy man, once a schoolmaster, but too fond of cold rum and water), kicked the captain down stairs? Who but he declared, striking a seraphine in Octave's shop, with virtuous vehemence, that he, Saint Sheddle, would call out and fight any man who dared to whisper a syllable against the maligned young lady?

Adolphus Butterbrod, Ph. Dr., of Schwindelburg, who has just passed Bompazek with so low a bow, although the basso scarcely acknowledged it, does not like Saint Sheddle : he says he is 'an indriguaud.' In days gone by, Butterbrod was confidential friend and agent to Bompazek, and had free right of warren over his pipes, his purse, his puddings, and his shirts; he arranged all the basso's engagements, and haughtily told concert-givers that he had 'roged'—or raised—his terms. But he was detected in flagrant delict of conspiring with Tonner von Heidelburg, Bompazek's enemy and rival; and cotemporary history records that the usually mild Bompazek (the rage of a sheep is terrible) beat the traitor violently with an umbrella, and banished him from the domains of Pickwinkle for ever. Saint Sheddle is Fidus Achates to the big basso now, and the Ph. Dr. would like to do him a good turn if he could.

Place aux Dames! Room for the stately lady in black velvet, who meanders gracefully along the pavement. Two smaller cygnets, in sea-green watered-silk and laced trousers, accompany the parent bird. This is Madame Perigord, the renowned contralto, and her youthful daughters. Lesbia Perigord has a beaming eye, a robe of silk velvet, long black ringlets, a chain of gold, a châtelaine, diamond rings, pearly teeth, faultless hands and feet, in little gloves and boots as faultless. Lesbia has a voice of liquid honey and passionate fire, poising itself for a moment on her ruby lips, and flying straightway into her hearers' hearts. Lesbia is a superb creature: but, oh! I will content myself with Camberwell and my Norah Creina—my gentle, simple Norah Creina, who cannot sing contralto, but can make Irish stew. For Lesbia has a temper. Let me whisper it; a deuce of a temper. Let me write it on paper and show it to you privately; a devil of a temper! I would rather not be Lesbia's sparrow, if I did not think my neck in want of wringing. I would rather not be one of Lesbia's sea-green children, if I preferred the law of kindness to the law of kicks and cuffs. I would rather not be Lesbia's maid, if I valued peace of mind or body; and I would decidedly not be Lesbia's husband upon any consideration whatever.

Madame Perigord was very nearly the death of Piccolo. Piccolo suffered much from rheumatism, and happening casually to mention the matter to the Perigord, she immediately insisted on sending to Paris to her doctor, one Mercantori, for a certain marvellous embrocation, which would cure Piccolo instantaneously. It was no use demurring to Mercantori's preparation. It had cured the Perigord when she was like that (pointing to a sideboard as an emblem of immobility), and he must take it. Besides, Piccolo is so accustomed to do what he is asked, that had Madame Perigord proposed sending for a white elephant from Siam, and boiling it up into broth as a remedy for rheumatism, it is not improbable that he would have assented to the proposition. So, the famous embrocation (for which Piccolo was to be charged cost price) was sent for from Paris. In the course of the week a deal case of considerable size, addressed to Lord Piccolo, arrived in London at the music-seller's residence, and he was gratified by having to pay one pound nine and sevenpence sterling for carriage. The case, being opened, was found to contain sundry bottles of a dark liquid resembling treacle-beer, several packages of mysterious-looking blue-paper tubes, closely approximating in appearance to the fireworks manufactured by the Chevalier Mortram, and a large pot of pomatum. One of the bottles being opened, emitted such a deadly and charnel-like odour that Mrs. Piccolo, who is rather a strong-minded woman, immediately condemned the whole paraphernalia as rubbish, and sentenced it to perpetual penal servitude in the dusthole: which sentence was as speedily put into execution, but not before a cunning document was found coiled up among the supposititious fireworks. This turned out to be a facture, or invoice, in which Lord Piccolo, of London, was debited to Vicesimo Mercantori, Pharmacien-Droguiste, in the sum of three hundred francs, otherwise, twelve pounds sterling, for goods by him supplied. Mrs. Piccolo went into hysterics. Piccolo was moved to call Doctor Mercantori injurious names; but as that learned pharmacien and druggist was some hundreds of miles away, the reproaches cannot have done him much harm. The worst was yet to come. Piccolo was rash enough to remonstrate with the Perigord. Miserable man! The Perigord incontinently proceeded to demolish him. She abused him in French—she abused him in Italian—she abused him in English. She wrote him letters in all sorts of languages. She stamped in his music-warehouse and shook the dust from off her feet on the threshold. She sent Girolamo Bastoggi, Avocato of Turin, to him, who spoke of *la giustizia*, and snuffed horribly. She even sent her mother (the Perigord had a mother at that time), a dreadful old female with a red cotton pocket-handkerchief tied round her head, and outrageously snuffy. The old lady's embassy was not fertile in conversation, but it was dreadfully contemptuous. After expressing her opinion that England was a 'fichu pays,' she looked round upon the assembled Piccolo family, said, '*Vous êtes toutes des —pouah!*' snapped her fingers, expectorated, and vanished. The unhappy Piccolo would only have been too happy to pay

tho disputed twelve pounds, but Mercantori's demands all
merged into the grievous wrong that had been done Madame
Perigord. She had been touched in her honour, her loyalty,
her good faith. She spoke of Piccolo as an *infâme*, a man of
nothing, a music-master, a gredin. She mocked herself of him.

There is a domestic animal attached to the Perigord's establishment in the capacity of husband : a poor, weak-eyed,
weak-minded man, in a long brown coat, who leads a sorry
life. He is supposed to have been, in early life, a dancing-
master in France ; and Madame married him (it can scarcely
be said that he married her) under the impression that he had
' *rentes*,' or income—which he had not. He fetches the beer ;
he transposes Madame Perigord's music ; he folds circulars and
seals tickets when she gives a concert. The maid patronises
him, and his children do not exactly know what to make of
him. They call him ' *ce drôle de papa.*' His principal consolation is in the society of a very large hairy dog, called
Coco, over which he maintains unbending authority, teaching
him the manual exercise with much sternness. The satirical
say that Madame Perigord's husband dines in the kitchen,
and varnishes his wife's boots when she plays male parts.
When she goes to Paris, it is reported that she puts him out
to board and lodge, at a cookshop in the Marais ; leaving him
behind while she visits Brussels or the Rhine with her daughters. It is certain that she made a long operatic tour in the
United States, leaving her husband in London, and that, as
she forgot to remit him any money, the unhappy man was
reduced to great straits.

Here come a face and a pair of legs I know very well.
How do you, Golopin ? Golopin is the first flautist of the
day. He is almost a dwarf. He is within a hair's breadth of
being humpbacked. He has a very old, large, white head,
under which is a little, old, tanned, yellow face. He plays
the flute admirably, but in private life he squeaks and
scratches himself. Golopin's chiefest reminiscence, greatest
glory, most favourite topic of conversation, is the fact that he
was once kicked by the Emperor Napoleon. ' In the year
nine,' he says, ' I find myself called to play of my instrument
at one of the musical entertainments give by the Emperor and
King at the Tuileries. Pending the evening, feeling myself
attained by an ardent thirst, I retire myself into the saloon at
refreshments prepared for the artists. In train to help myself
from the buffet, I perceive myself that the ribbon of my shoe
had become loose. It was justly then the fashion to wear the

culotte courte of white kerseymere, with silk stockings. 1
stoop myself down then to adjust my shoe-string, having my
back to the door, when I hear itself rolled upon the hinges
with a movement of authority. *Aussitôt* I receive a violent
kick in the kerseymeres. I recognised the *coup du maître*—
the master kick. Yes ; it was well him, the victor of Auster-
litz and Marengo, the crowned of the Pope, the Emperor. I
raise myself ; I salute ; I make the reverence ; I say, " Sire !"
" Ah, M. Golopin," cries the hero, " I demand pardon of you.
I took you for a *caniche*—a white poodle dog." I have those
kerseymeres still, my friend !'

Golopin is a worthy little creature, but is very irascible.
He boasts of unnumbered persons he has killed in single
combat abroad, and specially of a *maître d'armes* whom he
vanquished with the broadsword. He has great faith in his
flute, and generally carries it about with him. At Casserole's
restaurant in the Haymarket, one evening, having a violent
dispute with Klitzer, the cornet-à-pistonist, who had bantered
him into a state of frenzy, he positively struck that big
instrumentalist in the face, though he had to jump at least a
foot in the air to do so. He dismissed him with these mag-
niloquent words, ' Miserable ! You have neither the courage
of a bug nor the integrity of a lobster. Had I my instrument
with me I would chastise you.' People have been rather
chary of bantering Golopin since then. That bounteous,
kindly, consistent mother Nature of ours, whom we all abuse.
and yet should be so grateful to, scarcely ever fashions a
little deformed man but she implants in him a most valorous
stomach, a high disdain and sense of injured merit, a noble
pugnacity and irascibility that make it dangerous to ridicule
and insult him.

Who is this, that comes riding—not on a whirlwind like
Mr. Addison's angel (in a Ramilies wig) to direct the storm,
but on a peacefully ambling bay pony ? It is the well-known
amateur and *ami des artistes*, Sir Peddler Fugue. See ; he
has just stopped his little nag, and bends over the saddle to
talk to Trump, the composer. Sir Peddler Fugue is one of
a class not peculiar to the musical world, but common to all
the artistic professions. There is your fine-art amateur, who
pokes about studios, and advises you to kill that light, and
scumble that background, and glaze down that little finger;
who has just come from seeing Turpey's grand figure-piece
for next year's Exhibition ; who knows why the hanging
committee treated Maul so scurvily, and how much Pallet-

knife is to have for his commission from Slubber, the great Manchester cotton-spinner; and when Chizzle the sculptor will come back from Rome. There is your dramatic amateur, who has the *entrée* to all the green-rooms; who took Madame Spinosetti to Nice; paid for little Katty Tentoe's choregraphic education at the Conservatoire; lent Grogham his Justice Woodcock wig; lost a few hundreds in the Capsicum Street Theatre (under Pepper's management); wrote a very bad farce that was once played somewhere on a benefit night; and behaved like a father to Miss Haresfoot. There is your literary amateur, who was so good as to read over the proofs of Professor de Roots's bulky work upon the Integral Calculus (a service handsomely acknowledged by De Roots in his Preface); who found the money for the 'Comic Economist,' a humorous illustrated publication, with contributions by the first authors and artists of the day, which had an average circulation of twelve weekly, and lived five weeks; who edited the letters and remains of Twopenny the poet (poor fellow! few remains had he to leave save tavern scores, pawn-brokers' duplicates, and unpaid washing bills); and who is a member of the Goosequill Club, held at the Homer's Head, Grub Street. There is your musical amateur, the gentleman who ogles Euterpe through his eye-glass; goes to all the concerts; hangs about all the music-warehouses; and is the general friend, socius, and adviser of the artists. They are worthy fellows, mostly, these art amateurs, having little in common with the big-wigged patrons of old, who were wont to be addressed somewhat in this poetic strain:—

> Still shall my Muse the noble Mugmore sing,
> Friend of the arts and couns'llor of his king,

—and who paid for servile praise with a purse full of gold pieces, just as a provision-merchant would buy a tub of far wholesomer Dorset butter. They do not resemble the ridiculous dilettanti and cognoscenti of the last century, who meddled with artists' private affairs, and wrote them patronizing letters of advice, and suggested an alteration in a stanza, which spoilt it, and then left their *protégés* to starve. Thank heaven, Art wants no such patrons now! The *ami des artistes* of whom Sir Peddler Fugue is a type, likes and frequents artistic society for its own sake.

Sir Peddler Fugue, Bart., is very long and lean; and, but for the excellent condition and grooming of his horse, and that he himself is dressed as a quiet English gentleman, instead of a suit of rusty armour, he would bear no inconsiderable resemblance to that deathless knight of La Mancha who had a rueful countenance. If, again, it be Quixotic to be good, and brave, and generous, yet withal a little eccentric, somewhat pedantic, and occasionally (when his exquisite taste and finished appreciation of Art get the better of him) a bit of a bore, Sir Peddler Fugue is decidedly of the same mental mould as Cervantes' hero. Sir Peddler has a white moustache, grizzled hair, a chin tuft, and wears such spotless buckskin gloves, such lustrous boots, and has so noble and erect a carriage, that he has several times been mistaken, both at home and abroad, for the sovereign of a German principality. He is a bachelor, and lives in chambers in the Albany, where his sitting-room is hung round with M. Baugniet's lithographs of celebrated musicians, and, I verily believe, with a specimen of every musical instrument, ancient and modern, under the sun : from David's harp to Mr. Distin's sax-horns : from the lyre that Bruce brought from Abyssinia, to Straduarius's fiddles and Case's concertinas. The baronet plays a little on most of these instruments ; but he chiefly affects a brown old violoncello, with which, in the stillness of the night season, he holds grim and mysterious conferences : the instrument grumbling and groaning then, *sotto voce*, as if it were the repository of secrets which none might hear but he. Far in the recesses, moreover, of a gloomy street in the undiscovered countries lying between Baker Street and the Edgeware Road, there is a long, low, green-papered room, not unlike the inside of a fiddle-case. Thither, twice a week, during certain appointed months in the year, Sir Peddler Fugue repairs, preceded by his man-servant, carrying the brown old violoncello. There he meets a few other amateurs and professionals, reverent men with bald heads and spectacles : Viscount Cattegat (who elevated Miss Bowyer, the soprano, to the peerage, like a nobleman as he was) ; Francis Tuberose, M.P. (ætat. 80), who plays prettily on the viola ; Sir Thomas Keys, that time-honoured music-master, who taught music to the princesses, and was knighted by the revered George the Third himself ; and little old Doctor Sharp (Mus. Doc. Oxon.), who wears black smalls and gaiters, bless his heart, and composed a cantata for the Jubilee, goodness knows how many years ago. When these rare old boys meet, the wax candles are lighted, pinches from golden snuff-boxes are exchanged, voluminous music scores are produced, and the veterans plunge into a Saturnalia, of which Bach, Beethoven, Mendelssohn, Mozart, arc the high priests. Scrape away, yo valiant old men! Scrape, ye stout and kind old hearts! Thore aro resonant echoes to your harmony, far away; in drowsy little country towns, in remote villages, in German Schlossen, in Italian villas, in hot Indian bungalows, whore Lieutonant-Colonel Chutnee, Major Peppcrpot, and Mango the surgeon, may be oven now scraping tunefully for pure love of art, while dissolute Lieutenant Potts is muddling himself with brandy pawnce, and Ensigns Pockett and Cuc are quarrelling over billiards.

Sir Peddler Fugue lived very long abroad, I believe, before he succeeded to the baronetcy. While in Milan, he composed an opera, of course, the libretto of which was founded on the story of Hector and Andromache, Cephalus and Aurora, or some equally dreary subject. It is said to have been produced at Civitá Vecchia with considerable success as the work of the Cavaliere Maestro Pedlero Fugio, Principe Inglese. In Italy, the baronet acquired a habit of speaking his native language with such a foreign accent and manner that you are puzzled sometimes to determine his English or Italian extraction. 'Beautiful!' is his favourite expression. 'I have seen the Coggi,' he says; 'she is B-e-a-u-ti-ful! Your opera, my dear Tromp, is b-e-a-u-ti-ful. I shall nevare forget the b-e-a-u-tiful cabalet to in the third act. No!' Whereupon he lifts his hat in true foreign style, and rides away on his ambling pony, to stop or be stopped by a dozen more professionals with whom he is on terms of intimacy, in his course down Regent Street.

Still up and down the paving-stones the celebrities of the Musical World pass; and, like the fashionable lady of Banbury who rode the white horse, and had rings on her fingers and bells on her toes, a man, if he be so minded, can have music wherever he goes.

XXVI.

A LITTLE MORE HARMONY.

STILL must I hear! Shall the hoarse peripatetic ballad-singer bawl the creaking couplets of 'The Low-backed Car' beneath my window; shall the summer breeze waft the strains of 'Pop Goes the Weasel' upon my ears, and drive me to confusion, while I am endeavouring to master the difficulties of the

Turkish alphabet; shall the passing butcher-boy rattle his bones, and the theological beggar-man torture a psalm-tune into dolorous cadences; shall the young lady in the apartment next to mine string my nerves into the rigours, while she is practising 'Les Souvenirs de Cracovie,' with that ceaseless verbal accompaniment of one, and two, and three; one, and two, and three! Shall music in some shape or other resound from the distant costermonger and the proximate street boy; the brooding swallows sitting upon the eaves, and showing me 'their sunny backs'; the ill-ground organ in the next street; and the beaten tom-tom and execrable caterwauling of Howadjee Lall from Bombay! To say nothing of the deep-mouthed dog next door; the parrot at number eight which is always endeavouring to whistle 'Il Segreto,' and always trying back, and never succeeds in accomplishing more of the air than the first three-quarters of a bar; and Colonel Chumpfist's man-servant over the way, who sings valorously while he cleans his master's boots in the area! I say, shall all these things be, and I not sing, lest haply my readers think they have already had enough and to spare, of my musical reminiscences! No: the Musical World shall be again my theme,—a little more harmony my song.

I will take a morning concert. Say one given in the height of the season by Signor Papadaggi, the famous singing-master. Papadaggi is a little man, but he has done great things. Twenty years ago he came to England from Leghorn, very poor and humble. He dwelt in the neighbourhood of Golden Square in those days; smelt of smoke; was not without a strong suspicion of garlic; had many button-up or cloudy linen days, when he slunk rather than walked under the defunct Quadrant Colonnade, and made a tremendous deal of a clean shirt when he mounted one. Papadaggi was very hairy then, and dined off grease, and was hand and glove with Riffi the bass, and Raffi the tenor, and Taggragati the piccolo player. He does not know Riffi nor Raffi now. He was very down, financially speaking, when Lor Brown, banquier of the City, took him up and into Belgravia. This laid the foundation of Papadaggi's fortune; but the superstructure was of his own erection. The brightest of his Lamps of Architecture was this—he shaved. There was, as you are aware, previous to that momentous question, Why Shave? being asked, an almost insurmountable prejudice among English respectability against beards and mustachios. These hirsute appendages seemed always connected in the minds of the British Pater- and Mater-familias with dirt, revolution, immorality, poverty, atheism, and non-payment of rent. Every great singer, artist, or musician, who happened to be the rage, might barely be tolerated in wearing a beard, just as a captain in the Life Guards or a traveller just returned from the interior of Dahomey might be ; but to the unknown, the poor, the struggling, the ambitious abnegation of the razor was fatal. Papadaggi was wise in his generation, and shaved. Not to an utter state of barefacedness, however, for he left his whiskers, which were neatly trimmed into the form of truncated, and lay on his cheeks like black muttonchops. These whiskers were the making of Papadaggi. He was no longer a confounded foreigner. He went into the best houses, and taught the flower of the British aristocracy and moneyocracy. In the banking world he is amazingly popular. Roehampton, Putney, and Ham Common, where bankers' villas most do congregate, will hear of no other music-master than Papadaggi. He has long since abandoned the confoundedly foreign prefix of Signor, and has Mr. I. Papadaggi printed on his cards. When I state that he is a director of two assurance companies, has recently been elected a member of the Mousaion Club, and has taken to wearing a white neckcloth in the daytime, the conclusion will easily be arrived at that he has a comfortable balance at his banker's, and is a highly respectable man.

Papadaggi married an English lady, Miss Hammernell, of Birmingham, and though of the pontifical faith himself, will send his son to Oxford. He has a tremendous house at Tyburnia, with a footman—a real footman, in plush and powder. Why did not the paternal Papadaggi, dead in Leghorn yonder, live to see the day ? P. the Second and Great is a little man, but he drives a monumental cab drawn by a big brown horse—a very horse of Troy—that moves with ? sert of swelling cadence of motion, as if he were practising Mozart's Requiem to himself. It is good to see honest Papadaggi behind the big horse ; a regulation tiger hanging on behind, and the music-master's little body gently swaying with the curvetings of his steed.* It is good to hear the thundering knock of the regulation tiger at the door of number six hundred and six A, Plesiosaurus Gardens West, where Papadaggi is about to give three-quarters of an hour's singing lesson for a guinea. It is good to see Papadaggi toddle out of his cab in

* A.D. 1853. Papadaggi would ride in a neat little brougham now. Private cabriolets are fast becoming numbered among ' things departed.'

the lightest of varnished boots, and the brightest of lemon-coloured gloves, and to note the respect with which the golden footmen receive him, and the easy patronage with which he passes them, mounts the stairs, gives his lesson, and lunches with Madame la Comtesse and the youthful ladies.

Once a year, Papadaggi gives his Grand Morning Concert at the Nineveh Rooms, Arrow-head Street, Cuneiform Square, in which rooms, the Nineveh Subscription Balls are given—balls to which (without unimpeachable vouchers from the leaders of the world) admission is as difficult as of old to the Eleusinian mysteries. In the Nineveh Rooms, with their huge tarnished pier-glasses, walls of a pale dirty blue, with cracked stucco ornaments, and faded benches and ottomans: which two last articles of furniture are no strangers to a certain lively insect —the pulex superbus, or fashionable fleas—our friend's Grand Concert takes place. For some days previous, the doorway of the Nineveh Rooms is blockaded, to the profound disgust of the Ameliorated Young Men's Table-turning Association, and the Society for the Protection of Stewed-eel Sellers, with gigantic posting boards, in which a weak-minded printer has seemingly gone raving mad in different coloured inks and varieties of eccentric type : howling in large capitalled prime donne, babbling in fat-lettered instrumentalists, melancholy mad in smaller type respecting Papadaggi's residence and the principal music warehouses where tickets, price half a guinea each (stalls fifteen shillings), may be had, and a plan of the rooms is on view.

I don't think it would be an unpardonable vulgarism to call Papadaggi's poster a stunner. It literally stuns you, so tremendous is its size, so marvellous are the attractions it promises, so brilliant are the celebrities who are to appear. Papadaggi has everybody. The Opera stars ; the famous Lurliety, who was a fixed star last season, but has taken it into his head lately to become a meteor ; Basserclyffe ; little Miss Larke ; Nightingale, of course ; Soundinbord Smasherr, the world-renowned Swedish pianist, just returned from America ; Madame Katinka Kralski, who plays tunes nobody can find the beginning or end of, upon a new instrument, the pifferarinium, which has just been patented and completed, at the cost of some thousands of pounds by Piccolo, and which looks very much like a pianoforte turned inside out ; Herr Bompazek, the great German basso ; little Klitz, the flautist, who goes everywhere, and whom everybody knows ; and greatest attraction of all, the astonishing Panslavisco, that

Mogul of Harpists, that dark mysterious child of genius, whose present popularity exceeds the greatest ever achieved by Paganini, the Whistling Oyster, the Hippopotamus, the Great Ant-eater, or General Tom Thumb. Besides these, there are multitudes of smaller musical notorieties, native and foreign, vocalists and instrumentalists : from the Misses Gooch, of the Royal Academy of Music, the pleasing ballad singers, to hard-working Tom Muffler, who means to do something with the big drum yet.

I am afraid the bénéficiare does not pay many of his artists. You see he is so fashionable, so run after, that it is rather an honour than otherwise to sing for him gratis. The Misses Gooch can truly affirm themselves to be of the nobility's concerts when they go starring round the provinces in the autumn after they have sung for a year or two at P.'s Grand Musical Festival. A great many professionals sing for Papadaggi through pure friendship and goodwill, for the little man is universally liked and respected. A great many sing because others sing, and a great many more because they want to be heard at any risk. The bird that can sing and won't sing is a *rara avis*. I never knew a bird that could sing but that would sing, whether his hearers liked it or not ; and I even know a great many birds that can't sing and oughtn't to sing, who *will* sing. Papadaggi, however, does not get all the professionals gratuitously. Orpheus Basserelyffe, with whom fifteen guineas for a song is as much a fixed idea as the cultivation of his garden was with Candide, says, ' I'll sing, by all means, but I must have the cash, Pap, my boy ;' and Pap pays him : while old Grabbatoni, the renowned performer on the violoncello, contents himself with saying every year as he pockets his eight guineas, ' Next year, mio caro, I play for noting—for noting—yes !' but, somehow or other, with Grabbatoni that next year never comes.

We will suppose the momentous day to have arrived, and Papadaggi's Grand Concert to have commenced. The carriages of the nobility and gentry, and the cabs of the public in general, block up Nineveh Street ; the coachmen doze on their boxes ; the neighbouring public-houses are full of the silken calves and gilt-knobbed sticks of the splendid footmen. Within, the ladies are ranged upon the faded ottomans—a beautiful show. There are peeresses, bishopesses, judgesses, bankeresses, baronetesses, stock-brokeresses, and merchant-princesses. Papadaggi has just handed a duchess to a seat ; and is at this moment whispering soft compliments to a

cabinet-ministress, with admirable equanimity and self-pos-
session.   The whiskers are resplendent; the boots shine
like patent-leather stars accidentally fallen from Böotes.   The
room is very full and very hot, and many of the dandies,
unable to find seats, lean their all-round collars against walls,
so to support their weary frames.   A vicious family from
Peckham Rye (a mamma, three daughters, an aunt, and a
melancholy governess) have fallen upon and utterly routed an
imbecile young man in a feeble white neckcloth, who acts as
check-taker for the stalls, and who holds a crimson worsted
cord across the space between the last ottoman and the wall.
The vicious family have only tickets for the back seats ; but,
having thoroughly demolished the imbecile young man mentally, and driven him before them like chaff before the wind,
they make a razzia into the stalls, and nearly overthrow a stockbroker's colony from Maida Hill, the members of which gather
themselves up indignantly, and whisper among themselves
despairingly, 'City people !'   Old General Jupp, who has sent
his family to the concert before him, and has walked down
from the Cutcherry Club, has found that he has left his ticket
behind him, and has had to pay over again at the doors, and
can't find his party, and sits apart in a corner on a cane-
bottomed chair, muttering horribly.   A meek-eyed young
dandy, who has come in cloth boots, with his hair curled (he
must be an only son with a taste for music, who fancies he
can sing second in a quartett), can't find Thrummer, the
musical clerk in the Treasury, who sings 'The Wolf' so
capitally, and who promised to point out all the musical celebrities to him.   He cannot, indeed, find anybody that he
knows, nor a place anywhere, and is repining secretly on
the staircase, where he looks so miserable, that the money-
taker, a florid man who officiates as a waiter at the London
Tavern o' nights, and sometimes takes a spell in the black
work, or undertaking line of business, compassionates him, and
is half inclined, were he not so great a dandy, to offer him
some of the beer from the pint pot under his chair.   There are
a great many foreigners in the concert-room, who come with
free admissions, as it is the custom of musical foreigners to
do ; two or three critics attached to the morning newspapers,
who listen to the songs with a knowing air and their heads
on one side, as if they knew perfectly well what the next bar
was to be ; and a country gentleman, who has come up to
town to attend a meeting of the Ameliorated Young Men's
Table-turning Association, and has blundered into Papadaggi's

concert-room by mistake, where he sits listening to the performances with a bewildered air.

Papadaggi's concert proceeds swimmingly. To be sure, the order of the programme is not strictly observed—the song that should be first frequently coming last, and *vice versâ*. Such misadventures will, however, happen in the best regulated morning concerts. Codlinetti, the Italian buffo-singer, who is of a capricious and changeable temperament, suddenly changes the song for which he is put down, to one of an entirely different character: to the indignation of Peddle, who is the accompanyist (presides at the pianoforte we believe are the appropriate words), who is a morose man, and insists upon playing the symphony in the original song; upon which Codlinetti, under shadow of turning over the music and showing Peddle the proper place, manifests a strong desire to fling him over the orchestra among the duchesses. Fraulein Ninni Stolzappel, the charming warbler of German Lieds, has likewise objected to the unfortunate man's accompaniment to her song, and at the end of a cadence, and in a voice audible even to General Jupp in the corner, has called Peddle 'Pig,' in the German language; whereat life becomes a burden to Peddle, and as he pounds the keys as though they were his enemies, he devoutly wishes that he were back in his quiet attic in the Royal Academy of Music, Tenterden Street, Hanover Square. Papadaggi neither plays nor sings. He is too learned to do anything; but he hovers about the orchestra, and hands singers on and off, and pervades the concert with his whiskers and white neckcloth —so that a considerable portion of the applause is meant for Papadaggi, and is by Papadaggi taken unto himself with many bows and smiles. Did you never know people who somehow seem to have a vested interest in the fruits of everybody's labours? There is scarcely a great picture painted, a book written, a palace built, a good deed done, but it turns out that somebody is entitled to considerable praise, or must be honourably mentioned in connection with it, though as far as your judgment went he never put a finger to the work, or a stone to the edifice. The number of unknown benefactors and passive great men is astonishing. I see their names in the literary pension list; I find Parliament making them grants every session; I hear their healths proposed at public dinners, and see them get up covered with modesty, to return thanks, when they bashfully allude to the things they have been instrumental in carrying out, though for the life of me I can't make out what they ever had do with anything.

What the green-room is to the theatre, the robing-room to the assize court, the vestry to the church; so is the singers' room to the concert-hall. But, far more elegant, sprightly, and amusing, than the dramatic green-room, is the 'professional room' behind the ragged leaves of the screen at the bottom of the steps of the orchestra at Papadaggi's concert. There are no garish gas-lights here, no tinselled dresses; no rouge, bismuth, jaded faces, pantomime masks—no passing carpenters and call-boys:—all is fresh, sparkling, and gay. Fresh flowers, rosy bonnets, and rosier faces, cleanest of shirts, smartest of female toilettes, newest of white kid gloves, most odoriferous of scents. I don't pretend to know much about female fashions, though I have occasionally studied that sphinx-like journal the 'Follet'—every flounce in which is an enigma—with fear and trembling. I don't pretend to know much about dress; but I do think that the best dressed ladies in creation are the female singers at a morning concert. They unite the prettiest portions of the English and French styles of costume. They dress their hair exquisitely, and display their little jewelleries inimitably. There is a whole art in making the most of a ring, a brooch, a bracelet. I have seen born ladies covered with gems, on whom they produced no more elegant effect than a bright brass knocker would on a pigstye door. And, more than all this, my musical belles have the unmistakable appearance of having *dressed themselves*, and are ten times smarter, neater, prettier for it, scorning the adventitious femme-de-chambre. There is a table covered with fruit and wine in the singers' room. I regret to see Tom Muffler sitting thereat. Tom is not given to drinking; but when drink is given to him, he exceeds.

Who is that strange wild man lying dislocated over, rather than sitting upon, an ottoman, his long fingers twined together, his eyebrows bent into the form of a horse-shoe, his puissant head bent down? That is Panslavisco the harpist. The trumpet of fame is braying his name out to all Europe, like an impetuous inconsiderate trumpet as it is, blowing for dear life to make up for lost time. He is deaf to Fame's trumpet. Fortune is pelting him with golden marrow-bones. He heeds not Fortune. She has pelted him with bones without any gold or marrow in them before now. He stands, and walks, and works, and lives alone: he and his harp, for they are one. The professionals say he is dull. The ladies say

he is a brute. The multitude cry ' Io Panslavice ! Evoe Panslavice !' as they would to Bacchus. He lets them cry on.
He plays his harp, and there is silence, and a wild tumult at
the end ; and then he receives his money, sees his harp put
into a green-baize cover, and carried off by a dun-bearded
man as mysterious as his master, and goes away. No concert is complete without him. In town and country he is
sure to draw. He has no intimates, no places of resort save
a mouldy cigar shop—where he sits as silent, and apparently
as immovable, as one of the tobacco-chests—and a dreary
public-house in a court up Drury Lane, where he drinks
large quantities of beer, tacitly. He speaks seldom, and then
he does not seem to be quite certain in his mind as to which
is his mother tongue, and his speech is a garbled compromise
of many languages. Indeed, nobody knows for certain of
what nation he is. Some say he is an Italian, some say he is
a German, some say he is a Dane. His harp is of all nations,
and speaks all languages. Of course there are grim reports
about, of his having killed men, and negotiated a psychical
investment in an unholy office. His wealth is put down at a
fabulous amount, his crimes as unutterable. Little Miss
Larke, who is a brave body, as valorous as the young lady
whose virgin smile lighted her safely through the Green Isle,
once took courage to ask Panslavisco how he did. ' As well,'
he answered, ' as a man can be, who is eating his own liver.'
He looks indeed as if he were Prometheus, and, wishing to be
alone, had contracted to do the vulture's work vicariously.

Little Saint Sheddle, who lives no one knows how, but is
the very Captain Cook of the musical world, is supposed to
be the only man in Europe who has been sufficiently admitted
to Panslavisco's intimacy to dine with him. He describes
these dinners as if he were telling a ghost story. The table,
he says, is garnished with two plates, two pots of porter,
and one steak in a dish. Panslavisco cuts the steak into two
exact portions ; takes one half, pushes the other half towards
Saint Sheddle, and falls-to without saying a word, After
dinner he produces a cigar-box and a bottle of Hollands, and
smokes and drinks prodigiously, but with little more conversation ; then he will get up and go out, or go to bed, or begin to
play his harp wildly—all in a speechless manner. ' It's something to say one has dined with him,' whispers Saint Sheddle,
' but it's very queer.'

Panslavisco lies upon his ottoman, profoundly immobile,
until it is nearly time for him to play. Then he begins to

pat and smooth down his harp, as a man would adjust the girths of a wild horse he was about to ride. His turn in the programme arrives; the harp is carried into the orchestra; he follows it; throws his long sinuous hair back; sweeps his bony fingers over the strings, and begins to play. A wild horse and his rider are no bad images for him and his harp. He seems to ride upon it: to bestride it as a witch would a broomstick, making the air awful with the melody of a demoniacal Sabbath. He bows his head to the applause when he has done, more as if the blast of a tempest had smote him upon the head and compelled him to bow to it, than in reverence. Now he is gone, and the audience begin to breathe again, and whisper 'Wonderful!' He goes back to the singers' room, drinks one glass of wine, swallows a biscuit as though it were a pill, and falls into a stony sleep upon the ottoman, passive, inert, unstrung, as though he had been broken on a wheel of wild melody.

This man, with the sinewy vigorous frame worn into rocks and caverns of bone, as if by the volcanic upheaving of his soul within; with the huge, Medusa-like head; the swelling veins in his forehead; the eyes like abysses; the face seamed, and scarred, and worn in tempests of study, hunger, cold, and misery, looks as if he had newly come from some combat with the demon, and had been victorious, but had suffered horribly in the fray. A dozen years ago Panslavisco had as much genius, and played as learnedly, sweetly, gracefully, boldly, nervously, wildly, as he does now. But he played in a garret, where he had no friends, no fire, no body-linen, no bread, and where his landlady bullied him for his rent. Viragos squabbling over a disputed right in a wash-tub in a back slum, have heard as fascinating harmonies through a garret window held up by a bundle of fire-wood, as princesses of the blood hear now in the Nineveh Rooms. Panslavisco has taught the harp to butchers' daughters for scraps of meat; has fiddled in low dancing-rooms, and played the pianoforte at quadrille-parties for a morsel of bread. Now, they are all come. Fortune, fame, sycophants to admire, beautiful women to smile, lords to say 'Come and dine.' They are all too late. They cannot bring back the young wife, dead in a long slow agony; the little children who faded one by one; they cannot bring back the time when the man had a heart to love and hope, and was twenty-one years of age.

But Heaven be good to us all! What have I to do with this, unless to say with Montaigne, '*Que sais-je?*' If I go to a concert, and pay half a guinea to hear a man play upon the harp, am I to dogmatise upon his inward feelings or his life? For all I know, Panslavisco's morose, mysterious exterior may be but a fastidious envelope, and he may be, after all, a cheery, happy man. I hope so.

The last concerted piece in the programme has been performed, and the critics go home to write out their opinions on Papadaggi's grand morning concert. Much bonnet-adjusting, music-hunting-for, and a little flirtation take place in the singers' room. The imbecile young man falls savagely upon the remnants of the wine and biscuits, and becomes maudlin in a moment. Papadaggi flits about joyfully with a cash-box, and a slave of the lamp follows him with the check-boxes. The concert is over. Papadaggi asks the stars of the afternoon to come home and dine with him. Some accept; some plead other engagements. He wakes Panslavisco, and asks *him*. The harpist does not decline the invitation categorically. He simply says, 'Pay me, and let me go.'

Let me go too. *Licet?*

XXVII.

GIBBET STREET.

THE Ghetto is for the Jews, and the Fanal for the Greek merchants, the Cannebière for the Marseilles boatmen, and the Montaigne Sainte Geneviève for the rag pickers. Holywell Street is for the old clothes vendors, Chancery Lane for the lawyers, Fifth Avenue for the upper Ten Thousand, and GIBBET STREET is for the thieves. They reside there, when in town.

It is an ugly name for a street, and an uglier thing that the street should be a den of robbers; but—with the slightest veil of the imaginatively picturesque so as to wound nobody's sensitive feelings—it exists. Gibbet Street and the thieves— the thieves and Gibbet Street—are as manifest and apparent as the sun at noonday. Gibbet Street is just round the corner. It is only five minutes' walk from the office of ' Household Words.'* It is within the precincts of the police-station and the police courts of Bow Street. It is within an easy walk of the wealthy Strand; with its banking-houses, churches, and Exeter Hall. It is not far from the only National Theatre

* A.D. 1855.

now left to us, where her Majesty's servants are supposed to
hold the mirror up to nature nightly; and *veluti in speculum*
might be written with more advantage over the entrance to
Gibbet Street than over the proseenium of the play-house; for
vice and its image are in view there at any hour of the day or
night: a comfortable sight to see. Gibbet Street is contiguous
to where the lawyers have their chambers, and the high Courts
of Equity their sittings; and a beneher from Lincoln's Inn
might stroll into Gibbet Street in the spare ten minutes before
the Hall dinner, and see what nice work is being cut out for
the Central Criminal Court there; while an inhabitant of
Gibbet Street, too lazy to thieve that day, might wander into
the inn, and see the Lord High Chancellor sitting, all alive,
in his court, and saying that he will take time to consider that
little matter which has been under consideration a trifle less
than seventeen years.* A merry spectacle to view. The
Queen herself comes within bowshot of Gibbet Street many
times during the fashionable season, when it pleases her to
listen to the warblings of her Royal Italian Opera singers.
The tips of the blinkers of her satin-skinned horses were seen
from Gibbet Street; the ragged young thieves scampered from
it to stare at her emblazoned coaches; and, if one of the
ethereal footmen—transcendant being in the laced coat, large
cocked hat, bouquets, and golden garters—had but run the
risk of a stray splash or two of mud on his silk stockings, or a
stray onion at his powdered head, or a passing violence to his
refined nose, he might have spent an odd quarter of an hour
with great profit to himself in Gibbet Street: better, surely,
than bemusing himself with beer at the public-house in Bow
Street. He would have seen many things. Been eased, probably, of his gold-headed stick, his handkerchief, his
aiguillettes, and his buttons with the crown on them; and, on
his return, he might have told the sergeant flunkey, or the
yeoman footpage, or the esquire shoeblack, or the gentleman
stable-boy of the curious places he had visited. The Lord
Great Chamberlain might hear of it eventually. It might
come to the ears of Majesty at last. For the first time, I
wonder? Is anything of Gibbet Street and its forlorn population known in palatial Pimlico? Perchance: for hard by
that palace, too, there are streets full of dens, and dens full
of thieves. Do not Hulk Street and Handcuff Row, and
Dartmoor Terrace and the great Ticket-of-Leave Broadway,

---

* Such scandalous delays existed when I wrote this paper. Such delays, I am glad to acknowledge, exist, save in very rare cases, no longer.

all abut upon Victoria Street, Westminster; and is not that within sight of the upper windows of tho palace of Buckingham?

It is plain to me that a thief must live somewhere. He is a man like the rest of us. His head has a cranium, an os frontis, a cerebellum, and an occiput, although it be covered by a fur cap, and decorated with Newgate 'aggerwators,' instead of a shovel hat or a velvet cap with pearls and strawberry leaves. He is a ragged, deboshed, vicious, depraved, forsaken, hopeless vagabond; but he has a heart, and liver, and lungs: he feels the summer's sun and the winter's ice. If you prick him, he bleeds; if you beat him, he cries out; if you hang him, he chokes; if you tickle him, he laughs. He requires rest, food, shelter—not that I say he deserves them, but he must have them—as well as the best of citizens and ratepayers. Ferocity, dishonesty, are not the normal state. A lion cannot be always roaring, a bear cannot be always hugging; and, unless you make of every thief *caput lupinum*, and shoot him down wherever you find him, he must have his den, his hole, or his corner; his shinbone of beef, or his slain antelope. Being human, he is also gregarious; and thus Gibbet Street. If you leave holes, the foxes will come and inhabit them; if you suffer heaps of rubbish to accumulate, the bats and dragon-flies will make them their habitation; if you banish the broom from your ceiling corners, the spiders will come a-building there; if you flush not your sewers, the rats will hold high holiday in them; and if, to make an end of truisms, you are content to bear with rottenness and dirt in the heart of the city that has no equal, on the skirt of your kingly mantle a torn and muddy fringe; if your laws say, Dirt, you are an institution, and Vermin, you are vested, and Ignorance, you are our brother; if you make and keep up, and sweep and garnish a Thieves' Kitchen, with as much care and precaution as if it were a diplomatic mission to Ashantee, or a patent place, or an assistant commissionership, why the thieves will come and live in it. Which is the greatest scandal—a house infested with vermin, or the carelessness of the servant who has suffered them to accumulate there? Gibbet Street is a scandal—a burning shame; but it is not half so scandalous or shameful as the governmental dwellers in Armida's Garden, who have suffered the foul weeds to grow up; who have yawningly constructed succursal forcing-houses for crime and ignorance, and have had a greenhouse in every gaol, and a conservatory in every Gibbet Street. They may

x

say that it is not for them to interfere : some of them interfere
to obstruct national education ; others interfere to manufacture pet hypocrites in gorgeous gaols.

I notice that the principal argument of the police before the
magistrates when they wish to put down a penny theatre, a
penny dancing-saloon, concert-hall or beer-shop, lies in the
fact of the place inculpated being a resort for thieves and the
worst of characters.   Bless me, good Mr. Superintendents and
Inspectors, astute and practical as you are, where are the
thieves to go ?   What are they to do in the small hours ?   Is
the Clarendon open to them ?   Would they be welcome at
the Sacred Harmonic ?   Would Mr. Albert Smith be glad to
see them at the Egyptian Hall ?   Are their names down for
the house dinners at the Garrick or the Carlton ?   You will
have none of them even in your prisons or hulks, but you turn
them out with tickets of leave as soon as they have imposed on
the chaplain with sham repentance ; or as soon as your gamut
of reclaiming measures has been drummed over.   You empty
them on the streets and then, wall-eyed, moon-struck Society
holds up its hands and gapes, because astute Superintendent X,
practical Inspector Z, tell you that the thieves are gone back
to Gibbet Street ; that they are 'forty thieving like one' at the
corner ; and that they are careering about with life-preservers,
chloroform-bottles, crow-bars, and skeleton keys.   Where else
should they go ?   Where *can* they go ?   'Where !' echo the
six hundred and fifty-six slumberers in Armida's Garden,
waking up from a sodden trance ; 'but what a shocking place
this Gibbet Street is !   We shall really have to move for leave
to bring in a bill some day to put it down : meanwhile, let us
never, no never, give a thought to the practicability of putting
down thieves or thieving by moving one finger, by making one
snail's footstep towards the discountenance and destruction of
the teeming seed from which crime is grown,'—seed colported
and exposed as openly as the rhododendrons or ranunculuses
in the little brown paper bags in Covent Garden Market ; seed
that, with our eyes shut, and with a dreamy perseverance in
wrong-doing, we continue scattering broadcast over the fields ;
afterwards spending millions in steam-ploughs of penal laws,
and patent thrashing-machines of prison discipline, and improved harrows of legislation, and coercive drains, and criminal
subsoiling ; all for the furtherance of the goodly gibbet harvest.
What is the good of throwing away the cucumber when you
have oiled, and vinegared, and peppered, and salted it ?   Why
don't yo smuash the cucumber frames ?   Why don't you burn

the seed ? Hang me all the thieves in Gibbet Street to-morrow, and the place will be crammed with fresh tenants' in a
week ; but catch me up the young thieves from the gutter and
the doorsteps ; take Jonathan Wild from the breast ; send
Mrs. Sheppard to Bridewell, but take hale young Jack out of
her arms ; teach and wash me this unkempt vicious colt, and
he will run for the Virtue Stakes yet ; take the young child,
the little lamb, before the great Jack Sheppard ruddles him
and folds him for his own black flock in Hades ; give him
some soap instead of whipping him for stealing a cake of
brown Windsor ; teach him the Gospel, instead of sending him
to the treadmill for haunting chapels and purloining prayer-
books out of pews ; put him in the way of filling shop-tills,
instead of transporting him when he crawls on his hands and
knees to empty them ; let him know that he has a body fit and
made for something better than to be kicked, bruised, chained,
pinched with hunger, clad in rags or prison gray, or mangled
with gaoler's cat ; let him know that he has a soul to be saved.
In God's name, take care of the children, somebody ; and there
will soon be an oldest inhabitant in Gibbet Street, and never a
new one to succeed him !*

It is the thieves that made the place, not the place the
thieves. Who offers to build a new Fleet Prison, now arrest
on mesne process is abolished ? Is not Traitors' Gate bricked
up now that acts of attainder are passed no more ? Would
not the Lord Mayor's state-coach be broken up and sold for
old rubbish a month after the last Lord Mayoralty ? There
would be no need for such a place as Gibbet Street, if there
were no thieves to dwell in it ; but so long as you go hammering parchment act-of-parliament-drums, and beating up for
recruits for Satan's Light-fingered Brigade, so long will the
Gibbet Street barracks be open, and the Gibbet Street billeting
system flourish.

Near a shabby market, full of damaged vegetable stuff,
hedged in by gin-shops—a narrow, slimy, ill-paved, ill-smelling, worse-looking street, the majority of the houses private (!)
but with a sprinkling of marine-stores, rag-shops, chandlers'
and fried-fish warehouses, low-browed, doorless doorways,
leading to black rotten staircases, or to tainted backyards,
where corruption sits on the water-butt, and fever lives like
a house-dog in the dust-bin : with shattered windows, the
majority of them open with a sort of desperate resolve on the

* Reformatories, thank God ! have multiplied in the land since these
lines were first penned.

part of the wretched inmates to clutch at least some wandering fragment of pure light and air : this is Gibbet Street. Who said (and said wisely, and beautifully too), that a sunbeam passes through pollution unpolluted ? It cannot be true, here, in this abandoned place. If a sunbeam could permeate into the den, I verily believe it would be tarnished and would smell foully before it had searched into the abyss of all this vapour of decay. What manner of men save thieves, and what manner of women save drudges, bond-servants, yet loving helpmates to their brutal mates, live here ? It would be wholesome and profitable for those young ladies and gentlemen who imagine even the modern thief to be a rake, bejewelled, broadclothed, with his brougham, his park hack and his seraglio, to come and dwell here in Gibbet Street. Ask the police (when they are assured they have a sensible man to deal with, they tell him the plain truth), ask astute Superintendent X, practical Inspector Z, where the swell mob is to be found. They will laugh at you, and tell you that there is no swell mob now. Well-dressed thieves there are, of course ; robbers on a great scale ; well-educated men of the world ; cautious ; who live by themselves, or in twos or threes, and in luxury. But the thief, generically speaking, is an ignorant, coarse, brutalised, simple-minded, spendthrift, in spite of his thievish cunning. He is always hiding his head in the sand, like the imbecile ostrich ; coming back to hide where there is no concealment, in Gibbet Street after a great robbery, and pounced upon immediately by X, the astute, or Z, the practical. The thief is recklessly improvident. His net earnings, like the receipts of an usurer-ridden prodigal, are infinitesimally small in proportion to his gross plunder. The thieves' and leaving shops are his bill-discounters. He gorges tripe, and clods, and stickings. He is drunk with laudanumed beer and turpentined gin. He pays five hundred per cent. excess for his lodging, his raiment, and his food. He is robbed by his comrades ; for there is not always honour among thieves. He is as often obliged to thieve for his daily bread, as for the means of indulging his profligacy. There is no work so hard as thieving. Hours of patient watching, waiting, marching, countermarching, flight, skulking, exposure, and fatigue have to be passed, for often a reward of three-halfpence. The thief's nerves are always strung to the highest degree of tension ; he has no holidays ; he is always running away from somebody ; always seeking or being sought. The thief is as a man afflicted with a mortal disease. Like a person with disease of the heart, who knows that some day he will stagger and fall, the thief knows he has the great convict aneurism; that the apoplexy of arrest must come upon him. He knows not when. Ho gets drunk sometimes and forgets the skeleton; but he knows it must come some day—a skeleton with a glazed hat, a number and letter on his collar, and handcuffs in his pocket.

You need no further picture of Gibbet Street. Walk twenty yards and you can see the place itself—the stones, the gutters, the rags that hang out like banners; and the wretched, pale-faced population: some men's faces swollen by liquor, and some women's from bruises, and some women's and men's from both. It is safe enough to go down Gibbet Street in the day-time—at least you are safe enough from personal violence. If you are well dressed, of course you will be robbed; but, at night, you had better avoid it, though policemen patrol it, and the carriages of the nobility and gentry, who are patronising the theatres, are sometimes stationary at its upper entrance.

I have been acquainted with this Tartarus these dozen years; and, although I am a professional town traveller, and have frequented, of malice prepense, the lowest haunts of half a dozen European capitals, I never bestowed much notice upon Gibbet Street. I took it for granted as an abode of thieves, glanced curiously at its low-browed, bull-necked, thick-lipped inhabitants, and buttoned up my coat pockets when I was obliged to pass through it. Lately, however, it so happened, that Gibbet Street and I have been nearer acquaintances; and, curiously, my more intimate knowledge of this home of dishonesty has been due to the fine arts.

My friend Poundbrush—that celebrated but unassuming artist—paints Grecian temples, Egyptian pyramids, Oriental kiosks, panoramas of the Mediterranean, and bombardments of the Malakhoff tower—occupying many thousand leagues of landscape and square feet of canvas—at a great atelier or painting-room, spaciously erected for the purpose, in the very thick of Gibbet Street. How Messrs. Doublctie and Coverflats, the accomplished directors of this great scene-painting undertaking, could have selected Gibbet Street as a location for their studio seems, at the first blush, to pass comprehension; but the rent may have been moderate, or the premises convenient, or the situation central; at any rate there they are with thieves to right of them, thieves to left of them, thieves in front of them; volleying oaths and ribaldry all day long.

Under Poundbrush's auspices I have had many opportu-

nities lately of assisting at the At Homes of the Gibbet Street
thieves. Their interiors are not by any means difficult of
visual access; for their windows are, as I have said, mostly
open. Besides a great portion of their daily business is
transacted in the open street. They eat in the street, they
drink, fight, smoke, sing, and—when they have a chance—
thieve in the street. A very curious contemplation is presented by standing at the window of this studio. Turning
your back to the busy painters, who are pursuing a beautiful,
humanising art, revelling in fruits and flowers, sunny landscapes, and stately architecture, and then to turn your eyes
upon this human dunghill. What have we done to be
brought to this strait? Look into the black holes of rooms,
cast your eyes upon those ragged heaps where the creatures
sleep, hear the men curse, and see them strike the wretched,
wretched women.

It was in some of these latter-day contemplations of the
thieves in their domesticity in Gibbet Street, that I came to
my grand (!) conclusion that the thief is a man—and that he
must eat and drink and sleep; and I am gratified to be able to
chronicle one little trait of human nature in my human thief,
and that, too, of the kindlier sort. At one o'clock, post mere-
diem, lately, the waiter from some adjacent cookshop was
journeying through Gibbet Street (always a North-west passage of great peril and travail to waiters and potboys), and, in
his hands, he bore one of those stately pyramids of pewter-
covered dishes of meat and potatoes, which none but waiters
can balance, or cookshop keepers send out all hot. A thief
passing that way—a young thief, probably inexperienced,
new to Gibbet Street, who had not yet acquired its code of
etiquette—followed the waiter dexterously, and was about to
tilt the topmost dish from off the pyramid, with a view to
upsetting the whole edifice, scattering the viands, and
making off with the contents. I trembled for the result.
Two or three half-naked boys and a hungry dog of most
dishonest appearance, watched the proceedings with anxious
eyes. The nefarious purpose had nearly been accomplished,
when there issued suddenly from a doorway, a tall robber—
a black-whiskered Goliath. He, espying the intention of the
juvenescent footpad, suddenly cast him into the kennel; thus
allowing the waiter with his savoury cargo to pass safely by;
and roughly shaking the youth, cried out, 'What are you
up to? Don't yer know, yer fool! Them's for Painting
Room!'

What was this? Was it reverence for art, or can there be really some honour among thieves, some hidden good in this wretched Gibbet Street?

XXVIII.

STROLLERS AT DUMBLEDOWNDEARY.

THE strollers. Have not the righteous powers of law, reform, science, and sectarianism been directed for centuries against the strollers? There have been wise Justices in ruffs, and doublets, and trunk-hose, determined to put the strollers down, and most signally failing in so doing, ever since the time of the Spanish Armada; just as, I dare say, in the mythic time of San Apollo and all the gods and goddesses, the great Justice Midas—for all that he was squire, knight of the shire, and custos rotulorum—failed in putting the strollers of `his` epoch down. Strollers have been declared rogues and vagabonds by all sorts of statutes: pulpit thunder and quarter-sessions lightning have been levelled against them times out of number. No matter; the strollers have a principle of life in them stronger than the whole family of Shallows. Hunted from populous neighbourhoods, and threatened with all those legal perils which attend the dire English crime of being unlicensed, they are surely to be found, after apparently irretrievable extinguishment, cosily ensconced in some quiet little village, the marvel and delight of the unsophisticated, as they have been for ages.

Here they are, this blessed spring-tide afternoon, in my dear Dumbledowndeary. Their wheels have been new tired, some fresh stitches have been put into the buskin, an additional inch has been added to the cothurnus, and some extra dabs have been given to the scenery; but here in its entirety is the Thespian waggon at Dumbledowndeary.

Which Dumbledowndeary, I beg to remark, is thoroughly an out-of-the-way place. One of our magnates expresses his opinion that it is left out—at all events, you can't find it in —many maps of England, and it never rains or snows at the same time it does in other places. There is no mint (I mean the herb, not the Hotel de la Monnaie) in Dumbledowndeary, no turnip radishes, no salad oil, and there are very few carrots. *There is no lawyer;* there was one some time ago, but he made a most signal failure of it, and died.

There is very little clergyman; for the incumbent couldn't make the place out, so he spends his living of six hundred a year in Hastings, and the cure of souls is done in job-work by a succession of clerical nonentities, of whom very little indeed is seen, between service. There is never any cholera at Dumbledowndeary, and seldom any fever, and so little sickness and few accidents, that our doctor's principal amputations are confined to the plants in his greenhouse, and he is fain to eke out his time by taking photographic portraits, for pure love of science, of the inhabitants, to their immense delight : mute inglorious Miltons coming out under the process and on the prepared paper, as speaking likenesses, and ' Cromwells, guiltless of their country's blood,' all generally mild men with sandy whiskers, appearing beneath the influence of collodion and iodine, as the most truculent and black-bearded bravos. We have no crime, and no immorality (to speak of), and our only regret is, that more Londoners do not arrive at our natty railway station ; wander in our green lanes and voiceful woods, fill their eyes with the delicious prospect of wood and water and meadow around them ; taste our publicans' neat wines, and avail themselves of their commodious stabling, and at last be so delighted with the place as to buy, build, or hire houses, and settle in Dumbledowndeary altogether. But I am afraid that those who know of and love this queer, pleasant, little spot, keep the secret to themselves, as those Indians do who are aware of the city of gold in Central America, and tell no stranger, lest the profane vulgar should step in and spoil it.

Our taste for the drama in Dumbledowndeary, though not often indulged in, is vast. We take trips to town sometimes, and go to the play ; and mighty are the discussions that afterwards take place about the plays we have seen. We have settlers amongst us, hermits long since retired from the busy world, who can remember Siddons, the elder Kean, and Young. These ' shoulder their crutch and show how '—plays were acted. There was a dark man who lodged up the back lane last year, and was supposed to have been formerly a play-actor. It was mooted that he should read Shakspeare in the schoolroom ; and he said he would think about it ; which I suppose he has been doing ever since, for no more came of the proposition. We have frequent bets of fours and sixes of alcoholic fluids, respecting the exact readings of quotations from the dramatists ; and reference being made to the authors' works themselves, both parties are generally found to be in the wrong. Lastly, though we have no regular theatre (not even the smallest provincial one, within ten miles), we are visited, with tolerable regularity, once a year, by a band of those wandering histrionics called strollers. They omitted to visit us last year, and I grieved; thinking the dramatic element in Dumbledowndeary was on the decline; but a few days since, walking up street, the time being dinner time, and the object of my journey the fruitless one of procuring a ha'porth of mint, with a view to its conversion into sauce for lamb, I was greeted with the intelligence that the mummers were come.

The announcement was the more pleasant as it followed close on the heels of another class of amusements with which we have lately been favoured. We have seen a sight in Dumbledowndeary within the last fortnight not unfamiliar, I dare say, to my older and travelled readers, but which to the younger portion must be quite novel and surprising. What do you think of five wild and picturesque foreigners appearing in Dumbledowndeary, coming from no man knows where, and going no man knew whither; four of them leading two monstrous bears and two hideous wolves, with chains and muzzles, and the fifth man bearing a drum of uncouth make, which he smote continuously! Bears and wolves in England! They took us back to the time of King Egbert, and the Royal Bear, which lived in the Tower, and washed himself in the River Thames. The bears were brown beasts, with that pitiably half-human appearance, which bears have when on their hind-legs, of being distressed mariners in shaggy brown coats and trousers, much too loose for them: the name of one of them was Martin, and a most woe-begone Martin he was, with paws like very dirty driving-gloves, with the fingers coming through, a preposterous muzzle, and a general expression of the most infinite raggedness and wretchedness. He danced, did Martin, and went through the military exercise, and kissed his keeper at the word of command, with oh! such an unmistakable longing in his countenance to amplify the kiss into a hug, and a gnash, and a tear! Martin's brother was a young bear—Martin the foundling, perhaps—who, whether the major part of his sorrows were yet to come, according to the axiom, or not, seemed to have quite enough of them now, and abandoned himself to despair in the dust, at every convenient opportunity, till forced to assume the duopedal attitude by the cudgel of his master. As to the two wolves, they were not performing

wolves, nor dancing wolves, nor learned wolves, by any
means: they were simply wolves—lanky, brindled, savage-
looking creatures, whose existence was embittered by an
insufficiency of raw flesh, human or otherwise, and by the
necessity of wearing a muzzle, and being tugged about by a
chain. They viewed the performances of their ursine brethren
with profound disgust and contempt: their masters, whom
they unwillingly permitted to drag them along, with more
disgust still, mingled with fear and loathing. Man delighted
them not, nay, nor woman either; the one sole object on
which their attention seemed fixed, and to which their desires
were directed, lay in the amalgamated legs of the juvenile
population of Dumbledowndeary. For those tender, fleshy,
tearable, crunchable, howlable-for extremities did their fierce
mouths water, their teeth gnash, and their eyeballs glare,
and their bushy tails disport themselves, in a manner horrid
to behold.

If the bears and the wolves, and their strange keepers (the
man with the drum was a study in himself) were a source of
amusement, imagine what a fertile source of recreation the
strollers must have been. As soon as I heard that the mummers were come, I lost no time in repairing to the spot
where they had set up their theatre. It was not ill-chosen.
A green patch of land, with a natural amphitheatre of turf
around it, then a path, then another patch, whereon Mr.
Clewline, the sail-maker, spreads out his sails like gigantic
table-cloths, and pitches them, or waterproofs them, or does
something to them with a mysterious compound; and then
the broad shining river with the yachts dancing on its
bosom, like trim bits of nautical cabinet-making; the dusky
brick-laden barges with heavy sails, that would seem to be
impregnated with brick-dust too, so dusky red are they; the
squat Prussian and Swedish barks waiting . at the ballast
wharf; the Gravesend steamer puffing and smoking along the
channel on the Essex side; the unobtrusive, yet labouring
ant-like little tugs, pilot fishes to great sharks and whales of
Yankee liners, and Green's Indiamen and Australian packet-
ships, deep in the water with auriferous cargoes. There is
one-legged Barker in his little boat, his oars as he feathers
glancing in the wet spray and golden sun like priceless
gems, though they are but humble lancewood after all. There
is Mr. Thumb, the pilot, shoving off to board and pilot, *nolens
volens*, a homeward-bound ship; there is a neat little skiff
pulling in from a yacht with ladies deep in novel reading and

crochet work; there, opposite to me, in Essex, are flat marsh lands, and flatter meadows, and the white smoke of another train on another railway, and thereabouts, they tell me, lives the wicked contractor who sold the hay which the horses couldn't eat, and which it was very lucky they did not eat, under the circumstances of cold lamb connected with the forage in question; and here, at my feet, is the grassy patch with the strollers' booth upon it.

It is a very tumbledown edifice indeed, of old boards and canvas, which have evidently done service in countless grassy patches, to say nothing of fairs, all over England. There is an outer proscenium supported on a platform, about which there can be no mistake, for it simply consists of a few loose boards placed on the body of a van, which evidently serves for the conveyance of the paraphernalia of the company through the country. The proscenium itself, as a work of art, is abominable; as a curiosity it is laudable. All styles of decoration find representatives on its surface—the intensely Præ-Raphaelite prevailing; for the rules of perspective are wholly set aside, and the avidity of the artist for purity and brilliancy have caused him to throw aside all except the primary colours—red, blue, and yellow. There are two lateral doors, which mean nothing, inasmuch as they lead to nothing, and don't open, and upon which knockers in the Louis Quatorze style are planted in bitter mockery. There is a door, left centre, which is of some signification, inasmuch as it is the box, pit, and gallery entrance, and pay-place. The summit of the proscenium is occupied by those useful domestic animals, the lion and unicorn at issue, as usual, about the possession of the crown, and more frequently, I am afraid, getting more brown bread than white bread or plum cake during the progress of their hostilities; there are a quantity of flowers painted, which, if novelty of design and strangeness of colour met with their reward, would infallibly carry off the gold medal at Chiswick and all other horticultural shows; and, finally, there are the names of the proprietors of the booth—Messrs. Hayes and Walton—glaring in red lead, and yellow ochre, and blue verditer. The 'walk up' process to the booth is apparently effected by an inclined plane, with a few battens nailed across it at irregular intervals —an Avernus of which the descent will be, I opine, more facile than the ascent.

There is a side door of ingress, however—the stage door, I presume—to the Theatre Royal Dumbledowndeary. Close by it is another van with a hood or tilt—a sort of mixture of the Thespian and Rommaney, or Gipsy, very picturesque. There is a ladder leading up to this van or waggon. Between its shafts there is at this moment, smoking his pipe, an individual who, by his smock frock, might be a waggoner; by his tight-fitting trousers, a stableman; by his squab oilskin hat, a sailor; by his broken nose and scarred complexion, a fighting man; but who, by his wavy black hair (yet bearing the brand of the fillet), his shaven jaw, his stage eye, stage lip, stage step, is unmistakably a Thespian, a stroller, a mummer, if you will. Can this be Hayes? Walton, perhaps? No, Walton should be short and stout, and, if I mistake not, bald. He can't be both, may be one, is perchance neither. As I muse, another man who, in his blue frock coat, has a smack of the butcher, crosses him, bearing a pail of water, and enters the stage door. *He* puzzles me horribly! What can he want a pail of water for? Not for ablution—that would be too absurd; not for drinking—that were absurder still ; perhaps for some dramatic purpose, for something in the play. Anon comes forth from the booth, a female form, closely draped in a dingy shawl that might have been worn as a toga in one of the comedies of Meander, it looks so old. I cannot see her face; but, as she climbs into the waggon, I catch a glimpse of a cotton stocking—pink? Well, not very pink; say lavendered by dirt; and a red leather brodequin. 'Tis a dancer; and, as she disappears there protrudes for a second from under the tilt, a human face, and that face is white with chalk, red with paint, and bald, with a cockscomb, and is as the face of a clown, and I get excited.

So do some eighty or a hundred boys and girls, of various sizes and ages, who are standing, like me, on the turf or gambolling on the turf amphitheatre, some with the intention, as I have, of patronising Hayes and Walton, when their theatre opens. Others, oppressed by that perpetual want of pence that vexeth public children, contenting themselves with seeing as much as they can of the outside of the show, hopeless of internal admittance. It is very pleasant to see all these happy poor children, *not* ragged, but in the decent, homely, common clothes that country children wear; it is very good to hear this village murmur as

'The mingling notes come soften'd from below.'

I cannot hear

'The swain responsive as the milkmaid sung ;'

swains don't respond or milkmaids sing in these back parts. I cannot hear

> 'The watchdog's voice that bays the whispering wind;'

but I can hear

> 'The playful children just let loose from school,'

the noisy geese gabbling o'er the pool, the sober herd lowing to meet their young, and the loud laugh which speaks (not always, dear Goldsmith) the vacant mind.

Two sober horses feed quietly by the side of the tilted chariot, while the rest of the landscape is made up by a misanthropic donkey, which appears to have given up thistles altogether as gross and sensual luxuries, and browses contentedly on chalk and stunted thistles; and a big brown dog that seems to know everybody, and tumbles everybody, and makes a very fierce pretence of barking and biting, belying his fierceness all the time by the wagging of his tail and the leer on his honest countenance—a landscape of happiness and plenty, and quietude and the Queen's peace.

Of Peace, say I?* As I watch the strollers' booth, there comes across the field of the river a little black steamer, with a white funnel, towing a hulkish, outlandish bark, with her mainmast all gone to pieces, with an outlandish flag at her mizen, and floating proudly above it the English ensign. This is a Russian prize; and, as though looking through a camera, you suddenly drew a red slide between the lens and the eye, this field of peace becomes at once a field of war. See, transport No. 42 is just going down river; she is chock full of heavy guns and munitions of war; yonder little schooner, painted light-blue, a Fruiterer from the Azores, laden with peaceful oranges and lemons, has been chartered by Government for the conveyance of stores to the Black Sea; transport No. 19 is expected down shortly with artillery horses, and transport No. 70 with hussars and lancers. I begin to remember that, within a few miles of my quiet, peaceful, little Dumbledowndeary, are the most famous arsenals and dockyards to be found in this mortal world—fields of the balls of death—laboratories of destructive missiles. But the waters curl and are blue and sparkling, and the tides have their ebb and flow, whether their burdens be peaceful argosies or armed galleys; and the river-shores remember that they have seen the Danes in the Thames, and

* A.D. 1855.

the Dutch in the Medway, and the mutiny of the Nore, and that they were none the less green and smiling.

Messrs. Hayes and Walton do not trouble themselves about the war, save in so far as it affects the price of tallow candles and two-inch rope, or influences the minds of their audiences, leading them (H. and W.) to compose and perform pieces of a war turn or of a military tendency—all to suit the popular appetite for the drama pugnacious. Thus, though the piece originally announced for this evening was the Corsican Brothers, or the Fatal Resemblance and the Murdered Twins; H. and W., finding Dumbledowndeary to be partially a down-to-sea-going place, including among its population coast-guardsmen, bargemen, watermen, and fishermen—persons all supposed to have a lively interest in the progress of the war—changed the drama to the Russian War and the Gallant Turk; or, Death, the Danube, and the Tartar Bride.

We have waited a considerable time—so considerable, indeed, that Mr. Sprouts the peripatetic fishmonger and pur-veyor of sundries in general, has driven his little truck, drawn by a placid little ass, to the brink of the amphitheatre, and is driving quite a brisk trade in cakes, nuts, apples, oranges, and ginger beer. We almost feel inclined to ask for bills of the play.

By-and-by a little cheer directs my attention from the proscenium; and my spirits are raised to the highest pitch by the appearance on the platform of an Individual. He makes his appearance, curiously, much in the same manner as I have seen Mr. Calcraft make his appearance on a certain dreadful stage in front of one of Her Majesty's gaols, where he does the second tragedy business—cautiously advancing to the front and curiously peering into and scanning the populace. But he wears garments far different from the doomster's sables; having on a pair of gay boots, which I dare swear have been originally ankle-jacks, and are now covered with a coat of red paint; a pair of ample calico trousers, a broad leathern belt with a large brass buckle (pattern the Miller and his Men—size, Grindoff), a velveteen polka jacket with coarse gold lace sewn down all the seams, an imitation point-lace collar, and *such* a turban! a wondrous combination of a wide-awake hat with a dirty shawl twisted round it, and streamers of spangled gauze and a broken feather—a turban that would make any Cheltenham or Leamington spinster die of envy. This in-dividual, after a cursory but evidently efficient survey of his auditory—having reckoned them all up, and dividing the paying from the non-paying ones—disappears into the place from whence he came; soon, however, to re-appear with a long green drum, whose bruised parchments attest how long and often it has suffered the discipline of the stick. This drum ho discreetly proceeds to sling by a cord to the posts of the proscenium, and deliberately performs a solo upon it—a solo that has very little beginning and an elastic end—being capable of prolongation *ad infinitum;* or of being cut sharp off when necessity requires.

To him, presently, a man in private clothes, with a trombone. Next, a man with a horn, and a troublesome cough, which makes of his horn-blowing one continual catarrh. Next, a young lady in long black ringlets and long white calico; next, a ditto ditto in red hair braided and short pink calico spangled trousers to match, and blue boots; next a diminutive child-woman or woman-child, I scarcely know which, who, with her dark eyes and hair and slight figure, would be pretty but for a preternaturally large and concave forehead—a forehead that seems to argue wrong and mismanagement somewhere beyond the inevitable malformation of nature; next a magnificent creation full six feet high, with flowing black hair (or wig), a plumed hat, an imitation point-lace collar, a half modern military, half Elizabethan doublet, a fierce sword, trunk hose, buckskin (imitation) tights, and a pair of jack-boots—large, high in the thigh, acute in the peaks, lustrous with copal varnish or grease—a monarch pair of boots—such boots that had you dared displace them and they had been Bombastes', he would have had your life in a twinkling in King Artaxomines' time. These boots seem to oppress their wearer with a deep and awful sense of the responsibility they involve. They are perchance the only pair of jack-boots in the company, and to wear them, perhaps, is as precious a favour as it was of old to wear the king's robe of honour. This booted man moves with an alternate short step and stride. His eyes are bent downward, but not in humility —they are looking at his boots. He has no eyes, no ears, no thought apparently for anything beyond those nether casings. I look at him with fear and loathing, mingled with patriotic hatred; for I seem to recognise in him the Emperor of Russia, and already suspect him of nefarious designs connected with the Tartar Bride.

Two more personages appear in succession, and make up the effective strength of the company. There is an old man with feeble legs and a flaxen wig, ill-concealing a stubbly gray head of hair.   He wears a gray jerkin with hanging sleeves; beneath which there is a suspicion of Dirk Hatteraick's pink striped shirt, and hose to match.   Besides being the old man of the troupe, physically and dramatically, he is one of the orchestra likewise, and carries a battered old flageolet, of which the music comes out all at wrong holes and produces dismal discord.   The last histrionic who makes himself mani- fest, is a little man, who, by his particularly bandy legs, frill, cockscomb and painted face is of the clown, clowny—the clown I caught a glimpse of in the waggon; and who has a habit of rubbing his face continually with a blue pocket-handkerchief rolled up into a very small ball, which, taking his painted face into consideration, is, at the least, inconvenient.   The company range themselves on the platform, and there is dead silence in the amphitheatre.   You might hear a piece of sweetstuff drop.

I very soon find that the clown does not belie his appear- ance; for he advances to the front with the man in the won- derful turban, and is immediately addressed by him as Mr. Merriman and desired to be funny.

Upon which he at once stands upon his head.   Unfor- tunately, however, the boards upon which he stands being loose, it occurs to one of them to stand upon its head likewise, upon the fulcrum and lever principle, and Mr. Merriman is very nearly precipitated down the inclined plane, and into the midst of his admirers.   He as suddenly recovers himself, and makes a joke which is none the less happy for not having the remotest connection with the event which has just oc- curred.

'Merriman,' says the turbaned Turk, in a jaunty, off-hand manner, 'have you ever travelled?'

'All over the world,' answers Merriman.

'Have you been in 'Merrikar?'

'No, not there; I said all over the world, mind.'

'Well, in Afrikar, Europe, 'Stralia?'

'No, no, I said the world.'

'Well, where 'ave you been?'

Mr. Merriman scratches his head as if to refresh his geo- graphical reminiscences, and after a pause, answers, 'I've been in Dumbledowndeary.'

This is taken as a great joke, and is roared at accordingly.

'Merriman,' asks he of the turban again, 'what is non- sense?'

'Why,' to him replies the jocoso, 'to eat vinegar with a

fork 's nonsense. To try to stop the tide with a teaspoon 's nonsense. And to try to stop a woman's tongue when she's a talking 's nonsense.'

This is received as even a more exquisite witticism than the first, and is greeted with much haw-hawing and clapping of hands by the men, and much blushing and giggling by the women. The little folks laugh, as it is their happy privilege to laugh at everything at which they don't cry.

Merriman is proceeding to make another joke, when the Turk stops him.

'You had better, Merriman,' he says, 'hinform the company that this hevening we shall have the honour of pfromming the Rooshian War and the Gallant Turk; or, Death, the Danube, and the Tartar Bride.'

Merriman makes the announcement with many deliberate mistakes and transpositions of the original text.

' As the pfrommences will be raather long ' the Turk adds by way of rider, ' we will fust 'ave a shut dence on the outside, and the pfrommences will then kmence in the hinteriar. Hadmission sixpence to boxes, and thruppence to gallery.'

The 'shut dence' then takes place. But as the space is extremely limited on which its evolutions are performed, the dancers literally walk through the figures. The clown moves his legs a great deal, but his body not much, and is excessively active within a confined space. The old man, whose legs move naturally of themselves through feebleness, is paralytically nimble, and the young lady in white calico is as energetic as she can be under the circumstances. I look at her and the little child-woman with a sort of nervous interest, and observe that they cling to each other, and whisper together, and make much of one another. I imagine some relationship between them, or at least some strong sympathy and bond of love and suffering, often stronger, God knows, than ties of blood. As for the Emperor of Russia, he feels it plainly beneath the dignity of his boots to dance, and contents himself with an occasional grim bow to his partner.

There is rather a hitch at the end of the 'shut dence,' and to say the truth, rather a long wait before the 'pfrommences kmence in the hinteriar.' Perhaps the manager is waiting for the approach of dusk, for it is yet broad daylight; perhaps (and the noise of some hidden hammers would seem to bear out this view of the question) the arrangements are not yet completed. Meanwhile the solo on the drum is repeated, and an overture by the whole of the orchestra (any tune or time)

Y

and then there is another 'shut dence,' performed however
without the co-operation of the Emperor, who, probably disgusted at the levity of the proceedings, disappears altogether.
Just then I become sensible of the presence of young
Harry Bett, who is commonly known as the Young Squire,
and has made up his mind to drain the cup of delirious excitement known as Life in Dumbledowndeary to the very dregs.
Young Harry has a coat with many pockets, and trousers
fitting him much tighter than his skin, and, if the constant
perusal of a betting-book made a reading man, would take
a double first class at any university. He bets freely, does
young Harry, upon fights, races, hop-harvests, trotting mares,
cribbage, boating, ratting, cricketing, and general events. He
has brought with him a gallon of beer, in a flat stone bottle,
and a quantity of bird's-eye tobacco and short pipes. He
is quite an enthusiastic admirer of the minor drama, though in
rather a violent and turbulent phase.

He startles me at first somewhat by addressing the mighty
Emperor of Russia himself by his Christian name, and by
making derisive inquiries after his state of health. He alarms
me by gallantly offering beer to the lady in white ; by breaking into the very marrow of Mr. Merriman's witticisms with
adze-headed jokes of his own, and by pouring forth to me the
details of an irruption he had made into the dressing-room of
the company—which was the stage of the theatre, indeed—
and, according to his account, presented an exactly similar
appearance to the barn made famous in Hogarth's print. But,
when I find that his free-and-easiness is appreciated to the
fullest extent ; that Hayes evidently thinks him a bold fellow,
and Walton a dashing spirit, I begin to think that I have
been living behind the time somehow, and that life in Dumbledowndeary is the life for a rackety blade, after all.

Louder beats the drum, and louder still brays the music
through the inspiriting strains of 'Pop goes the Weasel,' which
dashing melody young Harry has called for, and is now supposed to be heard for the first time in Dumbledowndeary.
Hey for dissipation ! Let us throw aside the conventionalities
of society and be gay and rackety with a vengeance. We
spurn the inclined plane, with its servile battens nailed
across, and enter the Theatre Royal by the side-door, when
we immediately assume nine points of the law—possession of
a front seat—supposed to form part of the boxes ; young
Harry sternly tendering the gallery price, threepence, which
after some demur is accepted by the Tartar Bride, who

appears to be Argus-eyed; for though taking money at the gallery door outside, she spies us in the boxes, and is literally down upon us in a twinkling.

During an interval of from ten to fifteen minutes, some twenty score of our population come tumbling into the theatre. There is nothing but a coarse canvas covering, supported on poles, overhead, rough deal planks on tressels to sit upon, and the bare grass beneath. The theatre is—well not brilliantly, but—lighted with somebody's patent gas, which appears to be a remarkably pitchy compound, flaring away in tin cressets. We make ourselves very comfortable, however, with the gallon of beer (which young Harry liberally dispenses to his neighbours), and the tobacco-pipes, while above us rise tiers of seats occupied by brick-makers, ballast-heavers, sand-men, farm labourers, nursery-maids, decent young women (and in *that* respect my Dumbledown-deary is a very coronal of jewels of pure water), bargemen, boatmen, preventive men, children, and dogs. You would be puzzled to find a more motley assemblage at any other theatre in England, major or minor. The aristocracy of the place, such as the butcher, the farmers, and two or three worthy landlords, do not hold aloof from the entertainment altogether, but they are bashful, and will drop in by-and-by.

All in, and all ready to begin—in front, at least—though by a continued hammering behind all does not seem quite ready there. I see Mr. Merriman and the Turk in anxious confabulation over an old hat; which, from its tinkling when moved, I conjecture must contain coppers. Those coppers must be receipts, and Merriman and the Moslem must be Hayes and Walton. The convex-headed young lady (who is otherwise attired as a coryphée), laboriously brings down the much-enduring drum; and, placing it before that part of the proscenium where the orchestra should be but is not, grasps the sticks in her tiny little hands and begins battering away at it afresh. I begin to grow very sick of this very long wait, likewise of the continuous strophes of 'Pop goes the Weasel,' which the brass band drones forth; though I am somewhat diverted by the touching resignation with which the flageolet allows the trombone to wipe the mouthpiece of his instrument on his sleeve, and also by a survey of the coat and hat of the trombone himself. That musician is one diamond of grease, and his clothes form perfect facets of oleaginous matter. Young Harry, however, does not find the time hang heavily. He hands the foaming can about—at least its substitute, a broken mug—he converses familiarly with the ladies of the company who sit familiarly on the front benches till it be their turn to ascend the stage, and he holds earnest parley with some members of the upper gallery who are beguiling the time by pelting us with nut-shells, and broken pipes. Two or three 'hallos!' and 'now thens!' accompanied by a strong recommendation to 'cheese it' (*i. e.*, act of cessation), cause these trifling annoyances to cease. Meanwhile, the theatre is getting fuller. I need not say that the free-list is entirely suspended —no! not entirely : there is one exception—the policeman is admitted free. He surveys the assemblage municipally, the proscenium critically, the corps dramatique favourably. The performances have not long commenced before I observe him applauding the Emperor of Russia enthusiastically.

With that potentate, who is sitting majestic in his boots immediately before me, and condescendingly partaking of beer with the young Squire, I enter into brief conference. I am somewhat disappointed to find that he is merely a Russian field-marshal after all, but I still revere his boots. He tells me that I was right in my surmise respecting Hayes and Walton. They are the parties, he says, and very nice parties they are. He apologises for the thinness of the company, saying that it is not yet complete, but that it was very strong at Stepney Fair, where they were doing twenty houses a day. The lady in white is Mrs. Hayes. He thinks Dumbledowndeary a poor place. He anticipates but mediocre business, as the thing isn't known yet, and they haven't as much as sent a drum about. Do I think that the tradesmen would give a bespeak ? If so, they would have some bills printed, and—

Tinkle, tinkle, tinkle! A bell, which has been ringing about once in every half minute as a species of sop to the public impatience, now rings to some purpose, and the curtain rises.

The Russian War! The Tartar Bride! Death and the Danube! The Gallant Turk! Yes; let me see. Azarack (this Turk) is in love with Selima, pronounced Syllabub (lady in white), daughter to Chum-Chum, a Tartar peasant (the old man, and discovered to be a rank Irishman), but is coverted by a Russian Field-Marshal (Boots). There is an under-plot, treating of the loves of Hilda Chum-Chum's second daughter (Convex) and Wingo, a Wallachian peasant (played by a personage in a costume novel to me, but, if I mistake not, Mr. Merriman in buff boots). The drama is in three acts, averaging twelve minutes each. The scene varies between a woodman's hut, a modern drawing-room, and a dungeon, supposed to be the palace or castle of Field-Marshal Boots. I think I cannot better sum up the plot than by stating that in act the first there is one murder, two fights, Wingo up the chimney (which catches fire), one imprisonment of Chum-Chum, and three appeals (on her knees) by Selima to Boots, beginning with 'Ear me.' Act the second: three fights, two abductions of Selima, one elopement by Hilda, a torture undergone by Chum-Chum, a comic song by Wingo, and innumerable soliloquies by Boots. Act the third: three fights (one fatal), one ghost, one general reconciliation, and a dance by the characters, ending with the Triumph of the Turks, and Ruin of the Russians. I need not say that Boots is at last totally discomfited and brought to signal shame, and is dragged off, dead, by the toes of those very jack-boots he has done so much, by his ruffianly conduct, to disgrace. I may add that all these events appear to take place in that part of Turkey which borders on Tartary, close to the Danube, where it falls into the Baltic Sea; that the dialogue is all carried on in the purest vernacular, including such words as 'old Bloke,' 'blow me,' pickles,' 'go to Bermondsey,' and the like; that it is elevated, however, by sundry scraps from 'Othello,' 'Manfred,' 'Venice Preserved,' and 'Richard the Third,' sprinkled hither and thither like plums in a pudding, and spouted by Boots; and, to wind up, that there is not one single H in a right place among the whole company.

I must confess that, in my vagabond way, I find it all very pleasant notwithstanding; and that I am charmed with the audience, so charmed with the play, acted out upon the fresh green turf. So I sit through the laughable drama of 'A Day Well Spent' (not to speak of a variety of intermediate singing and dancing) with great content, and, at parting, promise the ex-Emperor (in private life at once a humble and familiar man) that I will interest myself with the tradesmen for a bespeak next Monday.

XXIX.

CHEERILY, CHEERILY

IF I had not been in London within the last month, and seen the wondrous tide of emigration setting out from the docks there; if I had not read in certain journals of the Jeremy Diddler and its teeming cargo; if I had not passed through the port of Southampton lately, and gazed upon the Hampshire folk singing loud emigratory pœans, and departing by whole tribes for the Diggings, with cradle, mattock, and spade; if many weeks had passed since at Havre I saw the Grand Bassin crammed—choked, with Yankee liners, with emigrant-ships for the States, for California, and for Australia (some of which, I make bold to tell you, in confidence, were in my private opinion no better than tubs); if I did not know that Plymouth, and Bristol, and Cork, yea, and the American seaboard far away (wheels within wheels) had each their exodus; that in remote South Sea islands and Pacific inlets, painted savages were packing up their wardrobes, consisting, I suppose, of a tomahawk and a toothpick, neatly folded in a plantain leaf; if I did not know that in swarming Canton and thieving Shanghae, and piratical little mud-and-thatch villages on the Yo-hang-ho and Yang-tse-Kiang, broad-hatted and long-tailed Chinamen were saving up pice and cash for passage-money and gold-digging tools; if I did not know that, from Indus to the Pole, blacks, whites, tawnies, and mulattos, were baking human heads, and polishing skulls, and carving concentric balls, and weaving gorgeous shawls, and curing reindeers' tongues, and fermenting champagne wine for the Australian market; that, wherever there were hearts to feel and tongues to express the fierce, raging lust for gold, the cry was, 'Off, off, and away!'—if I did not know this, I say, I should be tempted to think that from Liverpool alone the great army of voluntary exiles was setting forth; that there, and there alone, was the Red Sea and the host of Israel, with their gold, and silver, and precious stones; there, the pillar of fire and the pillar of cloud; there, the prospect of wandering in a watery desert not forty, but one hundred days: for, verily, all Liverpool seems to be off.

> 'A king stood on the rocky brow
> That looks o'er seaborn Salamis.

But I, poor, penniless plebeian, with never a regal bend in my scutcheon, stand on the stones of mud-born Liverpool; every stone of whose docks, and every brick of whose warehouses were wont to be cemented, according to Mr. George Frederick Cooke, 'by the blood and sweat of the enslaved and murdered African;' and from the brows of Prince's Dock, and Canning Dock, and Bramley Moore Dock—from the brows of that unequalled line of basins, reaching from the shore opposite Eastham to below Bootle and Waterloo—I gaze on the 'ships by thousands,' and the 'men in nations,' that lie below.

Oh, cheerily, cheerily! is the anchor-song, morning, noon, and night in the great docks where the vessels from the coast of Africa lie, which have come home laden with gold-dust, and palm-oil, and elephants' teeth, and which are off again, ere many days, with huge packages of Birmingham hardware and Manchester goods, coral necklaces, and gincrack ornaments for Mumbo Jumbo and Ashantee fetishes, slop rifles and cutlasses for the King of Dahomey's amazons. Bright blue or bright green, with brave streaks of white, are these vessels painted—hulls, masts, and yards; whether that the rays of the African sun fall less fiercely on them than on a black surface, or whether to dazzle and bewilder the simple savages with harlequin colours, deponent sayeth not. A strong, a very strong odour of palm-oil scents the breeze, pervades the decks, breaks out in a rich oleaginous dew on the apparel and faces of the bystanders. Here is a gruff mate, seated on a water-cask, teaching a parrot to swear, who is all oil—clogged and sticky with the luscious product. Talk of the Hull whalers! what are those train-oil-indued vessels to these greasy ships and greasier men? Gigantic tubs and casks of palm-oil, worth, they tell me, from thirty to forty pounds each, are being hoisted on shore, rolled about the quays, gauged by the vicious-looking boring-tools of the Custom-house officers, and carted away in greasy vans.

Empty casks there are also, and in plenty, which are to be conveyed back to Africa; then brought home full of oil again. How many voyages have these ill-coopered tubs made since they were hammered up by swarthy, black Kroomen, in some sweltering barracoon on the Guinea coast? What raging suns, what blustering hurricanes, what soaking deluges of rain, what legions of winged locusts and mosquitoes, must have shone, and blown, and battered against those crazy old staves, since they first held palm-oil! Coopered, too, by slaves; worked at to the music of cowhide-whips, or paid for in drams of rum, or lacquered buttons and scraps of red cloth. And yet, consoling thought! how many thousand pounds of candles and bars of soap have been made from the yellow grease these casks have held, and how little we reck, seeing them kicking about on this Liverpool quay, of what the Kroomen's cooperage and the greasy sap of the African tree have done for civilization and for Christianity. As I muse, come a flying horde of ragged wretches to scrape with oyster-shells and long nails what portions of coagulated oil yet adhere to the insides of the casks. But a stern dock policeman falls upon them and smites them.

If you think to cross that bridge leading from one dock to the other, my friend in the bombazine dress, the black triangular bonnet, and the big, flat, chequered basket like a wicker draught-board, you will be disappointed, as I have been. For while I was lingering on the Palm-Oil Quay, underground machinery was at work, strange noises were heard, some cog-wheels moved, and the bridge, gravely parting in the middle, disappeared into the dock walls, like a trick in a pantomime. A bold baker made a flying leap on one half, just as the water-parted operation took place; and he gained the opposite side, somehow, but how I know not, and now stands there exulting, though confessing that it was a 'close shave.' A dreary gulf flows between him and me; but a big ship is coming out of dock, they tell me, and I must make the best of it, and wait till she has passed, and the bridge is drawn to again.

A disappointment! No big ship is here, but a little leg-of-mutton-sailed, squat, grubby barge, full of—mercy on us!—chairs and tables. The 'Saucy Sally' of Lancaster, Flachey, master. There are chests of drawers for'ard, and four-post bedsteads aft; and the captain (five feet of tarpaulin, with a yellow oilskin hat, in the midst of which his brown face glows like a gigantic blister) commands his crew from a Pembroke table. The 'Saucy Sally' is not too proud to remove goods in town and country, and to enact the part of a spring van on the salt seas. Some Hegira from Liverpool to Lancaster is she favouring now, though I cannot, in connection with the railway and this Pickford and Chaplin and Horne era, discover the advantage of the long sea for so short a period of transit. I am reminded of that dear but old-fashioned friend of mine who, to this day, insists on coming from Margate by the hoy! A hoy from Margate in 1860; shade of Charles Lamb!

The 'Saucy Sally' has dropped down into the river, the captain bearing, with phlegmatic composure, some jocose criticisms on his singular cargo. But now, following her, comes the big ship in good earnest—the 'Zephaniah W. Caucus,' of New York, fifteen hundred tons, bound for Port Phillip. It may appear strange to you that an American vessel should carry British emigrants to a British colony, but stranger still will it seem, when I inform you (as I am informed by a politician with an umbrella and a shockingly bad tongue in the way of statistics, behind me) that British vessels can in no wise attempt the carrying trade in the American seaports, and would convey emigrants from New York to San Francisco at their peril. At which the statistical umbrella-carrier gets quite purple and inflamed with indignation against free-trade without reciprocity; so much so, that I move out of the way, being of the free-trade way of thinking.

The 'Zephaniah W. Caucus,' was a large cotton-ship once; but, no sooner did the exodus to Australia commence than she became suddenly, and without any prior training, one of the Blue Peter line of packet-ships, which, as the whole world knows, are all A 1's at Lloyd's, are all copper-bottomed and copper-fastened, all carry experienced surgeons, and all offer peculiar and unrivalled accommodation for cabin and steerage passengers. The three-quarter statuette of Z. W Caucus—probably a great transatlantic shipowner, or lawgiver, or speculator in town lots, or orator, or wild-beast tamer, or something famous—stands proudly, in wood and whitewash, at the head of the ship, surveying the hawse-holes with the eye of a monarch, and defying the bowsprit as he would an enemy. Looking at him I am fain to confess the very great family likeness between figure-heads generally. They all seem to have been chiselled from the same models, designed in the same train of thought. Caucus, now, with the addition of a cocked hat and epaulettes, and minus an eye or an arm, would be twin-brother to Admiral Nelson, bound to Singapore, close by; with a complete coat of gold-leaf, a fiercely-curled wig and a spiky crown, he would do excellently well for 'King Odin,' screw-steamer for Odessa; with an extra leer notched into his face, his whiskers shaved off, and in his hand a cornucopia resembling a horse's nosebag, twisted and filled with turnips, he would pass muster for Peace or Plenty; while with a black face, a golden crown and bust, and a trebly-gilt kitchen-poker or sceptre, he would be the very spit and fetch of Queen Cleopatra. Distressingly alike are they, these figure-heads, with the same perpetual unmeaning grin in their wooden faces, the same eyes, coats, hair, and noses in salient angles; the same presumptuous attitudes, as though the forecastle (save the mark!) were not good enough for them, and carrying, all, the same pervading expression of impertinent inanity—so much so, that I could almost find it in my heart to strike them. Among other departments of the Fine Arts as applied to practical uses, figure-heads stand specially in need

of reformation ; and some day or other, when Sir Edwin Landseer has taken that zoological abomination, the Royal Arms, in
hand ; when Mr. Grant or Mr. Thorburn have turned their
attention towards the pictorial amelioration of the Marquisses
of Granby and Heroes of Waterloo in the possession of the
Licensed Victuallers ⨍ the government will, perhaps, commission Mr. Bailey or Mr. Lough to apply the long-neglected
principles of ornamental statuary to the works of our nautical
sculptors ; and, rivalling that great benefactor who first re-
formed our tailors' bills, reform our figure-heads.

But to the Z. W. Caucus. Her accommodation. Well ; I
grant the copper bottom and copper fastenings, the experienced surgeon and the unrivalled cabins, but the steerage,
the commonalty's cabins—humph ! I look on the deck of
the big ship, and I see it alive with fevered, dusty, uncom-
fortable emigration at sixteen pounds a head : a desert of
heads, and tossing, struggling legs and arms, with an oasis of
poop, where the cabin passengers smile blandly from beneath
their *tegmine fagi*, and peer with spy-glasses and lorgnettes at
the crowded fore-deck, as they would at a curious show.
Why don't the steerage folk go down below instead of cum-
bering the decks ? is a question you will very naturally ask,
and which has been asked, too, several times within the last
ten minutes by the captain and his mates, with sundry energetic references connected with comparative anatomy, and the
invocation of strange deities. Why don't they go below ?
Well, poor creatures ! do you know what the below is they
have to go to, and to live in, for four months ? Erebus multiplied by Nox, divided by Limbo, multiplied again by a
chaos of trunks, and casks, and narrow berths and bruised
elbows—of pots, pans, kettles, and children's heads, that seem
to fulfil the office of the hempen fenders on board steamboats
and to be used to moderate the first sharp collision between
two hard surfaces—a chaos of slipping, stumbling, swearing,
groaning, overcrowding, and—no, not fighting. Let us be
just to the poor people. There is more law, and justice, and
kindly forbearance, and respect for age and feebleness in the
steerage of an emigrant ship, than in the Great Hall of Pleas
all the year round, with the great door wide open and all the
judges ranged. Men find their level here, in these darksome
wooden- dungeons ; but man's level, gentlemen, is not necessarily brutality, and violence, and selfishness. I have seen
kindness with never a shirt, and self-denial in rags ; and
down in noisome, sweltering steerages there is, I will make

bold to aver, many a Dorcas ministering barefoot, and many
a good Samaritan who has but what he stands upright in.

Smile away, gentlemen passengers on the poop. You have
but to smile, for your passages are paid, and your prospects
on arrival in the colony are bright. Smile away, for you
will have fresh meat during a great portion of the passage,
and preserved provisions during the remainder. For you are
those crates of ducks and geese, those festoons of vegetables,
those hundredweights of beef, and veal, and mutton, packed
in ice. Smile away, for you have cosy, airy little state-
rooms, with cheerful holes in the wall for beds, an elegant
saloon, an obsequious steward, books, flutes, accordions,
cards, dice, and book-learning. You can, if you have a mind,
write your memoirs or a novel, during the voyage, compose
an opera, study navigation, or learn the key-bugle. If you
must be sea-sick, you can retire to your state-rooms and be ill
there comfortably and elegantly. But, down in the steerage,
how are the poor folk to wile away the weary time? Fancy
the honest creatures during the first three days after the
Z. W. Caucus has sailed. Everybody ill, everybody groaning,
all the women whimpering, all the children crying. Everything unpacked, but nothing 'come-at-able.' Heavy trunks,
chests of drawers, and washhand-stands, breaking away, and becoming bulls of upholstery in ship-board china-shops. Knives
and forks and plates running wild, and drinking-horns going
clean out of their mind. 'That'll be it, sir,' says a sailor,
who has been 'out foreign,' to me; 'but bless you, when they
have been well shaken up for two or three days, they'll settle
down comfortably enough.' Ah! when they have 'settled
down,' and are bearing straight away across the great ocean,
what dreary days and nights they will pass! How bitterly
grandfather will regret that he is 'no scollard,' and that he
didn't 'take to his larning kindly;' and how little boy Ned,
who has thriven at school, reading from a torn and yellow
copy of the Weekly Blunderer (more prized there than the
newest, dampest, third edition of the 'Times' on London
breakfast tables), reading to a delighted gaping audience of
graybeards and matrons, babes and sucklings, will become
for that and many succeeding days a wonder and a prodigy!
Then, on fine Sunday evenings, they will lean quietly over
the bulwarks, and watch the rapid course of the good ship;
or, shading their eyes from the sun's rays, looking wistfully
ahead, and speculate where land may be, far, far away beyond the waste of blue. There will be gay fellows aboard

who will sing songs and crack jokes; there will be story-
tellers as indefatigible as that prince of barbers who had the
seven brothers; but, I am afraid also that there will be many
score passengers in that narrow steerage who will be in-
sufferably bored and wearied by the voyage: who will count
the time from breakfast to dinner, and so to supper, and so to
bed, wishing the good ship and her passengers, several times
during the twenty-four hours, at Jericho.

Still glides the Z. W. Caucus out of dock, somewhat slowly,
for she is heavily laden and lies deep in the water. A portion of her crew are busy at the capstan-bars—sallow, Yankee
fellows mostly, with elf-locks and red flannel shirts, and tarry
trousers. As they pace, they spit; and in the intervals of
spitting, they sing, or rather moan in chorus a dismal ditty
that hath neither tune nor words, but which means something, I suppose. Anon the strains are wild and fitful, like
the wailings of an Æolian harp; anon they rise to a loud and
vengeful *crescendo*, like a Highland coronach. Not all the
crew, though, are joining in this mysterious chant; a very
considerable portion of them are down below in their berths,
sleeping off a surfeit of rum and tobacco; and not a few will
be brought on board, while the Z. W Caucus is in the river,
also affected by rum and tobacco, and affectionately guarded
by a boarding-master, or proprietor of a sailors' lodging-house
(whom I should be sorry to say was two-fourths crimp and
the remainder extortioner), who has the greatest interest in
bringing sailors aboard, seeing that he is paid so much
a head for them in consideration of certain advances he
has made, or is supposed to have made to them, and
which are duly deducted from the pay of the unconscious
mariner.

Nearly out of dock, and the commander, Captain Paul W.
Blatherwick, of Forty-second Street, New York, who is standing amidships, turns his quid complacently. The captain
wears a white hat, with a very broad brim, and an obstinate
and rebellious nap, refusing pertinaciously to be brushed or
smoothed. He has a shirt of a wonderful and complicated
pattern, more like a paperhanging than a Christian shirt, and
with a collar which looms large, like the foresail of a yacht.
He has a profusion of hair and beard, and very little eyes, and
a liberal allowance of broad black ribbon and spy-glass.
Captain Blatherwick is part owner as well as commander, and
has therefore a paternal interest in his emigrants; but he is
rather pre-occupied just now, for two of his very best hands

—A. B.'s, stalwart, trusty reefers and steerers—are absent; and although he has searched all the low lodging-houses and all the low taverns in the town, he has been unable to find them. Just, however, as he has made a virtue of necessity, and, giving them up for lost, has shaped a fresh plug of tobacco for his capacious cheek, there is a stir and bustle in the crowd; its waves heave to and fro, and parting them like a strong steamer, come two men. One has his hammock on his head, large gold ear-rings, and his 'kit' in his hand. He flies like the nimble stag celebrated in Mr. Handel's Oratorio; but he is pursued by a Dalilah, a Circe, an enchantress, with a coral necklace, dishevelled hair, and a draggle-tailed dimity bedgown. She clings to his kit; she embraces his hammock; she passionately adjures him to leave her, were it only his ear-rings, as a souvenir. But he remembers that England (represented, for the moment, by his Yankee captain) expects every man to do his duty for fifty shillings a month and his victuals; and, shutting his ears to the voice of the charmer, he leaps on board. I say leaps, for there are ten good solid feet of muddy water between the quay edge and the side of the Z. W. Caucus; yet you have scarcely time to shudder and think he will be drowned, ere he is scrambling among the shrouds, as a playful kitten would skip about, if kittens wore red shirts and ear-rings. His companion is equally rapid in his motions—more so, perhaps, for he is impeded by no luggage, and clung to by no Dalilah. He has little wherewith to lure Dalilah; for, of all the notable equipments with which he landed at George's Dock, fifteen days ago, he has now remaining—what think you? a blanket! As I stand here, nothing but a sorry, patched, tattered blanket,—nor shirt, nor shoe, nor rag else. He wraps it about him sternly though, as though it were a toga; and, with a hurrah of defiance, a yell from the crowd, and a cheer from his shipmates, vaults on board. Then he falls down a ladder, very drunk, and I see him no more. They *will* be skinned, they will be fleeced, these foolish Jacks. They won't go to the admirable and palatial Sailors' Home. They *will* go down to Wapping, and Paradise Street, and fall among thieves. Who is to help them if they won't help themselves?

Oh, cheerily, cheerily! The big ship is fairly out of dock. The ropes are cast off, and she stands down the river, towed along by a steamer; the poor emigrants crowding the decks, the tops, the yards even, to take their fill of England, home, and beauty, seen for the last time. He who knows all **things** knows alone if they, or their children, or their children's children, will ever see the beloved land again.

The bridge will not be down for half an hour yet, for the 'King Odin,' Czernicheff master, screw-steamer for Odessa, is coming out laden with boiler-plates, and to come home again with wheat. She needs no 'tug,' but steams out stolidly on her own end, and with her own screw. There is another Yankee liner at anchor off Egremont, and just on the point of sailing. Shall we slip on board this grimy, uncouth, useful tug-steamer, and board her for a minute?

The 'Elizabeth Scradgers,' eight hundred tons, Captain Peleg J. Whittlestick, is a genuine 'liner.' She is bound for New York, with forty cabin passengers and two hundred steerage ditto. Sixteen guineas are demanded for the after-passage, the sum of two pounds ten is the ticket for the steerage multitude. And such a multitude! Three-fifths Irish, one-fifth Germans, and a timid, irresolute, scared, woe-begone fifth of English, who look as if they had gone to sleep in Liverpool and had been knocked up in the Tower of Babel. A confusion of tongues, a confusion of tubs, a confusion of boxes. A flux of barbarous words, a tangle of children settling on bulkheads and ladder-rounds like locusts. And an odour! ugh! let us go on deck, whither all the passengers follow us; for the muster-roll is being called, and as the authorities verify the name and passage-money receipt of each emigrant, the Government Emigration agent ascertains that there are no cases of infectious disease among the passengers; no lame, halt, and blind; no paralytics and no bed-ridden dotards. Andy O'Scullabogue of Ballyshandy, County Cork, is turned back for having a trifle of five children ill with a putrid fever. Judith Murphy can by no means be passed, for she is appallingly crippled. Florence M'Shane is sent on shore because he is blind, and Terence Rooney, because his mother has only one leg. These poor wretches have been scrambling and scraping their passage-money together for months. The two pounds ten have come, six-pence by sixpence—nay, penny by penny, from the peelings of diseased potatoes; from the troughs of gaunt, greyhound-like pigs; down long ladders in hods of mortar, in London or in Dublin; out of damaged oranges in Saint Giles's and Bethnal Green. They are the economies from relinquished gin glasses and eschewed tobacco; the savings of denied red herrings, and half rations of potatoes. Some of the emigrants have begged their passage-money; some are about to emi-

grate at the expense of the parish, and some have had their
passage-money remitted to them from their friends in America.

While the ceremony of 'passing' has been going on on
deck, the crew of the vessel have been below, searching for
stowaways—unfortunate creatures too poor to pay the necessary sum, who have concealed themselves in out-of-the-way
holes and corners, thinking to escape detection in the general
confusion, and to be conveyed across the Atlantic free of
expense. But they are mistaken. You must get up very
early in the morning if you would essay to get on the blind
side of an American sailor ; and not many minutes have
elapsed before two ragged women are discovered in some
hideous crevice, and a wretched dwarf, clutching a fiddle
under his shrunken arm, is detected in a cask, his heels
upwards, and coiled up into a perfect Gordian knot of deformity. I do not exaggerate, and I libel no one when I say,
that after they have been well hustled and bonnetted on the
deck, these forlorn beings are kicked over the side by the
chief mate, a gigantic mariner in a tail-coat, raised in Connec-
ticut, and with a huge brown fist, so hard, so horny, so corrugated with knotted veins, that it looks like the fist of that
slave-dealer alluded to by the authoress of 'Uncle Tom's
Cabin'—as if it 'had grown hard in knocking down niggers.'
'For,' says the mate, jerking a jet of tobacco juice and an
explanation to me across his shoulder, 'you must jest ketch
'em sharp, you must, these Irishers, and that's a fact. It's
a word and a blow here, and no flies.' And this latter axiom
the chief officer religiously carries out in all his dealings with
the steerage passengers, anathematizing the eyes of any refractory emigrant for the first offence, and knocking him down
like an ox for the second.

I stumble aft, as well as I can for luggage, human and inanimate, and take a peep into the saloon, where there is a
negro steward in a white jacket, and where there are soft
carpets, softer couches, gaily-decorated panels, comfortable
state-rooms, silken hangings, and a regiment of spittoons
carved and gilt in the Louis Quatorze style, and quite gorgeous to behold. A passenger I find below seems so delighted
with his bed, that he is continually lying down on it, then
jumping up, falling back half a dozen paces on the bright
Brussels carpet, and regarding the trim couch with rapt
ecstasy—rubbing his hands meanwhile with the anticipation
of quite a surfeit of luxuries for his sixteen guineas. But a
little bird which has accompanied me whispers that the

Elizabeth Scradgers will be no sooner out of the river than
the bright carpets will be rolled up, and the painted panels unscrewed, and that the silken hangings, and mahogany fittings,
and soft couches will disappear, to be replaced by bare boards,
and scrubby horsehair, and hard beds—the luxuries being reserved for the next departure from port.   What else the little
bird would tell me I know not, for at this moment comes Captain Peleg J. Whittlestick from his cabin, with loud and nasal
injunction for all strangers to 'clear!'   He is as like in voice,
person, and dress to the captain of the Z. W Caucus as two
cherries are like each other.   The Government Emigration
agent, the surgeon, the broker, the captain's friends, and I
who write, step on board the tug.   'Cheerily, cheerily, oh!'
begins that dismal windlass chorus as the anchor is being
hove up ; the emigrants give a sickly cheer, and another ship-
load of humanity is off.

The mysterious agency which whilom removed the dock
bridge from beneath my feet, has slowly ground it (with a
rusty grumble as of iron chains in torture) into its place again,
and I cross over to the other side.

Dock upon dock, quays after quays, 'quay berths,' loading
and unloading sheds, long lines of bonding warehouses, barrels,
bales, boxes, pitch, tar, ropes, preserved provisions, water-
casks, and exodus everywhere ! Whole tribes of north-country
people, and west-country people, and all sorts of country
people, darting off to the Antipodes with an eager, straining
rush.   As for New York, or Boston, or Philadelphia, those
seaports are only considered as being 'over the way,' easy
trips across the water, to be accomplished with a carpet-bag
and a hat-box, and with as little fuss and ceremony as a ride
in one of the little ferry steamers that ply between Liverpool
and Birkenhead, or Seacombe and Tranmere.   Gentlemen go
coolly off to Melbourne and Port Phillip in alpaca coats and
wide-awakes ; ladies, to Adelaide and Geelong with blue pokes
to their bonnets, and lapsful of crochet work as though they
were going picknicking.   Sunburnt captains, bound for the
other side of the world, set off in their shirt-sleeves, and tell
their smiling cheerful spouses just to mind the baby, and have
dinner ready at four o'clock in about eight months time or so.
Oh, cheerily, cheerily ! Cheerily, oh ! A thousand hammers
coopering water-casks take up the cry ; a thousand shovels
shovelling potatoes into the hold for stock re-echo it.   Stand
out of the way there ! Here is a waggon-load of preserved
provisions : mock-turtle soup and stewed mushrooms in tin

cases hermetically sealed; green peas and fresh mint, to be eaten under the line. Make way there for the live stock for the emigrant ship, 'Gold Nugget'—sheep, poultry, and a milch cow. Mind yourself! a bullock has broken loose from the 'Jack Robinson,' for Sydney. He is a patriotic beast : England, with all its faults, he loves it still; and if he is to be made steaks of, he prefers being eaten on this side the equinoctial line. Stand from under ! a giant crane is hoisting blocks of Wenham Lake ice on board the Melbourne packet 'Bushranger.' They are all pressed for time, they are all going, cheerily, cheerily ; they are all, if you will pardon me the expression, in such a devil of a hurry.

But the trunks, my dear sir, the trunks ! Can you, sensible, cautious, discreet, as I am sure you are, forbear, when you gaze on these trunks, forbear holding your head with your hands, or leaping into the air with a short howl, in sheer frenzy. The trunks! Roods, perches, acres of land covered with great sea-chests, trunks, bonnet-boxes, chaise-boxes, portmanteaus, valises, trunks of piebald leather, calf-skin, marble paper, morocco, Russia leather, oak, mahogany, and plain deal. Avalanches of trunks, with surely sufficient literature pasted inside to set up the schoolmaster abroad in Australia for years to come. As for such small articles as carpet bags, desks, hat-boxes, writing-cases, and railway rugs, they are as plentiful as ratafia cakes, twenty a penny. Children of tender years stagger by with trunks ; stalwart porters carry piles of them, as waiters at eating-houses carry the tin dishes and covers. Grim spectres hover about, moaning weird complaints of phantom boxes lost or mislaid, and point with skinny fingers to invisible crockery-ware packed in straw. I come upon the lone female in the bombazine dress and the triangular bonnet. She sits forlorn, 'remote, unfriended, melancholy, slow,' inexpressible misery on her wan face, stranded high and dry on a band-box. Her 'things' have departed from her ; an oak chest has been shipped bodily for Montevideo, and three mattresses and a palliasse went out to the best of her belief in the 'King Odin.' She is going to Celebes. Now what can this good woman be going to do at Celebes ? I puzzle myself mightily with this question, staring like one distraught at this lone woman, sitting under the dock shed like a Banshee on a band-box, till the edge of a hard-hearted oaken chest coming violently on my toes sufficiently admonishes me to mind my own concerns.

Still cheerily, cheerily, to all parts of the deep waters

z

whither ships go, till I stroll down to a remote quay to change
the scene, and see the Irish packets come in.   Yet even here
'tis but the old song to a somewhat fresher tune, for the mobs
of poor Irish who are landed, pell-mell, from the Dublin,
and Belfast, and Cork steamers, are off again for America to-
morrow or the next day.   Tumbling ashore they come—
ragged, dirty, draggle-tailed, and (to trust their looks) half-
starved.   Gaunt reapers and bogtrotters in those traditional
blue body-coats, leathern smalls, and bell-crowned hats, that
seem to be manufactured nowhere save in Ireland; grizzled
old women, bent double with age and infirmity; children who
seem to have sprung up like some crass fungus of decomposi-
tion rather than to have been born; and slatternly girls with
shawls huddled over their heads.   Some of the men have thick
shoes, passably holey; but three-fourths of the females and all
the children have neither shoes nor stockings.   Some of the
women carry heaps of what, at first sight, you might take
for foul rags, but which, moving and crying suddenly, you
discover to be babies.   Their luggage is on their backs, or
in despairingly small and dirty bundles slung on sticks.
They have a plurality of nothing save children.   They may
have money, some of these miserable objects—the bare price
of their passage to America—sewn up in tattered petticoats
and sleeve linings; but, whether they have or not, they have
no sooner set foot on the quay than they fall a-begging,
tendering the hand for charity mechanically, as a snuff-
taker's finger and thumb would seek his nose.   They sit
stolidly on posts, or crouch on the bare ground, staring around
with vacant listless eyes, as though they had landed in the
Moon and didn't know the way to the mountains in it.   And,
poor souls! for aught they know of the land they have now
set their weary feet upon, they might just as well be in the
Moon, I trow.   Presently come to them some of their own
countrymen in darned coats and patched smalls, keepers of
styes called lodging-houses and dens called taverns.   To these
are they consigned and carried away; and if they have anything to be robbed of, and are robbed, they have, at least, the
satisfaction of being robbed by their compatriots.

These woeful travellers have been gently pushed and
hustled on shore by hundreds, and when the last bell-crowned
hats have passed the gangway I am about departing, when I
am informed that there is yet more live stock to be landed.
More! What more can remain after all this misery and all these
rags, and all these walking typhus fever and small-pox hospitals?

As I have asked the question, I must answer it. There is a great deal more on the deck of the steamer yet. Pigs more. Cattle more. Sheep more. Stand on the extreme verge of the quay and peep over the deck of the steamer. Do not turn sick and rush away in horror, but look. Look at this Smithfield* in miniature; Smithfield, but infinitely more crowded in proportion; Smithfield, but ten times dirtier; Smithfield, with more cruelty, and wanton neglect, and shameful filth than you would find any Monday or Friday morning bewteen Cock Lane on the one side and Barbican on the other. Are you a Common Councilman? If so, snuff up the balmy, piggy, beefy, muttony gale with a relish. Are you a slavery abolitionist? Look on these beasts so scientifically and geometrically packed for economy of space, that every sheep's leg fits into its fellow's eye, and every bullock has a sheep between its horns, and you will have a very apt idea of how herrings are packed in a barrel, and how negroes are stowed for the Middle Passage. Are you a statist? Speculate on the exact amount of suffering, the nice quota of torture, the justly-balanced ratio of maddening thirst these miserable animals undergo during a twelve, a fifteen, or a twenty hours' passage. Are you a plain man with a plain English tongue? Lift it up, and with a will, against the shameful cruelties of the cattle transit system; against that monstrous inconsistency which can make governments and municipalities Argus-eyed to petty nuisances, and stone blind to these abominations; which can make mayors, and corporations, and police authorities, strain at the gnat of an orange-woman or a halfpenny candle sold on a Sunday, and swallow this enormous camel. To look at these dumb creatures panting with agony, their tongues hanging out, their eyes dilated, their every muscle throbbing; staggering on their legs, wallowing in filth, too stupified with agony to low, or bleat, or squeak, too sick to move, too cowed to struggle: is enough to rouse a man of adamant. Some of the animals are so wedged and packed together that they are suffocated, and not able even to lie down and die, die standing. Here is a wretched bullock—luckier than its fellows, for it has some two inches space on either side of it—lying desolate by the funnel, with its eyes piteously turned up, and seeming to entreat slaughter. Nor will slaughter be long in coming; for the deputed slaughterer, nice in such matters, and knowing to a hair the power of endurance in the beast, kills it just before

* *Fuit.*

z 2

it would otherwise die. The dead carcase would be unsale-
able, or at best would have to be surreptitiously disposed of;
but slaughtered alive, it is genuine imported meat, and fetches
its price.

Cheerily oh, cheerily !

XXX.

HOW I WENT TO SEA.

How many years ago is it, I wonder, when, resenting some
boyish grievance, deeply and irrecoverably irate at some
fancied injury, wounded and exacerbated in my tenderest feelings, I ran away from school with the hard, determined, unalterable intention of going on the tramp and then going to
sea? The curtain has fallen years ago, and the lights have
been put out long since, on that portion of my history. The
door of the theatre has been long locked and the key lost
where *that* play was acted. Let me break the door open now
and clear away the cobwebs.

About that time there must have been an epidemic, I think,
for running away at Mr. Bogryne's establishment, Bolting
House, Ealing. 'Chivying' we called it. We had three or
four Eton boys among us, who had carried out so well the
maxim of *Floreat Etona* at that classic establishment, that they
had flourished clean out of it; and—whether it was they
missed the daily flogging, (Mr. Bogryne was tender-hearted)
or the fagging, or the interminable treadmill on the *Gradus ad
Parnassum* (we were more commercial than classical)—they
were always running away. One boy 'chivied' in consequence of a compulsory small-tooth comb on Wednesday evenings—he wouldn't have minded it, he said, if it had been on
Saturdays. Another fled his *Alma Mater* because he was
obliged to eat fat, and another because he could not get fat
enough. Spewloe, our biggest boy,—who was the greatest
fool and the best carpenter of his age I ever knew—caught
the chivying disease of the Etonians, and was continually ab-
sconding. He was always being brought back in a chaise-cart
at breakfast-time, and spoiling our breakfast with his shrieks
(he was fifteen, and bellowed like a bull) while undergoing
punishment. They beat him, and he ran away the more.
They took away his clothes, and he ran away the next day in
the French master's pantaloons (crimson crossbars on an orange

ground), and the knife-boy's jacket. They tried kindness with him, and fed him with large blocks of plum cake and glasses of ginger wine, but still he ran away. They rivetted a chain on him with a huge wooden log attached to it, as if he had been a donkey; but he ran off next day, log and all, and was found browsing in a hedge, like an animal as he was. At last they sent for his Uncle, a fierce Being connected with the East Indies, in a blue surtout and white duck trousers; so starched and stiff and cutting, that his legs looked, as he walked, like a pair of shears. He took Spewloe away; but what he did with him I know not, for he never revealed the secrets of his prison-house. I saw him again, years afterwards, in a cab, with a tiger; his foolish face decorated with such tight whiskers and mustachios, such a tight neckcloth, such tight boots and gloves and stays, that he could scarcely move. I believe he went into the army and to India, to fight the Affghans. I hope they proved less terrible to him than Bogryne, and that he did not run away from them.

I think, were I to be put upon my affirmation relative to the cause of *my* running away from Mr. Bogryne's establishment, and going on tramp, that I should place it to the account of the Pie. There was a dreadful pie for dinner every Monday; a meat pie with a stony crust that did not break, but split into scaly layers, with horrible lumps of gristle inside, and such strings of sinew (alternated by lumps of flabby fat) as a ghoule might use as a rosary. We called it kitten pie—resurrection pie—rag pie—dead man's pie. We cursed it by night, we cursed it by day: we wouldn't stand it, we said; we would write to our friends; we would go to sea. Old Bogryne (we called him 'old' as an insulting adjective, as a disparaging adjective, and not at all with reference to the affection and respect due to age)—old Bogryne kept Giggleswick the monitor seven hours on a form with the pie before him; but Giggleswick held out bravely, and would not taste of the accursed food. He boxed the ears of Clitheroe (whose father supplied the groceries to the establishment, and who was called in consequence 'Ginger') like a sack, for remarking, sneeringly, to the cook, that he (Bogryne) never ate any of the pie himself, and *that he knew the reason why.* Candyman, my chum, found a tooth in the pie one day—a dreadful double-tooth. Who was going to stop in a school where they fed you with double-teeth? This, combined with the tyranny of the dancing-master, some difficulties connected with the size of the breakfast roll, and others respecting the conjugation of the verb τύπτω (for, though we were commercial, we learnt Greek, hang it!), and the confiscation of a favourite hocky stick—for which I had given no less a sum than fourpence and a copy of Philip Quarll—drove me to desperation. I 'chivied' with the full intention of walking to Portsmouth, and going to sea. Lord help me!

One bright moonlight night I rose stealthily from my bed, dressed, and stole down stairs. I held my breath, and trod softly as I passed dormitory after dormitory; but all slept soundly. The French master—who was wont to decorate himself hideously at night with a green handkerchief round his head, and a night-garment emblazoned like the *San benito* of a victim of the Inquisition—gurgled and moaned as I passed his door: but he had a habit of choking himself in his sleep, and I feared him not. Clitheroe, who slept under the last flight of stairs, was snoring like a barrel organ; and Runks, his bedfellow, who was the best story-teller in the school, was telling idiotic tales, full of sound and fury signifying nothing, to himself in his slumbers. I crept across the playground cautiously, in the shadow of the wall. The play-shed; the brick wall against which we were wont to play 'fives;' the trim little gardens, three feet by four, where we cultivated mustard and cress, and flowering plants which never flowered; somehow seemed to glance reproachfully at me as I stole out like a thief in the night. The tall gymnastic pole on which we climbed appeared to cast a loving, lingering shadow towards me, as if to bring me back. The sky was so clear, the moon was so bright, and the fleecy clouds were so calm and peaceful as they floated by, that I half repented of my design and began to blubber. But the clock of Ealing church striking, called to mind the bell I hated most—the 'getting-up bell.' The pie, the tooth, the dancing-master, the diminished roll, and the Greek verb, came trooping up; and, my unquenchable nautical ardour filling me with daring, I got over the low palings, and dropped into the high road on my way to sea.

Nobody was in my confidence. Such friends and relatives as I had were far away, and I felt that 'the world was all before me where to choose.' My capital was not extensive. I had jacket, waistcoat, and trousers with the etceteras, half a crown in money, a curiously-bladed knife with a boat-hook and a corkscrew by way of rider, and an accordion. I felt that, with these though, I had the riches of Peru.

To this day I cannot imagine what the New Police could have been about, that moonlight night, that they did not pounce upon me, many-bladed knife, accordion and all, long before I reached Hyde Park Corner. Nor can I discover why Mr. Bogryne pursued me in a chaise-cart and sent foot runners after me up and down all roads save the very one I was walking quietly along. I must have looked so very like a runaway boy. The ink was scarcely dry on my fingers; the traces of yesterday's ruler were yet fresh on my knuckles; the dust of the play-ground adhered to my knees.

A bed next night at a London coffee-shop; a breakfast and a wild debauch on raspberry tarts and ginger beer, very soon brought my half-crown to twopence, and I felt a lowness of spirits and the want of stimulants. A penny roll and a saveloy brought me to zero. The accordion was a bed the next night, and a sausage roll by way of breakfast, the next morning. The many-bladed knife produced a mouthful of bread and cheese and half a pint of beer for dinner. Then, having nothing, I felt independent.

By some strange intuitive education, I felt myself all at once a tramp, and looked at the journey to Portsmouth quite philosophically. Curiously, when the produce of the many-bladed knife had been consumed and forgotten, and the want of another repast began to be very unpleasantly remembered; it never once occurred to me to turn back, to seek assistance from any friend or friend's friend or boy's father with whom I had spent a holiday in London. It never struck me that if employment were to be found at sea, there were docks and ships in London. I was bound for Portsmouth—why I know not—but bound as irrevocably as though I had a passport made out for that particular seaport, and the route was not by any means to be deviated from. If the London Docks were situated in New York, and if Blackwall were the port of Bombay, they could not, in my mind, have been more unattainable for the purpose of going to sea, than they were, only a mile or so off. I was not afraid of Mr. Bogryne. I seemed to have done with him ages ago. I had quite finished and settled up accounts with him; so it appeared to me. He, and the days when I wore clean linen, and was Master Anybody, with a name written in the fly-leaf of a ciphering-book; with a playbox, and with friends to send me plum cakes and bright five-shilling pieces, were fifty thousand miles away. They loomed in the distance, just as the burning cities might have done to Lot's wife, very dimly indeed.

It was Saturday afternoon. I well remember loitering some time about Vauxhall, and wondering whether that hot dusty

road—with the odours of half a dozen bone-boiling establishments coursing up and down it like siroccos—could be near
the fairy establishment where there were always fifty thousand additional lamps, and to which young Simms at Bolting
House had been—marvellous boy!—twice during the Mid-
summer holidays. After listlessly counting the fat sluggish
barges on the river, and the tall dusty trees at Nine Elms
(there was no railway station there then), I set out walking,
doggedly. I caught a glimpse of myself in the polished plate-
glass window of a baker's shop, and found myself to be a very
black grimy boy. Vagabondism had already set its mark
upon me. I looked, so long and so earnestly, in at the baker's
window that the baker—a lean, spiky Scotchman (whose name,
McCorquodale, in lean spiky letters above his shop-front
ooked like himself), appeared to think I was meditating a
bold border foray on his stock in trade, and rushed at me so
fiercely round his counter with a bread-tin, that I fled like a
young gazelle. I plodded down the Wandsworth road;
blushing very much as I passed people in clean. shirts and
well-brushed clothes, and pretty servant-maids, dressed out in
ribbons like Maypoles, laughing and chattering in the gardens
and at the doors of suburban villas. I had a dreadful qualm,
too, on meeting a boarding-school for young gentlemen in full
force, walking in procession two and two. As I passed the
master—a stout man genteelly garotted in a white neckcloth,
and walking severely with the youngest pupil as if he had him
in custody—I shivered. Bolting House and Mr. Bogryne
loomed, for an instant, not in the distance, but close upon me.
Good gracious! I thought—What if there should be some
masonic intercourse between preceptors, relative to the recovery
of runaways; some scholastic hue-and-cry; some telegraphic
detection of chivying? But the schoolmaster passed me in
silence, merely giving me a glance, and then glancing at his
boys, as if he would say, 'See, young gentlemen, the advantage
of being boarded, washed, and educated, in an establishment
where moral suasion is combined with physical development
('Times,' August 20). If ever you neglect your use of the
globes, or sneer at your preceptors, or rebel at pies, you may
come, some day, to look like that.' The last and biggest boy,
in a checked neckcloth and a stand-up collar, as I made way
for him on the pavement, made a face at me. It was so like
the face I used to make at the ragged little boys, when Bogryne's
pupils went out walking, that I sat down on a dog's-meat
vendor's barrow and cried again.

By some circuitous route which took me, I think, over Wandsworth Common, and through Roehampton and Putney, I got that evening to Kingston-upon-Thames. The sun was setting, as I leaned over the bridge. I was tired and hungry ; but, dismissing the idea of supper, as something not sufficiently within the range of possibility to be discussed, I certainly began to feel anxious concerning bed. Where or how was it to be? Was it to be barn, or hay-rick, or out-house—or simply field, with the grass for a pillow, and the sky for a counterpane? My thoughts were interrupted by a stranger.

He was, like myself, a tramp : but, I think I may say without vanity, he was infinitely more hideous to look at. Short and squat and squarely built, he had the neck of a bull and the legs of a bandy tailor. His hands were as the hands of a prizefighter. They were so brown and horny that where the wrists joined on to his arm you might fancy the termination of a pair of leather gloves. His face was burnt, and tanned with exposure to sun and rain to a dull brickdust colour; purple-red on the cheek-bones and tips of the nose and chin. Both hands and face were inlaid with a curious chequer-work of dirt, warranted to stand the most vigorous application of a scrubbing-brush. His head was close cropped like a blighted stubble-field, and his flabby ears kept watch on either side of it like scarecrows. He had pigs' eyes of no particular colour ; no eyebrows, no beard save a stubbly mildew on his upper lip like unto the mildew on a pot of paste, a ' bashed ' nose, and a horrible hare-lip. He had an indefinite jacket with some letters—a W, I think, and an I—branded on one sleeve, a pair of doubtful trousers, and something that was intended for a shirt. None of these were ragged, nor could they be called patched, for they were one patch. Finally, he had a bundle in his hand, a cap like a disc cut out of a door-mat on his head, and something on his feet which I took to be a pair of fawn-coloured slippers, but which I subsequently found to be a coating of hardened mud and dust upon his skin.

He looked at me for a moment half curiously, half mena-cingly ; and then said, in a shrill falsetto voice that threw me into a violent perspiration :—

' Where wos you a going to ?'

I replied, trembling, that I was going to bed.

' And where wos you a going to sleep ?' he asked.

I said I didn't know.

He stroked the mildew on his lip and spoke again :—

'I s'pose now you'd be a young midshipmite?'

I am certain that I must have looked more like a young sweep, but I contented myself with saying that I did not belong to His Majesty's service ;—yet.

'What might you be adoing of, now?' he demanded.

It was a dreadful peculiarity of this man that when he spoke he scratched himself; and that when he didn't speak he gave his body an angular oscillatory wrench backwards and forwards from the shoulder to the hip, as if he had something to rasp between his jacket and his skin ; which there is no doubt he had. I was so fearful and fascinated by his uncouth gestures that he had to repeat his question twice before I answered ; then, not knowing what to describe myself, (for I could not even assume that most ambiguous of all titles, a gentleman), I said, at hazard, that I was a tailor.

'Where wos you a going to-morrow?'

I said, hesitatingly, to Portsmouth.

'Ah! to Portsmouth,' resumed the man, 'to Portsmouth, surely! Have you got thruppence?'

I replied, humbly, that I hadn't.

'No more haven't I,' said the tramp, conclusively; 'not a mag.'

There ensued an ambiguous, and, to me, somewhat terrifying silence. I feared that my companion was indignant at my poverty, and that, on the principle of having meal if he couldn't get malt, he would have three-pennorth of jacket, or three-pennorth of waistcoat, or three-pennorth of blood. But I was agreeably disappointed : the villanous countenance of my companion cleared up ; and he said condescendingly—

'I'm a traveller.'

'And a very evil-looking traveller, too,' I thought.

'If you had got thruppence, and I had got thruppence,' he went on to say, 'I knows a crib down yonder where we might a snoozed snug. But if you ain't got nuffin, and I ain't got nuffin,' the traveller continued, quite in a didactic style, 'we must turn in at the Union. Do you know what the Union is?'

I had heard of the repeal of the Union, and the Union Jack, and one of our boy's fathers was a member of the Union Club. I had an indistinct notion, too, of an Union workhouse ; but my fellow-tramp had some difficulty in explaining to me that the Union was a species of gratuitous hotel ; a caravansary kept by the Poor Law Commissioners for the special relief of the class of travellers known in ordinary parlance as tramps, and in the new Poor Law Act as 'casual paupers ;' and where in consideration of doing an hour's work in the morning, I could be provided with supper and a bed.

We walked together to the house of the relieving officer to obtain tickets of admission. The functionary in question lived in a pretty little cottage, with a shining brass door-plate much too large for the door, and a fierce bell ; which every time it pealed, shook the little house to its every honeysuckle. The parochial magnate was not at home ; but a rosy girl—with an illuminated ribbon and a species of petrified oyster as a brooch, and who was his daughter, I suppose—came to a little side window in the wall in answer to our summons; and, scarcely deigning to look at us, handed us the required tickets. Ah me! A twitch, a transient twitch came over me when I thought that there had been days when Master Somebody in a prodigious lay-down collar with white ducks, had walked with young ladies quite as rosy, with brooches quite as petrified, and had even been called by them 'a bold boy.'

Misery, they say, makes a man acquainted with strange bedfellows : but shall I ever again, I wonder, sleep in company with such strange characters as shared the trusses of straw, the lump of bread, and slab of Dutch cheese, that night, in the casual ward of Kingston workhouse? There was a hulking fellow in a smock-frock, who had been a navigator, but had fallen drunk into a lime-pit and burnt his eyes out, who was too lazy to beg for himself and was led about by a ragged, sharp-eyed boy. There were two lads who tramped in company ; they had been to sea and were walking from Gosport to London. My fellow, the man with the wrench, had been born a tramp and bred a tramp ; his father was a tramp before him, and I dare say his children are tramps now.

'Yer see,' he deigned to explain to me, after he had despatched his supper, 'I likes change. I summers in the country, and winters in London. There's refuges and "ressipockles," ' (by which, I presume, he meant receptacles) 'in winter time, and lots of coves as gives yer grub. Then comes spring time ; I gets passed to my parish—the farther off the better, and I gets a penny a mile. When I gets there I goes 'cross country on quite another tack. I knows every Union

in England. In some they gives you bread and cheese, and
in some broth, and in some skillygolee. In some they gives
you breakfast in the morning, and in some they doesn't. You
have to work your bed out. Here, Kingston way, you wheels
barrows ; at Guildford you pumps; at Richmond you breaks
stones ; at Farnham you picks oakum ; at Wandsworth they
makes you grind corn in a hand-mill till your fingers 'amost
drops off at yer wristés. At Brighton now they're a good
sort, and only makes you chop up firewood ; but Portsmouth's
the place ! You're a young un,' he pursued, looking at me
benignantly, 'and green. Now, I'll give you a wrinkle. If
you're a-going to Portsmouth, you manage to get there on a
Saturday night ; for they keeps you all day Sunday, and they
won't let you do no work; and they gives you the jolliest
blow out of beef and taters as ever passed your breastbone.
The taters is like dollops o' meal !'

With this enthusiastic eulogium on the way in which they
managed matters at Portsmouth, the traveller went to sleep—
not gradually, but with a sudden grunt and jerk backward.
The blind navigator and his guide had been snoring valorously for half an hour ; and the two sailor lads, after an
amicable kicking match for the biggest heap of straw, soon
dropped off to sleep, too. There was an unsociable tinker in
the corner, who had smuggled in a blacking-bottle full of gin,
notwithstanding the personal search of the workhouse porter.
He gave no one, however, any of the surreptitious cordial,
but muddled himself in silence ; merely throwing out a
general apothegm to the auditory that he preferred getting
drunk in bed, as ' he hadn't far to fall.' He did get drunk,
and he did fall. I was too tired, I think, to sleep ; but none
of my companions woke during the night, save an Irish
reaper who appeared more destitute than any of us ; but whom
I watched, in the dead of the night, tying up some gold and
silver in a dirty rag.

Next morning was Sunday—a glorious, sunshiny, bird-
singing, tree-waving Sunday. They turned us out at eight
o'clock with a meal of hot gruel, and without exacting any
work from us. The hereditary tramp and I walked together
from Kingston to Esher. The navigator stopped in Kingston,
having a genteel begging walk in the environs : and the
Irishman sallied forth London-ward with a slip-shod wife, and
a tribe of ragged children, who had slept in the women's
casual ward. With them went the two sailor lads ; one of
whom, with a rough kindness that would have made me give

him a penny if I had possessed one, carried the Irishwoman's sickly baby.

'Why don't you chuck them ere shooses off?' asked my friend as we plodded along. 'They wouldn't fetch nothing, to sell, and they're only a bother to walk in, unless you was to put some wet grass in 'em. Look at my trotters,' he continued, pointing to his feet, and tapping the sole of one of them with the blade of his knife, 'they'se as hard as bricks, they is. Go buff-steppered—that's the game.'

Some remnants of Master Somebody's pride in his neat Bluchers must have lingered about me, for I declined the invitation to walk barefoot.

'When shoes is shoes,' pursued the tramp argumentatively, 'they'se good for those as likes 'em, which I don't; but when they're "crab-shells," and leaky and gummy in the soles, and lark-heeled the sooner you get shut of 'em the better. There's togs, too,' he pursued, looking with proper pride at his own attire, 'the sooner you peels off them cloth kicksies the better. There ain't no wear in 'em, and they'se no good, if you ain't on the flash lay. My jacket 's Guildford gaol. My trousers is Dartford Union; and my flannel shirt is the Society for the 'Ouseless Poor. When I can't patch 'm no longer, and they gets all alive like, I tears up. Do you know what "tearing" up is? A course you don't. Well, I goes to a Union a night, and I rips up into bits every mortal bit I has upon me. Then they comes in the morning, and they puts me into a sack, and they puts me in a cart and takes me afore the beak. Tearing up is twenty-one days, and quod meals, which is mind ye reglar, is good for a cove, and freshens him up.'

Here he sat down on a milestone; and producing a remarkably neat housewife case, proceeded to overhaul all parts of his apparel with as much care and circumspection as if they had been of purple and fine linen, catching up any stray rents and 'Jacob's ladders' with a grave and deliberate countenance.

How long this man and I might have kept company I am not prepared to say; but we soon fell out. He descried, or fancied that he could descry, something in my face that would be sure to attract the sympathics of the benevolent, and loosen their purse-strings: or, as he phrased it 'nobble the flats;' and he urged me with great vehemence, not only to beg pecuniary relief from all passers by, but also to diverge from the high road, and go 'a grub cadging,' i.e., to beg broken victuals at small cottages and gentlemen's lodge-gates.

Finding that I was too shame-faced, he felt himself, I suppose, called upon to renounce and repudiate me as unworthy his distinguished company and advice ; and, telling me that I warn't fit for tramping nohow, he departed in great dudgeon down a cross road leading towards Reading. I never saw him again.

I walked that day—very slowly and painfully, for my feet had begun to swell—to Guildford. I was very hungry and faint when I arrived, but could not muster courage enough to beg. I had a drink or two of water at public-houses, going along, which was always readily granted ; and I comforted myself from milestone to milestone with the thought of a supper and bed at Guildford, where my ex-mentor had informed me there was a 'stunning Union.' But, woeful event ! when I got to Guildford, it was full nine o'clock in the evening. The good people of that pleasant market town were taking their walks abroad, after church-service ; good, easy, comfortable, family folk—fathers of families—sweethearts in loving couples—all, doubtless, with cosy suppers to go home to, and snug beds—and knowing and caring nothing for one poor, soiled, miserable tramp, toiling along the highway with his fainting spirit just kept breast high by the problematical reversion of a pauper's pallet and a pauper's crust. I soon found out the relieving officer, who gave me my ticket, and told me to look sharp or the Union would be closed ; but I mistook the way, and stumbled through dark lanes, and found myself, weeping piteously and praying incoherently, in quagmires, and when I did get at last to the grim, brick, castellated Union-house, the gates were closed, and admission to the casual ward was impossible. The porter, a fat, timid man, surveyed me through the grate, and drew back again as by the light of a lantern he scanned my gaunt, hunger-stricken mien. He thrust a piece of bread to me between the bars, and recommended me to seek the relieving officer again, who, he said, would find me a bed. Then, he wished me good night, and retreated into his little lodge or den with the air of a man who has got rid of a troublesome customer.

Good night ! It began to rain, and to menace a thunderstorm ; but I sat down in a ditch and devoured the bread. It was eleven o'clock, and I was wet to the skin ; when by dint of dodging up and down dark lanes, and knocking up against posts, and bruising my shins over mile-stones, I got to the relieving officer's again.

The relieving officer lived up a steep flight of steps ; and, as I approached the bottom thereof, was peeping out at the door to see what sort of a night it was. He shook his head, either at the dirty aspect of the weather or at that of your humble servant, and was just about closing his door, when I ran up the steps and caught him by the coat-tail.

'Dear-a deary me !' said the relieving officer when I had explained my errand to him, 'dear-a deary me !'

This was perplexing rather than encouraging ; and I waited some moments for a more definite communication. But none came, and the relieving officer kept staring at me with a bewildered expression, twitching nervously at a watch-ribbon meanwhile, and then whirling it round as if he intended presently to sling the seals at my head ; but I made bold to tell him what the porter had told me about his finding me a bed.

'Dear-a deary me !' said the relieving officer again, dropping the threatened missiles ; but, this time, with a shake of the head that gave solemn significance to his words. 'Where am I to find a bed ?'

This was a question that I could not answer ; nor, apparently, could the relieving officer. So he changed the theme.

'There *isn't* such a thing as a bed,' he remarked.

I don't think that he meant to deny the existence of such a thing as a bed, taken in the light of a bed ; but rather that he intended to convey the impossibility of there being such an institution as a bed for such as I was.

'You must go further,' he said.

'Where further ?' I asked desperately.

'Oh, I'm sure I can't say,' replied the relieving officer : 'you must go on. Yes,' he repeated with another stare of bewilderment and clutch at his watch appendages, 'go on— further—there's a good lad.'

Whatever I may have found inclination to respond to this invitation, was cut short by the relieving officer shutting the door precipitately, and putting up the chain. So I did go on ; but not much further. I wandered down to the banks of the canal, where I found a coal-barge just unladen. It was very hard, and black, and gritty ; but I found out the softest board, and, in that barge, in spite of all the rain and coal-dust, I slept soundly.

From Guildford to Farnham next day, through Alton ; where, if I remember right, the ale is brewed. My feet were terribly swollen and blistered ; but, with a sullen pride I kept to my shoes. I have those shoes to this day in a neat case. Such crabshells ! It was just one o'clock when I walked into Farnham ; but, I was so tired out, that, pending the opening of my hotel, the workhouse, I turned into a field, and slept there, under a hedge, until nearly eight o'clock.

I may remark as a noteworthy feature of the frame of mind I must have been in during my tramp, that although I was a sharp boy, with a taste for art and a keen eye for the beauties of nature, I observed nothing, admired nothing—nor smiling landscapes, nor picturesque villages, nor antique churches. I saw, felt, thought, of nothing but of the mortal miles I had to walk. The counties of Surrey and Hampshire were to me but vast deserts of coach-roads, diversified by oases of milestones, with a Mecca or Medina, in the shape of an Union workhouse, at the end of each day's weary travel. I met wayfarers like myself, but they were merely duplicates of the sunburnt tramp, the Irish reaper, and the drunken tinker. There was, now and then, a stray Italian boy, and an Alsatian broom-girl or so ; and once I met a philanthropist in a donkey-cart, who sold apples, onions, pots and pans, red herrings, Common Prayer Books, and flannel. He gave me a raw red herring—if, being already cured, that fishy esculent can be said to be raw. Raw or cooked, I ate it there and then.

I never begged. Stout farmers' wives, with good-humoured countenances, threw me a halfpenny sometimes, and one pleasant-spoken gentleman bade me wait till he saw whether he could find sixpence for me. But he had no change, he said ; and, bidding me good evening in quite a fatherly manner, rode away on his dapple gray steed. Has he change, now, I wonder ?

When I woke up I went straight to the workhouse. Farnham did not boast an Union, but had a workhouse of the old school. The master was a pleasant old man, with a large white apron, and gave me a liberal ration of bread and cheese. I happened to be the only occupant of the ward that evening ; and, being locked up early, I had time to look about me, and select the cleanest and softest-looking truss of straw. The whitewashed walls were covered with the names of former tramps ; their poetical effusions and their political sentiments were scratched with nails or scrawled in charcoal. John Hind had laboured hard to rhyme 'workhouse' with 'sorrow ;' but, although he had covered some six feet of wall with his efforts, he had not succeeded. Some anonymous hand had scrawled in desperate Roman capitals 'God help the poor;' to which I said 'Amen.' Mr. Jack Bullivant had recorded, in energetic but untranscribable terms, his disapproval of the quality of the cheese; and J. Naylor had given vent to his democratic enthusiasm in 'Hurrah for uni'—something which looked like unicorn, but was intended, I fancy, to mean 'universal suffrage.' Chartism was the great wall-cry in those days. Close to the door was the sign manual of 'Paul Sweeny, bound to London with Fore Kids.' Motherless, perhaps.

There had been one 'casual' in before me; but he was taken so violently ill immediately after his admission, that he had been removed into another out-house, on to a truckle bed: the rules of the establishment not permitting his being transferred to the infirmary. The poor wretch lay groaning piteously, as I could hear with painful distinctness through the thin wall that separated him from the casual ward. His groans became at last so appalling that they worked me into an agony of terror; and I clung to the locked door (in the centre of which there was a largish grating) and beat against it, to the great disgust and irritation of the porter; who, with a lantern at the end of a pitchfork, came in to look at the moribund occasionally, and who made a rush at me at last as he would have done at a young bull. 'It's all over with him,' he said to me in remonstrance; 'so where's the good? The doctor's gone to a birth; but we've give him a bottle of stuff till he comes, and made him comfable. So lie down.'

Whatever the 'stuff' was—doctors' stuff, kitchen stuff, or household stuff—the miserable man continued 'moaning of his life out' as the porter said querulously, until it was almost morning. Then the doctor (a pale, over-worked, under-paid young man with tight trousers, and spectacles, always in a chaise and a perspiration) came; and I heard him tell the porter that the man would 'go off easily.' He presently did.

They let me out at eight o'clock—sick, dizzy, and terrified. 'I told you so,' the porter said with apologetic complacency, 'he went off quite "comfable."' This was his epitaph. Who he was or what he was—where he came from or whither he was going—no man knew, and it was no man's business to inquire. I suppose they put him in the plain deal shell, which I saw the village carpenter tacking together as I turned down the street, and so lowered him under ground. They might have written 'comfable' on his tombstone, for any

2 ▲

purpose a word would serve—if they gave paupers tombstones; which they do not.

But, this poor dead unknown man did me a service. For, whether I was superstitious, or whether my nerves were unstrung, or whether repentance at my obdurate folly came tardily, but came at last, I went no farther on the way to Portsmouth, but thought I wouldn't go to sea, just at present, and tramped manfully back to Ealing, determined to take all Mr. Bogryne could give me, and be thankful. But I did not get what I expected and what I deserved. I found anxious friends just on the point of putting out bills of discovery as for a strayed puppy; I found a fatted calf already slaughtered —kindness, affection, forgiveness, and *Home.*

There was but one drawback to my happiness. With some strong preconceived notion of the dreadful company I must have been keeping, and the horrible dens I must have sojourned in, my relations and friends found it to be their bounden duty to wash me continually. When it wasn't warm bath, it was yellow soap and scrubbing-brushes; and when it wasn't that, it was foot-bath. I was washed half away. I was considerably chafed, and morally hustled, too, by good pious relatives in the country; who, for many months afterwards, were for ever sending me thick parcels; which, seeing, I thought to be cakes; which, opening, I found to be tracts.

I have walked a good deal to and fro on the surface of this globe since then; but I have never been to sea—on similar terms—since, any more.

XXXI.

FASHION.

WHEN a man applies himself soberly to reflect upon the fitness of things in general, and of their several tendencies towards the great End, of what a whirligig of vanity and inutility—of waste and glitter—the Great World seems to consist! All these flounces and furbelows; all this crinoline, bergamot, paste and jewellery, wax-chandlery, Brussels lace and Sèvres china; all those jobbed horses, silken squabs, double and triple knocks, tags and embroideries and fripperies of the Heralds' College, what are they good for?—what end do they serve? All these mountebank bowings and reverences; these kissings of hands and backing out of rooms of lath and plaster; these clatterings about streets for the purpose of bandying pieces of engraved pasteboard; these grinnings to your fellow worm of five feet long across a glass of grape juice; these bawlings out of names by lacqueys; these posturings and jumpings, and agonies of etiquette; and turning day into night and night into day, and eating when we are not hungry, and drinking when we are not thirsty: all these, the life-chords of the Great World, to what end are they? Who commanded them? Who promulgated the statutes that regulate them? If Fashion were a tangible idol with a frontal protuberance and a golden head, squatting on his hams in a pagoda like Juggernaut, we should not need to wonder at his votaries wearing absurd dresses and passing their lives in the performance of more absurd ceremonies. We might set down the worship to be a delusion; but we might concede the dresses and the ceremonies to be the offspring of a sincere though mistaken superstition, and to be typical or symbolic of something. But my lady Azalea, the Queen of the world of Fashion, is a member of the Church of England, as by law established, and she would be indignant if you were to ask her whether she worshipped a protuberant idol. Besides, Fashion is not tangible or palpable. No one ever saw Fashion, or drew his (or her?) portrait, or promulgated the conditions of his (or her?) creed, or taught what is heterodox or what orthodox; except one vulgar pretender who wrote a Handbook of Etiquette; which, for any authority it was grounded on, might as well have been a handbook to the Bear Garden.

What are the laws of Fashion, and who made them? Who regulates their absurdities and their proprieties? It was the height of fashion in Charles the Second's time to display about four inches of white shirt between the waistband and the vest; now if I were to enter a ball-room with my shirt bulging from the bottom of my waistcoat, I should be bowed down stairs. Why should Fashion in sixteen hundred and sixty-three be beauty, and impropriety in eighteen hundred and sixty? Can anything be absurder than the present chimney-pot hat? Nothing. Yet, if you were to meet me in Regent Street with a hunting cap, a shovel hat, a sombrero, or a fur porringer like that which Henry of Lancaster wore— would you speak to me? The day after to-morrow velvet skulls, shovel hats, flip-flaps, or rabbit-skin porringers may be the only wear. Why should the bishop have refused to ordain Oliver Goldsmith, because he wore scarlet breeches?

What are wigs, boots, colours, fashionable virtues, fashionable vices, *bon ton*, high breeding, worth, after all? Will they save 'the sprightliness of youth, the fair cheeks and full eyes of childhood, the vigorousness and strong flexure of the joints, of twenty-five,' from the 'hollowness and deadly paleness, the loathsomeness and horror of a three days' burial?' Will they avail us one jot in the day when you and I and all the world, 'nobles and learned, kings and priests, the wise and the foolish, the rich and the poor, the prevailing tyrant and the oppressed party shall all appear to receive their symbol?' Will Fashion and Madame Devy and the Red-book keep the 'storm from the ship or a wrinkle from the brow, or the plague from a King's house?' Is the world any better for Fashion, and could it not move towards its end without Fashion, do you think?

'A man,' says a divine I love to quote, 'may read a sermon the best and most passionate that ever man preached. if he shall but enter into the sepulchre of kings   *   *   *   * where our kings have been crowned, their ancestors lie interred, and the king must walk over his grandsire's head to take the crown.' Now what a homily might a man read over second-hand court dresses, over a Court Circular, or over a Red-book two years old! How sharp one might be upon the miserable vanities of superfluities, and the uselessness of luxuries. How easily we could do without them.

> 'Give but to nature that which nature needs,
> Man's life is cheap as beast's.'

You, and I, and the king, could live on sixpence a day, and never go hungry. But after all, in the very midst and flow of this our homilies and this sharpness of our exhortation, comes this thought to make us pause before we go with unwashed faces to live in a tub like Diogenes, or to hide ourselves in a cave, and cover ourselves with the skins of wild beasts, as Jean-Jacques Rousseau talked of doing, or to dig up pig-nuts for food, and shovel gold away as if it were mud, like Timon in the play. For we begin to think how many thousand men and women in England, and how many millions more throughout the world, earn their daily bread by making and vending Fashion's elegant trumpery;—gloves, fans, spangles, scents, and bon-bons: how ships, colonies, and commerce, are all mixed up in a curious yet congruous elaboration with these fal-lals: how one end of the chain may be my lady's boudoir and its knick-knacks in Belgravia, and the other end a sloppy ship-dock on the hot strand of the Hooghly; how the beginnings of a ball supper, with its artificial flowers, its trifles, its barley-sugar temples, its enamelled baskets and ratifia cakes, were the cheerless garret and the heated cellar : how the Immensities of the world—its workshops, and marts, and bourses, and chambers of commerce—are, after all, only an accumulation of these fashionable littlenesses in bulk; packed into huge bales and casks, registered in ledgers and day-books, and sent and re-sent in strong ships, with bills of lading and charter-parties, to the uttermost ends of the earth. Pause before you condemn Vanity Fair—reflect for a minute before you run to the justice's to have its charter taken away. Obadiah Broadbrim has helped to stock it; conventicles have been built from its profits; the crumbs that fall from its table feed millions of mouths. Nor does the beneficence of Fashion end here. After she has made one set of fortunes at first-hand, she showers her favours on trade at second-hand. From second-hand court dresses, and from second-hand fashion of all kinds, the moral of Fashion can be more strongly pointed, than from Fashion herself when arrayed in all her glory.

Let us instance Mrs. Brummus. She is the mysterious female who deals in second-hand ladies' apparel. I look upon Mrs. Brummus's vast silent repository of last season's varieties with the awe I have for a family vault; for the scenery of a worn-out pantomime; for undertakers' Latin (in oil colours); for last year's Belle Assemblée, or for the tailor's plate of the fashions and the Court Guide for the year eighteen hundred and fifty-nine.

Mrs. Brummus's repository nestles as Milton's fountain did, in 'the navel of a wood,' quite in the core of a cancer of dingy, second-hand streets and houses. Both Mrs. Brummus and her shop have, moreover, a dingy, faded, second-hand appearance. They remind you of the magnificent allocution of the lady to the quondam dealer in second-hand apparel in Congreve's comedy; 'You that I took from darning of old lace and washing of old gauze, with a blue-black nose over a chafing-dish full of starved embers, behind a traverse-rag, in a shop no bigger than a bird-cage!' The chafing-dish and the blue-black nose may be gone; but there is yet a marvellous touch of the bird-cage about Mrs. Brummus's shop: there is yet the traverse-rag, the torn lace to be darned, and the old gauze to be washed.

Enter. Here is the discarded wardrobe of those **enchanting**

actresses, those ravishing songtresses, those bewitching
dancers, who have so enthralled and delighted Fashion; who
have drawn rapturous plaudits from Fashion's kid-gloved
hands: melting sighs from under Fashion's white waistcoats;
tender glances from Fashion's double-barrelled lorgnettes;
lisps of praise from Fashion's mustachioed lips, when the
wearers of those dresses acted, and sang, and danced on Fashion's great chalked stage—upon that stage where there are
more sinks and rises, more drops, flats, borders, set pieces,
wings, and floats; where there are more changes of scene,
spangled vanities, more going down graves and vampire traps;
where there are more music, dancing, gay clothes, red and
white paint, hollow hearts and masks for them to wear, than
you would find on the stage of the largest playhouse in the
world.   Suspended and recumbent, folded up, stretched out,
singly and in heaps, in Mrs. Brummus's birdcage shop in
dimly distant crypts, and parlours, and crannies, and cupboards, and lumbering old presses, and groaning shelves,
are the crimson velvet dresses of duchesses, the lace that
queens have worn, our grandmothers' brocaded sacks and
hoops and high-heeled shoes, fans, feathers, silk stockings,
lace pocket-handkerchiefs, scent-bottles, the Brussels lace veil
of the bride, the sable bombazine of the widow, embroidered
parasols, black velvet mantles, pink satin slips; blue kid,
purple prunella, or white satin shoes; leg of mutton, bishop,
Mameluke sleeves; robes without bodies and bodies without
robes, and sleeves without either; the matron's apron and the
opera dancer's skirt.   Here is Fashion in undress, without its
whalebone, crinoline, false hair, paint, and pearl powder;
here she is tawdry, tarnished, helpless, inert, dislocated, like
Mr. Punch's company in the deal box, he carries strapped
behind his back.

If there be one article of commerce which Fashion delights
in more than another, it is Lace.   The rich products of
Mechlin, Valenciennes, Brussels, and Liège; the scarcely less
valuable wares of Nottingham and Honiton; the almost priceless remnants of 'old point'—'beggars' lace'—the lace that
Henrietta Maria loved to wear and Vandyck to paint.   Not
one of Mrs. Brummus's tattered morsels of lace but has
its history and its moral.   Here is the veil in which poor
Clara Rackleton was married to Captain Middleman.   They
had a grand estate (grandly encumbered) at Ballyragget in
the county Galway.   Charley Middleman kept hounds and
open house; and his widow lives now in a boarding-house at

Tours with her two daughters. Clara's Brussels lace veil was not sold by her lady's-maid nor by the bride herself. It was neither lost nor stolen ; but Captain Middleman, formerly of the twenty-fifth Hussars, privately conveyed Mrs. Middleman's veil, together with two ostrich feathers and a carved ivory Chinese fan, to Mrs. Brummus's emporium. He drove the bargain, he pocketed the money, and he lost that same money half an hour afterwards at chicken-hazard, at the Little Nick near Leicester Square.

A wedding-dress—all white satin, lace, and silver sprigs. Methinks I can see it now, glistening and sparkling in the August sun, and rustling and crumpling in the August air, as at the close of the London season its beautiful wearer descends that ugly narrow little staircase, which has been a ladder of delight to so many, a *via dolorosa* to so many more, and which leads from the vestry-room of St. George's, Hanover Square, into Maddox Street. The wearer of the satin dress comes down the shabby steps a wedded bride. She is married to a lord ; a duke has given her away. Fourteen young bridesmaids in white have wept at the responses. Two have fainted, and one has been carried into the vestry, to be sal-volatilized. A nervous clergyman has addressed the bride-expectant as 'Thomas, wilt thou have this man to be thy wedded wife ?' The bridegroom has been seized with the usual deadly perturbation, and offered to place the ring on the finger of the pew-opener ; and the clerk, while gravely correcting the errors of all parties, has viewed the whole proceedings with an air of deep misanthropy. At last, somehow or other, the right man has married the right woman ; the pew-opener and beadle have been feed, and the verger remembered ; the clergyman has had his rights and the clerk his dues. The licence has been conned over ; the register has been signed—by the bridegroom in character meant to be very valiant and decided, but in reality very timorous and indistinct ; by the bride with no pretence or compromise, but in a simply imbecile and hysterical manner ; by the father of the bride in a neat hand I should like to see at the bottom of a cheque ; and by big General Gwallyor of the Indian army (the additional witness) in a fierce military manner, with a dash at the end like an oath. The little boys have shouted, and the wedding-carriage, with its crimson-vested post-boys and spanking grays, has clattered up ; the policemen have put down an imaginary riot, threatened with their batons the crowd generally, and menaced with arrest one individual lamp-post; and then, shining out like a star among the silver favours and orange flowers, the snowy dresses and black dress coats, the smiles and tears, comes the bride: God bless her! Is there a sight more beautiful under heaven than a young bride coming out of church? Can you forget Sir John Suckling's beautiful lines in his ballad upon a wedding?—

> ' Her feet beneath her petticoat
> Like little mice stole in and out,
> As if they feared the light.
> And then she dances such a way,
> No sun upon an Easter-day
> Is half so fine a sight.' *

Now, alas! my lord is at Florence, my lady is in furnished lodgings in London, and the bride's dress is at Mrs. Brummus's. There was an action at law in the Court of Probate and Matrimonial Causes respecting them not long since; and numberless suits in all sorts of courts are pending between them now. My lord hates my lady, and my lady hates my lord; and they write abusive letters against each other to their mutual friends.

Fashion is born, is married, and dies every year, and Fashion is buried in Mrs. Brummus's dusky shop; she watches its funeral pyre, and superintends the process of its incineration; until, phœnix-like, it rises again from its ashes to die again.

Fashion dies. It is so far like a prince or a rich man that while it lives we dress it up in purple and fine linen, and fall down and worship it, and quarrel with and hate our brothers and sisters, for a smile from our demi-god, for a card for Fashion's balls or the *entrée* to Fashion's back-stairs. But no sooner is the demi-god dead than we utterly desert and forget it. We do not condescend, as in the case of dead humanity, to fold its rottenness in gold and crimson velvet, to build a marble monument above it, sculptured all over with lies; to state in an inscription that beneath reposed the ashes of such and such a most noble, high, mighty, powerful Prince Fashion, who was a father to his subjects, and a model to his compeers, and was in short the very best Fashion that ever was known, and the first fashionable gentleman in the world. No, we allow the corpse of Fashion to putrefy in the gutter, or to be eaten up by the vultures and the storks, and

---

* Founded on a beautiful old superstition of the English peasantry that the sun dances upon an Easter morning

adjutant birds. There have been kings even treated as cava-
lierly. When the luxurious Louis Quinze lay at the point of
death, the noise of the courtiers deserting their monarch to pay
their respects to the new king elect echoed through the long
galleries of Versailles *like thunder* When the old king was dead
they crammed his miserable body (he died of the most horrible
form of small-pox) into a box, and jolted him off in a post-
chaise by night to St. Denis, where they flung him into rather
than buried him in the sepulchre of his ancestors. So do we act
by our dead King Fashion—adding even insult to injury ; for,
after his death we scoff and jeer at him, and are tremendously
satirical upon the ridiculous, hideous, frightful, preposterous
fashion that he was. It is my opinion that if Messrs. Banting
and Prance were to confine themselves to performing the
funerals of Fashion, they would cease to be the fashionable
undertakers they are.

Fashion is greater than king or kaiser when he is alive ;
but dead, he is of no more account than a broken egg-shell.
Le roi est mort—vive le roi ! Leg-of-mutton sleeves and short
waists are dead. Long live tight sleeves and long waists !

XXXII.

YELLOWKNIGHTS.

WHEN Roscius was an actor in Rome, I think it highly
probable that private theatricals, imitative of the performances of the great dramatic exemplar of the day, were a
highly popular amusement among the juvenile Roman aristocracy. It is pleasant as well as reasonable to think so. I
would have given something to have been able to witness
such a celebration in the great city of men ; and that such
sights often took place I have very small doubts. That
amiable system of classical education under which you and I,
my dear Hopkins, were reared, but which our sons, let us
hope, will mercifully escape—that grand scheme of gram-
matical tuition which held chief among its axioms that the
mind of youth, like a walnut-tree, must be quickened by
blows in its advances to maturity ; that the waters of Helicon
were not wholesome unless duly mingled with brine ; and
that the birch and the bays were inextricably interwoven in
the poetical chaplet—that system, I say, taught us (among
irreproachable quantities and symmetrical feet) to look upon

everything appertaining to Rome and the Romans with something very much akin to horror ; to regard Plautus as a bugbear
and Terence as a tyrant ; to remember nothing of Horace but
the portrait of his schoolmaster—nothing of Virgil but the cruel
memory of Juno. But now that a new generation has grown up,
and we ourselves (according to an ingenious theory some time
propounded) have changed our cuticle, and have had provided
for us a new set of viscera, we can afford to look back without
bitterness or regret, without fear or trembling, upon the old
days of *verbum personale* and *studio grammaticæ.* Queer days !
They would have flogged us for reading Mr. Macaulay's
'Lays,' and caned us had we looked upon Lemprière, not as
a dull book of reference, but as the most charming collection
of fairy tales in the world. Now all our gerunds and supines,
our dactyls and spondees, our subjects and attributes, our
hexameters and pentameters, are mingled in a pleasant jumble
of dreamy memories : now that we quite forget what took
place in the thirty-sixth Olympiad, and don't know the names
of the forty tyrants, and can't remember the value of an As or
the number of stadia between Rome and Capri (I speak
for myself, Hopkins)—we can indulge in the fancy that the
Romans were not at all times frowning, awful spectres,
with hook-noses, laurel-bound brows, and flowing togas,
incessantly occupied in crossing the Rubicon, subduing
the Iceni, reviewing the tenth legion, striking Medusa-
like medals, standing behind chairs with hatchets and
bundles of rods, or marching about with S. P. Q. R. stuck on
the top of a pole. Cicero pleaded against Verres, but there
were other advocates to plead in the cause of a countryman's
pig. The geese were not always saving the Capitol—'bo' must
have been occasionally said to them, and they eaten with sage
and onions sometimes. The Cumæan sibyl must have taken
a little snack on her tripod from time to time. Mæcenas
must have made jokes, great Cæsar stooped to pun, and stern
Brutus played with his children. Yes ; among all this
solemn bigwiggery—these triumphs, ovations, sacrifices,
orations (in which a tremendous amount of false Latin
was talked, you may be sure), there must have been a
genial, social, homely, comic element among the Roman
citizens. Who shall say that there were not Cockney Romans
who pronounced vir, *wir*, and dropped the H in Horrida ?
Who shall say that there were no games at blindman's-buff,
forfeits, and hunt the slipper, on long winter evenings, in the
great Consular families ; that there was no kissings under

the mistletoe in the entertainments of the Roman knights ; that there were no private theatricals, blithesome, ridiculous, and innocent, what time Roscius was an actor in Rome ?

For that matter, I am persuaded that, long before, Thespis's little brothers and sisters performed tragedies in a go-cart, not in socks and buskins, but in socks and pinafores, before their big brother took to the legitimate business in a waggon ; and that Alcibiades got up a private pantomime among his friends, parodying Aristophanes' Knights, with himself (Alcibiades) for clown, Socrates for pantaloon, and Glycerium for columbine. But confining ourselves to Rome, would you not have delighted to have witnessed some ancient private theatrical entertainment in the now capital of the papal dominions ? It is good (confounding chronology) to fancy the largest lamp lit ; the Atrium fitted up, draped with some borrowed togas ; the *patres conscripti* in the front rows, the *matres conscripti* behind, among them, of course, the mother of the Gracchi, thinking the performances of her children the most wonderful that ever were seen, but entertaining no very exalted opinion of the dramatic efforts of Master Marcus Antonius Lepidus, aged nine, or of that conceited little upstart Fatua Fanna, who would not be allowed to play at all if she were not the niece of the Pontifex Maximus. See— there are the blushing, simpering young Roman virgins, all in fine white linen with silver hems, and their tresses powdered with gold-dust. There is pretty little Livia Ottilia, the great heiress, whose cruel papa wanted her to give up her large fortune towards the expenses of the Punic war, and become a vestal virgin ; but she knew better, and ran off to Brundsium with young Sextus Quintilius. There is demure little Miss Octavia Prima—she looks as though spikenard would not melt in her mouth ; who would think, now, that she sticks gold pins into the shoulders of her slaves, and beats her lady's-maid with the crumpling-irons ? There are the young Roman beaux, terrible fellows for fast chariot-driving, wild-beast fighting, gladiator backing : yonder is young Flavius, the president of the Whip Club ; his motto is *Quousque tandem :* there, ambergrised, powdered, perfumed, is that veteran toad-eater and tuft-hunter, but pretty poet, Q. Horatius Flaccus ; he will write a charming copy of Sapphics on the occasion, dedicated to his influential patron, the Marquis Mæcenas, who will probably ask him to dinner and give him roast pig stuffed with honey, garum, and slave-fed carp.

There is Ovidius Naso, who was a fine man once, but now goes among the gay youths by the name of Nosey. He has led a very dissipated life, and will be compelled to fly from his creditors by-and-by, to some remote corner of Asia Minor, attributing, of course, his forced absence to political reasons. There also, among the audience, you may see P. Virgilius Maro, in top-boots and a bottle-green toga. He, too, is a poet, but is a great authority on matters bucolic, breeds cattle, is a magistrate of his county, and president of the Campanian Agricultural Association. There is Curius Dentatus, that conceited fop, who is always showing his white teeth; and Aulus Gellius, who is a very Othello to his wife; and Pompeius Crassus, who is considered to be very like his friend Cæsar; and Mark Antony, who has incurred something like odium for his naughty conduct towards Mrs. Mark, and his shameful carryings on with a mulatto lady in Egypt; and there is Cato, the censor, who disapproves of theatricals, public and private, in the abstract, turning up his nose in a corner and pretending to read the last number of 'Sibylline Leaves.' But, mercy on us! what chronology is this! Mark Antony, Curius Dentatus, and Cato the censor! As well have Romulus and Remus with the wolf in for the last scene, Numa Pompilius to give the entertainment, and Horatius Cocles to announce that a shell-fish supper is ready. Away, pleasant and most ignorant fancies!

The mind of my life is as a cemetery, full of gravestones; but here and there are gay cenotaphs, airy temples of the composite order, with comic masks sculptured on the pediment,—flower-grown tombs, sacred to private theatricals. This pen shall be a key, and open one of them.

There was 'Yellowknights.' Yellowknights was the commodious family mansion of Hipkins Hawes, Esquire, a man of the richest, but of the merriest and the best. He had a prodigious number of daughters, all pretty; and envious people said that his private theatricals were only baits to lure young men on to matrimonial destruction. He must have been very indiscriminate in his lurings, be it as it may, for he was visited by a whole colony of sexagenarian gentlemen living in the vicinity, who cared, I think, much more about his rare old port than his performances, and by a host of children, among whom I can mention one youth, aged eight, who was decidedly not lured by any matrimonial snares with reference to the Miss Haweses, but by a juvenile predilection for plum cake, orange wine, trifle, a glorious grapery, an unrivalled nectarine wall, and a whole Tower armoury of toys, rocking-horses, cricket-bats, electric ducks, regiments of soldiers, and India-rubber balls like balloons. Of course I fell in love with all the Miss Haweses afterwards; but somehow they all married somebody else. Perhaps my hair didn't curl, so I couldn't come into wedlock with them. Hipkins Hawes took the young men exactly as they came, and as he found them. 'If the fellows,' he was wont to say (he was a plain-spoken man), 'come after my gals, let 'em. If Loo or Bell are sweet upon Jack or Dick, let them come to Hipkins Hawes and tell him what they mean, and he'll see what to do. Hipkins Hawes knows how many blue beans make five.' Hipkins Hawes did. Though he lived in that grand and commodious mansion Yellowknights, and kept horses, carriages, and footmen, he had formerly pursued no more elevated a calling than that of a coach-builder; and many and many a holiday afternoon have I spent in gazing at and admiring the wonderful lord mayors' and sheriffs' coaches that Hipkins Hawes built at his grand repository in Orchard Street, Portman Square. To be lifted into one of these carriages, and to sit for a moment on one of those imperial squabs, was to me then the *summum bonum* of human felicity. What would I give to be able to feel such a pleasure now!

We, the family of your informant, were humble neighbours of the wealthy Yellowknights people; dwelling, indeed, in a detached cottage, where an attempt at gentility was made by the existence of a coach-house and a two-stall stable, but the vehicular accommodation of the first of which was only called into requisition for a child's chaise, and in the second of which trunks, lumber, and odds and ends cumbered the manger, and refused not to abide by the crib. The great mansion and our genteel cottage were both in a small village some five miles from London, with which communication was kept up by a bi-daily stage-coach. I went down to the village the other day by rail. Our genteel *habitat* had been pulled down bodily, and our two-stall stable occupied perhaps a hundredth part of the ground on which a mighty circular stable for roaring locomotives had been built. Yellowknights —where was that commodious mansion? It had been converted into a ladies' school—no: the South-Southern Branch College for Ladies. Lecturer on physical astronomy, Professor Charles S. Wain! Hipkins Hawes is Sir Hipkins Hawes, Bart., now, and dwells in a mansion at Tyburnia as big as a barrack.

But in the old days Hipkins Hawes, the retired coach builder, was the merriest, most hospitable, charitable soul on the whole suburban country-side. He was always giving balls, suppers, *fêtes champêtres*, archery meetings, charades, fancy-dress *soirées*, and especially private theatricals. The Miss Haweses used to drive to London in carriages and four (it was not considered extravagant to drive four horses then, and I have .seen a great duchess, dead and gone, riding in a coach and six), convulse Holywell Street, and throw Vinegar Yard into an uproar, in voyages of discovery after theatrical costumes. They were quite costume-books themselves. I think I must have seen the eldest Miss Hawes as a Bayadère, Lady Macbeth, Columbine (in Turkish trousers), the Fair One with the Golden Locks, Zuleika, Clari the Maid of Milan, Ophelia (a very cheap costume, consisting in the last part merely of a bedgown and back hair), Mrs. Haller, and Flora Macdonald. As to the youngest Miss Hawes, she was so incessantly playing fairies, sylphs, and Ariels, that at this day I can't help picturing her to myself with wings, a silver-foil wand, and a short muslin skirt; though I know her to be married to Mr. Bearskin (of Bull and Bearskin, stockbrokers) and the mother of six children. Then the young Haweses (males), of whom there was a swarm, all six feet high, in the army, the navy, the Church, Cambridge University, Guy's Hospital, and the Charter House, were continually busy with private theatricals; painting scenes on the lawn, modelling comic masks in clay, putting the footboy to hard labour in whitewashing, pulling up the dining-room flooring for traps, purloining the sheets and table-cloths for ghosts, blowing up the greenhouse with badly-made fireworks, stifling the servants with premature red fire, and, in fact, as Mrs. Hipkins Hawes said (the only person at Yellowknights who did not approve of private theatricals), 'turning the house out of windows.' She was a weak lady, subject to headaches, and with an expressive but somewhat monotonous formula of reply to every remark, namely, 'stuff and nonsense.' Said the doctor to her, when at last she lay mortally sick, ' I fear, madam, that you are seriously indisposed,' Whereupon, ' Stuff and nonsense !' cried out Mrs. Hipkins Hawes, and died.

Hipkins Hawes himself did not take any active part in the private theatricals, save paying good round sums for the expenses incurred, and enjoying in a most beaming manner the enjoyments of the children he loved so well. His prin-

cipal employment was to sit at the great French windows
overlooking the lawn, drink old port, and tell funny stories to
young Bearskin, the stockbroker, and to Captain Chuff, who
had been a king's messenger, had travelled the wide world
over, had a wonderful potato snuff-box, presented to him by
the Emperor Alexander's aide-de-camp, and was reported to
be a gay man. I never knew any one seem happier, more
contented, more at peace with the world and himself than
Hipkins Hawes, the retired coach-builder, then a florid, bald-
headed, fair, round-bellied proprietor, aged fifty. He would
hold the prompt-book during the rehearsals of his children's
plays, and make tremendous mistakes in his self-imposed
task. He would laugh the loudest at the jokes, and clap his
fat hands, and take the little children who had played the
fairies on his knees and kiss them. Ah! those were the days
of pipe and tabour, of joy and gladness, of cake and wine ; of
the mirror before any of the quicksilver at the back is worn
off; of the plated service before whitening and chamois
leather have been too often used, and the copper begins to
show. We youngsters were frequent guests at Yellowknights,
partly, perhaps, because all youth was welcome at that
universal children's friend society ; partly because we were
considered to be (I say it without vanity—woe is me !) a
somewhat clever family. I had a brother who was a great
chemist, who always had particoloured fingers and stained
clothes, who burnt holes in all the blankets with noxious
acids, who once nearly blew the front of the house out with
some subtle chemical preparation, and who was always trying
experiments upon the cat.* I had a brother who had a wonderful genius for drawing ships. He drew so many of them
on the margins of his spelling-book, that he quite overlooked
the words ending in one or more syllables, or the book itself,
and turned out an egregious dunce. I had a brother who
made electrical machines out of cardboard and sealing-wax,
models of ships that wouldn't swim, and wooden clocks that
wouldn't go. His famous and favourite feat, however, was
borrowing sixpence of me, which he never gave back. I had
a sister—she is dead, dear girl !—who wrote the neatest,
prettiest hand that ever was seen, long, I am sure, before she

---

* What an inestimable boon has the invention of photography been
to heads of families whose younger branches are addicted to the study of
chemistry. You can't well blow a house up with a camera obscura,
iodine, collodion, and gallic acid, and you may produce a pretty portrait
of somebody.

could read. I have one of her books now, 'Lines to ——,
Morning. Psalm CIX.' I don't know what I was famous for
myself, beyond sore eyes, and an intense love for privi-
theatricals. This last attachment made me useful. I was
call-boy, under-prompter, mob (behind the scenes), Sir
Jeffery Hudson in the pie, one of the Children in the Wood,
Prince Arthur, one of Hop-o'-my-Thumb's brothers, a demon,
a fairy, a black footboy, and the Yellow Dwarf. I wonder I
never turned actor in after-life : so devoted was I to the
drama in those early days.

Our theatre was the great front drawing-room at Yellowknights, our stage, of course, the back drawing-room, the
folding-doors making the proscenium. The dining-room was
our favourite *salle de spectacle ;* but Hipkins, our host, fond
as he was of private theatricals, was fonder still of his dinner,
and was not to be cheated out of the enjoyment of his rare
old port by the French windows looking out upon the lawn.
I think Captain Chuff, Admiral Deadeyes (from the Priory),
old Mr. Puffweazle the retired solicitor, and others of his
port-wine friends, coincided in this view of matters : it was
the more annoying to us, as the dining-room was garnished by
two massive Corinthian pillars, and looked exactly like a real
stage proscenium.

We did the best with what we had though, the drawing-
rooms, and famously with those. Crowded audiences we used
to have in those cheerful apartments, deaf old ladies in the
front row, groups of happy children everywhere, and a grinning background of servants—' to see how Miss Louisa do take
her part to be sure !' I need not enter into a minute criticism of our performances. We played everything, tragedy,
comedy, farce, burlesque, and opera (all the Miss Huweses
played and sang). I am afraid I was not much of an actor
myself—I was so small and weak ; but not to be egotistical,
I imagine that I did once make something like a sensation as
the physician's head in Za-ze-zi-zo-zu.

I think if I had built coaches enough (mentally or bodily)
to be very rich, that I should like to have a commodious
family mansion, where my sons and daughters could play
their private theatricals out. I am sure I would not grudge
them the use of the dining-room, but would build a commodious summer-house on the lawn, where I could sip my old
port wine.

XXXIII.

THE SPORTING WORLD.

I TAKE it for granted that you are not a 'sporting man.' I take it for granted that you own no race-horses, yachts, or ratting terriers; that you have not 'backed the Slasher for a "fiver";' and that you 'have' nothing on any 'event.' I take it for granted that you are not prepared to bring forward a novice to run the Hampshire Stag; that you are not one of the contributors to the correspondents' column of 'Bell's Life,' anxiously awaiting a reply to your cribbage query last week, and feverish to know whether 'A. wins;' and, lastly, that though you may have a sufficient zest for the amenities of social intercourse, you are not to be 'heard of' at the bar of any sporting public-house, where you 'will be happy to see your friends.'

I propose to read 'Bell's Life'—a very honestly and respectably conducted weekly paper—with you, but I do not propose to read it in that spirit. There are thousands who read it as what it is—a sporting print, giving reliable information on all sporting subjects. It is the chronicle of what is called the Sporting World. A human eye never asleep (*nunquam dormio*), and six columns of advertisements greet us in the front page. Instanter we become denizens if not *habitués* of the sporting world. Have we horses?—here are saddles, bridles, harness, harness-paste, unrivallad nosebands, inimitably rowelled spurs, and patent 'bits,' to conterfeit the marks appended to which is felony. Have we dogs?—inventive tradesmen tempt us to purchase kennels, collars, dog-whips and specifics against the distemper and hydrophobia.

We are invited to peruse works on the dog, works on the horse, works on the management and treatment of every animal of which man—having exhausted the use and employment—has condescended to make the means or the end of the hydra-headed amusement known as 'sporting.' Foxes to replenish the hunting preserves, which by the too zealous ardour of their Nimrods have become denuded of their odoriferous vermin, are advertised in company with stud grooms who can bleed, sling and fire horses, and whippers-in who can be highly recommended. One gentleman wants twenty couple of deer to give a sylvan relish to the dells and

2 B

glades of his park; another has some prime ferrets to dispose
of 'Well up to trap;' a third wants to sell two bloodhounds;
a fourth to purchase some Cochin China fowls, and a real
Javanese bantam or two. Then there is a Siberian wolf and
her cubs to be sold—a bargain—by an amateur 'who has no
further occasion for them' (we should fancy not); and who,
apparently puzzled as to whether they are 'sporting' animals
or not, and consequently entitled to the freedom of 'Bell's
Life,' is perplexingly ambiguous in his description: hinting,
at the commencement, that they would be 'suitable for a
nobleman fond of zoology,' but subsiding, eventually, into a
vague alternative, 'or would do for a menagerie.' They
would be suitable there, I opine; but are not exactly the sort
of quadrupeds I should like to make drawing-room pets of, or
to win in a raffle.

Soon, however, a thoroughly sporting announcement comes
blazoned forth in conspicuous type. 'To be sold at Tattersall's, five-and-twenty couple and a half of fox-hounds, the
property of a gentleman relinquishing hunting.' Good; or
has hunting relinquished the gentleman: which is it? Shall
I mind my own business and take the sale as a sale and
nothing but a sale, or shall I be malicious and surmise that
the gentleman has ridden, neck or nothing, after the five-and-
twenty couple and a half of fox-hounds till he and they have
clean outridden and lost scent of the fox, and having started
another species of vermin called the 'constable,' which pursuing, the gentleman has managed to outrun, and has ended
by riding 'over hounds?' He has gone to the dogs, and his
dogs have gone to Tattersall's. Who can this gentleman relinquishing hunting be? Not the Honourable Billy Buff, third
son of Lord Riffington of Raff Hall, Rowdyshire, surely. Not
that gay scion of aristocracy—that frolicsome pilaster (if I
may call him so) of the state—whilom of ten successive regiments of cavalry, all 'crack' ones, out of which he was ten
times moved to exchange or sell by ten successive colonels.
Not Billy Buff, who was the worthy and emulous associate of
the Earl of Mohawk, of Sir Wrench Nocker, Bart., and of that
gay foreign spark, the Russian Count Bellpulloff, who laid a
wager of fifty to one with Lord Tommy Plantagenet (called
'facer' Plantagenet from his fondness for the ring), that he
would, while returning from the Derby on the summit of a
'drag,' fish off four old ladies' false fronts by means of a salmon
hook affixed to the end of a tandem whip within twenty
minutes, but happening, just on turning the quarter, to hook

a fierce butcher under the chin by mistake—lost his wager. The fifty was in five-pound notes, and Bellpulloff offered to make them peasants of the Ukraine (he had fifty thousand sheep and five thousand serfs on his paternal estate Tcharcshi-Bellpullofforgorod) if Tommy would bet again, but the 'facer' wouldn't. Not Billy Buff, the scourge and terror of the police, the Gordian knot and worse than Sphynx-like enigma to sitting magistrates, the possessor of a museum in his chambers in Great Turk Street, consisting solely of purloined goods—articles of vice rather than of *vertu :*—fifty brass plates inscribed with the name of Smith ; a gamut of knockers on which he could play 'God save the Queen ;' miles of bell-wire ; ill-gotten area railings like stands of spikes ; brewers' sign-boards —enough to set up fifty publicans ; good women without heads : goldbeaters' naked arms brandishing their auriferous hammers fiercely, as though they would like to be at their ravisher ; glovers' stiff fingered hands, little dustpans, original teapots, golden canisters, pounds of candles, sugar-loaves, and scarlet cocked hats and Hessian boots, adorned moreover with gold, and of gigantic proportions. Not this Billy ; the Billy who positively had two of his front teeth knocked out in order to be able to imitate a peculiar whistle he had heard among the refined denizens of Old Street, St. Luke's ; who made it his proud boast and self-glorification, that calling one morning on a friend who lived in an entresol in Regent Street, and in a house otherwise occupied as a fashionable millinery establishment, he did then and there, in the absence of the fair work-women at dinner, sit upon and utterly spoil and crush flat twenty-seven new bonnets, all ready trimmed, ordered, and wanted for the Chiswick Horticultural *fête* next day, whereby Mademoiselle Guipure (the millinery firm was Gimp, Guipure, and Gingham, and they went bankrupt last year) was driven to a state bordering on frenzy, and was only appeased by a cheque for a large amount. Yet Billy—this Billy—kept hounds, I know, and the old half-couple has a pleasant savour of his old familiar eccentricity. After that duel of his with Captain Trigghair of the Guards ; after the two consecutive fevers he caught at Pau in the Pyrenees ; and, notably, after that ugly wrestling-match in the coffee-room of Flimmer's Hotel, where Jack Langham (eight feet in height, and known as the 'baby') threw him, whereby he cut his hand open, and got rather more of the sand off the floor and a splintered champagne glass or two into the wound than was pleasant—Billy sowed his wild oats, sold his museum, and, marrying old Mrs. McMack (widow of General McMack, H.E.I.C.S., who died at Brighton of the modification of the East India Company's charter and an excess of curry), retired to Budgerow Park, near Godown, Dawkshire, fully determined to subside into a country gentleman. We heard of him at first as exceedingly devoted to Mrs. McMack (late), whose five poodle-dogs he much delighted to array in martial attire, and to instruct in the manual exercise : indeed—there was a report in town that each poodle slept in a four-post bed, and that Billy went round for the candlesticks. But the Honourable Mrs. Buff (late McMack) took to sitting under the Reverend Lachrymose Snivel, of St. Niobe's Chapel (belonging to the Primitive Weepers' connection), an ecclesiastic of such a watery and tearful nature and aqueous of doctrine, that his ministry, combined with an over-zealous attachment to the abstinence-from-any-food-save-water-melon system, and the hydropathic system, prompting her, as did this latter, to the hankering after strange pumps, and taking long journeys in quest of artesian wells of extraordinary repute, eventually brought on dropsy, of which she died. Then Billy took to hunting his part of the country, and keeping hounds and the rest of it. I never had a day with him, for, goodness help me ! I ride like a tailor's goose ; but those who have ridden with the Dawkshire hounds, of which Billy was master, assure me that he did the thing in first-rate style ; that he had a kennel built for his hounds in the *cinque-cento* or *renaissance* style of architecture, which, coupled with the fact of the dogs very nearly eating a whipper-in one night, made Billy quite fashionable among the gentlemen of the country side. He it was also, I believe, who made that sublime response to an indignant farmer, who reproached him with riding through a turnip-field, on the ground that it was always customary to 'ware turnips— to whom says Billy, ' How the deuce was I to know they were turnips, unless you stuck a boiled leg of mutton in the middle of 'em ?' But, alas ! I heard one day that Billy had been ' carrying on shameful ;' next, that he was ' shaky ;' next, that he was ' wanted ;' finally, that he was ' done up ;' and now who shall say that my surmise is chimerical, if I conjecture that the five-and-twenty couple and a half of fox-hounds, to be sold at Tattersall's, might once have formed the pack of the Honourable Billy Buff, Lord Riffington's third son ?

Poor Billy Buff ! sorrowful, sold-up scion of aristocracy, where art thou now, I wonder ? Hast thou gone down to the cities of refuge that are in Belgium ?—to sly little Spa, nestling among quasi-Prussian trees : to ' pale Brussels ;' or gaunt, grim,

silent Ghent? Or art thou at Kissingen, or Wiesbaden, or
Aix, making wry faces at some ill-smelling, rusty-keys-tasting
brunnen; or at Homburg, pricking on a limp printed card
how many times rouge has turned up; or at Boulogne, wistfully peering at the white cliffs of Albion through a telescope;
or at the prison of Clichy in Paris, otherwise known as the
Hôtel des Haricots; or art thou languishing at the suit of a
Gasthof-keeper in the *Constablerward* of some petty German
principality? Certain I am, that if in this country, thou wilt
never be at Tattersall's to see thy hounds sold. The memories
would come rushing over thee; it would be too much for thee
to contemplate Flora and Hector, that ran so evenly together,
and that carried their tails so bravely parallel, that, at a side
view, they looked like one dog. Nor unmoved couldst thou
view Blucher, the deep-mouthed hound, and Sandy, the old
liver-patched fellow that knew every move on Reynard's board,
and the half couple—that young dog that would give tongue,
for all a fierce whipper-in nearly cut the dumb brute in two
with his double thong. Ah! 'the southerly winds and the
cloudy skies' that proclaimed thy hunting mornings: where
are they now? Where are the gay young bucks from London,
with bran-new scarlet and leathers, the *chefs d'œuvres* of Nugee,
or Crellin, or Buckmaster: the lads that took the astonishing
leaps o'er hedges, and ditches, and stone walls, when bright
eyes were looking at them, and went round by gates and gaps,
like sensible fellows, when bright eyes were somewhere else?
They are gone like the smoke of the cigars they puffed as they
rode to cover; like the mighty breakfasts they consumed at
Budgerow House at thy expense; like the mightier dinners
and libations they achieved at ditto ditto, when the chase was
over, and the fox was caught. Who will realise *tableaux vivants*
of Luke Clennell's picture of a hunting dinner now?—who will
preside at joyous banquets in thy great dining-room, and stir
up the punch-bowl (nasty fellow!) with the fox's brush, and
give 'Tom Moody,' and fall first beneath the table among
black bottles and unsteady top-boots? The ancient huntsman
has transferred his stained scarlet frock and grog-blossomed
countenance to another master; they are going to build an
Agapemone, or a Sanatorium, or a Puseyite convent on the ruins
of thy *renaissance* kennel; the very ragged boy that followed
barefoot, in his torn red jacket, thy hounds, and begged for
coppers because he was in at the death; the pepper-and-salt
farmer, who began by swearing at the fox and then mounted
his cob and followed it; the parson on his big brown horse;

the staring red-haired children ; the old dames that hobbled
out from cottages ; the bumpkins with heads of hair that looked
like thatch, who put their hands beside their mouths, and
yelled a rustic Tallyho ! as the hunt swept by :—where are
they now ? Ichabod, Ichabod—enough. We have all been
sold up more or less, at some time or another. We have all
been bankrupt, or insolvent, or have compounded with our
creditors, in friendship, love, hopes, ambition, truth. Some of
us, too, have paid but little, very little, in the pound.

From dogs to horses. Tattersall's again ; but this time the
spirited auctioneers leave but little room to surmise. Thirteen
racers to be sold. All from irreproachable dams and by aristocratic sires. The Beauty, by Candlebox out of Sophronisba,
brother to Columbine, sire to Rhodomontade, to be sold by
auction : with all his engagements. With him are other horses
and mares, all of equally illustrious descent. Some have won
plates in canters, and others cups in hand-gallops, and others
again have walked over the course for purses full of sovereigns.
All are to be sold : with *their* engagements. It does not
require vision quite as acute as that necessary for seeing
through a millstone to discern who the gentleman going abroad
is. I think Sir Gybbe Roarer knows him : Sir G. Roarer,
Bart., whose horse, Ramoneur, won the Sootybridge sweep-
stakes. Sir G. R. Bart., whose filly, Spagnoletta, was scratched
just before the St. Rowels, last year. The same Baronet who
started Polly for the Pineapple stakes, and is supposed to have
given Jack Bellyband, his jockey, instructions not to win, he
having laid against himself considerably ; but Jack having
drunk too much champagne, forgot himself and *did* win, to the
Baronet's wrath and consternation. Sir G. R. had a share in
the horse which started for—what was it ?—the Bumblebury
Cup, entered under a certain name—was it Theodosius ?—and
as of a certain age, but which was subsequently discovered to
be a horse called Toby, two years older. Can Sir Gybbe
Roarer, Bart., be the gentleman who is going abroad ? I think
he is. He is always going abroad, and selling his horses and
buying fresh ones : with their engagements. He stands to
win a pretty sum on the next French steeple-chase : I hope he
may get it. Sir Gybbe Roarer dresses very like his groom,
and has a hoarse voice and an intensely shiny hat. When he
wins he treats everybody with champagne, beggars included,
and throws red-hot halfpence out of hotel windows ; when he
loses, he horsewhips his servants and swears. There is but
one book to him in the world,—his betting-book, for he wants

no Racing Calendar; he is that in himself. He has a penchant
for yachting sometimes, between Ascot and the Leger. His
yacht is called the Handicap. Will he ever go to the Levant
in her, I wonder?

Supposing that, looking at 'Bell's Life' as you and I do—
not as a mere chronicle of sporting occurrences, a calendar for
reference and information, but as a curiously accurate, though
perhaps unconscious mirror of what, from the amusement of
the mass of the people, has come to be the engrossing business and occupation of a very considerable section of that
people,—we ponder a moment over Sir Gybbe Roarer's race-
horses, stepping down in the spirit, if you like, to Tattersall's
yard, where they are to be sold.

Here they are, slender symmetrical creatures with satin
coats, with trim and polished hoofs, with plaited manes, with
tails so neatly cropped that not one hair is longer than
another. Full of blood, full of bone, full of mettle and action,
almost supernaturally speedy of foot, patient, brave, and
generous in spirit : high-mettled racers, in fact. Now, to
what cunning knave can it first have occurred to build on
these beautiful, generous animals a superstructure of fraud
and knavery, and low chicanery? Why should a horse be
used as the corner-stone of the Temple of Roguery? And
why, more than this, should these few stone-weight of horse-
flesh be capable of producing the mighty effects they do upon
the manners and morals of a great nation? The Beauty,
Sophronisba, Columbine : they are not war-horses ; their
necks are not clothed with thunder ; they say not among the
captains, 'Ha! ha!'—yet, on them has hung, and will hang
again, the lives and fortunes, not of scores but of hundreds,
not of hundreds, but of thousands and tens of thousands. A
wrinkle in the satin coat of Sophronisba ; a pail of water in-
advertently or maliciously administered to Columbine ; an ill-
hammered nail in Rhodomontade's shoe ; these are sufficient
to send clerks and shop-boys to the hulks, to bring happy
households to beggary and shame, and solid mercantile firms
down by the run. Sophronisba, Columbine, Rhodomontade,
though they know it not, have swallowed up the patrimony of
widows and orphans ; on their speed or tardiness depend
tedious law-suits : interminable mazes of litigation in Chancery
can be unravelled by their hoofs. They are powerful—all
unconsciously—for more good and evil than ever was stowed
away in all Pandora's box. If Sophronisba runs for the
Cup, Charley Lyle will marry the heiress. If Columbine is

scratched for the Trebor Handicap, young Bob Sabbertash must sell his commission in the Twenty-sixth Hussars. Stars and garters, wealth and honours, life and death, hang on the blind fiat of these horses.

And this is 'Bell's Life' (called in the sporting world 'The Life'), and this is man's life, too!

Great things are wrought from small beginnings, and mighty edifices stand upon comparatively slender foundations. According to Hindoo theology, the world stands on an elephant's back—which again stands on a tortoise; though what that stands on is not yet decided by the learned Pundits of the unchanging East. So, on the slender fetlocks and pasterns of these bay and chestnut horses in Tattersall's saleyard are erected the Great National festivals of the English people—the acknowledged British holidays: holidays for the due and catholic enjoyment of which grave legislative bodies suspend their sittings, dinner-parties of the loftiest and most solemn *haut ton* are postponed, and courtly *thés dansantes* put off. There was a professor of music I knew who was ruined through having fixed his morning concert to take place on the Derby Day.

The Derby Day! who would think these quiet, meek-eyed scions of the hippic race were the alls-in-all, the cynosures, the alphas and omegas of that momentous day? Yet so they are. Closely shrouded in checked or gaily-bordered horse-cloths—as jealously veiled from the prying public eye as was ever favourite Odalisque of Osmanli Pacha of three tails as on Sunday morning they take their long-expected, much-talked-of gallops—jealous and anxious eyes watch their every movement; a falter is eagerly foreshadowed as the forerunner of a 'scratch,' a stumble as the inevitable precursor of a string-halt, an over-vigorous whinny impetuously translated as a cold, fatal to next Wednesday's start. Readers of 'Bell's Life,' how you pluck at your long waistcoats; how you twitch at the brims of your low-crowned hats; how many entries and re-entries, and erasures and pencil-smudgings are made in those note-books of yours, with the patent metallic leaves and the everlasting pencils and all on the ups and downs, the on-goings and short-comings of these unconscious four-legged creatures. Early on the Wednesday morning, Newman and Quartermaine's retainers are as busy as hives of bees multiplied by infinity. Pails of water—resembling (in an inverse degree) the casks of the Danaïdes, inasmuch as they are always being emptied, and are never empty—dash refreshing streams against wheels numerous enough to furnish, it would seem, clock-work for the world. Strange barouches, unheard-of britzkas, phaetons that should properly have been sequestrated in the Greenyard of oblivion, or broken up in the coach factory of forgetfulness long since, suddenly start up from remote coach-houses: their wheels screaming horribly; their boxes anxious for the accommodating man who 'does not mind sitting there the least in the world,' and who always manages to get more champagne than anybody else; their boots panting for hampers of choice provisions, always securely tied up, and always dropping sprinklings of lobster salad and raised pie on the road in the 'Hop-o'my-thumb' manner—mad, in a word, to be down to the Derby, and to run their poles through adverse carriage panels. Small, weazen, silver-haired men who have vegetated during the winter in 'watering-houses,' and down strawy mews, where the coachmen's wives live, who take in washing, and the fifth footman dwells over the harness-room when he's out of place—these patriarchs of the saddle emerge in a weird and elf-like manner from stable-doors: their rheumatism-bowed frames swathed in crimson silk jackets, white cords on their shrunken legs, gamboge tops on their spindle-shanks, and great, white, fluffy hats, a world too large for them, on their poor bald heads—calling themselves, save us, Postboys—cracking their knotty whips with senile valour, and calling to Jim to 'let his head go,' and to Tom to 'take a squint at the mare's off foot.' And they get into the saddle, these rare old boys! And they hold up their whips warningly to their fellow boys when there is a 'dead lock' between Cheam and Sutton; and they untie hampers, and eat pies innumerable, and get very drunk indeed; yet drive home safely, and return the 'chaff' measured out to them with interest.

The Derby Day; do I require the limits of this paper to describe it thoroughly? Say, rather a volume—say, rather, the space occupied by the 'Encyclopædia Britannica,' or Mr. Alison's 'History of Europe.' The rushing, roaring, riving, rending, raving railway station full of the million of passengers, who, taking first-class tickets, are glad to leap into third-class carriages; the fifty thousand, who, wishing to go to Epsom, are compulsorily conveyed (howling the while) to Brighton or Dover instead. The twenty thousand that say that it is a shame, and that they will write to the 'Times,' together with the ten thousand that do write, and don't get their letters inserted. The hundreds that lose their handker-

chiefs, watches, and temper. The two or three benign men
who haven't anything on the race, and say that really, all
things considered, the Company have done as well as could
reasonably be expected for the public—as if any one expected
anything in reason on the Derby Day! The road with the
solemn drags full of, and surmounted by, solemn guardsmen—
hearses of the Household Cavalry. The open carriages, close
carriages, chaises, carts, omnibuses, stage coaches full of
familiar faces. Everybody there, on the rail and on the road,
on the Derby Day. The House of Lords, and the House of
Commons, the Bar, the Bench, the Army, the Navy, and the
Desk ; May Fair and Rag Fair, Park Lane and Petticoat Lane,
the Chapel Royal and Whitechapel, Saint James's and Saint
Giles's. Give me a pen plucked from the wing of a roc (the
most gigantic bird known, I think); give me a scroll of
papyrus as long as the documents in a Chancery suit; give
me a river for an ink-bottle, and then I should be scant of
space to describe the road that leads to the course, the hill, the
grand stand, the gipsies, the Ethiopian serenaders, the clouds
of horsemen, like Bedouins of the desert, flying towards
Tattenham Corner ; the correct cards that never are correct ;
the dog that always gets on the course and never can get off
again, and that creates as much amusement in his agony as
though he had been Mr. Merryman. The all-absorbing,
thrilling, soul-riveting race. The ' Now they're off !' 'Now
they're coming round !' 'Here they come !' ' Black cap !'
' Blue cap !' ' Green Jacket !' Red jacket !' 'Red jacket it
is, hurrah !' followed by the magic numbers at the grand
stand, the flight of the pigeons, and the changing of hands of
unnumbered thousand pounds. The throwing at the sticks.
The chickens, the salads, the fillings of young bodies with old
wine, the repasts on wheels, and hobnobbings over splinter-
bars. The broken glasses, cracked heads, rumpled bonnets,
flushed faces. The road home ! the Cock at Sutton, and a
' quiet ' cup of tea there. The chaffing, the abuse, the indict-
able language. The satirical crowd on Kennington Common.
The Derby Day, in a word : and all for what ? Where are the
causes to these most mighty effects ? Look around, student of
' Bell's Life,' and see them in the slender race-horses, the stud
of a gentleman going abroad, to be sold without reserve.

Change we the theme, for of horseflesh you must have had
more than enough. Else, had I space besides and time, I
would touch upon the *fatidici vati*, the sporting prophets, already
touched upon elsewhere. Else, should you hear strange stories

of stables, and nobbled horses, and rare feats of jockey-ship. Else, would I introduce you, 'Bell's Life' reading neophyte, to one of these same jockeys, a weary, haggard, slouching little man, all mummified in baggy great-coats, and drinking brandy and water tremulously—a very different spectacle from the trim, natty, spruce little jock, with the snowy leathers and the lustrous tops and the rainbow jacket, who is in earnest confab with his owner before the race; or, after it, and after winning, is cheered enthusiastically up and down the course, or who leans indolently over the balcony of the Grand Stand, flacking his horsewhip to shake hands with lords. But 'Bell's Life,' my friend, has as many phases as human life has, and we must hurry to another.

The Ring! Fights to come! Not many, thank Heaven—thank reading, writing, and arithmetic; and yet, one, two, three columns are devoted to the Ring. Jack Nimmo and the Grotto Passage Pet, for fifty pounds a side. The Nottingham Bruiser and Bandy Starling, at catch weight, for ten pounds a side. Tom Knuckles will fight Ned Lumsden (the Butcher) for twenty pounds, and his money is ready at Mr. Fibbs's, the Knowledge Box, Chancery Lane. Toby Nutts, of Birmingham, is surprised that the Sheffield Toddler has not made good the last deposit; he is to be heard of at the Bunch of Fives, Rampant Horse Street, Norwich. Tass Cokerconk writes to correct an error that has crept into your valuable paper, as I did not strike foul, and being at present out of town (Tass is wanted for a little matter of hocussing and card-sharping), and so on. We are delighted to see that our old friend, Frisky Wappem, is to be found every other evening at Jemmy Crab's, the Leg of Mutton Fist, Bell Alley, where he gives lessons in the noble art of self-defence to noblemen and gentlemen. N.B. Gloves provided. Sparring by the pick of the fancy; and every alternate evening devoted to harmony by first-rate pro-fessionals.

I take it for granted that you have never seen a prize fight. I hope you never will; yet, conscientiously pelligrinising as we are through 'Bell's Life,' I don't think I shall be wrong in showing you one, in the spirit—as a scarecrow and an example.

The fight between Lurky Snaggs and Dan Pepper—the Kiddy. A steam-boat—'The Pride of the River'—has been chartered for the momentous occasion, for the fight is to take place at some—to the uninitiated—carefully-concealed place on the Kent or Essex shore. A trip by rail was at first con-templated; a railway company, with an ardour and enthusiasm

for the P. R. which did them honour, having offered handsome
terms and every accommodation in the way of special trains;
but old Sol Abrams, the Nestor of the Ring, reminded the
promoters of the cheerful exhibition that a county magistrate,
determined to stop the fight, might balk their battle-ground
from station to station, and send for reinforcements of 'bobbies,'
or policemen, by the great tale-teller, the electric telegraph.
So the river was decided on. The steamer has been freighted
with bottled stout, wines, spirits, cigars, captains' biscuits, and
sandwiches; and, at an early hour, she receives a motley bevy
of passengers—all, however, respectable in the Thurtellian or
gig-keeping sense of respectability, for they have all paid a
guinea for their voyage and back. Several nobs, several first-
rate men, several City men—all peculiar and distinct varieties
of the *genus* sporting man, but on which I cannot stay to
descant now—are present; and I am compelled to acknowledge
the presence of many, very many of the gentlemen we met last
night—the chained and ringed dandies—the bucks who know
where Brixton is, and who sits at Bow Street on Monday
mornings. Take care of your pockets, oh! my young student
of ' Bell's Life,' for, of all the out-and-out thieves——

There are some temporary difficulties, occupying, indeed,
a considerable portion of the forenoon, before a battle-ground
can be finally selected. In one parish a fierce county
magistrate sallies forth against the Fancy, with the whole of
the *posse comitatus* he has been able to muster at his heels; in
another, a detachment of the rural police puts them to rout,
with the loss of a considerable portion of their baggage. At
last, a sweet little slip of waste land, skirted on one side by a
towing-path and on the other by a brickfield, is selected, and
possession taken, without molestation. There is a slight disturbance at first with a drunken horse-chaunter and a sporting
blacksmith, who persist in offering to fight Snaggs and Pepper
themselves for any number of pots of ale. These, however,
are speedily disposed of—the horse-chaunter by being settled
off-hand by three facers and a crack under the left ear, and sent
home in a cart with his bloody sconce wrapped round with
one of the staring shawls : the blacksmith by being tilted into
a wet ditch, and left to get sober at his leisure. Then,
business begins in right earnest. Sundry vans, omnibuses,
and knowing-looking livery-stable breaks have been following
the course of the steamboat down the river; together with a
locust crowd of chaise-carts, dog-carts, Hansom cabs, and a
few private cabriolets—one with the smallest tiger and the

largest gray mare to be found probably in England, and containing the Mæcenas of the Ring, rather pink about the eyes, and yellow about the cheek-bones from last night's champagne. An amateur trotting-match or two has been got up on the road, and Jack Cowcabbidge, the nobby greengrocer, of the Old Kent Road, has broken the knees of Handsome Charley's mare Peppermint, for which Charley swears that he will 'pull him.' All these vehicles cluster together in a widish outer ring, having sundry scouts or videttes posted, to give notice of the approach of inimical forces; and, in addition, there are several horsemen, hovering on the skirts of the ring, well-mounted gentlemen in garb, and apparently half interested and delighted with the prospect of the sport, and half ashamed to be seen in such company. Old Squire Nobsticks, of Nobstick Hall, close by, has come in spite of his gout in a roomy velocipede, and navigates into the inner ring amid the cheers of the Fancy. He never misses a fight. This inner ring I speak of is now formed. The stakes are firmly driven into the turf, the ropes passed through circular orifices in their tops, and all made snug and comfortable. Now, Monsieur Tyro, if you please, button up all your pockets, and essay not to enter the inner ring, for the swell mobsmen will stone you from it if you do, and hustle and rifle you as you come out. Stand on the top of this hackney cab, and you will be enabled to view the proceedings with greater ease and comfort. None but the veterans of the Fancy and the Mæcenasses (?) of the Ring have the privilege of sitting on the grass close to the ropes.

> ' 'Tis distance lends enchantment to the view.'

The heroes peel, and, divesting themselves of the grubby or chrysalis-like covering of great-coats and wrap-rascals, appear in the bright butterfly bravery of denuded *torsos*, white drawers and stockings, flaring waist-handkerchiefs and sparrow-bill shoes. We have no time to ponder on the magnificent muscular development of these men's chests and arms. The bottleholders are at their respective corners, with their bottles and sponges; the referee stands watch in hand (I hope he will not lose it ere the fight be done); the swell mobsmen make a desperate rush at anything they can lay hands on; and these two men proceed to pound each other's bodies.

I could describe the scene that follows, but *cui bono?* Content yourself with fancying who first drew claret; how often the referee cried time: who got down whom at the ropes; who put out cleverly with his left; whose face bore severe marks of punishment, hit out wildly, hung like a mass of butcher's meat on his second's knee; and, failing at last to come up to time, fell down senseless on the turf, caused the sponge to be thrown up, and victory to be declared for his opponent. What need is there for me to state who officiated for Snaggs, and who did the needful for the Kiddy; how there was a savage foray on this latter's party by the Nottingham Roughs; how there was a cry of 'Foul!' and how the swell mobsmen robbed right and left, hitting wildly meanwhile, till the Mæcenas of the Ring—fleeing from before them—fell into the ditch a-top of the tinker, and had an after-fight or fancy epilogue with him? We have had enough of it.

And I am not half through 'Bell's Life' yet, though you must be as weary of it and of me as ever was Mariana in the Moated Grange. But, as I said before, 'Bell's Life' is as the life of man, and how am I to despatch so important a subject in a dozen columns? Come we, however, to close quarters, and make an end on't.

There is the column devoted to pedestrianism—including walking, running, and leaping matches. Tyros as we may be in sporting matters, there are few of us but have occasionally met an individual in short cotton drawers and a linen jacket, with a printed handkerchief twisted round his head, after the manner of the French *poissardes*, walking manfully along a suburban turnpike road; his left arm kept on a level with his *sternum*, or breast bone, and his right hand clutching a short stick—walking for a wager. Or who has not seen the bold runner, skimming along the Queen's highway, with nimble legs and a stern and unmoved countenance, amid the clamours of riff-raff boys and the cheers of his supporters.

And fishing: fly, salmon, and jack? And wrestling? And 'cocking' (hid slily in an out-of-the-way corner, but existing and practised for all that). And quoits, and bowls? And cricket? And aquatics (yachting and sculling)? And change-ringing? And the mysterious game of Nurr and spell, goff, skating, hockey, quarter-staff, single-stick, fencing, dog-fancy-ing, pigeon-shooting, sparrow-shooting, archery, chess, draughts, billiards, ratting, otter-hunting? Have I nothing to say on all those subjects? I have, indeed, and to spare; but knowing that I could never finish were I once to begin, I will eschew the temptation and say nothing. These are bound up with us, these sports and pastimes—they are bone of our bone, and flesh of our flesh—they are crackling cinders at almost every Englishman's fireside.

One word, and an end. Of the phases of sporting life I have endeavoured to delineate, all offer some repulsive and humiliating traits. In these feeble sketches of some of the sports and pastimes of some of the English people, I have been compelled to bring into my canvas degraded human beings—to delineate base passions and appetites—to become the limner and biographer of scoundrels and dens. It may appear to some that I have been incoherent and fantastical—that I have sinned, like the painter in Horace, by joining horses' necks to human heads,

> '———— and wildly spread
> The various plumage of the feather'd kind
> O'er limbs of different beasts absurdly joined.'

Yet those who know the section of the world I have touched upon, know too, and will acknowledge, that to all the manly English sports that find a record in ' Bell's Life '—round all these fine sturdy oaks with their broad chests and brawny arms—there are obscene parasites and creepers of chicanery, roguery, and ruffian blackguardism—dead leaves of low gambling and vulgar debauchery—rotten limbs of intemperance, knavery, and violence. The potato fields of English sports are afflicted with something worse than a potato blight, an insect more deadly than the *aphis vastator :* by the betting blight : the foul scorpion of betting-shops, and racing-sweeps, and public-house tossing-matches.

I hope I have not said a word in ridicule or deprecation of the athletic sports of England—the sports that send our lads (from Eton to charity schools) forth to do yeoman's service all over the globe. Nor can I end this Paper without recognising the hopeful good that education, steam, cheap printing, cheap pictures, and cheap schools have done towards discouraging and discountenancing that brutal and savage wantonness in our sports, which was, until very lately, a scandal and disgrace to us as a nation. Every Englishman who numbers more than forty summers, can remember what formed the staple objects of amusement among the people in his youth. Bull-baiting, bear-baiting, duck-hunting, floating a cat in a bowl pursued by dogs ; fastening two cats together by their tails, and then swinging them across a horizontal pole to see which should first kill the other ; tying a cat and an owl together and throwing them into the water to fight it out ; cock-fighting (before lords in drawing-rooms, sometimes—the birds being provided with silver spurs) ; ratting ; and, as a climax of filthy savagery, worrying matches by men against bull-dogs, the man being on his knees having his hands tied behind him! These sports, thank Heaven! are nearly extinct among us, and though, from time to time, we hear of brutes indulging in nooks and corners in such miscalled sports, we look at them as ruffianly anachronisms, post-dated vagabonds who should have lived in the days when the Roman ladies made it a sport to thrust golden pins into the flesh of their female slaves, or when it was the pastime of the British people, from the sabbath before Palm Sunday to the last hour of the Tuesday before Easter, to stone and beat Jews. But we are not quite spotless in our sports, yet.

XXXIV.

WHERE ARE THEY?

I HAVE no desire to trench on the province or interfere with the circulation of the numerous compendious little works, the authors of which are so desirous to know Who's Who? What's What? or Which is Which? in eighteen hundred and fifty-three, four, five, or nine. I hope that the result of their inquiries will be eminently satisfactory to them; and that they will allow me to confine myself to the speculative query, 'Where are they?'

Yes; where are they? 'Whom?' you may ask. I answer —People. People who do and are doing the most extraordinary things around us daily and hourly; but with whom, our whole life long, we seem forbidden to come in contact, and regarding whose whereabouts we must needs be perpetually perplexed. They must be somewhere, these People, yet we never saw them, never shall see them, perhaps; we may have sat next to them at dinner yesterday, ridden in the same omnibus, occupied the next seat in the pit, the same pew at church, jostled against them in the City, five minutes ago, yet we are no wiser, and must ramble up and down the world till our span be accomplished, and our ramblings ended, still bootlessly repeating the query, 'Where are they?'

A chief cause for our distressing uncertainty as to where the people we are in search of are to be found, lies in the disagreeable uniformity of costume prevalent in the present day. We are worse off than were we placed as observers in some savage country where the inhabitants wore no clothes at all;

for there, at least, the Chief might be recognised by the extra
quantity of paint he adorned himself with ; and we might in
time become sufficiently initiated in the mysteries of tattoo to
tell the Medicine man from the Peon, the young Warrior from
the Old Brave.   But may I ask how are we to tell any one man
from another (our own immediate acquaintances excepted) by
his dress alone ?   The millionnaire may be walking past us in
an intense state of shabbiness, and the spendthrift may hustle
us half into the gutter in all the bravery of ' heavy-swelldom,'
cane and jewellery.   There is a Judge, I have heard, who
dresses like the frequenter of race-courses ; I have had pointed
out to me a Peer of the Realm whom I should have taken for
a waiter at a City chop-house ; and I know an actor—a very
humorous and jocular comedian indeed—who looks like a
professed member of the Society of Jesuits.   Really, what
with the moustache movement, the beard movement, the
detective police, the cheap clothing establishments, the shirt-
collar mania, the introduction and wearing, by peaceful
business every-day men, of the wildest and most incon-
gruously picturesque garments—such as ponchos, togas, vi-
cunas, siphonias, Inverness wrappers, &c.—nobody knows
who or what anybody else is ; and the father may go searching
for his children, and the child for his parent, and the wife for
her husband, all echoing and re-echoing, like Montaigne with
his *Que sais-je?*—the one frivolous and vexatious, yet recondite interrogation, ' Where are they ?'

Of course the public enunciation of this demand will lead
to the reception of some tons of letters by Messrs. Chapman
and Hall, from parties anxious to give full information of
' where' they are.   They will be astonished that I have been
so long ignorant of their whereabouts ; and my 'Where are
they ?' will be quite swamped and put to shame by a chorus of
' We are here ; we are there ; we are everywhere.'   None
will abstain from communicating their local habitations and
names save those who have some strong private and personal
reasons for keeping it a dead secret, where they are at all.
Meanwhile, pending the communicativeness of the one class,
and the reticence of the other, where are they all, nevertheless ?

Where, for instance, are the vast majority of the advertisers
and the people that are advertised for ? and, more than that,
what sort of people can they be ?   The ' Times' is full of such
subjects for speculation ; and I dare say the clerks who receive
the advertisements themselves, and the compositors who set

2 c

them up, and the press-readers who revise them, often pause
in the midst of their task to wonder where the seekers and
the sought may be.   Where is the 'gentleman who witnessed
the brutal assault' on the other gentleman getting out of a
Chelsea omnibus on Tuesday the twenty-second instant, and
who would confer an inestimable favour if he would look in at
No. 3, Muggleston Street, Pimlico?   Will he ever confer this
inestimable favour, this gentleman?   Alas, we may search the
reports of the police courts and the Middlesex Sessions for
months, years, and find no sign of him!   The assaulter and
the assaulted, the lawyers and the witnesses, may all have
settled their little business long since.   Lawyers may have
been instructed, and they in their turn may have instructed
counsel, costs may have been incurred, charged, taxed, paid,
not paid, sued for; the aggrieved party may at this very
moment be expiating his rash desire to obtain justice in
Whitecross Street or the Queen's Bench; the villain who
committed the gross assault may be coolly puffing his cigar
on the deck of the 'Lively Dolphin,' bound for Melbourne;
the gentleman who witnessed the affray may be (without the
slightest cognizance of the other's propinquity) sailing with
him on the salt sea, or in another ship on the same sea,
twin cherries on one stalk of coral for a shark to gnaw, or
lying near him at the bottom of the sea itself; the lawyers
may be dead, their daughters dowered with, or their sons
spending, the Costs; the Pimlico omnibus may be broken to
pieces or burnt, or we may be hailing it at this very moment.
The affair may have taken all, or any, or none of these turns.
How do we know? what do we know?   Nothing!   And we
have not even a definite knowledge of ' nothing '—nothingness
—the *néant* even.   What is nothing?   It it not a——? but soft.

Where is the party who called on Messrs. Ruggles and
Fuggles in the course of last September, and who is requested
to call again?   What did he call for?   Was it to tell Ruggles
that he was his long-lost son, supposed to have gone down
with all hands on board the 'Chowder-Ally,' outward-bound
East Indiaman, twenty years ago?   Was it to ask Ruggles and
Fuggles if they had heard anything of his (whose?) long-lost
daughter, supposed to have gone down with all hands in the
' Mango,' homeward-bound West Indiaman, ten years since?
Was it merely to pull Ruggles's nose or to call Fuggles a liar;
and do Ruggles and Fuggles desire to see him again in order
to serve him with a notice of action, or to confess that they
were in the wrong, and tender him the hand of reconciliation;

or to ask him to dinner, commend a poisoned chalice to his lips, present him with a service of plate, or smite him beneath the fifth rib? Where is he, finally? Reading the 'Times' at this very moment, perhaps, and in his anxiety to learn the latest news from the East, deliberately skipping the advertisements; troubled with a short memory, maybe, and with the paragraph beneath his eyes, quite forgetting Ruggles and Fuggles's names, and that he ever called on them at all; or, fully mindful of his September visit, but determined to see Ruggles and friend at Jeddo, in Japan, before he trusts himself within twenty miles of their house again. Perhaps, my dear reader, *you* may be the party who called, and when this meets your eye, will rush off to Ruggles's incontinent, or to Peele's Coffee-house, to consult the files of the 'Times' for the date of the advertisement—or without a moment's delay, will proceed to put the breadth of the British Channel—nay, the Atlantic—nay, the Southern Pacific Ocean—between Ruggles, Fuggles, and yourself.

Where are the 'descendants (if any) of Jean Baptiste Pierre Jouvin, who was supposed to have been a French Huguenot refugee in London, about the year sixteen hundred and eighty?' Wherever can the individual be, who seeks to find out descendants from so remote a stock? Is he Methusaleh, Sir Barnard Burke, the wandering Jew, Isaac Laquedem, or the laborious historian of the Revocation of the Edict of Nantes seeking to verify some document, to elicit some fact, to authenticate some date? Or is there perchance some Jouvin yet alive, a Protestant and a Frenchman, anxious to learn tidings of his old Huguenot ancestor—a rich Jouvin, a pious Jouvin, a kindly Jouvin, yearning to share his riches and his love with some one bearing his name, and descended from the race that suffered *pro Fide* in the bad days of old? Or does the advertisement emanate—dreadful thought!—from some wily Jesuit, or fierce Inquisitor's great grandson cherishing ancestral bigotry and traditional hatred—actuated by fanatical hostility towards Huguenotism in general and Jouvin in particular, and thirsting to decoy him into some private Inquisition, there to torture him on a private rack or burn him at a private stake. Where are the descendants (if any) of J. B. P. Jouvin? Have they kept their father's name, and Faith, and trade, and do they yet ply the shuttle and weave the rich silks in gloomy Spitalfields? Uncertainty, uncertainty! There may be Jouvins yet, but they may have re-emigrated—degenerated—

their very name may have become corrupted. One may be by this time an Irishman—say Father O'Jowler, consigning (in oratory) Protestants to torment, and on the little steps of his little altar fiercely denouncing the British Government, the Saxon race, and the theory of the earth's movement. One Jouvin may have emigrated to America, and in process of time transmuted himself into Colonel Gracchus Juvvins, that fierce pro-slavery Senator and (prior to his bankruptcy and 'absquatulation' from the State of New York) ardent Free Soiler. There may be descendants of Jouvin in England, debased into Joggins, and, all unconscious that their ancestors were silk-weavers in Spitalfields, be keeping coal and potato-sheds in Whitechapel.

Where on earth are the people who send conscience-money to the Chancellor of the Exchequer? Did you ever personally know any one who so sent cash or halves of bank-notes to Downing Street? Who takes the conscience-money in—the hall-porter, a money-taking clerk specially appointed for the purpose? Does the hall-porter wink? does the clerk lay his finger to his nose as the conscientious anonymous thrusts the precious envelope into their hand, and rushes through the rubbish into Fludyer Street—or is the conscience-money all sent by post? Can you point out to me one single gentleman with a white waistcoat, a broad-brimmed hat, and a watch and seals, and say—'There goes T. J., or L. B., who sent the Chancellor of the Exchequer fifty pounds yesterday on account of taxes unpaid?' Yet these men making restitution must be somewhere or other. What are they like? I have a fanciful theory—founded on what basis I am, I confess, quite at a loss to tell—that the majority of these men troubled with a conscience are men with white waistcoats, broad-brimmed hats, watches and seals; furthermore, that they all wear low shoes, and take snuff from massive golden boxes. They are all immensely rich, of course; and the conscience-dockets in their cheque-books are mingled with numerous others relating to donations to charitable institutions, police-court poor-boxes, and cases of real distress. I can fancy the entries in their diaries running somewhat thus: 'Attended board-meeting of orphan sympathizers at noon; relieved the destitute at half-past twelve; gave away soup-tickets at one; flannels and coals at two; drew cheque for fifty pounds, and enclosed it to the Chancellor of the Exchequer as conscience-money at three.' I wonder how long after they have defrauded the revenue to any considerable extent their conscience begins to prick them, and how long they battle with conscience, and hocuss him, and smother him, and refuse to listen to his still small voice. I wonder when it is they are at last persuaded to make restitution, and how they do it—whether with the ineffable felicity of well-doing, or with the uneasy satisfaction of atoning by a partial disgorgement for a grievous roguery, or with the tremor of detection, or the sullenness of self-reproach, or the horror of despair. Are the conscience-money senders, after all, not the white-waistcoated, low-shoed men I have figured to myself, but hard, stern, gaunt, grisly lawyers, bill-discounters, bailiffs to great landlords, speculators, guardians, committee men, trustees, and the like? Are they suddenly overtaken with such a sharp and quick remorse for the injuries they have inflicted on those over whom they have power, or who have trusted in them, for the widows they have been hard upon, and the orphans whose noses they have ground, that in sheer tremor and agony of mind they with their trembling hands adjust the salves of gold and plasters of bank-notes to the hidden sores of their hearts, and in a desperate hurry send tens and twenties and fifties all over the country; this to the widows' almshouse and this to the orphan's asylum; this to the water company for unpaid water-rate; this to the gas company for the falsified meter; this to the railway company for having travelled in first-class carriages with second-class tickets, or exceeded the allowed quantity of luggage, or smoked in defiance of the bye-laws; this to the Exchequer in part compensation of the abused commissioners and defrauded collectors of income-tax? Whether I am at all right or all wrong in these surmisings, I imagine the payments of conscience-money are generally payments on account—on very small account—of the sums due to individuals or to Government. I think if I had ten thousand a year, and a great many shares in a great many mines and railways, all purchased at a considerable discount, and all quoted, now, at a considerable premium; if I had a large house and many servants, and my aunt in Somersetshire had disinherited my disreputable brother Bob in my favour; if my brother Ned's children (he failed, poor fellow, shortly after I retired from the firm) were in a charity-school, and Ned's widow (her dowry started us in business) taking in needlework,—if my last little ventures in slaves in Cuba, and Brummagem guns in Caffraria, and bowie-knives in Arkansas, and rum, brandy, and abdominous idols on the Guinea coast had all been very successful,—I think, now and then, when I had begun to think that I was getting old, and that I had been a hard man, or that I had the gout, or a fit of indigestion, or the blues—that I could send the halves of a few notes to the Chancellor of the Exchequer as conscience-money:—reading the announcement of the enclosure in the next morning's 'Times' would help down my tea and toast a little. I think, too, that I should like to see my name in a few subscribers' lists, and committee lists, and stewards for public dinner lists.

Where are the people who advertise children's cauls for sale ? And where, more difficult to find still, are the people who buy them—ay, and give ten guineas for them ? It has occurred to me, sometimes, wandering through London, to lose my way, and in some unknown street in some little-known neighbourhood to come suddenly upon a dingy shop, in the window of which was the announcement: ' A child's caul to be sold here.' But I never had courage to enter. I never had courage to ask to inspect the weird article, possessing, according to popular superstition, more occultly nautical powers than the famed egg-shells in which, unless broken by the cautious egg-spoon at the morning breakfast-table, the unholy witches sail about in yachting expeditions on their hideous sabbath. I had never the courage to wait till the unknown customer with the ten guineas arrived. He does arrive, I believe, to this day ; but where he is I know not, neither where are the cauls or the children that are born with them. I wasn't born with a caul. The places where they are on sale are published in the advertisement, but don't believe that the original proprietors of the cauls come from or live there. The only place where I could imagine a child's caul to be indigenous, would be at a herbalist's, than which, with the solitary exception of a ladies' second-hand warehouse, I do not know a more mysterious and cloudy establishment.

There are two classes who, though their whereabouts is wrapped in much mystery, I am not very curious about. These are the writers of the cypher or puzzle advertisements commencing somewhat in this style :—

' Fxin5obtlmztyivk6oZithhho8tmqgllpTT55gglolYi9.'

And secondly, the monogrammatical advertisers :—the ' Pick-ackifaxes,' ' Boot-jacks,' ' No hearth-rug,' ' How about X. ?' and gentlemen adopting that style of literature. I don't think that much good would result to us or to anybody if we knew where those worthies were. Besides, they, and the makers of appointments, and the sayers of soft sayings and the talkers of drivelling nonsense in a newspaper, with forty thousand subscribers, and goodness knows how many million readers, enters into the category I mean to descant upon some of these days when I ask, Where are the Donkeys that are not on Hampstead Heath, Brighton Cliff, Smithfield Monday Market —not in costermongers' shallow broom-carts, or the Pound ?

Where are all the 'perpetual commissioners for witnessing the deeds to be executed by married women ?' The Lord Chancellor is as perpetually appointing them ; they have all curious names and addresses ; but where are they ? I never saw a perpetual commissioner ; I never knew a married woman who was doomed to go through the awful ordeal of executing a deed and having it witnessed by one of these dread beings. Are they perpetually sitting, these commissioners ? Do they never leave off witnessing the deeds I never saw ? There is one Hugh Harmer Hollowpenny, dwelling at Bettwys-y-boyd, in Wales. Fancy a commissioner having to sit perpetually at Bettwys-y-boyd, to witness the execution of the deeds never, under any circumstances whatever, executed by the married women of that ilk !

Where are three-fourths of the barristers who are called to the bar ? Do they practise ; do they earn anything ; does anybody ever see anything of them ? Are they born barristers of seven years' standing : or how do they like standing so long ?

The gentlemen who have commissions signed by the Lord-Lieutenant, where are they ? Where is the Court of Lieu-tenancy of London, and who belongs to it ? I have seen a deputy-lieutenant at a levée, but I want to know where he is when he is at home ; what he is lieutenant over, and why, and all about it ?

I don't care where the dissolute Initials are. My private opinion is, that if they are foolish enough to run away from home, their parents are well rid of them. I have more curiosity to know where the people are who are to call in Bedford Row or Southampton Buildings, or Lincoln's Inn, in order that they may hear something to their advantage. I wonder what it is ! My curiosity is checked by the knowledge that it will not be by any means to my advantage to find out ; yet selfishness notwithstanding, I can't give up reading this portion of the ' Times ' every morning, lest there should be by chance a stray notice hinting that a call on my part somewhere in the neighbourhood of the inns of court would be advantageous to me, or that there are some odd thousands of unclaimed stock or hundreds of unclaimed dividends standing in my name in the books of the Bank of England.

Where are the cases of real distress,—the people who write the appeals to the benevolent,—the daughters of beneficed clergymen,—the widows of distinguished officers? I should like to know how many of these cases are indeed in real distress, and how many are as near as first cousins to the honourable society of begging-letter writers.

Where are the 'Lord Mayor's sword-bearer's young man,' and the 'Lord Mayor's trumpeter's young man,' and the 'water-bailiff's young man,' when not officially engaged, and what are they like when not officially clothed? I wonder whether I ever dined at Greenwich with the water-bailiff's young man. Where are the yeomen of the guard, and the marshalmen, and the sergeant trumpeters, and the pursuivants-at-arms, when there are no coronation or marriage processions, no openings of the House, no state visits to the Opera. Do they wear in private life those resplendent crimson and gold doublets, those symmetrical trunk hose, those historical but hideous little hats with the red and white roses?* Where are they? Where are the innumerable mourning-coaches in long clothes that followed the Duke of Wellington's funeral? If there were another state funeral, would they come out again?

Where are all the thousands of Ladies of Glasgow, Abstainers of Lambeth, and Members of the Primitive Church of Bermondsey, who sign their so many thousand names to petitions for the redress of almost every imaginable worldly grievance, laid on the tables of the Houses of Parliament almost every night in the session? Where are the people who get up those petitions, and the people who write them? And tell me, oh tell me more than all, where are those petitions themselves at this present time?

Where are they? And who answers where? And where, by-the-by, are all the echoes that have been perpetually answering where, ever since people began to make frothy speeches? Where, again, are the people who read frothy speeches when they *are* made and reported? Where are the 'perhaps too partial friends' who have persuaded so many authors to publish? Did they know what they were at when

* Of even this costume, as worn at least by the Tower Yeomen, the question may now be asked 'Where is it?' Time *edax rerum* has shouldered the doublet from Tower Hill, and the Beefeaters' dress will soon be reckoned altogether, I fear, among ' Things departed.'

they took those courses? Where are nine-tenths of the books
so persuaded into existence? Do the friends read them until
they are all imbecile together? Where is the Blank, this ——
who has been the subject of all those verses? What does
Blank think of them? Is he as tired of them as I am, or as
you are of me?

Still, where are they? Where are, or is, that noun of
multitude signifying many, the Public? What sort of a
public is it? Is it the 'enlightened British,' the 'impatient-
of-taxation,' the 'generous,' the 'impartial,' the 'discriminating,' the 'indignant,' the 'exacting,' the 'ungrateful?' Have
these publics any consanguinity with the 'many-headed monster,' the 'mob,' the 'swinish multitude,' the 'masses,' the
'populace,' the 'million?' Has this public anything to do with
the Republic, and how much? Is this the public which has
so loud a Voice, and so strong an Opinion upon public topics,
and a Public Service for the advantage of which all our states-
men are so particularly anxious? Where is this highly-
favoured, highly-privileged, much-cared-for, much belauded,
much abused, always talked of, never seen public? I observe
that it is never present when it is the subject of a joke at the
theatre; which is always perceived to be a hit at some other
public richly deserving it, and not present. Is the public composed of the two or three thousand weak-minded individuals
who take Billierson's Liver Pills, and Muley Moloch's Treasures of the Oasis, and Timour the Tartar's Medicated Cream?
Are the people who read the Reverend Boanerges Bluderbuss's
Wickedness of Washing proved by Prophecy the public? Is
it the public that believes in the Mission, and Divinity, and
Angelic Nature of Thomas Towser, ex-shoemaker and prophet,
who renounces cleanliness and predicts the speedy destruction
of the world and the advent of the Millennium every Thursday
and every Sunday throughout the year, at the east end of
London?

I should like to be informed, if you have no objection,
where are the rogues who put red lead into my cayenne pepper, Venetian red, fuller's earth, and bad starch into my cocoa;
chicory, burnt beans, and chopped hay into my coffee; Prussian blue, gummed and varnished sloe-leaves, emerald green,
and bits of birch brooms in my tea; chalk, water, calves' and
horses' brains into my milk; alum, gypsum, and dead men's
bones into my bread; sand and clay into my sugar; cabbage-
leaves, lettuce-leaves, hay, and brown paper into my tobacco
and cigars; glass into my snuff; devil's dust, rotten thread,

and evil odours into my clothes ; cotton into my silk handkerchiefs ; cast iron into my razors ; charcoal into my lead pencils ; bad brandy, sloe-juice, and logwood into my port wine ;
turpentine, mastic, and water into my gin ; pyroligneous and
oxalic acids into my pickle jar ; ground sealing-wax and
pounded sprats into my anchovy sauce ; treacle, salt, cocculus
indicus, and laudanum into my porter ; dogs, cats, and horses
into my sausages ; and drowned puppies and kittens into my
mutton pies.   Where are they, the great tribe of Adulterators ?
—the scoundrels who put villanous nastinesses into wholesome
food ?   Mr. Accum may have warned us that there is ' death
in the pot ;' the ' Lancet ' may have sent forth its commissioners
to analyse samples of teas and sugars ; a miscreant may be detected once in four years or so, filling up cases of preserved
meat with the vilest offal, and neatly packing the interior of
forage trusses of hay with shavings, stones, and dead lambs ;
these hang-dogs—who have in their murderous frauds endeavoured to send out death and disease with the fleets and
armies of England—may have their names gibbeted (in a
quiet gentlemanly manner) once or twice in a session during
a languid debate in the golden House of Lords ;—but where
are they ?   There is another public whose whereabout I am
exceedingly anxious to find out,—the virtuously ' indignant '
public,—the public that applauds so vehemently in the galleries of criminal courts,—that ' with difficulty are restrained
from tearing to pieces ' notorious criminals, on their emerging
from Bow Street after their examination and committal for
trial.   Now, nothing would please me so much as to introduce
this public, the virtuous and indignant public, to the villanous
and adulterating public ; and 'gin a public meet a public
putting red lead into pepper, or sloe-leaves into tea, or offal
into hay—and 'gin a public beat a public, and kick a public,
and pelt a public, it seems to me that the two publics would be
very appropriately brought together.
    Where are the people who ' go about saying things ?' *I*
never go about saying things about other people ; yet other
people are always going about saying things about me.   They
say (I merely adduce myself as an embodiment of Anybody)
that I have a wife alive in Bermuda, and that I ill-treat the
Mrs. Present Writer, alive and resident with me in England,
dreadfully.   They say I don't pay my rent, and that I have
invested fifty-five thousand pounds in the French funds.
They say that my plate is all pawned, and that bailiffs in
livery wait at my table.   They say that I am about to invade

England with ninety thousand men next week; and that I
was here, disguised as a Lascar crossing-sweeper, last Tuesday, reconnoitering. They say I have taken to drinking;
that I can't paint any more pictures; that I have written
myself out; that I lost four thousand pounds on the last
Chester Cup; that I have exercised a sinister influence over
the foreign policy of the country, opened despatch-boxes, and
tampered with despatches. They say I eat an ounce and a
half of opium every day, and that Blims wrote my last
pamphlet on Electoral Reform. They say I am about to
become lessee of her Majesty's Theatre; that I set my house
on fire ten years ago; that I am the 'Septimus Brown' who
was taken into custody in the last gambling-house razzia;
that I have shares in the Turkish loan, and the Russian railways; that I have presented a gold snuff-box to the ex-beadle
of St. Clement Danes; that I murdered my aunt, my cousin,
and my brother-in-law years before the commission of the
crime for which I am now condemned to death; that I am an
atheist; that I am a Jesuit; that my father was hanged; that
I am illicitly related to royalty; that I am to be the new
governor of Yellow Jack Island; and that I cut Thistlewood's
head off. Now, where are the people who say all these things
about me, about you, about kings, queens, princes, and
chandlers'-shop keepers? *You* dont 'go about' saying such
things; *I* don't go about saying them; yet somebody goes
about saying them. Where is your somebody and my somebody? Where are they?

Where are the Parties in the City to whom your money-
lender is always obliged to apply to obtain the money he
lends you? Where is the party who does not like the last
name on the bill, and would prefer an additional name?
Where is the Other Party, the only implacable party, who
won't hear of any delay in your being sued, sold up, and
arrested? Where is the Third Party, who is always obliged to
be consulted, 'squared,' spoken to; who always holds the
bill, and won't give it up; who was so unfortunately present
when your friend wished to mention that little matter privately
to the other party, and who consequently prevented its satisfactory adjustment? Where is he? I ask again, where is
he? Where are they? Everybody!

Where is the 'gentleman' who has called for us during our
absence from home; but who returns no more than the hat,
umbrella, and thermometer which he is supposed to have
taken from the entrance hall? Where is the gentleman for

whom the silk-lined overcoat, or the patent-leather boots were
made, but whom they did not fit; which is the sole reason of
their being offered to us at so reduced a rate? Where is that
unflinching friend of the auctioneer, the gentleman who has
such a number and such a variety of articles of property—
from ready-furnished freehold shooting-boxes, to copies of
Luther's Bible—and who is always going abroad, or is lately
deceased? Where is the lady who is always relinquishing
housekeeping, and is so strenuously anxious to recommend
her late cook or housekeeper? Whereabouts, I wonder, are
the two pounds per week which can with facility be realized
by painting on papier-mâché, or by ornamental leather-work?
or by the accomplishment easy of acquirement and 'connected
with the Crystal Palace?' Where is the fortune that is so
liberally offered for five shillings? Where are the smart
young men who want a hat? Where are all the bad writers
whom the professors of penmanship in six lessons are so
anxious to improve? Where are the fifty thousand cures
warranted to have been effected by De Pompadour's Flour of
Haricoes? Where are all the wonderfully afflicted people
who suffered such excruciating agonies for several years, and
were at last relieved and cured by two boxes of the pills, or
two bottles of the mixture; and who order, in a postscript,
four dozen of each to be sent to them immediately, for which
they enclose postage stamps? Where are the gentlemen of
good education, who offer five hundred thanks for Government
appointments, legally transferable? Where are the other
gentlemen who have the Government appointments, and do
transfer them legally, and accept the thanks, and keep the
inviolable secrecy which is always to be observed, and where,
WHERE, I say, are the Government appointments which are
' legally transferable'?

Where are the First-Rate Men, the Rich City Men, The
Twenty Thousand Pound Men, who are sure to 'come into'
every new project the moment it is fairly launched? Where
are the buyers of all those eligible investments—the partakers
(for five hundred pounds down) in fortune-making patents for
articles in universal demand? Whereabouts, in the daily,
evening, or weekly papers, am I to find the enthusiastically
laudatory criticisms of new novels (such as 'A delightful
work.'—*Times*. 'The best novel of the day.'—*Chronicle*. 'An
admirable book.'—*Examiner*. 'Worthy of Fielding.'—*Globe*)
appended to the booksellers' advertisements? Where are the
purchasers of the cerulean neck-ties with crimson and gold

bars, the death's-head shirts, the pea-green gloves that we see displayed in hosiers' shops? Where are the libraries which would be incomplete without nearly all the new books criticised in the weekly papers?—and which, of course, have got them? Where are those hereditary bondsmen, who to free themselves must strike the blow; where is the blow to be struck, and how are the bondsmen to strike it?

One question more, and I have done. Where are all the people whom we are to know some of these days? Where is the dear friend to whom, ten years hence, we shall recount what an atrocious villain our dear friend of to-day turned out to be? Where are they all hidden—the new connections we shall form, quite forgetting our present ties of blood and friendship? Where are the wives unknown, uncourted yet; the children unborn, unthought of, who are to delight or grieve us? Where are the after-years that may come, and where is all that they may, and all that we already know they must, bring?

THE END.

LONDON:

ROBSON AND SONS, PRINTERS, PANCRAS ROAD, N.W.

CHATTO & WINDUS'S

LIST OF BOOKS.

IMPORTANT VOLUME OF ETCHINGS.

Folio, cloth extra, £1 11s. 6d.

Examples of Contemporary Art

ETCHINGS from Representative Works by living English and Foreign Artists. Edited, with Critical Notes, by J. COMYNS CARR.

"*It would not be easy to meet with a more sumptuous, and at the same time a more tasteful and instructive drawing-room book.*"—NONCONFORMIST.

Folio, half-bound boards, India proofs, 21s.

William Blake

ETCHINGS from his Works. By WILLIAM BELL SCOTT. With descriptive Text.

"*The best side of Blake's work is given here, and makes a really attractive volume, which all can enjoy . . . The etching is of the best kind, more refined and delicate than the original work.*"—SATURDAY REVIEW.

NEW VOLUME OF HUNTING SKETCHES.

Oblong 4to, half-bound boards, 21s.

Canters in Crampshire.

By G. BOWERS. I. Gallops from Gorseborough. II. Scrambles with Scratch Packs. III. Studies with Stag Hounds.

Square 8vo, cloth, extra gilt, gilt edges, with Coloured Frontispiece
and numerous Illustrations, 10s. 6d.

The Art of Beauty.

By Mrs. H. R. HAWEIS, Author of "Chaucer for Children."
With nearly One Hundred Illustrations by the Author.

*"A most interesting book, full of valuable hints and suggestions. . If
young ladies would but lend their ears for a little to Mrs. Haweis, we are quite
sure that it would result in their being at once more tasteful, more happy, and more
healthy than they now often are, with their false hair, high heels, tight corsets, and
ever so much else, of the same sort."—*NONCONFORMIST.

Crown 4to, containing 24 Plates beautifully printed in Colours, with
descriptive Text, cloth extra, gilt, 6s. ; illustrated boards, 3s. 6d.

Æsop's Fables

Translated into Human Nature. By C. H. BENNETT.

*"For fun and frolic the new version of Æsop's Fables must bear away the
palm. There are plenty of grown-up children who like to be amused ; and if this
new version of old stories does not amuse them they must be very dull indeed,
and their situation one much to be commiserated."—*MORNING POST.

Crown 8vo, cloth extra, with 639 Illustrations, 7s. 6d., a New Edition
(uniform with "The Englishman's House") of

A Handbook of Architectural Styles.

Translated from the German of A. ROSENGARTEN by W.
COLLETT-SANDARS. With 639 Illustrations.

Crown 8vo, Coloured Frontispiece and Illustrations, cloth gilt, 7s. 6d.

A History of Advertising,

From the Earliest Times. Illustrated by Anecdotes, Curious
Specimens, and Biographical Notes of Successful Advertisers.
By HENRY SAMPSON.

Crown 8vo, with Portrait and Facsimile, cloth extra, 7s. 6d.

Artemus Ward's Works

The Works of CHARLES FARRER BROWNE, better known as
ARTEMUS WARD. With Portrait, facsimile of Handwriting, &c.

*"The author combines the powers of Thackeray with those of Albert Smith.
The salt is rubbed in with a native hand—one which has the gift of tickling."—*
SATURDAY REVIEW.

Small 4to, green and gold, 6s. 6d.; gilt edges, 7s. 6d.

As Pretty as Seven,

and other Popular German Stories. Collected by LUDWIG
BECHSTEIN. With Additional Tales by the Brothers GRIMM,
and 100 Illustrations by RICHTER.

Crown 8vo, cloth extra, 7s. 6d.

A Handbook of London Bankers;

With some Account of their Predecessors, the Early Goldsmiths ; together with Lists of Bankers, from 1677 to 1876. By F G. HILTON PRICE.

"*An interesting and unpretending little work, which may prove a useful contribution towards the history of a difficult subject. Mr. Price's anecdotes are entertaining. . . There is something fascinating, almost romantic, in the details given us of Child's Bank. . . There is a great deal of amusing reading and some valuable information in this book.*"—SATURDAY REVIEW.

Crown 8vo, cloth extra, 9s.

Bardsley's Our English Surnames ·

Their Sources and Significations. By CHARLES WAREING BARDSLEY, M.A. Second Edition, revised throughout, considerably enlarged, and partially rewritten.

" *Mr. Bardsley has faithfully consulted the original mediæval documents and works from which the origin and development of surnames can alone be satisfactorily traced. He has furnished a valuable contribution to the literature of surnames, and we hope to hear more of him in this field.*"—TIMES.

Demy 8vo, illustrated, 1s. each.

Henry Blackburn's Art Handbooks ·

Academy Notes for 1877.

With 143 Illustrations of the Principal Pictures at Burlington House: more than One Hundred being Facsimiles of Sketches drawn by the Artists.

*** ACADEMY NOTES *for 1875 and 1876 may also be had, price* One *Shilling each.*

" *We at once take an opportunity of offering our thanks, as well as those of all visitors to the Exhibition, to Mr. Blackburn for his very carefully executed review of the Academy pictures, illustrated by some 100 woodcut memoranda of the principal pictures, almost half of them from the pencils of the painters themselves. A cheaper, prettier, or more convenient souvenir of the Exhibition it would be difficult to conceive and unreasonable to expect.*"—TIMES.

Pictorial Notes in the National Gallery.

THE BRITISH SCHOOL. With upwards of 100 Illustrations of the principal Pictures at Trafalgar Square ; forming a complete Catalogue of the British Section.

The Old Masters at Trafalgar Square.

With numerous Illustrations. [*In the press.*

Pictures at South Kensington.

With 80 Illustrations of the Raphael Cartoons, the Sheepshanks Collection, &c.

Grosvenor Notes, 1878.

With numerous Illustrations, contributed by the Artists themselves. [*In the press.*

Demy 8vo, cloth extra, with Illustrations, 18s.

Baker's Clouds in the East ·

Travels and Adventures on the Perso-Turkoman Frontier. By
VALENTINE BAKER. With Maps and Illustrations, coloured
and plain, from Original Sketches. Second Edition, revised and
corrected.

"*A man who not only thinks for himself, but who has risked his life in order to
gain information. . . A most graphic and lively narrative of travels and adventures which have nothing of the commonplace about them.*"—LEEDS MERCURY.

Crown 8vo, cloth extra, gilt, with Illustrations, 7s. 6d.

Boccaccio's Decameron;

or, Ten Days' Entertainment. Translated into English, with an
Introduction by THOMAS WRIGHT, Esq., M.A., F.S.A. With
Portrait, and STOTHARD'S beautiful Copperplates.

Price One Shilling Monthly, with Four Illustrations.

Belgravia Magazine.

*That the purpose with which "BELGRAVIA" was originated has been
fulfilled, is shown by the popularity that has attended it since its first appearance. Aiming, as may be inferred from its name, at supplying the most
refined and cultivated section of London society with intellectual pabulum suited
to its requirements, it sprang at once into public favour, and has since remained
one of the most extensively read and widely circulated of periodicals. In passing
into new hands it has experienced no structural change or modification. Increased energy and increased capital have been employed in elevating it to the
highest standard of excellence, but all the features that had won public appreciation have been retained, and the Magazine still seeks its principal support in the
homes of Belgravia. As the means through which the writer most readily reaches
the heart of the general public, and in consequence as the most important of aids
in the establishment of morals and the formation of character, fiction still remains
a principal feature in the Magazine. Two Serial Stories accordingly run through
its pages ; supplemented by short Stories, Novelettes, and narrative or dramatic
Sketches : whilst Essays, Social, Biographical, and Humorous ; Scientific Discoveries brought to the level of popular comprehension, and treated with a light
touch ; Poetry, of the highest character ; and records of Adventure and Travel,
form the remaining portion of the contents. Especial care is now bestowed
upon the illustrations, of which no fewer than four appear in each number.
Beyond the design of illustrating the article they accompany, these aim at maintaining a position as works of art, both as regards drawing and engraving.
In short, whatever claims the Magazine before possessed to favour have now been
enhanced, and the Publishers can but leave the result to a public that has seldom
failed to appreciate all earnest, persistent, and well-directed efforts for its amusement and benefit.*

*** The THIRTY-FOURTH Volume of BELGRAVIA (which in-
cludes the BELGRAVIA ANNUAL), elegantly bound in crimson cloth, full
gilt side and back, gilt edges, price 7s. 6d., is now ready.—Handsome
Cases for binding the volume can be had at 2s. each.*

THIRD EDITION, crown 8vo, cloth extra, gilt, 6s.

Boudoir Ballads ·

Vers de Société. By J. ASHBY-STERRY.

Imperial 4to, cloth extra, gilt and gilt edges, price 21s. per volume.

Beautiful Pictures by British Artists :

A Gathering of Favourites from our Picture Galleries. In 2 Series.

The FIRST SERIES including Examples by WILKIE, CON-STABLE, TURNER, MULREADY, LANDSEER, MACLISE, E. M. WARD, FRITH, Sir JOHN GILBERT, LESLIE, ANSDELL, MARCUS STONE, Sir NOEL PATON, FAED, EYRE CROWE, GAVIN O'NEIL, and MADOX BROWN.

The SECOND SERIES containing Pictures by ARMYTAGE, FAED, GOODALL, HEMSLEY, HORSLEY, MARKS, NICHOLLS, Sir NOEL PATON, PICKERSGILL, G. SMITH, MARCUS STONE, SOLOMON, STRAIGHT, E. M. WARD, and WARREN.

All engraved on Steel in the highest style of Art. Edited, with Notices of the Artists, by SYDNEY ARMYTAGE, M.A.

" This book is well got up, and good engravings by Jeens, Lumb Stocks, and others, bring back to us pictures of Royal Academy Exhibitions of past years." —TIMES.

Crown 8vo, with Photographic Portrait, cloth extra, 9s.

Blanchard's (Laman) Poems.

Now first Collected. Edited, with a Life of the Author (includ-ing numerous hitherto unpublished Letters from Lord LYTTON, LAMB, DICKENS, ROBERT BROWNING, and others), by BLAN-CHARD JERROLD.

" His humorous verse is much of it admirable — sparkling with genuine 'esprit,' and as polished and pointed as Praed's."—SCOTSMAN.

Crown 8vo, cloth extra, 7s. 6d.

Bret Harte's Select Works,

in Prose and Poetry. With Introductory Essay by J. M. BEL-LEW, Portrait of the Author, and 50 Illustrations.

" Not many months before my friend's death, he had sent me two sketches of a young American writer (Bret Harte), far away in California (' The Out-casts of Poker Flat,' and another), in which he had found such subtle strokes of character as he had not anywhere else in late years discovered ; the manner resembling himself, but the matter fresh to a degree that had surprised him ; the painting in all respects masterly, and the wild rude thing painted a quite wonderful reality. I have rarely known him more honestly moved."—FORSTER'S LIFE OF DICKENS.

Crown 8vo, cloth extra, gilt, 7s. 6d.

Brand's Observations on Popular Anti-

quities, chiefly Illustrating the Origin of our Vulgar Customs, Ceremonies, and Superstitions. With the Additions of Sir HENRY ELLIS. An entirely New and Revised Edition, with fine full-page Illustrations.

Small crown 8vo, cloth extra, gilt, with full-page Portraits, 4s. 6d.

Brewster's (Sir David) Martyrs of Science.

Small crown 8vo, cloth extra, gilt, with Astronomical Plates, 4s. 6d.

Brewster's (Sir David) More Worlds
than One, the Creed of the Philosopher and the Hope of the Christian.

Small crown 8vo, cloth extra, 6s.

Brillat-Savarin's Gastronomy as a Fine
Art; or, The Science of Good Living. A Translation of the "Physiologie du Goût" of BRILLAT-SAVARIN, with an Introduction and Explanatory Notes by R. E. ANDERSON, M.A.

" We have read it with rare enjoyment, just as we have delightedly read and re-read quaint old Izaak. Mr. Anderson has done his work of translation daintily, with true appreciation of the points in his original; and altogether, though late, we cannot but believe that this book will be welcomed and much read by many."—NONCONFORMIST.

Demy 8vo, profusely Illustrated in Colours, price 30s.

The British Flora Medica ·
A History of the Medicinal Plants of Great Britain. Illustrated by a Figure of each Plant, COLOURED BY HAND. By BENJAMIN H. BARTON, F.L.S., and THOMAS CASTLE, M.D., F.R.S. A New Edition, revised, condensed, and partly re-written, by JOHN R. JACKSON, A.L.S., Curator of the Museums of Economic Botany, Royal Gardens, Kew.

THE STOTHARD BUNYAN.—Crown 8vo, cloth extra, gilt, 7s. 6d.

Bunyan's Pilgrim's Progress.
Edited by Rev. T. SCOTT. With 17 beautiful Steel Plates by STOTHARD, engraved by GOODALL ; and numerous Woodcuts.

Crown 8vo, cloth extra, gilt, with Illustrations, 7s. 6d.

Byron's Letters and Journals.
With Notices of his Life. By THOMAS MOORE. A Reprint of the Original Edition, newly revised, Complete in One thick Volume, with Twelve full-page Plates.

" We have read this book with the greatest pleasure. Considered merely as a composition, it deserves to be classed among the best specimens of English prose which our age has produced. The style is agreeable, clear, and manly, and when it rises into eloquence, rises without effort or ostentation. It would be difficult to name a book which exhibits more kindness, fairness, and modesty."—MACAULAY, in the EDINBURGH REVIEW.|

Demy 4to, cloth extra, gilt edges, 31s. 6d.

Canova's Works in Sculpture and Model-
ling. 150 Plates, exquisitely engraved in Outline by MOSES, and
printed on an India tint. With Descriptions by the Countess
ALBRIZZI, a Biographical Memoir by CICOGNARA, and Portrait by WORTHINGTON.

"*The fertility of this master's resources is amazing, and the manual labour
expended on his works would have worn out many an ordinary workman. The
outline engravings are finely executed. The descriptive notes are discriminating,
and in the main exact.*"—SPECTATOR.

Two Vols. imperial 8vo, cloth extra, gilt, the Plates beautifully
printed in Colours, £3 3s.

Catlin's Illustrations of the Manners,
Customs, and Condition of the North American Indians : the result of Eight Years of Travel and Adventure among the Wildest
and most Remarkable Tribes now existing. Containing 360
Coloured Engravings from the Author's original Paintings.

Small 4to, cloth gilt, with Coloured Illustrations, 10s. 6d.

Chaucer for Children :
A Golden Key. By Mrs. H. R. HAWEIS. With Eight Coloured
Pictures and numerous Woodcuts by the Author.

"*It must not only take a high place among the Christmas and New Year books
of this season, but is also of permanent value as an introduction to the study of
Chaucer, whose works, in selections of some kind or other, are now text-books in
every school that aspires to give sound instruction in English.*"—ACADEMY.

Demy 8vo, cloth extra, with Coloured Illustrations and Maps, 24s.

Cope's History of the Rifle Brigade
(The Prince Consort's Own), formerly the 95th. By Sir WILLIAM
H. COPE, formerly Lieutenant, Rifle Brigade.

"*This latest contribution to the history of the British army is a work of the
most varied information regarding the distinguished regiment whose life it nar-
rates, and also of facts interesting to the student in military affairs. .
Great credit is due to Sir W. Cope for the patience and labour, extending over
many years, which he has given to the work. . . In many cases well-executed plans of actions are given.*"—MORNING POST.

"*Even a bare record of a corps which has so often been under fire, and has
borne a part in important engagements all over the world, could not prove
otherwise than full of matter acceptable to the military reader.*"—ATHENÆUM.

Crown 8vo, cloth gilt, Two very thick Volumes, 7s. 6d. each.

Cruikshank's Comic Almanack.
Complete in Two SERIES : The FIRST from 1835 to 1843 ; the
SECOND from 1844 to 1853. A Gathering of the BEST HUMOUR
of THACKERAY, HOOD, MAYHEW, ALBERT SMITH, A'BECK-
ETT, ROBERT BROUGH, &c. With 2000 Woodcuts and Steel
Engravings by CRUIKSHANK, HINE, LANDELLS, &c.

Crown 8vo, cloth extra, gilt, 7s. 6d.

Colman's Humorous Works:

"Broad Grins," "My Nightgown and Slippers," and other Humorous Works, Prose and Poetical, of GEORGE COLMAN. With Life by G. B. BUCKSTONE, and Frontispiece by HOGARTH.

Crown 8vo, cloth extra, gilt, with Portraits, 7s. 6d.

Creasy's Memoirs of Eminent Etonians,

with Notices of the Early History of Eton College. By Sir EDWARD CREASY, Author of "The Fifteen Decisive Battles of the World." A New Edition, brought down to the Present Time, with 13 Illustrations.

"*A new edition of 'Creasy's Etonians' will be welcome. The book was a favourite a quarter of a century ago, and it has maintained its reputation. The value of this new edition is enhanced by the fact that Sir Edward Creasy has added to it several memoirs of Etonians who have died since the first edition appeared. The work is eminently interesting.*"—SCOTSMAN.

To be Completed in Twenty-four Parts, quarto, at 5s. each, profusely illustrated by Coloured and Plain Plates and Wood Engravings,

Cyclopædia of Costume,

or, A Dictionary of Dress—Regal, Ecclesiastical, Civil, and Military—from the Earliest Period in England to the reign of George the Third. Including Notices of Contemporaneous Fashions on the Continent, and preceded by a General History of the Costumes of the Principal Countries of Europe. By J. R. PLANCHÉ, Somerset Herald.— A Prospectus will be sent upon application. Part XIX. now ready.

"*A most readable and interesting work—and it can scarcely be consulted in vain, whether the reader is in search for information as to military, court, ecclesiastical, legal, or professional costume. All the chromo-lithographs, and most of the woodcut illustrations—the latter amounting to several thousands—are very elaborately executed; and the work forms a livre de luxe which renders it equally suited to the library and the ladies' drawing-room.*"—TIMES.

** *Part XIV. contains the Completion of the DICTIONARY, which, as Vol. I. of the Book, forms a Complete Work in itself. This volume may now be had, handsomely bound in half red morocco, gilt top, price £3 13s. 6d. Cases for binding the volume may also be had, price 5s. each.*

The remaining Parts will be occupied by the GENERAL HISTORY OF THE COSTUMES OF EUROPE, arranged Chronologically.

Demy 8vo, half-bound morocco, 21s.

Dibdin's Bibliomania;

or, Book-Madness : A Bibliographical Romance. With numerous Illustrations. A New Edition, with a Supplement, including a Key to the Assumed Characters in the Drama.

Parts I. to XII. now ready, 21*s.* each.

Cussans' History of Hertfordshire.

By JOHN E. CUSSANS. Illustrated with full-page Plates on Copper and Stone, and a profusion of small Woodcuts.

" Mr. Cussans has, from sources not accessible to Clutterbuck, made most valuable additions to the manorial history of the county from the earliest period downwards, cleared up many doubtful points, and given original details concerning various subjects untouched or imperfectly treated by that writer. The pedigrees seem to have been constructed with great care, and are a valuable addition to the genealogical history of the county. Mr. Cussans appears to have done his work conscientiously, and to have spared neither time, labour, nor expense to render his volumes worthy of ranking in the highest class of County Histories.' —ACADEMY.

Demy 8vo, cloth extra, 12*s.* 6*d.*

Doran's Memories of our Great Towns.

With Anecdotic Gleanings concerning their Worthies and their Oddities. By Dr. JOHN DORAN, F.S.A.

SECOND EDITION, demy 8vo, cloth gilt, with Illustrations, 18*s.*

Dunraven's The Great Divide ·

A Narrative of Travels in the Upper Yellowstone in the Summer of 1874. By the EARL of DUNRAVEN. With Maps and numerous striking full-page Illustrations by VALENTINE W. BROMLEY.

" There has not for a long time appeared a better book of travel than Lord Dunraven's ' The Great Divide.' . . The book is full of clever observation, and both narrative and illustrations are thoroughly good." —ATHENÆUM.

Demy 8vo, cloth extra, with Illustrations, 24*s.*

Dodge's (Colonel) The Hunting Grounds

of the Great West: A Description of the Plains, Game, and Indians of the Great North American Desert. By RICHARD IRVING DODGE, Lieutenant-Colonel of the United States Army. With an Introduction by WILLIAM BLACKMORE; Map, and numerous Illustrations drawn by ERNEST GRISET.

" This magnificent volume is one of the most able and most interesting works which has ever proceeded from an American pen, while its freshness is equal to that of any similar book. Colonel Dodge has chosen a subject of which he is master, and treated it with a fulness that leaves nothing more to be desired, and in a style which is charming equally for its picturesqueness and its purity." —NONCONFORMIST.

Crown 8vo, cloth extra, gilt, with Illustrations, 6*s.*

Emanuel On Diamonds and Precious

Stones: their History, Value, and Properties; with Simple Tests for ascertaining their Reality. By HARRY EMANUEL, F.R.G.S. With numerous Illustrations, Tinted and Plain.

Crown 8vo, cloth extra, with Illustrations, 7s. 6d.

The Englishman's House:

A Practical Guide to all interested in Selecting or Building a House, with full Estimates of Cost, Quantities, &c. By C. J. RICHARDSON. Third Edition. With nearly 600 Illustrations.

₊ *This book is intended to supply a long-felt want, viz., a plain, non-technical account of every style of house, with the cost and manner of building ; it gives every variety, from a workman's cottage to a nobleman's palace.*

Crown 8vo, cloth boards, 6s. per Volume ; a few Large Paper copies (only 50 printed), at 12s. per Vol.

Early English Poets.

Edited, with Introductions and Annotations, by Rev. A. B. GROSART.

*"Mr. Grosart has spent the most laborious and the most enthusiastic care on the perfect restoration and preservation of the text ; and it is very unlikely that any other edition of the poet can ever be called for. From Mr. Grosart we always expect and always receive the final results of most patient and competent scholarship."—*EXAMINER.

1. *Fletcher's (Giles, B.D.)* Complete Poems : Christ's Victorie in Heaven, Christ's Victorie on Earth, Christ's Triumph over Death, and Minor Poems. With Memorial-Introduction and Notes. One Vol.

2. *Davies' (Sir John)* Complete Poetical Works, including Psalms I. to L. in Verse, and other hitherto Unpublished MSS., for the first time Collected and Edited. With Memorial-Introduction and Notes. Two Vols.

3. *Herrick's (Robert) Hes*perides, Noble Numbers, and Complete Collected Poems. With Memorial-Introduction and Notes, Steel Portrait, Index of First Lines, and Glossarial Index, &c. Three Vols.

4. *Sidney's (Sir Philip)* Complete Poetical Works, including all those in "Arcadia." With Portrait, Memorial-Introduction, Essay on the Poetry of Sidney, and Notes. Three Vols.

5. *Donne's (Dr. John)* Complete Poetical Works, including the Satires and various from MSS. With Memorial-Introduction and Notes.

[*In the press.*

₊ *Other volumes are in active preparation.*

Crown 8vo, cloth extra, with Illustrations, 6s.

Fairholt's Tobacco ·

Its History and Associations ; with an Account of the Plant and its Manufacture, and its Modes of Use in all Ages and Countries. By F. W. FAIRHOLT, F.S.A. A New Edition, with Coloured Frontispiece and upwards of 100 Illustrations by the Author.

*" A very pleasant and instructive history of tobacco and its associations, which we cordially recommend alike to the votaries and to the enemies of the much-maligned but certainly not neglected weed. Full of interest and information."—*DAILY NEWS.

Crown 8vo, cloth extra, with Illustrations, 4s. 6d.

Faraday's Chemical History of a Candle.
Lectures delivered to a Juvenile Audience. A New Edition.
Edited by W. CROOKES, F.C.S. With numerous Illustrations.

Crown 8vo, cloth extra, with Illustrations, 4s. 6d.

Faraday's Various Forces of Nature.
A New Edition. Edited by W. CROOKES, F.C.S. With numerous
Illustrations.

Crown 8vo, cloth extra, with Illustrations, 7s. 6d.

Finger-Ring Lore:
Historical, Legendary, and Anecdotal.—Earliest Notices; Supersti-
tions ; Ring Investiture, Secular and Ecclesiastical ; Betrothal and
Wedding Rings ; Ring-tokens ; Memorial and Mortuary Rings ;
Posy-Rings ; Customs and Incidents in Connection with Rings ;
Remarkable Rings, &c. By WILLIAM JONES, F.S.A. With Hun-
dreds of Illustrations of Curious Rings of all Ages and Countries.

"*Enters fully into the whole subject, and gives an amount of information
and general reading in reference thereto which is of very high interest. The
book is not only a sort of history of finger-rings, but is a collection of anecdotes
in connection with them. The volume is admirably illustrated, and
altogether affords an amount of amusement and information which is not otherwise easily accessible.*"—SCOTSMAN.

"*One of those gossiping books which are as full of amusement as of instruction.*"—ATHENÆUM.

THE RUSKIN GRIMM.—Square crown 8vo, cloth extra, 6s. 6d.;
gilt edges, 7s. 6d.

German Popular Stories.
Collected by the Brothers GRIMM, and Translated by EDGAR
TAYLOR. Edited, with an Introduction, by JOHN RUSKIN.
With 22 Illustrations after the inimitable designs of GEORGE
CRUIKSHANK. Both Series Complete.

"*The illustrations of this volume   . are of quite sterling and admirable
art, of a class precisely parallel in elevation to the character of the tales which
they illustrate; and the original etchings, as I have before said in the Appendix to
my 'Elements of Drawing,' were unrivalled in masterfulness of touch since Rembrandt (in some qualities of delineation, unrivalled even by him).   . To make
somewhat enlarged copies of them, looking at them through a magnifying glass,
and never putting two lines where Cruikshank has put only one, would be an exercise in decision and severe drawing which would leave afterwards little to be learnt
in schools.*"—Extract from Introduction by JOHN RUSKIN.

One Vol. crown 8vo, cloth extra, 9s.

Gilbert's (W. S.) Original Plays:
"A Wicked World," "Charity," "The Palace of Truth,"
"Pygmalion," "Trial by Jury," &c.

"*His workmanship is in its way perfect ; it is very sound, very even, very
well sustained, and excellently balanced throughout.*"—OBSERVER.

One Shilling Monthly, Illustrated by ARTHUR HOPKINS.

The Gentleman's Magazine.

Edited by SYLVANUS URBAN, Gentleman.

In seeking to restore the "GENTLEMAN'S MAGAZINE" to the position it formerly held, the Publishers do not lose sight of the changed conditions under which it now appears. While maintaining an historical continuity which dates back to the reign of George the Second, there will be no attempt to burden the present with the weight of a distant past, or to adhere slavishly to traditions the application of which is unsuited to the altered conditions of society at the present time. It is sought to render the Magazine to the gentleman of to-day what in earlier times it proved to the gentleman of a past generation. New features will be introduced to take the place of those which disappear; in the most important respects, however, the connecting links between the present and the past will be closest. Biography and History, which have always formed a conspicuous portion of the contents, will retain the prominence assigned them, and will be treated with the added breadth that springs from increased familiarity with authorities and more exact appreciation of the province of the Biographer and the Historian. Science, which confers upon the age special eminence, will have its latest conclusions and forecasts presented in a manner which shall bring them within the grasp of the general reader. The philosophical aspect of Politics, the matters which affect Imperial interests, will be separated from the rivalries of party, and will receive a due share of attention. Archæology (under which comprehensive head may be included Genealogy, Topography, and other similar matters), Natural History, Sport and Adventure, Poetry, Belles Lettres, Art in all its manifestations, will constitute a portion of the contents; and Essays upon social subjects will, as heretofore, be interspersed. Under the head of Table Talk matters of current interest will be discussed, and facts of historic value will be preserved. A Work of Fiction by some novelist of highest position will run through the pages of the Magazine, and will be illustrated by artists of known excellence. With a full sense of what is involved in their promise, and with a firm resolution to abide by their pledges, the Publishers undertake to spare no exertion that is necessary to secure the highest class of contributions, to place the Magazine in the first rank of serials, and to fit it to take its place on the table and on the shelves of all classes of cultivated Englishmen.

. *Now ready, the Volume for* JULY *to* DECEMBER, 1877, *cloth extra, price* 8s. 6d.; *and Cases for binding, price* 2s. *each.*

Demy 4to, cloth extra, with Illustrations, 31s. 6d.

Gillray the Caricaturist

The Story of his Life and Times, with Anecdotal Descriptions of his Engravings. Edited by THOMAS WRIGHT, Esq., M.A., F.S.A. With 83 full-page Plates, and numerous Wood Engravings.

Crown 8vo, cloth extra, with a Map, 3s. 6d.

Gold,

or, Legal Regulations for the Standard of Gold and Silver Ware in the different Countries of the World. Translated from the German of STUDNITZ by Mrs. BREWER, and Edited, with additions, by EDWIN W. STREETER.

Crown 8vo, cloth gilt and gilt edges, 7s. 6d.

The Golden Treasury of Thought:

AN ENCYCLOPÆDIA OF QUOTATIONS from Writers of all Times and Countries. Selected and Edited by THEODORE TAYLOR.

Square 16mo (Tauchnitz size), cloth extra, 2s. per volume.

The Golden Library:

Bayard Taylor's Diver-
sions of the Echo Club.

The Book of Clerical Anec-
dotes.

Byron's Don Juan.

Carlyle (Thomas) on the
Choice of Books. With a Memoir. 1s. 6d.

Emerson's Letters and
Social Aims.

Godwin's(William)Lives
of the Necromancers.

Holmes's Autocrat of the
Breakfast Table. With an Introduction by G. A. SALA.

Holmes's Professor at the
Breakfast Table.

Hood's Whims and Oddi-
ties. Complete. With all the
original Illustrations.

Irving's (Washington)
Tales of a Traveller.

Irving's (Washington)
Tales of the Alhambra.

Jesse's (Edward) Scenes
and Occupations of Country Life.

Lamb's Essays of Elia.
Both Series Complete in One Vol.

Leigh Hunt's Essays : A
Tale for a Chimney Corner, and
other Pieces. With Portrait, and
Introduction by EDMUND OLLIER

Mallory's (Sir Thomas)
Mort d'Arthur : The Stories of
King Arthur and of the Knights
of the Round Table. Edited by
B. MONTGOMERIE RANKING.

Pascal's Provincial Let-
ters. A New Translation, with
Historical Introduction and
Notes, by T. M'CRIE, D.D.,
LL.D.

Pope's Complete Poetical
Works.

Rochefoucauld's Maxims
and Moral Reflections. With
Notes, and an Introductory
Essay by SAINTE-BEUVE.

St. Pierre's Paul and
Virginia, and the Indian Cot-
tage. Edited, with Life, by the
Rev. E. CLARKE.

Shelley's Early Poems
and Queen Mab, with Essay by
LEIGH HUNT.

Shelley's Later Poems :
Laon and Cythna, &c.

Shelley's Posthumous
Poems, the Shelley Papers, &c.

Shelley's Prose Works,
including A Refutation of Deism,
Zastrozzi, St. Irvyne, &c.

White's Natural History
of Selborne. Edited, with additions, by THOMAS BROWN,
F.L.S.

" A series of excellently printed and carefully annotated volumes, handy in size, and altogether attractive."—BOOKSELLER.

Small 8vo, cloth gilt, 6s.

Gosse's King Erik:

A Tragedy. By EDMUND W. GOSSE. Vignette by W. B. SCOTT.
" We have seldom seen so marked an advance in a second book beyond a first. Its merits are solid and of a very high order."—ACADEMY.

Small 8vo, cloth gilt, 5s.

Gosse's On Viol and Flute.

Second Edition. With a Vignette by W. B. Scott.

Half-bound, paper boards, 21s.; or elegantly half-bound crimson
morocco, gilt, 25s.

The Graphic Portfolio.

Fifty Engravings from "The Graphic," most carefully printed on the finest plate paper (18 in. by 15 in.) from the Original Engravings. The Drawings are by S. L. FILDES, HELEN PATERSON, HUBERT HERKOMER, SYDNEY HALL, E. J. GREGORY, G. D. LESLIE, W. SMALL, G. DU MAURIER, Sir JOHN GILBERT, G. J. PIN-WELL, CHARLES GREEN, G. DURAND, M. E. EDWARDS, A. B. HOUGHTON, H. S. MARKS, F. W. LAWSON, H. WEIGALL, and others.

"Contains some of the choicest specimens, both of drawing and wood-engraving. Admirable in details and expression, and engraved with rare delicacy."—DAILY NEWS.

Crown 8vo, cloth extra, gilt, with Illustrations, 7s. 6d.

Greenwood's Low-Life Deeps:

An Account of the Strange Fish to be found there; including "The Man and Dog Fight," with much additional and confirmatory evidence; "With a Tally-Man," "A Fallen Star," "The Betting Barber," "A Coal Marriage," &c. By JAMES GREENWOOD. With Illustrations in tint by ALFRED CONCANEN.

Crown 8vo, cloth extra, gilt, with Illustrations, 7s. 6d.

Greenwood's Wilds of London:

Descriptive Sketches, from Personal Observations and Experience, of Remarkable Scenes, People, and Places in London. By JAMES GREENWOOD. With 12 Tinted Illustrations by ALFRED CONCANEN.

" Mr. James Greenwood presents himself once more in the character of 'one whose delight it is to do his humble endeavour towards exposing and extirpating social abuses and those hole-and-corner evils which afflict society.'"—SATURDAY REVIEW.

Crown 8vo, cloth extra, gilt, with Illustrations, 4s. 6d.

Guyot's Earth and Man;

or, Physical Geography in its Relation to the History of Mankind. With Additions by Professors AGASSIZ, PIERCE, and GRAY. 12 Maps and Engravings on Steel, some Coloured, and a copious Index.

Crown 8vo, cloth extra, 6s.

Hake's New Symbols :

Poems. By THOMAS GORDON HAKE.

"*The entire book breathes a pure and ennobling influence, shows welcome originality of idea and illustration, and yields the highest proof of imaginative faculty and mature power of expression.*"—ATHENÆUM.

Medium 8vo, cloth extra, gilt, with Illustrations, 7s. 6d.

Hall's (Mrs. S. C.) Sketches of Irish

Character. With numerous Illustrations on Steel and Wood by DANIEL MACLISE, Sir JOHN GILBERT, W. HARVEY, and G. CRUIKSHANK.

"*The Irish Sketches of this lady resemble Miss Mitford's beautiful English Sketches in 'Our Village,' but they are far more vigorous and picturesque and bright.*"—BLACKWOOD'S MAGAZINE.

Three Vols. royal 4to, cloth boards, £6 6s.

Historical Portraits ;

Upwards of 430 Engravings of Rare Prints. Comprising the Collections of RODD, RICHARDSON, CAULFIELD, &c. With Descriptive Text to every Plate, giving a brief outline of the most important Historical and Biographical Facts and Dates connected with each Portrait, and references to original Authorities.

Small 8vo, cloth limp, with Illustrations, 2s. 6d.

The House of Life ;

Human Physiology, with its Applications to the Preservation of Health. For use in Classes, and Popular Reading. With numerous Illustrations. By Mrs. F. FENWICK MILLER.

Two Vols. royal 8vo, with Coloured Frontispieces, cloth extra, £2 5s.

Hope's Costume of the Ancients.

Illustrated in upwards of 320 Outline Engravings, containing Representations of Egyptian, Greek, and Roman Habits and Dresses.

"*The substance of many expensive works, containing all that may be necessary to give to artists, and even to dramatic performers and to others engaged in classical representations, an idea of ancient costumes sufficiently ample to prevent their offending in their performances by gross and obvious blunders.*"

Crown 8vo, cloth extra, gilt, 7s. 6d.

Hood's (Thomas) Choice Works,

In Prose and Verse. Including the CREAM OF THE COMIC
ANNUALS. With Life of the Author, Portrait, and over Two
Hundred original Illustrations.

*" Not only does the volume include the better-known poems by the author, but
also what is happily described as ' the Cream of the Comic Annuals.' Such delicious
things as ' Don't you smell Fire ? ' ' The Parish Revolution,' and ' Huggins and
Duggins, will never want readers."*—GRAPHIC.

Crown 8vo, cloth extra, with Photographic Portrait, 6s.

Hood's (Tom) Poems, Humorous and

Pathetic. Edited, with a Memoir, by his Sister, FRANCES FREE-
LING BRODERIP.

*" There are many poems in the volume which the very best judge might well
mistake for his father's work."*—STANDARD.

Square crown 8vo, in a handsome and specially-designed binding,
gilt edges, 6s.

Hood's (Tom) From Nowhere to the

North Pole: A Noah's Arkæological Narrative. With 25 Illustrations by W. BRUNTON and E. C. BARNES.

*" The amusing letterpress is profusely interspersed with the jingling rhymes
which children love and learn so easily. Messrs. Brunton and Barnes do full
justice to the writer's meaning, and a pleasanter result of the harmonious co-
operation of author and artist could not be desired."*—TIMES.

Crown 8vo, cloth extra, gilt, 7s. 6d.

Hook's (Theodore) Choice Humorous

Works, including his Ludicrous Adventures, Bons-mots, Puns,
and Hoaxes. With a new Life of the Author, Portraits, Facsimiles, and Illustrations.

Demy 8vo, cloth extra, 12s. 6d.

Hueffer's The Troubadours:

A History of Provençal Life and Literature in the Middle Ages.
By FRANCIS HUEFFER.

Crown 8vo, cloth extra, 7s.

Horne's Orion ·

An Epic Poem, in Three Books. By RICHARD HENGIST HORNE.
Tenth Edition.

*" Orion will be admitted, by every man of genius, to be one of the noblest, if not
the very noblest, poetical work of the age. Its defects are trivial and conventional,
its beauties intrinsic and supreme."*—EDGAR ALLAN POE.

Crown 8vo, cloth extra, 7s. 6d.

Howell's The Conflicts of Capital and

Labour. Including Chapters on the History of Guilds; Trades Unions; Apprentices; Technical Education; Intimidation and Picketing; Restraints on Trade; Strikes—their Objects, Aims, and Results; Trade Councils; Arbitration; Co-operation; Friendly Societies; the Labour Laws, &c. By GEORGE HOWELL, Author of "A Handy Book of the Labour Laws," late Parliamentary Secretary to the Trades Unions of Great Britain.

Atlas folio, half morocco, gilt, £5 5s.

The Italian Masters ·

Autotype Facsimiles of Original Drawings in the British Museum. With Critical and Descriptive Notes, Biographical and Artistic, by J. COMYNS CARR.

" *This splendid volume.* *Mr. Carr's choice of examples has been dictated by wide knowledge and fine tact.* . *The majority have been reproduced with remarkable accuracy. Of the criticism which accompanies the drawings we have not hitherto spoken, but it is this which gives the book its special value.*"—PALL MALL GAZETTE.

Small 8vo, cloth extra, 6s.

Jeux d'Esprit,

Written and Spoken, of the Later Wits and Humourists. Collected and Edited by HENRY S. LEIGH.

" *This thoroughly congenial piece of work* *Mr. Leigh's claim to praise is threefold: he has performed the duty of taster with care and judgment; he has restored many stolen or strayed bons-mots to their rightful owners; and he has exercised his editorial functions delicately and sparingly.*"—DAILY TELEGRAPH.

Two Vols. 8vo, with 52 Illustrations and Maps, cloth extra, gilt, 14s.

Josephus's Complete Works.

Translated by WHISTON. ˙Containing both "The Antiquities of the Jews," and "The Wars of the Jews."

Small 8vo, cloth, full gilt, gilt edges, with Illustrations, 6s.

Kavanaghs' Pearl Fountain,

And other Fairy Stories. By BRIDGET and JULIA KAVANAGH. With Thirty Illustrations by J. MOYR SMITH.

" *Genuine new fairy stories of the old type, some of them as delightful as the best of Grimm's ' German Popular Stories.'* . . . *For the most part, the stories are downright, thorough-going fairy stories of the most admirable kind.* . *Mr. Moyr Smith's illustrations, too, are admirable. Look at that white rabbit. Anyone would see at the first glance that he is a rabbit with a mind, and a very uncommon mind too—that he is a fairy rabbit, and that he is posing as chief adviser to some one—without reading even a word of the story. Again, notice the fairy-like effect of the little picture of the fairy-bird ' Don't-forget-me,' flying away back into fairy-land. A more perfectly dream-like impression of fairy-land has hardly been given in any illustration of fairy tales within our knowledge.*"—SPECTATOR.

Small 8vo, cloth extra, 5*s*.

Lamb's Poetry for Children, and Prince

Dorus. Carefully reprinted from unique copies.

"*The quaint and delightful little book, over the recovery of which all the hearts of his lovers are yet warm with rejoicing.*"—Mr. SWINBURNE, in the ATHENÆUM.

Crown 8vo, cloth extra, gilt, with Portraits, 7*s*. 6*d*.

Lamb's Complete Works,

In Prose and Verse, reprinted from the Original Editions, with many Pieces hitherto unpublished. Edited, with Notes and Introduction, by R. H. SHEPHERD. With Two Portraits and Facsimile of a page of the "Essay on Roast Pig."

"*A complete edition of Lamb's writings, in prose and verse, has long been wanted, and is now supplied. The editor appears to have taken great pains to bring together Lamb's scattered contributions, and his collection contains a number of pieces which are now reproduced for the first time since their original appearance in various old periodicals.*"—SATURDAY REVIEW.

Crown 8vo, cloth extra, with numerous Illustrations, 10*s*. 6*d*.

Mary & Charles Lamb.

Their Poems, Letters, and Remains. With Reminiscences and Notes by W. CAREW HAZLITT. With HANCOCK'S Portrait of the Essayist, Facsimiles of the Title-pages of the rare First Editions of Lamb's and Coleridge's Works, and numerous Illustrations.

"*Very many passages will delight those fond of literary trifles; hardly any portion will fail in interest for lovers of Charles Lamb and his sister.*"—STANDARD.

Demy 8vo, cloth extra, with Maps and Illustrations, 18*s*.

Lamont's Yachting in the Arctic Seas;

or, Notes of Five Voyages of Sport and Discovery in the Neighbourhood of Spitzbergen and Novaya Zemlya. By JAMES LAMONT, F.R.G.S. With numerous full-page Illustrations by Dr. LIVESAY.

"*After wading through numberless volumes of icy fiction, concocted narrative, and spurious biography of Arctic voyagers, it is pleasant to meet with a real and genuine volume.   He shows much tact in recounting his adventures, and they are so interspersed with anecdotes and information as to make them anything but wearisome. . .   The book, as a whole, is the most important addition made to our Arctic literature for a long time.*"—ATHENÆUM.

Crown 8vo, cloth gilt, 7*s*. 6*d*.

Latter-Day Lyrics:

Poems of Sentiment and Reflection by Living Writers; selected and arranged, with Notes, by W. DAVENPORT ADAMS. With a Note "On some Old French Forms of Verse" by AUSTIN DOBSON.

Crown 8vo, cloth extra, 8s. 6d.

Lee's More Glimpses of the World Unseen.

Edited by the Rev. FREDERICK GEORGE LEE, D.C.L., Vicar of All Saints', Lambeth; Editor of "The Other World; or, Glimpses of the Supernatural," &c.

Crown 8vo, cloth extra, with Illustrations, 7s. 6d.

Life in London;

or, The History of Jerry Hawthorn and Corinthian Tom. With the whole of CRUIKSHANK'S Illustrations, in Colours, after the Originals.

Small crown 8vo, cloth extra, 4s. 6d.

Linton's Joshua Davidson,

Christian and Communist. By E. LYNN LINTON. Sixth Edition, with a New Preface.

Crown 8vo, cloth extra, with Illustrations, 7s. 6d.

Longfellow's Complete Prose Works.

Including "Outre Mer," "Hyperion," "Kavanagh," "The Poets and Poetry of Europe," and "Driftwood." With Portrait and Illustrations by VALENTINE BROMLEY.

Crown 8vo, cloth extra, gilt, with Illustrations, 7s. 6d.

Longfellow's Poetical Works.

Carefully Reprinted from the Original Editions. With numerous fine Illustrations on Steel and Wood.

" *Mr. Longfellow has for many years been the best known and the most read of American poets ; and his popularity is of the right kind, and rightly and fairly won. He has not stooped to catch attention by artifice, nor striven to force it by violence. His works have faced the test of parody and burlesque (which in these days is almost the common lot of writings of any mark), and have come off unharmed.*"—SATURDAY REVIEW.

THE FRASER PORTRAITS.—Demy 4to, cloth gilt and gilt edges, with 83 characteristic Portraits, 31s. 6d.

Maclise's Gallery of Illustrious Literary

Characters. With Notes by Dr. MAGINN. Edited, with copious Additional Notes, by WILLIAM BATES, B.A.

" *One of the most interesting volumes of this year's literature.*"—TIMES.

" *Deserves a place on every drawing-room table, and may not unfitly be removed from the drawing-room to the library.*"—SPECTATOR.

Crown 8vo, cloth extra, with Illustrations, 2s. 6d.

Madre Natura v. The Moloch of Fashion.

By LUKE LIMNER. With 32 Illustrations by the Author. FOURTH EDITION, revised and enlarged.

" *Agreeably written and amusingly illustrated. Common sense and erudition are brought to bear on the subjects discussed in it.*"—LANCET.

Handsomely printed in facsimile, price 5*s.*

Magna Charta.

An exact Facsimile of the Original Document in the British Museum, printed on fine plate paper, nearly 3 feet long by 2 feet wide, with the Arms and Seals of the Barons emblazoned in Gold and Colours.

*** A full Translation, with Notes, on a large sheet, 6*d.*

Crown 8vo, cloth extra, 7*s.* 6*d.*

Maid of Norway (The).

Translated from the German by Mrs. BIRKBECK. With Pen and Ink Sketches of Norwegian Scenery.

NEW COPYRIGHT WORK BY MARK TWAIN.

Post 8vo, illustrated boards, 2*s.*

An Idle Excursion, and other Papers.

By MARK TWAIN.

Small 8vo, cloth extra, with Illustrations, 7*s.* 6*d.*

Mark Twain's Adventures of Tom Sawyer.

With One Hundred Illustrations.

" A book to be read. There is a certain freshness and novelty about it, a practically romantic character, so to speak, which will make it very attractive."— SPECTATOR.

*** Also a Popular Edition, post 8vo, illustrated boards, 2s.

Crown 8vo, cloth extra, with Illustrations, 7*s.* 6*d.*

Mark Twain's Choice Works.

Revised and Corrected throughout by the Author. With Life, Portrait, and numerous Illustrations.

Post 8vo, illustrated boards, 2*s.*

Mark Twain's Pleasure Trip on the

Continent of Europe. ("The Innocents Abroad," and "The New Pilgrim's Progress.")

Two Vols. crown 8vo, cloth extra, 18*s.*

Marston's (Dr. Westland) Dramatic

and Poetical Works. Collected Library Edition.

" The ' Patrician's Daughter' is an oasis in the desert of modern dramatic literature, a real emanation of mind. We do not recollect any modern work in which states of thought are so freely developed, except the ' Torquato Tasso' of Goethe. The play is a work of art in the same sense that a play of Sophocles is a work of art ; it is one simple idea in a state of gradual development . . ' The Favourite of Fortune' is one of the most important additions to the stock of English prose comedy that has been made during the present century."— TIMES.

Crown 8vo, cloth extra, 8s.

Marston's (Philip B.) All in All:
Poems and Sonnets.

Crown 8vo, cloth extra, 8s.

Marston's (Philip B.) Song Tide,
And other Poems.   Second Edition.

Handsomely half-bound, India Proofs, royal folio, £10 ; Large Paper copies, Artists' India Proofs, elephant folio, £20.

Modern Art ·
A Series of superb Line Engravings, from the Works of Distinguished Painters of the English and Foreign Schools, selected from Galleries and Private Collections in Great Britain.   With descriptive Text by JAMES DAFFORNE.

Crown 8vo, cloth extra, gilt, gilt edges, 7s. 6d.

Muses of Mayfair :
Vers de Société of the Nineteenth Century.   Including Selections from TENNYSON, BROWNING, SWINBURNE, ROSSETTI, JEAN INGELOW, LOCKER, INGOLDSBY, HOOD, LYTTON, C. S. C.; LANDOR, AUSTIN DOBSON, &c.   Edited by H. C. PENNELL.

Crown 8vo, cloth extra, 6s., a New and Cheaper Edition of

The New Republic;
or, Culture, Faith, and Philosophy in an English Country House. By W. H. MALLOCK.

"*The great charm of the book lies in the clever and artistic way the dialogue is managed, and the diverse and various expedients by which, whilst the love of thought on every page is kept at a high pitch, it never loses its realistic aspect. It is giving high praise to a work of this sort to say that it absolutely needs to be taken as a whole, and that disjointed extracts here and there would entirely fail to convey any idea of the artistic unity, the careful and conscientious sequence of what is evidently the brilliant outcome of much patient thought and study. . Enough has now been said to recommend these volumes to any reader who desires something above the usual novel, something which will open up lanes of thought in his own mind, and insensibly introduce a higher standard into his daily life. . Here is novelty indeed, as well as originality, and to anyone who can appreciate or understand 'The New Republic,' it cannot fail to be a rare treat.*"—OBSERVER.

*** The ORIGINAL EDITION, *in Two Vols. crown 8vo,* 21s., *may also be had.*

Square 8vo, cloth extra, with numerous Illustrations, 9s.

North Italian Folk.
By Mrs. COMYNS CARR.   With Illustrations by RANDOLPH CALDECOTT.

MOORE'S HITHERTO UNCOLLECTED WRITINGS.
Crown 8vo, cloth extra, with Frontispiece, 9s.

Prose and Verse—Humorous, Satirical,

and Sentimental—by THOMAS MOORE. Including Suppressed
Passages from the Memoirs of Lord Byron. Chiefly from the
Author's MSS., and all hitherto Inedited and Uncollected. Edited,
with Notes, by RICHARD HERNE SHEPHERD.

"*Hitherto Thomas Moore has been mostly regarded as one of the lighter writers
merely—a sentimental poet par excellence, in whom the 'rapture of love and of
wine' determined him strictly to certain modes of sympathy and of utterance, and
these to a large extent of a slightly artificial character. This volume will serve to
show him in other, and certainly as attractive, aspects, while, at the same time,
enabling us to a considerable extent to see how faithfully he developed himself on
the poetical or fanciful side. . This is a book which claims, as it ought to
obtain, various classes of readers, and we trust that the very mixed elements of
interest in it may not conflict with its obtaining them. For the lightest reader
there is much to enjoy; for the most thoughtful something to ponder over; and the
thanks of both are due to editor and publisher alike.*"—NONCONFORMIST.

Crown 8vo, cloth extra, with Vignette Portraits, price 6s. per Vol.

The Old Dramatists:

Ben Jonson's Works.
With Notes, Critical and Explanatory, and a Biographical Memoir by WILLIAM GIFFORD. Edited by Col. CUNNINGHAM. Three Vols.

Chapman's Works.
Now First Collected. Complete in Three Vols. Vol. I. contains the Plays complete, including the doubtful ones; Vol. II. the Poems and Minor Translations, with an Introductory Essay by

ALGERNON CHARLES SWINBURNE; Vol. III. the Translations of the Iliad and Odyssey.

Marlowe's Works.
Including his Translations. Edited, with Notes and Introduction, by Col. CUNNINGHAM. One Vol.

Massinger's Plays.
From the Text of WILLIAM GIFFORD. With the addition of the Tragedy of "Believe as you List." Edited by Col. CUNNINGHAM. One Vol.

Fcap. 8vo, cloth extra, 6s.

O'Shaughnessy's (Arthur) An Epic of
Women, and other Poems. Second Edition.

Crown 8vo, cloth extra, 10s. 6d.

O'Shaughnessy's Lays of France.
(Founded on the "Lays of Marie.") Second Edition.

Fcap. 8vo, cloth extra, 7s. 6d.

O'Shaughnessy's Music and Moonlight:
Poems and Songs.

Crown 8vo, illustrated boards, with numerous Plates, 2s. 6d.

Old Point Lace, and How to Copy and
Imitate It. By DAISY WATERHOUSE HAWKINS. With 17
Illustrations by the Author.

Crown 8vo, carefully printed on creamy paper, and tastefully
bound in cloth for the Library, price 6s. each.

The Piccadilly Novels:
Popular Stories by the Best Authors.

Antonina. By WILKIE COLLINS.
Illustrated by Sir J. GILBERT and ALFRED CONCANEN.

Basil. By WILKIE COLLINS.
Illustrated by Sir JOHN GILBERT and J. MAHONEY.

Hide and Seek. By WILKIE COLLINS.
Illustrated by Sir JOHN GILBERT and J. MAHONEY.

The Dead Secret. By WILKIE COLLINS.
Illustrated by Sir JOHN GILBERT and H. FURNISS.

Queen of Hearts. By WILKIE COLLINS.
Illustrated by Sir J. GILBERT and A. CONCANEN.

My Miscellanies. By WILKIE COLLINS.
With Steel Portrait, and Illustrations by A. CONCANEN.

The Woman in White. By WILKIE COLLINS.
Illustrated by Sir J. GILBERT and F. A. FRASER.

The Moonstone. By WILKIE COLLINS.
Illustrated by G. DU MAURIER and F. A. FRASER.

Man and Wife. By WILKIE COLLINS.
Illustrated by WILLIAM SMALL.

Poor Miss Finch. By WILKIE COLLINS.
Illustrated by G. DU MAURIER and EDWARD HUGHES.

Miss or Mrs.? By WILKIE COLLINS.
Illustrated by S. L. FILDES and HENRY WOODS.

The New Magdalen. By WILKIE COLLINS.
Illustrated by G. DU MAURIER and C. S. RANDS.

The Frozen Deep. By WILKIE COLLINS.
Illustrated by G. DU MAURIER and J. MAHONEY.

The Law and the Lady. By WILKIE COLLINS.
Illustrated by S. L. FILDES and SYDNEY HALL.

The Two Destinies. By WILKIE COLLINS.

*** Also a **POPULAR EDITION of WILKIE COLLINS'S
NOVELS**, post 8vo, illustrated boards, 2s. each.

Felicia. By M. BETHAM-EDWARDS.
With a Frontispiece by W. BOWLES.

"*A noble novel. Its teaching is elevated, its story is sympathetic, and the kind
of feeling its perusal leaves behind is that more ordinarily derived from music or
poetry than from prose fiction. Few works in modern fiction stand as high in our
estimation as this.*"—SUNDAY TIMES.

Olympia. By R. E. FRANCILLON.

THE PICCADILLY NOVELS—*continued.*

Under the Greenwood Tree.   By THOMAS HARDY.

Fated to be Free.   By JEAN INGELOW.

The Queen of Connaught.   By HARRIETT JAY.

The Dark Colleen.   By HARRIETT JAY.

" *A novel which possesses the rare and valuable quality of novelty. . . . The scenery will be strange to most readers, and in many passages the aspects of Nature are very cleverly described. Moreover, the book is a study of a very curious and interesting state of society. A novel which no novel-reader should miss, and which people who generally shun novels may enjoy.*"—SATURDAY REVIEW.

Patricia Kemball.   By E. LYNN LINTON.

With Frontispiece by G. DU MAURIER.

" *Displays genuine humour, as well as keen social observation. Enough graphic portraiture and witty observation to furnish materials for half-a-dozen novels of the ordinary kind.*"—SATURDAY REVIEW.

The Atonement of Leam Dundas.   By E. LYNN LINTON.

With a Frontispiece by HENRY WOODS.

" *In her narrowness and her depth, in her boundless loyalty, her self-forgetting passion, that exclusiveness of love which is akin to cruelty, and the fierce humility which is vicarious pride, Leam Dundas is a striking figure. In one quality the authoress has in some measure surpassed herself.*"—PALL MALL GAZ.

The Waterdale Neighbours.   By JUSTIN MCCARTHY.

My Enemy's Daughter.   By JUSTIN MCCARTHY.

Linley Rochford.   By JUSTIN MCCARTHY.

A Fair Saxon.   By JUSTIN MCCARTHY.

Dear Lady Disdain.   By JUSTIN MCCARTHY.

The Evil Eye, and other Stories. By KATHARINE S. MACQUOID.

Illustrated by THOMAS R. MACQUOID and PERCY MACQUOID.

" *Cameos delicately, if not very minutely or vividly, wrought, and quite finished enough to give a pleasurable sense of artistic ease and faculty. A word of commendation is merited by the illustrations.*"—ACADEMY.

Number Seventeen.   By HENRY KINGSLEY.

Oakshott Castle.   By HENRY KINGSLEY.

With a Frontispiece by SHIRLEY HODSON.

" *A brisk and clear north wind of sentiment—sentiment that braces instead of enervating—blows through all his works, and makes all their readers at once healthier and more glad.*"—SPECTATOR.

Open! Sesame!   By FLORENCE MARRYAT.

Illustrated by F. A. FRASER.

" *A story which arouses and sustains the reader's interest to a higher degree than, perhaps, any of its author's former works.*"—GRAPHIC.

Whiteladies.   By Mrs. OLIPHANT.

With Illustrations by A. HOPKINS and H. WOODS.

" *A pleasant and readable book, written with practical ease and grace.*"—TIMES.

The Best of Husbands.   By JAMES PAYN.

Illustrated by J. MOYR SMITH.

Fallen Fortunes.   By JAMES PAYN.

The Piccadilly Novels—*continued.*

Halves.　　　　　　　　　　　By James Payn.
　With a Frontispiece by J. Mahoney.

Walter's Word.　　　　　　　By James Payn.
　Illustrated by J. Moyr Smith.

What he Cost her.　　　　　　By James Payn.

"*His novels are always commendable in the sense of art. They also possess another distinct claim to our liking: the girls in them are remarkably charming and true to nature, as most people, we believe, have the good fortune to observe nature represented by girls.*"—Spectator.

Her Mother's Darling.　　　　By Mrs. J. H. Riddell.

The Way we Live Now.　　　　By Anthony Trollope.
　With Illustrations.

The American Senator.　　　　By Anthony Trollope.

"*Mr. Trollope has a true artist's idea of tone, of colour, of harmony: his pictures are one, and seldom out of drawing; he never strains after effect, is fidelity itself in expressing English life, is never guilty of caricature.*"—Fortnightly Review.

Diamond Cut Diamond.　　　By T. A. Trollope.

"*Full of life, of interest, of close observation, and sympathy. . . . When Mr. Trollope paints a scene it is sure to be a scene worth painting.*"—Saturday Review.

Bound to the Wheel.　　　　By John Saunders.

Guy Waterman.　　　　　　By John Saunders.

One Against the World.　　　By John Saunders.

The Lion in the Path.　　　　By John Saunders.

"*A carefully written and beautiful story—a story of goodness and truth, which is yet as interesting as though it dealt with the opposite qualities. . . . The author of this really clever story has been at great pains to work out all its details with elaborate conscientiousness, and the result is a very vivid picture of the ways of life and habits of thought of a hundred and fifty years ago. Certainly a very interesting book.*"—Times.

Ready-Money Mortiboy.　　By W. Besant and James Rice.

My Little Girl.　　　　　　By W. Besant and James Rice.

The Case of Mr. Lucraft.　　By W. Besant and James Rice.

This Son of Vulcan.　　　　By W. Besant and James Rice.

With Harp and Crown.　　　By W. Besant and James Rice.

The Golden Butterfly.　　　By W. Besant and James Rice.
　With a Frontispiece by F. S. Walker.

"' *The Golden Butterfly* ' *will certainly add to the happiness of mankind, for we defy anybody to read it with a gloomy countenance.*"—Times.

NEW NOVEL BY JUSTIN M^CCARTHY
Two vols. 8vo, cloth extra, Illustrated, 21*s*., the SECOND EDITION of

Miss Misanthrope.

By JUSTIN MCCARTHY, Author of "Dear Lady Disdain," &c.
With 12 Illustrations by ARTHUR HOPKINS.

"*In 'Miss Misanthrope' Mr. McCarthy has added a new and delightful portrait to his gallery of Englishwomen.   It is a novel which may be sipped like choice wine ; it is one to linger over and ponder ; to be enjoyed like fine, sweet air, or good company, for it is pervaded by a perfume of honesty and humour, of high feeling, of kindly penetrating humour, of good sense, and wide knowledge of the world, of a mind richly cultivated and amply stored.   There is scarcely a page in these volumes in which we do not find some fine remark or felicitous reflection of piercing, yet gentle and indulgent irony.*"—DAILY NEWS.

MRS. LINTON'S NEW NOVEL.
Two Vols. 8vo, cloth extra, Illustrated, 21*s*., the SECOND EDITION of

The World Well Lost.

By E. LYNN LINTON, Author of "Patricia Kemball," &c. With
12 Illustrations by HENRY FRENCH and J. LAWSON.

"*We are inclined to think that in this novel Mrs. Lynn Linton has reached a higher artistic mark than in any former one.*"—NONCONFORMIST.
"*If Mrs. Linton had not already won a place among our foremost living novelists, she would have been entitled to it by her latest work of fiction—a book of singularly high and varied merit.   The story rivets the attention of the reader at the outset, and holds him absorbed until the close.*"—SCOTSMAN.

NEW NOVEL BY THE AUTHOR OF "JULIET'S GUARDIAN."
Three Vols., crown 8vo, 31*s*. 6*d*.

Deceivers Ever.

By Mrs. H. LOVETT CAMERON.

Crown 8vo, red cloth, extra, 5*s*. each.

Ouida's Novels.—Uniform Edition.

Folle Farine.	By OUIDA.	*Pascarel.*	By OUIDA.
Idalia.	By OUIDA.	*Puck.*	By OUIDA.
Chandos.	By OUIDA.	*Dog of Flanders.*	By OUIDA.
Under Two Flags.	By OUIDA.	*Strathmore.*	By OUIDA.
Tricotrin.	By OUIDA.	*Two Wooden Shoes*	By OUIDA.
Cecil Castlemaine's Gage.	By OUIDA.	*Signa.*	By OUIDA.
Held in Bondage.	By OUIDA.	*In a Winter City.*	By OUIDA.
		Ariadnê.	By OUIDA.

NEW NOVEL BY MR. JAMES GRANT.
Shortly, Three Vols., crown 8vo, 31*s*. 6*d*.

The Lord Hermitage.

By JAMES GRANT, Author of "The Romance of War," &c.

Post 8vo, illustrated boards, 2s. each.

Cheap Editions of Popular Novels.

[WILKIE COLLINS' NOVELS may also be had in cloth limp at 2s. 6d. See, too, the PICCADILLY NOVELS, *for Library Editions.*]

Under the Greenwood Tree.   By THOMAS HARDY

Ready-Money Mortiboy. By WALTER BESANT and JAMES RICE.

The Golden Butterfly.   By Authors of " Ready-Money Mortiboy."

This Son of Vulcan. By the Authors of " Ready-Money Mortiboy."

My Little Girl.   By the Authors of " Ready-Money Mortiboy."

The Case of Mr. Lucraft. Authors of " Ready-Money Mortiboy."

With Harp and Crown.   Authors of " Ready-Money Mortiboy."

The Woman in White.   By WILKIE COLLINS.

Antonina.   By WILKIE COLLINS.

Basil.   By WILKIE COLLINS.

Hide and Seek.   By WILKIE COLLINS.

The Dead Secret.   By WILKIE COLLINS.

The Queen of Hearts.   By WILKIE COLLINS.

My Miscellanies.   By WILKIE COLLINS.

The Moonstone.   By WILKIE COLLINS.

Man and Wife.   By WILKIE COLLINS.

Poor Miss Finch.   By WILKIE COLLINS.

Miss or Mrs. ?   By WILKIE COLLINS.

The New Magdalen.   By WILKIE COLLINS.

The Frozen Deep.   By WILKIE COLLINS.

The Law and the Lady.   By WILKIE COLLINS.

Gaslight and Daylight.   By GEORGE AUGUSTUS SALA.

The Waterdale Neighbours.   By JUSTIN McCARTHY.

My Enemy's Daughter.   By JUSTIN McCARTHY.

Linley Rochford.   By JUSTIN McCARTHY.

A Fair Saxon.   By JUSTIN McCARTHY.

Dear Lady Disdain.   By JUSTIN McCARTHY.

An Idle Excursion.   By MARK TWAIN.

The Adventures of Tom Sawyer.   By MARK TWAIN.

A Pleasure Trip on the Continent of Europe. M. TWAIN.

Oakshott Castle.   By HENRY KINGSLEY.

Bound to the Wheel.   By JOHN SAUNDERS.

Guy Waterman.   By JOHN SAUNDERS.

One Against the World.   By JOHN SAUNDERS.

The Lion in the Path.   By JOHN and KATHERINE SAUNDERS.

Surly Tim.   By the Author of " That Lass o' Lowrie's,"

Two Vols. 8vo, cloth extra, with Illustrations, 10*s*. 6*d*.

Plutarch's Lives of Illustrious Men.

Translated from the Greek, with Notes Critical and Historical,
and a Life of Plutarch, by JOHN and WILLIAM LANGHORNE.
New Edition, with Medallion Portraits.

Crown 8vo, cloth extra, with Portrait and Illustrations, 7*s*. 6*d*.

Poe's Choice Prose and Poetical Works.

With BAUDELAIRE'S "Essay."

" *Poe stands as much alone among verse-writers as Salvator Rosa among
painters.*"—SPECTATOR.

Crown 8vo, cloth extra, Illustrated, 7*s*. 6*d*.

The Life of Edgar Allan Poe.

By WILLIAM F. GILL. With numerous Illustrations and
Facsimiles.

Small 8vo, cloth extra, with Illustrations, 3*s*. 6*d*.

The Prince of Argolis :

A Story of the Old Greek Fairy Time. By J. MOYR SMITH.
With 130 Illustrations by the Author.

Demy 8vo, cloth extra, 12*s*. 6*d*.

Proctor's Myths and Marvels of Astro-

nomy. By RICHARD A. PROCTOR, Author of "Other Worlds
than Ours," &c.

" *Mr. Proctor, who is well and widely known for his faculty of popularising the
latest results of the science of which he is a master, has brought together in these
fascinating chapters a curious collection of popular beliefs concerning divination by
the stars, the influences of the moon, the destination of the comets, the constellation
figures, and the habitation of other worlds than ours.*"—DAILY NEWS.

" *The reader who begins this charming volume—a dozen chapters to as many
instances of erroneous observation or superstitious credulity—will hardly fail to
peruse it to the end.*"—GRAPHIC.

Crown 8vo, cloth extra, 5*s*.

Prometheus the Fire-Giver.

An attempted Restoration of the Lost First Part of the Trilogy
of Æschylus.

" *Another illustration of that classical revival which is due in no small degree
to the influence of Mr. Swinburne. . Much really fine writing, and much
appreciation of the Æschylean spirit.*"— HOME NEWS.

" *Well written in parts—soft, spirited, and vigorous, according to requirement.*"
—ILLUSTRATED LONDON NEWS.

Crown 8vo, cloth extra, with Portrait and Facsimile, 12s. 6d.

The Final Reliques of Father Prout.

Collected and Edited, from MSS. supplied by the family of the Rev. FRANCIS MAHONY, by BLANCHARD JERROLD.

In Two Series, small 4to, blue and gold, gilt edges, 6s. each.

Puniana;

or, Thoughts Wise and Other-Why's. A New Collection of Riddles, Conundrums, Jokes, Sells, &c. In Two Series, each containing 3000 of the best Riddles, 10,000 most outrageous Puns, and upwards of Fifty beautifully executed Drawings by the Editor, the Hon. HUGH ROWLEY. Each Series is Complete in itself.

" A witty, droll, and most amusing work, profusely and elegantly illustrated." —STANDARD.

Crown 8vo, cloth extra, gilt, 7s. 6d.

The Pursuivant of Arms;

or, Heraldry founded upon Facts. A Popular Guide to the Science of Heraldry. By J. R. PLANCHÉ, Esq., Somerset Herald. With Coloured Frontispiece, Plates, and 200 Illustrations.

Crown 8vo, cloth extra, 7s. 6d.

Rabelais' Works.

Faithfully Translated from the French, with variorum Notes, and numerous Characteristic Illustrations by GUSTAVE DORÉ.

Crown 8vo, cloth gilt, with numerous Illustrations, and a beautifully executed Chart of the various Spectra, 7s. 6d., a New Edition of

Rambosson's Astronomy.

By J. RAMBOSSON, Laureate of the Institute of France. Translated by C. B. PITMAN. Profusely Illustrated.

Crown 8vo, cloth extra, 6s.

Red-Spinner's By Stream and Sea :

A Book for Wanderers and Anglers. By WILLIAM SENIOR (RED-SPINNER).

" Mr. Senior has long been known as an interesting and original essayist. He is a keen observer, a confessed lover of ' the gentle sport,' and combines with a fine picturesque touch a quaint and efficient humour. All these qualities come out in a most attractive manner in this delightful volume. . It is pre-eminently a bright and breezy book, full of nature and odd out-of-the-way references. . We can conceive of no better book for the holiday tour or the seaside." —NONCONFORMIST.

" Very delightful reading; just the sort of book which an angler or a rambler will be glad to have in the side pocket of his jacket. Altogether, ' By Stream and Sea ' is one of the best books of its kind which we have come across for many a long day." —OXFORD UNIVERSITY HERALD.

Handsomely printed, price 5*s*.

The Roll of Battle Abbey ;

or, A List of the Principal Warriors who came over from Nor-
mandy with William the Conqueror, and Settled in this Country,
A.D. 1066–7.   Printed on fine plate paper, nearly three feet by
two, with the principal Arms emblazoned in Gold and Colours.

In 4to, very handsomely printed, extra gold cloth, 12*s*.

The Roll of Caerlaverock.

The Oldest Heraldic Roll ; including the Original Anglo-Norman
Poem, and an English Translation of the MS. in the British
Museum.   By THOMAS WRIGHT, M.A.   The Arms emblazoned
in Gold and Colours.

Crown 8vo, cloth extra, 7*s*. 6*d*.

Memoirs of the Sanson Family ·

Seven Generations of Executioners.   By HENRI SANSON.   Translated from the French, with Introduction, by CAMILLE BARRÈRE.
*"A faithful translation of this curious work, which will certainly repay perusal
—not on the ground of its being full of horrors, for the original author seems to
be rather ashamed of the technical aspect of his profession, and is commendably
reticent as to its details, but because it contains a lucid account of the most notable
causes célèbres from the time of Louis XIV. to a period within the memory of
persons still living.   .   Can scarcely fail to be extremely entertaining."—*
DAILY TELEGRAPH.

Crown 8vo, cloth extra, profusely Illustrated, 4*s*, 6*d*. each.

The "Secret Out" Series.

The Art of Amusing :
A Collection of Graceful Arts,
Games, Tricks, Puzzles, and Cha-
rades. By FRANK BELLEW. 300
Illustrations.

Hanky-Panky :
Very Easy Tricks, Very Difficult
Tricks, White Magic, Sleight of
Hand. Edited by W. H. CRE-
MER. 200 Illustrations.

Magician's Own Book :
Performances with Cups and Balls,
Eggs, Hats, Handkerchiefs, &c.
All from Actual Experience.
Edited by W. H. CREMER. 200
Illustrations.

Magic No Mystery :
Tricks with Cards, Dice, Balls,
&c., with fully descriptive Directions ; the Art of Secret Writing ;
the Training of Performing Animals, &c.   With Coloured Frontispiece and many Illustrations.

The Merry Circle :
A Book of New Intellectual Games
and Amusements.   By CLARA
BELLEW.   Many Illustrations.

The Secret Out :
One Thousand Tricks with Cards,
and other Recreations ; with Entertaining Experiments in Drawing-room or "White Magic." By
W. H. CREMER. 300 Engravings.

NEW VOLUME OF THE "SECRET OUT" SERIES.
Crown 8vo, cloth extra, with numerous Plates, 4*s*. 6*d*.

The Pyrotechnist's Treasury ;

or, Complete Art of Making Fireworks.   By THOMAS KENTISH

In reduced facsimile, small 8vo, half Roxburghe, 10s. 6d.

The First Folio Shakespeare.

Mr. WILLIAM SHAKESPEARE's Comedies, Histories, and Tragedies. Published according to the true Originall Copies. London,
Printed by ISAAC IAGGARD and ED. BLOUNT, 1623.—An exact
Reproduction of the extremely rare original, in reduced facsimile
by a photographic process—ensuring the strictest accuracy in every
detail. *A full Prospectus will be sent upon application.*

"*To Messrs. Chatto and Windus belongs the merit of having done more to
facilitate the critical study of the text of our great dramatist than all the Shakespeare clubs and societies put together. A complete facsimile of the celebrated
First Folio edition of 1623 for half-a-guinea is at once a miracle of cheapness and
enterprise. Being in a reduced form, the type is necessarily rather diminutive,
but it is as distinct as in a genuine copy of the original, and will be found to be as
useful and far more handy to the student than the latter.*"—ATHENÆUM.

Post 8vo, with Illustrations, cloth extra, gilt edges, 18s.

The Lansdowne Shakespeare.

Beautifully printed in red and black, in small but very clear type.
With engraved facsimile of DROESHOUT's Portrait, and 37 beautiful
Steel Plates, after STOTHARD.

Two Vols. crown 8vo, cloth extra, 18s.

The School of Shakspere.

Including "The Life and Death of Captain Thomas Stukeley,"
with a New Life of Stucley, from Unpublished Sources ; "No-
body and Somebody," "Histriomastix," "The Prodigal Son,"
"Jack Drum's Entertainement," "A Warning for Fair Women,"
with Reprints of the Accounts of the Murder ; and "Faire Em."
Edited, with Introductions and Notes, and an Account of Robert
Green and his Quarrels with Shakspere, by RICHARD SIMPSON,
B.A., Author of "The Philosophy of Shakspere's Sonnets," "The
Life of Campion," &c. With an Introduction by F. J. FURNIVALL.

Crown 8vo, cloth extra, with Illustrations, 7s. 6d.

Signboards :

Their History. With Anecdotes of Famous Taverns and Remarkable Characters. By JACOB LARWOOD and JOHN CAMDEN
HOTTEN. With nearly 100 Illustrations.

"*Even if we were ever so maliciously inclined, we could not pick out all Messrs.
Larwood and Hotten's plums, because the good things are so numerous as to defy
the most wholesale depredation.*"—TIMES.

Exquisitely printed in miniature, cloth extra, gilt edges, 2s. 6d.

The Smoker's Text-Book.

By J. HAMER, F.R.S.L.

Crown 8vo, cloth extra, gilt, with 10 full-page Tinted
Illustrations, 7s. 6d.

Sheridan's Complete Works,

with Life and Anecdotes. Including his Dramatic Writings,
printed from the Original Editions, his Works in Prose and
Poetry, Translations, Speeches, Jokes, Puns, &c. ; with a Collection of Sheridaniana.

"*The editor has brought together within a manageable compass not only the
seven plays by which Sheridan is best known, but a collection also of his poetical
pieces which are less familiar to the public, sketches of unfinished dramas, selections
from his reported witticisms, and extracts from his principal speeches. To these
is prefixed a short but well-written memoir, giving the chief facts in Sheridan's
literary and political career ; so that, with this volume in his hand, the student
may consider himself tolerably well furnished with all that is necessary for a
general comprehension of the subject of it.*"— PALL MALL GAZETTE.

Crown 8vo, cloth extra, gilt, 6s. 6d.

The Slang Dictionary.

Etymological, Historical, and Anecdotal. An ENTIRELY NEW
EDITION, revised throughout, and considerably Enlarged.

"*We are glad to see the Slang Dictionary reprinted and enlarged. From a high
scientific point of view this book is not to be despised. Of course it cannot fail to
be amusing also. It contains the very vocabulary of unrestrained humour, and
oddity, and grotesqueness. In a word, it provides valuable material both for the
student of language and the student of human nature.*"—ACADEMY.

Crown 4to, uniform with "Chaucer for Children," with Coloured
Illustrations, cloth gilt, 10s. 6d.

Spenser for Children.

By M. H. TOWRY. With Illustrations in Colours by WALTER
J. MORGAN.

"*In these transcripts the writer has endeavoured to preserve the thoughts and
language of Spenser, while presenting the tales in a simple and continuous form.
The work of one of our greatest poets has not been approached in an irreverent
spirit, nor with any intention of vulgarizing his fictions by relating them in a
familiar and mocking manner—a style too often supposed to be that most attractive
to the young.*"

Imperial 4to, containing 150 beautifully-finished full-page Engravings
and Nine Vignettes, all tinted, and some illuminated in gold and
colours, half-morocco, £9 9s.

Stothard's Monumental Effigies of Great

Britain. With Historical Description and Introduction by JOHN
KEMPE, F.S.A. A NEW EDITION, with a large body of Additional
Notes by JOHN HEWITT.

*** A few Large Paper copies, royal folio, with the arms illuminated
in gold and colours, and the plates very carefully finished in body-colours,
heightened with gold in the very finest style, half-morocco, £15 15s.

Crown 8vo, cloth extra, 9s.
Stedman's Victorian Poets

Critical Essays. By EDMUND CLARENCE STEDMAN.

" We ought to be thankful to those who do critical work with competent skill and understanding, with honesty of purpose, and with diligence and thoroughness of execution. And Mr. Stedman, having chosen to work in this line, deserves the thanks of English scholars by these qualities and by something more ; he is faithful, studious, and discerning."—SATURDAY REVIEW.

Large 8vo, half-Roxburghe, with Illustrations, price 9s.
Stow's Survey of London.

Edited by W. J. THOMS, F.S.A. A New Edition, with Copper-plate Illustrations.

Crown 8vo, cloth extra, with Illustrations, 7s. 6d.
Swift's Choice Works,

in Prose and Verse. With Memoir, Portrait, and Facsimiles of the Maps in the Original Edition of " Gulliver's Travels."

" The ' Tale of a Tub ' is, in my apprehension, the masterpiece of Swift ; certainly Rabelais has nothing superior, even in invention, nor anything so condensed, so pointed, so full of real meaning, of biting satire, of felicitous analogy. The ' Battle of the Books ' is such an improvement on the similar combat in the Lutrin, that we can hardly own it as an imitation."—HALLAM.

" Swift's reputation as a poet has been in a manner obscured by the greater splendour, by the natural force and inventive genius, of his prose writings ; but, if he had never written either the ' Tale of a Tub ' or ' Gulliver's Travels,' his name merely as a poet would have come down to us, and have gone down to posterity, with well-earned honours."—HAZLITT.

Mr Swinburne's Works.

The Queen Mother and Rosamond. Fcap. 8vo, 5s.

Atalanta in Calydon.
A New Edition. Crown 8vo, 6s.

Chastelard.
A Tragedy. Fcap. 8vo, 7s.

Poems and Ballads.
Fcap. 8vo, 9s.

Notes on "Poems and Ballads." 8vo, 1s.

William Blake :
A Critical Essay. With Facsimile Paintings. Demy 8vo, 16s.

Songs before Sunrise.
Crown 8vo, 10s. 6d.

Bothwell :
A Tragedy. Two Vols. crown 8vo, 12s. 6d.

George Chapman :
An Essay. Crown 8vo, 7s.

Songs of Two Nations.
Crown 8vo, 6s.

Essays and Studies.
Crown 8vo, 12s.

Erechtheus :
A Tragedy. Crown 8vo, 6s.

Note of an English Republican on the Muscovite Crusade. 8vo, 1s.

A Note on Charlotte Brontë.
Crown 8vo, 6s.

MR. SWINBURNE'S NEW WORK.

Crown 8vo, cloth extra, 9s.

Poems and Ballads. SECOND SERIES.

By ALGERNON CHARLES SWINBURNE.

. Also in fcap. 8vo, at same price, uniform with the FIRST SERIES.

Fcap. 8vo, cloth extra, 3s. 6d.

Rossetti's (W. M.) Criticism upon Swin-

burne's " Poems and Ballads."

Crown 8vo, cloth extra, with Illustrations, 7s. 6d.

Strutt's Sports and Pastimes of the

People of England ; including the Rural and Domestic Recreations, May Games, Mummeries, Shows, Processions, Pageants,
and Pompous Spectacles, from the Earliest Period to the Present
Time.   With 140 Illustrations.   Edited by WILLIAM HONE.

. A few Large Paper Copies, with an extra set of Copperplate
Illustrations, carefully Coloured by Hand, from the Originals, 50s.

Medium 8vo, cloth extra, with Illustrations, 7s. 6d.

Dr. Syntax's Three Tours,

in Search of the Picturesque, in Search of Consolation, and in
Search of a Wife.   With the whole of ROWLANDSON's droll page
Illustrations, in Colours, and Life of the Author by J. C. HOTTEN.

Large post 8vo, cloth, full gilt, gilt top, with Illustrations, 12s. 6d.

Thackerayana :

Notes and Anecdotes   Illustrated by a profusion of Sketches by
WILLIAM MAKEPEACE THACKERAY, depicting Humorous Incidents in his School-life, and Favourite Characters in the books of
his everyday reading.   With Hundreds of Wood Engravings and
Five Coloured Plates, from Mr. Thackeray's Original Drawings.

" *It would have been a real loss to bibliographical literature had copyright
difficulties deprived the general public of this very amusing collection. One of
Thackeray's habits, from his schoolboy days, was to ornament the margins and
blank pages of the books he had in use with caricature illustrations of their
contents. This gave special value to the sale of his library, and is almost cause
for regret that it could not have been preserved in its integrity. Thackeray's
place in literature is eminent enough to have made this an interest to future
generations. The anonymous editor has done the best that he could to compensate for the lack of this. It is an admirable addendum, not only to his collected
works, but also to any memoir of him that has been, or that is likely to be,
written.*"—BRITISH QUARTERLY REVIEW.

Crown 8vo, cloth extra, gilt edges, with Illustrations, 7s. 6d.

Thomson's Seasons and Castle of In-

dolence.   With a Biographical and Critical Introduction by ALLAN
CUNNINGHAM, and over 50 fine Illustrations on Steel and Wood.

Two Vols. crown 8vo, cloth boards, 18*s.*; Large Paper copies
(only 50 printed), 36*s.*

Cyril Tourneur's Collected Works,

Plays and Poems. Edited, with Critical Introduction and Notes,
by J. CHURTON COLLINS.

Crown 8vo, cloth extra, with Coloured Illustrations, 7*s.* 6*d.*

J. M. W. Turner's Life and Correspond-

ence. Founded upon Letters and Papers furnished by his Friends
and fellow Academicians. By WALTER THORNBURY. A New
Edition, considerably Enlarged. With numerous Illustrations
in Colours, facsimiled from Turner's original Drawings.

Taine's History of English Literature.

Translated by HENRY VAN LAUN. Four Vols. small 8vo, 30*s.*

*** Also a New and Cheaper Edition, in Two Vols., crown
8vo, cloth extra, 15*s.*

Small 8vo, cloth gilt, with Portrait, 6*s.*

Thoreau : His Life and Aims.

A Study. By H. A. PAGE, Author of "The Life of Thomas
De Quincey," &c.

EXTRACT FROM PREFACE.—"*The nature-instinct in Thoreau was so strong
that, as I believe, it may even do something to aid in the interpretation of certain
phenomena of so distant a period as the Middle Age. I see a kind of real likeness
between this so-called ' Stoic' of America, with his unaffected love for the slave, his
wonderful sympathies and attractions for the lower creatures, his simplicities,
and his liking for the labour of the hand, and that St. Francis whose life has
recently been made fresh and real to us by the skilful pen of Mrs. Oliphant. All I
claim for Thoreau is a disinterested and not a one-sided and prejudiced hearing.'*

Crown 8vo, cloth extra, with Illustrations, 7*s.* 6*d.*

Timbs' Clubs and Club Life in London.

With Anecdotes of its famous Coffee-houses, Hostelries, and
Taverns. By JOHN TIMBS, F.S.A. With numerous Illustrations.

Crown 8vo, cloth extra, with Illustrations, 7*s.* 6*d.*

Timbs' English Eccentrics and Ec-

centricities : Stories of Wealth and Fashion, Delusions, Impos-
tures, and Fanatic Missions, Strange Sights and Sporting Scenes,
Eccentric Artists, Theatrical Folks, Men of Letters, &c. By JOHN
TIMBS, F.S.A. With nearly 50 Illustrations.

One Vol. crown 8vo, cloth extra, 7s. 6d.

Tom Taylor's Historical Plays.

"Clancarty," "Jeanne d'Arc," "'Twixt Axe and Crown," "The Fool's Revenge," "Arkwright's Wife," "Anne Boleyn," "Plot and Passion."

** The Plays may also be had separately, at 1s. each.

Crown 4to, half-Roxburghe, 12s. 6d.

Vagabondiana,

or, Anecdotes of Mendicant Wanderers through the Streets of London ; with Portraits of the most Remarkable, drawn from the Life by JOHN THOMAS SMITH, late Keeper of the Prints in the British Museum. With Introduction by FRANCIS DOUCE, and Descriptive Text. With the Woodcuts and the 32 Plates, from the original Coppers.

Large crown 8vo, cloth antique, with Illustrations, 7s. 6d.

Walton and Cotton's Complete Angler ;

or, The Contemplative Man's Recreation : being a Discourse of Rivers, Fishponds, Fish and Fishing, written by IZAAK WALTON ; and Instructions how to Angle for a Trout or Grayling in a clear Stream, by CHARLES COTTON. With Original Memoirs and Notes by Sir HARRIS NICOLAS, and 61 Copperplate Illustrations.

Carefully printed on paper to imitate the Original, 22 in. by 14 in., 2s.

Warrant to Execute Charles I

An exact Facsimile of this important Document, with the Fifty-nine Signatures of the Regicides, and corresponding Seals.

Beautifully printed on paper to imitate the Original MS., price 2s.

Warrant to Execute Mary Q. of Scots.

An exact Facsimile, including the Signature of Queen Elizabeth, and a Facsimile of the Great Seal.

Crown 8vo, cloth extra, with Illustrations, 7s. 6d.

Wright's Caricature History of the

Georges. (The House of Hanover.) With 400 Pictures, Caricatures, Squibs, Broadsides, Window Pictures, &c. By THOMAS WRIGHT, Esq., M.A., F.S.A.

Large post 8vo, cloth extra, gilt, with Illustrations, 7s. 6d.

Wright's History of Caricature and of

the Grotesque in Art, Literature, Sculpture, and Painting, from the Earliest Times to the Present Day. By THOMAS WRIGHT, M.A., F.S.A. Profusely illustrated by F. W. FAIRHOLT, F.S.A.

J. OGDEN AND CO., PRINTERS, 172, ST. JOHN STREET, E.C.